D0076544

Introduction to Indo-European Linguistics

OSWALD J. L. SZEMERÉNYI

Introduction to Indo-European Linguistics

Translated from

Einführung in die vergleichende Sprachwissenschaft

4th edition, 1990

with additional notes and references

OXFORD
UNIVERSITY PRESS

OXFORD
UNIVERSITY PRESS

Great Clarendon Street, Oxford OX2 6DP

Oxford University Press is a department of the University of Oxford.
It furthers the University's objective of excellence in research, scholarship,
and education by publishing worldwide in

Oxford New York

Athens Auckland Bangkok Bogotá Buenos Aires Calcutta
Cape Town Chennai Dar es Salaam Delhi Florence Hong Kong Istanbul
Karachi Kuala Lumpur Madrid Melbourne Mexico City Mumbai
Nairobi Paris São Paulo Singapore Taipei Tokyo Toronto Warsaw

with associated companies in Berlin Ibadan

Oxford is a registered trade mark of Oxford University Press
in the UK and in certain other countries

Published in the United States
by Oxford University Press Inc., New York

Oswald Szemerényi, *Einführung in die vergleic' ıde*
sprachwissenschaft, 4., revised edition
© Wissenschaftliche Buchgesellschaft, Darmstadt, 1990
This translation © Oxford University Press 1996

The moral rights of the author have been asserted

Database right Oxford University Press (maker)

First published in paperback 1999

All rights reserved. No part of this publication may be reproduced,
stored in a retrieval system, or transmitted, in any form or by any means,
without the prior permission in writing of Oxford University Press,
or as expressly permitted by law, or under terms agreed with the appropriate
reprographics rights organization. Enquiries concerning reproduction
outside the scope of the above should be sent to the Rights Department,
Oxford University Press, at the address above

You must not circulate this book in any other binding or cover
and you must impose this same condition on any acquirer

British Library Cataloguing in Publication Data
Data available

Library of Congress Cataloging in Publication Data
[Einführung in die vergleichende Sprachwissenschaft. English]
Introduction to Indo-European linguistics
Oswald J. L. Szemerényi.—[4th rev. ed.]
Includes bibliographical references.
1. Indo-European languages—Grammar, Comparative. 2. Comparative
linguistics. I. Title.
P575.S913 1996 415-dc20 96-14370

ISBN 0-19-823870-3

1 3 5 7 9 10 8 6 4 2

Typeset by Regent Typesetting, London
Printed in Great Britain
on acid-free paper by
Bookcraft (Bath) Ltd., Midsomer Norton

Preface to the English Translation

This work was first published in 1970—in German, since it had been commissioned by the well-known German publisher Wissenschaftliche Buchgesellschaft (WB) of Darmstadt. In due course the German original was followed by translations into various other languages, obviously because the work was felt to fill a gap in the literature available for the study of Indo-European linguistics. First came a Spanish translation in 1978, no doubt helped by the weighty recommendation of Professor Eugenio Coseriu, followed by a Russian translation in 1980 and by an Italian translation in 1985, which was in fact a revised and enlarged edition, the basis of the thoroughly revised third German edition of 1989. The second edition of 1980 brought only the correction of the numerous misprints of the first edition, as did the fourth edition of 1991 in relation to the third edition. The details of this long and complex story can now be read in my *Summing Up a Life* of 1991, (pp. 45 f.)

The appearance of translations into a number of important world languages raises at once the question how it has come about that there has been so far no English translation, especially as the author is known to be proud of having been born in London city and has been a British citizen by birth for eighty years now. It can be stated right away that an attempt to produce an independent work, an *Introduction to IE Philology*, was actually started in the mid-1950s, long before the German *Einführung*. I worked on this book quite hard, and I still have 346 typewritten quarto pages to show the seriousness of the effort: 168 pages present a survey of the IE languages, and pp. 169–346 give a thorough phonology, (see *Summing Up*, pp. 49 f.). But it remains true that, although I worked hard, I did not work hard enough, and when the request of the WB came in January 1965 to write for them a German *Einführung*, the English plan was naturally shelved, at least for the time being.

In these circumstances it came as a great surprise when, after the publication of the *Einführung* in 1970, the WB informed me in March

1972 that a civil engineer in California had offered to produce an English translation and in support of his offer had referred to Dr Madison Beeler, professor at Berkeley, who had said that the book was an excellent introduction to the subject. I wrote at once to Professor Beeler and recalled that, as stated in the *Einführung* (p. 12), I was working on an (English) *Introduction*, and went on to say: 'It can hardly be expected this year but it will certainly be published next year, in England'—a dream that was never to be fulfilled.

This could have meant the end of all hope of ever seeing my ideas about IE linguistics in an English garb. But miracles have not ceased altogether. In December 1990 Anna Morpurgo Davies, since 1971 Professor of IE Philology in Oxford, drew the attention of the Oxford University Press to my *Einführung* and suggested that a translation into English might be a useful addition to their programme.

The result is now in the hands of the reader. One of my earliest friends in England, David Morgan Jones, since 1953 Professor of Classics at Westfield College, University of London, and now in retirement in Penzance, was willing to shoulder the task of translation with his wife Irene. I owe them profound gratitude for solving a difficult task so successfully. I also hope that the Oxford University Press will find the venture a not unrewarding undertaking.

As was the case with the Italian translation, my book has again benefited from the years which have passed up to the time of its publication. I have once again tried to include everything that seemed profitable. I trust that a new generation of readers, representing English speakers throughout the world, will feel that it has been well served by myself and my excellent collaborators.

Freiburg i. Br. Oswald Szemerényi
2 July 1994

Preface to the First Edition

This work was conceived by the publishers as an introduction to comparative Indo-European linguistics, and the author has carried out their intention to the best of his ability. The introductory chapters 1–3 are of a more general nature, but the main part provides a comparative phonology and morphology of the Indo-European languages.

In the treatment of problems, importance has been attached to making a clear distinction between the Indo-European situation as reconstructed by the comparative method and the diachronic interpretation of this situation. In this way it was hoped to ensure that the student would always keep these two problems separate, and train himself not to tackle the second until the first was resolved.

The work is envisaged as a genuine introduction to the subject. For this reason every effort has been made to set out facts, problems, and conclusions as simply as possible. Even a beginner, however, should be put in a position to acquaint himself with the intricacies of the various problems. In contrast to the practice of some well-known introductions, which provide only a summary bibliography at the end, references to further literature are given throughout, not in footnotes but at the end of each section. Since Indo-European linguistics is a world-wide discipline cultivated in many countries, I have sought to include everything of importance available to me, especially recent and contemporary literature, while for the earlier period the reader is for the most part referred to the bibliographical collections in older standard works.

Regarding the references to the literature of the subject, I have had the advantage of working for many years in research establishments plentifully equipped in this field of study. Special thanks are due to my former home, University College London, to the other institutions of London University, especially Bedford College, and to the British Museum, to all of which with their rich treasures I had continuous access for fifteen years. In the last five years, through the generous support of the Land of Baden-Württemberg and of my new university, I have been able to establish a research centre here in Freiburg also. In a few cases it has seemed desirable to mention works which I have not seen: these are identified by an asterisk. In the months since the end of 1968 when the manuscript was sent to the publishers, a number of important works have appeared. These have been cited at least once, but it was unfortunately impossible to treat them with the same thoroughness as earlier publications. If a work is not mentioned, this does not necessarily mean that it is unknown to me. I should, however, be grateful if authors who do not find their works used here would send them to me; they would be of advantage in the event of a second edition. I should like also to mention that the major part of the research within the last half-century has been treated by me in a historical review to appear in *Current Trends in Linguistics* 9 [1972, 119–95].

There remains only the pleasant duty of expressing my gratitude to those who have helped me with this work. Special thanks are due to my former secretary, Miss Ingrid Lang, and to Dr Utz Maas and Dr Alfred Bammesberger.

Freiburg i. Br.
4 August 1970 Oswald Szemerényi

Preface to the Third Edition

This work first appeared over fifteen years ago. If it has the same good fortune in its new revised form, after another fifteen years it will have entered the third millennium, a prospect which brings home to its author the great responsibility inherent in his undertaking. If his book was to do justice to this difficult but noble task, it required a thorough revision in order to absorb and critically reflect the many new ideas which have matured in our field of study during fifteen years. It has consequently undergone many changes.

These changes have in part been made in the text itself. This was necessary where I have changed my views or found it desirable to formulate them more precisely, and, much more often, where the reader had to be given information on recent developments, since only in this way could the original aims of the work be safeguarded. This was unavoidable, for example, in the case of the so-called glottal theory (6.9), or of the verbal aspect (9.4.4.5); the latter in particular required a more detailed and decided treatment. But even beyond these major problems it has been necessary to include much new matter: to mention only one example, recent views on the accentuation of nouns and verbs, etc. Such additional sections have been indicated, where possible, in the Table of Contents.

Furthermore, the rapid progress of world-wide research has, of course, necessitated changes in the notes. The author is more than ever convinced (and this conviction has been strengthened by many oral and written communications received from others) that an introduction can fulfil its purpose only if it helps the beginner to gain a foothold by opening up for him the many ways of ongoing research. In the present writer's opinion, such help may be impaired or even rendered wholly ineffective in two ways. First, no more than a bibliographical appendix may be given, listing important works; as a result all doctrines appear to be peculiarly those of the author, whereas in fact by and large they represent the *communis opinio* of his time. This is the case with Meillet's *Introduction* and accounts for certain peculiarities of French works on Indo-European. Secondly, there are those who, like Brugmann in his *Grundriss*, provide an ample bibliography for each separate chapter, but not step by step for each point at issue. In my own case, from the first edition onward, it has seemed more honest and more helpful to make the reader aware from the outset that we have had many precursors and to show especially what they achieved. I have also sought to avoid as far as possible a one-sided presentation: to mention not only those writers whose views coincided with mine but also those who held other opinions, and often to indicate briefly how their work should be judged. I have also felt it appropriate to give due prominence to old views alongside the new, thus making clear and maintaining the link with the founders of our science.

The great number of references makes it necessary radically to abbreviate the titles of the more frequently cited books and periodicals. If only a name (obviously that of an author) and year are given, the work will in all probability be found listed under 'Abbreviations'. For abbreviations of names of languages there is a separate list. Abbreviated names of journals are included in the main index, but it is possible that a few rarely cited periodicals have been omitted; these can easily be found in the list of abbreviations at the beginning of each volume of the international *Bibliographie Linguistique*. Old abbreviations these days are often superseded by new ones, which are usually such as to reveal that their inventors have no feeling for historical continuity. For me, an abbreviation such as *BGDSL* can only imply a deliberate rejection of the historical fact that the journal in question was founded and for many years edited by Hermann Paul and Wilhelm Braune, and was accordingly for a whole century until recently referred to only as *PBB*. Equally unhistorical, or even antihistorical, to my mind is the use of *ZVS* for the venerable *KZ*, which constantly reminded us of the journal's founder Adalbert Kuhn.* No less unpleasant is the frequent changing of numeration in periodical series, a practice which takes no account of the pride a contributor should feel at seeing that his work decorates, say, vol. 112 and not merely vol. 3. It is with equal pleasure that one sees that *AJPh* reached its hundredth volume in 1979 and likewise *JAOS* in 1980; that in 1985 *BSL* reached its eightieth and *KZ* its ninety-eighth volume. Much greater are the difficulties of finding one's way in the French *RPh*, in which new series are introduced at ever shorter intervals; *proxime accessit* the British *ArchL*.

* 5 October 1988. I have today learnt that the old *KZ* (founded in 1851; see R. Schmitt, *KZ* 100 (1987), 205 f.), after a transitional period as *ZVS*, is to appear in future as *HS* (*Historische Sprachforschung*). Cf. Gusmani, 'La fine della KZ', *InL* 12, 1987/8, 173–4; R. Schmitt, *ZRP* 105, 1989, 636–7.

Finally, it should perhaps be mentioned that within the book numerous cross-references are provided to other passages dealing with a particular problem.

I had almost completed the long task of revision when, through the kindness of one of its authors, I received a new and copious work of which, regrettably, I was not able to take full account but which, for that very reason, I must emphatically recommend here (as also at 1.6 fin. and 3 fin.). I refer to vol. i of the *Indogermanische Grammatik* founded by Jerzy Kuryłowicz, which contains the introduction to the Indo-European languages by the late Warren Cowgill, so early departed, and the phonology by his very active collaborator, Manfred Mayrhofer.

After this lengthy discourse I can only say: *dixi et saluaui animam meam*.

Freiburg i. Br.
19 May 1986 Oswald Szemerényi

Contents

Abbreviations, etc.

The following list includes mainly, but not only, periodicals, books, and other works which are referred to in the text, mostly in abbreviated form.

AAntHung = *Acta Antiqua Hungarica*, Budapest.
AA(rm)L = *Annual of Armenian Linguistics*, Cleveland, Ohio.
ABäG = *Amsterdamer Beiträge zur älteren Germanistik*, Amsterdam.
Abraham, Werner (ed.), *Kasustheorie*, Frankfurt am Main, 1971.
AC = *L'Antiquité Classique*, Brussels.
Adrados, F. Rodriguez, *Laringales* = *Estudios sobre las laringales indoeuropeas*, Madrid, 1961; 2nd enlarged edn. 1973.
——*Verbo* =*Evolución y estructura del verbo indoeuropeo*, Madrid, 1963.
——'The new image of IE: the history of a revolution', *IF* 97, 1993, 1–28.
AGI = *Archivio Glottologico Italiano*, Florence.
AIED = *Ancient Indo-European Dialects*, ed. H. Birnbaum and J. Puhvel, Los Angeles, 1966.
AION-L = *Annali dell'Istituto Orientale di Napoli, Sezione Linguistica* 1–9, 1959–70.
AIΩN = *Annali del Seminario di Studi del Mondo Classico, Sezione Linguistica*, Pisa 1979– (14, 1994).
AJGLL = *American Journal for Germanic Languages and Literatures*, Honolulu.
AJP(h) = *American Journal of Philology*, Baltimore.
AKUP = Arbeiten zum Kölner Universalien Projekt, Cologne.
ALH = *Acta Linguistica Hungarica*, Budapest.
AL(Hafn) = *Acta Linguistica (Hafniensia)*, Copenhagen.
ANRW = *Aufstieg und Niedergang der römischen Welt*, ed. H. Temporini and W. Haase, Berlin, 1972– (29/1–2, 1983).
Anttila, Raimo, *An Introduction to Historical and Comparative Linguistics*, 1972; 2nd edn. 1989.
AO = *Archív Orientální*, Prague.
APILKU = *Arbejdspapirer udsendt af Institut for Lingvistik*, University of Copenhagen.
Arbeitman, Yoel L. (ed.), *In Memoriam Ben Schwartz*, 1988.
ArchL = *Archivum Linguisticum*, Glasgow and Menston, Yorks, 1949–80.
Arens[2] = H. Arens, *Sprachwissenschaft: Der Gang ihrer Entwicklung von der*

Antike bis zur Gegenwart, 2nd edn., Freiburg i. Br. 1969.
Arqritica, Madrid.
ASGM = *Atti del Sodalizio Glottologico Milanese*, Milan.
ASNP = *Annali della Scuola Normale Superiore di Pisa*.
Auroux, Sylvain (ed.), 'Antoine Meillet et la linguistique de son temps', *HEL* 10/2, 1988, 1–348.
Back, Michael, *Die synchrone Prozessbasis des natürlichen Lautwandels*, Stuttgart 1991; see review by Householder, *Krat* 38, 1993, 17–24.
BalkE = *Balkansko Ezikoznanie/Linguistique Balkanique*, Sofia.
Bammesberger, Alfred, *Studien zur Laryngaltheorie*, 1984.
——*Der Aufbau des germanischen Verbalsystems*, 1986.
——(ed.), *Die Laryngaltheorie*, 1988.
——*Die Morphologie des urgermanischen Nomens*, 1990.
BB = *(Bezzenbergers) Beiträge zur Kunde der idg. Sprachen*, 1877–1906.
BBCS = *Bulletin of the Board of Celtic Studies*, Cardiff.
BDPhS = *Biographical Dictionary of the Phonetic Sciences*, ed. A. J. Bronstein, L. J. Raphael, and C. J. Stevens, New York 1977.
Beekes, R. S. P., *Laryngeals* = *The Development of the Proto-IE Laryngeals in Greek*, The Hague 1969.
——*Origins* = *The Origins of the IE Nominal Inflection*, Innsbruck 1985.
——*A Grammar of Gatha-Avestan*, 1988.
——'Wackernagel's explanation of the lengthened grade', in *Wackernagel Kolloquium*, 1990, 33–53.
Benveniste, Émile, *Origines* = *Origines de la formation des noms en indo-européen*, 1935.
——*HIE* = *Hittite et indo-européen*, 1962.
Berger, Hermann, *Einige Ergebnisse der Phonemstatistik*, Abhandlungen der Heidelberger Akademie, 1986/1, 1987; see Ternes, *Kraṭ* 33, 1988, 164–7.
BiOr = *Bibliotheca Orientalis*, Leyden.
Birnbaum, Henrik, *Problems of Typological and Genetic Linguistics Viewed in a Generative Framework*, The Hague 1970.
BJL = *Belgian Journal of Linguistics*, 1985–.
Bomhard, Allan R., *Nostratic* = *Towards Proto-Nostratic*, Amsterdam 1984.
——and J. C. Kerns, *The Nostratic Macrofamily: A Study in Distant Linguistic Relationship*, Berlin 1994.
Bopp, Franz, *Konjugationssystem* = *Über das Conjugationssystem der Sanskritsprache in Vergleichung mit jenem der griechischen, lateinischen, persischen und germanischen Sprache*, Frankfurt am Main 1816.
BPTJ = *Biuletyn Polskiego Towarzystwa Językoznawczego/Bulletin de la Société Polonaise de Linguistique*, Wrocław.
Bréal, M., *The Beginnings of Semantics*, ed. and trans. G. Wolf, London 1991; the French original, *Essai de sémantique*, first appeared in 1897.
Brugmann, Karl, *Grundriss*² = *Grundriss der vergleichenden Grammatik der indogermanischen Sprachen*, 2nd edn., i, ii 1–3, 1897–1916.
——*KVG* = *Kurze vergleichende Grammatik*, 1902–4.
——and Hermann Osthoff, *Morphologische Untersuchungen auf den Gebiete der indogermanischen Sprachen* i-vi, 1878–1910.

BSL = *Bulletin de la Société de Linguistique*, Paris 1867– .
BSO(A)S = *Bulletin of the School of Oriental (and African) Studies*, London.
BzN = *Beiträge zur Namenforschung*, Heidelberg.
Cardona, George, et al. (eds.), *Indo-European and Indo-Europeans*, 1971.
Carruba, Onofrio (ed.), *Towards a Hittite Grammar*, Pavia 1992.
CFC = *Cuadernos de Filología Clásica*, Madrid.
CFS = *Cahiers Ferdinand de Saussure*, Geneva.
Chadwick, Studies = *Studies in Mycenaean and Classical Greek Presented to John Chadwick*, (*Minos* 20–2), 1987.
Chantraine, Pierre, *Parf.* = *Histoire du parfait grec*, 1927.
——*Morph.* = *Morphologie historique du grec*, 2nd edn., 1964.
——*DELG* = *Dictionnaire étymologique de la langue grecque* i-iv, Paris, 1968–80; cf. Szemerényi, *Gn* 43 (1971), 641–75; 49 (1977), 1–10; 53 (1981), 113–16 (=*SM* 1559–1607).
CHD = *Chicago Hittite Dictionary* iii (L–N), 1980–9.
CILL = *Cahiers de l'Institut de Linguistique de Louvain.*
Coll. Myc. = *(International) Colloquium on Mycenaean Studies* 1–9, 1956–93.
Collinge, N. E., *Laws* = *The Laws of Indo-European*, Amsterdam 1985.
——(ed.), *An Encyclopaedia of Language*, London 1990.
Coloquio = *Actas del (X) Coloquio sobre lenguas y culturas prerromanas de la peninsula iberica* 1–6, 1976–93.
Convegno = *Atti del Convegno Internazionale di Linguisti, Sodalizio Glottologico Milanese* 1–9, 1950–93.
Cowgill, W., and Mayrhofer, M., *Indogermanische Grammatik* i/1–2, Heidelberg 1986.
Cowgill, W., In Memory of = *Studies in Memory of Warren Cowgill*, Berlin 1987.
CQ = *Classical Quarterly*.
Crystal, David, *The Cambridge Encyclopedia of Language*, 1987.
CTL = *Current Trends in Linguistics* i–xiv, ed. T. A. Sebeok, 1963–76. For some especially interesting volumes see Szemerényi, *Krat* 20 (1976), 1–12 (esp. on xi, 1973), and *Phonetica* 36 (1979), 158–68 (on xiii/1–2, 1975), both repr. in *SM* 513–24, 541–51.
Delbrück, B., *Einleitung in das Studium der indogermanischen Sprachen*, Leipzig 1880.
Desnickaja, A.V. (ed.), *Aktual'nyje voprosy sravnitel'nogo jazykoznanija*, 1989.
Directions, see Lehmann and Malkiel.
Duhoux, Yves, *Le verbe grec ancien*, Louvain 1992.
——'L'aspect verbal: du mycénien à l'ie.', in *Coll. Myc.* 9 (1993), 215–36.
——'L'aspect verbal en grec ancien', *Syntaktika* 7 (1994), 9–18.
Dyen 1992 = Isidore Dyen, Joseph B. Kruskal, and Paul Black, *An IE Classification: A Lexico-statistical Experiment*, Philadelphia 1992.
EC = *Études Celtiques*, Paris.
EIE = *Études Indo-européennes*, Lyon.
Einhauser, Eveline, *Die Junggrammatiker*, Trier, 1990; see Collinge, *HL* 18, 1991.

Elementa, ed. V. V. Ivanov (new periodical), Moscow, 1993–
Em = *Emerita*, Madrid.
Erhart, Adolf, 'Die ie. Dualendung -*ō(u)* und die Zahlwörter', *Sbornik Brno*, 1965/A-13.
——*Studien zur ie. Morphologie*, Brno 1970.
——*Zur Entwicklung der Kategorien Tempus und Modus im Indogermanischen*, 1985.
——*Das ie. Verbalsystem*, Brno, 1989; see Klein, *Lg* 69, 1993, 204.
——*Die idg. Nominalflexion und ihre Genese*, Innsbruck 1993.
Ethnogenese = *Studien zur Ethnogenese*, Opladen, i (1985), ii (1988).
Etimologija, ed. O. N. Trubačev, annual publication, Moscow.
Euler, Wolfram, *Indoiranisch-Griechische Gemeinsamkeiten der Nominalbildung und deren idg. Grundlagen*, Innsbruck 1979.
——'Präteritaltempora für Vergangenheit in älteren idg. Sprachen', in *Wackernagel Kolloquium*, 1990, 131–49.
Evidence = *Evidence for Laryngeals*, ed. W. Winter, The Hague 1965.
Fachtagung = *Akten der ... Fachtagung der Indogermanischen Gesellschaft* 1–9, 1955–94.
Fanning, B. M., *Verbal Aspect in New Testament Greek*, Oxford 1990.
FBA = Fellow of the British Academy.
Festus = Festus, *De verborum significatu*, ed. W. M. Lindsay, in *Glossaria Latina iussu Academiae Britannicae edita* iv, 71–507, Paris 1930; repr. Hildesheim 1965.
FF, *FuF* = *Forschungen (und) Fortschritte.*
Fillmore, Charles J., 'The case for case', in E. Bach and R. T. Harms (eds.), *Universals in Linguistic Theory*, 1968, 1–88; an easily accessible German version is available in Abraham 1971, 1–118.
Fischer-Jørgensen, Eli, *Trends in Phonological Theory*, Copenhagen, 1975.
Fisiak, Jacek (ed.), *Recent Developments in Historical Phonology*, The Hague 1978.
——(ed.), *Historical Morphology*, The Hague 1980.
FL = *Foundations of Language.*
FoL(H) = *Folia Linguistica (Historica).*
Fs = *Festschrift.*
Fulk, R. D., *The Origins of IE Quantitative Ablaut*, Innsbruck 1986.
Gamkrelidze–Ivanov = Thomas V. Gamkrelidze and Vjačeslav V. Ivanov, *Indoevropejskij jazyk i indoevropejcy: Rekonstrukcija i istoriko-tipologičeskij analiz prajazyka i protokul'tury* i–ii, Tblisi, 1984. An English translation planned by Mouton since 1987 may appear in 1995.
Gamkrelidze, Fs. = *Istoričeskaja lingvistika i tipologija*, Moscow 1991.
Garde, Paul, *Histoire de l'accentuation slave* i–ii, Paris 1976.
Gauger et al. = Hans-Martin Gauger, Wulf Oesterreicher, and Rudolph Windisch, *Einführung in die romanische Sprachwissenschaft*, Darmstadt 1981.
Georgiev, Vladimir, *Introduction to the History of the IE Languages*, Sofia 1981 (first published in Russian 1958).
GGA/GGN = *Göttingische Gelehrte Anzeigen/Nachrichten.*

GL = *General Linguistics*, University Park, Pa.
Glotta, Göttingen.
Gn = *Gnomon*, Munich.
Godel, Robert, *An Introduction to the Study of Classical Armenian*, Wiesbaden 1975.
Gonda, Jan, *Moods* = *The Character of the IE Moods*, Wiesbaden 1956.
——*The Aspectual Function of the Rigvedic Present and Aorist*, 1962.
——*Old Indian*, 1971.
——*Vedic Literature*, 1975.
GR = *Greece and Rome*.
Grammont, Maurice, *Traité de phonétique*, Paris 1933; 5th edn. 1956.
GURT = Georgetown University Round Table on Languages and Linguistics, Washington, DC.
Hahn, Adelaide, *Subjunctive* = *Subjunctive and Optative*, New York 1953.
Harðarson, Jón A., *Studien zum idg. Wurzelaorist*, Innsbruck 1993.
Haudry, Jean, *Préhistoire de la flexion nominale ie.*, 1982.
Hawaii Papers = *Working Papers in Linguistics, University of Hawaii*, Honolulu.
Heger, Klaus, *Monem, Wort, Satz und Text*, 2nd enlarged edn., 1976 (on its relation to the 1st edn., see 344–7).
——*Flexionsformen, Vokabeln und Wortarten*, Heidelberg 1985.
HEL = *Histoire, Epistémologie, Langage*, Lille.
Heth. und Idg. = *Hethitisch und Indogermanisch*, see Neu and Meid.
Hirt, Hermann, *IG* = *Indogermanische Grammatik* i–vii, Heidelberg 1921–37.
HL = *Historiographia Linguistica*, Amsterdam.
Hock, Hans Henrich, *Principles of Historical Linguistics*, Berlin 1986.
Hockett, Charles F., *A Manual of Phonology*, Baltimore 1955.
——*Course* = *A Course in Modern Linguistics*, New York 1958.
Hoenigswald, Fs. = *Festschrift for Henry Hoenigswald on the Occasion of his Seventieth Birthday*, Tübingen 1987.
Hoffmann, Karl, *Injunctiv* = *Der Injunctiv im Veda*, 1967.
——*Aufsätze zur Indoiranistik* i–ii (1975–6); iii (1993).
Hofmann–Szantyr = J. B. Hofmann and A. Szantyr, *Lateinische Syntax und Stilistik*, 2nd edn., Munich 1965.
HS = *Historische Sprachforschung*, new title of *KZ* since vol. 101, 1988; see the note in the Preface to the 3rd edn. of this *Introduction*, 1989, and on the *KZ* in the nineteenth century Szemerényi, in *Fs. Strunk*, 1995, n. 7.
HSCP = *Harvard Studies in Classical Philology*.
Hübschmann, Heinrich, *Armenische Grammatik, Armenische Etymologie*, Leipzig 1907; repr. Hildesheim 1962.
IAN(OLJ) = *Izvestija Akademii Nauk (Otdelenija Literatury i Jazyka)*, Moscow.
IC = *Indogermanische Chronik*, bibliographical supplement of *Sprache*, 13–34 (1969–92), when it had to cease publication.
ICHL = *International Conference on Historical Linguistics*.
idg. = indogermanisch.

IE = Indo-European.
IE and IEs, see Cardona.
IF = Indogermanische Forschungen, Berlin.
IIJ = Indo-Iranian Journal, Dordrecht.
Illyč-Svityč, V. M., *Akc. = Imennaja akcentuacija v baltijskom i slavjanskom*, Moscow 1963; English translation by R. L. Leed and R. F. Feldstein, *Nominal Accentuation in Baltic and Slavic*, Cambridge, Mass., 1979.
Indogermanisch und Keltisch, see K. H. Schmidt 1977.
InL = Incontri Linguistici, Trieste.
Isebaert, Lambert, see *van Windekens, Memoriae.*
——(ed.), *Miscellanea Linguistica Graeco-Latina*, 1993.
IULC = Indiana University Linguistic Club.
Ivanov, V. V., *Obščeind. = Obšče-indoevropejskaja, praslavjanskaja i anatolijskaja jazykovyje sistemy*, Moscow 1965.
——*Glagol = Slavjanskij, baltijskij i rannebalkanskij glagol*, Moscow 1981.
IZ = (Techmers) Internationale Zeitschrift für Allgemeine Sprachwissenschaft, founded and edited by F. Techmer (1843–91), saw only five volumes (plus one supplement) between 1884 and 1890; on its importance see K. Koerner, in *BDPhS* 206–7, 'The importance of *IZ* in the development of general linguistics' (1973); Barozzi, *SSL* 24 (1984), 11–78.
IzvAN, see *IAN*.
JA = Journal Asiatique, Paris.
Jamison, Stephanie W., *Function and Form in the '-áya-' Formations of the Rig Veda and Atharva Veda*, 1983.
JAOS = Journal of the American Oriental Society, New Haven, Conn.
Jasanoff, Jay, *Stative = Stative and Middle*, Innsbruck 1978.
JCL = Journal of Celtic Linguistics, Cardiff 1992– .
JCS = Journal of Cuneiform Studies, Cambridge, Mass.
JEGP(h) = Journal of English and Germanic Philology, Leeds.
Jespersen, Otto, *Language = Language, Its Nature, Development and Origin*, London 1922; 11th edn., 1959 (paperback, New York, 1964).
JHLP = Journal of Historical Linguistics and Philology, 1983– .
JHS = Journal of Hellenic Studies, London.
JIES = Journal of IE Studies, Hattiesburg, Miss.
JL = Journal of Linguistics, Cambridge.
Jonsson, H., *The Laryngeal Theory: A Critical Survey*, 1978.
JRAS = Journal of the Royal Asiatic Society, London.
Kahane, Fs. = Festschrift Henry Kahane, ed. H. H. Hock, 1973.
Kammenhuber, Annelies, 'Hethitisch' = 'Hethitisch, Palaisch, Luwisch und Hieroglyphenluwisch', in *Altkleinasiatische Sprachen*, Leiden 1969, 119–357.
KBS = Klagenfurter Beiträge zur Sprachwissenschaft, Klagenfurt.
Kellens, Jean, *Les noms racines de l'Avesta*, Wiesbaden 1974.
——*Le verbe avestique*, 1984.
——(ed.), *La reconstruction des laryngales*, Liège, 1990; cf. Lindeman, *Krat* 37 (1992), 58–62.
——and Pirart, Eric, *Les textes vieil-avestiques* i–iii, Wiesbaden, 1988–91.

Kerns, J. A., In Memory of: *Bono Homini Donum: Essays in Historical Linguistics in Memory of J. Alexander Kerns* i–ii, ed. Y. L. Arbeitman and A. R. Bomhard, Amsterdam 1981.
Kilani-Schoch, M., *Introduction à la morphologie naturelle*, Berne 1988.
Kilian, Lothar, *Zum Ursprung der Indogermanen*, Bonn 1983; cf. Lochner von Hüttenbach, *Krat* 29, 1985, 160–3; A. Häusler, *Jahresschrift für mitteldeutsche Vorgeschichte* 68, 1985, 390–3.
King, R. D., *Historical Linguistics and Generative Grammar*, Englewood Cliffs, NJ, 1969.
Kiparsky, Paul, *Explanation in Phonology*, Dordrecht 1982.
Koerner, E. F. Konrad, *Western Histories of Linguistic Thought: An Annotated Chronological Bibliography 1822–1976*, Amsterdam 1978.
Krahe, Hans, *Idg. Sprw.* = *Indogermanische Sprachwissenschaft*, 3rd edn., i–ii, 1958–9; iii (Krahe and Meid), 1972.
Krat = *Kratylos*, Wiesbaden.
Kronasser, Heinz, *Etymologie der hethitischen Sprache* i (pts. 1–6), 1962–6; ii (ed. E. Neu), 1987.
KSchr. = *Kleine Schriften.*
Kuhn, Thomas S., *The Structure of Scientific Revolutions*, 2nd edn. 1970.
Kuryłowicz, Jerzy, *Études* = *Études indo-européennes* i, 1935.
—*Accentuation* = L'accentuation des langues ie., 1952; 2nd edn. 1958.
—*Apophonie* = *L'apophonie en indo-européen*, 1956.
—*Esquisses* = *Esquisses linguistiques* i, Munich 1960; 2nd edn. 1973; ii, 1975.
—*Categories* = *The Inflectional Categories of IE*, 1964.
—*IG* = *Indogermanische Grammatik* ii: *Akzent, Ablaut*, 1968.
—*Metrik* = *Metrik und Sprachgeschichte*, 1975.
—*Problèmes* = *Problèmes de linguistique ie.*, 1977.
KZ = *(Kuhns) Zeitschrift für vergleichende Sprachforschung*; see *HS*.
La Linguistique, Paris.
Labov, William, 'Building on empirical foundations', in Lehmann and Malkiel 1982, 17–92.
LACUS = *The Lacus Forum*, Columbia, SC, 1975–(14th, 1990).
LALIES = *Actes des Sessions de Linguistique et de Littérature*, Paris.
Latein und Indogermanisch, see Panagl and Krisch.
LB = *Leuvense Bijdragen*, Louvain.
LBer = *Linguistische Berichte*, Brunswick.
Lehmann, W. P., *PIE* = *Proto-IE Phonology*, 1952.
—*Historical Linguistics: An Introduction*, New York, 1962, 3rd edn. 1992.
—*PIE Syntax*, 1974.
—(ed.), *Language Typology*, 1990.
—*Theoretical Bases of Indo-European Linguistics*, New York 1993.
—and Y. Malkiel (eds.), *Directions for Historical Linguistics*, Austin, Tex., 1969; see Szemerényi, *GL* 10 (1970), 121–32.
—(eds.), *Perspectives on Historical Linguistics*, 1982.
LeS = *Lingua e Stile*, Bologna.
Leumann[2] = Manu Leumann, *Lateinische Laut- und Formenlehre*, 2nd edn., 1977 (1st edn. 1926–8).

Lewis, Henry and Pedersen, Holger, *CCCG* = *A Concise Comparative Celtic Grammar*, 1937; repr. 1961.
Lg = *Language: Journal of the Linguistic Society of America*, Baltimore 1925– .
LIn = *Linguistic Inquiry*, Cambridge, Mass.
Lindeman, Fredrik Otto, *Einführung in die Laryngaltheorie*, Berlin 1970.
——*The Triple Representation of Shwa in Greek and Some Related Problems of IE Phonology*, Oslo 1982.
——*Introduction to the Laryngeal Theory*, Oslo 1987.
Lings = *Linguistics*, Berlin.
Lockwood, W. B., *IE Philology: Historical and Comparative*, London 1969.
——*A Panorama of IE Languages*, London 1972.
LPosn = *Lingua Posnaniensis*, Poznań.
LSci = *Language Sciences*, Bloomington, Ind.; since 1979, Tokyo.
Lüdtke, Helmut (ed.), *Kommunikationstheoretische Grundlagen des Sprachwandels*, Berlin 1980.
Makajev, E. A., *Struktura* = *Struktura slova v ie. i germanskix jazykax*, Moscow, 1970.
Malkiel, Yakov, *Etymology*, Cambridge 1993.
——(ed.), see Lehmann and Malkiel (eds.)
Mallory, J. P., *In Search of the Indo-Europeans*, 1989.
Martinet, André, *Économie* = *Économie des changements phonétiques*, Berne 1955.
——*A Functional View of Language*, Oxford 1962.
——*Évolution des langues et reconstruction*, Paris 1975.
——*Studies in Functional Syntax*, Munich 1975.
——(ed.), *Grammaire fonctionnelle du français*, Paris 1979.
——*Syntaxe générale*, Paris, 1985; see Lazard, *BSL* 81/2, 1986, 17–21.
——*Des steppes aux océans: l'indo-européen et les indo-européens*, Paris 1986.
Mayrhofer, Manfred, *KEWA*: *Kurzgefasstes etymologisches Wörterbuch des Altindischen* i–iv, Heidelberg 1953–80.
——*Nach hundert Jahren: Ferdinand de Saussures Frühwerk und seine Rezeption*, 1981; see Szemerényi, *Krat* 28, 1984, 54–9.
——*EWA* = *Etymologisches Wörterbuch des Altindoiranischen* i–, 1986.
——1986, see Cowgill and Mayrhofer.
McCone, Kim, *The IE Origins of the Old Irish Nasal Presents*, Innsbruck 1991; see *IC* 34, 353*t*.
MDOG, see *ZDMG*.
Meid, Wolfgang, *Das germanische Präteritum*, Innsbruck 1971.
——*Das Problem von idg. /b/*, Innsbruck 1989.
Meier-Brügger, Michael, *Griechische Sprachwissenschaft* i–ii (Sammlung Göschen), 1992.
Meillet, Antoine, *Introduction à l'étude comparative des langues ie.*, Paris 1903; 8th edn. 1937.
——*Esquisse d'une grammaire comparée de l'arménien classique*, Vienna, 1903; 2nd rev. edn. 1936.
——*Dialectes* = *Les dialectes ie.*, 1908, 2nd edn. 1922.
——*Altarmenisches Elementarbuch*, Heidelberg 1913.
——*LHLG* = *Linguistique historique et linguistique générale* i–ii, 1921–36.

——and Marcel Cohen, *Les langues du monde*, Paris 1924; 2nd edn. 1952. (repr. 2 vols., 1981). It will be replaced by J. Perrot (ed.), *Les langues dans le monde ancien et moderne*, Paris; the first volume on sub-Saharian Africa and pidgins and creoles appeared in 1981.
——and Vendryes, Joseph, *Traité de grammaire comparée des langues classiques*, 1924; 2nd edn. 1953.
Meiser, Gerhard, *Lautgeschichte der umbrischen Sprache*, Innsbruck 1986.
MH = *Museum Helveticum*, Basle.
Michelini, Guido, *La linguistica testuale e l'indoeuropeo: il passivo*, Brescia 1981.
Minos = *Minos: Revista de Filología Egea*, Salamanca.
MIT = Massachusetts Institute of Technology, Cambridge, Mass.
Mnem = *Mnemosyne*, Leiden.
Mounin, Georges, *Histoire de la linguistique des origines au XX*[è] siècle, Paris 1967.
——*La linguistique du XX*[è] siècle, Paris 1972.
MSL = *Mémoires de la Société de Linguistique de Paris.*
MSS = *Münchener Studien zur Sprachwissenschaft.*
MTA(T) = (a) Magyar Tudomanyos Akademia (Tagja).
MU = *Morphologische Untersuchungen*, see Brugmann and Osthoff.
Myc. Colloquium, see *Coll. Myc.*
Nagy, Gregory, *Greek Dialects and the Transformation of an IE Process*, Harvard, Mass., 1970; see Szemerényi, *Krat* 14, 1972, 157–65 (=*SM* 1608–16).
Neu, Erich (1) = *Interpretation der hethitischen mediopassiven Verbalformen*, 1968.
——(2) = *Das hethitische Mediopassiv und seine idg. Grundlagen*, 1968
——and Meid, W. (eds.), *Hethitisch und Indogermanisch*, Innsbruck 1979.
Newmeyer, F. J. (ed.), *Linguistics: The Cambridge Survey* i–iv, Cambridge 1988.
NJL = *Nordic Journal of Linguistics*, Oslo.
NOWELE = *North-Western European Language Evolution*, Odense.
NTS = *Norsk Tidsskrift for Sprogvidenskab*, Oslo.
Nussbaum, A. J., *Head and Horn in IE*, Berlin 1986.
ÖA(W)Anz = *Österreichische Akademie (der Wissenschaften), Anzeiger.*
ÖAWSb = *Österreichische Akademie der Wissenschaften, Sitzungberichte.*
Oettinger, Norbert, *Die Stammbildung des hethitischen Verbums, 1979.*
ÖLT = *Österreichische Linguistentagung.*
OLZ = *Orientalistische Literaturzeitung.*
Osthoff, see Brugmann and Osthoff.
Palmer, Frank R., *Mood and Modality*, Cambridge, 1986; see Hagège, *BSL* 84/2, 1989, 77–84.
Palmer, Leonard R., *The Latin Language*, London 1954.
——*Descriptive and Comparative Linguistics*, London 1972.
——*The Greek Language*, London 1980.
Panagl, Oswald, and Krisch, Thomas (eds.), *Latein und Indogermanisch*, Innsbruck, 1992.

PBB = *Paul und Braune: Beiträge zur Geschichte der deutschen Sprache und Literatur*, 1874–. *T/H*: Tübingen/Halle.
PCLS(P) = *Proceedings of the Chicago Linguistic Society (Parasession)*.
Pedersen, Holger, *VKG* = *Vergleichende Grammatik der keltischen Sprachen* i–ii, 1908–13.
——*Linguistic Science in the Nineteenth Century*, 1931; paperback: *The Discovery of Language*, Bloomington, Ind., 1962.
——*Hittitisch* = *Hittitisch und die anderen ie. Sprachen*, 1938.
——*Tocharisch vom Gesichtspunkt der ie. Sprachvergleichung*, 1941.
Perrot, see Meillet and Cohen.
Peters, Martin, *Untersuchungen zur Vertretung der idg. Laryngale im Griechischen*, Vienna, 1980.
Petersson, Herbert, *Studien über die idg. Heteroklisie*, Lund 1921.
——*Zur Kenntis der idg. Heteroklisie*, Lund and Leipzig 1922.
PICCS = *Proceedings of the International Conference of Celtic Studies*.
PICHL = *Papers from the International Conference on Historical Linguistics*.
PICL = *Proceedings of the International Congress of Linguists* 1–12, 1928–78; 13 (Tokyo 1982), 1983; 14 (Berlin 1987), pts. 1–3, 1990.
PICO = *Proceedings of the International Congress of Orientalists*.
PICPS = *Proceedings of the International Congress of Phonetic Sciences* 1–11, 1932–87.
PIE = Proto-Indo-European.
Pilch, Herbert, *Phonemtheorie* i, 3rd edn., 1974.
Pinkster, Harm, *Latin Syntax and Semantics*, London, 1990; considerable changes from Dutch original of 1984. German version, *Lateinische Syntax und Semantik*, 1988.
Pisani, Vittore, *Studi sulla preistoria delle lingue ie.*, Rome 1933.
——*Geolinguistica e indeuropeo*, Rome, 1940; see Specht, *Gn* 19 (1943), 155–61.
——*L'etimologia*, 2nd edn. 1967.
——*Le lingue indeuropee*, 3rd edn. 1971.
Pokorny, Julius, *IEW* = *Indogermanisches etymologisches Wörterbuch* i, 1949–59; ii, 1965–9.
Polomé, Edgar C. (ed.), *Research Guide on Language Change*, Berlin 1990.
——(ed.), *Perspectives on IE Language, Culture and Religion*, *JIES* Monograph 7, 1991.
Polomé, Studies = *Studies in Honor of Edgar C. Polomé*, ed. M. A. Jazayery and Werner Winter, Berlin and New York 1988; see Lamberterie, *BSL* 84/2, 1989, 204–11.
Porzig, Walter, *Gliederung des idg. Sprachgebiets*, 1954.
Porzio Gernia, M. L., *La sorte di M e D finali* [in the history of Latin], Rome 1974.
PP = *La Parola del Passato*, Naples.
Prat, Louis C., *Morphosyntaxe de l'ablatif en latin archaique*, Paris 1975.
Prokosch, E., *A Comparative Germanic Grammar*, 1939.
Proc. Brit. Acad. = *Proceedings of the British Academy* (London).
Puhvel, Jaan, *Laryngeals and the IE Verb*, 1960.
——(ed.), *Substance and Structure of Language*, 1969.

——1991a = *Hittite Etymological Dictionary* i–ii (*a*-, *e*-, *i*-), Berlin, 1984; iii (*h*-), 1991. All in a strange nineteenth-century style.
——1991b = *Homer and Hittite*, Innsbruck, 1991.
——and Birnbaum, Henrik (eds.), *Ancient IE Dialects*, 1966.
QPL = *Quaderni Patavini di Linguistica*, Padua.
Quattordio Moreschini, Adriana (ed.), *L'opera Scientifica di Antoine Meillet*, Pisa, 1987.
RAL = *Rendiconti dell'Accademia dei Lincei*, or *Reale Accademia dei Lincei*.
Rasmussen, Jens Elmegård, *Haeretica Indogermanica*, Copenhagen 1974.
——'IE ablaut *i~e/o*', *APILKU* 7 (1988), 125–42.
——*Studien zur Morphophonemik der idg. Grundsprache*, Innsbruck 1989.
RBPh = *Revue Belge de Philologie et d'Histoire*, Brussels.
RC = *Revue Celtique*, Paris.
REA = *Revue des Études Anciennes*, Bordeaux.
REArm = *Revue des Études Arméniennes*, Paris.
REG = *Revue des Études Grecques*, Paris.
REGC = *Revue des Études Géorgiennes et Caucasiennes*, Paris.
REIE = *Revue des Études Indo-européennes*, Bucharest, 1–4, 1938–47.
REL = *Revue des Études Latines*, Paris.
RES = *Revue des Études Slaves*, Paris.
RHA = *Revue Hittite et Asianique*, Paris.
RIGI = *Rivista Indo-Greco-Italica*, Rome 1917–38.
RIL = *Rendiconti dell'Istituto Lombardo*, Milan.
Risch, Fs. = *-o-pe-ro-si*: *Fs. Ernst Risch*, Berlin 1986.
Rivara, René, *Le système de la comparaison*, Paris 1990.
RivLing = *Rivista di Linguistica*, 1989– .
Rix, Helmut, *Historische Grammatik des Griechischen*, 1976.
——*Zur Entstehung des uridg. Modussystems*, Innsbruck 1986.
——'The *PIE* Middle', *MSS* 49 (1988), 101–19.
——(ed.), *Oskisch-umbrische Inschriften*, 1993.
Rix, Fs. = *Indogermanica et Italica*, Innsbruck 1993.
RLaR = *Revue des Langues Romanes*, Montpellier.
RO = *Rocznik Orientalisticzny*, Warsaw.
Robins, R. H., *Ancient and Mediaeval Grammatical Theory in Europe*, London, 1951.
——*General Linguistics: An Introductory Survey*, London 1964.
——*A Short History of Linguistics*, London 1967.
——*The Byzantine Grammarians: Their Place in History*, Berlin 1993.
RPh = *Revue de Philologie*, Paris.
RPhon = *Revue de Phonétique*, Paris.
RSEL = *Revista (de la Sociedad) Española de Lingüística*, Madrid.
Ruipérez, Martin S., *Sistema de aspectos*, Salamanca, 1954; French translation, 1982.
Saussure, Ferdinand de, *Cours* = *Cours de linguistique générale*, 1916; 2nd edn. 1922.
——*Recueil* = *Recueil des publications scientifiques* (1–268 the famous *Mémoire*, see 5. 3. 5. n.1 and 6.4 in the main text), Geneva, 1922; see Mayrhofer 1981.

SCelt = *Studia Celtica*, Cardiff.
Scherer, Anton, *Gestirnnamen bei den idg. Völkern*, 1953.
——(ed.), *Die Urheimat der Indogermanen*, 1968.
——*Handbuch der lateinischen Syntax*, 1975.
Scherer, Fs. = *Donum Indogermanicum: Festgabe für A. Scherer*, 1971.
Schmalstieg, William R., *Indo-European Linguistics: A New Synthesis*, Penn., 1980.
Schmid, Wolfgang P., *Studien zum baltischen und indogermanischen Verbum*, 1963.
Schmidt, Gernot, *Studien zum germanischen Adverb*, diss., Berlin, 1962.
——*Stammbildung und Flexion der idg. Personalpronomina*, 1978; see Seebold, *Krat* 23, 1979, 63–71.
Schmidt, Johannes, *Die Verwandtschaftsverhältnisse der idg. Sprachen*, 1872.
——*Die Pluralbildungen der idg. Neutra*, 1889; repr. Hildesheim, 1980.
——*Die Urheimath der Indogermanen und das europäische Zahlsystem*, 1891.
——*Kritik der Sonantentheorie*, 1895.
Schmidt, Karl Horst, *Die Komposition in gallischen Personennamen*, Tübingen, 1957 (= *ZCP* 26, 33–301).
——(ed.), *Indogermanisch und Keltisch*, Wiesbaden 1977.
Schmidt, K. H., Fs. = *Indogermanica et Caucasica, Fs. K.H.S.*, 1994.
Schmitt, Rüdiger, *Dichtung und Dichtersprache in indogermanischer Zeit*, Wiesbaden, 1967.
——(ed.), *Indogermanische Dichtersprache*, Darmstadt, 1968.
——*Indogermanische Dichtersprache und Namengebung*, Innsbruck, 1973.
——*Einführung in die griechischen Dialekte*, Darmstadt, 1977.
——(ed.), *Etymologie*, Darmstadt, 1977.
——*Grammatik des Klassisch-Armenischen*, Innsbruck, 1981.
Schmitt-Brandt, Robert, *Die Entwicklung des idg. Vokalsystems*, 1967.
Schmoekel, Reinhard, *Die Hirten, die die Welt veränderten: Die Geschichte der frühen Indo-Europäer*, Hamburg 1985.
Schramm, G., *Namenschatz und Dichtersprache*, Göttingen, 1957.
Schrijver, Peter, *The Reflexes of the PIE Laryngeals in Latin*, Amsterdam 1991.
Schwyzer, Eduard, *Delectus*[3] = *Dialectorum Graecarum exempla epigraphica potiora* (3rd edn. of *Delectus inscriptionum Graecarum propter dialectum memorabilium*, ed. P. Cauer), Leipzig, 1923.
——*GG* = *Griechische Grammatik* i, 1934–9, ii (ed. A. Debrunner), Munich 1950.
SCO = *Studi Classici e Orientali*, Pisa.
ScSl = *Scando-Slavica*, Copenhagen.
SE = *Studi Etruschi*, Florence.
Seebold, Elmar, *Das System der idg. Halbvokale*, 1972; see Schindler, *Sprache* 23, 1977, 56–65.
——*Das System der Personalpronomina in den frühgermanischen Sprachen*, 1984.
SEEJ = *The Slavic and East European Journal*, Madison, Wis.
SEER = *The Slavonic and East European Review*, London.

Seiler, Hansjakob, *Steigerung* = *Die primären griechischen Steigerungsformen*, diss., Zurich, 1950.
——*L'aspect et le temps dans le verbe néo-grec*, Paris 1952.
——*Relativsatz, Attribut und Apposition*, Wiesbaden 1960; see Regula, *IF* 66, 1961, 279–88; C. Smith, 'Determiners and relative clauses', *Lg* 40, 1964, 37–52; Szemerényi, *Krat* 12. 1967, 41–52.
——(ed.), *Linguistic Workshop* i: *Vorarbeiten zu einem Universalienprojekt*, Munich, 1973; iii, 1975.
——*Sprache und Sprachen* (collected papers), Munich, 1977.
——(ed.), *Language Universals* (conference, 1976), Tübingen 1978.
SGGJ = *Sravnitel'naja grammatika germanskix jazykov*, Moscow, i–ii (1962), iii (1963), iv (1966).
SiL = *Studies in Linguistics.*
SILTA = *Studi Italiani di Linguistica Teorica ed Applicata*, Padua.
Sintagma, Madrid 1989–.
SL = *Studia Linguistica*, Lund.
SLang = *Studies in Language*, Amsterdam.
SLS = *Studies in the Linguistic Sciences*, Urbana, Ill.
SMEA = *Studi Micenei ed Egeo-Anatolici*, Rome.
SO = *Symbolae Osloenses.*
SOL = *Studi Orientali e Linguistici*, Bologna.
Sommer, Ferdinand, *Handbuch der lateinischen Laut- und Formenlehre*, 2nd edn., 1914; pt. i was re-edited in 1977 as F. Sommer and Raimund Pfister, *Handbuch* i, *Lautlehre.*
——*Kritische Erläuterungen zur lat. Laut- und Formenlehre*, 1914.
——*Hethiter und Hethitisch*, 1947.
——*Zur Geschichte der griechischen Nominalkomposita*, 1948.
Sommer, Fs. = *Corolla Linguistica, Fs. für F.S.*, Wiesbaden 1955.
SPAW = *Sitzungsberichte der Preussischen Akademie der Wissenschaften*, Berlin.
Specht, Franz, *Ursprung* = *Ursprung der idg. Deklination*, 1944; repr. 1962.
SPIL = *Stellenbosch Papers in Linguistics.*
Sprache, Vienna, 1949– .
SS = *Slovo a Slovesnost*, Prague.
SSL = *Studi e Saggi Linguistici*, Pisa.
Stang, Christian S., *Vgl. Gram.* = *Vergleichende Grammatik der baltischen Sprachen*, Oslo 1966.
Starke, Frank, *Die Funktionen der dimensionalen Kasus und Adverbien im Althethitischen*, Wiesbaden 1977.
——*Untersuchung zur Stammbildung des keilschrift-luwischen Nomens*, Wiesbaden 1990; see Melchert, *HS* 105 (1993), 309–12.
Strunk, Klaus, *Nas.* = *Nasalpräsentien und Aoriste*, 1967.
——*Zum Postulat 'vorhersagbaren' Sprachwandels bei unregelmässigen oder komplexen Flexionsparadigmen*, Munich, 1991.
——'Rekonstruktionsprobleme', *Fachtagung* 9, 1994, 374–402.
——(ed.), *Probleme der lateinischen Grammatik*, 1973.
Sturtevant, Edgar H., *The Pronunciation of Greek and Latin*, Philadelphia,

1940; 2nd edn. Groningen 1968.

——*The Indo-Hittite Laryngeals*, Baltimore 1942.

——1951 = E. H. Sturtevant and E. Adelaide Hahn, *A Comparative Grammar of the Hittite Language* i; rev. edn. New Haven, Conn., 1951. In *Lg* 28, 1952, 422 n. 19, Hahn warns that this volume was entirely Sturtevant's; she was to have written ii on Syntax.

Szemerényi, Oswald John Louis, *Numerals* = *Studies in the IE System of Numerals*, Heidelberg 1960.

——'*Auhuma*' = 'Gothic *auhuma* and the so-called comparatives in *-uma*', *PBB(T)* 82, 1960, 1–30 (=*SM* 2212–41).

——'Principles of etymological research in the IE languages', *Fachtagung* 2 (1962), 175–212; repr. in R. Schmitt, *Etymologie*, 1977, 286–346 (=*SM* 40–77).

——*Trends* = *Trends and Tasks in Comparative Philology* (inaugural lecture, 23 Oct. 1961), London 1962 (=*SM* 21–39).

——'Structuralism' = 'Structuralism and Substratum: Indo-Europeans and Semites in the Ancient Near East', *Lingua* 13, 1964, 1–29 (=*SM* 78–106).

——*Syncope in Greek and IE and the Nature of IE Accent*, Naples, 1964.

——'Development of the *-o-/-ā-* stems in the light of the Mycenaean evidence', *Coll. Myc.* 4, 1966, 217–25 (=*SM* 1244–52).

——'New Look' = 'The new look of IE: reconstruction and typology' (inaugural lecture, 25 Nov. 1966), *Phonetica* 17, 1967, 65–99 (=*SM* 123–57).

——'Comparative' = 'The Mycenaean and the historical Greek comparative and their IE background', in *Studia Mycenaea*, ed. A. Bartoněk, Brno 1968, 25–36 (=*SM* 1326–37).

——'Methodology' = 'Methodology of Genetic Linguistics', in *Enzyklopädie der geisteswissenschaftlichen Arbeitsmethoden*, pt. 4: *Methoden der Sprachwissenschaft*, Munich and Oldenburg 1968, 3–38.

——'Rückverwandlung' = 'The Attic "Rückverwandlung", or Atomism and Structuralism in action', in *Gedenkschrift für W. Brandenstein*, 1968, 139–57 (=*SM* 1338–56).

——*Einführung in die vergleichende Sprachwissenschaft*, Darmstadt 1970; 3rd completely rev. edn. 1989; 4th edn. 1991. Spanish translation 1978; Russian, 1980; Italian, 1985.

——*kēr* = 'The name of the "heart"', in *Donum Balticum to C. S. Stang*, Stockholm 1970, 515–33 (=*SM* 172–90).

——*Richtungen der modernen Sprachwissenschaft* i (1916–50), Heidelberg, 1971; Spanish translation 1979.

——'Comparative linguistics', in *CTL* ix, 1972, 119–95.

——'La théorie des laryngales de Saussure à Kuryłowicz et à Benveniste: essai de réévaluation', *BSL* 68, 1973, 1–25 (=*SM* 191–215).

——'A Gaulish dedicatory formula', *KZ* 88, 1975, 246–86 (=*SM* 216–56).

——'Problems of the formation and gradation of Latin adjectives', in *Studies L. R. Palmer*, 1976, 401–24 (=*SM* 978–1001).

——'Kinship' = 'Studies in the kinship terminology of the IE languages', *Varia* 1977 (= *Acta Iranica* 16), 1978, 1–240.

——Review of K. H. Schmidt, *Die festlandkeltischen Sprachen*, Innsbruck

1977, *ZCP* 36, 1978, 293–7.
——'Vedic *šam* ...', *InL* 4, 1978, 159–84 (=*SM* 1725–50).
——'About unrewriting the history of linguistics', *Fs. Hj. Seiler*, 1980, 151–62 (=*SM* 355–66).
——*Richtungen der modernen Sprachwissenschaft* ii (1950–60), 1982; Spanish translation 1986.
——1985 = 'Recent developments in IE linguistics', *TPS* 1985, 1–71 (= *SM* 396–466, *Addenda* 466).
——'Syntax, meaning and origin of the IE particle k^we', *Fs. H. Gipper* ii, 1985, 747–75 (= *SM* 367–95).
——*SM* = *Scripta Minora* i–iii, Innsbruck 1987; iv and v (*Word Index*), 1992.
——*An den Quellen des lateinischen Wortschatzes*, Innsbruck 1989.
——*Summing Up a Life*, HochschulVerlag, Freiburg 1992.
Szemerényi, Fs.[1] =*Festschrift* i–ii, ed. B. Brogyanyi, 1979.
Szemerényi, Fs.[2] =*Festschrift* i–iii, ed. B. Brogyanyi and R. Lipp, 1992–3.
TAPA = *Transactions and Proceedings of the American Philological Association*, Chico, Calif.
TCLP = *Travaux du Cercle Linguistique de Prague*, 1929–39.
Thumb, Albert, and Hauschild, Richard, *Handbuch des Sanskrit* i/1–2, 1958–9.
Thurneysen, Rudolph, *GOI* = *Grammar of Old Irish*, Dublin 1946.
TIES = *Tocharian and IE Studies*, Reykjavik, 1–6, 1987–93.
Tipologija = *Tipologija i vzaimodeistvije slavjanskix i germanskix jazykov*, Minsk 1969.
TL = *Theoretical Linguistics*, Berlin.
TLL = *Travaux de Linguistique et de Littérature*, Strasburg.
TLP = *Travaux Linguistiques de Prague*, 1966–.
TPS = *Transactions of the Philological Society*, Oxford.
Trubetzkoy, N. S., *Grundzüge der Phonologie*, 1939; 3rd edn. 1962.
Tucker, Elizabeth Fawcett, *The Creation of Morphological Regularity: Early Greek Verbs in -éō, -áō, -óō, -úō and -íō*, Göttingen 1990.
UAJb = *Ural-Altaische Jahrbücher*, Wiesbaden and Bloomington, Ind.
Untermann, Jürgen, Fs. = *Sprachen und Schriften des antiken Mittelmeerraums, Fs. für J. U.*, Innsbruck 1993.
Vaillant, André, *Gram. comp.* = *Grammaire comparée des langues slaves* i–v, 1950–77.
VDI = *Vestnik Drevnej Istorii*, Moscow.
Vennemann, Theo, *Preference Laws for Syllable Structure and the Explanation of Sound Change*, Berlin 1988.
——(ed.), *The New Sound of IE*, Berlin 1989; see Szemerényi, *Diachronica* 6/2, 1990, 237–69.
Villar Liebana, Francisco, *Orígen de la flexión nominal indoeuropea*, Madrid 1974.
——*Dativo y locativo en el singular de la flexión indoeuropea*, Salamanca 1981.
——*Ergatividad, acusatividad y género en la familia lingüística indoeuropea*, Salamanca 1983.
——*Los indoeuropeos y los orígenes de Europa: lenguaje e historia*, Madrid 1991.

Vineis, E. (ed.), *Le lingue ie. di frammentaria attestazione/Die idg. Restsprachen*, Pisa 1983.
VJ = *Voprosy Jazykoznanija*, Moscow.
VSJ = *Voprosy Slavjanskogo Jazykoznanija*, Moscow.
Wackernagel, J. and Debrunner, A., *Ai. Gr.* = *Altindische Grammatik* i, ii/1–2, iii, Göttingen, 1896–1954.
Wackernagel Kolloquium (1988), 1990; see *Krat* 37, 1992, 45–53.
Wagner, Heinrich, *Das Hethitische vom Standpunkte der typologischen Sprachgeographie*, Pisa 1985.
Watkins, Calvert, *Origins* = *The Origins of the Celtic Verb* i, Dublin 1962.
——*Verb* = *Indogermanische Grammatik* iii/1: *Geschichte der idg. Verbalflexion*, 1969; cf. 3. 2 n. 7 in the main text.
——'The language of the Trojans', in M. J. Mellink (ed.), *Troy and the Trojan War*, 1986, 45–62.
——*Selected Writings* i: *Language and Linguistics*; ii: *Etymology, Culture and Poetics*, 1994.
van Windekens, Memoriae = *Studia etymologica Indoeuropea memoriae A. J. van Windekens (1915–1989) dicata*, ed. L. Isebaert, Louvain 1991.
Windisch, Rudolf, 'Zwischen Substratomanie und Substratophobie', in *Fs. Szemerényi*[2] ii, (1992), 339–52; for the question whether Lat. *ū* > Fr. *ü* is due to Celtic influence, note (against) that in my view a similar change is taking place in English—without any Celtic influence.
Winter, Werner, 'Vocative' = 'Vocative and Imperative', in Puhvel 1969, 205–23.
WJA = *Würzburger Jahrbücher für die Altertumswissenschaft*.
Woudhuizen, Fred, *The Language of the Sea Peoples*, Amsterdam 1992.
WPLUH, see *Hawaii Papers*.
WuS = *Wörter und Sachen*, Heidelberg, 1–23, 1909–44.
Wyatt, William F., *IE /a/*, Philadelphia 1970.
Yoshida, Kazuhiko, *The Hittite Medio-passive Endings in '-ri'*, Amsterdam, 1990; see Eichner, *IC* 34, 1992, 388–90.
ZA = *Zeitschrift für Assyriologie*, Berlin.
ŽA = *Živa Antika*, Skopje.
ZCP = *Zeitschrift für celtische Philologie*, Tübingen.
ZDL = *Zeitschrift für Dialektologie und Linguistik*, Wiesbaden.
ZDMG = *Zeitschrift der Deutschen Morgenländischen Gesellschaft*, Stuttgart.
ZDS = *Zeitschrift für deutsche Sprache*, Berlin.
ZFSL = *Zeitschrift für französische Sprache und Literatur*, Wiesbaden.
ZII = *Zeitschrift für Indologie und Iranistik*, Leipzig, 1–10, 1922–36.
ZMf = *Zeitschrift für Mundartforschung*, Wiesbaden; from 1969 changed to *ZDL*.
ZPhon, *ZPSK* = *Zeitschrift für Phonetik, Sprachwissenschaft und Kommunikationsforschung*, Berlin.
ZRP(h) = *Zeitschrift für romanische Philologie*, Tübingen.
ZSP = *Zeitschrift für slavische Philologie*, Heidelberg.
Zwolanek, Renée, *'Vā́yav Índraśca': Studien zu Anrufungsformen*, Munich 1970.

Languages Cited

Aeol.	Aeolic
Ar.	Aryan
Arc.	Arcadian
Arm.	Armenian
Att.	Attic
Avest.	Avestan
Balt.	Baltic
Boeot.	Boeotian
Celt.	Celtic
CLuw.	Cuneiform Luwian
Cypr.	Cyprian
Dor.	Doric
Eng.	English
Falisc.	Faliscan
Finn.	Finnish
Fr.	French
Gath.	Gathic
Gaul.	Gaulish
Gmc.	Germanic
Goth.	Gothic
Gr.	Greek
Grm.	German
Hitt.	Hittite
Hom.	Homeric
Idg.	Indogermanisch
IE	Indo-European
Iran.	Iranian
Ital.	Italian
Lat.	Latin
Lett.	Lettish
Lith.	Lithuanian
Luw.	Luwian
MDu.	Middle Dutch
MHG	Middle High German
MIr.	Middle Irish
MLG	Middle Low German
MW	Middle Welsh
Myc.	Mycenaean
NE	New English
NHG	New High German
NPers.	New Persian
OCS	Old Church Slavic
OE	Old English
OHG	Old High German
OIce.	Old Icelandic
OInd.	Old Indic
OIr.	Old Irish
OIran.	Old Iranian
OLat.	Old Latin
OLith.	Old Lithuanian
ON	Old Norse
OPers.	Old Persian
OPrus.	Old Prussian
ORuss.	Old Russian
OSax.	Old Saxon
Osc.	Oscan
OW	Old Welsh
Pamph.	Pamphylian
Phryg.	Phrygian
Russ.	Russian
Semit.	Semitic
Serb.	Serbian
Serb.-Cr.	Serbo-Croat
Skt.	Sanskrit
Slav.	Slavic
Thess.	Thessalian
Toch.	Tocharian
Umbr.	Umbrian
Ved.	Vedic
W.	Welsh

1

Introduction

1.1. SIMILARITIES BETWEEN LANGUAGES IN VOCABULARY

Anyone who in addition to his own language is familiar with a foreign language will, in suitable cases, perceive not only unsurprising dissimilarities but also remarkable similarities between them. An English speaker studying German needs no instruction to observe that German *Vater*, *Mutter*, *Hand*, *Eis* sound very much like *father*, *mother*, *hand*, *ice* in his own language. In the same way, an Italian learning Spanish cannot long remain unaware that Spanish *padre*, *madre*, *mano*, *pie* are identical, or nearly so, with the corresponding words in Italian. A Russian travelling in other Slavonic countries will soon notice that the words *ruka* 'hand', *noga* 'foot', *zima* 'winter', etc., of his native speech are the same or similar in most other Slavic languages.

In view of the early Greeks' reputation for unbounded curiosity we should, on the basis of our own experience, expect them to have made similar observations. We are, however, disappointed in this respect. It is, of course, not surprising that they failed to discover resemblances, obvious as these are to us, between their language and Latin, since Latin came too late into their field of view. They might, however, with justice have been expected to detect similarities between their own language and that of their inveterate enemies, the Persians. Nothing of the sort is recorded, although, as we now know, such resemblances could easily have been recognized: to Greek πατήρ, μάτηρ, ἐστί correspond Persian *pitā* (acc. *pitar-am*), *mātā* (acc. *mātar-am*), *asti*. Even so, it is interesting that Plato in his dialogue *Kratylos* (410[a]) proposes to derive Greek πῦρ, ὕδωρ, κύων and 'many other words' from Phrygian, on the grounds that they had almost the same form in that language and were not easily explicable within Greek. The linguistic achievement of the general Epaminondas is, however, much more impressive. According to Athenaeus (13, 650f.) he based the claim of his native city, Thebes, to the district of Sidai on the boundary of

Boeotia and Attica on the fact that *σίδα* 'pomegranate' was a Boeotian word, for which the Athenians used *ῥοιά*. This shows, as do various dialect scenes in Aristophanes' comedies, that the Greeks had a keen ear for language distinctions, at least within the field of Greek, and we can only regret that, unlike Napoleon, who took scholars with him on his Egyptian campaign, Alexander the Great included no expert in linguistics among the men of learning who accompanied him to Asia as members of his staff.

What was said above about the Greeks in relation to Latin applies only to the pre-Hellenistic period. When the Greeks really came to know the new language, they must have quickly recognized its resemblances to their own. The Romans, too, saw that Latin *sex septem* corresponded to Greek *ἕξ ἑπτά*, and, assuming that the early Romans substituted *s* for the Greek aspirate, regarded *silua* as corresponding to *ὕλη*: '*ὕλας* dicunt et nos *siluas*, item *ἕξ sex* et *ἑπτά septem*' (Festus, 392). Hence some drew the conclusion that Latin was a Greek dialect. A few went further, considering Latin to be an Aeolic dialect, since the so-called recessive accent of Aeolic ('barytonesis') was very similar to that of Latin.[1]

[1] Cf. Athenaeus 10, 425[a]. On this point see also Gabba, 'Il latino come dialetto greco' in *Miscellanea A. Rostagni*, 1965, 188–94; I. Opelt, 'La coscienza linguistica dei Romani', *Atene e Roma* 14, 1969, 21–37, esp. 33f.; Leumann in Hofman–Szantyr 1965, *Allgemeiner Teil*, 23* §15; Pisani, *L'etimologia*[2], 34; M. Tavoni, 'On the Renaissance idea that Latin derives from Greek', *ASNP* 18, 1986, 205–38.

1.2. SIMILARITIES IN GRAMMATICAL STRUCTURE

In the languages mentioned it is possible to establish similarities not only of vocabulary (the so-called lexical correspondences) but also of grammar. Clearly the correspondence between English *love–loved–loved* and German *lieben–liebte–geliebt* is no less striking than that between *father* and *Vater* or *ice* and *Eis*. When an Italian uses the construction *ho cantato* as the past tense of *cantare* 'to sing' and a Spaniard says *he cantado*, the agreement in structure is obvious, as it is in another form of the past tense, Italian *cantavo/cantavi/cantava* and Spanish *cantaba/cantabas/cantaba*.

It is surprising that such structural similarities passed so long unnoticed, or at least unrecorded. We hear of no observations of this kind in ancient times. The medieval and early modern periods also simply ignored them.[1] Even the astonishing Joseph Justus Scaliger (1540–1609), who had the insight to anticipate the idea of linguistic relationship and accordingly recognized in Europe eleven mutually independent 'mother tongues' (including a 'deus-language', i.e.

Romance, and a 'god-language', i.e. Germanic), did not go beyond lexical comparisons (Arens[2], 74). The time had not yet come for a true understanding of the idea of language comparison.

In the same way, the idea of historical development was no more than a promise for the future. The changes occurring in the development of Latin word forms to Romance continued to be formulated in the artificial terminology of antiquity, and in the seventeenth century and even later the use of terms such as addition, subtraction, transposition, and inversion of letters (see 2.1) was taken for granted, as it had been by Quintilian. Before him, Aristotle had shown a similar lack of perceptivity in dealing with language changes in the historical period (*Poetics* 1458[a]). Finding in Homer πόληος, Πηληιάδεω, he explains them as produced by lengthening from πόλεως, Πηλείδου, the forms of his own day; Homeric κρῖ, δῶ, and ὄψ were in his view shortened from κριθή, δῶμα, ὄψις. It does not trouble him that Homeric forms, in use at least five centuries before his own time, are thus derived from later forms. In fact for him language is unchangeable, and if in spite of this changes appear to occur they are to be explained as instances of arbitrary poetic licence.

[1] The statement of H. Ludolf (d. 1704) that linguistic relationship is revealed by the grammar, not the vocabulary (see *H. Schuchardt-Brevier*, 1928, 198), is an exception; a doctrine still fairly generally held, it has been repeatedly disputed by Mańczak (e.g. *HS* 103, 1991, 178f.).

1.3. THE FOUNDATION OF COMPARATIVE LINGUISTICS

This was the position until the end of the eighteenth and beginning of the nineteenth century. Two circumstances contributed to changing it. First, the idea of comparison had established itself in a number of disciplines, most conspicuously in 'comparative anatomy'. In 1787 Christian Jakob Kraus (1753–1807) postulated that in all languages 'the main general features of structure as well as the particular case endings of nouns, degrees of comparison of adjectives, conjugation of verbs, word order in affirmative and negative statements and questions' should be collected and set out (most aptly on loose cards, perhaps!) in such a way that 'each language may be compared with each other language in any way desired' (Arens[2], 143).

As early as 1781 Johann Christoph Adelung (1732–1806) had laid down precise criteria for different degrees of language relationship:

If two languages agree with one another in their root words and inflexional and derivational syllables, overall with only a few exceptions, and the differences affect only vowels ... and related consonants, they are merely *dialects* of one another. ... If there are marked differences in their inflexional and derivational syllables, they are merely *related* languages. Completely different kinds of derivation and inflexion together with a marked difference in the roots and their meaning indicate more or less *distinct* languages. (Arens[2], 149f.)

This doctrine requires comparison of grammatical structure as well as of the 'roots and their meaning', i.e. of vocabulary; the resemblances and discrepancies in structure, not as hitherto in vocabulary alone, are decisive for the degree of relationship.[1]

The second factor leading to the overthrow of traditional concepts, and so to the foundation of modern linguistics, was the intensive study of Sanskrit, the old literary language of India. After many occasional references by other writers to similarities with European languages, Sir William Jones (1746–94), High Court Judge in Fort William, Bengal, succeeded in reaching a truly novel and liberating view. In a lecture of 1786, but not published until 1788, he briefly summarized the new discovery:

The Sanscrit language, whatever be its antiquity, is of a wonderful structure; more perfect than the Greek, more copious than the Latin, and more exquisitely refined than either; yet bearing to both of them a stronger affinity, both in the roots of verbs and in the forms of grammar, than could possibly have been produced by accident; so strong, indeed, that no philologer could examine all three without believing them to have sprung from some common source which, perhaps, no longer exists. There is a similar reason, though not quite so forcible, for supposing that both the Gothick and the Celtick, though blended with a very different idiom, had the same origin with the Sanscrit; and the old Persian might be added to the same family.

Research on vocabulary (which is what Jones means by 'roots of verbs', since in his view nouns are derived from these) and on grammatical structure thus leads to the true interpretation of language relationship: if a number of languages agree to an adequate extent in both these respects, the only possible explanation is that they derive from a common ancestral source, which itself may no longer exist, and are in this sense genetically related. In other words, genetically related languages are divergent developments of a common original language.

In spite of these discoveries, Sir William Jones was not seen by his contemporaries and subsequent generations as the founder of the new science. The reason lies not only in the circumstances of the time—the French Revolution and the Napoleonic Wars—and his own early death, but in the fact that the idea he put forward was a preliminary outline rather than a thesis fully supported by evidence and argument. The same must be said of Friedrich von Schlegel (1772–1829), who, similarly enlightened by the study of Sanskrit, employed the name 'comparative grammar' (*vergleichende Grammatik*) for the new science in his book *Über die Sprache und Weisheit der Indier* (1808):[2]

The old Indian Sonskrito [*sic*] has the closest relationship with the Roman and Greek as well as with the Germanic and Persian languages. The similarity is not merely found in the great number of roots which it has in common with them, but extends to the innermost structure and grammar. The correspondence is therefore not accidental, to be explained as due to intermixture, but essential, pointing to a common origin. (Arens², 160)

This is in much the same terms as Jones's statement. Schlegel goes further, however; he gives an indication, brief though it is, of the method of the new comparative grammar, using Persian to exemplify it:

The declension offers very little or, more precisely, nothing. ... The conjugation much more; the mark of the first person is *m*, which has disappeared in Latin but has the fuller form *mi* in Indic and Greek; from *si* of the second person in Indic and Greek only *i* remains; the mark of the third person is *t* or *d*, plural *nd*, as in Latin and German; Greek has the fuller *ti* and *nti*, following the earlier form. The Persian present active participle in *ndeh* is like the German in *nd*, early *nde*. (Arens², 162)

The method presented in this passage, and what follows it, in a sketchy and programmatic form was set out by a younger scholar who left nothing to be desired in his full and convincing treatment of the subject. It is no wonder that contemporaries and subsequent generations alike have celebrated Franz Bopp (1791–1867) as the true founder of comparative linguistics. In his renowned work *Konjugationssystem*, published in 1816, Bopp set himself the aim of showing how, in the Old Indic conjugation, 'the determinations of relationship are expressed by corresponding modifications of the roots, and how at times the *uerbum abstractum* [i.e. "to be"] coalesces with the stem syllable to form a single word', and that the same was the case in Greek and Latin, and finally, of proving 'that in all those languages which derive from Sanskrit or together with Sanskrit from a common mother, no determination of a relationship is expressed by an inflexion which they do not have in common with that ancestral language'. It is indispensable, he says, 'above all to familiarize ourselves with the conjugational system of the Old Indic language and then to make a thorough comparison of the conjugations of the Greek, Roman, Germanic, and Persian languages, whereby we perceive their identity' (Arens², 176).

It is evident that Bopp is no theoretician. He offers no general reflections on how language relationship is to be understood and how it is to be proved. He treats as established and requiring no proof not only the concept of language relationship but also the existence of such a relationship, in the sense of a common origin, between the languages which he has investigated. What he seeks to prove is something quite different. It is that all these languages exhibit a common structure, and furthermore that all the material components of that structure, roots, endings, etc., are identical. The concept of language relation, as can be seen from the statements of C. J. Kraus and J. C. Adelung quoted above, had long been in the air. Instead of these vague theoretic generalities Bopp erected a firm edifice which by its very existence—an existence which it owes to Bopp—became the compelling proof of a language relationship which had formerly been a mere assumption. As a method, its influence continues to the present day.

The two supporting pillars of Bopp's teaching, agreement in grammatical structure and in the language material which bears the structure, still stand. The relationship of, say, the Polynesian languages or certain Amerindian languages can, even today, be demonstrated only with the aid of these principles. Both are of equal importance. Agreement in grammatical structure alone, without agreement in the language material embodying it, as we can see, for example, in a comparison of Hungarian with Turkish noun inflexion, is inadequate to prove genetic connections.[3]

[1] It must, however, be pointed out that the basic truths concerning linguistic relationship were clearly established, and in particular the closeness, even identity, of Hungarian and Lappish (the language of the Lapps in the far north) was demonstrated, with the help of grammatical structure and lexicon, as far back as 1770 by the Hungarian Jesuit János Sajnovics in *Demonstratio idioma Ungarorum et Lapponum idem esse* (Copenhagen). In 1799 Samuel Gyarmathi published his much more comprehensive work, *Affinitas linguae Hungaricae cum linguis Fennicae originis grammatice demonstrata* (Göttingen), which extended the relationship to the whole of the Finno-Ugric group. The two Hungarian scholars are now generally recognized as the founders of the historico-comparative method; see Robins, *A Short History of Linguistics*, 170 (but erroneous on Gyarmathi); Szemerényi, *SM* i, 514; B. Wickman, *UAJb* NS 4, 1984, 224. According to G. J. Stipa, *Finnisch-Ugrische Sprachforschung: Von der Renaissance bis zum Neopositivismus*, Helsinki 1990, Sebastian Münster discovered in 1544 that Finnish, Estonian, and Lappish were related; see L. Campbell, *Lg* 68, 1992, 186f.

[2] The term 'comparative grammar' (*vergleichende Grammatik*) was not, however, coined by Friedrich von Schlegel, but occurs as early as 1803 in a review by his brother August Wilhelm; see Aarsleff, *The Study of Language in England 1780–1860*, 1967, 157 n. 115. The expressions *vergleichende Sprachlehre* and *vergleichendes Sprachstudium* used by Vater (see Koerner, *LeS* 22, 1987, 347) have a different meaning.

[3] On the roles of Jones and Bopp, see Szemerényi 1980; R. Sternemann, *Franz Bopp und die vgl. ie. Sprachwissenschaft*, Innsbruck 1984; R. H. Robins, 'The life and work of Sir William Jones', *TPS* 1987, 1–23; Schlerath, 'Franz Bopp', in M. Erbe (ed.), *Berlinische Lebensbilder Geisteswissenschaftler*, 1989, 55–72; Garland Cannon, *The Life and Mind of Oriental Jones*, Cambridge, 1990; and, in general, S. N. Mukherjee, *Sir William Jones: A Study in Eighteenth Century British Attitudes to India*², London 1987.

On etymology and language comparison before Bopp, see Hiersche, *Fs. Knobloch*, 1985, 157–65.

On the significance of Sanskrit—the first extensive comparison of which with Latin and several oriental languages by Paulinus a S. Bartholomaeo (*Dissertatio*, 1802) was republished in 1977 by L. Rocher—see Mayrhofer, 'Sanskrit und die Sprachen Alteuropas', *GGN* 1983 (5); its 'liberating' effect is (wrongly) disputed by Bernabé, 'El descubrimiento del sánscrito', *RSEL* 13, 1983, 41–62.

On measuring linguistic relationship, see J. Kristophson, 'Zur Messbarkeit von Sprachverwandtschaft', *FoLH* 4/2, 1984, 311–20.

1.4. THE FOUNDATION OF HISTORICAL LINGUISTICS

Language comparison cannot, however, be the first step in our endeavours. Anyone with a command of English and German alone might, on the basis of the principles established above, be tempted to conclude from the current forms *house*, *mouse*, *louse* and *Haus*, *Maus*, *laus* that the common original forms were *haus*, *maus*, *laus*. Thanks to the availability, however, of copious linguistic evidence covering a period of more than a thousand years, we know that the ancient forms had *ū*, not *au*, and must in consequence have been *hūs*, *mūs*, *lūs*.

It can accordingly be stated as a general methodological principle that language comparison in the sense indicated above can be undertaken only when the fullest possible use has been made of the historical study of language. The importance of this viewpoint was already recognized by Schlegel in *Über die Sprache und Weisheit der Indier*, where he allows in etymological research 'no kind of rules for the changing or transposition of letters' such as had been the practice in antiquity and still was in his own time, but demands 'complete similarity of the word for proof of derivation. Of course, if the intermediate stages can be historically demonstrated, then *giorno* can be derived from *dies*. ... But one must, as has been said, be able to prove by historical methods the intermediate forms or the general analogy; there must be no inventing of fictions on the basis of principles.' He recognized equally clearly that for the purpose of language comparison the earliest stages of languages are to be used. Modern English or German is not to be compared with Latin or Greek, but recourse must be had to Old English or Gothic (Arens², 161f.).

The true founder of historical linguistics is rightly considered to have been Jacob Grimm (1785–1863). In his four-volume work *Deutsche Grammatik* (1819–37) he had the clear aim of producing a 'historical grammar of the German language' (he here uses 'German' in the sense of 'Germanic'). Consequently he deals with all the Germanic languages, and gives a systematic account one after another of the earliest, middle, and modern phases of the various Germanic languages, beginning with Gothic and ending with Modern English. The result is, in fact, a grammar both historical and comparative. (See D. Cherubim, 'Hat J. Grimm die historische Sprachwissenschaft begründet?' *ZPSK* 38 (1985), 672–85.)

Quite different was the development of research in the field of the classical languages. Initially and for many decades Latin and Greek were compared with Sanskrit and other languages, while their internal history was neglected and left to classical scholars. Not until the end of the last century was it recognized and repeatedly emphasized, especially by Paul Kretschmer (1866–1956), that a historical study of these languages was the natural prerequisite for their comparative study.[1]

[1] The slow and tentative progress of the struggle with the problems of language, which goes back more than 2,000 years, can be followed with the help of the large selection of aptly chosen excerpts from the original authorities in H. Arens, *Sprachwissenschaft: der Gang ihrer Entwicklung von der Antike bis zur Gegenwart*[2], Freiburg 1969. See also Mounin, *Histoire de la linguistique des origines au XXe siècle*, and *La linguistique du XXe siècle*; Robins, *A Short History of linguistics*, London 1967, and *Ancient and Mediaeval Grammatical Theory in Europe*, London 1951; G. Sampson, *Schools of Linguistics*, London 1980; O. Amsterdamska, *Schools of Thought (from Bopp to Saussure)*, Dordrecht 1987.

Among earlier works, special mention should be made of Pedersen, *Linguistic Science in the Nineteenth Century*, Cambridge, Mass., 1931, (repr. in paperback as *The Discovery of Language*, Bloomington, Ind., 1962). See also G. Lepschy, *A Survey of Structural Linguistics*, London 1970; Milka Ivić, *Trends in Linguistics* (from Serbian), 1965; on the German translation (1971), see Christmann, *Krat* 18, 1976, 6–11 (numerous mistakes); M. Leroy, *Les grands courants de la linguistique moderne*[2], Brussels 1971 (see Koerner, *GL* 13, 1973, 54–6, and on the English translation of 1967 Lyons, *Lg* 45, 1969, 105–8). On histories published 1962–74, see Koerner, *HL* 1. 1974.

Leading personalities seen through the eyes of later generations are presented in T. A. Sebeok, *Portraits of Linguists* i–ii, 1966.

For Indo-European studies the distinguished work of Gauger et al., *Einführung in die romanische Sprachwissenschaft*, provides significant parallels; for the subjects discussed above, see there 17–28, 45f.

1.5. AIMS OF COMPARATIVE LINGUISTICS

These two complementary lines of research have also a common character, in that both make use of the comparative method. While historical study involves comparison of different chronological sections of the same language, comparative linguistics investigates different languages with regard to their earlier, prehistoric connections.[1]

Such researches have a twofold aim. The first is to restore or reconstruct the hypothetical original language, using the comparative method. When this has been achieved as far as possible, it is the researcher's second task to show how the individual languages have evolved from it in a development lasting for centuries or even millennia. The dual direction of this objective recalls a famous passage in Plato's *Republic*. In the unforgettable section on the Divided Line (509^{d}–511^{e}) he describes how the seeker after truth is able to rise 'as far as the underived first principle and starting-point of all, and after grasping that ... descends again to the conclusion' (511^{b}). So for the comparative linguist the individual languages are the 'footholds and starting-points', by means of which he can make his way back to the beginning of them all and then, having taken hold of the beginning, can understand and explain the special features of each.[2]

[1] On the comparative method down to the Neogrammarians, see Szemerényi 1971, 11–17; R. Wells in H. Hoenigswald (ed.), *The European Background of American Linguistics*, 1979, 23–61; on views about linguistic change, see R. Windisch, *Zum Sprachwandel: Von den Junggrammatikern zu Labov*, Berne 1988.

[2] On the terms 'comparative', 'diachronic', 'historical', see Heger, *Fs. Winter*, 1985, 333–45.

1.6. ITS SUBJECT-MATTER: THE INDO-EUROPEAN LANGUAGES

Now that we have sketched in broad outline the aim of the comparative study which is the main concern of this book, we must proceed to define more closely its subject-matter, namely the languages which are to be compared.

In his earliest work Bopp dealt with only five languages, Sanskrit (Indic), Persian (Iranian), Greek, Latin, and Germanic, which can be regarded as the founder-members, so to speak, of the language family named after them 'Indo-Germanic', and which even today constitute the basic equipment of the Indo-Europeanist.[1] Later, but in some cases by Bopp himself, many other languages were recognized as belonging to the family, including Celtic and Albanian. Our century has added a number of languages, the former existence of which was previously unknown. Of especial significance is the discovery of the Anatolian group in Asia Minor, of which Hittite is the chief representative, and of Tocharian in Central Asia.

Although it is impossible to review here in any detail the members of the Indo-European language family, it seems appropriate at least to enumerate them briefly.[2]

1. *Aryan* includes *Indic* (more accurately *Indo-Aryan*, since not all the languages of India are Indo-European) and *Iranian*, both known at least from the middle of the first millennium BC. On their background see A. Parpola, 'The coming of the Aryans', *Studia Orientalia* 64, 1988, 195–302; cf. Tischler, *ZDMG* 140, 1990, 397–8; Kuiper, *Aryans in the Rigveda* Amsterdam 1991. Note also Gamkrelidze and Ivanov, 'Die Indo-Europäer', in *Ursprache und Urheimat*, Moscow and Leipzig 1990, 80: 'Biology confirms that Indo-Iranians came to India from the Near East. Only in this case could malaria [!] not have harmed them.' On *Ossetic*, see Christol, *LALIES* 8, 1990, 7–50.

2. *Armenian*, known from a translation of the Bible and other works since the fifth century AD.

3. *Anatolian* is the earliest attested branch of Indo-European. Its

documents go back to the Hittite Old Kingdom, some perhaps as far as the eighteenth century BC. The best-known and therefore for us the most important language of this group is *Hittite*, but the more archaic *Luwian* is also historically significant and now more readily accessible. Closely related to Luwian is *Hieroglyphic Hittite*, a language used in hieroglyphic inscriptions of the late Hittite and post-Hittite periods, especially in northern Syria. In the northern area of the Hittite empire in Asia Minor, with its centre at Hattusa (modern Boghazköy) to the east of Ankara, *Palaic* was spoken. Recent researches have revealed that the languages of western Asia Minor known from the first millennium BC, *Lycian*, *Lydian*, and probably also *Carian*, were likewise descendants of Hittite or Luwian. Recently there have even been attempts to connect *Etruscan*, directly or at least indirectly, with Anatolian (cf. Beekes, *Fs. Rix*, 1993, 46–51, and for the texts Rix, *Etruskische Texte*, ed. minor, i–ii, Tübingen 1991), and the language of the Trojans (!) has also been claimed as a member of the Anatolian group (Watkins 1986; see Bader, *BSL* 82/2, 1987, 202f.). On the so-called 'sea peoples', see Woudhuizen 1992.

4. *Tocharian* is known in two dialects designated A and B or East and West Tocharian, or Agnean (=A, language of Agni, Turfan-Quarašahr area) and Kuchean (=B, language of Kučva). They are attested in manuscripts of the second half of the first millennium AD from Chinese Turkestan.

5. *Greek*, recorded in a multiplicity of dialects, of which the literary dialects, above all Attic-Ionic, are of especial importance for Indo-European studies. Until the early 1950s the history of Greek began with Homer; since then the decipherment of the Linear B script has pushed back our horizon by half a millennium. For general literature see Schwyzer, *GG* i–ii; L. R. Palmer, *The Greek Language*, London, 1980.

6. *Italic* is principally represented by *Latin*, whose beginnings have long been seen in two inscriptions of the sixth century BC; but the Praenestine brooch, formerly dated *c.*600 BC, has turned out to be a forgery. Most closely related to Latin is *Faliscan*, on which see B. D. Joseph and R. E. Wallace, 'Is Faliscan a local Latin patois?' *Diachronica* 8/2 (1991), 159–86. The so-called Italic dialects, likewise known from inscriptions, are also important, especially *Oscan* and *Umbrian*; on *Sabine* see Negri, 'La lingua di Numa', in *Fs. Szemerényi*[2] ii, 229–65. On all problems of Italic see Leumann[2]; Meiser 1986; Rix (ed.) 1993.

7. *Venetic*, formerly treated as a dialect of Illyrian, has only recently been recognized as an independent language. It is now know from about 275 inscriptions. It is very closely related to the Italic group, to

which some scholars in fact assign it; cf. T. Hirunuma, 'The dialects of ancient northern Italy', *JIES* 14, 1986, 205–17 (Raetic, Venetic, Ligurian, Lepontic). For the texts, see Pellegrini and Prosdocimi, *La lingua venetica* i–ii, 1967; Anna Marinetti, *Le iscrizioni sudpicene* i: *Testi*, 1985; S. Schumacher, *Die rätischen Inschriften* Innsbruck, 1992.

8. *Celtic* embraces *Continental Celtic*—represented by *Gaulish* and now also by *Hispano-Celtic*[3]—and *Insular Celtic*, which similarly has two branches: *Goidelic*, comprising *Irish*, *Scottish Gaelic*, and the recently (since 1974) extinct *Manx*, and *Brythonic* (or simply *British*), which includes *Welsh*, *Breton*, and *Cornish*, of which the last has been extinct since 1777, when Mrs Dolly Pentreath, the last speaker of Cornish, died.[4] For British see R. W. Elsie, *The Position of Brittonic*, Bonn, 1979. On the origin of the Ogam writing of Old Irish see P. Sims-Williams, 'Deciphering the Early Irish Ogam alphabet', *TPS* 91, 1993, 133–80.

9. *Germanic*, traditionally divided into three branches:

(*a*) *East Germanic*, of which the main representative is *Gothic*, chiefly known from Wulfila's translation of the New Testament (fourth century AD).

(*b*) *West Germanic*: *High German*, *Low German*, together with *Dutch*, *English*, and *Frisian*.

(*c*) *North Germanic*: *Norwegian* and *Icelandic* (*West Norse*), *Swedish* and *Danish* (*East Norse*). Until about AD 700 the so-called *Proto-Norse* shows scarcely any dialectal divergences.

More recent theory brings (*a*) and (*c*) together in a single group to which the name *North Germanic* is given, and (*b*) above is correspondingly named *South Germanic*. For a further variant see Mańczak, *HS* 103, 1991, 95, with references.

10. *Baltic* comprises *Old Prussian*, extinct[4] since 1700 and known[5] only from a few texts (*West Baltic*), and *Lithuanian* and *Lettish* (*East Baltic*), both recorded from the sixteenth century and now enjoying a revival.

11. *Slavic* is divided into three great groups:

(*a*) *East Slavic*: *(Great) Russian*, *Ukranian* and *White Russian*.

(*b*) *West Slavic*: *Czech* and *Slovak*, *Polish*, *Sorbian*, and some minor, partly extinct, languages.

(*c*) *South Slavic*: *Bulgarian*, *Macedonian*, *Serbo-Croat*, and *Slovene*.

The oldest form of Slavic, and the most important for the comparatist, is *Old Church Slavic*, with records going back to the ninth century. In spite of displaying distinct features of Bulgarian (and also Macedonian), it is so archaic as to serve virtually as the original common Slavic.

12. *Albanian*, with two main dialects, *Tosk* and *Geg*, known since the fifteenth century.

To this round dozen of main branches of Indo-European may be added other languages attested in an extremely fragmentary state[6] from inscriptions or merely from names: *Phrygian*, *Thracian*, *Daco-Mysian*, *Illyrian* with *Messapic*, *Ligurian* (?), *Ancient Macedonian*.[7]

It is self-evident that for the purpose of language comparison the earliest period of each of these groups is the most important; e.g. Old Indic, or even the 'Oldest Indic' of the Vedas, and not the modern Indian languages such as Bengali or Hindi; Old Persian and Avestan, the sacred language of the Zarathustrian religion, and not modern Persian; Old High German, Old English, etc.

Anyone who wishes to become familiar with the problems of the Indo-European languages and to work in this field will need to start with a basic equipment of Latin, Greek, Old Indic, and Gothic, and in the course of time to add further important languages such as Hittite, Old Church Slavic, etc.

[1] As a comprehensive term for this language family, *Indo-European* was first proposed (and probably coined) in 1813 by the well-known physician Dr Thomas Young in the *London Quarterly Review* 10/2 (=no. 19), 255f., 264f.; see F. Norman, *Modern Language Review* 24, 1929, 317; Siegert, *WuS* 22, 1942, 75f. The term *Indo-Germanic* ('indogermanisch'), current especially in Germany, was until recently assumed to have its origin in the work *Asia Polyglotta* (1823) by J. Klaproth, possibly as his own abridgement of the clumsy designation 'Indisch-Medisch-Sclavisch-Germanisch', which he had used in 1810 (Siegert, 80, 89). It was shown, however, by Fred Shapiro in 1981 (*HL* 8, 165–70; cf. Koerner, *IF* 86, 1982, 13f.) that *indogermanique* had been used and perhaps actually coined as early as 1810 by a French geographer of Danish origin, Conrad Malte-Brun, as an inclusive term for the languages 'qui règnent depuis les bords du Gange jusqu'aux rivages de l'Islande'. The form *indisch-europäisch* or *indo-europäisch* is often used by Bopp (from 1833, see Siegert, 77f.) and later scholars; similarly, *Indo-Germanic* often occurs in England from 1830 onwards (Norman, 318f.). Modern usage shows a sharp division: in German *indogermanisch* is used almost without exception, in all other languages the alternative (Eng. *Indo-European*, Fr. *indo-européen*, Ital. *ind(o)europeo*, etc.). In the last century Max Müller in England preferred the term *Aryan* ('arisch'), and this was used also by H. Zimmer in Germany: 'The term Aryan is used by him instead of Indo-Germanic or Indo-European, not implying that it is more correct than they, but that it is in any event shorter and more convenient' (cited from Osthoff, *PBB* 3, 1876, 6 n.). The term is, however, legitimate only for the Indo-Iranian group (see Norman, 319; Siegert, 84f.; Szemerényi 1978, 125f.; 1992, 70), and is to be avoided as incorrect in the sense of Indo-European.

[2] A more detailed survey of the Indo-European languages and their earliest records is to be found in Meillet, *Introduction*, ch. 2; Krahe, *Idg. Sprw.* i, 9f.; Pisani, *Le lingue indeuropee*; Vendryes and Benveniste, in Meillet and Cohen², 1–80; F. Villar, *Lenguas y pueblos indoeuropeos*, Madrid, 1971; *Los indoeuropeos y los orígenes de Europa: lenguaje e historia*, Madrid 1991; Lockwood, *A Panorama of Indo-European Languages*, London 1972; Kilian 1983; P. Baldi, *An Introduction to the Indo-European Languages*, Carbondale, Ill., 1983; (on this work see Duhoux, *CILL* 11/1–2, 1985, 322–3: 'un livre à prendre avec les plus extrêmes réserves, et dont on souhaitera qu'il ne soit pas trop lu par les étudiants auxquels il s'adresse'); Gamkrelidze—Ivanov, pp. xlvi–lxii; Cowgill and Mayrhofer 1986, 11–71; J. P. Mallory, *In Search of the Indoeuropeans*, London 1989; F. Bader (ed.), *Langues indo-européennes*, Paris 1994, an excellent work, which not only enumerates the IE languages and their documents

but also briefly sketches their structure (the kind of work which I myself completed on a smaller scale some ten years ago). The same can be said of *Języki indoeuropejskie*, the first volume of which (published in Warsaw 1986) treats Indic, Iranian, Tocharian, Anatolian, Armenian, Greek, and the Balkan languages, while a second volume, published in 1988, deals with the remaining IE languages of Europe, i.e. Italic, Romance, Celtic, Germanic, Baltic, Slavic.

On attempts to associate the IE family with other language groups (under a denominator *Nostratic*), see Bomhard 1994.

[3] For this name, see Szemerényi, *KZ* 88, 1974, 267; *ZCP* 36 1979, 294; D. E. Evans, 'The labyrinth of Continental Celtic' (*Proc. Brit. Acad.* 65, 1979, 497–538), 502f., 514f.; 'The identification of Continental Celtic with special reference to Hispano-Celtic', in *Coloquio* 5 (1989), 1993, 563–608; C. J. Crowley in *In Memory of J. A. Kerns*, 1981, 73–85; and note the title of J. F. Eska's book *Towards an Interpretation of the Hispano-Celtic Inscription of Botorrita*, Innsbruck 1989, with the important n. 2, p. 181. (On this inscription, see Meid, *Die erste Botorrita Inschrift*, Innsbruck 1993).

For the alternative designation *Celtiberian*, see K. H. Schmidt, 'Problems of Celtiberian', (*Celtic Society of Japan*, 5, 1992, 37–75), 41, 54f.

[4] On the general problem of 'extinct' languages, see Szemerényi, 'Sprachverfall und Sprachtod', in *In Memory of J. A. Kerns*, 1981, 281–310; Dressler, 'Language death', in Newmeyer iv, 1988 184–92; R. Rindler-Schjerve, 'Sprachverschiebung und Sprachtod', in H. Beck (ed.), *Germanische Rest- und Trummersprachen*, Berlin 1989, 1–4.

On *Language Attrition in Progress* (1986) see Swiggers' review in *Krat* 34, 1989, 169f.; on R. Hindley, *The Death of the Irish Language*, the review by N. C. Dorian, *Lg* 67, 1991, 823–8; and cf. the discussion note 'Another view of endangered languages' by P. Ladefoged, *Lg* 68, 1992, 809–11.

[5] See W. Euler, *Das Altpreussische als Volkssprache*, Innsbruck 1988 (cf. *Krat* 36, 1991, 171–4).

[6] For 'fragmentary' languages, see E. Vineis (ed.), *Le lingue ie. di frammentaria attestazione*, Pisa 1983; Prosdocimi, 'Riflessioni sulle lingue di frammentaria attestazione', *Quaderni dell'Ist. di Linguistica* vi, Urbino, 1989, 131–63.

[7] On these languages, see R. Katičić, *Ancient Languages of the Balkans*, The Hague 1976; R. Solta, *Einführung in die Balkanlinguistik*, 1980, esp. ch. 2; G. Neumann and J. Untermann, *Die Sprachen im Römischen Reich der Kaiserzeit*, Cologne and Bonn 1980; P. di Giovine, 'Tracio, dacio ed albanese', *RAL* 34, 1980, 397–412; *ANRW* 29/2, 1983; Rădulescu, 'Illyrian, Thracian, Daco-Mysian', *JIES* 12, 1984, 77–131; 15, 1988, 239–71; (for Messapic) Lejeune, *AIΩN* 13, 1992, 211–31 (find-places and transcription); Duridanov, *Die Sprache der Thraker*, Neuried 1985; Babiniotis, 'The question of Mediae in Ancient Macedonian', *Fs. Szemerényi*[2] ii, 29–40. In the above-mentioned *Języki indoeuropejskie* the Balkan languages are treated by L. Bednarczuk, 469–513. On Phrygian and its relation to Greek see G. Neumann, *ÖAWSb* 499, 1988, with the note on p. 4 against the assumption of a *Mysian* language. Djakonoff and Neroznak, *Phrygian*, New York, 1985, is rather disappointing; see the damning reviews of Neumann (*Krat* 32, 1987, 88–93), Klein (*Lg* 64, 1988, 199–200) and Mayrhofer (*Archiv für Orientforschung* 36/37, 1992, 182f.). The *Corpus des inscriptions paléo-phrygiennes* iii, (ed. Brixhe and Lejeune), Paris 1984, is indispensable.

2

Language in Change

2.1. DIVERGENCES IN FORM

How, then, is the task of language comparison to be undertaken? What can be compared, and how?

In the first place, it is evident that word units, which can be isolated fairly easily, invite comparison. If the same idea is expressed by (virtually) identical words, as for example *ice* and Grm. *Eis*, the impulse to compare them is irresistible. It thus appears that comparison is natural when meaning and expression both coincide. It is surely inconceivable that Lat. *pater* and Gr. *πατήρ* should have arisen independently and have no connection with one another. But even in cases where identity of form and meaning is not complete, comparison, in the sense of an attempt to establish a connection, is hard to avoid. Lat. *ferō* and Gr. *φέρω* are today, both in Britain and in Germany, pronounced alike, and one could therefore be tempted to take the same view of this instance as of *pater/πατήρ* etc. We know, however, that in the classical period, and even until approximately the beginning of the Christian era, *φέρω* was pronounced *pherō*, with *ph* denoting not *f* but an aspirated labial *p* + *h*, as in Swiss German *phange*, from *behangen*. Is the comparison, then, of *ferō* and *pherō* to be abandoned? Clearly not.

How far, then, is a discrepancy in form and/or meaning admissible? At what point will the limit of tolerance be reached? The ancient scholars were permissive in this respect. It is sufficient to quote here the note on *deus* from Festus (ed. Lindsay, p. 181):

> deus dictus quod ei nihil desit; uel quia omnia commoda hominibus dat; siue a Graeco δέος quod significat metum, eo quod hominibus metus sit. sed magis constat id uocabulum ex Graeco esse dictum, aspiratione dempta qui mos antiquis nostris frequens erat.

Of the four explanations offered only two are internal, based on Latin. The first is of the type *lucus a non lucendo*, and takes account only of the element *de* in *deus*. In the second the same element provides the basis for a quite different etymology. The other two explanations have recourse to Greek. In the third the formal agreement is complete, but, as in the first two, the meaning is laboriously tailored to fit. Only the fourth explanation can be regarded as plausible from the point of view of meaning, but the question then arises whether the procedure here adopted, the modification of Gr. *θεός* by omission of the aspiration, is really admissible. According to our current knowledge, it is impossible: omission of the aspiration could have given only **teos*, whence Lat. **teus*, not *deus*; cf. *tūs* from *θύος*, *tunnus* from *θύννος*.

This objection rests, of course, on the assumption that *in linguistic change* there exists a certain *regularity*, and that particularly in sound changes there is no place for the various liberties which the ancient scholars, followed by those of the Middle Ages and early modern times, took for granted. Thus according to Varro (*De Lingua Latina* 5, 6; cf. 7, 1) word change occurs 'by omission or addition of letters and through their transposition or change' ('litterarum enim fit demptione aut additione et propter earum traiectionem aut commutationem . . .'). Quintilian (1.6.32) gives a similar but somewhat fuller description of the methods of etymologists of his own day: 'qui uerba paulum declinata uarie et multipliciter ad ueritatem reducunt [i.e. etymologize] aut correptis aut porrectis aut adiectis aut detractis aut permutatis litteris syllabisue' (cf. 1.5.10f.).

As to the extent to which formal discrepancies can be admitted, it was not until the nineteenth century that a fundamentally new conception was reached. It can be formulated, rather paradoxically, as follows: no limits are set to *divergences* so long as they can be shown to be *regular*. To give an extreme but by no means untypical example: the correspondence between Eng. *wheel*, Gr. *κύκλος*, and OInd. *čakra-*, despite appearances to the contrary, is exact to a hair (as we shall see later, 4.7.5.1).

2.2. DIVERGENCES IN MEANING

With regard to meaning, however, the facts themselves compel us to adopt a much more liberal attitude. It is, for instance, far from obvious that Fr. *chrétien* 'Christian' and '*crétin*' 'idiot' have any connection, yet both derive from Lat. *Christianus*, which became *crétin* in the dialect of Valais (Switzerland). Similarly, Eng. *silly* and Grm. *selig* are formally identical; in Old English *sǣlig* still meant 'happy, blessed'. Ital. *formaggio* and Fr. *fromage* (earlier *formage*) both mean 'cheese' and come from Lat. **formaticus*, a derivative of *forma*. The original expression was *caseus formaticus* 'cheese made in a mould', from which the meaning 'cheese' was absorbed by *formaticus*, and *caseus* could be omitted as superfluous.

This is not to say that in the development of meaning, only irregular and unaccountable changes are to be found. Certain general tendencies are recognizable even in semantic change. It does not, however, follow, if in one well-authenticated instance a word meaning 'fence' comes to mean 'town' (as can be seen from the pair Grm. *Zaun* and Eng. *town*), that 'fence' always becomes 'town' or 'town' always comes from 'fence'[1].

It follows that, in language comparison, priority must be given unconditionally to the form. If two forms correspond exactly or according to the rules, this compensates for some degree of discrepancy in the meaning. On the other hand, if two forms cannot be referred to a 'common denominator', this is not offset even by total agreement in meaning. For reasons of form, *deus* (still *deiuos* in early Latin) can no more be connected with *θεός* than with English *god*.

[1] The principles of semantics and semantic development were first treated by M. Bréal (1897); see now *The Beginnings of Semantics*; also S. Ullmann, *The Principles of Semantics*[2], Glasgow 1957; *Semantics: An Introduction to the Science of Meaning*, Oxford 1964; *Précis de sémantique française*[2], Berne 1959; all three are provided with copious bibliographies. H. Kronasser, *Handbuch der Semasiologie*[2], Heidelberg 1968, is also useful. For recent theories see P. Ziff, *Semantic Analysis*, Ithaca, New York, 1967; J. J. Katz and J. A. Fodor, 'The structure of a semantic theory', *Lg* 39, 1963, 170–210 (repr. with minor changes in Fodor and Katz, *Structure of Language: Readings in the Philosophy of Language*, Englewood Cliffs, NJ 1964, 479–518); U. Weinreich, 'Explorations in semantic theory', in *CTL* iii, 1966, 395–477; De Mauro, *Introduzione alla semantica*, Rome 1966; J. J. Katz, 'Recent issues in semantic theory', *FL* 3, 1967, 124–94; J. Lyons, 'Firth's theory of meaning', in *In Memoriam J. R. Firth*, London 1966, 288–302; B. Campbell, 'Linguistic meaning', *Lings* 33, 1967, 5–23.

Surveys of recent research are provided by G. Lepschy, *Lings* 15, 1965, 40–65; K. Baumgärtner, *ZDS* 20, 1965, 79–90; R. Simone, *LeS* 1, 1966, 355–86.

On semantic change: E. Coseriu, 'Pour une sémantique diachronique structurale', TLL 2/1, 1964, 139–86; B. Pottier, 'Vers une sémantique moderne', ibid. 107–38. See also W. L. Chafe, *Meaning and the Structure of Language*, Chicago 1970; K. Baldinger, *Teoría semántica*, Madrid 1970; J. J. Katz, *Semantic Theory*, New York 1972; H. E. Brekle, *Semantik*, Munich 1972; G. Leech, *Semantics*, Harmondsworth 1974; Fillmore, 'The future of semantics', in Austerlitz (ed.), *The Scope of American Linguistics*, 1975, 135–57; F. R. Palmer, *Semantics*, Cambridge 1977; 2nd enlarged edn. 1981; J. Lyons, *Semantics* i–ii, Cambridge 1977; R. M. Kempson, *Semantic Theory*, Cambridge 1977; H.-J. Heringer et al., *Einführung in die praktische Semantik*, Heidelberg 1977; S. C. Dik, 'Inductive generalizations in semantic change', in *Fs. Lehmann*, 1977, 283–300; R. Jackendoff, 'Katz's autonomous semantics', *Lg* 57, 1981, 425–35; H. Parret and J. Bouveresse (eds.), *Meaning and Understanding*, Berlin 1981; K. Allan, *Linguistic Meaning* i–ii, London 1986 (cf. *Lg* 64, 1988, 155–8); R. Schleifer, *A. J. Greimas and the Nature of Meaning*, London 1987; U. Eco et al. (eds.), *Meaning and Mental Representation*, Bloomington, Ind., 1988 (see *Lg* 68, 1992, 224–5); R. Jackendoff, *Semantic Structures*, Cambridge, Mass., 1990 (see *Lg* 68, 1992, 399–402). For a historical survey, see B. Nerlich, *Semantic Theories in Europe 1830–1930*, Amsterdam 1992.

For the basic problem, note Mignot, 'Les mots ont-ils un sens?', *BSL* 83, 1988, 21–39.

On the semantic field, see Oesterreicher, in Gauger et al., 274–85.

A very useful work is D. D. Steinberg and L. A. Jakobovits (eds.), *Semantics: An Interdisciplinary Reader*, Cambridge 1971.

2.3. REGULARITY IN SOUND CHANGE

To make the comparison of forms from different languages at all possible scientifically, they must be split up into smaller, indeed into the smallest possible, units. A general impression, while it may provide the impulse for a comparison, is not accessible to scientific verification. The minimal components of the word units are the speech sounds. Instead of a vague comparison of two or more words which give a general impression of 'sounding alike' and also have the same or similar meaning, a methodical comparison is therefore made of all the sounds of which each word is made up. Though this may seem self-evident now, at the beginning of the nineteenth century it was a revolutionary change of attitude, leading two generations later to consequences which are still felt today.

After a few long since forgotten predecessors, the Danish scholar Rasmus Kristian Rask (1787–1832) established in 1818 that in many Germanic words which could be compared with corresponding words in Latin and Greek, the 'letters' had undergone changes in such a way that certain 'rules' could be set up. For example, a regular transition from *p* to *f* is to be observed between Gr. πατήρ, Lat. *pater*, and OIce. *faðir*, and between πούς, *pēs*, and *fōtr*, etc. The same regularity can be seen in the case of Gr. τ κ, δ γ, φ θ χ, which become in Germanic þ *h*, *t k*, *b d g*.

These observations, correct with one exception (Rask had wrongly judged the development of IE *b*), were taken over by Jacob Grimm in the second edition of the first volume of his *Deutsche Grammatik* (1822, pp. 56, 161) and expanded into an impressive system. By attributing to Greek φ θ χ the modern pronunciation he could make them equivalent to the Germanic *f* þ χ, and thus represent the whole development as circular. If M is used to denote the voiced stops (*mediae*) *b d g*, *T* to denote the voiceless stops (*tenues*) *p t k*, A the aspirates (*aspiratae*) φ θ χ and the spirants *f* þ χ with which they were equated, the Germanic changes indicated above (adding the connection of IE *b* with Gmc. *p*) can be set out as follows:

T becomes A
A becomes M
M becomes T

or, still more simply:

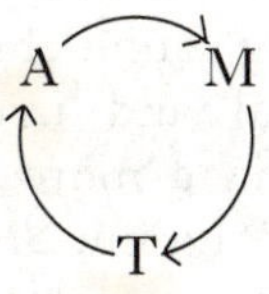

The regularity of these changes, the extent of which Grimm increased by the discovery of a similar circular development in Old High German, so impressed his contemporaries that what he himself had called *Lautverschiebung* ('sound shift') they named, after its discoverer, 'Grimm's Law', 'loi de Grimm'. For the first time not only had a large number of phonetic correspondences, or rather phonetic divergences, between different languages been precisely formulated, but also it had been shown that the various partial developments stood in a coherent relationship to each other. It was this that constituted Grimm's originality and so powerfully impressed his contemporaries. That Grimm made some errors, even in essential points such as the nature of the aspirates, makes no difference at all to his historical significance.[1]

[1]The account in O. Jespersen, *Language* 43f., is marred by an astonishing lack of historical perspective: Grimm is severely taken to task for his mistakes, as though in the case of so great a personality in the field of research what mattered was the degree of correctness and not the influence of his work. A truer estimate is given by another Danish scholar, H. Pedersen, *Linguistic Science in the Nineteenth Century*, 258–62. See also E. Prokosch, *A Comparative Germanic Grammar*, 47–9, 304–5.

Rask's researches appear in a completely new light in P. Diderichsen, *R. Rask og den grammatiske tradition*, Copenhagen 1960 (German summary, 233–8), who also discusses Hjelmslev's judgement of Rask (included as the truth in Mounin, *Histoire* 162f.).

For a survey of modern research, see Collinge, *Laws* 63f., 259f.; *G. I. Alexander, Fortis *and* Lenis *in Germanic*, Berne 1983; Birkhan, *Das 'Zipfsche Gesetz', das schwache Präteritum und die germanische Lautverschiebung*, Vienna 1979. On the theory of glottalization, see 6.9 below and Gamkrelidze–Ivanov, 40, 79, 962, 1321.

A new approach in Davenport and Staun, 'Dependency phonology and the first Germanic consonant shift', *FoLH* 4, 1984, 219–40; important for the whole problem is R. Schrodt, *Die germanische Lautverschiebung im Kreise der idg. Sprachen*, Vienna 1973; 2nd edn. 1976.

2.4. EXCEPTIONS AND THEIR EXPLANATION

It is interesting that neither Rask nor Grimm considered the regularities which they discovered in sound change to be generally valid. Rask held that the consonants 'often' change in accordance with the stated rules, while according to Grimm the sound shift is carried through 'in the mass' but 'is never tidily finished off in the individual case. Some words remain in the early state; the stream of change has passed them by' (Arens[2], 193, 202). Even forty years later, G. Curtius could lay down that 'in the life of sounds . . . fixed laws can be recognized which have a validity almost as consistent as that of natural forces', but nevertheless added that among sound changes two kinds are to be distinguished, 'regular or general' and 'irregular or sporadic', of which the latter type occurs 'only in a more or less restricted number of instances' (Arens[2], 268f.; cf. Pulgram, *Studi Bolelli* (1985), 275–9).

This was understandable at that period, since it was an undeniable fact that alongside the many cases in which development took place according to the rules, there were cases in which it was observed to follow a different course.

For example, clear cases of correspondence such as Goth. *ist hafts fisks nahts* with Lat. *est captus piscis nox* were in breach of the rules of the sound shift, since, in Gothic, *t* and *k* had not been shifted. It was, however, easy to realize that in all these instances the unshifted sound was preceded by a spirant, whether inherited (*s*) or produced by the sound shift (*f h*). The reason, therefore, that the sound shift had not taken place was to avoid a sequence of two spirants (*sf sχ fþ* etc.). The importance of this explanation lay in the recognition that an *exception* to the regularity of the sound shift was itself *regular*.[1]

A further group of exceptions is represented by those words which in Germanic have two voiced stops, e.g. Goth. *bindan* 'to bind'. It seems beyond doubt that this corresponds to Skt. *bandh-* 'to bind'. We come up against difficulties, however, when we examine the comparison more precisely. The correspondence Goth. *-d-*: Skt. *-dh-* is as expected according to the rules of the sound shift, but Goth. *b-*: Skt. *b-* in initial position seems to contradict the rules; to Skt. *b* a *p* should correspond in Germanic. As long as it was taken for granted that in all cases Sanskrit shows the earlier form, a plausible explanation for the irregularity could not be found. If, however, the evidence of Germanic is given equal weight, *bindan* points to IE *bh-dh*. Grassmann realized in 1862 that the 'irregularity' in such cases lies on the side of Sanskrit and Greek: both languages show dissimilation in a succession of two aspirates, by which the first loses its aspiration. A good example is found among the reduplicated verbs in these languages. In Indic the 1st s. of the present tense of *dhā*-'put' has the form *da-dhā-mi*; in Greek, from the corresponding *θη-* (*t+h+ē*), it is *τί-θη-μι*. But for the dissimilation of the aspirate, one would have expected **dha-dhā-mi*, **thi-thē-mi*.[2]

[1] Rasmussen (*AL* 18 (1983), 208) takes the view that *sp st sk* and *pt* were initially shifted to *sf sþ sχ* and *fþ*, and that later these became by dissimilation *sp st sk* and *ft*; this possibility had already been considered by Meillet (*MSL* 12, 1901, 24). On this theory all exceptions to the sound shift would be eliminated. On the problem of exceptions see *W. Zonneveld, *A Formal Theory of Exceptions in Generative Phonology*, 1978 (cf. Booij, *Lingua* 48, 1979, 255–64); Collinge, 'Exceptions', *TPS* 1978, 61–86.

[2] H. Grassmann, 'Über die Aspiraten und ihr gleichzeitiges Vorhandensein im An- und Auslaute der Wurzeln', *KZ* 12, 1863, 81–138; cf. 4.7 below.

2.4.1.

In this group, then, it turned out that there was no question of exceptions to the sound shift: the irregularity was on the side of the other languages, and even this was found to be a regularity. There now still remained one larger group of exceptions. According to the general rules, the IE voiceless stops gave in Germanic the corresponding voiceless spirants: *p* changed to *f*, *t* to þ, *k* to *χ* (and beyond this to *h*). There are, however, a great number of cases in which, instead of *f* þ *h*, the voiced *b d g* appear, apparently without any reason. For example, to Lat. *frāter* corresponds Goth. *brōþar*, but to Lat. *pater* the corresponding Gothic word is *fadar*. Similarly, where Lat. *socer/socrus* have the single *k*, Old High German shows two contrasting correspondences in *swehur/swigar*; cf. modern *Schwäher* and *Schwieger(mutter)*.

The explanation of this twofold development was discovered in 1875 by the Danish scholar Karl Verner (1846–1896). Starting from the fact that the irregular development was particularly conspicuous in the conjugation of the so-called strong verbs, he concluded that 'the cause of the differentiation must be sought in some particular phonetic factor which undergoes variation in the course of conjugation.' After excluding all other possibilities the only factor remaining was 'the variable IE accent', which appeared with particular clarity in Old Indic. The 'grammatical alternation', which survives today as an opposition between present and past tense in Grm. *schneiden/schnitt* 'cut', *ziehen/zog* 'pull(ed)', was formerly found in the past tense between the 1st and 3rd s. on the one hand and the pl. (with 2nd s.) on the other: OHG *sneid/snitum, zōh/zugum,* OE *wearþ/wurdon* 'became', etc. To this corresponds in Old Indic a change not only in the grade of the vowel but also in the position of the accent: from *vart-* 'turn' the 1st s. perfect is *va-várt-a*, the 1st pl. *va-vṛt-imá*. From these correspondences, which could be observed in large categories of forms, Verner drew the conclusion that *f* þ *χ*, arising in the first place from IE *p t k*, in medial position became the voiced spirants ƀ đ ǥ when not immediately preceded by the accent. This explanation is valid also for *brōþar/fadar*, *swehur/swigar*, since the corresponding OInd. forms are *bhrā́tar-/pitár-*, *śváśura-/śvaśrū́-*. Further confirmation is provided by the fact that the inherited IE voiceless spirant *s* was differentiated in the same way in Germanic: after the accent it was kept (possibly to become voiced later); elsewhere it became voiced and later changed to *r*. Consequently the past tense of OE *wesan* 'to be' was *wæs/wǣron* from earlier **wás/*wēsúm*; this alternation survives in NE *was/were*.[1]

[1] Verner's essay 'Eine Ausnahme der ersten Lautverschiebung', written with classical clarity and still worth reading, was published in the spring of the following year (*KZ* 23, 1876, 97–130). The exceptions to the sound shift had already been collected by C. Lottner, *KZ* 11, 1862, 161–205. See recent work by E. Rooth, *Das Vernersche Gesetz in Forschung und Lehre 1875–1975*, Lund 1974; Normier, *KZ* 91, 1978, 191f.; A. Szulc, 'Zur relativen Chronologie des Vernerschen Gesetzes', *Kopenhagener Beiträge zur germanistischen Linguistik* 10, 1978, 5–17; Milroy, *ICHL* 5, 1982, 223–9; Gamkrelidze–Ivanov, 39 n. 1, 195, 960; Collinge, *Laws* 203f.; H. Eichner (below, 2.5 fin.); Mańczak, 'La restriction de la règle de Verner', *HS* 103, 1990, 92–101.

2.5. SOUND LAWS

These results of persevering and ever more accurate research led inevitably to a reappraisal of Curtius' dichotomy of regular and sporadic sound change (see 2.4). If the alleged sporadic changes are time and again revealed as simply another kind of regularity, the conclusion can only be that every sound change is properly to be regarded as regular. This new doctrine, first announced by W. Scherer in 1875, found its most enduring expression in 1878 in the words of the leading Neogrammarians, Hermann Osthoff (1847–1909) and Karl Brugmann (1849–1919):

Every sound change, in so far as it proceeds mechanically, is completed in accordance with laws admitting of no exceptions; i.e. the direction in which the change takes place is always the same for all members of a language community, apart from the case of dialect division, and all words in which the sound subject to change occurs in the same conditions are affected by the change without exception.

This programmatic statement is to be found in the preface of H. Osthoff and K. Brugmann, *Morphologische Untersuchungen auf dem Gebiete der idg. Sprachen* i, Leipzig, 1878, p. xiii. The whole preface was a confession of faith of immense acuity and effectiveness, in which the Neogrammarians took issue with their predecessors—a new chapter in the never-ending drama of the quarrel between Ancients and Moderns.[1]

The concept of *sound law* brought to an end the final phase of pre-scientific linguistics. If a sound law seems to be ineffective, it is because of interference by another sound law or the operation of analogy (see 2.8).

It is evident that the theory of the sound law is not scientifically proved; it is a postulate of scientific research. It can certainly be said that it was positively required by a whole series of observations—and not only those concerned with the sound shift—and so had a certain inductive basis. Thanks to the work of Karl Popper, however, we now understand that by induction no hypothesis can be verified;[2] indeed, the value of hypotheses lies in the attempt, through further continued use and testing, to falsify them. So long as this does not happen, they retain their full usefulness.[3]

On the technique of setting up sound laws, see Eichner, 'Wie stellt man ein Lautgesetz auf', *KBS* 13–14, 1987–8, 83–105.

[1] On the Neogrammarians, see Putschke, 'Zur forschungsgeschichtlichen Stellung der junggrammatischen Schule', *ZDL* 36, 1969, 19–48; K. J. Jankowsky. *The Neogrammarians*, 1972; T. Wilbur (ed.), *The Lautgesetz Controversy*, 1977 (the most important writings, and pp. lx–xcv a review of the whole period); the commemorative volume of *TPS*, 1978, esp. 17–35, Hoenigswald, 'The *annus mirabilis* 1876 and posterity'; Koerner, 'The Neogrammarian

doctrine', *ICHL* 3, 1978, 129–52 (esp. 136 on Schleicher); Kiparsky, *ICHL* 4, 1980, 416. See also above, 1.5 n. 1, and Szemerényi, *Phonetica* 36, 1979, 162–5; more recently A. Quattordio Moreschini (ed.). *Un periodo di storia linguistica: i Neogrammatici*, Pisa 1986; G. Graffi, 'Luoghi comuni su H. Paul (e la scuola neogrammatica)', *LeS* 23, 1988, 211–34; A. Manaster-Ramer, 'Lautgesetzlichkeit and morphologization', *FoLH* 7/2, 1988, 363–70 (369: Neogrammarians live!); Eveline Einhauser, *Die Junggrammatiker*, Trier 1990. Cf. also Labov (below, 2.6 n.2 (*c*)); Swiggers, 'A propos du terme "junggrammatisch"', *HS* 105, 1992, 155–60.

[2] On induction, see K. R. Popper, *The Logic of Scientific Discovery*, London 1959 (an enlarged translation of *Logik der Forschung*, Vienna 1934), repr. 1992, esp. 309f., and *The Poverty of Historicism*, London 1957, repr. 1991, esp. 130f. Cf. Ruwet, *Introduction à la grammaire générative*, 1967, 12f.; Grünbaum, 'Can we ascertain the falsity of a scientific hypothesis?' *Studium Generale* 22, 1969, 1061–93; Putschke (n. 1 above), 31f.

[3] From the abundant literature on the cause(s) of linguistic change I mention only a few recent works: Samuels, *Linguistic Evolution*, 1972; Itkonen, 'Rationality as an explanatory principle in linguistics', in *Studia Coseriu* ii, 1979, 77–87; 'On the rationalist conception of linguistic change', *Diachronica* 1/2, 1984, 203–16; *Causality in Linguistic Theory*, Bloomington, Ind., 1984; Mańczak, 'Frequenz und Sprachwandel', in Lüdtke 1980, 37–9; R. Lass, *On Explaining Language Change*, Cambridge 1980; I. Rauch, 'What is cause?' *JIES* 9, 1981, 319–28 (modern theories); L. Campbell and J. Ringen, 'Teleology and the explanation of sound change', *Phonologica* 4, 1981, 57–68 (in favour, but proposals must be explicit); G. Drachmann, 'Teleological explanation in phonology', ibid. 101–11 (also in favour); Lass, 'Explaining sound change: the future of an illusion', ibid. 257–73 (against); J. Aitchison, *Language Change: Progress or Decay?*, London 1981; M. Harris, 'On explaining language change', *ICHL* 5, 1982, 1–14; Itkonen, 'Change of language as a prototype for change in linguistics', ibid. 142–8; Vizmuller, 'Evidence and explanation in historical linguistics', ibid. 374–84; Vennemann, 'Causality in language change: theories of linguistic preference as a basis for linguistic explanations', *FoLH* 4, 1983, 5–26 (24: historical linguists not only *will* but *may* go on looking for explanations); Lehmann, 'Typology and the study of language change', *Diachronica* 2, 1985, 35–49; J. Harris, *Phonological Variation and Change*, Cambridge 1985 (cf. *FoLH* 7/2, 1987, 409–13); J. Gvozdanović, *Language System and Its Change: On Theory and Testability*, Berlin 1985; L. Agostiniani and P. Bellucci Maffei (eds.), *Linguistica storica e cambiamento linguistico*, Rome 1985; H. Lüdtke, 'Esquisse d'une théorie du changement langagier', *La Linguistique* 22, 1986, 3–46; W. Koopman et al., *Explanation and Linguistic Change*, Amsterdam 1987; Vennemann 1988; L. E. Breivik and E. H. Jahr (eds.), *Language Change: Contributions to the Study of its Causes*, Berlin 1989; P. Baldi (ed.), *Linguistic Change and Reconstructional Methodology*, Berlin 1990; J. D. Collins, 'A theory for language change: Barnett's theory of cultural change', *LACUS* 14, 1990, 347–63; Polomé (ed.) 1990; J. Herman, 'Conscience linguistique et diachronie', *BSL* 84, 1990, 1–11; J. J. Ohala, 'What's cognitive, what's not, in sound change', *LeS* 27, 1992, 321–62.

2.6. ARE THEY VALID OR NOT?

This does not mean that the concept of sound law has not since 1878 often been challenged. Particularly impressive were the results obtained by 'dialect geography' (*géographie linguistique*). The programmatic statement that each word has its own history appeared to assert that there could be no generally valid sound developments, no sound laws. This interpretation, however, overlooked the fact that the study of the history of the individual word (concluding, for instance, that *abeille* 'bee' is an intruder in Parisian French) is possible only because the sound laws provide a sure means of establishing whether a word in a particular region is native or an immigrant from outside, i.e.

a loan word—even if from the same language. It must also be noted that the slogan of dialect geography, 'Each word has its own history', is a gross exaggeration; it should rather be said, with Malkiel, that 'Many (or some, or just a few) words seem to have truly unique histories'. Thus the statistical basis of the objection and its degree of probability are fundamentally altered.[1]

The other objection raised by dialect geography, that the boundary within which the sound law operates is different for each word, also has little validity, since it in fact relates only to the transitional zones between well-defined dialects and not to the central areas, in which in fact 'each' word is affected by a given sound change.

Dauzat is therefore quite right when he says: 'Avec le recul d'une trentaine d'années, il n'apparaît pas que la géographie linguistique ait sérieusement sapé le solide édifice élevé par la rigoureuse méthode des néogrammairiens', and: 'La constance des lois phonétiques reste donc, en principe, hors de tout atteinte'.[2]

[1] Introductions to dialect geography: E. Gamillscheg, *Die Sprachgeographie und ihre Ergebnisse für die allgemeine Sprachwissenschaft*, 1928; K. Jaberg, *Aspects géographiques du langage*, 1936; A. Dauzat, *La géographie linguistique*[2], 1948 (the quotations are from pp. 50 and 58); A. Bach, *Deutsche Mundartforschung*[2], 1950. Its methods are well illustrated by the material discussed in Th. Frings, *Grundlegung einer Geschichte der deutschen Sprache*[3], 1957. Application to Ancient Greek: E. Risch, *MH* 6, 1949, 19–28; 12, 1955, 61–76; *Krat* 11, 1967, 142–55. Y. Malkiel's formulation is taken from his article 'Each word has a history of its own' contributed to the Wenner-Gren Symposium (1964), now in *Glossa* 1, 1967, 137–49, quotation from 145. On Jules Gilliéron (1854–1926), the founder of the theory (among whose works is *Généalogie des mots qui désignent l'abeille*, Paris 1918), see Windisch in Gauger et al. 117–33.

[2] A number of new directions are to be noted in the treatment of these questions since the mid-1960s.

(*a*) The consequences of *generative grammar* have been worked out mainly by three researchers: P. Kiparsky, *Explanation in Phonology*, 1982 (a collection of 11 important and often pioneering works, cf. *Lg* 60, 1984, 416f.), P. Postal, *Aspects of Phonological Theory*, 1968, and R. D. King, *Historical Linguistics and Generative Grammar*, 1969. An impressive restatement of the old views is to be found in U. Weinrich et al., 'Empirical foundations for a theory of language change', in Lehmann and Malkiel, *Directions for Historical Linguistics*, 97–195 (cf. Szemerényi, *GL* 10, 1970, 121–32).

(*b*) A *sociological* direction is mainly represented by William Labov, e.g. 'The social motivation of a sound change', *Word* 19, 1963, 273–309; *The Social Stratification of English in New York City*, 1966; 'The social setting of linguistic change', *CTL* xi, 1973, 195–251.

(*c*) The doctrine of *lexical diffusion* was founded by Wang, *Lg* 45, 1969, 9–25; cf. Chen and Wang, 'Sound change', *Lg* 51, 1975, 255–81 (256: 'a phonological rule gradually extends its scope of operation to a larger and larger portion of the lexicon'); Phillips, 'Word frequency and the actuation of sound change', *Lg* 60, 1984, 320–42. On this, see also Labov, 'Resolving the Neogrammatical controversy', *Lg* 57, 1981, 267–308.

(*d*) The developmentalist view of *linguistic change and variation* is represented by C.-J. N. Bailey, 'The integration of linguistic theory', in Stockwell and Macaulay (eds.), *Linguistic Change and Generative Theory*, 1972, 22–31; *Variation and Linguistic Theory*, 1973; Bailey and R. W. Shuy, *New Ways of Analyzing Variation in English*, 1973; Bailey, 'Old and new views on language history and language relationships', in Lüdtke 1980, 139–81; these were followed by 'Developmental linguistics', *FoL* 15, 1982, 29–37; *On the Yin and Yang Nature of Language*, 1982 (cf. *Lg* 61, 1985, 241–2); 'The proper job of the historical-comparative linguist', *Fachtagung* 7, 1985, 58–70; also L. R. Waugh and S. Rudy (eds.), *New Vistas in Grammar: Invariance and Variation*, Amsterdam 1989; R. Fasold and D. Schiffrin (eds.), *Language Change and Variation*, Amsterdam 1989.

(*e*) The importance of *frequency* as a factor leading to irregular developments has in recent years been repeatedly stressed by the Polish linguist Witold Mańczak, e.g. *Le développement phonétique des langues romanes et la fréquence*, Cracow 1969; *Frequenzbedingter unregelmässiger Lautwandel in den germanischen Sprachen*, Warsaw 1987.

2.7. CONFIRMATION BY PHONOLOGY

The concept of sound law has gained fresh support from modern developments in linguistics, especially in the field of phonology.

2.7.1

The old *phonetics* had investigated the articulation of speech sounds minutely down to the smallest detail. As a reaction against this fragmenting and atomizing procedure there arose in the late 1920s the science of *phonology*, which directed its aim at the function of speech sounds.[1] From this point of view it became evident that minute differences of pronunciation as such are of no significance or relevance for the linguist. Only those differences are significant and relevant which have a function in language, i.e. which serve to differentiate between units of speech. For example, the German *ch* sounds in *nicht* and *Nacht* are for the phonetician two different sounds. The speaker, however, is unaware of the difference, since it has no significance for his language; these pronunciation variants are not used to distinguish words. On the other hand, the two sounds which in English are denoted by *s*, as in *loose* and *lose*, can in German, if at all, differentiate words only in medial position, e.g. *reisen* 'travel' and *reissen* 'tear', but in French, as in English, the difference is significant in any position: *coussin* and *cousin*, *Saône* and *zone* differ only in this respect; cf. *sabre–zabre*; *sel, scel, selle, celle–zèle*; *sain, saint, sein–zain*.

The linguistically significant sounds, or *phonemes*,[2] of a language can be most easily established by the use of 'minimal pairs', i.e. pairs of words distinguished by a single speech sound, as *cat mat*, *cat cut, cat can*. By this method of *commutation*, i.e. changing one sound at a time, any word can be broken up into its component phonemes. Thus the phonemes of Eng. *bread* can be identified as *b* (by comparing *tread*), *r* (cf. *bled*), *e* (cf. *broad*: the spelling variant *e*/*ea* has no phonemic relevance), *d* (cf. *breath*, in which *th* denotes a single sound þ).

As the stream of speech is divided into ever smaller units—continuous speech, sentences, phrases, words . . .—the phonemes constitute the last in the series, distinguished from the rest by the fact that they have no meaning in themselves but only serve to differentiate other units: they are just diacritical signs. They are not, however, the last in the sense of being incapable of further analysis; they can be described in terms of certain articulatory features. If the sounds *p t k*, *b d g*, which function as phonemes in many languages, are compared with one another, it will be found that the second series is distinguished from the first only by the fact that all its members are voiced, whereas the members of the first series are voiceless. The phonemes *p* and *b* differ from each other only in respect of voicing and are otherwise identical, but they differ from the other members of both series in being labials—sounds articulated with the lips. In contrast to other labials, *m* or *f* or *v*, it can be seen that *p b* are characterized by a closure of the lips, which is released in the process of articulation. Thus the phonemes *p* and *b* each have three distinctive features (closure, labial articulation, presence or absence of voice), which taken together differentiate them from all other phonemes, including each other; they are characterized and, as it were, constituted by these features, so that in general it can be said that *the phoneme is a bundle of distinctive features*.[3]

[1] The term 'phonology' was coined by Sechehaye in 1908, but its fortune was made when it was adopted (and adapted) by Jakobson (and other Prague scholars) in 1923; see R. Jakobson, *Selected Writings* i[2], 1971, 467, and cf. Jakobson and L. R. Waugh, *The Sound Shape of Language*, 1979, 17.

[2] The term was coined by the French linguist A. Dufriche-Desgenettes in 1873, adopted by Havet and (from him) by Saussure, then helped to wide acceptance by the Kazan school; see Jakobson, *SW* ii, 396f.; Fischer-Jørgensen 1975, 8f.; Szemerényi 1971, 88f.; Amacker, *CFS* 41, 1987, 7–20; Mayrhofer, *Krat* 33, 1988, 2f.

[3] We cannot pursue here the further ramifications of phonology. One point only need be stressed: alongside *function*, an equally important role is played by the aspects of *system* and *structure*. Basic are: N. S. Trubetzkoy, *Grundzüge der Phonologie*[3], 1962; Ch. F. Hockett, *A Manual of Phonology*, 1955; A. Martinet, *Éléments de linguistique générale* (1960), ch. 3. See also Pilch, *Phonemtheorie* i[3]; W. Mayerthaler, *Einführung in die generative Phonologie* Tübingen, 1974; S. R. Anderson, *The Organization of Phonology,* New York 1974; M. Kenstowicz and C. Kisseberth, *Generative Phonology: Description and Theory*, New York 1974; L. M. Hyman, *Phonology: Theory and Analysis*, New York 1975; A. H. Sommerstein, *Modern Phonology*, London 1977; C. Sloat, S. A. Taylor, and J. E. Hoard, *Introduction to Phonology*, Englewood Cliffs, NJ, 1978; P. Ladefoged, *A Course in Phonetics*[2], New York 1982; R. Lass, *Phonology: An Introduction to Basic Concepts*, Cambridge 1984; E. Ternes, *Einführung in die Phonologie*, Darmstadt 1987. For a defence of the place of the phoneme in generative phonology (long disputed), see Schane, 'The Phoneme revisited', *Lg* 47, 1971, 503–21. A collection of 13 studies presented in J. J. Ohala and J. J. Jaeger (eds.), *Experimental Phonology*, Orlando, Fla., 1986, is meant to demonstrate 'the viability of experimentation in phonology' (cf. *Lg* 66, 1990, 826–31). On *natural phonology*, see D. Stampe, *A Dissertation on Natural Phonology*, New York 1979; J. B. Hooper, *An Introduction to Natural Generative Phonology*, New York 1976. For those interested in typological questions the following are important: M. Ruhlen, *A Guide to the Languages of the World*, Stanford, Calif., 1977 (embraces 700 languages); I. Maddieson, *Patterns of Sounds*, Cambridge, 1984.

An excellent survey of the development of phonological theories is E. Fischer-Jørgensen, *Trends in Phonological Theory*, Copenhagen 1975. Almost 60 of the most important contributions in this field, from Sapir to Lamb, are contained in the reader of V. B. Makkai, *Phonological Theory*, New York 1972. See also S. R. Anderson, *Phonology in the Twentieth*

Century, Chicago 1985. Various recent trends in phonology are discussed by Dressler (natural), Durand (dependency), and Kenstowicz (generative) in the new *RivLing* 1, 1989, and in the paper by Davenport and Staun (dependency) (above, 2.3 n. 1 fin.); in book-length studies by e.g. J. Durand, *Dependency and Non-linear Phonology*, London 1985, and others. Practical help is offered in M. Halle and G. N. Clements, *Problem Book in Phonology: A Workbook*, Cambridge, Mass., 1983. A handy inventory of the large number of signs used is G. K. Pullum and W. A. Ladusaw, *Phonetic Symbol Guide*, Chicago, 1986. On *The Revised International Phonetic Alphabet* of 1989, see Ladefoged, *Lg* 66, 1990, 550–2 (551 for the revised chart).

2.7.2

The results gained from the *synchronic* study of languages in their modern state must, of course, be applicable to their *diachronic* or historical study, especially in the field of sound change.

The phoneme is, as has been said, a collective concept: it brings together all those phonetically distinguishable but still similar sounds, the *allophones*, which do not serve to differentiate meaning. A phoneme is simply the sum (or class) of its allophones, which can either stand in free exchange (their use determined by non-linguistic factors) or occur in complementary distribution, in so far as they are bound to certain positions and conditions. Thus the English phoneme *t* is aspirated before the stress (*table, top*), but not when it is preceded by *s* (*stable, stop*). An allophonic situation of this kind is described in Verner's Law (see 2.4.1): the new voiced spirants were allophones of the originally voiceless spirants, with which they alternated in complementary distribution.

Even more significant for sound change is the interpretation of the phoneme as a 'bundle of distinctive features'. If a phoneme, say *b*, changes, it means that one of its distinctive features changes. For example, the feature of closure can change: the lips, instead of being completely closed, are carelessly left half-open, thus producing a spirant. This change took place in Ancient Greek about the beginning of the Christian era, so that in modern times *β* is pronounced *v* not *b*. Similarly, there can be a change in voicing: if the vocal chords are no longer in vibration during the articulation, the result is a change of *b* to voiceless *p*. This happened, for example, in Germanic, in which *p* corresponds to IE *b*. Phonemes are not, however, isolated in the phoneme system; it is normal to find sets of phonemes sharing a common distinctive feature. Of the three features which characterize *b*, two, closure and voice, occur also in *d* and *g*, which differ from *b* (and each other) only in their place of articulation. It follows that if a distinctive feature changes in a particular phoneme, the same change (since it is made unconsciously) must take place not only in all instances of that phoneme but also in all phonemes exhibiting the same distinctive feature. Thus in the Germanic sound shift the change in the feature *voice* led to the common shift of IE *b d g* to Gmc. *p t k*. Sound change is accordingly regular, and indeed systematic, from this standpoint also.[1]

In conclusion, it should be noted here that the various kinds of sound change can be classified in the following manner:

(*a*) regular sound changes, i.e. regular changes of single phonemes;
(*b*) regular group changes, i.e. regular changes of distant phonemes (assimilation and dissimilation, e.g. *e-i*>*i-i*, *l-l*>*l-r*);
(*c*) irregular (sporadic) group changes, e.g. Attic *Κόρκυρα* from *Κέρκυρα*.[2]

[1] This is only a small sample of the many complicated procedures treated in an elegant and impressive manner by A. Martinet, *Économie des changements phonétiques*, 1955. The pioneering works of R. Jakobson are now readily accessible in his *Selected Writings* i², 1971. See also Szemerényi, 'Methodology', where further literature is cited. New views are advanced in Dressler and Grosu, 'Generative Phonologie und idg. Lautgeschichte', *IF* 77 (1972), 19–72; Dressler, 'A semiotic model of diachronic process phonology', in Lehmann and Malkiel 1982, 93–131; Szemerényi 1971, 53–97; 1982, 59–78; Back 1991.

[2] See Szemerényi, *Lg* 46, 1970, 140–6 (=*SM* 472–8).

2.8. ANALOGY

What we have said so far about the sound laws requires an additional note. The Neogrammarians themselves had emphasized (in that part of their manifesto quoted above) that their statement applied to sound change 'in so far as it proceeds mechanically'. It is clear that sound laws can be interfered with, not only by other sound laws, but by a further powerful factor in language change, that of *analogy*.

It was, indeed, in contrast to the concept of sound laws that this term, which goes back to ancient times, gained the precise meaning that it has in modern linguistics. Analogy denotes a morphological transformation on the model of forms already existing in the language. When this occurs, purely phonetic developments in accordance with the sound laws are for the most part suppressed and obscured.

In German, at the end of the MHG and beginning of the NHG periods, the earlier paradigms *stīgen: steic/stigen, biegen: bouc/bugen, binden: bant/bunden* gave place to NHG *stieg/stiegen, bog/bogen, band/banden*. The assimilation of the s. and pl. forms was simply a case of analogical change, not the result of phonetic processes. A phonetic development from *steic* to *stieg* or from *bunden* to *banden* is in fact impossible, in the sense that it could not be reconciled with our other knowledge.[1]

[1] Analogical changes, like semantic changes, can only with difficulty be brought under general formulae. Attempts in this direction have been made in recent times by J. Kuryłowicz, 'La nature des procès dits analogiques', *AL* 5, 1949, 15–37; W. Mańczak, 'Tendances générales des changements analogiques', *Lingua* 7, 1958, 298–325, 387–420; 'A propos de l'analogie

progressive', *Lings* 33, 1967, 8–26; 'Les lois du développement analogique', *Lings* 205, 1978, 53–60; in 'Laws of analogy', in Fisiak 1980, 283–8, he defends his 5 laws against Best (see below). (On both these scholars, see Szemerényi 1982, 134f.; Collinge, *Laws* 249f.). See further H. Höfding, *Der Begriff der Analogie*, Teubner 1924; repr. Darmstadt 1967; G. Lerchner and Th. Frings, 'Analogie', *PBBH* 84, 1962, 48–57; Lehmann 1962, 177–92; Trnka, 'On Analogy', *ZPhon* 21, 1968, 345–51; K.-H. Best, *Probleme der Analogieforschung*, 1973; E. A. Esper, *Analogy and Association*, 1973; Anttila, *Analogy*, 1977; Mayerthaler, in Lüdtke 1980, 80–130; F. J. Zamora Salamanca, 'La tradición histórica de la analogía lingüística', *RSEL* 14, 1985, 367–419; T. Krisch, 'Analogische Prozesse in der lat. Sprachgeschichte', in *Latein und Indogermanisch*, 1992, 155–81.

On analogy in generative grammar, see R. D. King, *Historical Linguistics and Generative Grammar*, 1969, 127f.; Vennemann and Wilbur, *Schuchardt, the Neogrammarians and the Transformational Theory of Phonological Change*, 1972, 183f., esp. 202; Kiparsky 1982, chs. 10, 11; Zamora Salamanca, op. cit., 394f. On the beginnings of modern research on analogy, see Vallini, *Analogia dal periodo Schleicheriano a F. de Saussure*, Pisa 1972; Morpurgo Davies, *TPS* 1978, 36–60 (47: proportional analogy was introduced in 1875 by Havet; cf. García-Ramón, *Wackernagel Kolloquium*, 1990, 150–9); H. H. Christmann, 'Zum Begriff der Analogie in der Sprachwissenschaft des 19. Jahrhunderts', *Fs. K. Baldinger*, 1979, 102–15. For the period 1816–1977 an almost complete bibliography exists in R. Anttila and W. A. Brewer, *Analogy: A Basic Bibliography*, Amsterdam, 1977.

2.9. COMPARISON OF HIGHER UNITS

What has been said in this chapter about sound change is valid *mutatis mutandis* for language as a whole—morphology, syntax,[1] vocabulary.[2] We can and must follow the same principles for the larger units as for the smaller and smallest. The foundation must always be material identity or similarity, which maintains its power of support even when forms or meanings show wider divergences. The contrary is not tenable and can lead to nothing but unfounded assumptions and confusion. The measure of material identity or similarity—a question which was left in abeyance at the beginning of this chapter (2.1 fin.)—can now also be defined more precisely: the divergence must be in agreement with the sound laws. Many almost incredible correspondences are found in this way which are nevertheless exact from the point of view of linguistics. An often quoted example of such divergent development is the Armenian numeral *erku* 'two' in relation to the forms in the other IE languages, e.g. Lat. *duo*. A comparison with IE **dwō* arouses in the uninitiated the unpleasant feeling that in this instance not a single sound fits, and rightly so; nevertheless, it can be demonstrated that the comparison is correct. The proof can, however, be established only by the most careful observation and determination of the phonetic developments, i.e. of the sound laws.[3] For this reason phonology remains the surest foundation for all comparative linguistics and can never be neglected, however unwelcome some may find this. Here too the truth of the proverb is confirmed: *per aspera ad astra*.

[1] Since this book has no section on syntax, it may be useful to give some references to

modern works, e.g. W. P. Lehmann, *Proto-IE Syntax*, 1974; (ed.), *Syntactic Typology*, 1978; G. Lakoff, *Irregularity in Syntax*, 1970; P. W. Culicover, *Syntax*, 1976; R. P. Stockwell, *Foundations of Syntactic Theory*, 1977; idem et al., *Workbook in Syntactic Theory and Analysis*, 1977; Ch. Li (ed.), *Mechanisms of Syntactic Change*, 1977; D. W. Lightfoot, *Principles of Diachronic Syntax*, 1979; E. A. Moravcsik and J. R. Wirth, *Current Approaches to Syntax*, 1980; E. K. Brown and J. E. Miller, *Syntax: A Linguistic Introduction to Sentence Structure*, 1980; *Syntax: Generative Grammar*, 1982; P. H. Mathews, *Syntax*, 1981; T. Givón, *Syntax: A Functional-typological Introduction* i, 1984, ii, 1991; J. Haiman, *Natural Syntax*, 1985; I. A. Mel'čuk, *Dependency Syntax*, 1988 (see Hagège, *BSL* 84/2, 1990, 63–71). For general problems see H. B. Rosén, *Is a Comparative IE Syntax Possible?*, Innsbruck 1993 (in Russian, *VJ* 1993 (1), 5–21); Lehmann, 'Responsibilities in Syntax', *AJGLL* 1/2, 1989, 101–32; 'Syntactic Residues', in Lehmann (ed.) 1990, 171–87; 'Syntactic Change', in Polomé (ed.) 1990, 365–88.

Special fields: P. Ramat (ed.), *Linguistic Reconstruction and IE Syntax*, 1980; Th. Krisch, *Konstruktionsmuster und Bedeutungswandel indogermanischer Verben*, 1984; Ch. Touratier (ed.). *Syntaxe et latin*, 1985; H. Pinkster, *Latin Syntax and Semantics*, 1990 (Dutch original 1984); M. Baratin, *La naissance de la syntaxe à Rome*, 1989; H. Hettrich, *Untersuchungen zur Hypotaxe im Vedischen*, 1988. For the problems of the passive note G. Stein, *Studies in the Function of the Passive*, 1979; A. Siewierska, *The Passive: A Comparative Linguistic Analysis*, 1984. A selection of 23 articles on syntax from a non-generative viewpoint is available in F. W. Householder, *Syntactic Theory* i: *Structuralist*, 1972 (Penguin). On Martinet's *functional syntax* see his *Studies in Functional Syntax*, 1975, and *Syntaxe générale*, Paris 1985.

[2] For etymology, the science of the origins of vocabulary, note V. Pisani, *L'etimologia*[2], 1967; E. Seebold, *Etymologie*, 1981; M. Pfister, *Einführung in die romanische Etymologie*, 1980; A. Bammesberger, *English Etymology*, 1984; Szemerényi 1989; Malkiel 1993. A handy reader, with 18 selections, is R. Schmitt, *Etymologie*, 1977. On the closely connected problems of *glottochronology*, see Dyen 1992.

[3] On Arm. *erku*, see 8.5.2, n. 2. For the *substratum* problems, note Windisch 1992.

2.10. A FINAL WORD ON THE SOUND LAWS

As we have seen, the principle that sound laws admit no exception was first established by the Neogrammarians (*c.*1878). In contrast to former practice, they also emphasized that a correct understanding of the life of a language can only be gained by one who 'out of the gloom, thick with theories, of the workshop in which the Indo-European basic forms are forged, one day steps forth into the clear air of palpable reality', and entrusts himself to the guidance of later, even the most recent, times and, above all, of living dialects (see pp. ix–x of their preface, referred to in 2.5). In the hundred years since their time these ideas have been developed further in various directions (see 2.6, n. 2), and today have reached a point where the synchronic situation is dissolving into a mass of facts which cannot be brought under rules—corresponding, one might say, to the state of society, or at least of western society.

It is time, therefore, to point out that this picture of things does not necessarily apply to earlier periods, or rather, only with strict limitations. Since in earlier times society was itself much smaller, more united, and, owing to measures of central control, much more strongly cohesive than today, the language situation also was much more unified.[1] This difference is clearly significant for the problems of phonetic development and unexceptional sound laws.

[1] The importance of *time* is rightly stressed by Lehmann (*ICHL* 7, 1987, 339–348) with the postulate (341): 'linguistics must examine any language in its social situation with reference to the passage of time.' Note also Meid's paper on *early–middle–late* IE (*Fachtagung* 5, 1975, 204–19) with the emphatic statement (207) that in the early period 'Indo-European must have been so small a language community that dialect differentiation on a spatial basis played no part', an idea further developed by Eichner, *ÖLT* 13, 1985, 15f.

3

Tasks of Indo-European Linguistics

3.1. THE RECONSTRUCTION OF INDO-EUROPEAN

The fact that so many languages of Europe and south-west Asia show widespread agreements in their grammatical structure and vocabulary can be explained, as we have seen, only by the assumption that they all spring from a common basic language, which we call Indo-European, and are all nothing other than independently developed variants of this original language, the *Ursprache*.[1]

It follows that the first task of the Indo-Europeanist is to work back to the fullest possible reconstruction of Indo-European. The *phonological* system, which was of course a closed system, can be reassembled to a satisfactory extent and with a fair degree of certainty. The *morphological* system, although likewise closed, presents significantly greater difficulties, but this also can be recovered to a large extent. Much more problematic is the *syntax*. Here the units with which we have to work are larger, and consequently it is only with much less confidence that the historical variations can be used as a basis for recovering a prehistoric system. Finally, the *vocabulary* can be recognized in its main outlines with considerable success, especially on a regional basis, but as vocabulary does not form a closed system in any language, it is only partially discoverable for Indo-European also.[2]

Next, the reconstructed Indo-European language system can and must be used as a starting-point for the interpretation of the system and its prehistory.[3] For this we are in a particularly favourable position: a great deal can be established about the prehistory of reconstructed Indo-European.

A further important task of the Indo-Europeanist is to use the reconstructed original language as a starting-point and with its help throw light on the prehistory and early history of the individual languages derived from it. The main historical periods of these languages are, of course, outside the scope of the Indo-Europeanist's work, which illuminates only their origins; see above, 1.5.

In the treatment of both these tasks there are two positions which in theory are sharply divided. In the view of some scholars, the comparative method can do no more than establish *correspondences*. If we are compelled by the facts to recognize that, for example, Latin *deus*, Old Irish *día*, Lithuanian *dievas*, Old Indic *devas*, etc., which all mean 'god', are genetically related, this means only that we can say that Lat. *d* corresponds to OIr. *d*, Lith. *d*, OInd. *d*, etc.; we cannot go further and claim to know what sound they all come from. The reconstruction of a form in the original language, in this case **deiwos*, should be thought of as merely providing a formula to simplify and sum up the clumsy and long-winded statement of the established correspondences.[4] In opposition to this, others hold that the comparative method enables us to recover an extinct phase of a language. A reconstructed form, e.g. **deiwos*, is the reality which underlies the forms in the individual languages, from which all of them have developed in accordance with their own sound laws.[5] It must, of course, be admitted that the reconstruction reflects the state of linguistics at a given time. Thus it can, like a theory in natural science, be modified and improved by fresh discoveries. In fact our present reconstructions (as is recognized also by the supporters of the first position mentioned above) are 'better' than those current a century ago, i.e. they correspond better to the historical facts.[6] But it is only when we acknowledge the reality of the various reconstructed forms that we can meaningfully occupy ourselves with the question how they are related to each other, i.e. how the system was built up. From the outset realism, a realistic approach, plays a decisive part in reconstruction, since the reconstruction of phonetically impossible sounds and sound sequences (=words) can be considered nothing but an idle game.[7] In this *Introduction*, therefore, we adopt the second of the two positions outlined above, that of *realism*.[8]

To indicate that a form is reconstructed, not attested, it is preceded by an asterisk: **deiwos*.[9] This applies not only to IE forms but also to reconstructed forms in the individual languages.

[1] On the progress of research, see Drosdowski, 'Die Erforschung des idg. Altertums (1816–1966)', *Die wissenschaftliche Redaktion* 2, 1966, 51–69; Mallory, 'A short history of the IE problem', *JIES* 1, 1973, 21–65; idem 1989, ch. 1.

[2] R. A. Hall Jr. estimates (*LeS* 4, 1969, 402 n. 19, and still more optimistically *LACUS* 6, 1980, 95) that for Proto-Romance it is possible to reconstruct 95–98% of the phonological system, 80–85% of the morphology, 60% of the syntax, and 70–75% of the vocabulary. For a model of an evaluation of the (Greek) lexicon, see Morpurgo Davies, 'The linguistic evidence', in G. Cadogan (ed.), *The End of the Early Bronze Age in the Aegean*, 1986, 93–123, who shows (p. 105) on a sample of 578 words from Chantraine's *DELG* that '*ca.* 52.2% . . . have an *étymologie obscure*. Of the remaining 47.8% almost one sixth (i.e. *ca.* 8%) consists of clear . . . borrowings . . .. This leaves us with less than 40% of words which have an IE etymology.' In this context the thesis advanced by R. Hudson, *Lg* 70, 1994, 331–9, would—if proved right—be of great general interest, namely that about 37% of word tokens are nouns *in all languages*.

[3] According to Meillet (*Introduction*[8], 1937, 49 f.) this kind of interpretation—today called *internal reconstruction*—is impossible; it would become possible only if other languages, related to IE, were to be discovered.

[4] See e.g. Delbrück, *Einleitung*, 1880, 52 f.; Meillet, *Introduction*, 1st edn., pp. viii, 27, 29; Hjelmslev, *Le langage*, 1966, 37. In his well-known article on reconstruction (*KZ* 41, 1907, 1–64), Hermann goes even further (p. 62): complete forms (e.g. **deiwos*) cannot be reconstructed at all, only single sounds, and even these are meant as approximations only, not as phonetically completely correct reconstructions.

[5] See Hockett, *Lg* 24, 1948, 128 f.; *Course* 506; Hall, 'On realism in reconstruction', *Lg* 36, 1960, 203–6; 'Coerenza e realismo nella ricostruzione', *LeS* 4, 1969, 399–404; Hoenigswald, *Language Change and Linguistic Reconstruction*, 1960, 134 f.; 'Phonetic reconstruction', *PICPS* 5, 1965, 25–42; Nehring, 'Zur "Realität" des Urindogermanischen', *Lingua* 10, 1961, 357–68; M. R. Haas, 'Historical linguistics and the genetic relationship', *CTL* iii, 1966, 113–53, esp. 124, 130.

[6] For 'successive reconstructions of the phonological system of PIE', see Lehmann, in *Fs. Hoenigswald*, 1987, 225–35 (from Schleicher on); Mallory 1989, 17.

[7] Note that the two 'positions' outlined are denoted by Wyatt (*Lg* 48, 1972, 688) *formulist* and *realist* respectively.

[8] On the methods of reconstruction see, since the last war: Bonfante, 'On reconstructions and linguistic method', *Word* 1, 1945, 83–94, 132–61; J. W. Marchand, 'Internal reconstruction of phonemic split', *Lg* 32, 1956, 245–53; Michelena, *Lenguas y protolenguas*, 1963; Kuryłowicz, 'On the methods of internal reconstruction', *PICL* 9, 1964, 9–31; *CTL* xi, 1973, 63–92; Martinet, 'Les problèmes de la phonétique évolutive', *PICPS* 5, 1965, 82–102; Szemerényi, 'New Look', 1967; 'Methodology', 1968; Adrados, 'Die Rekonstruktion des Indogermanischen und die strukturelle Sprachwissenschaft', *IF* 73, 1968, 1–47; Michelena, 'Comparación y reconstrucción', *Em* 37, 1969, 99–135; Dyen, *Lg* 45, 1969, 499–518; King 1969, 154 f.; Anttila, *Introduction* 264 f., 335–88; Ambrosini, 'On linguistic reconstruction', *Studi Bolelli*, 1974, 17–37; Neu, in Arnold and Sinemus (eds.), *Sprachwissenschaft*, 1974, 319 f.; Miranda, *Lingua* 36, 1975, 289–305; Szemerényi, 'Rekonstruktion in der idg. Flexion: Prinzipien und Probleme', *Fachtagung* 5, 1975, 325–45; 'On reconstruction in morphology', *Studies A. A. Hill* iii, 1978, 267–83; 'Strukturelle Probleme der idg. Flexion', *Fachtagung* 7, 1985, 515–33; T. Bynon, *Historical Linguistics*, Cambridge 1977, 45–75; **Problemy rekonstrukcii*, Moscow 1978; H. Birnbaum, *Linguistic Reconstruction*, Washington, DC 1978; Prosdocimi, 'Diacronia: ricostruzione', *LeS* 13, 1979, 335–71, 501–2 (cf. Szemerényi, *Krat* 30, 1985, 9); Klimov, 'K tipologičeskoj rekonstrukcii', *VJ* 1980 (1), 3–12; Mayrhofer, 'Über sprachliche Rekonstruktionsmethoden', *ÖAWAnz* 117, 1981, 357–66; D. M. Job, in *Gedenkschrift Kronasser*, 1982, 46–71; Haudry, 'La reconstruction', *La Linguistique* 21, 1985, 91–107; Gamkrelidze—Ivanov 457f.; Belardi, 'Sulla ricostruzione dell' ie.' in *Scritti in onore di T. Bolelli*, 1985, 39–66, and cf. Cipriano, 'Implicazioni metodologiche e fattuali della teoria di W. Belardi sull' ie.', *SSL* 28, 1989, 101–26; Hock 1986, 717 s.v. *realism*, esp. 568f.; Meid, *Reconstructing IE: a Methodological Approach*, Innsbruck 1987. One number of *InL* (9, 1986, 67–152) is devoted to 9 articles on the problems of reconstruction (by e.g. Campanile, Neu, Strunk). A useful survey of recent trends in IE studies, esp. concerning noun and verb, is given in Adrados 1993; more self-centred is Lehmann, 'The current thrust of IE studies', *GL* 30, 1990, 1–52 (German version: *Die gegenwärtige Richtung der indogermanistischen Forschung*, Innsbruck 1992). For practical purposes W. Cowan, *Workbook in Comparative Reconstruction*, New York 1971, and the 2nd edn. by W. Cowan and J. Rakušan, *Source Book for Linguistics*, Amsterdam 1985, are very useful. With special reference to syntax: Krisch, *Konstruktionsmuster und Bedeutungswandel indogermanischer Verben*, 1984, esp. 26f., 99f.; 191f.

[9] On the introduction of the asterisk, see Koerner, *KZ* 89, 1976, 185–90.

3.2. FURTHER QUESTIONS

The reconstruction sets a number of further tasks. When a good part of the vocabulary has been restored, various questions can be answered which are of great interest to the student of early history.

What was the structure of the 'family' and of society in general?[1] What were the beliefs of the Indo-Europeans, what did they know? Did they worship gods?[2] What knowledge did they possess of metals, animals, plants?[3] What can answers to these last questions contribute to solving the problem of their homeland and period?[4] Did they already possess an elevated poetic diction and perhaps also poetic forms?[5]

There also arise further linguistic questions. Can we discover dialect differences within Indo-European? What can be established about the process of differentiation which led to the formation of the individual languages?[6]

To discuss all these questions would require a larger book than the present one. This *Introduction* is on so limited a scale that it is only possible either to touch on all of them superficially or to investigate more thoroughly just a few problem areas. We have adopted the latter course in the hope that the reader who has gained a secure basis will extend his interest to further problems.[7]

[1] See Szemerényi, 'Kinship', 1978; Gamkrelidze—Ivanov, 755–75; H. Hettrich, 'IE kinship terminology', *Anthropological Linguistics* 27, 1987, 453–80; McCone, in Meid (ed.) *Studien zum idg. Wortschatz*, 1987, 144f. As regards the structure of IE society, since 1930 an increasing and, in spite of some objections, overwhelming influence has been exercised by George Dumézil's doctrine of a threefold division of the IE peoples, the *three classes* being formed by *priests*, *warriors*, and *herder-cultivators*. Of his many works note *L'idéologie tripartie des indo-européens*, Brussels 1958 (a synthesis of his views since 1930); *Mythe et épopé* i: *L'idéologie des trois fonctions*, Paris 1968. A general survey may be found in J.-C. Rivière (ed.), *George Dumézil à la découverte des indo-européens*, Paris 1979.

[2] For religion, see F. Cornelius, *Idg. Religionsgeschichte*, Munich 1942; W. Euler, 'Gab es eine idg. Götterfamilie?' in Meid (n. 1 above), 35–56; Polomé, ibid. 201–17; Haudry, *La religion cosmique des indo-européens*, Paris 1987; Mallory, *In Search of the Indo-Europeans*, London 1989, ch. 5; Meid, *Aspekte der germanischen und keltischen Religion*, 1991. For the Dumézilian doctrine see his *Les dieux souverains des indo-européens*, Paris 1977; G. J. Larson (ed.), *Myth in IE Antiquity*, Berkeley, Calif., 1974; C. S. Littleton, *The New Comparative Mythology*, Berkeley, Calif., 1966, 3rd edn. 1982; J. G. Oosten, *The War of the Gods: The Social Code in IE Mythology*, London 1985; for a critique, A. Momigliano, 'George Dumézil and the trifunctional approach to Roman civilization', *History and Theory* 23/3, 1984, 312–30.

[3] On metals, see V. V. Ivanov, *Istorija slavjanskix i balkanskix nazvanij metallov*, Moscow 1983; Makkay, 'Ancient metal names and the first use of metals', *Balcanica* 23, 1992, 311–18. For animals and plants, note S. Bökönyi, *History of Domestic Mammals*, 1974; *Pferdedomestikation, Haustierhaltung und Ernährung*, Innsbruck 1992; D. Zohary and M. Hopf, *Domestication of Plants in the Old World: The Origin and Spread of Cultivated Plants in West Asia, Europe, and the Nile Valley*, Oxford 1988.

[4] See Dressler, 'Methodische Vorfragen bei der Bestimmung der Urheimat', *Sprache* 11, 1965, 25–60; Scherer (ed.), *Die Urheimat der Indogermanen*, 1968; Mallory, 'A history of the IE problem', *JIES* 1, 1973, 21–65; *Paleontologia Linguistica: VI Convegno Internazionale di Linguisti*, Milan 1977; Szemerényi 1985, 44–54; *Ethnogenese* i, 1985 (Untermann on IEs, Risch on Greeks); Strunk, *InL* 9, 1986, 136 f.; Mallory 1989, ch. 6 (traditional), and for the Near East Gamkrelidze and Ivanov, *JIES* 13, 1985, 3–91; Gamkrelidze, 'Asiatic homeland', in *Studies Polomé*, 1988, 161–7; *KZ* 100, 1988, 371 f.; critique by I. M. D'yakanoff, *JIES* 13, 1985, 92–174, and M. Kaiser and V. Shevoroshkin, *JIES* 14, 1986, 365–78; Shevoroshkin, 'IE homeland and migrations', *FoLH* 7, 1988, 227–50; Dolgopolskij, *FoL* 8, 1989, 10 n. 4, 11 n. 5 (Anatolia, Balkans); Mańczak, *HS* 103, 1991, 178–92 (against Gamkrelidze, for

Poland!); *De la préhistoire des peuples ie.*, Cracow 1992, esp. 70–107; S. Zimmer, *Ursprache, Urvolk und Indogermanisierung*, 1990; in general, W. Nagel, 'Indogermanen und Alter Orient', *MDOG* 119, 1989, 157–213.

But at present a lively discussion exercises the experts centring around C. Renfrew, *Archaeology and Language: The Puzzle of IE Origins*, London 1986; in his view the IE language originated in the Near East and was spread to Europe by the first farmers beginning *c.*7000 BC, partly via Anatolia, partly via Central Asia. For criticism, see Meid, *Archäologie und Sprachwissenschaft*, Innsbruck 1989, and (apart from a large number of mostly negative reviews) Renfrew, Szemerényi et al. in *TPS* 87/2, 1989, 101–78. By a curious coincidence, about the same time a so far largely unnoticed study was published by G. S. Krantz, *Geographical Development of European Languages*, Berne 1988, which advanced the same basic views. The author stated that a preliminary version went back to 1981, but Renfrew (in a letter to me) declared that his theory had been adumbrated in 1973 in R. A. Crossland and A. Birchall (eds.), *Bronze Age Migrations in the Aegean*, 263–76, esp. 270. The linguistic discussion proper centres more promisingly on the developmental and temporal sequence of *early–middle–late* IE; see Meid, 'Probleme der räumlichen und zeitlichen Gliederung des Indogermanischen', *Fachtagung* 5, 1975, 204–19, and recently Adrados 1993, 1–28. The *Palaeo-European* long advocated by H. Krahe has been disposed of by his pupil W. P. Schmid, 'Indogermanische Modelle und osteuropäische Frühgeschichte', *Akad. Mainz* 1978/1, 1–24, who thinks that the centre of the IE community was in the Baltic area.

The archaeological facts and problems are expertly presented by two specialists: A. Häusler, 'Archaeologie und Ursprung der Indogermanen', *Das Altertum* 38, 1992, 3–16 (autocthonous in Europe); id., 'Zur Frage nach dem Ursprung der Griechen', in J. Herrmann (ed.), *Heinrich Schliemann*, 1992, 253–66; J. Makkay, 'About the archaeology of the IE problem', *Acta Arch. Acad. Hung.* 44, 1992, 213–37; 'A neolithic model of IE prehistory', *JIES* 20/3–4, 1992, 193–238. Both give ample references, as does Villar, 'La teoría de la IE-eización neolítica', *Arqritica* 3, 1992, 14–16.

5 Humbach, 'Idg. Dichtersprache?' *MSS* 21, 1967, 21–31; R. Schmitt, *Dichtung und Dichtersprache in idg. Zeit*, 1967; idem (ed.), *Idg. Dichtersprache*, 1968; Meid, *Dichter und Dichtkunst*, Innsbruck 1978; Nagy, 'On the origins of the Greek hexameter', *Fs. Szemerényi*, 1979, 611–31; Campanile, 'Idg. Metrik und altirische Metrik', *ZCP* 37, 1980, 174–202; Toporov, 'Die Ursprünge der indoeuropäischen Poetik', *Poetica* 13, 1981, 189–251; Gamkrelidze–Ivanov, 832 f. On the verse form, see Vigorita, 'The IE twelve-syllable line', *KZ* 90, 1977, 37–46; M. West, *Greek Metre*, Oxford 1982; Watkins, 'Aspects of IE poetics', in Polomé (ed.), *The Indo-Europeans in the 4th and 3rd Millennia*, Ann Arbor, Mich., 1982, 104–20; F. Bader, 'Meillet et la poésie ie.', *CFS* 42, 1988, 97–125; Meid, *Formen dichterischer Sprache im Keltischen und Germanischen*, 1990; Swiggers, 'The origin of the Greek meter: A. Meillet's views and their reception by É. Benveniste and N. Trubetskoj', in *Studies E. C. Polomé* i, 1991, 199–215; also Isebaert (ed.) 1993, 350 (on Benveniste). On Schleicher's fable, see Lehmann and Zgusta, in *Fs. Szemerényi*[1], 1979, 455–66; Koerner, in Vennemann 1989, 3f. For Mesopotamian influence, see G. Costa, *SSL* 27, 1987, 151–75; M. Reichel, 'Gräzistische Bemerkungen zur Struktur des Gilgamesch', *Fs. Szemerényi*[2], 1992, 187–208.

6 Porzig, *Gliederung*; Milewski, 'Die Differenzierungen der ie. Sprachen', *LPosn* 12/13, 1968, 37–54; Scherer, 'Die Indogermanisierung Europae', in *Convegno* 5, 1972, 21–36.

7 A short survey of comprehensive works on IE linguistics may be appended here. From the period preceding the Neogrammarians, note F. Bopp, *Vergleichende Grammatik des Sanskrit, Zend, Armenischen, Griechischen, Lateinischen, Litauischen, Altslavischen, Gotischen und Deutschen* i–iii, Berlin 1833–52 (with two further edns., 1857–61, 1864–71); A. Schleicher, *Compendium der vergleichenden Grammatik der idg. Sprachen*, Weimar 1861–2 (with 3 further edns.); R. Westphal, *Vergleichende Grammatik der idg. Sprachen*, Jena 1873 (on this see L. Farmini, *RIL* 116, 1983, 167–80). With the new era came Brugmann, *Grundriss; KVG*; Meillet, *Introduction*; Hirt, *IG*; Pisani, *Glottologia ie.*, 1961. Of the *Idg. Grammatik* in several volumes founded by Kuryłowicz the following are now available: ii *Akzent, Ablaut* (Kuryłowicz), 1968; iii/1 *Geschichte der idg. Verbalflexion* (Watkins), 1969; i/1–2 *Einleitung* (Cowgill), *Lautlehre* (Mayrhofer), 1986; on further projected volumes, see Mayrhofer, *Fachtagung* 7, 1985, 258 f. The latest comprehensive treatment is this *Introduction*; less detailed and rather unsystematic is Lockwood 1969. Not readily accessible because of the

languages are A. N. Savčenko, *Sravnitel'naja grammatika ie. jazykov*, Moscow 1974, and Th. Simenschy and Gh. Ivănescu, *Grammatica comparată a limbilor indoeuropene*, Bucharest 1981. Novel in approach: G. Décsy, *The IE Protolanguage: A Computational Reconstruction*, Bloomington, Ind., 1991.

4

Phonology: Reconstruction of the System

4.1. VOWELS

From comparison of the individual languages it appears that Indo-European possessed the five basic vowels, both short and long:

i		*u*		*ī*		*ū*
	e *o*				*ē* *ō*	
	a				*ā*	

In Greek this vowel system remains intact in most dialects. In Attic and Ionic, however, long *ā* was raised to *ǟ*, which later coalesced with inherited *ē* to give *η*, but was in Attic changed back to *ā* after *e*, *i*, and *r* (see Szemerényi, 'Rückverwandlung').[1] In both dialects short and long *u* were shifted forwards to give *ü*. In Latin the long-vowel system is fairly well preserved, whereas the short vowels, except in initial syllables, were subject to extensive weakening, and even in initial syllables were often affected by their phonetic environment. In Aryan the system was completely changed by the falling together of the three lower vowels *a*, *e*, *o* in *a*, and of the corresponding long vowels in *ā*, resulting in a three-vowel system.[2] In Germanic a partial coalescence took place: *a* and *o* fell together in *a*, *ā* and *ō* in *ō*, OHG *uo*; in Gothic there was a further coalescence of *e* and *i* in *ĭ*, while the long *ī* and *ē* remained separate. In Slavic the development was the opposite of Germanic: *a* and *o* fell together in *o*, *ā* and *ō* in *a*. In Lithuanian *a* and *o* gave *a*, *ā* and *ō* gave *ō* or *uo*. In Slavic *i* and *u* became the ultra-short *ĭ*, *ŭ*, long *ī* and *ū* becoming *i* and *y*.

[1] See Laroche, *Mél. Chantraine*, 1972, 83f. (date too late); Sommerstein, *Sound Pattern of Ancient Greek*, 1973, 52f.; Mignot, 'La genèse du vocalisme en grec ancien', *Estudios a E. Alarcos Llorach* i, 1976, 193–206; Gusmani, in *Studies Palmer*, 1976, 77–82; Gates, *Glotta* 54, 1976, 44–52; Messing, *Illinois Classical Studies* 1, 1976, 1–6; Miller, *Sprache* 22, 1977, 137f.; Crespo, *Cuadernos de Filología Clásica* 12, 1977, 187f.; 13, 1978, 309f. For the early history of research, see B. H. Davis, 'A history of the research on IE vocalism 1868–1892', diss., U. of N. Carolina, 1972. For more general problems, note Catford, 'The recent history of vowel classification', in *Towards a History of Phonetics: In Honour of D. A. Abercrombie*, Edinburgh 1981, 19–32.

[2] For Semitic influence, see Szemerényi 1985, 41f. (with references). According to the so-called'Brugmann's Law' (see Curtius' *Studien* 9, 1876, 367f., 380f.), IE *o* became Aryan *ā* in open syllables. This law was abandoned by Brugmann himself (see *IF* 32, 1913, 191 n. 2) and others (see Gonda, *Old Indian*, 1971, 25, 102), but has its supporters even today, e.g. Dressler, *IF* 77, 1973, 51; Burrow, *BSOAS* 38, 1975, 55–80; Kuryłowicz, *Problèmes* 163f., esp. 169f.; Jamison 1983, 11–24, 200–12. Cf. also Collinge, *Laws* 13f.; Sihler,'Further evidence in support of Brugmann's Law', *Fs. Hoenigswald*, 1987, 367–73; Cowgill and Mayrhofer 1986, 146–8 (on and for the law); Lubotsky, *IIJ* 32, 1989, 105–7, and in Kellens 1990, 129–36 (for); accepted by Beekes, *Fs. Meid*, 1989, 36. According to Prosdocimi and Marchese (*Fs. Szemerényi*, 1992), Saussure gave a laryngeal account of Brugmann's Law before 1890.

The former presence of *e* in Aryan was proved by the law of palatalization: velars and labiovelars became affricates before original *e* and *i/y*; see further below, 4.7.4.7, and Szemerényi 1964, 4;'New Look' 68; Mayrhofer,'Sanskrit und die Sprachen Alteuropas', *GGN* 1983, 137–42; Collinge, *Laws* 133f., and'Who did discover the law of palatals?' in *Fs. Hoenigswald*, 1987, 73–80; R. Schmitt, *Ernst Kuhn und Vilhelm Thomsen*, Copenhagen 1990, 12–18.

This short survey cannot, of course, include all the details, but gives a general picture. Further details concerning Latin are given below (4.1.12). The developments mentioned are illustrated by the examples which follow (4.1.1–10).

4.1.1. *a*

**agō* 'I drive': Gr. ἄγω, Lat. *agō*, Skt. *ajāmi*, ON *aka* 'drive, travel';
**agros* 'pasture, field': Gr. ἀγρός, Lat. *ager*, Skt. *ajras*, Goth. *akrs*;
**dakru* 'tear': Gr. δάκρυ, Lat. *dacruma* (later *lacrima*), Goth. *tagr*, OHG *zahar*;
**ghans-* 'goose': Gr. χᾱν (Att. χήν), Lat. *anser*, Skt. *haṁsa-* 'goose, swan', OHG *gans*; see *Symbolae Mitxelena* i, 1985, 265–73.

4.1.2. *ā*

**swādu-* 'sweet': Gr. ἁδύς (Att. ἡδύς), Lat. *suāuis*, Skt. *svādu-*, OHG *s(w)uozi*;
**bhāghu-*'arm': Gr. πᾶχυς (Att. πῆχυς), Skt. *bāhu-*, OHG *buog* 'bow, bend';
**mātēr* 'mother': Gr. μᾱ́τηρ (Att. μήτηρ), Lat. *māter*, Skt. *mātar-*, OE *mōdor*, OHG *muoter*, Lith. *motė* 'woman, wife', OCS *mati, mater-*;
**bhrātēr* 'brother': Gr. φρᾱ́τηρ 'member of a phratry', Lat. *frāter*, Skt. *bhrātar-*, Goth. *brōþar*, OHG *bruoder*.

4.1.3. *e*

**bher-* 'carry': Gr. φέρω, Lat. *ferō*, Skt. *bharāmi*, Goth. *bairan* (*ai=e*, for *i* before *r* and *h*), OHG *beran* (Grm. *ge-bären*, Eng. *bear*);
**esti* 'is': Gr. ἐστί, Lat. *est*, Skt. *asti*, Goth. *ist*;
**genos* 'race, family, kind': Gr. γένος, Lat. *genus*, Skt.*janas-*;
**nebhos, nebhelā* 'cloud, sky': Gr. νέφος νεφέλη, Lat. *nebula*, Skt. *nabhas-*, OCS *nebo, nebes-*.

4.1.4. *ē* (became *ā* in Germanic, except Gothic, *ī* in Celtic)

**rēg-s* 'king', Lat. *rēx*, Skt. *rājā* 'king, rajah', OIr. *rī* (gen. *rīg*);

**sē-* 'to sow'; Lat. *sēmen*, Goth. *mana-sēþs* 'mankind, world', OHG *sāmo*, OCS *sěmę*, OIr. *sīl* 'seed';

**dhē-* 'put, do, make': Gr. *τί-θη-μι*, Skt. *da-dhā-mi*, Lat. *fē-cī*, Goth. *missa-dēds* 'misdeed', OHG *tāt*;

**plē-* 'full': Gr. *πλή-ρης*, Lat. *plē-nus*, Skt. *prā-tas*.[1]

[1] According to Koivulehto (see Brogyanyi and Krömmelbein (eds.), *Germanic Dialects*, 1986, 249–94, English summary 293), the NWGmc. change *ē* > *ā* was in Scandinavia completed by the 3rd cent. BC at the latest. Beside this *ē* (more correctly $ē_1$) there was also an $ē_2$ which was kept unchanged in all Germanic languages; cf. Goth. OSax. *hēr* 'here', OIce. *hér*, and see Knapp, *PBB(T)* 96, 1974, 207–40; Polomé, in Bammesberger 1988, 384–401.

4.1.5. *o*

**oktō* 'eight': Gr. *ὀκτώ*, Lat. *octō*, Skt. *aṣṭā*, Goth. *ahtau*, OIr. *ocht*;

**owis* 'sheep': Gr. *ὄϝις οἶς*, Lat. *ouis*, Skt. *avis*, Goth. *awistr-is* (gen.) 'sheepfold', OHG *ou(wi)*, Lith. *avis*, OCS *ovĭca*;

**potis* 'lord, master, husband': Gr. *πόσις* (*δεσπότης*), Lat. *potis potior*, Skt. *patis*, Goth. *brūþ-faþs*'bridegroom', Lith. *pats* (early *patis*) 'husband';

orbhos* 'orphan, destitute': Gr. *ὀρφανός*, Lat. *orbus*, Arm. *orb* 'orphan', Goth. *arbi* 'inheritance' (orbhyom*), OHG *arbi*, *erbi*, OIr. *orb* 'heir, inheritance'.

4.1.6. *ō*

**gnō-* 'know': Gr. *ἔγνων γι-γνώ-σκω*, Lat. *gnōscō* (pre-class.), *nōuī*, Skt. *jñāta-* (cf. Lat. *(g)nōtus*), OCS *znati*;

**dō-* 'give', **dō-no-m*, **dō-ro-m* 'gift': Gr. *ἔδωκα δί-δω-μι δῶρον*, Lat. *dō*, *dōnum*, Skt. *da-dā-mi*, *dānam*, OCS *dati*, *darŭ*, Lith. *dúoti*;

**ōku-* 'quick': Gr. *ὠκύς*, Lat. *ōcior*, Skt. *āšu-*;

**yōs-* 'gird oneself': Gr. *ζωστός ζώννυμι ζώνη*, Avest. *yāsta-* 'girt', Lith. *júostas* 'girt', OCS *po-jas-ŭ* 'girdle'.

4.1.7. *i*

**wid-* 'know': Hom. Gr. (ϝ)*ίδ-μεν*, Skt. *vid-ma*, Goth. *witum*;

**widhewā* 'widow': Lat. *uidua*, Skt. *vidhavā*, Goth. *widuwō*, OHG *wituwa*, OCS *vĭdova*;

**misdho-* 'pay': Gr. *μισθός*, Skt. *mīḍha-* (*mīḷha-*) 'prize'; Avest. *mižda-* 'pay', OCS *mĭzda*, Goth. *mizdō*, NHG *Miete*;

*k^wis, *k^wid 'who, what': Lat. *quis quid*, Hitt. *kwis kwid*, Gr. *τίς τί* (from **τιδ*).

4.1.8. *ī*

**gʷīwos* 'alive, living': Lat. *uīuos*, Skt. *jīva*, Lith. *gývas* (*y*=*ī*), OCS *živŭ*;
**wīs* 'strength': Gr. *(ϝ)ῖς, Lat. uīs*;
**pīwon-* 'fat': Gr. πίων, Skt. *pīvan-*;
**pī-* 'to drink': Gr. πίνω πῖθι, Skt. *pīta-* 'drunk', OCS *pivo* 'beer'.

4.1.9. *u*[1]

**yugom* 'yoke': Gr. ζυγόν, Lat. *iugum*, Skt. *yugam*, Goth. *juk*, OCS *igo* (*yŭ-* to *yĭ-*, then *i*);
**rudhros* 'red': Gr. ἐ-ρυθρός, Lat. *ruber*, Skt. *rudhira-*, OCS *rŭdrŭ*;
**medhu* 'honey', mead'; Gr. μέθυ, Skt. *madhu* 'sweet drink, honey', OCS *medŭ* 'honey', *OE medu*, OHG *metu* 'mead';
**snusūs* 'daughter-in-law'; Gr. νυός, Lat. *nurus*, Skt. *snuṣā*, OHG *snur*; see Szemerényi, *Syncope* 318f.

[1] See Adams, 'Change of *u* to *i* after a labial', *MSS* 46, 1985, 5–11.

4.1.10. *ū*

**mūs* 'mouse': Gr. μῦς, Lat. *mūs*, Skt. *mūṣ-*, OCS *myšĭ*, OE OHG *mūs*;
**bhrū-* 'brow': Gr. ὀφρῦς (*οπ-φρῦς 'eye-brow'), Skt. *bhrū-*, OE *brū*;
**ūdher* 'udder': Lat. *ūber*, Skt. *ūdhar*, OE *ūder*, OHG *ūtar*;
**dhūmos* 'smoke': Skt. *dhūma-*, Lat. *fūmus*, Lith. *dúmai*, OCS *dymŭ*; cf. also Gr. θῡμός.

4.1.11. Schwa.[1]

An additional vowel is inferred from clear morphological correspondences such as

Skt. *sthi-ta-* 'standing': Gr. στατός, Lat. *stătus*
Skt. *a-di-ta* (3rd s. aor. mid. of *dā-* 'give'): Gr. ἔ-δο-το
Skt. *pitar-*: Gr. πατήρ, Lat. *pater*, etc.

in which Aryan *i* stands in contrast to *a* in the other Indo-European languages (in Greek, also to ε or ο, which often appear in place of α on the analogy of related forms with η or ω, e.g. τίθεμεν τίθημι, δίδομεν δίδωμι). Since neither IE *i* nor *a*, discussed above, can account for these correspondences, it is usually assumed that an Indo-European murmured vowel (perhaps similar to the sound of *a* in Eng. *alone*, *sofa*) must be posited. This vowel is called *schwa* (*indogermanicum*), a term borrowed from Hebrew grammar (*šwā* 'emptiness', for the murmured vowel between consonants), and is usually denoted by an inverted *e* (ə). Its nature and functional role in the vowel system as a whole will be treated in more detail later (5.3.4).

Parallel to this *schwa indogermanicum primum* some scholars posit a *schwa indogermanicum secundum*: whereas the former is a weakening of a long vowel, the latter is held to represent the weakening of short vowels. The factual base of this hypothesis is, however, inadequate (see 6.6.15).

[1] Schwa does not appear in Mayrhofer's phonology (*IG* i/2, 90); it is replaced by the putative laryngeal source. On the development of schwa to Gmc. *u*, see below, 5.3.4 n. 1. On the general problems of schwa, see R. Lass, 'On *schwa*', *SPIL* 15, 1986, 1–30; for a useful parallel from a living language, see S. P. Verluyten (ed.), *La phonologie du schwa français*, 1988.

4.1.12.

In Latin the inherited system of short vowels is subject to changes, especially in respect of the middle vowels *e* and *o*.

(i) IE *e* becomes *o*

(*a*) before *w*: **newos* 'new', Gr. νε(ϝ)ός: OLat. *nouos*; **tewos* 'thy', **sewos* 'his/hers/its' (reflexive), Gr. τεός ἑός: OLat. *touos souos*; cf. Szemerényi 1976, 421f.;

(*b*) after *sw*-: *swe*- becomes first *swo*-, then *so*-: **swesōr* 'sister', Skt. *svasar*-, Goth. *swistar*: Lat. *soror*; **swekuros* 'father-in-law', Gr. ἑκυρός: Lat. *socer*; **sweneti* 'sounds', Skt. *svanati*: OLat. *sonit*; **swepnos* 'sleep', OE *swefn* 'sleep, dream': Lat. *somnus* (from **sopnos*);

(*c*) before velar *l*, i.e. *l* preceding the back vowels *a o u* and consonants other than a second *l*: **wel*- 'wish', retained in *uelim uelle*, appears as *uol*- in *uolō uolt* from **welō* **welti*; **welu*- 'turn' (cf. Gr. ἐλύω) gives *uoluō uolūtus*, and similarly **se-luō* (cf. λύω) *soluō solūtus*.

(ii) IE *e* becomes *i* before a velar nasal, i.e. before *ng*, *nk*: **tengō* (cf. τέγγω) gave *tingō*; **k^{w}enk^{w}e*, from IE **penk^{w}e* with assimilation of *p* to *k^{w}*, became *quīnque* (*i* lengthened by analogy with *quīntus*).

(iii) IE *o* becomes *u* before a velar nasal: Gr. ὄγκος 'hook', Lat. *uncus*; also before *mb*: Lat. *umbo umbilīcus*, Gr. ὀμφαλός; before velar *l*: *sulcus*, Gr. ὁλκός; *ulcus* from **olkos*, itself from **elkos* by (i)(*c*) above, cf. Gr. ἕλκος.

(iv) *wo* before *r s t* became *ue*- about 150 BC: OLat. *uortō uorsus uoster uotāre* became *uertō uersus uester uetāre*; cf. Eichner, in *Latein und Indogermanisch*, 1992, 67 n. 48.

In non-initial syllables general closing of short vowels, i.e. raising in the direction of *i u*, took place. Cf. *faciō*: *afficiō affectus*, *premō*: *comprimō compressus* (in closed syllables this raising stops at *e*). The extreme point of this tendency is syllable loss (syncope): Gr. δεξιτερός, Lat. *dexter*; **wiros* became **wirs*, **wirr*, finally *uir*. In cases of syncope following postconsonantal *r*, another vowel develops between the consonants: OLat. *sakros* (5th cent. BC) was syncopated to **sakrs*, whence **sakers*, **sakerr*, *sacer*; in the same way **agros* became *ager*.

4.2. DIPHTHONGS

Combinations of the more open vowels *a e o* with a close vowel, *i* or *u*, within a single syllable (tautosyllabic combinations) are also present in Indo-European:

ei *oi* *eu* *ou*
ai *au*

These spellings represent the pronunciation of the IE diphthong; i.e. in each case the short sound of *a, e,* or *o* is combined with that of *i* or *u* (*ai* as in *night*, *ei* as in *they*, *oi* as in *joy*, *au* as in *cow*, *ou* as in *go*, *eu* as in Welsh *blew*). Latin *ae* was pronounced *ai* until AD 200.[1]

The development of the diphthongs at first corresponds to that of the independent vowels. Thus in languages in which *o* became *a*, *oi* and *ou* became *ai* and *au*. Further on there appeared a tendency for them sooner or later to become monophthongs. In Latin this stage was reached as early as the first half of the second century BC: *ei* became *ī*, *oi* became *ū*, and *ou*, with which *eu* had fallen together some centuries earlier, became *ū*. Only *ai* (written *ae*) and *au* survived the classical period. In Greek the diphthongs were preserved in the classical period with the exception of *ou*, which became *ū* although it continued to be written *ου*. In Germanic *ei* became *ī* at an early date. Of the other diphthongs, *ai* and *au* in Gothic became as a rule open *ę̄* and *ǭ*;[2] in Old High German *ai* became *ē* before *r w h* but *ei* in other positions; *au* became *ō* before *h* and the dentals *d t z s n r l*, elsewhere *ou*. In Slavic *ei* became *ī*, *ai* and *oi* gave *ē*, the *u*-diphthongs *ū*. In Lithuanian the diphthongs have been preserved until the present day, except that the *i*-diphthongs have partly become *ie*. In Aryan all diphthongs fell together to give *ai* and *au* in the first place; these still survive in Old Iranian, but in Indic appear from the earliest records monophthongized to *ē* and *ō*.

[1] See Szemerényi in K. Büchner (ed.), *Latein in Europa*, 1978, 29f. and 43 nn. 21 (against Blümel) and 25 (=*SM* 1005f. and 1019 nn. 21, 25); Coleman, *CFC* 20, 1987, 156f.; Eichner (above, 4.1.12).

[2] Cf. D'Alquen, *Gothic AI and AU*, 1974.

A few examples for each diphthong can illustrate these developments:

4.2.1. *ai*

**aidh*- 'burn': Gr. αἴθω, Lat. *aedēs* 'shrine, house' (originally 'hearth'), *aestus*, *aestās*, Skt. *ēdha*- 'tinder', OHG *eit* 'funeral pyre';

**kaiko*- 'blind': Lat. *caecus*, OIr. *caích* 'one-eyed', Goth. *haihs* (id.); cf. Gr. καικίας 'north-east wind' (the 'dark one');

**daiwēr* 'husband's brother': Gr. δαήρ, Skt. *dēvar*-, Arm. *taigr*, OCS

dēverĭ, OHG *zeihur*; also Lat. *lēuir* from **dēuir* under the influence of *laeuus* ('quasi laeuus uir') with non-Roman *ē*;
**ghaido-* 'goat': Lat. *haedus*, Goth. *gaits*, OHG *geiz*.

4.2.2. *ei*

**deik-* 'show, say': Gr. δείκνυμι, Lat. *dīcō*, Goth. *ga-teihan* 'announce, inform', OHG *zīhan* 'accuse';
**deiwos* 'god': Lat. *deus*, *dīuus*, Skt. *dēvas*, OPrus. *deiws*, Lith. *dievas*;
**ei-ti* 'goes': Gr. εἶσι, Lat. *it*, Skt. *ēti*, Lith. *eit(i)*;
**sneigʷh-* 'to snow': Gr. νείφει, OLat. *nīuit*, OHG *snīwan* (cf. 4.7.5.3).

4.2.3. *oi*

**woida* 'I know': Gr. (ϝ)οἶδα, Skt. *véda*, OCS *vēdē, Goth.* wait, OHG *weiz*;
**oinos* 'one': Gr. οἴνη 'the one on a dice', Lat. *ūnus* (OLat. *oino*), Goth. *ains*, OIr. *oín*;
**snoigʷhos* 'snow': OPrus. *snaygis*, Lith. *sniegas*, OCS *snēgŭ*, Goth. *snaiws*, OHG *snēo*;
**toi* 'those, they': Gr. (Dor.) τοί, Lat. *is-tī*, Skt. *tē*, Goth. *þai*.

4.2.4. *au*

**aug-* 'to increase': Lat. *augeō*, Gr. αὔξω αὐξάνω, Goth. *aukan* (intrans.), Lith. *áugti* 'grow';
**sausos* 'dry': Gr. αὖος, Skt. *šōṣa-* (from *sōṣa-*), Lith. *sausas*, OCS *suxŭ*, OHG *sōrēn* 'to dry up';
**aus-* 'ear': Lat. *auris*, *auscultō*, Goth. *ausō*, Lith. *ausis*; on these and Gr. οὖς see Szemerényi, *SMEA* 3 (1967), 47f. (=*SM* 1273f.).
**aus-* 'to draw (water)': Gr. αὔω ἐξαύω, Lat. *hauriō*, ON *ausa*.

4.2.5. *eu*

**deuk-* 'draw, lead': Lat. *ducō (*OLat. *doucit*), Goth. *tiuhan*, OHG *ziohan*;
**geusō* 'I taste': Gr. γεύομαι, Goth. *kiusan*;
**eusō* 'I burn': Gr εὕω, Lat. *ūrō*, Skt. *ōṣāmi*;
**leuk-* 'give light, shine': Gr. λευκός, Goth. *liuhaþ* 'light, Skt. *rōčati* 'shines'.

4.2.6. *ou*

**roudhos* 'red': Lat. *rōbīgō* and (dialectal) *rūfus*,[1] Goth. *rauds*, OHG *rōt*, Lith. *raudas*, *raudonas*;
**loukos* 'glade, clearing': Lat. *lūcus* (OLat. *loucom*), Skt. *lōka-* 'space, world', Lith. *laukas* 'field', OHG *lōh* 'overgrown clearing', cf. *Water-loo*;

**klounis* 'buttock': Lat. *clūnis*, Lith. *šlaunis* 'thigh, hip', Skt. *śrōṇi-*, ON *hlaun*;

**louksno-* 'shining': Lat. *lūna* (Praenestine *losna*), OPrus. *lauxnos* (pl.) 'group of stars, constellation', Avest. *raoxšna- 'gleaming'*.

[1] See Risch, *Fs. Szemerényi*, 1979, 705–24.

4.2.7.

Indo-European had also long diphthongs such as *āi ōi*. These, however, are found almost exclusively in case endings, and will accordingly be discussed under morphology; see also 6.6.14.

4.3. SEMIVOWELS

The semivowels *y* and *w* can easily be reconstructed on the basis of the overwhelming evidence of the Indo-European languages. In the case of *w*, however, the original bilabial articulation (as in Eng. *w*) was already replaced in the earliest tradition of many languages by the labiodental (as in Eng. *v*, Grm. *w*). The old pronunciation was retained in classical Latin and Old Iranian; also in English, where it has survived to the present day. In Old Indic, however, the labiodental articulation was already noted by the earliest grammarians.

4.3.1.

The semivowel *y* was lost in Greek. In initial position it became the aspirate *h* or ζ; in intervocalic position it disappeared altogether; in consonant groups it led to a variety of developments,[1] e.g. *py>pt*, *ty>ss* or *tt*, etc. In Latin *y* was mostly preserved, but it disappeared in intervocalic position and after a consonant generally became the vowel *i*. In Germanic it was kept, except that in Old Norse initial *y* was lost, as also in Old Irish.[2] Examples:

**yek^{w}r̥t* 'liver': Skt. *yakr̥t*, Lat. *iecur*, Gr. ἧπαρ, Lith. *jeknos*;

**yugom* 'yoke': Skt. *yugam*, Lat. *iugum*, Gr. ζυγόν, Goth. *juk*, ON *ok*;

**treyes* 'three' (m.f.): Skt. *trayas*, Lat. *trēs* (from **tre(y)es*), likewise Gr. τρεῖς (with ει=ẹ̄), Goth. *þreis* (=*þrīs* contracted from *þrijis*); cf. 8.5.2;

**alyos* 'other': Gr. ἄλλος (with assimilation of *ly* to *ll*), Lat. *alius* (trisyllabic), Goth. *aljis*;

**medhyos* '(in the) middle': Skt. *madhya-*, Gr. μέσ(σ)ος (*ss* from *thy*), Lat. *medius* (trisyllabic), Goth. *midjis*.

[1] See Wyatt, *Glotta* 46, 1969, 229–37; 54, 1976, 1–11; Leroy, *Mél. Chantraine*, 1972, 105–17; Nocentini, *AGI* 57, 1972, 24–43; *Glotta* 56, 1979, 157f.; Billigmeier, *JIES* 4, 1977, 221–31; Peters, *Sprache* 22, 1977, 161; van Windekens, *JIES* 7, 1979, 129–32; Brixhe, *BSL* 74, 1979,

249–54; 77, 1982, 209–49; Huld, *AJP* 101, 1980, 324–30; Christie, *ICHL* 5, 1982, 421–5; Ambrosini, *Scritti Bolelli*, 1985, 27–9; Forssman, *Fs. Hoenigswald*, 1987, 118; Negri, *Convegno* 8 (1991), 55, 66, 71, 73. On Mycenaean, see Brixhe, *BSL* 84, 1989, 48–52, but esp. Duhoux, *BSL* 85, 1990, 359–65 (*yod* . . . en cours d'aspiration).

[2] For Albanian, see Orel, *FoLH* 8, 1989, 37–49.

4.3.2.

The semivowel *w* is unknown in Attic-Ionic from the earliest records onward. It survives, however, in many other dialects as late as the classical period, and in Mycenaean is still preserved generally.[1] In Old Irish it has become *f* in initial position, in Welsh *gw*. Examples:

**wīro-*, **wiro-* 'man': Skt. *vīras* 'hero', Lat. *uir*, Lith. *výras*, Goth. *wair*, OIr. *fer*;

**woida* 'I know': Skt. *vēda*, Gr. (ϝ)οἶδα, Goth. *wait*, OCS *vēdē;*

**owis* 'sheep': Skt. *avis*, Gr. ὄ(ϝ)ις, Lat. *ouis*;

**newos* 'new': Gr. νε(ϝ)ός, Lat. *nouus*, Skt. *navas*, OCS *novŭ*, Goth. *niujis*.

[1] For the Greek developments, see Meier-Brügger 1992, ii, 112.

4.4. NASALS AND LIQUIDS

These sounds are among the most stable elements of Indo-European. In all the languages they are preserved in general unchanged. The only significant exception is Aryan, in which *l* and *r* often coalesce: in Old Iranian *l* became *r* throughout, while in Old Indic dialect mixture has confused the original situation to such an extent that *l* and *r* can each represent IE *l* or *r*.[1] The nasal denoted by *n* can, of course, differ phonetically according to the following consonant: in *nt n* is dental, in *nk* velar. But this difference is not phonemic: the variants are allophones of the phoneme *n*. On the other hand, *m* is not determined by the phonemic environment; it comes in all positions and is an independent phoneme. It is further to be noted that in Old Indic *n* often becomes a cerebral (*ṇ*). In Greek, as in Hittite and Armenian, a prothetic vowel appears before initial *r*; see below 6.4.7.3, and for Hittite, Tischler, *KZ* 86 (1973), 267–86.

[1] On *l* in the Rigveda, see Ortolani-Barletta, *SOL* 3, 1986, 109f.

Accordingly the phonemes *m n l r* must be posited for Indo-European. Examples:

4.4.1. *m*

**mātēr*: Gr. μάτηρ, Lat. *māter*, Skt. *mātar-*;

**wem-* 'to vomit': Gr. ἐμέω, Lat. *uomō*, Skt. *vamiti* 'vomits'.

4.4.2. *n*

**nokʷt-* 'night': Gr. νύξ (gen. νυκτός), Lat. *nox*, Skt. *nak* (acc. *nakt-am*), Lith. *naktis*, Goth. *nahts*, Hitt. *nekut-* 'evening';
**seno-* 'old': Gr. ἕνος 'last year's', Lat. *senex*, Skt. *sana-* 'old, former', Lith. *sẽnas*, Goth. *sineigs*.

4.4.3. *l*

**leuk-* 'shine, give light': Gr. λευκός 'white', Lat. *lūx*, *lūcēre*, Goth. *liuhaþ* 'light', Skt. *rōčatē* 'shines', but also *lōka-* 'world';
**leubh-* 'to love': Lat. *lubet libet*, Skt. *lubh-* 'to desire', Goth. *liuba-* 'dear', OCS *ljubŭ*;
**pl̥u-*, **pelu-* 'much, many': Gr. πολύς, Goth. *filu*, OHG *filu*, OIr. *il*, Skt. *puru-* and *pulu-*, OPers. *paru* (see 4.5.4 and 5.3.5*b*).

4.4.4. *r*

**reudh-*, **rudh-* 'red': ἐρεύθω, 'redden', ἐρυθρός 'red', Lat. *ruber*, *rōbīgō*, *rūfus* (see 4.2.6), Lith. *raudas*, OCS *rudŭ*, *rŭdrŭ*, Goth. *rauda-*, OHG *rōt*, Skt. *rohit(a)-* but also *lohita-*;
**dhwer-*, **dhur-* 'door': Gr. θύρα, Lat. *forēs*, Goth. *daur*, OHG *tor*, Lith. *durys*, Skt. *dvāras*;
**bher-* 'carry': Gr. φέρω, Lat. *ferō*, Goth. *bairan*, Skt. *bhar-*.

4.5. SYLLABIC NASALS AND LIQUIDS

Up to this point we have reconstructed for Indo-European only such sounds as are actually attested, if not in all, at least in some Indo-European languages. A more careful comparison, however, of certain forms in the individual languages compels us to posit sounds which are nowhere preserved as such. Osthoff was the first, in 1876, to put forward the idea that, as the relationship of the Skt. dat. s. *pitre* 'to the father' to the loc. pl. *pitr̥ṣu* suggested, the same *r*-sound could function at one time as a consonant, at another (between consonants) as a vowel; further, that this syllabic or sonant *r̥* was retained only in Aryan, and that there was an obvious correspondence between it and the sequence ρα in Gr. πατράσι. In the same year Brugmann was led to assume the existence of syllabic nasals (*n̥ m̥*) and of syllabic liquids generally (*l̥* as well as *r̥*). Since that time these sounds have become firmly established as constituents of the Indo-European phonological system. They are also well known from many modern languages, including English, in which the final syllables of *button*, *bottom*, *bottle* contain *n̥ m̥ l̥*. In Slavic languages, e.g. Czech and Serbian, such sounds are recognized in spelling; they are written without a vowel, e.g. Czech *prst* 'finger', *vlk* 'wolf'.[1]

[1] The character of these sounds was well expressed by Lawrence Durrell in his 'Alexandria Quartet' (*Balthazar*, ch. 9): the one-eyed Hamid pronounced the name of Mr Pombal 'as if it contained no vowels: thus: Pmbl'. The African language Swahili even has stressed syllabic nasals, e.g. *ḿtu* 'man', a point of special importance in view of Jespersen's surprising attack in *Language*, 317f. On Osthoff, Brugmann, and others, see further below, 4.5.1, n. 1.

4.5.1

If we consider the word for 100 in the Indo-European languages, e.g.

Lat. *centum*, Gr. ἑκατόν, Goth. *hund*, Skt. *śatám*, Lith. *šimtas*,

we see that, leaving out of account the Greek ἑ-, they all begin with a sound derived from an Indo-European palatal (see 4.7.4) followed after an interval by the voiceless dental *t*; Gothic *d* arose from this by Verner's Law (2.4.1), thus attesting the originality of the accent position in the Greek and Old Indic forms. Between these two stops, however, appear sounds or sound groups which differ from one language to another, and which cannot correspond to any vowel discussed so far, nor to any group of vowel + nasal. We can, therefore, reach only the preliminary conclusion that the forms cited display the following correspondences:

Lat. *en* = Gr. α = Goth. *un* = Skt. *a* = Lith. *im*.

These correspondences are by no means isolated. They are not confined to this word, but occur quite regularly in a large number of words, e.g. in the forms for ten:

Lat. *decem*, Gr. δέκα, Goth. *taihun*, Skt. *dáša*, Lith. *dešimt*.

The way to a solution of the problem posed by such correspondences is indicated by, *inter alia*, certain Greek verb forms. The mediopassive present and imperfect 3rd pl. end usually in -νται and -ντο respectively; cf. the forms παιδεύονται ἐπαιδεύοντο from παιδεύω. In contrast to this, the so-called athematic verbs have forms like Homeric κείαται κείατο from κεῖμαι 'I lie'. Thus in such cases the athematic -αται -ατο correspond to the thematic -νται -ντο. A few years before Brugmann's discovery Saussure, who was still a schoolboy at the time, drew the conclusion that -αται -ατο must have arisen from -νται -ντο, which meant that in certain circumstances *n* could appear as *a*. The condition for this sound change is simply that *n* stood between two consonants (*key-n-tai*): it could not, therefore, be articulated as a consonant, but required a syllabic pronunciation. In general it can be said that a syllabic nasal, whether *n̥* or *m̥*, as they are now written, became α in Greek.

Similarly the verbal adjective of τείνω 'stretch', with root τεν-, has the form τατός because from the root *ten-* with loss of the root vowel *tntós*, i.e. **tn̥tós*, was formed. That the verbal adjective was originally formed with loss of the root vowel is clear from the archaic forms φυκτός ἄπυστος ἐπίσσυτος.

The same development is also found in Aryan. The verbal adjective of Skt. *tanōmi* 'I stretch', root *tan-*, is *tatas*, which arose like Gr. τατός from IE **tn̥tós*.[1]

By noting the correspondences *en*=α=*un*=*a*=*im* set out above, the developments of IE *n̥* and *m̥* can be tabulated as follows:

	Aryan	Gr.	Lat.	Gmc.	Lith.	Slav.	OIr.
n̥	*a*	α	*en*	*un*	*in*	*ę* (< *in*)	*an*, *en*
m̥	*a*	α	*em*	*um*	*im*	*ę* (< *im*)	*am*, *em*

The examples discussed (100, 10) thus go back to IE **km̥tóm*, **dekm̥(t)*. Further examples:

**mn̥tis* 'thought': Skt. *matís*, Lat. *mēns* (gen. *mentis*), Goth. *ga-munds* (*mundi-*) 'memory', Lith. *mintìs* 'thought', OCS *pa-mętĭ* 'memory';

**yuwn̥kos* 'young, young animal': Skt. *yuvaśa-* 'young', Lat. *iuuencus*, Goth. *juggs* (=*jungs*, contracted from **yuwungas*), W. *ieuanc*, OIr. *óac* (=*ōag*, with *g* < *nk*);

**g$^{\omega}$m̥tos* '(having) come': Skt. *gata-*, Gr. -βατος, Lat. *-uentus*, Lith. *gimtas* 'innate, native, natal' (see 4.7.5.2);

**septm̥* 'seven': Skt. *sapta*, Gr. ἑπτά, Lat. *septem*.

Note. In Old Church Slavic final *-n̥ -m̥* became *-ĭ*; cf. *kamenĭ* (acc.) 'stone', from *-m̥*.

[1] Following Osthoff's identification in 1876 (*PBB* 3, 52, 61f.) of Gr. πατράσι with OInd. *pitr̥ṣu*, i.e. of ρα with *r̥*, Brugmann in the same year generalized this and also discovered the *nasalis sonans* (Curtius' *Studien* 9, 324f. and 303f., 469f.); on this see Saussure's statements in the *Mémoire* (=*Recueil* 7, 40 n. 1, and 265) and in an early essay (ibid. 356f.). Saussure frequently stated that when barely 15 years old (1873) he had himself discovered the sonant nasal (see *CFS* 17, 1940, 13, 18f., 23f., and cf. the remarks in the Italian edn. of the *Mémoire* by G. C. Vincenzi, Bologna 1978, 339f.). The discovery had in fact already been made by Ahrens in 1838; see his *Kleine Schriften* i, 1891, 12, and cf. Fick, *GGA* 1881, 1418. From evidence available today it appears that Ahrens too had been anticipated by the French Indianist Bournouf (see Wackernagel, *Kleine Schriften* iii, 1979, 1709f.), who in 1823 (*JA* 3, 372), by comparison with Gr. τετύφαται from *τετυφνται, had derived Skt. *śāsati*, *dadatē* from **śāsnti*, **dadntē*. The now usual practice of denoting syllabic sonants by a small circle below the line was introduced by Saussure in his *Mémoire* (=*Recueil* 8, n. 1) but Mayrhofer could show (*Krat* 33, 1988, 12 n. 69) that Saussure had taken it from Lepsius; he also mentions (4, n. 23) that in the discovery of the sonant liquid Brugmann was anticipated by Benfey.

4.5.2

The syllabic liquids can be established in the same way. Their continuations are as follows:

	OInd.	Gr.	Lat.	Gmc.	Lith.	Slav.	OIr.
r̥	*r̥*	ρα/αρ	*or*, *ur*	*ur*	*ir*/*ur*	*ĭr*/*ŭr*	*ri*,*ar*
l̥	*r̥*	λα/αλ	*ol*, *ul*	*ul*	*il*/*ul*	*ĭl*/*ŭl*	*li*,*al*

Note. In Old Church Slavic the spellings *rĭ rŭ, lĭ lŭ* appear for these sounds; see P. Diels, *Altkirchenslavische Grammatik* i, 1932, 61f). Examples:

**kr̥d* (beside **kerd*) 'heart': Gr. *καρδία*, Lat. *cor*, OIr. *cride* (from **kr̥dyom*), Lith. *širdis*, OCS *srŭdĭce* (from *sird-*); from **kerd* Goth. *hairtō*, OS *herta* = OE *heorte*, OHG *herza*;

**dhr̥s-* 'dare': Skt. *dhr̥ṣṇōti* 'he dares', Gr. *θρασύς* 'bold', Goth. *gadaursan* 'dare'.

**dr̥k-* 'see': Skt. *dr̥š-* 'look', Gr. *δρακεῖν* 'catch sight of', OIr. *drech* 'face' (from **drikā*), Gmc. **turhta-* in OE *torht*, OHG *zoraht* 'bright';

**wl̥kʷos* 'wolf': Skt. *vr̥ka-*, Lith. *vilkas*, OCS *vlĭkŭ*, Goth. *wulfs* (see 4.7.5.1);

**pl̥t(h)u-* 'wide': Skt. *pr̥thu-*, Gr. *πλατύς*, Gaul. *Litana (*silua), OIr. *lethan*;

**ml̥du-* 'soft': Skt. *mr̥du-*, Gr. (Hsch.) *βλαδεῖς· ἀδύνατοι* (*βλα-* from *mla-*), Lat. *mollis* from **moldwis*[1].

[1] On the sonants in Slavic, see Moszyński, *VJ* 1969 (5), 3–10; in Greek, O'Neil, *Glotta* 47, 1970, 8–46; Wyatt, *SMEA* 13, 1971, 106–22; in Celtic, P. de Bernardo Stempel, *Die Vertretung der idg. Liquiden und Nasalen Sonanten im Keltischen*, 1987 (cf. Szemerényi, *ZCP* 44, 1991, 299f.).

4.5.3

Corresponding to these short syllabic nasals and liquids, a number of clear comparisons seem to attest the existence of long syllabic liquids and nasals.

Thus the OInd. verbal adjective *jātas* 'born', from the verb root *jan(i)-*, corresponds to Lat. *(g)nātus*, Gaul. *Cintu-gnātus* 'first-born' and Goth. *kunds*. It follows that in these instances *ā–nā–nā–un* correspond to one another, and have their common origin in a syllabic nasal which cannot, however, be identical with the short syllabic nasal. We can therefore infer a set of long syllabic nasals and liquids, which are represented as follows in the individual languages:[1]

	OInd.	Gr.	Lat.	Celt.	Gmc.	Lith.	Slav.
n̥̄	*ā*	*νā*	*nā*	*nā*	*un*	*in*	*ę*
m̥̄	*ā*	*μā*	*mā*	*mā*	*um*	*im*	*ę*
r̥̄	*īr, ūr*	*ρā*	*rā*	*rā*	*ur*	*ir*	*ĭr*
l̥̄	*īr, ūr*	*λā*	*lā*	*lā*	*ul*	*il*	*ĭl*

In the OInd. forms of the liquids, the vowel is *ū* if preceded by a labial or former labiovelar; in Iranian, *ar* appears throughout. In Baltic and Slavic, some instances of *u* instead of *i* occur, as in the case of the short sonants. In Germanic, Baltic, and Slavic, the continuations of the long syllabic sounds are identical with those of the short, i.e. they have been shortened; in Lithuanian and Slavic, however, the original distinction is still shown by different accentuation (see 5.2.6).[2] Examples for the long sonants:

**gn̥̄tos* 'born': Skt. *jātas*, Lat. *gnātus*, Gaul. *Cintugnātus*, Goth. *airþakunds* 'earthborn, earthy';

**wl̥̄nā* 'wool': Lith. *vilna*, ORuss. *vŭlna* (Russ. *vólna*), Goth. *wulla* (*ll* from *ln*), Avest. *varənā*, OInd. *ūrṇā* (from *wūr-*), Lat. *lāna* (from *wl-*), Gr. λᾶνος, λῆνος, W. *gwlan*;

**pl̥̄nos* 'full': Skt. *pūrṇa-*, Lith. *pilnas*, OCS *plŭnŭ*, Goth. *fulls*, OIr. *lān* (with loss of *p-*);

**gʷr̥̄tos* 'welcome, pleasing': Skt. *gūrta-*, Lat. *grātus* (Oscan *brātom*), Lith. *girtas* 'praised'; see Szemerényi, *KZ* 88 (1974), 252–65 (=*SM* i, 222–35);

gr̥̄nom 'ground (adj.), grain': Lat. *grānum*, OIr. *grān*, Goth. *kaurn* 'corn, wheat', *kaurnō* 'grain', OCS *zrĭno* 'grain', Lith. *žirnis* 'pea', Skt. *jīrṇa-* 'ground'.

**pr̥̄wo-* **pr̥̄mo-* 'fore-, first': Skt. *pūrva-*, OCS *prĭvŭ*, Lith. *pirmas*, Goth. *fruma*, OE *forma*; cf. also Dor. πρᾶτος.

In some cases Gr. ανα αμα αρα αλα,[3] Lat. *an(a) am(a) ar(a) al(a)* seem to occur as representatives of the long sonants. For example:

**pl̥̄mā* 'palm (of the hand)': OIr. *lām*, OHG *folma*, Gr. παλάμη, Lat. *palma*;

**sp(h)r̥̄g-* 'to sprout, crackle': Skt. *sphūrjati* 'breaks forth, crackles', Avest. *fra-sparəγa-* 'shoot, branch', Gr. σφαραγέομαι 'burst, crackle', Lat. *spargō*.

[1] Lehmann, *PIE* 86f.; Beekes, *Laryngeals* 186f., and others hold that Greek never had long syllabic sonants. This view was held long before by F. Bechtel, who, in his important study *Die Hauptprobleme der idg. Lautlehre seit Schleicher* (1892), also maintained (p. 217) that Saussure had not managed to prove in *Mémoire* 247f. (=*Recueil* 231f.) that long sonants existed in IE. See, however, Edgerton, *Lg* 19, 1943, 107f., and note that e.g. *r̥̄* can also derive from *r̥d* (see 6.2.8, Addendum 1). On some other instances, see Szemerényi, *Krat* 28, 1984, 75 (Skt. **pulun-* *pūrṇa-* from **pVlVn-* not **plHno-*; similarly **diligh-* *dīrgh-* from **dVlVgh-*).

[2] On long sonants in Slavic and elsewhere, see Vaillant, *Gram. comp.* i, 175f.; Schwyzer, *GG* i, 171 n. 1; Vachek, *To Honor R. Jakobson* iii, 1967, 2112; Lehiste and Popov, *Phonetica* 21, 1970, 40.

[3] A special Greek development to -ολι- is advocated by Strunk, *Glotta* 47, 1970, 1–8; *MSS* 28, 1970, 109–26; *PICL* 11/1, 1974, 375–81.

4.5.4

Indo-European *n̥* as a privative particle is attested in many languages, e.g. Skt. *a-jñātas*, Gr. ἄ-γνωτος, Lat. *ignōtus* (=*in-gn*, in which *in* arose from *en* according to 4.1.12(ii) and was then generalized), Goth. *un-kunþs* 'unknown', opposed to *jñātas*, γνωτός, *(g)nōtus*, *kunþs*. Such privatives can also be based on words with initial vowel; the particle then takes a different form in some languages, e.g. Gr. *ἄν-υδρος* 'waterless' = Skt. *an-udra-*. Thus it is customary to speak of syllabic nasals and liquids in prevocalic position (denoted by *m̥m* or *m̥ᵐ*, etc.), which in fact involves a contradiction, as these sounds can become syllabic only between consonants; it is a question here of the appearance, conditioned by the phonetic environment, of anaptyctic vowels, which in various ways became stable elements of the phonological system (cf. 6.6.15). Since the denotation *m̥m* is misleading—giving the impression of a syllabic followed by a consonantal *m*—we shall use *m̥ n̥*, etc. for the prevocalic position also. In most languages their representation is the same as in the other positions, but divergent developments are seen in Gr. *αν αμ αρ αλ*, OInd. *an am ir* and (after labials and former labiovelars) *ur*, Iran. *an am ar*, Slav. *ĭn ĭm ĭr ĭl*. Examples:

**tn̥u-* 'thin': Skt. *tanu-*, Gr. *τανύ* 'long-', OIr. *tanae*, OHG *dunni*, OCS *tĭnŭ-kŭ*;

**sm̥o-* 'some(one)': Skt. *sama-*, Iran. *hama-* 'any', Gr. *ἀμό-θεν, οὐδ-αμοί*, Goth. *sums*, Eng. *some*;

**gʷr̥u-* 'heavy': Skt. *guru-*, Gr. *βαρύς*, Goth. *kaurus* (from **kurus*); on Lat. *grauis* see Szemerényi 1976, 403f. (=*SM* 980).

**pl̥u-* 'much, many'; Skt. *puru-*, OPers. *paru-* (see 4.4.3; Szemerényi, *KZ* 88, 1974, 1–31 = *SM* 1410–40).

4.6. SPIRANTS

For Indo-European only one spirant can be established with certainty, voiceless *s*. Voiced *z* also occurs, but only as an allophone of *s* before voiced stops.

In general *s* is preserved in Old Indic, Lithuanian, and Old Church Slavic. In Greek it is kept before and after stops and when final; in other positions it becomes an aspirate (*h*), which is lost between vowels and in a number of so-called psilotic dialects, e.g. Ionic, in initial position also. In Iranian almost the same development is found.[1] In Latin *s* is kept in most positions, but between vowels it is 'rhotacized' to *r*.[2] In Germanic *s* gave *z* by Verner's Law (2.4.1); this is kept unchanged only in Gothic, becoming *r* in the other Germanic languages. A peculiarity of the eastern languages (Aryan, Slavic, and in part Baltic) is a change of *s* to *ś* after *i u r k*. This underwent further change in Old Indic to the cerebral *ṣ*, while in Slavic before velar vowels *x* (= *ch* as in *loch*) appears. For these cases the term 'RUKI [i.e. *r*, *u*, *k*, *i*] Law' is used. Examples:

**senos* 'old'; see 4.4.2.

**wes-* 'clothe': Skt. *vas-tē* 'puts on', Lat. *uestis uestiō*, Gr. *ἕννυμι*, *ἐσθής*, *ἐφεστρίς* 'outer garment', Hitt. *wes-* 'put on', Goth. *wasti* 'garment', *wasjan* 'clothe';

**eusō* 'I burn': Gr. *εὕω* (from **euhō* with anticipation of the aspirate), Lat. *ūrō ustus*, Skt. *ōṣāmi*;

**eso*, 1st s. subj. of **es-* 'be': Gr. *ἔω*, contracted Att. *ὦ*, Lat. *erō* (fut.), Skt. *asāni*.[3]

[1] Szemerényi, *Sprache* 12, 1966, 190f.; 14, 1968, 161f.; *Krat* 11, 1967, 219 n. 51; Gusmani, *AGI* 57, 1972, 10–23; Doria, *Studia Meriggi* i, 1979, 134–9; Szemerényi, *Fs. Winter*, 1985, 783f.

[2] On the Latin developments, see Touratier, *Glotta* 53, 1975, 246–81.

[3] On *s* in general, see Gamkrelidze–Ivanov, 116f.

4.6.1

The eastern development is seen, for example, in the locative plural, of which the ending was *-su*: Skt. *aśvā-su* 'in the mares', but *agni-ṣu* 'in the fires', *sūnu-ṣu* 'in the sons', *vāk-ṣu* 'in the words', *pitr̥-ṣu* 'in the fathers'; OCS *trĭ-xŭ* 'in three', *synŭ-xŭ* 'in the sons'. Also in the following:

**ters-* 'dry': Gr. *τέρσομαι* 'become dry', Lat. *tostus* (from **torsitos*), Goth. *ga-þairsan 'dry up'*, *þaurstei* 'thirst', OE *þurst*, OHG *durst*, Skt. *tr̥ṣyati* 'thirsts', Avest. *taršna-* 'thirst', Lith. *tirštas*;

**wers-* 'high place': Lat. *uerrūca* 'locus ēditus et asper' (Cato), 'wart', Skt. *varṣman-* 'height, peak', Lith. *viršus* 'summit', OCS *vrĭxŭ* 'summit, height'.[1]

[1] See Andersen, *ALHafn* 11, 1969, 171–90; Kiparsky, *ZSP* 34, 1969, 433; Birnbaum, *SS* 17, 1971, 235–47; Allen, *TPS* 1973, 102f.; Burrow, *Studies Palmer*, 1976, 33f.; Hock, 'Retroflection rules in Sanskrit', *South Asian Languages Analysis* 1, 1979, 47–62; Collinge, *Laws* 143f.; Gamkrelidze–Ivanov, 127f.; Vraciu, in Brogyanyi and Krömmelbein, *Germanic Dialects*, 1986, 609–13; Emmerick, *Fs. Humbach*, 1986, 71f. (Khotanese).

4.6.2

The variant *z* is well exemplified in the following:

**mizdho-* 'reward, pay': Goth. *mizdo*, OCS *mĭzda*; also Gr. *μισθός*, Avest. *mižda-* (*-iz->-iž-* as *-is-* > *-iš-*), Skt. *mīḍha-*;

**ozdos* 'branch': Gr. *ὄζος*, Aeol. *ὕσδος*, Goth. *asts*, Arm. *ost*;

**nizdos* 'nest': Lat. *nīdus*, OHG *nest*, Skt. *nīḍa-* (from *nizda->niẓḍa-*), Arm. *nist*; probably also Lith. *lìzdas* with analogically modified initial consonant.

4.6.3

Further spirants have been assumed for Indo-European on the basis of a few comparisons in which a Greek dental corresponds to an Aryan *s*. It is clear, for instance, that Skt. *r̥kṣa-* 'bear' corresponds to Gr.

ἄρκτος (also cognate are Lat. *ursus* and OIr. *art*), as does Skt. *takṣan-* 'carpenter' to Gr. τέκτων. As neither an IE dental nor IE *s* appears to explain the relationship, it has been common practice since Brugmann to posit an interdental spirant þ (=*th* in *thin*), together with its voiced counterpart ð (=*th* in *this*), and even aspirated *þh ðh*.

From the structural point of view this assumption can hardly be justified. The securely attested IE spirant *s* has no voiced counterpart (since *z* is allophonic), and it would be strange if an interdental series were more fully developed. An interdental series would, moreover, have a very curious distribution, occurring only after gutturals. It is more probable, therefore, that in such cases we have to do, not with independent phonemes, but with special developments arising in certain sound groups. This interpretation gains further support from the fact that in cases where the material for comparison is more extensive, the assumption of interdentals is contradicted by the evidence.

Thus the equation Gr. χθών, χθαμαλός = Skt. *kṣam-* 'earth' is set in a new light by the discovery of Hitt. *tekan*, gen. *taknas*, Toch. *tkaṁ*. The starting point was a form **dheghōm*, with variants **dheghom-*, **dhghem-/*dhghom-* as determined by the inflexion. From **dheghom-* arose the Hittite form, while from **dhghom-* by inversion of the initial consonant group came Gr. *χθομ-, later χθον-. Lat. *humus*, OCS *zemlja*, Gr. χαμαί are to be explained as due to simplification of *dhgh-* to *gh-*. Skt. *kṣ* is a special development of the same difficult initial group.

The equation ἄρκτος = *ṛkṣa-* also appears in a new light now that Hitt. *hartagga-* probably belongs to this group of words. In this case the starting-point must be a form **(H)ṛtko-* which appears to lie behind the clumsy Hittite spelling; in Greek it gave ἄρκτος by metathesis, in Indic it underwent a special development.[1]

[1] See Wright, *Omagiu Rosetti*, 1965, 1017–22, Schindler, *Sprache* 13, 1967, 191–205 and 23, 1977, 25–35, who give copious references to the literature; Ivanov, *Obščeind.* 24f.; Szemerényi, 'New Look' 85, and below, 7.1.4.4 n. 4; Gunnarsson, *NTS* 24, 1971, 21–82; Kuryłowicz, *BSL* 68, 1973, 93–103; Mayrhofer, *ÖAAnz* 119, 1982, 240–55; Fulk 1986, 216f.; Martinet 1986, 166f. Delamarre (*HS* 105, 1992, 151–4) suggests that Finn. *karhu* 'bear' represents an Aryan prototype **Hṛkṣas* from **H₂ṛtkos*; its *k* is from hardening of the initial laryngeal. According to Rix 1976, 31, for late IE a phoneme þ must be assumed, beside the metathetic instances mentioned above. See also Martinet 1986, 167f.

4.6.4

The attempt to ascribe to Indo-European an affricate *c* (=*ts*) can be considered a failure.[1]

[1] Benveniste, *BSL* 50, 1955, 30f.; *Hitt. et ie.*, 1962, 8; against, Lazzeroni, *SSL* 2, 1962, 12–22; Kronasser, *Etymologie* 52; Ivanov, *Obščeind.* 35f.; Szemerényi, 'New Look' 85; Kammenhuber, 'Hethitisch' 303.

4.7 STOPS

A cursory comparison of the phonological systems of the individual languages shows that they have inherited from Indo-European at least labial, dental, and guttural stops. It can just as easily be established that, in addition to the opposition voiced: voiceless, at least one other mode of articulation was in use at each of the articulatory positions mentioned above. Greek has a system of three series: voiced–voiceless–voiceless aspirate, e.g. *β π φ*. To this corresponds in Old Indic mainly the system voiced–voiceless–voiced aspirate, e.g. *b p bh*. These three series are also represented in many of the other languages, even if not in the same way. In Germanic, for example, *p f b* are found corresponding to Old Indic *b p bh*, i.e. to OInd. *bh* corresponds Gmc. *b*, a voiced sound, not a voiceless as in Greek. In other languages, e.g. Lithuanian and Slavic, the correspondences to OInd. *b* and *bh* fall together in *b*, so that in them too a voiced sound corresponds to OInd. *bh*. For the reconstruction of the third mode of articulation, therefore, two indicators are available: (*a*) Greek and Old Indic agree in pointing to aspiration as a main characteristic; (*b*) they differ in respect of voicing, and the evidence of Old Indic in favour of a voiced articulation is supported by the majority of the other languages.[1]

From this the traditional conclusion can provisionally be drawn that Old Indic has most faithfully preserved the original situation. Accordingly we must set up for the IE subsystem of stops the following phonemes:

p	*t*	*k*
b	*d*	*g*
bh	*dh*	*gh*

The question whether such a system of three series is possible and acceptable on general grounds will occupy us later (6.7.1).

Furthermore, it must be noted that Old Indic possesses a closed four-series system: not only *p b bh* but a symmetrical set *p ph b bh*. And so the question arises whether this does not more faithfully reflect the original state of affairs than the three-series system of other languages, and whether correspondences to the Old Indic fourth series are not to be found elsewhere. There are in fact a number of examples which seem to point to a fourth series also in Greek and other languages, and formerly the existence of such a series in Indo-European was taken for granted. More recent research has abandoned this point of view on the grounds that the fourth series is only weakly attested, for the most part in Aryan, so that it is not unreasonable to assume that it was an innovation. This question too must be treated in more detail later (4.8, 6.7.1.4). For the time being we may accept the phoneme types represented by *p b bh* as the three main types for Indo-European. Their existence, apart from initial *b*, is proved by a large number of correspondences.

In the case of the voiced aspirates we may ask whether they were monophonematic (i.e. single phonemes) or diphonematic (combinations of two phonemes). The question can be decided only on the basis of their distribution. In Indo-European there were sequences such as _*prek- *plāg-*drem-_ and also _*bhrāter- *dhreugh-_, etc., i.e. sequences of voiceless/voiced stop+liquid and voiced aspirate+liquid, but not sequences of three consonants, stop+spirant+liquid (e.g. not *psrem-*). This implies that in distributional terms *bhr* and *dhr* can count only as a sequence of two phonemes, not three, so that *bh* and *dh* are monophonematic.[2]

The development of the series of stops in the individual languages may now be traced in a descending line from Indo-European. The original classes are preserved only in Old Indic. In Greek the voiced aspirates, the so-called *mediae aspiratae* (MA), became voiceless aspirates, the so-called *tenues aspiratae* (TA), thus *bh* > *ph* (=ϕ), etc.[3] The Germanic development is revolutionary and complex, but can be summarized very simply by the laws of the sound shift (2.3):

p	*f*	*t*	*þ*	*k*	*χ, attested *h*
b became	*p*	*d* became	*t*	*g* became	*k*
bh	*b*	*dh*	*d*	*gh*	*g*

It should be noted that in the early historical period Gmc. *b d g* still had pronunciations similar to the corresponding Spanish phonemes: in intervocalic position they were voiced spirants; initially and after nasals and *z* they were voiced stops. Subsequently the voiced variants arising by Verner's Law (2.4.1) fell together with them.[4]

Old High German differs from the general Germanic situation as the result of the second or OHG sound shift. By this shift the Germanic voiceless stops, when double or after consonants and initially, became affricates (*p*>*pf*, *t*>*z*=*ts* and in the southern dialects also *k*>*kχ*), while between vowels and when final after a vowel they became long spirants (*p*>*ff*, *t*>*z*=*ss*, *k*>*hh*). Gmc. þ and *d* gave *d* and *t* respectively.[5]

In Latin the development of the third series is complicated, and passes through many intermediate stages which are still in part controversial. But the final result is clear.[6] In initial position the voiced aspirates become voiceless spirants: *bh-*>*f-*, *dh-*>*f-*, *gh-*>*h-*. In internal position they gave voiced stops (without aspiration): *-bh-*>*-b-*, *-dh-*>*-d-*, or in certain conditions *-b-*, *-gh-*>*-g-*, but between vowels, departing from the general trend, *-h-*. In Iranian, Lithuanian, Slavic, and Celtic the voiced aspirates fell together with the unaspirated voiced stops. In Armenian a sound shift very similar to that of Germanic took place.[4] It is interesting that *p* is lost in Celtic but in Armenian becomes *h*, which disappears before *o*.

For the development of the voiced aspirates in Greek and Old Indic, Grassmann's Law of Dissimilation (2.4) must also be taken into account: in a sequence containing two aspirated sounds, the first loses its aspiration. From IE **bheudh-* comes OInd. **baudh-*, then *bōdh-*, in Greek, first **pheuth-*, whence πευθ-.[7,8]

[1] For the general problems, see C. Peeters, 'A phonemic description of IE *bh dh gh*', *KZ* 85, 1971, 1–4; Martinet 1986, 160f.; Bomhard, 'The aspirated stops of PIE', *Diachronica* 3, 1986, 67–79. On aspiration, see B. Hurch, *Über Aspiration: Ein Kapitel aus der natürlichen Phonologie*, 1988.

[2] Cf. Szemerényi, *Phonetica* 17, 1967, 95. R. Jakobson answers a similar question on Bengali with the aid of the distinctive features, *Selected Writings* i², 1971, 647f.

[3] On the terms M(A), T(A), see Belardi, *In memoria A. Pagliaro*, 1984, 158: since *tenuis* (=ψιλός) denotes unaspirated consonants, it is absurd, he maintains, to speak of *tenues* or *mediae aspiratae*; for a quaternary system he suggests the following terms; *sorde tenui–sorde aspirate*, *sonore tenui–sonore aspirate*.

[4] On the sound shifts in the light of the new theory of glottalized sounds see below, 6.9, and cf. Szemerényi 1985, 9 (§2.6–7), 14.

[5] On the Germanic and OHG sound shifts, see the novel theories of Vennemann, 'Germanic and German consonant shifts', *ICHL* 6, 1985, 527–47; idem (ed.), *The New Sound of IE*, 1989, 231–44: IE consonant shifts (on the volume, see Szemerényi, *Diachronica* 6, 1990, 237–69); 'The relative chronology of the HG consonant shift', *Diachronica* 8, 1991, 45–57.

[6] On the Latin development of the voiced aspirates, see Szemerényi, 'The development of the IE Mediae Aspiratae in Latin and Italic', *ArchL* 4, 1952, 27–53, 99–116; 5, 1953, 1–21; Serbat, *RPh* 42, 1968, 78–90; Untermann, *Word* 24, 1971, 479f., esp. 485f.; *D. Fassunke (= Steinbauer), *Die Vertretung der urindogermanischen MA im Latein*, Magistr. Regensburg 1979; Eichner, in *Latein und Indogermanisch*, 1992, 58–62. On (Faliscan?) variation of initial *f-/h-* see Leumann², 168f.; Wallace and Joseph, *Glotta* 69, 1991, 84–93; L. Biondi, 'Osco CULCFNAM e l'alternanza F/H', *PP* 272, 1993, 374–92. Risch (*Rhein.-Westfäl. Akad. Abhg.* 72, 1984, 184) is of the opinion that the voiceless pronunciation of the aspirates in Greek and Latin could be due to the influence of the pre-Greek and pre-Latin populations respectively.

[7] See Hoenigswald, *JAOS* 85, 1965, 59f.; Langendoen, *Lg* 42, 1966, 7–9; Lejeune, *REA* 69, 1967, 280, 282; Levin, *SMEA* 8, 1969, 66–75; Lightner, *Studies M. Halle*, 1973, 128–30; Dressler, *Fs. J. Hamm*, 1975, 53–67; Schindler, *LIn* 7, 1976, 622–37; Szemerényi, *Krat* 20, 1977, 6–9 (=*SM* 518–21); Miller, *KZ* 91, 1978, 131–58; Vennemann, *Essays H. Penzl*, 1979, 557–84, esp. 557f.; Stemberger, *Glossa* 14, 1980, 113–35; Gamkrelidze, *In Memory of J. A. Kerns*, 1981, 607f.; Borowsky and Mester, *PCLS* 19, 1983, 52–63; Collinge, *Laws* 47f.; Gamkrelidze–Ivanov, 21f.; Salmons, 'Motivating Grassmann's Law', *HS* 104, 1991, 46–51.

[8] It should be noted here that, in addition to Old Indic and Greek, Hittite also probably attests the existence of the *voiced aspirates*. Sturtevant observed very early (e.g. *JAOS* 52, 1932, 10f.; definitively Sturtevant 1951, 58f.) that Hittite orthography consistently distinguishes between single writing and double writing of consonants, the former indicating a voiced stop or voiced aspirate, the latter an unvoiced stop, e.g. *i-ú-kán*, *i-ú-ga-an* 'yoke' (IE **yugom*), *te-(e-)kán* 'earth' (**dheghom*), and *lu-uk-ki-iz-zi* 'kindle, grow light' (**leuk-*). 'Sturtevant's rule' (or 'law') has often been discussed, most recently by A. R. Bomhard in several papers, e.g. 'Recent trends in the reconstruction of the PIE consonant system', *HS* 101, 1988, 2–25; 'Sturtevant's law in Hittite: a reassessment', in *Gedenkschrift for Charles Carter* (ed. Y. I. Arbeitman), 1992, 1–12; '"Zakon Stertevanta" v xettskom: reinterpretacija', *VJ* 1992 (4), 5–11 (*pp* indicates aspirated phonemes, *p* the non-aspirated consonants).

4.7.1. Labials

4.7.1.1. *p*

**ped*-, **pod*- 'foot': Gr. πούς ποδ-ός, Lat. *pēs ped-is*, Skt. *pad*-,Goth. *fōtus*, Arm. *otn*;

**spek*- 'to look': Lat. *speciō spectō*, Gr. σκέπ-τομαι (with inversion of *p-k*), Avest. *spas*-, OHG *spehōn* 'to spy';

**tep*- 'warm': Lat. *tepeō*, Skt. *tapati* 'warms, chastens himself', OCS *teplostĭ* 'warmth';

**uper(i)* 'over, above': Skt. *upari*, Gr. ὑπέρ, Lat. *s-uper*, Goth. *ufar*, OHG *ubir*.

4.7.1.2. *b*

(See 6.7.1.8 and Cowgill and Mayrhofer, *IG* i/2, 99f.).

**belo*- 'strength': Skt. *balam*, Gr. βέλ-τερος 'stronger, better', OCS *boljijĭ* 'bigger', Lat. *dē-bilis* 'strengthless, weak' (?); see Burrow, *Fs. Hoenigswald*, 63;

**pibeti* 'drinks': Skt. *pibati*, Lat. *bibit* (by assimilation), OIr. *ibid*;

**dheub*- 'deep, hollow': Goth. *diups*, Lith. *dubus*, OCS *dŭbrĭ* 'gorge, ravine', Gaul. *Dubno-rīx* 'World-king', OIr. *domun* 'world', W. *dwfn* 'world'; Cowgill and Mayrhofer, op. cit. 100 (doubts on Celtic members).

4.7.1.3. *bh*

**bher*- 'bear, carry': Skt. *bhar*-, Gr. φέρω, Lat. *ferō*, Goth. *bairan*;

**bhendh*- 'bind': Goth. *bindan*, Skt. *bandh*-, *bandhu*- 'relation', Lat. *of-fend-ix* 'chin-strap on a priest's cap', Gr. πεῖσμα 'rope, cable' (from *πενθ-σμα), πενθερός 'father-in-law, relation by marriage';

**albho*- 'white': Gr. (Hsch.) ἀλφούς· λευκούς, Lat. *albus*, OE *ælbitu* 'swan';

**gombho*- 'tooth, row of teeth': Gr. γόμφος 'peg, nail', γομφίος 'molar', Skt. *jambhas* 'tooth', *jambhya*- 'molar', OCS *zǫbŭ* 'tooth', OHG *kamb*, OE *comb* 'comb' ('toothed'), Toch. A *kam*, B *keme* 'tooth'; see Narten, *KZ* 79 (1966), 255f.

4.7.2. Dentals

4.7.2.1. *t*

**treyes* 'three': Skt. *trayas*, Gr. τρεῖς, Lat. *trēs* (see 4.3.1);

**teutā* 'race, people': OLith. *tauta* 'people', Osc. *touto* 'state, city', OIr. *tuath* 'people, land', Goth. *þiuda*, OHG *diot* (whence *diut-isc*, today *deutsch*), Hitt. *tuzzi*- 'army'; see Szemerényi 1978, 101–8;

**tres*- 'tremble, fear': Skt. *trasati*, Gr. τρέω (Hom. aor. τρέσ-σα) 'fear, flee', Lat. *terreō*, MIr. *tarrach* 'timid', Lith. *trišu* 'I tremble';

pet-* 'rush, fly, fall': Lat. *petō* (intrans. *iam uēr appetēbat*), Gr. *πέτομαι* 'fly', *πίπτω* 'fall', Skt. *patati* 'flies, hastens, falls', *patra-* 'feather, wing' (cf. Lat. *penna* from **pet-nā*), OE *feðer*, OHG *fedara* 'feather, plumage' (pet-rā*), MIr. *ethait* 'bird' (**pet-ontī*).

4.7.2.2. *d*

**domos* 'house': Gr. *δόμος*, Lat. *domus*, Skt. *damas*;
**ed-* 'eat': Lat. *edō*, Gr. *ἔδομαι* (fut.), *ἔδμεναι* (Hom.), *ἔδοντι* (Dor.), Skt. *ad-mi* 'I eat';
sed-* 'sit': Lat. *sedeō*, Gr. *ἕζομαι* (sed-y-*), *ἕδρα* 'seat', Skt. *asadat* 'sat down', Goth. *sitan*, ON *sitja*, OHG *sitzen*;
**reud-* 'to shout, howl': Lat. *rudō*, Skt. *rudati* 'wails, weeps', Lith. *raudoti* 'lament', OE *rēotan*, OHG *riozan* 'lament, weep'.

4.7.2.3. *dh*

As already indicated, *dh* becomes Lat. *d* in internal position, but *b* after *u* and *r* and before *r* and *l*.

**dhūmos* 'smoke': Skt. *dhūma-*, Lat. *fūmus* (see 4.1.10);
**medhyos* 'middle': Skt. *madhyas*, Lat. *medius* (see 4.3.1);
**widhewā* 'widow': Skit. *vidhavā*, Lat. *uidua* (see 4.1.7);
**ūdher* 'udder': Skt. *ūdhar*, Lat. *ūber*, OE *ūder*, OHG *ūtar*;
**werdho-*, **wr̥dho-* 'word': Goth. *waurd*, OHG *wort*, Lat. *uerbum*;
**bhardhā* 'beard': Lett. *barda*, OCS *brada*, OHG *bart*, Lat. *barba* (from **farbā* by assimilation);
**rudhro-* 'red': Gr. *ἐρυθρός*, Lat. *ruber*;
**stədhlo-* 'stall': Lat. *stabulum* (with anaptyxis of *-bl-* to *-bul-*).

4.7.3. Gutturals[1]

See also 4.7.4.

[1] I have retained the traditional term *guttural*, although it is manifestly false since these sounds are not articulated in the *guttur*. After various unsuccessful attempts a growing body of consensus seems to be building up in favour of *tectal*; cf. e.g. Lehmann 1993, 100f.

4.7.3.1. *k*

**kerd-*, **kr̥d-* 'heart': Gr. *καρδία*, Hom. *κῆρ*, Lat. *cor* (gen. *cordis*). Goth. *hairtō*, OIr. *cride*, Lith. *širdis*, OCS *srŭdĭce*;
**porkos* 'young pig': Lat. *porcus*, MIr. *orc*, OHG *far(a)h*, Lith. *paršas*;
**ekwos* 'horse': Lat. *equus*, Goth. *aihwa-tundi* 'bramble' (lit. 'horse-tooth'), OSax. *ehu-skalk* 'groom', Skt. *ašvas*;
**ōku-* 'swift': Gr. *ὠκύς*, Lat. *ōcior*, Skt. *āšu-*.

4.7.3.2. *g*

**agō* 'drive': Gr. *ἄγω*, Lat. *agō, Skt. ajāmi*;

**agros* 'field': Gr. ἀγρός, Lat. *ager*, Goth. *akrs*, Skt. *ajras*;
**genu*, **gonu* 'knee': Gr. γόνυ, Lat. *genu*, Hitt. *genu*, Skt. *jānu*;
**geus-* 'to taste': Gr. γεύομαι, Lat. *gustō*, Goth. *kiusan* 'try, test', Skt. *jōṣati* 'likes, enjoys'.

4.7.3.3. *gh*
**gheim-*, **gh(i)yem-* 'winter, snow': Gr. χιών, Lat. *hiems*, *bīmus* (lit. 'of two winters', from **bi-himos*), Lith. *žiema*, OCS *zima* 'winter', Skt. *hēman* (loc.) 'in winter', *śata-hima-* 'a hundred years old';
**anghu-* 'narrow': Lat. *angi-portus* 'narrow street, alley', Goth. *aggwus* (*gg*=*ng*), OHG *angi*, *engi*, OCS *ǫzŭ-kŭ*, Skt. *aṁhu-*;
**dheigh-* 'to mould (from mud)': Gr. τεῖχος 'wall' (dissimilated from **theikhos*), Lat. *fingō*, *figulus*, *figūra*, Goth. *ga-digan* 'knead, fashion from clay', *daigs* 'dough', OHG *teig*, Arm. *dizanem 'heap up'*, Avest. *pairi-daēza-* 'enclosure' (cf. Gr. παράδεισος 'garden, park', a loanword from Iranian, whence Eng. *paradise*, etc.), Skt. *dēhmi* 'smear', *dēhī* 'wall, dam';
**wegh-* 'to travel (in a conveyance), convey': Gr. ϝεχέτω (Pamph.) 'let him bring', (ϝ)ὄχος 'carriage, chariot', Lat. *uehō*, Goth. *ga-wigan* 'move, shake', OHG *wegan* 'move' (intrans.), OCS *vezǫ* 'convey', Avest. *vazaiti* 'travels', Skt. *vahati*.

4.7.4. Centum and satem; palatals, velars, labiovelars

4.7.4.1
In the examples given above, a guttural in the western languages regularly corresponds to a spirant (type *s* or *ś*) in the eastern languages. This applies to the majority of cases in which western IE languages present or, like Germanic, formerly presented a guttural. On the basis of this criterion a 'western' group, consisting of Greek,[1] Latin with the Italic dialects, Venetic, Celtic, Germanic, and now also Hittite and Tocharian (although not appearing in the West), was set up in contrast to an 'eastern' group – Baltic, Slavic, Albanian, Armenian, and Aryan; these two groups were named respectively *centum* and *satem* languages, from the form taken by the word for 'hundred' in Latin and Avestan.[2]

[1] See M. M. Todorović, 'IE gutturals in Mycenaean', *ŽA* 40, 1992, 29–38.
[2] These terms make their first appearance in P. von Bradke, *Methode und Ergebnisse der arischen [indogermanischen] Altertumswissenschaft*, 1890, 63f., 107f., and not, as many have asserted (e.g. Porzig, *Gliederung* 29 n. 4), in his earlier works, *Beiträge zur Kenntnis der vorhistorischen Entwickelung unseres Sprachstammes* (1888), or *Über die arische Alterthumswissenschaft und die Eigenart unseres Sprachstammes* (1888); in these works he speaks only of a 'clear rift' which caused a division into 'Eastern and Western Indo-Europeans', or into 'Western and Eastern Aryans', etc. (27, cf. 15, 17, 19f., 22, 30). Cf. Schwyzer, *GG* i, 54 (correct on von Bradke).

4.7.4.2
Alongside this type of correspondence, however, there are also cases in which a guttural occurs both in the western and in the eastern group. Examples:

**kreu*- 'bloody, raw; flesh': Gr. *κρέ(ϝ)ας* 'flesh', Lat. *cruor cruentus*, MIr. *crú* 'blood', OE *hrēaw*, OHG *(h)rawēr (h)rō* 'raw'—Lith. *kraujas* 'blood', OCS *kry*, Skt. *kraviṣ- kravyam* 'raw flesh';
**(s)ker(t)*- 'to cut': Gr. *κείρω*, Lat. *carō* (orig. 'cut, portion'), OHG *skeran*—Lith. *skiriù* 'divide', *kertù* 'cut, hew', Skt. *kr̥ntati kartati* 'cuts';
**loukos* 'grove': Lat. *lūcus*—Skt. *lōka*- 'open space, world', Lith. *laukas* (4.2.6);
**yugom* 'yoke': Lat. *iugum*—OCS *igo*, Skt. *yugam* (4.1.9);
**aug*- 'grow, increase': Lat. *augeō*—Lith. *áugti* (4.2.4);
**(s)teg*- 'to cover': Gr. *στέγω*, Lat. *tegō*—Skt. *sthaga(ya)ti* 'covers, veils', OCS *ostegŭ* 'garment';
**steigh*- 'go': Gr. *στείχω*, Goth. *steigan*—Skt. *stighnoti* 'steps, strides', OCS *stignǫ* 'come';
**mighlā* 'mist': Gr. *ὀμίχλη*—Lith. *miglà*, OCS *mĭgla*; also Skt. *mēgha*- from **moigh*-;
**nogho*- 'claw, foot': Gr. *ὄνυξ* (gen. *ὄνυχος*), Lat. *unguis*, OHG *nagal*—Lith. *nagas* 'nail', *nagà* 'hoof', OCS *noga* 'foot', *nogŭtĭ* 'nail'.

4.7.4.3
Since the first type of correspondence (4.7.4.1) cannot be explained as the result of development within individual languages, we are driven to the assumption that both types have their origins in the Indo-European period. To judge from historical parallels, such as Ital. *cento*, Fr. *cent* from Lat. *centum* (=*kentum*), the spirants involved in the first type of correspondence (types *s*/*š*) arose from earlier gutturals, which, however, in the final phase of Indo-European cannot have been identical with the gutturals which featured in the second type (4.7.4.2), since these were kept as such in the satem languages also. It is therefore inferred that there were *two kinds of gutturals* in Indo-European, a front series and a back series. The former were pronounced with closure of the tongue against the middle of the roof of the mouth (*palatum*, hard palate), the latter with closure of the tongue against the back of the roof of the mouth (*velum*, soft palate). The two series are therefore distinguished as *palatals* and *velars*, and it is the palatals which are involved in the first type of correspondence. Where it is important to mark the distinction, this is indicated by the use of e.g. *k* and *q*, or *k̂* and *k*, or *k'* and *k*, for palatals and velars respectively. Usually, however, as in the preceding part of this chapter, the dif-

ference can be disregarded; in the individual languages either it does not exist, as in the centum languages, or else, as in the satem languages, it is expressed by sharply distinct sound types, *s/š* and *k*, etc.

4.7.4.4

Indo-European had, however, yet *a third guttural series*, since in the majority of instances in which the satem languages show the *k* type, the corresponding type in the centum languages is not *k*, as in the case of the velars, but one represented by Latin *qu* or other sounds obviously developed from this type.

This is very clear in the case of the interrogative and indefinite pronoun. To OInd. *kas*, Lith, *kas* 'who' correspond Lat. *quis quo-* and Hitt. *kwis*. To these belong also Goth. *hwas hwa*, OHG *(h)wer (h)waz*. In the Italic dialects, on the other hand, such cases show a labial, e.g. Oscan *pis* 'quis', *pod* 'quod', and a similar development is found in Greek when the consonant in question stands before *a* or *o*, e.g. *πό-τερος* 'which (of two)', *πό-θεν* 'whence', etc.; before *e* or *i*, however, it is normally represented by a dental, e.g. *τίς* as opposed to Lat. *quis*.

There can be no doubt that here the centum type represents the original articulation, which in the satem languages lost the *w-* element as did Latin *qu* in the Romance languages, e.g. in Fr. *qui* or Ital. *chi che*, whereas in certain centum languages it changed to different sounds (type *p*, *t*). The velar and the labial elements were originally of equal importance. It is Latin which seems to have remained nearest to the Indo-European articulation. Consequently the Indo-European phoneme type is defined in general as a velar with simultaneous lip-rounding and denoted by the term *labiovelar*, written k^{ω}, g^{ω}, and $g^{\omega}h$. It need hardly be emphasized that the phonetic descriptions given above for the three series are not to be regarded as absolutely precise but as approximations.[1]

[1] Since the simultaneous existence in a synchronous system of three series of the sort just described is generally considered to be unattested in the Indo-European domain, and therefore to be actually impossible, reference must be made at this point to D. I. Edel'man, 'K tipologii ie. guttural'nyx', *IANOLJ* 32, 1973, 540–6, who demonstrates the existence of a triple opposition of three articulatory types (simple, palatalized, labialized) in Yazghulami, an East Iranian dialect in the North Pamir, and perhaps also in other neighbouring dialects. Even more important is the fact that recent research has succeeded in establishing reflexes of three series even in Anatolian, esp. in Luwian; see Melchert, *Studies in Memory of W. Cowgill*, 1987, 182–204; *HS* 102, 1989, 23 (also on Lycian); Morpurgo and Hawkins, *Studi G. Pugliese Carratelli*, 1988, 169–82 (esp. on Luw. *zart-* 'heart' from **kerd-*); Tischler, *Fs. Meid*, 1989, 429; *IF* 95, 1990, 74; Mayrhofer, *Lg* 65, 1989, 138; Otkupščikov, 'The IE guttural series', in A. V. Desnickaja (ed.), *Aktual'nye voprosy sravnitel'nogo jazykoznanija*, 1989, 39–69. Lehmann's system of two tectals (1993, 101) fails to account for the facts here given.

4.7.4.5

The representation of the labiovelars in the satem languages is fairly simple: they generally lose the labial element and thus fall together with the plain velars. Certain modifications will be discussed in 4.7.4.7. In the centum languages the developments are more complicated.

In Greek, as already indicated, the development depends on the phonetic environment: labials appear before *a*, *o*, and consonants, dentals before *e* and *i*, plain velars (κ γ χ) before and after *u*; g^{ω} and $g^{\omega}h$, however, become dentals only before *e*, giving labials β and φ before *i*.[1] In Latin k^{ω} is kept (written *qu*), but before *o*, *u*, and consonants the labial element is lost and only *k* (written *c*) remains: cf. *quis cuius*, *relinquō relictus*; exceptions are due to analogy (*quod*, *relinquunt*). In initial position before a vowel g^{ω}- and $g^{\omega}h$- became *w*- and *f*- respectively; internally both became *w* between vowels and *gw* (written *gu*) after *n*. Before liquids and nasals g^{ω} gave *g* and $g^{\omega}h$ gave *b*. In the Italic dialects (Oscan, Umbrian, etc.) k^{ω} changed to *p*, g^{ω} to *b* and $g^{\omega}h$ to *f*, but before consonants the labial element was lost. In Germanic the labiovelars were affected by the sound shift, so that from IE k^{ω} g^{ω} $g^{\omega}h$ Gmc. *hw*, *kw*, and *gw* are to be expected in the first instance. Of these *hw* and *kw* are still kept in Gothic, but in the other Germanic languages *hw* in internal position loses the labial element (Goth. *saihwan*, OHG *sehan* 'see'). The continuation of IE $g^{\omega}h$ is complicated and disputed.[2] It is certain that Gmc. *gw* was kept after nasals and became *g* before *u*, but *u* after a vowel in the same syllable, otherwise *w*; it appears to have become *b* in initial position except before *u*, and *g* after consonants.[2] The Celtic development is also disputed,[3] as are the labiovelars in general.[4]

[1] See Szemerényi, *SMEA* 1, 1966, 29–52; Stephens and Woodard, *IF* 91, 1986, 129–54; Uguzzoni, ibid. 155–85.

[2] See Seebold, *KZ* 81, 1967, 104–33; *Fachtagung* 6, 1980, 431–84 (442f. Gmc. *bōnis 'request, prayer' is traced to *ghwā- 'invoke', but see Szemerényi, *KZ* 93, 1979, 122–3=*SM* 2271–2); *Krat* 34, 1989, 124. Meid, in Untermann and Brogyanyi (below, 9.4.1.1 n. 3), 109f., and Polomé, *Fs. Hoenigswald*, 1987, 303–13, are both against Seebold, while Watkins, *In Memory of W. Cowgill*, 1987, 292f., sides with him; cf. OE *bona* 'killer' from *g^{w}*hono-n*. Note also Bammesberger, *JIES* 16, 1989, 234–5.

[3] See Cowgill, 'The outcome of *$g^{\omega}h$ in Celtic', *Fachtagung* 6, 1980, 49–78; P. Sims-Williams, 'The development of the IE voiced labiovelars in Celtic', *BBCS* 29, 1981, 201–29.

[4] See A. G. E. Speirs, *The PIE Labiovelars*, 1978; Mayrhofer 1986, 108f.

4.7.4.6

The developments of the IE palatals in the satem languages, some of which were illustrated in 4.7.3, are as follows:

IE	OInd.	Avest.	Slav.	Lith.	Arm.
k	*š*	*s*	*s*	*š*	*s*
g	*ǰ*	*z*	*z*	*ž*	*c* (=*ts*)

IE	OInd.	Avest.	Slav.	Lith.	Arm.
gh	*h*	*z*	*z*	*ž*	*j* (=*dz*), -*z*-

Note. OInd. *h* is simplified from earlier *ǰh*.

4·7·4·7

In these languages the velars and labiovelars gave plain gutturals, in OInd. *k g gh*, elsewhere *k g g*; in Armenian they were further changed by its 'sound shift' to *kh k g*.

In Aryan and Slavic, however, as well as to a lesser extent in Armenian, these sounds underwent further changes which can be summed up as *palatalization*. These changes are also familiar from the Romance languages in their development from Latin. Just as in the western Romance languages the affricates č ǰ (Eng. *ch j*) arose from Lat. *c* (=*k*) and *g* before the front vowels *e i* and the semivowel *y*, so the gutturals which resulted from the falling together of velars and labiovelars in the satem languages became affricates of the type *č* (=Eng. *ch*) or *c* (=*ts*).

In Aryan *k g gh* were palatalized to *č ǰ ǰh* before *e* (which later became *a*), *i*, and *y*. In Iranian the aspiration was lost, so that only *č ǰ* remained. In OInd. *ǰh* developed further to *h*, so that *č ǰ h* are found. Thus in OInd. the palatalized gutturals *ǰ h* fall together with the *ǰ h* which continue the IE palatals. For example:

k^{w}e 'and': Lat. -*que*, Gr. τε—Skt. Avest. *ča*;
g^{w}en- 'woman': Gr. γυνή, Goth. *qinō* (*q*=*kw*), OHG *quena*—Skt. Avest. *ǰani*-;
g^{w}hen- 'strike, kill': Gr. θείνω 'strike', φόνος 'murder', Hitt. *kwen*- 'strike, kill'—Skt. *hanti* 'strikes', Avest. *ǰan*-.

In Slavic the development was at first the same, but later *ǰ* (=*dž*) was simplified to *ž* (as *z* in *azure*);[1] since voiced aspirates and non-aspirates fell together, only the pair *č ž* are found. For example:

k^{w}id 'what': Lat. *quid*, Hitt. *kwid*, Gr. τί—OCS *čĭ-to*;
g^{w}en- 'woman': OHG *quena*—OPrus. *genna*, OCS *žena*;
g^{w}hen- 'strike': Hitt. *kwen*-—Lith. *genù* 'drive', OCS *ženǫ*.

In Slavic, however, a second palatalization took place.[1] Following the monophthongization of the diphthongs *ai oi* to *ē* (sometimes *i*), a preceding *k g* came again before a front vowel and became *c* (=*ts*) and *dz* (later *z*) by palatalization. For example:

**koilu* 'whole, undamaged': Gr. (Hsch.) κοῖλυ· τὸ καλόν, Goth. *hails*—OPrus. *kailūstiskan* 'health', OCS *cělŭ* 'whole, complete';
**ghoilo*- 'violent, high-spirited': Goth. *gailjan* 'rejoice', OHG *geil* 'wanton, exuberant'—OLith. *gailas* 'high-spirited', OCS *dzělŭ*.

In Armenian palatalization took place only in the case of the IE voiceless stops and voiced aspirates (*čhor-kh* 'four': Gr. τέτταρες, *ǰerm* 'warm': Gr. θερμός), not the voiced stops (*kin* 'woman': IE *g^{ω}*en*-, *keam* 'I live': IE *g^{ω}*i*-).

[1] See R. Channon, *The Progressive Palatalization of Velars in the Relative Chronology of Slavic*, 1979.

4.7.4.8
The development of the labiovelars can be summarized as follows:

IE	Gr.	Lat.	Gmc.	OIr.	OW
k^{ω}	π τ κ	*qu, c*	*hw*	*c*	*p*
g^{ω}	β δ γ	*gu, u, g*	*kw*	*b, g*	*b*
$g^{\omega}h$	φ θ χ	*f, b, gu, u*	*b, g, gw, w*	*g*	*g*, -ƀ-

IE	OInd.	Avest.	OCS	Lith.	Arm.
k^{ω}	*k, č*	*k, č*	*k, č, c*	*k*	*kh, čh*
g^{ω}	*g, ǰ*	*g, ǰ, -ž-*	*g, ž, (d)z*	*g*	*k*
$g^{\omega}h$	*gh, h*	*g, ǰ, -ž-*	g, *ž*, (*d*)*z*	*g*	*g, ǰ*

4.7.5

These developments are illustrated by the following examples:

4.7.5.1. k^{ω}

*k^{ω}*i*-, *k^{ω}*o*- 'who, what': Gr. τίς ποῦ 'who, where', Lat. *quis quod*, Hitt. *kwis*, Goth. *hwa(s)*—Skt. *kas*, *čid* (weakened to a particle 'even'), OCS *kŭ-to* 'who', *čĭ-to* 'what', Lith. *kas* 'who';

*k^{ω}*i*- 'atone': Gr. τίνω 'pay', τίνομαι 'punish, avenge'—Skt. *čayatē* 'avenges, punishes', *apa-či-ti-* 'reprisal'; hence

*k^{ω}*oinā* 'penalty': Gr. ποινή (as a loan word Lat. *poena*)—Avest. *kaēnā* 'punishment', Lith. *káina* 'price', OCS *cēna* 'price, value';

*k^{ω}*elo*-, *k^{ω}*e*k^{ω}*lo*- 'wheel' (*k^{ω}*el*- 'to turn'): Gr. κύκλος, ON *hvel*, OE *hwēol* (from **hweula*-, earlier **hwegwla*-) 'wheel'—Skt. *čakra*-, OPrus. *kelan*, OCS *kolo*;

**wl̥*k^{ω}os 'wolf': Gr. λύκος (from **wluk*$^{\omega}$os), Lat. *lupus* (dialectal), Goth. *wulfs* (from **wulhwas*, cf. with grammatical change ON *ylgr* 'female wolf' from **wulgwis*, IE **wl̥*k^{ω}*ī*; see Mayrhofer, op. cit. (below, 7.7.3, n. 3)—Skt. *vr̥kas*, OCS *vlĭkŭ*, Lith. *vilkas*;

penk*$^{\omega}$*e* 'five': Gr. πέντε, Lat. *quinque* (from **pinque* after *quattuor*), Goth. *fimf* (<finhw*, cf. *wulfs*)—Skt. *pañča*, Lith. *penkì*; see 8.5.2;

**sek*$^{\omega}$- 'follow': Lat. *sequor*, Gr. ἕπομαι—Skt. *sačatē*, *Avest*. *hačaitē*, Lith. *sekù*; here belongs also Lat. *socius* from **sok*$^{\omega}$*-yos*;

sek*$^{\omega}$- 'see': Hitt. *sakuwa* 'eyes', Goth. *saihwan*, *siuns* 'sight, appearance' (<seunis*, earlier **segwnis*), OIr. *rosc* 'eye, look' (< **pro-sk*$^{\omega}$*-o*), *sūil* 'eye' (< *sok^w-li-); see Szemerényi, *Fachtagung* 2, (1962), 191f.;

*pek^w- 'cook, bake'; Gr. πέσσω (from *pek^{w}yō), fut. πέψω, πέψις 'digestion', Lat. *coquō* (from *k^{w}ek^{w}ō by assimilation from *pek^{w}ō), W. *pobi* 'bake' (from *pop-*,*k^{w}ok^w-)—Skt. *pačati*, OCS *pekǫ* 'I roast' (2nd s. *pečeši*), Lith. (with transposition of *p* and *k*) *kepù*; on *coquō* see Szemerényi, *Lg* 48 (1972), 9 (=*SM* 2250).

4.7.5.2. g^w

*g^{w}en- 'woman': Gr. γυνή, OIr. *ben*, Goth. *qinō*, *qēns*—Skt. *ǰani-*, *gnā* ('goddess'), OPrus. *genna*, OCS *žena*; for Anatolian see Gusmani, 'Lydisch *kāna-* und luwisch *wana-*', *Fs. Knobloch*, 1985, and esp. Neu, *HS* 103 (1990), 208–17, who finds a Hitt. cognate in *kwin-*, a view rejected by Güterbock, *HS* 105 (1992), 1–3; cf. also 7.3.1 n. 1.

*g^{w}īwos, *g^{w}iwos 'living'; Gr. βίος 'life', Lat. *uīuos*, Osc. *bivus* (nom. pl.), Goth. *qius*, OHG *quek*, OE *cwic* (cf. *quick*='living', *quicksilver*), OIr. *beo* 'living'—Skt. *ǰīvas*, Lith. *gývas*, OCS *živŭ*;

*g^{w}em- 'come': Goth. *qiman*, OHG *queman*, whence *coman*, Lat. *ueniō* (from *wemyō), Gr. βαίνω (from *banyō, *bamyō)—Skt. *agamam* (1st s. aor.), *gamat* (3rd s. subj.), Avest. *ǰamaiti*, probably also Lith. *gemù* 'am born';

*g^{w}ou- 'cow, ox': Gr. βοῦς, Lat. *bōs* (dialectal), OIr. *bō* 'cow', OE *cū*, OHG *chuo*—Skt. *gaus*, Arm. *kov* 'cow', Slav. *gov-ędo* 'cattle'.

*bheg^w- 'to run': Gr. Hom. φέβομαι 'flee, fear'—Lith. *bēgu* 'run', OCS *bēgati*, *bēžati*;

*nog^w- 'naked': Goth. *naqaþs*, OE *nacod*, OHG *nackut*, Lat. *nūdus* (all from *nog^{w}odhos)—Skt. *nagna-*, OCS *nagŭ*, Lith. *núogas* (the last two from *nōg^{w}os);

*g^{w}el-n- 'acorn': Gr. βάλανος, Lat. *glāns* (gen. *glandis*)—Arm. *kałin*, Lith. *gilė*, OCS *želǫdĭ*;

*reg^{w}os 'darkness': Goth. *riqis*, Gr. ἔρεβος—Skt. *raǰas* (and *raǰanī* 'night'), Arm. *erek* 'evening'.

4.7.5.3. g^wh

*g^{w}her-, *g^{w}hormo- 'hot, heat': Gr. θερμός, Lat. *formus* 'hot', MIr. *gorim* 'I heat'—Skt. *gharma-* 'heat', Arm. *ǰerm* 'warm', OCS *gorēti* 'burn', *žeravŭ* 'glowing', Lith. *garas* 'steam', OPrus. *gorme* 'heat';

*g^{w}hedh- 'desire, ask for': Gr. θέσσασθαι 'pray for' (*g^{w}hedh-s-), πόθος (by dissimilation from *phothos), OIr. *guidiu* 'ask for' (*g^{w}hodheyō)[1]—OPers. *ǰadiyāmi* 'ask for', Lith. *gedù* 'long for, mourn', *godùs* 'greedy', OCS *žędati* 'to desire';

*g^{w}hen- 'strike, kill': Hitt. *kwen-*, Gr. θείνω, φόνος, Lat. *dēfendō* 'ward off', OIr. *gonim* 'wound, kill', OE *gūþ* 'battle' (from *gunþjō, *g^{w}hn̥tyā), OHG *gund-fano* 'battle standard' (as loan word Fr. *gon-*

falon)—Skt. *han-ti* 'strikes', *ghn-anti* 'they strike', OPers. *ajanam* 'I struck', Arm. *ǰnem* 'I strike' (earlier *ǰinem*), Lith. *genù* 'I drive', OCS *ženǫ* 'id.', *goniti* 'to hunt';

**snig*^{w}*h-* 'snow': Gr. νίφα, Lat. *niuem*, acc. (nom. *nix* from **sniks* from **snig*^{w}*h-s*), *ninguit* from **sning*^{w}*heti*; cf. 4.2.2;

**snoig*^{w}*hos* 'snow': Goth. *snaiws* from **snaigwas*, OIr, *snigid* 'drips, rains', W. *nyf* 'snow'—OPrus. *snaygis*, Lith. *sniegas*, OCS *snĕgŭ*;

**seng*^{w}*h-* 'proclaim': Goth. *siggwan* (*gg=ng*), OHG *singan* 'sing'; hence noun **song*^{w}*h-*, Goth. *saggws*, Gr. ὀμφή 'voice, prophecy', cf. Lat. *singultus*;

**neg*^{w}*hro-* 'kidney': Gr. νεφροί, Lat. (Lanuvium) *nebrundinēs*, (Praeneste) *nefrōnēs*, OHG *nioro* from **neuran-*, **negwr-*;

**dheg*^{w}*h-* 'to burn, warm'; Lat. *foueō* 'warm, foster', *fōmentum* (from *foui-*) 'poultice', *febris*, MIr. *daig* 'fire'—Skt. *dahati* (by dissimilation from *dhah-*) 'burns', Avest. *dažaiti*, Lith. *degù*.

[1] But from **g*^{w}*hedheyō* according to Cowgill; see above, 4.7.4.5 n. 3.

4.7.6. Note on the IE voiced gutturals

In a few instances Old Indic presents a voiced aspirate (*h*) where the other languages, in so far as they contribute anything, attest a plain voiced stop. The most certain examples are:

Skt. *hanu-* 'jaw(bone)'—Gr. γένυς, Lat. *gena*, Goth. *kinnus*;

Skt. *aham* 'I'—Gr. ἐγώ, Lat. *ego*, Goth. *ik*;

Skt. *mahi* 'big'—Gr. μέγας, Lat. *magnus*, Goth. *mikils*, Arm. *mec*;

Skt. *duhitar-* 'daughter'—Gr. θυγάτηρ; in this instance a velar is indicated by Avest. *dugədar-*, Lith. *duktē*.[1]

In one instance an Aryan voiced aspirate corresponds to a voiceless palatal in the other languages:

Skt. *hr̥d(aya)*, Iran. *zr̥d-* 'heart'—Gr. καρδία, Lat. *cor*, Lith. *širdis*.[2]

[1] See W. Winter, *Papers in Honor of M. S. Beeler*, 1980, 487–95; for 'daughter', see Szemerényi 1978, 19f. (original form **dhug-*); *Krat* 28, 1984, 71.

[2] Szemerényi, *Fs. Stang*, 1970, 513–33.

4.7.7. Note on the labiovelars

It is generally assumed that in the satem languages the labiovelars fell together with the velars completely, i.e. that they can no longer be distinguished from the velars. There are nevertheless a few clear traces of the former presence of labiovelars even within the satem group. In Old Indic the *ū* or *u* of such forms as *gūrta-* 'welcome' and *guru-* 'heavy' reveals that the guttural was formerly followed by a labial element, since the sonant liquid develops a *u*-timbre only after labials (elsewhere *i*). In Armenian the original labiovelars (with the exception of g^{ω}) are palatalized before *e i*, but not the plain velars. The infinitive of OCS *žengǫ* (IE *$*g^{\omega}hen$-*) is *gŭnati*, in which *ŭ* can be explained only as a reflex of the labial element of the IE labiovelar. These instances, few as they are, are sufficient to refute the thesis that labiovelars had never existed in the satem languages.[1]

[1] Cf. T. Burrow, *BSOAS* 20, 1957, 133–44; V. Pisani, *AGI* 46, 1961, 19–23; Szemerényi, *Syncope* 401–2 (first in 1948 and 1952). See also below, 6.7.2.1.1.

4.7.8. The nature of the labiovelars

It is the general view that k^{ω} etc. represent single phonemes, not phoneme groups (*k+w*). This view was originally based on the fact that in Latin verse a syllable containing a short vowel is normally short before *qu*, which cannot therefore represent a consonant group. This metrical usage, however, applies also to some consonant groups and so proves nothing for *qu*. Since *sequor* owes its new participle *secūtus* (the old form survives in *secta, sectārī*) to the analogy of *uoluō uolūtus*, it is clear that *qu* was felt as analogous to *lu* (with consonantal *u*), i.e. as no less a group. On this basis, therefore, it cannot be decided whether the IE labiovelar was one phoneme or two.[1]

Of greater weight is the observation that the development of a labiovelar, e.g. in Gr. ἕπομαι, is a single *p*, whereas the group *k'w* gives *šv* in Skt. *ašvas* 'horse', to which Gr. ἵππος corresponds. Unfortunately the Greek form poses a further problem with its *i*, and is hardly a suitable basis for such an argument. More significant would be a demonstration that in Indo-European k^{ω} and *kw* (i.e. plain velar+*w*) stood in opposition, so that e.g. $k^{\omega}ap$- and *kwap-* would be different words. Here too, however, it is unfortunate that the few examples of *kv-* in the satem languages are probably innovations.

There seems to remain only one way to decide this question: the structure of the IE syllable and word. As we have seen, Indo-European contained words such as *$*k^{\omega}ek^{w}lo$-* 'wheel', in which the sequence $k^{\omega}C$ occurs. In contrast, no groups such as *C+w+C* are found, no *twl, dwl, twn*, etc. It follows, therefore, that $k^{\omega}C$ cannot be taken as a group of three consonants, i.e. that k^{ω} is a single phoneme. Whether it had been so in early Indo-European is, however, another question.

[1] According to Coleman, *CQ* 13, 1963, 13–17, Lat. *qu* had two allophones, k^{ω} and *kw*. Against this a unitary view is put forward by Allen, *Vox Latina*, 1965, 16 (k^{ω}) and Wyatt, *Lg* 42, 1966, 666 (*kw*); the latter seems to be supported only by *sequor secūtus*, but *qu* could also count as a single sound in verse on the analogy of the Greek metrical rule for stop+liquid. Touratier's solution (*BSL* 66, 1972, 229f.), that monophonematic k^{ω} was realized in speech as the sequence *kw*, is a rather unsatisfactory play on words; cf. Leumann², 150. The case for a monophonematic interpretation is argued by A. M. Devine and L. D. Stephens, *Two Studies in Latin Phonology*, Saratoga, Calif., 1977, esp. 46–81; cf. Dressler's review, *IC* 24, 1978, 104 no. 584. For a sociological solution (Oscan-Umbrian influence), see Giannini, *AIΩN* 9, 1987, 239–52.

4.8. VOICELESS ASPIRATES

There exists in Aryan a fourth series of stops (see 4.7), which in Old Indic is represented by voiceless aspirated stops (*ph th kh*) and in Iranian by the corresponding voiceless spirants (*f* þ *x*). Conforming to the general principles of comparative method, it seems therefore appropriate to set up a similar series for Indo-European, although in the other languages it has for the most part merged with the other series. Recent attempts to prove that this series is an Aryan innovation will be considered later (6.7.1.4).

4.8.1

The most certain instances of a voiceless aspirate series are the following:

Skt. *phalaka-* 'board, lathe': OCS *polica* 'staff', ON *fjǫl* 'board';
Skt. *panthās*, gen. *pathas* 'way, road': Gr. πάτος 'path', πόντος 'sea', Lat. *pōns*, OCS *pǫtĭ* 'road';
Skt. *ratha-* 'chariot': Lat. *rota* 'wheel', OHG *rad*, Lith. *ratas*;
Skt. *vēttha* 'knowest'; Gr. οἶσθα, Lat. *uīdi-st-ī*, Goth. *waist*;
Skt. *pṛthu-ka-* 'young animal': Arm. *orth* 'calf', Gr. πόρτις 'heifer';
Skt. *pṛthu-* 'wide': Gr. πλατύς Lith. *platùs*;
Skt. *manthati* 'twirls': Lith. *mentùrė* 'whisk, ladle', OCS *mętǫ* 'stir up, tangle'; also Gr. μόθος 'press of battle' (?);
Skt. *asthi* 'bone'; Gr. ὀστέον, Lat. *os*, Hitt. *hastai*(?); cf. 5.4.5, 6.6.10.
Skt. *śaṅkha-* 'conch, shell': Gr. κόγχος 'mussel shell';
Skt. *śākhā* 'branch': Arm. *chax* (*ch*=*ts*+*h*) 'branch', ORuss. *soxa* 'stake, cudgel' (today 'plough'), Lith. *šakà* 'branch, prong', Goth. *hōha* 'plough'.

As regards distribution, it is remarkable that in Vedic *th* is not found in initial position, though it occurs much more frequently than the other voiceless aspirates taken together.

From the comparisons given above it is evident that in Greek *th* is represented by τ or θ, *kh* by χ. In Armenian the reflexes are *th* and *x*, and probably *ph*. In Germanic and Baltic the voiceless aspirates fall together with the corresponding unaspirated sounds, as also in Slavic with the exception of *kh*, which becomes *x*.[1]

[1] Cf. Meillet, *Dialectes* 78–83; Frisk, *Suffixales* th *im Indogermanischen*, 1936; Szemerényi, *ArchL* 4, 1952, 41–3; Hiersche, *Untersuchungen zur Frage der Tenues Aspiratae im Indogermanischen*, 1964; *REA* 80, 1978, 5–15; Villar, 'El problema de las sordas aspiradas ie.', *RSEL* 1, 1971, 129–60; Kuryłowicz, *BPTJ* 31, 1973, 3–9 (Aryan innovation); *Problèmes* 197–205; Michelini, 'Esisteva in ie. una serie di occlusive sorde aspirate?' *SILTA* 4, 1975, 49f.; Bomhard, *Nostratic* 18–20; 'The aspirated stops of PIE', *Diachronica* 3, 1986, 67–79; Rasmussen, in Vennemann 1989, 154f., 169 n. 7.

4.8.2

The frequency of voiceless aspirates after *s* in Old Indic is striking:

Skt. *sphūrjati*: Gr. σφαραγέομαι (see 4.5.3);
Skt. *sphurati* 'kicks away, tosses, springs': Gr. ἀσπαίρω 'struggle, twitch', Lat. *spernō*;
Skt. *sph(i)ya-* 'paddle, spade, shoulder blade' (see Janert, *KZ* 79 (1964), 89f.): Gr. σφήν 'wedge', OHG *spān* 'shaving' (?);
Skt. *sthā-* 'to stand': Gr. ἵστημι, Lat. *stāre*, etc.
Skt. *sthag-* 'to cover': Gr. στέγω, Lat. *tegō*;
Skt. *-iṣṭha-* (from *-istha-*, superlative suffix): Gr. -ιστος, Gmc. *-ista-*;
Skt. *čhid-* (*ch* from *skh*) 'cut off': Gr. σχίζω, Lat. *scindō*.

Instances also occur, as in the case of *sthag-* cited above, in which *s* is not present in all languages. These may include Sanskrit: Skt. *phēna-* 'foam': OCS: *pēna*, OHG *feim*, Lat. *spūma*.[1]

[1] This group is the main subject of Hiersche's book; see 4.8.1 n. 1.

4.8.3

In some cases a voiceless aspirate seems to be required by non-Aryan languages also; cf. Gr. ἀσκηθής 'unharmed' from *σκῆθος 'harm', Goth. *skaþis*.[1]

[1] According to Lamboni (*IF* 91, 1986, 227), Leumann[2] ignores Peruzzi's papers in which voiceless aspirates were found in Old Latin.

4.8.4

Instances such as the following are clearly onomatopoeic:

Skt. *kakhati* 'laughs': Gr. καχάζω, OCS *xoxotu*;
Skt. *phūt-karōti* 'puffs, blows': Gr. φῦσα 'breath, blast'; cf. Arm. *phukh* 'breath'.

4.9. THE PHONOLOGICAL SYSTEM OF INDO-EUROPEAN

We can now set out the following table for that phase of Indo-European which immediately preceded the individual languages:

4.9.1 Consonants

	Stops				Nasals	Liquids	Semivowels	Spirants
Labials	*b*	*p*	*bh*	*ph*				
Dentals	*d*	*t*	*dh*	*th*	*n*	*l*	*y*	*s*
Palatals	*g'*	*k'*	*g'h*	*k'h*	*m*	*r*	*w*	
Velars	*g*	*k*	*gh*	*kh*				
Labiovelars	g^{w}	k^{w}	$g^{w}h$	$k^{w}h$				

4.9.2. Vowels, diphthongs, sonants

i *u*	*ī* *ū*		
e *ə* o	*ē* *ō*	*ei* *oi* *eu* *ou*	*n̥* *m̥* *n̥̄* *m̥̄*
a	*ā*	*ai* *au*	*l̥* *r̥* *l̥̄* *r̥̄*

In inflexional endings long diphthongs *āi* *ōi* *ēu* *ōu* also occur.[1]

[1] For further discussion of the IE system, see below, 6. 8–9.

5

Morphonology

5.1. BASIC CONCEPTS

5.1.1

Phonemes are the constituent elements of larger linguistic units. The first of these larger units is generally understood by non-specialists to be the word, and the study of the changes in word forms, e.g. in declension or conjugation, to be the task of morphology. Variations such as Lat. *mēnsa/mēnsam/mēnsae* and *abōminātiō/abōminātiōnem/abōminātiōnis* are thus placed on the same level. Yet it is as clear now as it was for the Roman Christians that there is a great difference between *mēnsa* and *abōminātiō*. For the Latin speaker *mēnsa* cannot be analysed further, whereas *abōminātiō* both admits and invites analysis. In the first place, it is clearly derived from *abōminārī* by means of the suffix *-tiō(n-)* in the same way as *ōrātiō* from *ōrāre*, *laudātiō* from *laudāre*, etc. Secondly, *abōminārī* is obviously made up of further units, namely the preposition *ab*, the noun *ōmen ōminis*, and the verbal suffix *-ā*, for each of which, again, parallels are to hand. If we use the term *morpheme* for the smallest meaningful units of speech, *abōminātiō* can be considered as consisting of four morphemes. As this example shows, morpheme and word are not identical. A word can consist of a single morpheme, e.g. *uir*, but usually it comprises more than one. The construction of words from morphemes, or *word formation*, is as much a fundamental part of morphology as the study of inflexion, with which it is usually identified; cf. below, 7.1.4.7.

5.1.2

The example used above also shows that a morpheme is not necessarily an unchanging form. It may indeed be so: the morpheme *class-* retains its form in inflexion (*class/-es*) and word formation (*class-ify*). Often, however, various changes take place. For example, Grm. *geb-e* 'give', *gib-t* 'gives', *gab* 'gave', *gäb-e* (subj.) clearly contain the same morpheme, though in the different forms *geb-/gib-/gab/gäb-*. The morpheme, therefore, has *allomorphs*: in other words it is a collective concept for the allomorphs, just as the phoneme is the collective concept of its allophones. The type of morpheme variation illustrated by *geben* is of great importance in the German language and is known as *ablaut*. Equally important is the type called *umlaut*. These variations affect vowels, but in German, as in other languages, consonantal variations are also found. For example, in Russian the allomorph *ruk-* (nom. s. *ruk-á* 'hand') alternates with *ruč-* in *rúčka* 'little hand, handle', *ručnój* 'hand-, tame'; in English *house* (noun) with *house* (verb, *s*=*z*), or *knife* with *knive-s*.

5.1.3

Such alternations could be included either in phonology or in morphology. In phonology, following the treatment of the phonological system, they could form the material for a separate chapter on the combinatory possibilities of the phonemes in the stream of speech; they would represent the syntagmatic aspect of successive sounds in contrast to the paradigmatic arrangement of the system. On the other hand, they could be a subject in morphology, since they occur in inflexion and derivation. From the practical point of view, however, it seems expedient to deal with such alternations as border ground between the two main areas, as an interweaving of morphology and phonology, or, to use a term coined by Trubetzkoy, as *morphonology*.[1]

[1] In a fundamental essay, 'Gedanken über Morphonologie' (*TCLP* 4 (1931), 160–3), N. S. Trubetzkoy defined the task of morphonology as 'the investigation of the morphological utilization of the phonological material of a language', and assigned it a 'place of honour' between phonology and morphology. This standpoint is theoretically untenable; see esp. L. Ďurovič, 'Das Problem der Morphonologie', in *To Honor R. Jakobson* i, 1967, 556–68; like Kuryłowicz (*Phonologie der Gegenwart*, Vienna 1967, 158–69), he would like to see most of the problems relevant to this field discussed under phonology, and a few under morphology. In contrast A. Martinet (*La Linguistique* 1, 1965, 15–30) would allocate most of these topics to morphology, though recently (see *FL* 10, 1973, 349) he refers some to phonology. American (and Russian) linguistics is at present untouched by these theoretical doubts: cf. C. F. Hockett, *A Course in Modern Linguistics*, 1958, 271f.; R. A. Hall Jr., *Introductory Linguistics*, 1964, 138–44; O. Axmanova, *Fonologija, morfonologija, morfologija*, Moscow 1966, 52–62. See also Lamb, *Lg* 42, 1966, 550f., and (in opposition to Martinet's view) Postal, *FL* 2, 1966, 168f.; cf. Komárek, *TLP* 1, 1966, 145–61; Smith, 'The concept of the morphophone', *Lg* 43, 1968, 306–41; Newman, 'The reality of the morphophoneme', *Lg* 44, 1968, 507–15; Kuryłowicz, 'The notion of the morpho(pho)neme', in *Directions* 67–81; *Karlsson, *Phonology, Morphology and Morphophonemics*, Göteborg 1974; Kilbury, *The Development of Morphophonemic Theory*, Amsterdam 1976; Bergan, 'The morphophone', *LACUS* 3, 1977, 580–93; Dressler, *Grundfragen der Morphonologie*, Vienna 1977; L. Moessner, *Morphonologie*, Tübingen 1978; Anttila, 'Totality, relation and the autonomous phoneme', *CILL* 6/3–4, 1980, 49–64, esp. 58–60; Dressler, 'A model of morphonology', *Phonologica* 4, 1981, 113–22; Wurzel, 'Problems in morphonology', ibid. 413–34; Ford and Singh, 'On the status of morphonology', *PCLSP* 19, 1983, 63–78 (separation from morphology a failure); W. Lehfeldt, 'Überlegungen zum Gegenstandsbereich und zum Status der Morphonologie', *Fs. P. Hartmann*, 1983, 41–5 (44: belongs in different subdivisions of morphology); Dressler, *Morphonology: the Dynamics of Derivation*, Ann Arbor 1985 (4: belongs

neither to morphology nor to phonology; it mediates between both components without being itself a basic component); Migačev, 'O rekonstrukcii morfonologičeskix processov', *VJ* 1991 (5), 1992, 55–71 (on Germanic); Brixhe, 'Morphonologie', *BSL* 84, 1989, 21–54.

5.1.4

In addition to vowel and consonant alternations the *structure of the morpheme* will also be treated in this chapter. Furthermore a discussion of *accent*, which is bound up with the word but does not properly form part of morphology, belongs here.

5.2. ACCENT

Word accent is the emphasizing of one syllable within a word in contrast to the other syllables. The most important means of emphasizing a syllable are expiratory force (intensity), pitch, and duration. These are all employed in every type of accent, so that the long-prevalent practice of dividing languages into those with expiratory or dynamic accent and others with musical or pitch accent, as though in the former only intensity, in the latter only pitch played a part, is now obsolete. The attempt to counter this objection by drawing a distinction between 'predominantly' dynamic and 'predominantly' musical accent fails to meet the essence of the case, and the view that every accent is dynamic, the only difference being whether it is 'strongly' or 'weakly' centralizing, similarly overlooks the point at issue. Jakobson has shown that the essential difference between the two traditional types of accent is that in the one the extent of the accent is equal to the duration of the whole syllabic phoneme, in the other the accent affects only a part of the syllable, the mora. The former type is perceived as an accent of intensity, e.g. in English and Russian. The other can be illustrated from Lithuanian, in which a long vowel, which consists of two morae, can take an accent either on the first mora (falling accent) or on the second (rising accent), e.g. *súnui* 'son' (dat. s.)=*súunui*, but *bũdas* 'sort, kind'=*buúdas*. Accordingly we must speak of *syllabic accent* and *mora accent*.[1]

[1] R. Jakobson, 'Die Betonung und ihre Rolle in der Wort- und Syntagmaphonologie', 1931, in *SW* I², 1971, 117–36, esp. 119, 123; Trubetzkoy, *Grundzüge der Phonologie*³, 1962, 169–75; P. Garde, *L'accent*, 1968, esp. 50f. See also Szemerényi, *Syncope* 279f.; Garde, 'Principes de description synchronique des faits d'accent', in *Phonologie der Gegenwart*, 1967, 32–43; Pulgram, *Lingua* 23, 1969, 372–96; Rossi, 'L'accent, le mot et ses limites', *PICL* 10/4, 1970, 175–80; I. Lehiste, *Suprasegmentals*, 1970; Halle, 'On Slavic accentology', *LIn* 2, 1971, 1–19; Allen, *Accent and Rhythm*, Cambridge 1973, 74f. (stress 74f., pitch 83f., accent 86f.); Fromkin (ed.), *Tone: a Linguistic Survey*, 1978; Weidert, *Tonologie*, Tübingen 1981 (cf. Ladd, *Krat* 27, 1983, 36–40); Light, 'Tonogenesis', *Lingua* 46, 1978, 115–31; Henderson, 'Tonogenesis', *TPS* 1982, 1–24; D. Steriade, *Greek Prosodies and the Nature of Syllabification*, Diss., MIT, 1982; special no. *Prosody*, *FoL* 17/1–2, 1983, 1–285 (10 articles); Torsujeva, 'Sovremennaja problematika intonacionnyx issledovanij', *VJ* 1984 (1), 116–26;

Szemerényi, *TPS* 1985, 15–18; M. E. Beckman, *Stress and Non-stress Accent*, Berlin 1986; P. Ivić, 'Nature and functions of the prosodic phenomena in languages', *FoL* 22, 1988, 229–37; P. Auer, 'Zur More in der Phonologie', *ZfSprw* 10, 1991; H. van der Hulst and K. van der Snider, *The Phonology of Tone*, 1993.

On the early period of research, see Balázs, 'The forerunners of structural analysis and phonemics', *ALH* 15, 1965, 229–86. On the correlation of the terms tone, accent, intonation to syllable, word, syntagma, see Pilch, *Cahiers de linguistique théorique et appliquée* 3, 1966, 131–36. On intonation in particular, note the works of D. Bolinger, *Intonation and Its Parts*, Stanford 1986, and *Intonation and Its Uses*, 1989.

5.2.1

Languages differ, moreover, in the position of the accent within the word. In many languages the accent position is governed by mechanical rules; it is tied to a fixed place in the word. In Czech and Hungarian the accent always falls on the first syllable, in French on the last, in Polish on the penultimate. In Latin the accent position is determined by the penultimate syllable: if this is long, it takes the accent; if it is short, the preceding syllable is accented. There are, however, languages in which accent position is not fixed in this way. In Spanish, for example, the form *termino* can be accented in three different ways: *término* 'end', *termíno* 'I end', *terminó* 'has ended'; in English *prój̲ect* is a noun, *projéct* a verb. In contrast to the former type of 'bound' accent, the position of which is fixed by general and/or phonological rules, the latter type is said to be 'free', varying in position not, of course, at the whim of the speaker but in accordance with grammatical and morphematic peculiarities.[1]

[1] In 1977 L. Hyman found that, out of 444 languages, 114 (25%) had a main accent on the first syllable, 97 (20%) on the last syllable, and 77 (18%) on the penultimate syllable; primary accent on the second syllable is rare, occurring in only 12 (2.7%) of the languages. For these details, see Dogil, 'Elementary accent systems', *Phonologica* 4, 1981, 89–99. Note also M. Halle and J.-R. Vergnaud, *An Essay on Stress*, Cambridge, Mass., 1987 (cf. *Lg* 68, 1992, 159–65: 'a universal theory characterizing stress patterns of the world's languages').

5.2.2

Even a free accent can, nevertheless, be confined by particular restrictions, i.e. it is *free within limits*. A typical case is the Ancient Greek accent in the Attic dialect. This can fall on any one of the last three syllables of the word, but subject to certain conditions. Usually three kinds of accent are distinguished, which have been represented in writing since Byzantine times: the *acute*, the *circumflex*, and the *grave*. The grave, however, is positionally fixed: except before an enclitic, an acute accent on the final syllable becomes a grave if the word is not at the end of a sentence. This is often taken to mean that a word bearing an acute accent on the last syllable loses it in the run of the sentence (i.e. the accent is neutralized); it could, however, denote merely 'a lowered variant of the high tone'.[1] Thus only acute and circumflex remain as true accent types. On a long final syllable they are free: nom. s. *τιμή*, gen. s. *τιμῆς* show that *η* can take acute (*é*=*eé*) or circumflex (*é*=*ée*) according to grammatical function. A final syllable with a short vowel can take only the acute (which is lost). On the two preceding syllables (the penultimate and the antepenult), the accent is determined by the quantity of the final vowel or diphthong. If this is long, the penultimate can have only an acute accent, if short, a penultimate syllable with a long vowel or diphthong, if accented, takes only the circumflex, e.g. *φέρω δώρου*, but *δῶρον*. If the final syllable contains a long vowel or a diphthong counted as long, the antepenult cannot be accented at all. If it contains a short vowel or a diphthong counted as short, the antepenult can be accented but only with the acute: *φέρομεν φέρομαι*.

To describe these rules recourse is often had to a 'law of three morae', according to which the possible accentuations, starting from the final syllable, are as follows: (*a*) ⏑́ or ⏑⏑́ or ⏑́⏑, (*b*) ⏑́/⏑ or ⏑́⏑/⏑ ⏑́/⏑⏑ or ⏑⏑́/⏑⏑, (*c*) (⏑)⏑́/⏑/⏑; thus the accent cannot precede the third mora from the end of the word. This is contradicted by the fact that in the type *ἄνθρωπος* the accent falls on the fourth mora from the end (⏑́/⏑⏑/⏑). This difficulty cannot be evaded by reckoning a long middle syllable as 'half-long' (Schwyzer, *GG* i, 378) or by assuming that the penultimate syllable 'n'est pas intonable et ne renferme donc qu'une more' (Garde, *L'accent*, 145). The type *δῶρον δώρου* proves that a long penultimate also consists of two morae, and moreover it is unthinkable on general grounds that in an accentual system based on the mora a long vowel should have a value less than two morae. Justice is done to these facts by Jakobson's new formulation of the 'law of three syllables': 'The vocalic morae between the accented mora and the final mora cannot belong to different syllables, i.e. the distance between the accented mora and the final mora may not exceed one syllable'.[2]

[1] This is Allen's view, 'A problem of Greek accentuation', *In Memory of J. R. Firth*, 1966, 8–14, esp. 9; Carsson, *JHS* 89, 1969. 24–37, esp. 32; cf. Sommerstein, *The Sound Pattern of Ancient Greek*, 1973, 160f.; Allen, *Accent and Rhythm*, 1973, 244f.; D. G. Miller, *Glotta* 54, 1976, 11–24; Steriade, *LIn* 19, 1988, 271–81.

[2] For this formulation, see R. Jakobson, 'On Ancient Greek Prosody', 1937 (now *SW* i², 1971, 262–71); also Allen's modification, op. cit. (1966), esp. 12; 'Prosody and prosodies in Greek', *TPS* 1966, 107–48, 'Correlations of tone and stress in Ancient Greek', *To Honor R. Jakobson* i, 1967, 46–62. On the grave, see also H. Galton, 'The fixation of the accent in Latin and Greek', *ZPhon* 15, 1962, 273–99, esp. 286f. On the *ἄνθρωπος* problem, see Szemerényi, *Syncope* 234f. and the work there cited (238 n. 1) of M. Lucidi (now also in his *Saggi linguistici*, 1966, 77–102, with Belardi's preface, pp. xxf.), and Lurja, *VJ* 1964 (1), 116–22. On the mora see also Steriade (n. 1 above), 281–3.

5.2.3

Among the Indo-European languages, some show a bound accent from the beginning of their tradition (e.g. Armenian, Celtic, etc.), in others the accent is free or free within limits (e.g. Greek, Sanskrit, Lithuanian, and some Slavic languages). It is clear that the bound accent represents an innovation in contrast to the free, so that reconstruction of the Indo-European accent must be based on the languages with free accent.[1] Nevertheless Germanic, though it has a bound accent, is often of decisive importance in establishing the position of the Indo-European accent, since Verner's Law (as has been seen, 2.4.1) presupposes a stage in which the IE accent position was still preserved.

On the whole, however, it can be maintained that, next to Greek, Old Indic is the most important witness for the IE accent. The Old Indic accent of the Vedic period is substantially different from the Greek.[2] In the first place, it is free without restriction. In contrast to Greek, the Vedic accent can appear on any syllable: *tatás* 'stretched', *jā́nu* 'knee', *bhárata* 'carry' (2nd pl.), *bháramāṇas* 'carried', gen. *bháramāṇasya*. Secondly there are different kinds of accent, though it is to be noted that in referring to them the Indian grammarians always use the terminology of pitch, never of stress, from which it is generally inferred that the Old Indic accent was (predominantly) musical. The main accent is called *udātta* 'raised'. A syllable immediately following it has the *svarita* 'intoned', a falling tone, while all syllables preceding the *udātta* or following the *svarita* have the *anudātta* 'not raised', or low tone. For comparative purposes only the *udātta* is significant, together with the so-called independent *svarita*, which has become the main accent through loss of an earlier accented *i* or *u*, e.g. *nadyàs* 'rivers' from *nadíàs*.

[1] See A. M. Lubotsky, *The System of Nominal Accentuation in Sanskrit and PIE*, Leiden 1988 (22–119 Sanskrit evidence, 120–49 Greek evidence, 150–67 Germanic evidence); cf. *Krat* 36, 1991, 99–104.

[2] W. S. Allen, *Phonetics in Ancient India* (1953), repr. 1965, 87f.; J. Klein, *On Verbal Accentuation in the Rigveda*, New Haven, Conn., 1992. On the Old Indic terms, see also Cardona, *Fs. Kuiper*, 1969, 448f.

Note. It is interesting that in post-Vedic Indic the accent developed on the same lines as in Latin. The new 'dynamic' accent follows a four-syllable rule: it falls on the penultimate syllable if this is long, on the antepenult if the penultimate is short, and on the fourth from the end if the antepenult is also short. In some cases, however, the last syllable is accented. On Iranian see D. I. Edel'man, 'K xarakteristike obščeiranskoj akcentnoj sistemy', in *Iranskoe jazykoznanije: Ežegodnik 1981* (Moscow, 1985), 75–85.

5.2.4

The *position of the Indo-European accent* can be inferred in many cases from the agreement of Greek and Vedic both in individual words and in categories that can be systematically compared. Alongside isolated instances such as Ved. *dhūmás* 'smoke': Gr. θυμός, accent shifts such as Ved. *pā́t* 'foot', acc. *pā́dam*, gen. *padás*, corresponding to Gr. πούς πόδα ποδός, are highly significant. The IE accent position thus reconstructed is often confirmed by Germanic, e.g. Ved. *pitā́* but *bhrā́tā*, Gr. πατήρ but φράτηρ, Goth. *fadar* but *brōþar*; cf. the alternation in the perfect tense: Ved. *didḗśa* 'I showed': *didiśimá* 'we showed', OHG *zēh*: *zigum*, OE *tāh*: *tigon*. Sometimes the evidence of Slavic and/or Baltic can be added, though here in most cases account must first be taken of their various innovations; cf., nevertheless, Ved. *nábhas*, Gr. νέφος, Russ. *nébo* 'sky'.[1]

[1] Among fairly recent works mention should be made of Stang, *Slavonic Accentuation*, 1957; Dybo, *VSJ* 5, 1961, 30f.; *Slavjanskaja akcentologija*, Moscow 1981; Kuryłowicz, *IG* 7–197; Kiparsky, 'The inflexional accent in IE', *Lg* 49, 1973, 794–849 (cf. Garde 1976, 463–9); 'A compositional approach to Vedic [and IE] word accent', *R. N. Dandekar Felicitation Volume*, Delhi 1984, 201–10; Kiparsky and Halle, 'Towards a reconstruction of the IE accent', in L. Hyman (ed.), *Studies in Stress and Accent*, 1977, 209–38; a new version of this in *Lg* 57, 1981, 161–80. General survey in Szemerényi 1985, 15f. A change of the type *k^{w}étwores* to *k^{w}etwóres* is assumed by Rix (*Fs. Knobloch*, 1985, 348), but only in words of three or more syllables.

5.2.5

As regards the *nature of the Indo-European accent*, the fact that both the Vedic accent and until the end of the classical period the Greek accent were described in terms of pitch led to the inference that the IE accent was (at least predominantly) *musical*. As was explained earlier, however, it is more important to decide whether it was a *syllable accent* or a *mora accent*.[1]

Greek, with its opposition of acute and circumflex, appears to support a mora accent. Vedic has nothing comparable to this, but it has been noticed that in Vedic verse long *ā* is often treated as disyllabic, especially in the gen. pl. *-ām* and certain accusative forms in *-ām -ās*; compare, for example, disyllabic *gām* and (?) *dyām* with βῶν βοῦν and Ζῆν(α), and the genitive ending *-ām* with -ῶν. The Lithuanian gen. pl. ending *-ų̃*, with its circumflex, also agrees with this.[2]

The numerous agreements between Greek and Lithuanian are even more striking. In this connection it must be noted that the Lithuanian falling accent or acute (*ú*=*úu*) and the rising accent or circumflex (*ũ*=*uú*) have nothing in common with the similarly named Greek accents except the written signs; in pitch sequence they are the exact opposite. The Slavic accentuation, however, which also has these two kinds of accent, proves that in Lithuanian a reversal has taken place, so that the signs can be equated. Among the accent correspondences the following types are especially noteworthy:

Lith.	Greek
algà 'pay', gen. *algõs*	θεά, θεᾶς
nãmas 'house', loc. *namiẽ* 'at home'	οἴκοι 'at home' (=*οἴκοῐ)
gẽras 'good', nom. pl. *gerì*	οἶκοι 'houses' (=*οἶκοί)[3]
nom. dual *gerù*	θεώ
kálnas 'mountain', instr. pl. *kalnaĩs*	θεοῖς[3]

Thus it seems to be proved that the opposition of acute and circumflex in Greek has an exact correspondence in Lithuanian (and in Slavic), and consequently that this opposition of syllabic intonations is inherited from Indo-European. This would also entail that the Indo-European accent was mora-based.[4]

This essentially traditional view of the Indo-European accent has been challenged by the Polish scholar J. Kuryłowicz in a series of impressive works.[5] He begins by pointing out that a language which has a free accent, quantity (i.e. long and short vowels and diphthongs), and intonation on each syllable is typologically unknown; therefore no such system can be assumed for Indo-European. Next he finds that the alleged agreements between Greek and Balto-Slavic do not in fact exist, since in Greek the intonation is phonological only on the final syllable, whereas in Baltic it simply does not exist on the final, but only on the first, syllable. The Greek intonation is, he maintains, the result of contractions in the final syllable: here, and here only, the opposition αέ and άε (ά and ᾶ) acquired phonological significance. The Baltic development, on the other hand, rests on the fact that the accent was shifted from a short middle syllable to the first syllable, and the newly accented vowel, if long, received an acute, whereas an originally accented long vowel changed over to a circumflex: IE **mātérm̥* (acc.) and **bhrā́term̥* became Balt. **mõterim* **brõterim*. The alleged agreements of the type *algõs*: θεᾶς are merely illusory. Such intonations cannot be established for Indo-European.[6]

These conclusions have, however, been almost unanimously rejected by Baltic and Slavic specialists.[7] In particular the agreements in the intonation of final syllables still make a strong impression, and their dismissal as representing innovations is not convincing. A connection continues to be upheld, and with it the validity of the evidence provided by these languages for Indo-European.[8]

[1] Cf. Voyles, *Glotta* 52, 1974, 81: 'The question is not whether IE had tone but whether it was polytonous or monotonous; IE may have been monotonous, and Greek, Lithuanian polytony may be innovated.'

[2] The OInd. phenomenon is explained differently by Kuryłowicz, *IG* 15f.

[3] On the problem how Greek diphthongs in final position can have two kinds of intonation, see Kherlakian, *BSL* 79, 1984, 213–27 (in opposition to Kuryłowicz and Kiparsky). Differently Bonfante, *BSL* 81, 1986, 374–6; Mańczak, ibid. 377–84 (frequency!); Meier-Brügger, *Fachtagung* 8, 1992, 285f.; A. W. Grundt, 'Tonal accents in Basque and Greek', *ICHL* 4, 1980, 371–9.

[4] The old theory of Bezzenberger (*BB* 7, 1883, 66f.) and Hirt (*IF* 1, 1891, 1f. and *IG* v, 1929, 199f.) is still defended by Garde 1976, 340f., 458f., but cf. Kuryłowicz, *BSL* 72/2, 1977, 287.

[5] The works of Kuryłowicz extend from the early articles, 'Le problème des intonations balto-slaves', *Rocznik Slawistyczny* 10, 1931, 1–80, and 'L'indépendence historique des intonations baltiques et grecques', *BSL* 35, 1934, 24–34, to the comprehensive works *L'accentuation* (1952, 2nd edn. 1958, see pp. 162f.) and *IG*, 1968, 83f., 111f.

[6] On other grounds Kiparsky, *Lg* 49, 1973, 832, and Kortlandt, *JIES* 14, 1986, 153–60, also reject the IE intonations.

[7] Especially important are: Vaillant, *BSL* 37, 1936, 109–15, esp. 115; C. S. Stang, *Slavonic Accentuation*, 1957, 5f. (for the comparisons, 14); *Vgl. Gram.* 125f., esp. 130f.; L. Sadnik, *Slavische Akzentuation*, i, 1959; G. Y. Shevelov, *A Prehistory of Slavic*, 1964, 38–80, esp. 65f. Cf. also Illič-Svityč, *Akc.*, esp. 15f.; Kortlandt, *Slavic Accentuation*, Lisse 1975. A useful research report for 1957–77 by Kortlandt appeared in *KZ* 92, 1979, 269–81; see also *FoLH* 4 1983, 27–43; Collinge, *Laws* 271f.; W. R. Vermeer, 'PIE vowel quantity in Slavic', *Fachtagung* 8, 1992, 115–36. For IE, Hirt, *IG* v, *Der Akzent*, 1929, still remains important; also Loewe, *Der freie Akzent des Indogermanischen*, 1929; Campbell, 'The IE accent', *TPS* 1936, 1–42; and more recently Gercenberg, 'Rekonstrukcija ie. slogovyx intonacij', in Kacnel'son (ed.), *Issledovanija v oblasti sravitel'noj akcentologii*, Leningrad 1979, 3–89; and *Voprosy rekonstrukcii ie. prosodiki*, Leningrad 1981 (see Erhart, *Krat* 27, 1983, 74–8); Bomhard, *Nostratic* 61–73.

[8] For Germanic, the so-called *Auslautsgesetze* ('sound laws in word-final position') are important; see Hamp, *SL* 13, 1959, 29–48; Makajev, in *SGGJ* ii, 1962, 290–338; Lane, *JEGP* 62, 1963, 155–70; Hollifield, *Sprache* 26, 1980, 19–53, 145–78; 30, 1984, 73–9. For the difference between final bimoric and trimoric long vowels, see Stiles, *TPS* 86, 1988, 115–43. On the Germanic accent, see also Bennett, 'Prosodic features in Proto-Germanic', in van Coetsem and Kufner (eds.), *Towards a Grammar of Proto-Germanic*, 1972, 99–116, esp. 115; *A. Liberman, *Germanic Accentology* i, *The Scandinavian Languages*, Minneapolis 1982; Lubotsky (above, 5.2.3 n. 1), 150f.

5.2.6

An important phonological distinction must be briefly mentioned again here, since it receives unexpected confirmation from the Balto-Slavic accent. As was seen earlier (4.5.3), the IE short and long syllabic nasals and liquids had identical developments in Germanic and Balto-Slavic; the result in both series was *ur* or *ir*, etc. In Balto-Slavic, however, the old difference between short and long is still detectable in the accent.[1] Thus in Lithuanian the short sonants have given diphthongs with circumflex:

IE **dekm̥tos* 'tenth', Gr. δέκατος	Lith. *dešim̃tas*
**newn̥tos* 'ninth', Goth. *niunda*	*deviñtas*
mr̥-ti- 'death', Skt. *mr̥ty-u-*	*mir̃ti* 'die'
**wl̥kʷos* 'wolf', Skt. *vr̥kas*	*vil̃kas*

In contrast, the long sonants are represented by diphthongs with acute accent, now written *ìm ìn ìl ìr*:

IE *pl̥̄nos 'full', Skt. *pūrṇa-* Lith. *pìlnas*
*wl̥̄nā 'wool', Skt. *ūrṇā* *vìlna*
*gr̥̄no- 'ground', Lat. *grānum* *žìrnis* 'pea'
*gʷr̥̄tos 'agreeable', Lat. *grātus* *gìrtas* 'praised'
*gn̥̄tos 'known', Goth. *kunþs* *pa-žìntas*

[1] See Lindeman 1987, 86–8; E. Stankiewicz, 'The nominal accentuation of Common Slavic and Lithuanian', in *American Contributions, 10th Congress of Slavists*, Columbus, Oh., 1988, 385–400; Lubotsky (above, 5.2.3 n. 1), 18f.; Sklyarenko, 'The origin of Lithuanian intonations', *Baltistica* 26, 1990, 39–53 (Russ.); also *VJ* 1991 (6), 64–77.

5.2.7

In Greek, as the account given above shows, the IE accent position has been well preserved in nominal categories. In the verb, on the other hand, the original system has, with a few exceptions, been radically changed by the shifting of the accent towards the beginning of the word to the full extent allowed by the three-syllable rule: φέρομεν, φερόμεθα.[1]

A number of other changes are grouped together as *Wheeler's Law*. A polysyllabic word with dactylic ending (– ⏑ ⏑) shifts the accent from the final syllable to the penultimate: πατράσι from *πατρασί (cf. ποδῶν ποσί), ποικίλος ἀγκύλος in contrast to the more original Skt. *pēšalá- ankurá-*. Compounds of the type στρατηγός ἱπποφορβός show an accented penultimate in cases of dactylic ending: αἰπόλος βουκόλος πατροκτόνος etc.[2]

Vendryes' Law affects Attic only. By this law a circumflex accent on the penultimate syllable is replaced by an acute on the preceding syllable if this is short: ⏑ ⁀ ⏑ becomes ⏑́ – ⏑; hence ἀρχαῖος σπουδαῖος αἰδοῖος but τέλειος γέλοιος τρόπαιον ἔρημος. This is the explanation of ἔγωγε ἔμοιγε in contrast to ἐγώ ἐμοί from *ἐγῶγε *ἐμοῖγε, in which the long penultimate could bear only the circumflex.[3]

[1] On the problems of Greek accentuation, see Schwyzer, *GG* i, 371f.; Vendryes, *Traité d' accentuation grecque*, 1945; Lejeune, *Traité de phonétique grecque*^{2}, 1955, 265–72; *Phonétique historique du mycénien et du grec ancien*, 1972, 293–300; Kuryłowicz, *Accentuation*^{2}, 106–61; Garde, *L'accent*, 93f., 144–8; Allen, *Vox Graeca*, 1968, 106f.; Kiparsky, 'A propos de l' histoire de l'accentuation grecque', *Langages* 8, 1967, 73–93. See also 5.2.2 and Bailey, *Lg* 45, 1969, 644f.; Mouraviev, *CQ* 22, 1972, 113–20 (new rules for position of accent); Allen, *Accent and Rhythm*, 1973, 230f.; Sommerstein (above, 5.2.2 n.1), 122–79; Voyles, 'Ancient Greek accentuation', *Glotta* 52, 1974, 65–91; Lubotsky (above, 5.2.3 n. 1).

A dynamic element in addition to the predominantly musical accent is posited by Sealey, *GR* 10, 1963, 11–25; Szemerényi, *Syncope* 280f. (syncopes even with musical accent, e.g. in Greek; Mańczak, *BPTJ* 42, 1989, 129–37, accepts my examples but ascribes them to frequency); Allen, *TPS* 1966, 107–48, and *To Honor R. Jakobson* i, 1967, 46–62; against, Newton, *Phoenix* 23, 1969, 359–71, but cf. Allen, *Fs. Hoenigswald*, 1987, 11–18. Bubenik, *IF* 84, 1980, 90–106, supposes an expiratory accent for Proto-Greek and Mycenaean: this is certainly impossible.

[2] In support, Hirt, *IG* v, 1929, 50; Schwyzer, *GG* i, 379; against, Kuryłowicz, *Accentuation*^{2}, 147f.; *IG* 105; *Mél. Benveniste*, 1975, 327; Miller, *Glotta* 54, 1976, 15f.; cf. also Collinge, *Laws* 221f.

[3] Vendryes, *MSL* 13, 1906, 218f., conceding priority to Hirt, *IF* 16, 1905, 88, cf. *IG* v, 55f.; Schwyzer, *GG* i, 381; against, Kuryłowicz, *Mél. Benveniste*, 328f.; Miller, op. cit., 19f. (no limitation to Attic); Collinge, *Laws* 199f.; Meier-Brügger, *Fachtagung* 8, 1992, 283–9.

5.2.8

Latin has completely abandoned the original system, but between the prehistoric free accent and the three-syllable accentuation of the historical period there is a transitional stage.[1] After the middle of the first millennium BC the IE free accent was replaced by a bound dynamic accent on the first syllable,[2] which led to the weakening and even to the loss of short vowels in non-initial position: *faciō*, but *conficiō confectus*; *regō*, but *surgō pergō*; *sēmis*, but *sē(mi)stertius*, etc.; cf. 4.1.12 fin. In inscriptions of *c.*500 BC there is still no trace of these changes. The second accent change probably took place during the third century BC, and is not completed even by the time of Plautus, when words consisting of four short syllables were still accented on the first, e.g. *fácilia*.

[1] On the Latin accent, see Leumann², 235–54; Kuryłowicz, *Accentuation*², 381–9 (also on Romance); Galton (above, 5.2.2 n. 2), esp. 291f.; Lepscky, *ASNP* 31, 1962, 199–246; Kuryłowicz, *IG* 190f.; Allen, *JL* 5, 1969, 193f.; Mignot, *Mél. Benveniste*, 1975, 419–26; Pulgram, *Latin–Romance Phonology: Prosodics and Metrics*, 1975; 'The accent in spoken Latin', *Fs. Baldinger*, 1979, 139–44; Mignot, 'La place de l'accent en latin', *BSL* 75, 1980, 285–308; Rix, in G. Vogt-Spira (ed.), *Studien zur vorliterarischen Periode im frühen Rom*, 1989, 23–39: 'in about the 4th cent. the initial accent was superseded by the penultimate rule'.

On the old controversy whether the accent of classical Latin was musical or dynamic, see (against the musical accent) Allen, 'On quantity and quantitative verse', *In Honour of Daniel Jones*, 1964, 3–15, esp. 4; *Vox Latina*, 1965, 85f.; Pulgram, *AJPh* 84, 1965, 143.

[2] Against the initial accent, Untermann, *Word* 24, 1971, 489f.; it is also doubted by Pulgram, op. cit. (1975), 92–113.

5.2.9

So far only word accent has been discussed, as though each word had its own accent. This is not, of course, entirely the case. In all languages words are found which, because of their weaker meaning, have no accent of their own but 'lean on' other words and form an accentual unity with them. Such words are called *clitics* (from Gr. κλιτικός 'leaning');[1] if they are attached to the preceding word they are known as *enclitics*, if to the following word, *proclitics*. Examples of enclitics are Lat. *que ue*, inherited from Indo-European, and also pronouns like the indefinite *quis*, Gr. τις or με μου μοι in contrast to the emphatic non-enclitic ἐμέ ἐμοῦ ἐμοί. Proclitic were the so-called prepositions, which in Greek, if disyllabic, take the grave accent on the second syllable to denote loss of tone; the original accented form is seen in what is incorrectly termed anastrophe, e.g. πέρι ἔνι ἄπο. Even a syntagm such as ὁδὸς εἰς ἄστυ has only a single accent (Garde, *L'accent*, 93). It is interesting that in Old Indic the verb in a main clause, except in first position, is unaccented, whereas in first position and in subordinate clauses it is accented; whatever the explanation, we may suppose that the prevailing recessive accent of the Greek verb is connected with it.[2]

One of the most important observations on the position of enclitics is summed up in the so-called *Law of Wackernagel*, according to which they occupy the second place in the sentence.[3]

Such details apart, nothing is known about the accentuation of syntagms and sentences in the old Indo-European languages, nor, therefore, in Indo-European. It is, however, probable that interrogative sentences were marked in the usual way by a rising intonation.[4]

[1] On clitics, see Zwicky, *Phonologica*, 1976, 29–39; *On Clitics*, IULC 1977; Jeffers and Zwicky, 'The evolution of clitics', *ICHL* 4, 1980, 221–41; Berendsen and Zonneveld, 'Properties of clitics', *FoL* 18, 1984, 3–21; also Jucquois, *Muséon* 83, 1970, 535–40. For Slavic, see Jakobson, 'Les enclitiques slaves', 1933, now *SW* ii, 1971, 16–22. For the Latin accent before enclitics, see R. W. Tucker, *TAPA* 96, 1965, 449–61; Steriade, *LIn* 19, 1988, 296–8. On enclisis in Greek, see Barrett, *Euripides' Hippolytos*, Oxford 1964, 424–7; Allen, *Accent and Rhythm*, 1973, 240f.; Sommerstein (above, 5.2.2 n.1), 159–66; Steriade, op. cit., 283–96.

In an important general study, 'The independence of syntax and phonology', *Lg* 61, 1985, 95–120, and earlier, *Some Problems in a Theory of Clitics*, IULC 1982, J. L. Klavans has proposed three parameters for the placing of clitics: the structural factors *dominance* (initial/final) and *precedence* (before/after), and the phonological factor *liaison* (proclitic/enclitic). On this see also Zwicky, 'Clitics and particles', *Lg* 61, 1985, 283–305. For the syntax of clitics see F. Esvan and L. Renzi, *RivLing* 1/2, 1989.

[2] On the accent of the compound verb see Kuryłowicz, 'L'accentuation du verbe composé', *BSL* 59, 1964, 1–10.

[3] See Wackernagel, 'Ein Gesetz der idg. Wortstellung', *IF* 1, 1892, 333–436, repr. *Kleine Schriften* i, 1955, 1–104, and the important article of Watkins, *PICL* 9, 1964, 1035–42; also Blomqvist, *MH* 28, 1971, 145–55; Berrettoni, *SSL* 11, 1971, 170–99; Collinge, *Laws* 217f. Against Wackernagel: Hock, *Studies in the Linguistic Sciences* 12/2, 1982, 1–38. Recent studies: M. Hale, 'Notes on Wackernagel's Law in the language of the RV', *In Memory of W. Cowgill*, 1987, 38–50; G. Dunn, 'Enclitic pronoun movement and the Ancient Greek sentence accent', *Glotta* 67, 1989, 1–19 (16: from Homer to St Matthew a steady trend away from Wackernagel's Law); Ruijgh, 'La place des enclitiques', *Wackernagel Kolloquium*, 1990, 213–33 (233 reference to I. Hajdú, *Stellung der Enklitika . . . bei Pindar und Bacchylides*, Lund 1989); S. Luraghi, 'Sulla legge di Wackernagel', in *Dimensioni della linguistica*, 1990, 31–60 (see *Lg* 68, 1992, 222: some exceptions in Greek and Hittite); P. H. Miller, *Clitics and Constituents in Phrase Structure Grammar*, New York 1992; S. R. Anderson, 'Wackernagel's revenge', *Lg* 69/1, 1993, 68–98.

Parallels from Romance are examined by D. Wanner, *ICHL* 7, 1987, 575–90, and in book form, *The Development of Clitic Pronouns*, 1987 (see Pignatelli, *AGI* 76, 1991, 137–45); A. G. Ramat, 'Clitici latini e romanzi', in *Dimensioni della linguistica* (above), 11–30.

[4] The Old Indic position is thoroughly examined by Strunk, *Typische Merkmale von Fragesätzen und die aind. 'Pluti'*, Munich, Bayr. Akad. 1983 (cf. Szemerényi 1985, 18), and A. M. Etter, *Die Fragesätze im R̥gveda*, 1985, esp. 14, 122. The applicability to Avestan is disputed by Strunk, *Fs. Knobloch*, 1985, 466. It is interesting that in Akkadian in interrogative sentences the accent is shifted, with secondary vowel lengthening, to the penultimate or final syllable: *ippǖšū* or *ippušū́* 'will they do?' instead of *íppušū*; see Moscati, *Comparative Grammar of the Semitic Languages*, 1969, 70.

5.3. VOWEL ALTERNATIONS: ABLAUT

Change of consonants and/or vowels within a morpheme is a feature of the most diverse languages. Some examples of both have been given above (5.1.2). Here we propose to examine more closely a particular type of vowel alternation.

In Latin the allomorphs *fac-*, *fec-*, *fic-* (5.2.8) clearly belong together: *fac-* represents the original form, from which *fec-* and *fic-* arose at a certain time under certain conditions. We know also that this time was not earlier than about 500 BC. In such cases we have to do with a Latin vowel alternation, one which arose within the history of the Latin language.

There are, however, vowel alternations which can be shown not to have arisen during the history of Latin. It is clear that *tĕgō tŏga tēgula* represent the same root morpheme *teg-*, and equally so that the alternation *ĕ/ŏ/ē* would not be explicable within the history of Latin. In the same way the alternation between *deikō* (class. *dīcō*, but OLat. DEICERENT) and *dik-* in *dĭctus* is left unexplained. These alternations find correspondences in Greek, where they are even more richly represented. To the type *ĕ/ŏ/ē* belong, for example, πατέρα εὐπάτορα πατήρ, to the type *ei/i* λείπω ἔλιπον, with which in Greek *oi* is frequently associated, e.g. λοιπός. Precise equivalents are also found in Germanic: e.g. *ĕ/ŏ/ē* in Goth. *bairan* (*ai=ĕ*) *bar bērum* 'to bear, I/he bore, we bore'; *ei/oi/i* in *steigan staig stigum* 'to go up, I/he went up, we went up'.

Vowel alternations of this kind are found in the other Indo-European languages also. As they correspond exactly in their basic scheme and cannot be explained within the histories of the individual languages, they must necessarily be *inherited from Indo-European.* They appear both in lexical morphemes, the so-called roots, and in grammatical morphemes, the various suffixes. Since Jacob Grimm, this type of IE vowel alternation has been denoted in German by the word *Ablaut*, which is often used also in English alongside the (less convenient) term *vowel gradation*; in French *apophonie* (a loan translation with Greek components) is used.[1]

[1] For the basic problems, see Brugmann, *Grundriss*[2] i, 1897, 482–505; *KVG*, 1904, 138–50; Meillet, *Introduction* 153–68; Hirt, *IG* ii, 1921; Schwyzer, *GG* i, 353–64; Kuryłowicz, *Apophonie*; *IG* 199–338; J. Gil, 'L'apofonia en ie.', *Estúdios Clásicos* 14, 1970, 1–111; Szemerényi 1972, 138–43; Leumann[2], 29–41.

5.3.1

Our first task will be to give a purely descriptive account of the ablaut system. In the series *ĕ/ŏ/ē*, if *ĕ* is taken as the basis, the *normal grade*, *o* can be designated as its *o-grade* and *ē* as its *long* (or *lengthened*) *grade.* The type *ei/oi* thus shows normal grade and *o*-grade. In the series *ei/oi/i* the grade represented by *i* can be treated in a descriptive account as having arisen through the elimination or loss of *e*, and can be designated as a *nil-grade* or *zero grade*. In the series *e/o/ē* the representation of this grade is in fact zero, as in e.g. *ἐ-πτ-όμην* 'I flew' beside *πέτ-ομαι* 'I fly'. In contrast to this grade the normal grade can also be designated *full grade*. Finally, beside the long grade *ē* is found long grade *ō*, so that the basic scheme of vowel gradations comprises *five grades*: full grade, *o*-grade, zero grade, long grade, long *ō*-grade; all five are represented in the following Greek example:

F	O	Z	L	LO
πα-τέρ-α	*εὐπά-τορ-α*	*πα-τρ-ός*	*πα-τήρ*	*εὐπά-τωρ*

Not all grades are attested for every root, as the following selection shows:

F	O	Z	L	LO
πέτομαι	*ποτέομαι*	*ἐπτόμην*	–	*πωτάομαι*
ἔχω	*ὄχος*	*ἔσχον*	–	*εὐωχέω*
(<**σέχω*)	('holder')	*ἴσχω* (<**σί-σχ-ω*)		
sedeō	*solium* (if	*nīdus*	*sēdēs*	–
	<**sodiom*)	(<**ni-zd-os*	*sēdāre*	
		<*-sd-*)		
regō	*rogus*	–	*rēgula*	–
			rēx	
necō	*noceō*	–	–	–
decet	*doceō*	–	–	–
pater	–	*patris*	–	–
–	–	*uic-tr-īx*	–	*uic-tōr*

Very often only full grade, *o*-grade and zero grade are attested:

F	O	Z
λείπω	*λέ-λοιπ-α*	*ἔλιπον*
	λοιπ-ός	
ἐλεύσομαι	*εἰλήλουθα*	*ἤλυθον*

—the second example with prothetic *ϵ-* from IE **leudh-* (cf. OIr. *luid* <**ludh-et* 'he went', Goth. *liudan*<**leudh-* 'grow'), i.e.

**leudh-*   **loudh-*   **ludh-*.

Just as here the zero grade of the diphthongs *ei eu*, after loss of the full grade *e*, is the second component of the diphthong as vocalic *i u*, so the second component of the groups *en em er el* remains in the zero grade as sonant *n̥ m̥ r̥ l̥*, e.g.

δέρκομαι 'see'	*δέδορκα*	*ἔ-δρακ-ον*	(from **dr̥k-*)

πένθος	πέπονθα	ἔ-παθ-ον	(from **pn̥th-*)
'grief'			
πείσομαι	(<πενθ-σ-)	πάσχω	(from **pn̥th-sk-ō*)

From the structural point of view it is important to observe here that in all clear cases the syllabic sonants represent a zero grade.

The change in vocalic timbre from full to *o*-grade is called *qualitative ablaut*, while the change in quantity to zero or long grade is termed *quantitative ablaut*.

The ablaut series so far adduced have a monosyllabic basic form with *e* as the basic vowel. Most IE roots are of this type. But *a* and *o* also occur as basic vowels, as do *ā ē ō*. Thus we speak of short-vowel and long-vowel ablaut series. Further, there are disyllabic as well as monosyllabic roots. Roots may therefore be classified as

I. Monosyllabic: (*a*) with short vowel
(*b*) with long vowel

II. Disyllabic.

5.3.2. Monosyllabic short-vowel ablaut series

Most roots of this type contain, as has been said, the basic vowel *e*. If *C* is used to denote a consonant, roots of the type *CeC*, *CeCC*, *CCeC*, and *CCeCC* are possible and attested. Most of these types have been illustrated above; here only a few additional examples are given:

F	O	Z	L
**kel*- 'hide'			
Lat. *occulō*	**kolyā* in	Lat. *clam*	Lat. *cēlāre*
(< **kelō*)	Goth. *halja*		
OIr. *celim*	OE *hell*		
OHG *helan*	OHG *hella* 'hell'		
Grm. *ver-hehlen*			
**kerd*- 'heart'			
Goth. *hairtō*	Lat. *cor(d-)*	Lith. *širdìs*	Gr. κῆρ
		Gr. καρδία	
**melg*- 'strip off, milk'			
Gr. ἀμέλγω	Lat. *mulgeō*	Skt. *mr̥ṣṭa-*	Skt. *mārṣṭi*
Grm. *melken*	(< **molgeyō*)		'wipes'
**men*- 'think'			
Skt. *manas* 'mind'	Lat. *moneō*	Skt. *manyate*	
=Gr. μένος	*meminī*	Gr. μαίνομαι (< *man-y-*)	
	(< **me-mon-ai*)	Skt. *matas* (<**mn̥-to-*)	

The monosyllabic short-vowel ablaut series came to be of unique importance in Germanic. They form the foundation and framework for five of the seven classes of the so-called strong verbs, which survive with extraordinary tenacity right through to the modern Germanic languages. They correspond basically to the types which have been reviewed above. The following examples illustrate this for German:

I. IE *CeiC-/CoiC-/CiC-*: Gmc. *CīC-/CaiC-/CiC*

IE **steigh-*	Goth. *steigan*	*staig*	*stigum*	*stigans*
'climb'	OHG *stīgan*	*steig*	*stigum*	*gistigan*
	NHG *steigen*	(*stieg*)	*stiegen*	*gestiegen*

II. IE *CeuC-/CouC-/CuC-*: Gmc. *CeuC-/CauC-/CuC-*

IE **gheud-*	Goth. *giutan*	*gaut*	*gutum*	*gutans*
'pour'	OHG *giozan*	*gōz*	*guzzum*	*gigozzan*
	NHG *giessen*	*goss*	*gossen*	*gegossen*

Note IE *eu* becomes *iu* throughout in Gothic, *io* before *a e o* in the following syllable but otherwise *iu* in OHG.

III. The basic vowel is followed by nasal or liquid and a consonant (*R*=nasal or liquid):

IE *CeRC-/CoRC-/CR̥C-*: Gmc. *CeRC-/CaRC-/CuRC-*

IE **bhergh-*	Goth. *bairgan*	*barg*	*baurgum*	*baurgans*
'conceal'	OHG *bergan*	*barg*	*burgum*	*giborgan*
	NHG *bergen*	*barg*	(*bargen*)	*geborgen*

IV. The root is as in III but without the final consonant:

IE *CeR-/CoR-/CR̥-/CēR-*: Gmc. *CeR-/CaR-/CuR-/CēR-*

IE **bher-*	Goth. *bairan*	*bar*	*bērum*	*baurans*
'carry'	OHG *beran*	*bar*	*bārum*	*giboran*
	NHG *(ge)bären*	*-bar*	*-baren*	*geboren*

Note. In this class the syllabic sonant appears before a vowel (see 4.5.4), but in Germanic the reflex is the same as before a consonant in III. The earlier alternation in the preterite, corresponding to that of classes I–III, is preserved only in the preterite-presents Goth. *man munum* and *skal skulum*, OE *man munon*, OHG *scal sculum*; otherwise the long grade is substituted for the zero grade.[1]

[1] On this see Fourquet, *Festgabe L. L. Hammerich*, 1962, 64; Polomé, *PICL* 9, 1964, 872.

V. The structure of the root is the same as in IV, but the basic vowel is followed by a stop or spirant (here denoted by *T*):

IE *CeT-/CoT-*: Gmc. *CeT-/CaT-*

IE *sek^{ω}-	Goth. *saihwan*	*sahw*	*sēhwum*	*saihwans*
'see'	OHG *sehan*	*sah*	*sāhum*	*gisehan*
	NHG *sehen*	*sah*	*sahen*	*gesehen*

ADDENDUM. Loss of *e* in the zero grade of roots with *-we- -re-* etc. gives *-u- -r̥-* etc.:
**swep-* 'to sleep': ON *svefn* 'sleep', **swop-*: Lith. *sapnas*, **sup-*: Gr. ὕπνος.
**prek-* 'ask for': Goth. *fraihnan*, **prok-*: Lat. *procus* 'suitor', **pr̥k-sk-ō*: Skt. *pr̥ččhati*, Lat. *poscō*.[1]

[1] Cf. Levin 'A reclassification of the OE strong verbs', *Lg* 40, 1964, 156–61; Motsch, 'Zum Ablaut der Verben in der Frühperiode germanischer Sprachen', *Studia Grammatica* 6, 1967, 119–44; Hinderling, *Studien zu den starken Verbalabstrakta des Germanischen*, 1967, 10f.; Boggs, *Orbis* 15, 1967, 501–4; Campanile, 'La classificazione dei verbi forti in gotico', *SSL* 10, 1970, 174–83; Anderson, 'Ablaut in . . . the OE strong verb', *IF* 75, 1971, 166–97; Barnes and Esau, 'Germanic strong verb', *Lingua* 31, 1973, 1–34; E. van der Rhee, 'Vokalalternanzen im germanischen starken Verbum', *ABäG* 5, 1973, 11–31; F. van Coetsem, 'Germanic verbal ablaut and its development', in F. van Coetsem and L. R. Waugh (eds.), *Contributions to Historical Linguistics*, Leiden 1980, 281–339; U. Hempen, *Die starken Verben im Deutschen und Niederländischen*, Tübingen 1988; F. van Coetsem, *Ablaut and Reduplication in the Germanic Verb*, Heidelberg 1990. For the general trend in the Germanic languages, note the conclusion of O. Werner, *German Life and Letters* 43, 1990, 182–9: in the dialect of Luxemburg only 18 strong verbs still have a preterite.

5·3·3

A small number of monosyllabic roots have *a* or *o* as basic vowel:

F	O	Z	L	LO
**ag-* 'drive'				
Gr. ἄγω	ὄγμος 'swathe'	–	Lat. *amb-āg-ēs*	Gr. ἀγ-ωγ-ή
**ak-* 'sharp'				
Gr. ἄκρος	ὄκρις 'point'	–	–	–
Lat. *aciēs*	*ocris* 'hill'	–	*ācer*	–

When the basic vowel is *o*, there can be no distinct *o*-grade:

**od-* 'to smell'				
Lat. *odor*		–		
Gr. ὄζω		–	Gr. ὄδ-ωδ-α[1]	

[1] According to Kuryłowicz, *Apophonie* 185f., *IG* 251f., there was no *a/o* ablaut: a new *oi* could only be formed from the zero grade *i* on the pattern of *ai/i*; e.g. the root *ait-* had the zero grade *it-*, from which a new *o*-grade *oit-* was formed.

5.3.4. Monosyllabic long-vowel ablaut series

In a number of roots the long vowels *ā ē ō* occur as basic vowels of ablaut series. That they are basic vowels and not merely the long grade of short-vowel ablaut series can be seen not only from the absence of short-vowel forms but also from the following structural relationships.

Where in the short-vowel series there is a zero grade, e.g. in the formation of the verbal adjective with suffix *-to-*, in the long-vowel series there appears a schwa. Further, corresponding to *mi*-verbs with full-grade short-vowel singular forms and zero-grade plural forms, e.g. Gr. *εἶμι* 'I go', *ἴ-μεν* 'we go', the long-vowel roots show the alternance long vowel/schwa, e.g. *δί-δω-μι* 'I give', *δί-δο-μεν* 'we give', with the same zero-grade vowel as in the verbal adjective *δο-τός*. From the point of view of structure it should be added that long-vowel roots always end in the long vowel (*dō-*), whereas in short-vowel roots at least one consonant always follows the basic vowel.

Obviously long-vowel roots cannot be expected to have long-grade forms. Even if such forms once existed, we could not recognize them.

The best-attested long-vowel roots are **dhē-* 'put', **stā-* 'stand', **dō-* 'give'. The ablaut grades are as follows:

F	Z	O
**dhē-*		
Gr. *τί-θη-μι*	*τί-θε-μεν*	*θω-μός* 'heap'
Lat. *fēcī*	*factus*	
Goth. *ga-dē-ps* 'deed'		Goth. *dōms* 'judgement'
Skt. *da-dhā-mi*	Skt. *hi-ta-*	OE *dōn* 'do'
**stā-*		
Gr. ἵ-στᾱ-μι	*στᾰ-τός*	
Lat. *stāre*	*stă-tus*	*Lith. stuomuo, stuomas* 'growth'
Skt. sthā	*Skt. sthi-ta-*	
**dō-*		
Gr. δί-δω-μι	*δί-δο-μεν*	–
Lat. dōnum	*dă-tus*	–
Skt. da-dā-mi		

In the zero grade Greek has respectively *ε α ο*; Old Indic (and Aryan generally) has *i*; Latin and all other Indo-European languages always have *a*. It was precisely this opposition between Aryan *i* and *a* of the other IE languages which led in the first place to the supposition of schwa (see 4.1.11); in Greek this unstable neutral vowel would have been assimilated to the corresponding basic long vowel in each case, i.e. *θε-* on the analogy of *θη-*, etc. It is also theoretically possible that only Greek had retained an original multiplicity which had been reduced to a single timbre in the other languages;[1] on this see 6.4.7.2.

[1] On the situation in Old Indic (*ā/a* but in a few cases also *ā/i*) see Tischler, *In Memory of J. A. Kerns*, 1981, 311–23.

ADDENDUM. Some hold that schwa in medial position was lost in certain languages, cf. OInd. *duhitar-*, Gr. *θυγάτηρ*, but Iran. *dugdar*, *duxtar*, Lith. *duktė*, Goth. *dauhtar*. See (in favour): Meillet, *Dialectes* 63f.; Kuryłowicz, *IG* 225f., 235f.; Insler, *Lg* 47, 1971, 573–85; G. Schmidt, 'Tochter und Vater . . .', *KZ* 87, 1973, 36–83; Bennett, *Studies A. A. Hill* iii, 1978, 13–18; Pinault, 'The reduction of the IE laryngeals in internal syllables before yod', *ICHL* 5, 1982, 265–72; Bammesberger, *Studien zur Laryngaltheorie*, 1984, 94f.; according to Ringe, in Bammesberger 1988, 429, 'Germanic drops all laryngeals in medial syllables but apparently merges them with *u* in final syllables' (see Bennett, loc. cit.); see also Fulk, ibid. 153–77, esp. 171f., and cf. Matzel, *Krat* 34, 1989, 137. Against: in Iranian, Reichelt, *Iranisch* (=*Geschichte der idg. Sprachwissenschaft* ii 4/2, 1929), 51f.; Kuiper, *IIJ* 18, 1976, 241–53; in Armenian, Hamp, *JAOS* 90, 1970, 228–31, but in *Etimologija*, 1985, 64, he holds that schwa in medial position was lost in the whole northern branch of Indo-European. On Burrow's views, see Szemerényi, *Krat* 28, 1984, 68f.

5.3.5. Disyllabic ablaut series

That Indo-European had disyllabic as well as monosyllabic forms as the basis for ablaut variations can be seen most clearly from Old Indic. In the morphological system of that language the infinitive with suffix *-tum* (acc. of a stem in *-tu-* corresponding to the Latin supine) and the agent noun in *-tar-* are formed from the full grade of the root, whereas the verbal adjective in *-ta-* (=Lat. *-tus*) and the abstract noun in *-ti-* take the zero grade. In the present indicative also the full grade often occurs. Examples for monosyllabic roots:

	Present	Inf.	-ta-	-ti-
bhar- 'carry'	*bhárati*	*bhár-tum*	*bhr̥-tá-*	*bhr̥-tí-*
han- 'strike'	*hánti*	*hán-tum*	*ha-tá-*	*ha-ti-*
gam- 'go'	*gámati* (aor. subj.)	*gán-tum*	*ga-tá-*	*gá-ti-*
śru- 'hear'	(*śr̥ṇōti*)	*śró-tum*	*śru-tá-*	*śrú-ti-*

To these can be added the agent nouns from the same roots: *bhar-tar-*, *han-tar-*, *gan-tar-*, *śrō-tar-*.

In another group of verbs, however, we find a quite different situation, though the present may appear identical. Examples:

Present	Inf.	-tar-	-ta-	-ti-
jaratē 'sings, welcomes'		*jari-tar-*	*gūr-tá-*	*gūr-tí-*
janati 'produces'	*jani-tōs*	*jani-tar-*	*jā-tá-*	*jā-ti-*
sanōti 'gains'	*sani-tum*	*sani-tar-*	*sā-tá-*	*sā-tí-*
pavatē 'cleans'	*pavi-tum*	*pavi-tar-*	*pū-tá-*	*pū-ti-*
bhávati 'becomes, is'	*bhavi-tum*	*bhavi-tar-*	*bhū-tá-*	*bhū-tí-*

In this group, then, the full grade is disyllabic, and the second syllable always contains *i*. For this reason the Old Indic grammarians, often followed by their western successors, speak of roots without *i* (*an-iṭ*) and with *i* (*sa-iṭ*>*sēṭ*). There is the further difference that in this group *ūr*, *ā*, and *ū* appear in the zero grade, in contrast to the *ṛ*, *a*, and *u* of the *aniṭ*-roots (illustrated above); *ūr* and *ā* have already been noted as the Old Indic reflexes of the IE long sonants *r̥̄*, *n̥̄* (4.5.3).

It is clear that in these instances OInd. *i* cannot represent IE *i*, since if it had done so it could not have been lost. It must therefore represent IE schwa. Accordingly the full grade of the *sēṭ*-roots presupposes a type *CeRə*-, and the zero grade *CR̥̄*-. Since the zero grade of *CeR*- is *CR̥*-, it is easy to infer that *R̥̄* in *CR̥̄*- reflects the combination of *R*+*ə*. The presents *janati pavatē bhavati* must also contain **genə*- **pewə*- **bhewə*-, from which it follows that schwa is lost before a following vowel. It is also clear that *ū* in *pūta*- *bhūta*- represents the combination of the zero grade *pu*- *bhu*- (from **pew*- **bhew*-) with schwa, i.e. *ū*=*uə*, and examples like *nayati* 'leads', *nayi-tum*, *nī-tá*-, *nī-tí*-, or *bháyatē* 'fears', *bhī-tá*-, show that *ī* in such forms=*iə*.

In a number of instances, therefore, it can be seen that the long sonants (*n̥̄ m̥̄ r̥̄ l̥̄*) and also *ī ū* are of secondary origin, arising from the coalescence of the corresponding short sonants and *i u* with schwa. Since schwa itself is in clear cases the zero grade of a long basic vowel (see 5.3.4), one is led to conclude that the ablaut alternations in question involve disyllabic 'bases' such as **bhewā*- **pewā*- **genē*-, etc., in the reduced grades of which sometimes only the long vowel appears in zero grade form, giving **bhewə*- **pewə*- **genə*-, etc., and sometimes both syllables appear in the zero grade, giving **bhū*- **pū*- **gn̥̄*-, etc. Which long vowel was thus included in the base cannot be discovered from Old Indic, in which *ā ē ō* all become *ā*; to answer this question the testimony of the other languages, especially the classical languages, is needed.

Forms corresponding to the Old Indic *sēṭ*-roots are, of course, also found in the other languages. It is clear that Gr. *γενέτωρ*, Lat. *genitōr*, in contrast with e.g. Lat. *fer-tōr*=Skt. *bhar-tar*-, have not acquired an *ϵ* or *i* after the 'root' *gen*- as an arbitrary addition; a monosyllabic root *gen*- is also contradicted by the fact that its verbal adjective would necessarily have been *gentus*, instead of the actual form *(g)nātus* which exactly corresponds to Skt. *ǰāta*- and like the Sanskrit form goes back to IE **gn̥̄tos*. Further examples will be given below.

So far it has been shown that the disyllabic root type **CeRā*- occurs in the forms **CeRə*- and **CR̥̄*-, e.g. IE **gʷerə*- and **gʷr̥̄*- *in Skt. ǰaritar*- and *gūr-ta*-. IE **gʷerə*- presents full grade of the first syllable with zero grade of the second syllable, i.e. F_1Z_2; similarly **gʷr̥̄*- is Z_1Z_2.

The full-grade vowel of the second syllable can only be determined if a form with full-grade second syllable is attested, and in that case the first syllable is in zero grade, giving Z_1F_2. Such a form appears in Gr. *γνήσιος* 'born in wedlock', and accordingly Gr. *γενέτωρ*, Lat. *genitōr* (from **genatōr*) and Skt. *ǰanitar-* with their *ε a i* represent the zero grade of *ē*. The basic ablaut variants of **genē-*, which is never attested with full grade in both syllables, are therefore F_1Z_2 **genə-*, Z_1F_2 **gnē-*, Z_1Z_2 **gn̥̄-*. To these can be added the forms with (full) *o*-grade FO_1Z_2 and Z_1FO_2, i.e. **gonə-* and **gnō-*, and with long grades (in the first syllable only) **gēnə-* and **gōnə-*; schwa is lost before a vowel, so that forms of the type **gen- *gon- *gēn-* can occur. The following examples will serve to illustrate these points:

(*a*) **genē-*, 'beget, bear, be born':

F_1Z_2: Skt. *ǰani-tar*, Gr. *γενέ-τωρ*, Lat. *geni-tōr*; Skt. *ǰan-as*, Gr. *γέν-ος*, Lat. *gen-us*;
FO_1Z_2: Gr. *γόν-ος*, Skt. *ǰan-a-*; Gr. *γέ-γον-α*, Skt. *ǰa-ǰan-a*;
Z_1F_2: Gr. *γνή-σιος*;
Z_1FO_2: Gr. *γνω-τός* 'kinsman', Goth. *knō-dai* (dat. s. f.) 'race';
Z_1Z_2: Skt. *ǰā-ta-*, Lat. *(g)nātus*, Goth. *(airþa-)kunds* '(earth)born'.

(*b*) **pelē-* 'fill, be full':

F_1Z_2: Skt. *parī-man-i* (loc.) 'in plenty', *parī-ṇas-* 'excess'; Goth. *filu*, OE *fela*, OIr. *il* 'much, many';
FO_1Z_2: Gr. *πολ-ύς* (?), see 4.4.3, 5.4;
Z_1F_2: Lat. *plē-nus*, Gr. *ἔ-πλη-το*;
Z_1Z_2: Skt. *pūr-ṇa-*, Lith. *pìl-nas*, Goth. *fulls*; Skt. *pur-u-* 'much, many' (4.4.3).

(*c*) **gʷeyē-* 'live':

F_1Z_2: Gr. *βεί-ομαι* (fut.);
FO_1Z_2: Avest. *gay-a* 'life', Serb. *goj* 'peace';
Z_1F_2: Avest. *ǰyā-tu* 'life', Gr. *ζῆν*;
Z_1FO_2: Gr. *ζω-ός* 'alive'; Gr. *ἐ-βίω-ν*, *βιῶ-ναι*;
Z_1Z_2: IE **gʷī-wos* (see 4.7.5.2; cf. Bammesberger, *IF* 88, 1984, 227–34; Lindeman, *IF* 90, 1986, 62–4).

(*d*) **gheyā-* 'yawn':

FO_1Z_2: OHG *gei-nōn*;
Z_1F_2: Lat. *hiā-re*, OCS *zija-ti*;
Z_1Z_2: Lat. *hī-scō*.

(*e*) **gʷerō-* 'swallow':

F_1Z_2: Gr. *βάραθρον*, Arc. *ζέρεθρον* (both from **gʷerə*; see Szemerényi, *Syncope* 215); Arm. *ker* (*o*-stem *kero-*) 'food';

FO_1Z_2: Gr. βορ-ός, Lat. *uor-āre*;
Z_1F_2: Gr. ἔ-βρω-ν, βι-βρώ-σκω;
Z_1Z_2: Skt. *gīr-ṇa-* 'swallowed' (part.), Lith. *gìr-tas* 'drunk(en)'.

In the forms with zero grade of the first syllable the alternation between variants such as **gʷyō-*: **gʷiyō-* (*c*) should be noted. This and also *Cw-*: *Cuw-* are parallel to the alternation *mn-*: *mn̥-* discussed above (4.5.4; cf. 5.7.2.2–4).

Examples of disyllabic ablaut in noun inflexion are provided by the words for 'husband's brother's wife' (*f*) and 'duck' (*g*).

(*f*) F_1Z_2: Gr. ἐνάτηρ (Hom. εἰνάτερες has metrical lengthening of the first syllable), Lat. *ianitrīcēs* (from **yenatres*, with assimilation of **yena-* to **yana-*, vowel weakening in the second syllable, and *-īc* on the analogy of *genitrīcēs*), Phryg. ιανατερα, Lith. *jéntė*;
Z_1Z_2: Skt. *yātar-*.

The paradigm was thus nom. **yénə-tēr*, acc. **yénə-ter-m̥*, gen. **yn̥̄-trós*; cf. W. Schulze, *Quaestiones epicae*, 1894, 157f.; Kuryłowicz, *Accentuation*² 31; Beekes, *KZ* 86 (1972), 34; Neumann, *Glotta* 65 (1987), 33–7.

(*g*) F_1Z_2: Lat. *anas*, Lith. *ántis*, OHG *anut*; on this see Fulk, cited in 5.3.4, Addendum;
Z_1Z_2: Gr. νῆσσα, Ar. *ātī-*; see (against Rix) Lindeman, *HS* 103 (1990), 19.

The paradigm was thus nom. **anə-tī*, gen. *n̥̄-tiyās*; see Hollifield, *Sprache* 30 (1984), 34f., and again Rix, *HS* 104 (1991), 186–98[1].

[1] There is today no purely descriptive account of IE ablaut. We can still profit from Saussure's youthful work, the famous *Mémoire sur le système primitif des voyelles dans les langues indo-européennes*, 1878, reprinted in *Recueil des publications scientifiques de F. de Saussure*, 1922, and published in an Italian translation with commentary by G. C. Vincenzi, *Saggio sul vocalismo indoeuropeo*, Bologna 1978; see Szemerényi, *Krat* 24, 1980, 43–6; Prosdocimi, *IF* 89, 1985, 329–35. For the modern literature, esp. on the question of origin, see below, 6. 1–4.

5.3.6

Vowel gradation has a function in the Indo-European grammatical system the importance of which cannot be overstated. In the verb system, for example, full grade is for the most part associated with the present tense, zero grade with the aorist, and *o*-grade with the perfect (λείπω–ἔλιπον–λέλοιπα). Noun formations show originally a similar close connection with particular ablaut grades. In the course of inflexion also certain ablaut grades undergo a lively exchange; in many tenses of the verb full grade appears in the singular only, while dual and plural show the zero grade. As such alternations of grade are often coupled with alternations of accentuation, it may be said that the ablaut is redundant, e.g. that in the verbal adjective **klu-tós* (Gr. κλυτός, Lat. *inclutus*) the accented suffix *-tó-* is 'the sole carrier of the semantic function'. Since, however, the same accentuation could be used with different ablaut grades as early as Indo-European, i.e. there was no automatically correlated change, this statement is of limited significance.[1]

[1] On the redundancy of vowel gradation, see Kuryłowicz, *Phonologie der Gegenwart*, 1967, 160f.

5.3.7

Vowel alternations in addition to those involved in ablaut also seem to occur. These are of various types:

(*a*) Contractions, e.g. dat. s. *-ōi* from *-o+ei*, nom. pl. *-ōs* from *-o+es*; see 7.6.2 and 7.6.5.

(*b*) Alternations of vowel length in final position, e.g. **me/mē* 'me'; see Brugmann, *KVG* 145; Szemerényi, *Fs. Gipper*, 1985, 753f.; Strunk, 'Wortumfang und Wortform', *KZ* 100, 1988, 323f.

(*c*) Alternations of vowel length in internal position, especially *ī/i*, *ū/u* e.g. **wīro-*/**wiro-* 'man', **sūnu*/**sunu-* 'son'; cf. M. Leumann, *Kleine Schriften* 362 (first in 1952); Szemerényi, *Syncope* 328f. (also on Dybo); Kortlandt, *Slavic Accentuation*, 1975, 76f.; Leumann², 41.

(*d*) Obscure alternations such as **syū-*/**sīw-* 'to sew', **sp(h)yū-*/**sp(h)īw-* 'to spit'; see Kuryłowicz, *IG* 218; Rasmussen 1989, 109–19; below, 5.4.2.

(*e*) The alternations *wr̥ wl̥ wn̥*/*ru lu nu*, e.g. OInd. *vr̥kas*, Goth. *wulfs*: Gr. λύκος 'wolf'; cf. McCone, *Ériu* 36 (1985), 171–6.

(*f*) Shortening of long vowel before sonant+consonant, the so-called *Osthoff's Law*; see Osthoff, *Philologische Rundschau* 1, 1881, 1593f.; Schwyzer, *GG* i, 279; Collinge, *Laws* 127f.: e.g. ἔγνον<*ἔγνω-ντ; πτέρνη, OInd. *pārṣṇi-*, Lat. *perna* 'thigh'; κῆρ 'heart' is not, however, from **kērd* but from **kēr*, preserved in Hittite *kēr* (see Szemerényi, *Fs. Stang*, 1970, 520f.; *Fachtagung* 5, 1975, 336f., and below, 6.2.7.5).

5.4. CONSONANT ALTERNATIONS

Parallel to the vowel alternations there are a number of consonant alternations, which, in contrast to vowel gradation, have no functional significance.

5.4.1. *s* mobile

A number of roots appear in the different Indo-European languages, and sometimes even within the same language, with or without initial *s*.

In such cases the terms *movable s* or *s mobile* are used. Examples:

**teg-* 'to cover': Gr. τέγος τέγη 'roof, house', Lat. *tegō tēctum teges toga*, OIr. *tech* 'house', ON *þekja* 'to cover', *þak* 'roof', OHG *decchen dah*; but

**steg-* 'to cover': Skt. *sthagayati* 'veils', Gr. στέγω 'cover, keep off, protect', στέγος στέγη 'roof, house', ON *staka* 'coat, skin', OCS *o-stegŭ* 'garment, coat', Lith. *stíegti* 'to roof', *stógas* 'roof'.

**pek-* 'to see': Skt. *páśyati* 'sees', Avest. *pašne* 'in view of'; but

**spek-* 'to see': Skt. *spaś-* 'spy', Avest. *spasyeiti*, OLat. *speciō*, OHG *spehōn* 'to spy'.

**nē-* 'to sew': Goth. *nēþla*, OHG *nādala* 'needle'; but

**snē-* 'to spin': Skt. *snāvan-* 'sinew', OIr. *snīm* 'to spin', OHG *snuor* 'cord', probably also Gr. ἔ-ννη 'nēbat'.

In the interpretation of these variations there are two main lines of approach: *s-* is an originally meaningful prefix;[1] loss, or perhaps addition, of *s-* is a sandhi phenomenon: an immediately preceding word with final *s* caused a relocation of the boundary between the two words.[2] A third explanation of *s* as an infix has been proposed by Karstien (*Infixe im Indogermanischen*, 1971).[3]

[1] J. Schrijnen, *Études sur le phénomène de l's mobile*, 1891; 'Autour de l'*s* mobile', *BSL* 38, 1937, 117f.; Hirt, *IG* i, 318f., 329–33; Erhart, 'Sur le rôle des préfixes dans les langues ie.', *Sbornik, Univ. Brno*, 1966, A.14, 13–25; Makajev, *Struktura* 217f.; accepted by Kuryłowicz, *VJ* 1971 (3), 125f.

[2] F. Edgerton, 'IE *s* movable', *Lg* 34, 1958, 445–53.

[3] See further Schwyzer, *GG* i, 334; Benveniste, *Origines* 164f.; E. Fränkel, *IF* 59, 1949, 295f.; H. Wanner, 'Wortpaare vom Typus recken-strecken', *Sprachleben der Schweiz: Fs. R. Hotzenköcherle*, 1963, 133–40; Schindler, *Sprache* 15, 1969, 159; Hoenigswald, *Lg* 28, 1952, 182–5; J. Gleasure, *Ériu* 24, 1973, 190f. (suggests an origin in children's speech); Dunkel, in *In Memory of W. Cowgill*, 1987, 20. A *z* movable is assumed by H. W. Bailey (*Adyar Library Bulletin* 31/32, 1968, 11) in three cases, IE **zgʷes-*, Avest. *zgr̥t-*, Iran. *zgar-*; since *z* appears in all three instances before a voiced stop, however, it can only be, at the most, an allophone of *s* movable.

5.4.2

An alternation *w/zero* is found in initial groups, especially *tw- sw-*. It is widespread in the 2nd s. pronoun and the reflexive pronoun:

**twe* 'thee': Skt. *tvā(m)*, Gr. σε, Arm. *khe-z* (*kh*<*tw*);

**te*: Lat. *tē*, OE *þe(c)*, OHG *dih*, OCS *tę*;

**swe* '-self, -selves': Skt. *svayam*, Gr. (ϝ) ἑ;

**se*: Lat. *sē*, Goth. *sik*, OCS *sę*.

In the word for 'six' there is a similar alternation:

**sweks*: Gr. (ϝ)ἕξ, W. *chwech*, Avest. *xšvaš*;

**seks*: Lat. *sex*, Goth. *saihs*.[1]

An alternation *sy-/s-* is found in Skt. *syūtas* 'sewn', Lith. *siúti* 'sew', OCS *šiti* (< **syū-*): Skt. *sūtram* 'yarn', Lat. *suō* (see 5.3.7 *d*). Similarly, *py-/(s)p-* in Gr. πτύω 'spit' (from **pyū-*): Lat. *spuō*; also *ghy-/gh-* in Skt. *hyas* 'yesterday': Lat. *hes-ternus heri*, Grm. *gestern*.[2]

[1] A prefix *w-* is postulated by Miller, *Lingua* 37, 1975, 40, for cases such as *(w)esu*, *(w)ersen-*, *(w)es-*, *(v)arṣati*, *(v)ardh-*.

[2] An alternation *d-/zero* appears in **dakru/*akru* 'tear'; see Hamp, *Studies G. S. Lane*, Chapel Hill, 1967, 146f.; Makajev, *Struktura* 270f.; Dunkel (above, 5.4.1.n3), 14. An alternation *k-/zero* is discussed below, 6.4.4.2.

5·4·3

Interchange between different series of stops occurs at the end of morphemes and, more rarely, at the beginning of morphemes. Examples:

**pō-* 'to drink': Skt. *pāti* 'drinks', *pā-tram*=Lat. *pō-culum* (both from **pō-tlom*), *pōtus*, but reduplicated pres. Skt. *pibati*, Lat. *bibit*, OIr. *ibid* (all from **pibeti*);

**ap-* 'water': Skt. *āp-as*, but OIr. *abann* 'river' from **ab-* (or **abh-*?);

**dhwer-/*dhur-* 'door, gate': Gk. θύρα, Goth. *daur*, etc., but Skt. *dvār-*;

**bhudh-* 'ground': Skt. *budhna-*, Gr. πυθμήν, Lat. *fundus*, but OE *botm* from **bhud-*;

**wedh-* 'lead (home)': Skt. *vadhū-* 'wife', but Gr. ἔεδνον ἕδνον 'dowry', OE *weotuma* 'bride price' from **wed-* (but see Szemerényi, 'Kinship' 199f.);

**kap-* 'take hold of': Lat. *capiō*, Goth. *hafjan*, but OIr. *gabim* 'I take';

**ghabh-* 'take hold of': Lat. *habeō*, but Goth. *haban* from **kabh* (or from preceding **kap-*?);

**deik-* 'to show': Gr. δείκνυμι, Lat. *dīcō*, Goth. *teihan*, but Goth. *taikns* 'sign' from **deig-*;

**pak-* 'fix, fasten': Lat. *paciscōr pāx*, but *pangō pēgī*, Gr. πήγνυμι.[1]

The interchange of guttural voiced stops and voiced aspirate stops has already been mentioned, as has the isolated alternation between voiceless and voiced aspirate stops in **kerd-* 'heart': Gr. καρδία, Lat. *cor*, etc., but Skt. *hr̥d-*, Iran. *zr̥d-* from **ghr̥d-* (see for both 4.7.6).

[1] In the case of consonant variation in final position an obvious starting-point to be considered is combinatory change. See Stang, 'L'alternance des consonnes sourdes et sonores en indo-européen', *To Honor R. Jakobson* iii, 1967, 1890–4, who takes it as having arisen in verb inflexion, while Fourquet, *Sprachwissenschaft* 1, 1976, 108–114, sees in **kap-/*ghabh-* an alternation between unvoiced stop and voiced aspirate. Swadesh, 'The problem of consonant doublets in IE', *Word* 26, 1965, 1–16, offers a *rudis indigestaque moles*.

5·4·4

In some cases an initial stop seems to alternate with zero. The most interesting examples are:

**kost-* 'bone': OCS *kostĭ*, Lat. *costa* 'rib', but

**ost*- 'bone': Gr. ὀστέον, Lat. *os* (gen. *ossis*), Skt. *asthi*;
**kag*- 'goat': OCS *koza*, OE *hēcen* 'kid', MLG *hōken* (both from **hōkīna*), but
**ag*-: Skt. *aja*- 'he-goat', Lith. *ožys* (from **āgiyos*).[1]

[1] For attempts at explanation, see below, 6.4.4.2.

5.4.5. Sandhi phenomena

'Sandhi' is the name given, originally by Indian grammarians (Skt. *sandhi* 'putting together'), to sound changes occurring at the boundaries of adjacent words or morphemes.

In final position, sonants are lost after a long vowel in certain Indo-European languages.[1] In the nom. s. m. and f. of the *r*-stems we find Aryan *pitā mātā*, Lith. mótė, OCS *mati* in contrast to Gr. μήτηρ, Lat. *māter*. Similarly in the *n*-stems Skt. *aśmā* 'stone', Lith. *akmuo*, and even Lat. *(hom)ō* 'man' appear in contrast to Gr. ἄκμων; Skt. *ś(u)vā* 'dog', Lith. *šuo*, OIr. *cú* (from **kwō*), but Gr. κύων.[2] In the case of final -*u* doublets are found even within Old Indic: *d(u)vāu* or *d(u)vā* 'two', but Hom. δύω, OCS *dŭva*; cf. 8.5.2, and Strunk, *PBB* 114 (1992), 194–200.

Probably the loss of sonants in this position depended on sandhi conditions, i.e. it occurred before certain initial consonants in the following word. Thus variants arose in Indo-European of which one or other was generalized in each of the individual languages.

In some IE languages and presumably in Indo-European itself the frequent devoicing of final consonants (as in Grm. *Kind* pron. *kint*) is matched by a marked tendency in the opposite direction, e.g. Lat. *sub* < **(s)up*, IE **tod* < **to-t(o)*.[3]

In a group of consonants in final position one (or more) could be lost by assimilation, e.g. **mātēr* < **māters* (see 6.2.7.1). Where a consonant group was restored, a difficult group could be lightened by the development of a supporting vowel, normally schwa, at the end; e.g. OInd. *asthi* 'bone' from **asth* (by metathesis from **Hast*; cf. 6.6.10) via **asth-ə*.[4]

Vowels in final position can vary between long and short, e.g. **we*/**wē* 'or' (see 5.3.7*b*); the starting-point for this is certainly the shortening of an original long in sandhi before a following initial vowel.[5]

Finally, the frequent variation of forms with and without final -*s*, e.g. Lat. *ab*/*abs*, should be mentioned.[6] [7]

[1] G. S. Lane, *KZ* 81, 1968, 198–202, takes the view that loss originally occurred only before an initial sonant. Cf. Dunkel, 'A typology of metanalysis', *In Memory of W. Cowgill*, 1987, 7–37.

[2] See Szemerényi, *SMEA* 20, 1980, 220f. (on δῶ). Note that, according to Meillet, *MSL* 9, 1896, 365–72 (followed by Gauthiot, *Fin de mot*, 1913, 158f.), the IE final nasal was -*n*, not

-*m*. He also thought at one time (see *Hawaii Papers* 2/7, 1970, 33) that the final nasal was facultative, a view echoed by Bader, *BSL* 68, 1973, 69f.

[3] Szemerényi, *TPS* 1973, 55–74 (in spite of Normier, *KZ* 91, 1978, 207), esp. 60 (=*SM* 930). Cf. Shannon, 'The rise and fall of final devoicing', *ICHL* 7, 1987, 545–59; Rasmussen, in Vennemann 1989, 157, 251; M. Back, *Die synchrone Prozessbasis des natürlichen Lautwandels*, 1991, 202. For the Latin finals, note M. L. Porzio Gernia, *La sorte di M e D finali*, Rome Lincei, 1974.

[4] Szemerényi, *SMEA* 20, 224f. (with references); cf. further Gr. ἄλφα βῆτα from Semitic *alp bēt*. Differently Beekes, *Fs. Hoenigswald*, 1987, 53f.

[5] Szemerényi, 'The IE particle *kʷe*', *Fs. Gipper*, ii, 1985, 753f.

[6] See P. Russell, 'Preverbs, prepositions and adverbs: sigmatic and asigmatic', *TPS* 86, 1988, 144–72.

[7] For sandhi in general see Dunkel (n. 1 above); H. Andersen (ed.), *Sandhi Phenomena in the Languages of Europe*, Berlin 1986; and (?) *E. García Domingo, *Sandhi en indoeuropeo*, Burgos 1985 (but note *BSL* 82/2, 1987, 208–11).

5.4.6. Initial variation of *pt-/p-* in Greek

Some seventeen Greek words show an alternation of πτ-/π- in initial position, e.g. πτόλις πόλις, πτόλεμος πόλεμος. In some it may be due to the etymology. This would apply to *ptol-* if it was metathesized from **plot-*, originally **pl̥t-*, related to Skt. *pr̥t-* 'battle'; *pol-* would then somehow have lost *t*. In others it may have been caused by sandhi metathesis, by which, for instance, ἔλυθετ πόλιν became ἔλυθε τπόλιν, and this in the end became πτόλιν.[1]

[1] See Szemerényi, 'The consonant alternations *pt/p* in Early Greek', *Coll. Myc.* 6, 1979, 323–40 (=*SM* 1476–93); and cf. Michelena, in *Studia in honorem R. Lapesa* iii, 1975, 348f.; Brixhe, *BSL* 74, 1979, 237–59; Greppin, 'Armenian *t*', Greek *pt-*', *JIES* 10, 1984, 347–54; Fulk 1986, 218f.; Aloni and Negri, *Minos* 24, 1989, 139–44; Negri, *Convegno* 8, 1991, 66f.; Dunkel, 'Two old problems in Greek: *ptólemos* and *terpsímbrotos*', *Glotta* 70, 1993, 197–225.

5.5. MORPHEME STRUCTURE

The basic morphemes with fuller meaning, as compared with the grammatical morphemes, have also for the most part greater size. Investigation into the structure of such morphemes shows that they lie within definite limits. The basic types, or canonical forms as they are called, can often be brought under a very simple formula. For example, the canonical form in Chinese is the monosyllable, in the Semitic languages the triconsonantal root.[1] If *C* and *V* are used to indicate any consonant and vowel respectively, the possible basic morphemes of e.g. German can be represented as follows: *V*, *VC*, *CV*, *VCC*, *CCV*, *CVC*, *VCCC*, *CCCV*, *CCVC*, etc.[2]

[1] See e.g. Belova, 'Struktura semitskogo kornja', *VJ* 1991 (1), 79–90; but according to Ehret the third consonant was originally a suffix—see Bomhard, 'The root in IE and Afroasiatic', *Gedenkschrift Ch. Carter*, 1991, 7, and earlier, 'The reconstruction of the Proto-Semitic consonant system', *In Remembrance of A. Ehrman*, 1988, 113–40.

[2] Cf. Hockett, *Course* 284f.; Pilch, *Phonemtheorie* i, 22f.; L. Schmidt, 'Über den Gebrauch des Terminus "Wurzel"', in *Gedenkschrift J. Trier*, 1975, 63–84. On the development of the concept of root and the importance of Bopp's contribution to it, see J. Rousseau, *BSL* 79,

1984, 285–321, esp. 308f.; and earlier, Jucquois, 'The concept of root (Bopp–Schleicher–Saussure–Brugmann)', in *Studies A. A. Hill* iii, 1978; idem, *La reconstruction linguistique*, 1976, 12–173.

5.5.1

As early as the first century BC the Alexandrian grammarian Philoxenos held that all Greek words could be traced back to a fixed number of monosyllabic roots.[1] This doctrine survives in modern times; it is found, for example, in Adelung and W. von Humboldt (Arens[2] 151, 217).[2] It is applied to Indo-European by Bopp (see Delbrück, *Einleitung*[4] (1904), 59–61), and developed in greater detail by A. Schleicher (1821–68), who sets out the following forms:[3]

V, CV, VC, CVC, CCV, VCC, CCVC, CVCC, CCVCC

If account is taken of the distinction between monosyllabic and disyllabic roots which was noted under vowel gradation, the following canonical forms can be established (*e* represents *e*, *a*, or *o*):[4]

Monosyllabic	Disyllabic
VC **ed*- 'eat'	*CeCē* **pelē* 'fill'
CVC **med*- 'measure'	*CeCēC* **temāg*- 'cut'
CCVC **trem*- 'tremble'	
CVCC **serp*- 'creep'	
CCVCC **dhreugh*- 'deceive'	
CCCVC **strep*- 'make a noise'	
CCCVCC **spreig*- 'abound'	
CV̄ **dō*- 'give'	
CCV̄ **drā*- 'run'	

For those monosyllabic roots in which consonant groups are possible, a very simple structural formula can be set up. If stops are represented by *T*, sonants (*m n l r* and *i u* as components of diphthongs) by *R*, and the spirant *s* by *S*, the following general formula is obtained:

(*S*) (*T*) (*R*) *e* (*R*) (*T*/*S*)

which embraces the possibilities *eT*, *TeT*, *TReT*, *TReS*, *TeRT*, *TeRS*, etc. and *SeT*, *SeS*, *SReT*, *SReS*, *SeRT*, etc. If the phonemes are in order of increasing sonority *T*/*S*–*R*–*V*, it can be stated even more simply that *the phonemes on each side of a vowel are arranged in order of decreasing sonority* (from the centre outwards), so that *klep* is possible but not *lkep*, *stret* but not *rset*, *kers* but not *kesr*, etc. A root **pster*- for 'sneeze', which would depart from the normal structure, could therefore be tolerated only as an onomatopoeia; in fact, however, only **pter*- (Gr. πτάρνυμαι) and **ster*- (Lat. *sternuō*) are found. The initial group *ST(R)e* occurs very often, e.g. **ster*- **spek*- **skeid*- and

**splei-* **skrei-*, etc. By contrast *TTe-* is very rare (*πτερόν*), and so too is *TSe-*.[5] The maximum number of consonants found in a morpheme is five.[6]

[1] See A. F. Bernhardi, *Anfangsgründe der Sprachwissenschaft*, 1805, 106: 'All root words are monosyllabic', and cf. Bopp, *Analytical Comparison*, 1820, 8f., both quoted in Techmer's *IZ* 4, 1889, 8 n. 1, 19. At the beginning of this century a book like A. L. Snell, *The Beginning of Speech: A Treatise on the Uni-radical Origin of IE Words*, London 1910, could still be published. When barely 15 years old Saussure invented a system in which every root was built from *K P T* and internal *A*, giving triliteral structures like *KAP*, *TAK*, etc.; see *CFS* 32, 1979, 73–101.

[2] See Jucquois, 'Monosyllabisme originel, fonction et reconstruction', *Diachronica* 8, 1991, 17–44: the development was from monosyllabics to polysyllabics.

[3] See A. Schleicher, *Kompendium der vergleichenden Grammatik der idg. Sprachen*⁴, 1876, 332.

[4] On the structure of the syllable, see Jespersen, *Elementarbuch der Phonetik*, 1912, 145f.; Saussure, *Cours* 70–95; Kuryłowicz, *Études* 121; Scholes, *Lings* 36, 1968, 55–77; see further below 5.7.

[5] Perhaps commoner at an earlier period; see Gunnarsson, *NTS* 24, 1971, 80.

[6] See Szemerényi 1972, 143; Lehmann, *PIE Syntax*, 203f.

5.5.2

Within this structural formula further restrictions affecting the stops can be observed:[1]

Possible		Impossible
1. Voiced–voiced asp.	*bedh-*	I. Voiced–voiced (*bed-*)[2]
2. Voiced–voiceless	*dek-*	II. Voiced asp.–voiceless (*bhet-*)[3]
3. Voiced asp.–voiced	*bheid-*	III. Voiceless–voiced asp. (*tebh-*)[3]
4. Voiced asp.–voiced asp.	*bheidh-*	III is, however, possible after
5. Voiceless–voiced	*ped-*	*s*: **steigh-* 'go up'.
6. Voiceless–voiceless	*pet-*	

Note. (A) The sequence voiced—voiced occurs in Skt. *gad-ati* 'speaks', but this is confined to Old Indic.[4]

(B) Identical stops (type *pep-*) are excluded, but identical spirants are attested in **ses-* 'lie': Hitt. *ses-*, Skt. *sas-*.[5]

Furthermore, the nucleus of the root, i.e. the vowel, may not be followed by two sonants or two stops: thus e.g. *teurk-* and *tekt-* are impossible.[6] If nevertheless such a sequence seems to occur, there is a morpheme boundary between the two sonants or stops: Lat. *mūnus* from **moinos* is not formed from a root *moin-*, but from **moi-/mei-* (cf. Skt. *mayatē* 'exchanges') with the suffix *-nos* as in *fēnus*, *facinus*.

[1] Meillet, *Introduction* 173f.; A. Cuny, *RPhon* 2, 1912, 128f.; *Recherches sur le vocalisme, le consonantisme et la formation des racines en nostratique, ancêtre de l'indo-européen et du chamito-sémitique*, 1943, 113–59; cf. Borgstrøm, *Word* 10, 1954, 278f.; Stanley, *Lg* 43, 1968, 432f.; Chomsky and Halle, *Sound Pattern of English*, 1968, 386 (an alpha rule); Bechert, *LBer* 2, 1969, 28–46; *IF* 76, 1972, 15–19; Gercenberg, 'Teorija ie. kornja', *VJ* 1973 (2), 102–10; Gamkrelidze–Ivanov, 17f., 139f.; Penney, 'Laryngeals and the IE root', in Bammesberger 1988, 361–72. See further below, 6.5.4.

[2] Grassmann, *KZ* 12, 1863, 115, was the first to notice the absence of voiced stop–voiced stop; see Szemerényi 1985, 8.
[3] Cf. Saussure's observation quoted by Meillet, *MSL* 18, 1912, 60f.; Benveniste, *Origines* 171 n. 1; also Scherer in *Convegno* 5, 1972, 25 (loan words?); Miller, *Lings* 178, 1976, 58f.; *JIES* 5, 1977, 31–40; Szemerényi 1985, 8, 13. According to Cuny, *RPhon* 2, 129f., Pre-IE had both type II (*bhet-*) and type III (*tebh-*), but IE assimilated them to 6 and 4 respectively.
[4] Cuny, loc. cit., assumed that this type (I) was missing because it had been dissimilated to 2, e.g. *gʷed-* to *gʷet-*. For Skt. *gadati*, Thieme, *KZ* 86, 1972, 80, conjectured onomatopoeia, but the form might have been due to crossing with another root; cf. Mayrhofer, *KEWA* s.v.; Cowgill and Mayrhofer, *IG* i/2, 95 n. 19.
[5] Rix, *HS* 104, 1992, 191, has suggested that identical laryngeals, at least the type H_2, were also tolerated.
[6] See Saussure, *Recueil* 118, Meillet, *Introduction* 157; *BSL* 35/2, 1934, 54; Schwyzer, *GG* i, 238f.; Kuryłowicz, *IG* 203; Lehmann, *PIE Syntax*, 17.

5.5.3

The structural limitation of the simplest type of morpheme to *V̆C* or *CV̄* is not wholly valid. Morphemes of the type *CV̆* are in fact numerous. It is correct, however, that they all belong to a particular category: particles (**de*, **ghe*, **kʷe*) and pronominal stems (**to-* 'this', **me* 'I', **kʷi-* 'who'). Even simple *V* is possible, cf. the pronominal stem **e-* 'this'.[1] Note also in this connection Benveniste's root theory (6.5.1).

[1] *kʷe* is from the case form **kʷē*; see 8.3.3 n. 8.

5.5.4. Root determinatives

Comparison of Goth. *giutan* 'pour' with Lat. *fundō fūdī* leads to IE **gheud-*. But this root cannot be separated from **gheu-* 'pour' in Gr. *χέω* (<*χέϝω*) *χυ-τός*, Skt. *hu-* in pres. *ju-hō-ti* 'pours, sacrifices'. This means that **gheud-* was formed within Indo-European from the simpler **gheu-* by means of a suffix which no longer has any clearly perceptible meaning. Formative elements of this kind have been known since Curtius as root determinatives.

It often happens that a number of roots are derived from the same simple root by means of different determinatives. For example, Gr. *ἔλπομαι*, Hom. *ἐέλπομαι ἐλπίς* 'hope' lead to a root **welp-*. Parallel to these occur *ἔλδομαι ἐέλδομαι ἐέλδωρ* 'wish, longing', which come from a root **weld-*. It is obvious that **welp-* and **weld-* must belong together, in fact that they both derive from a simpler root **wel-*; this is confirmed by Lith. *vil-iúos* 'I hope', *vil-tìs* 'hope', to which Lat. *uelle* can be added.

Sometimes the simple root is not, or not certainly, attested, but is required by different parallel formations. For example, **drā-* 'run' is found in Skt. *drā-ti* 'runs, hastens', Gr. *ἀπο-δι-δρά-σκω*, aor. *ἀπ-έ-δρᾱν*; **drem-* is attested by Skt. *dram-ati* 'runs', Gr. aor. *ἔ-δραμ-ον*, and **dreu-* by Skt. *drav-ati* 'runs' and many European river names, including *Dravos* 'Drau/Drava', Gaul. *Druentia*, Fr. 'Drouance'. It is clear that **drā- *drem- *dreu-*, which all have the same basic meaning, cannot be independent of one another; all are derived from a basic root **dr-/*der-*, although this root is no longer attested. The existence of **trem-* in Gr. τρέμω, Lat. *tremō*, **trep-* in Lat. *trepidus*, OCS *trepetŭ* 'tremble', **tres-/*ters-* in Skt. *trasati* 'trembles', Gr. τρέω (<**tres-ō*), Hom. ἔ-τρεσ-σαν, Lat. *terreō* (<**ters-*) presupposes a basic root **tr-/*ter-* which survives as such only in Skt. *tarala-* 'trembling'. Gr. μέλπω 'sing', Hitt. *mald-* 'recite, vow', Gmc. *meldan* 'announce' (Grm. *melden*), Lat. *promulgāre*, Russ. *molvit'* 'say', Avest. *mrav-* = Skt. *brav-* 'say' go back to **melp-*, **meldh-*, **melg*, **melw-/*mleu-*, and these presuppose an original root **mel-* 'proclaim',[1] which probably still survives in Gr. μέλος 'song', Hitt. *mallai-* 'approve'.

[1] Cf. Szemerényi, *Em* 22, 1954, 159–74 (on **mel-*).

5.5.5

Root determinatives are an obvious solution for certain root structures which would otherwise contravene the restrictions judged valid for simple roots. Thus beside the above-mentioned **drā- *drem- *dreu-* 'run' a form **dreb-* is found in OE *treppan* 'to step' (from **trapjan*), NHG *trippeln* 'to trip', *Treppe* 'stairs', Lith. *drebù* 'tremble'. As a simple root this would have an 'impossible' structure, because it contains voiced stop–voiced stop. In this case, the existence of the other variants shows it to be a derived form containing a root determinative.

On the basis of such cases, irregular morpheme structure can be treated as being in itself proof of the presence of a root determinative. The root **kerdh-* 'row, herd' is 'impossible' as it contains unvoiced stop—voiced aspirate, and must therefore be understood as **ker-dh-*, cf. Schmitt-Brandt, 20.[1]

[1] The most important work in this field is still P. Persson, *Beiträge zur idg. Wortforschung* i–ii, 1912. See also *PICL* 7, 1956, 481f.; Kronasser, *Etymologie*, 1965, 420f.; Kuryłowicz, *IG* 222; Makajev, *VJ* 1969 (1), 3–21; *Struktura* 182f. Others are willing to admit only contaminations: see M. Bloomfield, *IF* 4, 1894, 66f. (cf. Persson, 594); Petersen, *Lg* 4, 1928, 11; Schmitt-Brandt, 12f., 25.

5.6. COMBINATORY CHANGES IN MORPHEME SEQUENCES

At the boundaries of morphemes in combination, certain sound changes take place which cannot normally appear within the morpheme itself, since the consonant groups concerned do not occur there.

5.6.1

Before an unvoiced stop at the beginning of a morpheme a voiced stop at the end of the preceding morpheme is assimilated, becoming unvoiced. This change occurs with especial frequency before suffixes with initial *t*. For example the root **yeug*- 'bind, yoke' with the suffix -*to*- of the verbal adjective gives Skt. *yuk-tá*-, Gr. *ζευκ-τός*.

Conversely an unvoiced stop or *s* becomes voiced before a voiced stop. Examples of this are also found within the morpheme, though even here the consonant group is first made possible by a preceding morpheme: Skt. *upabda*- 'trampling noise' from -*pda*- formed to *padyatē* 'falls'; Avest. *fra-bda*- 'forefoot' from *pad*- 'foot'; IE **nizdos* 'nest' (4.6.2) from **ni-sd-os*<**sed*-, Lat. *sedēre* etc.

Note. In Old Indic *t*(*h*) following cerebral *ṣ* (4.6) also becomes cerebral; e.g. the verbal adjective of *piṣ*- 'to crush' (from **pis*-, cf. Lat. *pinsere*, *pistor*) is *piṣṭa*- from *piṣ*+*ta*. Indo-European palatals, which appear in Sanskrit as *š ǰ*, followed by *t* give the group *ṣṭ*; cf. Skt. *aṣṭā* 'eight' (in contrast to Iran. *aštā*), *rāṣṭi* 'reigns' from **rēg-ti*.

5.6.2. Bartholomae's Law

In conformity with the above, the sequence voiced aspirate–unvoiced stop appears in most languages as unvoiced stop–unvoiced stop. Thus *gh*+*t* gives *kt* in Gr. *λέκτρον*, Lat. *lectus*, from the root **legh*- 'lie' which appears in Gr. *λέχος*, Goth. *ligan*, OHG *liggen*.

Diverging from this, Old Indic and indeed Aryan in general shows in such cases retention of the voicing, which is even extended to the unvoiced stops; Indic also retains the aspiration, transposing it to the end of the group. The original group voiced aspirate+unvoiced stop thus becomes voiced stop+voiced aspirate: e.g.

Skt. *labh*- 'seize': verbal adj. *labdha*-<*labh*+*ta*;
Skt. *budh*- 'wake': verbal adj. *buddha*- 'awakened'<*budh*+*ta*;
Skt. *dah*- 'burn' (palatalized from **dagh*-; see 4.7.4.7 and 4.7.5.3): verbal adj. *dagdha*-<*dagh*+*ta*.

If, instead of a (labio)velar as in the last example, a palatal was originally present (4.7.4.6), *ǰh-t* gave first *ždh* and later (5.6.1) cerebralized *ẓḍh*, in which *ẓ* finally disappeared with lengthening of the preceding vowel; for example *lih*- 'lick', verbal adj. *līḍha*- from IE **lîĝhto*-; *sah*- 'overpower', verbal adj. *sāḍha*-. The same occurs with verbal endings in -*t*-, e.g. *lēḍhi* from **lēh-ti* 'licks'.[1]

Originally this law was regarded as valid for Indo-European as a whole. In that case the Greek and Latin examples cited above would have to be a secondary development. There are, however, no convin cing examples outside Aryan; it is therefore more reasonable to limit the law to Aryan. It is certainly valid for Avestan: cf. *augda* (written *aogədā)* 'he said' from **augh-ta*, and even *augža* 'thou saidst' from **augh-sa*, which became *augzha*, then *augžha* (see 4.6), and finally with loss of aspiration *augža*; to Skt. *duhitar-* 'daughter' corresponds Avest. *dugdar-* (written *dugədar-*) from **dugh-tar-*.[2]

[1] This change was first described by C. Bartholomae, *Arische Forschungen* 1, 1882, 3f.; *KZ* 27, 1885, 206f., and is called after him Bartholomae's Law of Aspirates. See also below, 6.7.1.4–5.

[2] The law is still regarded as of Indo-European date by Kuryłowicz, *Études* 51 (cf. *Apophonie* 379f.); *PICL* 9, 1964, 13; *IG* 339; *BPTJ* 31, 1973, 8; Cuny, *RPhon* 2, 1912, 126f.; *BSL* 32, 1931, 43f.; Puhvel, 'Bartholomae's law in Hittite', *KZ* 86, 1972, 111–15; Hamp, *ZCP* 37, 1980, 169. See further Pisani, *Geolinguistica e indeuropeo*, 1940, 346f.; Mey, *NTS* 26, 1972, 81–9; G. Miller, *Fs. Lehmann*, 1977, 365–92 (contradicted by Rasmussen, in Vennemann 1989, 165); Vennemann, *Essays Penzl*, 1979, 557–84; Collinge, *Laws* 7f.; Gamkrelidze–Ivanov, 32f., 405. On the Germanic 'bits of proof' ('Beweisstücke') see W. H. Bennett, *Lg* 42, 1967, 733–7.

5.6.3

Special developments are found when a dental at the end of a morpheme meets a dental at the beginning of the following morpheme.

The sequence *-tt-* (also when derived from *-d-t-*) is particularly well attested in verbal adjectives with the suffix *-to-* and in abstract nouns formed from verbs by means of the suffixes *-ti-* and *-tu-*. E.g.:

IE **weid-* 'see'—**wid-to-* 'seen, known': Skt. *vitta-*, Avest. *vista-*, Gr. ἄ-(ϝ)ιστος 'unseen', Lat. *uīsus* (after *uīdī* instead of **uissus*), OIr. *fess* 'scita' (n. pl. from **wittā* with vowel mutation; cf. *fiss* 'knowledge' from **wid-tu-s*), Goth. *un-wiss* 'uncertain', OE *wiss*, OHG *gi-wiss* (modern *gewiss*), Serb.-Cr. *vēstŭ* 'clear', modified from **vĭstŭ* on the analogy of *vēdē* 'know'.

IE **sed-* 'sit'—**sed-to-*: Skt. *satta-*, Avest. *hasta-*, Lat. *-sessus*, OIr. *sess* 'seat', ON OE *sess* 'seat'; cf. OCS *sēsti*, Lith. *sėsti* 'sit'.

As can be seen, *-tt-* became *-ss-* in the West (Italic, Celtic, Germanic), *-st-* in the centre and East (Greek, Baltic, Slavic, Iranian), but appeared as *-tt-* in the extreme East (Old Indic). In order to reconcile these different developments, it was assumed quite early[1] that Indo-European *-tt-* first acquired an affricate pronunciation, i.e. *-t^{s}t-*, which by dissimilation gave *-ts-* and then *-ss-* in the West, but *-st-* in the centre and East, while in Old Indic *s* in *tst* was lost in the same way as in the historic compounds such as *utthā-* from *ut-sthā-* (i.e. *ud-sthā-*) 'stand up', etc. This explanation received fresh support from Hittite, in which e.g. *ets-teni* 'you eat' (written *ezzatteni*) shows the assumed Indo-European development from **ed-t-*.

Against this, in more recent times the stage *-t^s*t- has been held to be unnecessary, and it has been supposed[2] that by a dissimilatory 'breaking up of double consonants', with no intermediate stage, *-tt-*

gave partly *-ts->-ss-*, partly *-st-*. This is possible only if the special development of *-tt-* is taken as later than Indo-European. Avest. *hištaiti* 'stands' from IE **si-st-*, in contrast to *vista-* from **wid-to*, proves that *-tt-* had not yet become *-st-* at the time when *s* after *i* (and *u r k*, see 4.6) became *š*. For this reason an explanation[3] which requires *-tt-* to have become *-st-* or *-ss-*[4] within Indo-European is impossible.

That the OInd. *-tt-* does not point to a retention of the Indo-European situation is shown by the fact that, for *-ddh-*, traces remain in Old Indic too of a development to *-zdh-*, clearly by way of *-dzdh-*. Thus the imperatives *dēhi* 'give', *dhēhi* 'put' have arisen from **dazdhi* **dhazdhi*, which is proved not only by *ēdhi* 'be' from **az-dhi* (<**as-dhi*) but also directly by Avest. *dazdi* 'give'.[5]

The group *-ddh-*, if from *-dh-t-*, represents only a special case of Bartholomae's Law. Here too there is nothing comparable in the languages other than Aryan. Cf. Lat. *iussus* from **yudh-to-s* with loss of aspiration by way of **yuttos*.

It seems, therefore, safe to conclude that the dental groups *-tt-* and *-ddh-* acquired an affricate character in Indo-European, and that the *-tst-* and *-dzdh-* which originated in this way were dissimilated to *-ts-* or *-st-* in the individual languages, perhaps to some extent while these were still associated in regional groupings, while in Old Indic they were for the most part reconstituted as *-tt-* and *-ddh-*.

[1] Cf. Meillet, *Dialectes* 57–61; R. G. Kent, *The Sounds of Latin*[3], 1945, 117f.; Porzig, *Gliederung* 76–8; A. Schmitt, *KZ* 72, 1955, 234–5; Shevelov, *A Prehistory of Slavic*, 1964, 182–4; Strunk, *MSS* 25, 1969, 113–29; Leumann[2], 197.

[2] Schwyzer, *KZ* 61, 1934, 234, 248; Hammerich, *PBB(T)* 77, 1955, 127f.

[3] Johansson, *IF* 14, 1903, 310f.; Meid, *IF* 69, 1965, 226f., 236 (rejected by Makajev, *Struktura* 187); Hamp, *Ériu* 24, 1973, 162; Sihler, *IF* 84, 1980, 163f.

[4] L. Heller, *Word* 12, 1956, 7; Strunk (n. 1 above).

[5] Wackernagel, *Ai. Gr.* i, 1957, 177f., with Debrunner's additions. Against this, Tedesco, *Lg* 44, 1968, 1f.; but see Szemerényi, *Sprache* 12, 1967, 203f. on *azdā* (=*SM* 1868f.).

5.6.4. Siebs' Law

Particularly in Germanic, but also in other languages, variation can be observed in initial position between voiced stop and *s*+unvoiced stop or between voiced aspirate and *s*+unvoiced (aspirate) stop: e.g. Gmc. **dauma-* (MDu. *doom*) and **stauma-* (Eng. *steam*), MHG *briezen*= *spriezen* 'to sprout'. From such correspondences Siebs inferred that in Indo-European a voiced stop became unvoiced and a voiced aspirate became an unvoiced aspirate or non-aspirate when an *s*, presumably a prefix, came before it. The Russian scholar Illič-Svityč gave the law a more precise formulation: *s*+*k* and *s*+*g* in initial position generally become *sk-*, whereas *s*+*gh* appear as Skt. *skh-*, Gr. *σχ-*, and *sk-* in the other languages.[1]

[1] Cf. Th. Siebs (1862–1941), 'Anlautstudien', *KZ* 37, 1901, 277–324; V. M. Illič-Svityč, *VJ* 1961 (4), 93–8; H. Andersen, *Fs. Stang*, 1970, 18f. Kuryłowicz, *Études* 53f., *Apophonie* 378, also defends Siebs' Law and uses it to draw far-reaching conclusions, see below, 6.7.1.4. Cuny, *REA* 38, 1936, 73, assumes also a change of *s+bh* to *sph-*. See further Miller, *Fs. Lehmann*, 1977, 376f.; Collinge, *Laws* 155f.; Gamkrelidze–Ivanov, 56, 118, 140.

5.6.5. Haplology

A few examples support the possibility that, in sequences of phonemes consisting of like consonants separated by like or unlike vowels, so-called haplological simplifications, which are well known in historical periods, occurred in prehistoric Indo-European also. The future imperative offers particularly convincing examples: cf. e.g. 2nd pl. **bheretōd* from **bherete-tōd*, 3rd s. and pl. **agetōd *agontōd* from **age(tu)tōd *agon(tu)tōd*.[1]

[1] See 9.2.5*b*, with nn. 6, 10, for the references to Szemerényi and Forssman.

5.7. SYLLABLE STRUCTURE (SIEVERS' LAW)

An intermediate unit is usually placed between phoneme and word, namely the syllable. In monosyllabic languages, e.g. Chinese, this concept is superfluous, since syllable and word coincide. In all other language types, however, and consequently in the Indo-European languages and Indo-European, the syllable is a natural higher unit. Unfortunately there is, even today, *no generally accepted definition of the syllable*. But this much is clear: the syllable contains a core or nucleus, usually a vowel or sonant, and this is usually preceded and/or followed by certain elements, the so-called consonants. In a monosyllable such as 'fast' the boundaries of the syllable, beginning and end, are unambiguous. In a word of more than one syllable, e.g. 'fasten', the boundaries cannot always be determined by experimental and mechanical means, although Malmberg has found in sonagrams some help towards demarcating syllables. But the important point is that, whereas the syllabic nucleus can be determined phonetically, definition of the boundaries, as Kloster Jensen's discussion makes clear, requires a phonological approach, by which, however, they can be determined with certainty. This determination depends on the possibilities of phoneme combination at the beginning of syllables and in medial position that are valid for the language in question, and on prosodic factors.

For the history of a language and also for metrical usage the difference between open and closed syllables is important. A syllable is open if it ends with a nucleus, closed if it ends with a consonant. Open syllables with a short nucleus are reckoned as short in quantitative verse, while open syllables with long nucleus, and also closed syllables with short nucleus, even when this is followed by only a single consonant, are reckoned as long.

Note. Syllable and morpheme must not be confused. They may coincide, but need not and for the most part do not. For example the IE morpheme **bheidh-* can with the addition of another morpheme give the word **bheidhō*, of which the syllabic division is **bhei-dhō*.[1]

[1] On the problems of the syllable, see O. von Essen, *Allgemeine und angewandte Phonetik*[4], 1966, 126–36 (on syllabic boundaries 131f.); also Kuryłowicz, 'Contribution à la théorie de la syllabe', *Esquisses* 193–220 (first 1948), and B. Hála, 'La syllabe, sa nature, son origine et ses transformations', *Orbis* 10, 1961, 69–143. Cf. B. Malmberg, 'The phonetic basis for syllable division', *SL* 9, 1956, 80–7; also 15, 1961, 1–9; J. Laziczius, *Lehrbuch der Phonetik*, Berlin 1961 (156–93: history of the problem of the syllable); M. Kloster Jensen, 'Die Silbe in der Phonetik und Phonemik', *Phonetica* 9, 1963, 17–38; Rosetti, *Sur la théorie de la syllabe*, 1963; D. B. Fry, 'The functions of the syllable', *ZPhon* 17, 1964, 215–37; Delattre, *SL* 18, 1965, 13; Pilch, *Phonetica* 14, 1966, 238; Lebrun, ibid. 1–15; K. J. Kohler, 'Is the syllable a phonological universal?' *JL* 2, 1966, 207–8; I. Kunert, 'Zur Theorie der Silbe', *Dankesgabe an E. Koschmieder*, 1967, 82–95; R. J. Scholes, 'Syllable segmentation and identification in American English', *Lings* 36, 1968, 55–77; E. C. Fudge, 'Syllables', *JL* 5, 1969, 253–86 (against Kohler); G. Brown, *JL* 6, 1969, 1–17; Pulgram, *Syllable, Word, Nexus, Cursus*, 1970, 48f.; Krámský, 'The functional conception of the syllable', *Lings* 70, 1971, 45–56; Awedyk, 'A contribution to the theory of the syllable', *Bull. Fonolog.* 12, 1971, 49–56; Vennemann, 'The theory of syllabic phonology', *LBer* 18, 1972, 1–18; Hooper, 'The syllable in phonological theory', *Lg* 48, 1972, 525–40; Allen, *Accent and Rhythm*, 1973, 27f.; Pilch 1974, 16f.; Pulgram, *Latin–Romance Phonology*, 1975, 72f.; Porzio Gernia, 'Tendenze strutturali della sillaba latina', *Studi Bonfante*, 1976, 757–79; Danielsen, 'The problem of the syllable', *Sprachwissenschaft* 4, 1979, 13–23; Bell, 'The syllable', *PCLSP* 1979, 11–20; Kiparsky, 'Remarks on the metrical structure of syllable', *Phonologica* 4, 1981, 245–56; Steriade (above, 5.2, n. 1); *G. N. Clements and S. J. Keyser, *CV Phonology: A Generative Theory of the Syllable*, 1983 (cf. Steriade, *Lg* 64, 1988, 118–29); Lass, 'Quantity, resolution, and syllable geometry', *FoLH* 4, 1984, 151–80; W. Kreit-Mair, *Untersuchungen zur Silbenstruktur des Standarddeutschen*, Magistr. Munich, 1984; Vennemann, *Preference Laws for Syllable Structure and the Explanation of Sound Change*, 1988; Carmen Pensado, 'How do unnatural syllabifics arise?' *FoL* 8, 1989, 115–42; R. W. Murray and T. Vennemann, 'Syllable contact change in Germanic, Greek and Sidamo', *KBS* 8, 1982, 321–49; R. Noske, *A Theory of Syllabification and Segmented Alternation*, Tübingen 1993.

5.7.1

The syllabic structure of Indo-European, as of all languages, can be described by specifying the phoneme combinations possible before and after the syllabic nucleus. If the beginning of the syllable coincides with that of the word, we find the same possibilities of combination as set out above in the discussion of morpheme structure (5.5.1), and similarly when syllable-end and word-end coincide. If, however, the beginning and/or end of the syllable fall within the word, the conditions are altered. Although *kt- gr-* are possible at the beginning of a word, the words **aktos* (from **ag-tos*) and **agros* are not divided as *a-ktos* and *a-gros* but as *ak-tos* and *ag-ros*, and in general, when two syllabic nuclei are separated by two consonants, the syllabic boundary falls between the two consonants; if three consonants lie between the two nuclei, the boundary falls generally after the first consonant.

5.7.2.1. But there are certain modifications of the syllabic structure, particularly characteristic of Indo-European, which occur if the final member of a consonant group is a sonant, i.e. in groups such as *dy dw pty ptr*, etc. First recognized by E. Sievers (1850–1932), these were carefully studied and formulated by F. Edgerton (1885–1963), so that we can speak of the *Sievers–Edgerton Law*.[1]

On the basis of certain facts in Germanic and Vedic, Sievers established that in these languages, and probably in Indo-European also, *y* and *w* after a short syllable alternate with *i* and *u* (more precisely *iy* and *uw*) after a long syllable. Thus the same suffix appears as *-ja-* in Goth. *harjis* 'army' and as *-ija-* in *hairdeis* (from *-dijis*) 'herdsman'. Similarly in verbs *-ja-* in *satjiþ* 'sets' alternates with *-ija-* in *sōkeiþ* 'seeks' (from **sōkijiþ*) or *sandeiþ* 'sends' (from **sandijiþ*). The preceding long syllable need not be in the same word: it can be constituted by a preceding pause or the final syllable of the preceding word. Vedic does in fact show variation at the beginning of words of the type *dyaus/diyaus* 'daylight sky', *syām/siyām* 'I might be'; to this clearly corresponds the Latin alternation of *diēs/Iuppiter*, *Iouem*, of which the last two have *y-* from *dy-*.

Sievers' Law was later elaborated by Edgerton, in two admirable articles, into an impressive system embracing not only *y w* but also *n m l r*, i.e. the sounds which we call sonants. It has already been shown (4.4 and 4.5) that the nasals and liquids can function not only as consonants but also as vowels, and in the latter capacity they can by a secondary development occur even before vowels. These phonemes have therefore three allophones: *r*, for example, appears as *r* and *r̥*, the second of which has two variants, *Cr̥C* and *Cr̥V*. From this point of view, the vowels *i u* and the semi-vowels *y w* function as though they were allophones of one another: we find, corresponding to the variants of *r* just described, *y/i/iy* and *w/u/uw*. If *y/i/iy* is taken to represent any sonant, and any second sonant is represented by *w/u/uw*, any stop or *s* by *T*, any two stops or *s*+stop by *KT*, a short or long vowel by *a* or *ā* respectively, and finally a pause by |, the following variations are possible, according to Edgerton, for Indo-European:

<table>
<tr><td>one sonant</td><td>(1) aTya</td><td>but āTiya, KTiya, | Tiya</td></tr>
<tr><td>two sonants</td><td>(2) aywa</td><td>but āyuwa</td></tr>
<tr><td></td><td>(3) ayuT, ayu |</td><td></td></tr>
<tr><td></td><td>(4) aTyuT, aTyu |</td><td>but āTiyuT, āTiyu |
KTiyuT, KTiyu |
| TiyuT, | Tiyu |</td></tr>
<tr><td></td><td>(5) aTyuwa</td><td>but āTiwa, KTiwa, | Tiwa</td></tr>
<tr><td></td><td>(6) yuwa (or iwa?)</td><td></td></tr>
</table>

This means, if the sonant *y* follows *T*, e.g. *dy*, only *dy* can stand after a short vowel, whereas *dy* is inadmissible and *diy* arises automatically after a long vowel, or two consonants, or a consonant preceded by a pause: thus *edyo* but *ēdiyo*, *gdiyo*, and |*diyo*, and similarly for *dw*: *edwo* but *ēduwo*, *gduwo*, and |*duwo*.

In the case of two sonants, e.g. *r* and *y*, *ry* appears after a short vowel, but only *riy* is possible after a long vowel (e.g. *aryo*, *āriyo*); if a consonant follows, e.g. *d*, *ry* is impossible and *ri* develops automatically (*arid* not *aryd*); if a consonant also precedes, *ri* arises after a short vowel and *r̥i* after a long vowel (*adrid*, *ādr̥id*); similarly *r̥i* after two consonants (*ptr̥id* not *ptrid*).

[1] Cf. Sievers, *PPB* 5, 1877, 129f.; Wackernagel, *Ai. Gr.* i, 197f.; Edgerton, *Lg* 10, 1934, 235–65, and (improved version) 19, 1943, 83–124 (108f. summary of his rules); further, 38, 1962, 352–9, where he admits with characteristic frankness (353) 'my phonetic rules are not fully alive even in the Rigveda, still less are they in any other of the IE languages'; he claims, however, that the situation prevailing in the Rigveda, which verges on regularity, shows that 'the phonemic law was still operating at a time not extremely long before the beginning of the RV hymnal composition'. On this see also Kuryłowicz, *Apophonie* 171f., 340f., 348f.; Nagy 1970; Sihler, *Lg* 45, 1969, 248–73; 47, 1971, 53–78; Vennemann, ibid. 104f.; Seebold 1972; Erdmann, *Lg* 48, 1972, 407–15 (extends Sievers' Law to polysyllables); Beade, *Lingua* 30, 1972, 449–59; Kiparsky, 'Metrics and morphophonemics in the RV', in Brame (ed.), *Contributions to Generative Phonology*, 1972, 171–200; Horowitz, *Sievers' Law and the Evidence of the RV*, 1974 (11–38 'historique'); Kuryłowicz, *Metrik* 55f.; id., in *K. Ammer zum Gedenken*, 1976, 94f. (against Edgerton); Migron, 'Vedic trimeter verse and the Sievers–Edgerton Law', *IIJ* 18, 1976, 179–93; Collinge, *Laws* 159f.; Cowgill and Mayrhofer 1986, 164–8; Koivulehto, 'Die Sieverssche Regel im Lichte der germanisch-finnischen Lehnbeziehungen', in Brogyanyi and Krömmelbein (eds.), *Germanic Dialects*, 1986, 249–94 (at an early stage of Germanic Sievers' Law was not yet in force!); de Bernardo (above, 4.5.2 n. 1), 15–22, 47f.; Prosdocimi, 'Syllabicity and Sievers' Law', *ICHL* 7, 1987, 483–505; 'La legge di Sievers', *AGI* 74, 1990, 146–62; Prosdocimi and Marchese, 'Saussure as an Indoeuropeanist and phoneticist', in Brogyanyi and Lipp (eds.), *Symbolae O. Szemerényi oblatae* i, 1992, 89–111. Note also the survey by C. M. Barrack, 'Keyser, Kiparsky, O'Neil, and Postal vs. Sievers', *Lingua* 77, 1989, 223–96.

5.7.2.2. In the Vedic corpus the regularity of this law can also be shown statistically. The dat.-abl. pl. ending *-bhyas* occurs as *-bhiyas* 120 times, but only twice after a short vowel. In the first cycle of hymns the pronoun *tuvam* 'thou' appears after a pause or long vowel 105 times, *tvam* only eleven times; after a short syllable *tuvam* never occurs, whereas *tvam* occurs in that position thirteen times. Examples of the alternation well known from other languages also are the already mentioned *diyaus/dyaus*, *siyām/syām* (cf. OLat. *siem*), to which may be added **kwōn/*kuwōn* 'dog' (*šuvā/švā*, Gr. κύων), **dwō/*duwō* 'two' (cf. Hom. δύω but δώδεκα from δϝω-), **g*$^{\omega}$*nā*/**g*$^{\omega}$*n̥ā* 'woman' (Skt. *gnā*, Boeot. βάνα).[1]

[1] See Kuryłowicz, *Apophonie* 172; *IG* 217 fn.; Sihler, *Lg* 47, 1971, 69–73; Seebold 1972, 155–65, 301–6; Horowitz (above, 5.7.2.1 n.1), 62; and cf. 5.3.5 *e-g*.

5.7.2.3. Edgerton considered it the final proof of his thesis that the converse of Sievers' Law also held good in cases where the sequences *iy uw* had arisen through combinations of morphemes: thus from *su-varṇa-* 'gold' ('well-coloured') the variant *svarṇa-* had arisen, from *antariyāt*, *antaryāt*, from *anu-vartitā*, *anvartitā*, simply because the type *iy uw* was impossible after short vowel and single consonant, no matter how this sequence had arisen.[1]

[1] Lehmann, *Lg* 31, 1955, 355–66; Marchand, *Lg* 32, 1956, 285–7 (against); Horowitz (above, 5.7.2.1, n. 1) 39–48; cf. Klein, *Lg* 53, 1977, 428–31.

5.7.2.4. In checking this theory the Norwegian scholar F. O. Lindeman found that (*a*) the converse of Sievers' Law, if correct at all, is a relatively recent Indic, certainly not Indo-European, phenomenon; (*b*) the variations at the beginning of words occur only in monosyllables, whereas in polysyllables the initial sequence consonant+sonant is invariable; cf. the well-authenticated IE words **swekuros* 'father-in-law', **swesōr* 'sister', **swādu-* 'sweet', **dhwer-* 'door', **treyes* 'three', etc., which never alternate with forms having initial *suw-*, *dhuw-*, *tr̥e-*, etc. For monosyllabics note also Gr. *φάρυξ* and Lat. *frūmen* 'throat', Arm. *erbuc* 'breast' (from **bruc*), which point to an IE alternation **bhrug-/*bhr̥ug-*, and an alternation **sl̥ei-/*slei-* is shown by Lat. *saliua* as compared with Slav. *slina* 'spittle' and OE *slīm* 'slime'.[1]

[1] See Lindeman, 'La loi de Sievers et le début du mot en ie.', *NTS* 20, 1965, 38–108; Jamison, '*tvac* etc.', *IIJ* 29, 1986, 161–81; Kuiper, '*suar* and *tvam*', *IIJ* 30, 1967, 1–8.

5.7.2.5. Even if there is much that needs correction in Edgerton's perhaps over-precise formulations,[1] he still deserves credit for having extended Sievers' Law to the other sonants. That longer words should offer greater resistance to variation, and so generalize a single form, is remarkable but also understandable. It is also noteworthy that Edgerton's a priori formulae respecting two sonants agree strikingly well with Meillet's empirical rules (*Introduction* 134f.).[2]

[1] Edgerton is also opposed by Borgstrøm, *NTS* 15, 1949, 152; Sihler, *Lg* 45, 1969, 248–73; he is supported by Lehmann, *PIE* 10f.; *Fs. Kuiper*, 1969, 39–45. The possibility that the law is prior to our Rigveda is considered by Atkins, *JAOS* 88, 1969, 679–709.

[2] The impression is gaining ground that Sievers' Law is not a phonetic law, and that the phenomenon is confined to particular lexemes and morphological categories; see Horowitz (above, 5.7.2.1 n. 1), 60f.; Migron, *IIJ* 18, 193.

5.7.3

It is an interesting feature of Indo-European syllabic structure that long (so-called double) consonants do not occur in roots, although, at least in the case of *-tt-* and *-ss-*, they fairly often find a place at morpheme boundaries. In the old IE languages too, long consonants are something unusual: they are characteristic of pet names and expressive words, often including baby language. Whether the agreement of Hitt. *attas* 'father', Gr. *ἄττα*, etc. implies an IE **atta* (already a baby word in IE?) must, in view of the syllabic structure, remain doubtful.[1]

[1] On expressive gemination, see Kuryłowicz, *BSL* 62, 1968, 1–8, and *IG* 342f.; O. Masson, 'Géminations expressives dans l'anthroponymie grecque', *BSL* 81, 1986, 217–29. On Gmc. *jj, ww* from *jH, wH* see Kortlandt, in *Studies Polomé*, 1988, 356.

6

Prehistory of the Indo-European Phonological System

In the preceding chapters we have sought to reconstruct the phonological system of Indo-European as it appeared shortly before the end of IE linguistic unity. This situation can now be analysed in accordance with the methods of internal reconstruction (see Chapter 3), whereby we can in certain important points recover a still earlier situation, Proto-Indo-European.

6.1. ORIGIN OF THE ABLAUT GRADES: ZERO GRADE

With regard to the ablaut alternations, it is in the first place clear that loss of the basic vowel is connected with the position of the accent. Forms like Skt. *ás-mi* 'I am': *s-ánti* 'they are' from IE **és-mi*: **s-énti* (cf. Dor. *ἠμί*: *ἐντί*, Goth. *im*: *sind*, OCS *esmĭ*: *sǫtŭ*) can only be understood on the assumption that the root **es-* lost *e* and became *s* in the plural because of the shift of the accent from the root to the ending (cf. also Skt. 1st pl. *s-más*, 2nd pl. *s-thá* from IE **s-més*, **s-t(h)é*); in any case, one can only reach *s-* from *es-* and not vice versa.

This is important, because the Indian grammarians in their theory of vowel gradation started from the zero grade as the basic form and accounted for the other two grades as arising from it by successive additions of *a*: thus basic grade *diš-* 'show', *guṇa* ('secondary quality') *dēš-*<**d-a-iš-*, and *vṛddhi* ('increase') *daiš-*<**d-a-a-iš-*. In fact, the only possible basic form is the full grade, the *guṇa*-grade of the Indians, even if in isolated cases a zero grade can acquire a new full grade formed on the analogy of existing alternations (see 6.5.5).

The same connection between zero grade and accent shift is shown in the verb **ei-* 'go': 1st s. **éi-mi*: 1st pl. **i-més*, 3rd pl. **y-énti* (cf. Skt. *ḗmi imás yánti*). In noun forms the connection is seen in Gr. *πατέρα πατέρες* in contrast to *πατρός πατρῶν*; in verbal adjectives with the accented suffix *-tó-*, e.g. **gʷhen-* 'strike, kill': **gʷhn̥-tó-* (Skt. *hán-ti* 'strikes': *hatá-* 'struck'), **kleu-* 'hear': **klu-tó-* 'famous' (Skt. *śrutá-*, Gr. *κλυτός*), etc.

In all these cases the shift of accent to the word-end seems to result in the loss of the root vowel. There are, however, instances in which moving the accent back onto the first part of a compound word has the same effect. The full-grade word **genu* 'knee' (Lat. *genū*, Hitt. *genu*), for example, appears as **gnu* in Skt. *pra-j̆ñu-* 'bow-legged', Avest. *fra-šnu-* 'holding the knees forward', Gr. *πρόχνυ* (from **πρόγνυ*) 'kneeling, crouching (with knees forward)'.

This weakening extended also to long vowels. Corresponding to the difference of length it can be expected that, while short vowels disappear altogether, long vowels become short, at least in the first instance. In conformity with this is the fact that the zero grade of the long vowels is the short murmured vowel schwa.

It thus appears that the zero grade, the loss of the basic vowel in unaccented position, arose mostly before but also after the accent. Since such vowel weakenings and losses are known only in languages with a predominantly expiratory or dynamic accent, an accent of this kind is assumed for the Proto-Indo-European period in which the zero grade arose.[1]

[1] Cf. Hirt, *Der idg. Ablaut*, 1900, 20f.; *IG* ii, 9f., 192f.; Kuryłowicz, *Études* 77f.; *Apophonie* 97f.; Lehmann, *PIE* 111; Burrow, *The Sanskrit Language*, London 1955, 110. The claim that 'le ton est lié à l'alternance, il ne la provoque pas' (Benveniste, *Origines* 52) sounds strange when one considers the changes produced in the vowel system by the French or German accent. It was no doubt taken over from Meillet (e.g. *BSL* 27, 1926, 124–8; 31, 1931, 1–7), but is rejected even in France by e.g. Garde 1976, 461; Meillet's main argument was that the Greek and Indic accents show no sign of *intensité*, but this was precisely the reason why the German school assumed a different accent for the period of ablaut weakenings. The Western European view was (*sauf erreur*) formulated for the first time by L. Geiger, *Ursprung und Entwicklung der menschlichen Sprache* i, 1868, 164f.; then came L. Meyer, *KZ* 21, 1873, 343; Fick, *BB* 4, 1878, 191; Saussure, *Recueil* 117 (if *bhudh-* is the basic form, then so are *pt- t-*, which is clearly impossible; the correct forms are *pet- at-*); Delbrück, *Die neueste Sprachforschung*, 1885, 43f. Nevertheless the Indian theory has been defended in the West by e.g. Schmitt-Brandt, 23; Rundgren, *Studia Pagliaro* iii, 1969, 185f.; Wyatt, *IE /a/*, 1970, 58, 77 n. 24 (see Szemerényi, *Lg* 48, 1972, 169f.).

ADDENDUM 1. A quite different path is taken by C. H. Borgstrøm ('Thoughts about IE vowel gradation', *NTS* 15, 1949, 137–87). He assumes for Proto-Indo-European a stage with only open syllables and a single 'vowel' *ä*; in this system a mechanical rule had caused the disappearance of every second *ä* from the end. Thus 3rd s. **häsä-tä* became **hästä*, later **est*, while 3rd pl. **häsä-nätä* became **hsäntä*, later **sent*, from which arose **esti*, **senti*. But the 1st and 2nd pl. **smes*, **ste* are inconsistent with this rule: a form **häsä-mä* would have given *esm-*, while **häsä-mäsä* would have resulted in *sems-*. The type Skt. *dveṣṭi* from **dweis-ti* also remains a puzzle on this theory (**däwäyäsätä*>**deuyest*?). The basic error is, however, the assumption of a stage with open syllables only (see below). Cf. Borgstrøm's later version in *Word* 10, 1954, 275–87, esp. 282, and 'Tonkawa and IE vowel gradation', *NTS* 17, 1956, 119–28.

ADDENDUM 2. Loss by syncope can affect *i* and *u* also; see my *Syncope* and below, 6.7.2.2.5; also Fulk 1986, 40f., esp. 49 (at an early stage every second vowel before and after the vowel bearing the primary stress received a secondary stress; later every unstressed vowel was syncopated).

6.2. LONG GRADE

This grade is found in the first place in many nominative formations in consonant stems, not only in the animate class (m. f.) but also in the inanimate (n.): cf. Gr. πατήρ, ποιμήν, (Dor.) πώς, but also n. κῆρ (stem **kerd*). To these must be added certain aorist and perfect formations, e.g. Lat. *uehō uēxī*, *uenio uēnī*, and certain noun formations which are characterized as derivative by their long grade, e.g. OHG *swāgur* 'brother-in-law' from **swēkuros*, a long-grade derivative (i.e. *vr̥ddhi* formation) from **swekuros* 'father-in-law'. In some languages the long grade is used also in verbal derivatives, e.g. Lat. *cēlāre* from **celere* (preserved in *oc-culere*).

6.2.1

As regards the origin of the long grade, Streitberg's explanation was for a long time in favour, according to which the disappearance of a vowel, if combined with syllable loss, led to the lengthening of the vowel of a preceding accented syllable. Thus from a stem **pətéro* arose the nom. **pətēr*, whereas the acc. **pətérom* became **pətem̥* without lengthening, since no syllable loss was involved. In the same way **dyēus* arose from **dyéwos*, **gʷōus* 'cow' from **gʷówos*, **pēs* from **pédos*, **rēks* from **régos*, etc.[1]

[1] W. Streitberg, *TAPA* 24, 1893, 29–49; *IF* 3, 1893, 305–416; Hirt, *Der idg. Ablaut*, 1900, 175f.; *IG* ii, 37f.; Kuryłowicz, *Études* 92f., 160f., 234f.; Lehmann, *PIE* 111; Borgstrøm, *NTS* 15, 1949, 138; *Word* 10, 1954, 280; and recently again Purczinsky, *Word* 26, 1974, 386–94.

6.2.2

Not long afterwards, however, the objection was raised by M. Bloomfield that on this theory Indo-European could originally have had no monosyllabic words at all. Further, if the long grade in athematic verbs arose from thematic forms (e.g. Skt. *tāṣṭi* 'makes from wood' from **tekseti*), then, as Persson emphasized, one would expect the same in all instances, which is not the case; cf. Skt. *bharti* 'carries', *vaṣṭi* 'wishes', etc. Moreover, to take nouns, if **kērd* 'heart' is to be derived from **kerede*, then **deyewos* 'god' should have given **dēiwos*, not the form based on actual evidence, **deiwos*.[1]

[1] M. Bloomfield, *TAPA* 26, 1895, 5f.; Wackernagel, *Ai. Gr.* i, 68; M. van Blankenstein, *Untersuchungen zu den langen Vokalen in der* e-*Reihe*, 1911; P. Persson, *Beiträge zur idg. Wortforschung* i–ii, 1912, 625f.; M. Leumann, *KSchr.* 360, 367; Kortlandt, *Slavic Accentuation*, 1975, 84–6.

6.2.3

Since the possibility of a phonetic explanation of the long grade seemed to be vanishing, many scholars fell back on a non-phonetic explanation: the lengthening was a case of *sound symbolism* or had a *rhythmic-expressive* character. Loewe, for example, wrote: 'The IE lengthening had in the main a symbolic and specially dynamic character, in so far as the intensity of the conception was reflected in the length of the vowel'.[1]

[1] R. Loewe, *Germanische Sprachwissenschaft* i^4, 1933, 60, 62; Pisani, *RAL* 6/10, 1934, 394–421; Schwyzer, *GG* i, 355f.; Specht, *Ursprung* 338, 360. Against, Leumann, *KSchr.* 367f. Without any evidence, lengthening of *eR* to *ēR* is assumed by some, e.g. by Kortlandt, *Slavic Accentuation*, 85 ('phonetic lengthening before word-final resonant'), followed by Beekes, *Origins* 152, and, rather differently (following Schmalstieg), by Villar (see Szemerényi 1985, 29f.); Dunkel, in *In Memory of W. Cowgill*, 1987, 20: 'probably compensatory'—but of what?

6.2.4

An entirely new type of explanation, though one essentially in keeping with the Indian *guṇa*-theory, was put forward by Kuryłowicz. According to this, the lengthening was quite generally not of a phonetic but of a morphological nature. Thus the nominative of the consonant stems is explained as follows: the ending *-er*, which represents the original form without case ending of the nominative and survives later as vocative, became ambiguous, because tautosyllabic *-ēr* had been shortened to *-er*, whereas noun stems ending in a non-sonant consonant (*-ēT*) kept the long vowel; on the analogy of this the nominative character of *-er* was clarified by lengthening it to *-ēr*. In other instances of long grade (*vr̥ddhi* in noun formations like **swēkuros*, *s*-aorists like Lat. *rēxī tēxī*), we have to do with transformations on the analogy of the basic model *ei*/*i*, in which *i* was seen as the basic form, *ei* as the derivative, so leading to a derivative *ē* formed to a basic *e*.[1]

[1] Kuryłowicz, *Apophonie* 142–65, and on the extension of the long grade 264f.; *Categories* 198, 209f.; *IG* 298f. See also Nagy 1970 (cf. Szemerényi, *Krat* 14, 1972, 165); T. Mathiassen, *Studien zum slavischen und ie. Langvokalismus*, 1974; W. P. Schmid, 'Zur Dehnstufe im Baltischen und Slavischen', *Fs. H. Bräuer*, 1986, 457–66.

6.2.5

That this theory, ingenious though it is, is unsatisfactory and offers no real solution is due not only to its all too mathematical formulation, but also to the fact that it requires the development through analogical procedures of new phonemes and relationships not previously present in the language. And yet it is the case that analogical processes can take place only within the bounds of what is already present and available, precisely because they are directed in accordance with existing models. Even if a few *vṛddhi* formations could be explained in this way, it could only be so if models for them already existed, i.e. if the long grade was already present. The same is true of the long grade in the nominative, and it should also be noted that on this theory a neuter like κῆρ remains inexplicable.

Still less attractive is the psychological approach. Lengthening of consonants (Fr. *épppouvantable*) and vowels (Grm. *schäääbig*) is known in expressive speech, but not as developing into a generally applicable feature of normal speech.[1]

[1] The view (Schmitt-Brandt, 15f.) that **dyēus* 'sky', **kwēn* (*sic*) 'dog', and **Hnēr* 'man' developed by transposition and lengthening from **deiws*, **keun*, and **Hanr* is unacceptably odd.

6.2.6

A really satisfactory solution can only be reached if the basis of the long-grade formations can be traced back to phonetically explicable differences. The preparatory work of analysis was carried out by M. Leumann. In a brilliant essay Leumann showed that the origin of the *vṛddhi* formations (type **swēkuros* 'belonging to **swekuros*') is to be found in monosyllabic words which presented the long grade in the nominative singular. A good example is Skt. *nārī* 'woman', formed to m. *nā(r)* 'man'; in the same way a *vṛddhi* adjective **nēros* 'belonging to the man' would have been formed to **nēr* 'man'. Leumann could not, however, answer the final question how the long grade of the nominative had arisen.[1]

[1] M. Leumann, 'Vokaldehnung, Dehnstufe und Vrddhi', *IF* 61, 1952, 1–16, repr. in *KSchr.* 360–71. In the last sentence Leumann points out that the long grade in the nom. s. of monosyllabic nouns can be compared to the lengthening of *u* to *ū* mentioned on p. 362 of the reprint; on this, see below, 6.2.7.4. See further Kuryłowicz, *IG* 308f.; *Problèmes* 19f., 175f.; Campanile, *InL* 1, 1974, 52f.; Darms, *Schwäher und Schwager . . . Die Vrddhi-Ableitung im Germanischen*, Munich 1978; Ward, *Word* 29, 1978, 18–21. Hamp, *ZCP* 36, 1979, 8, is wholly negative. See further below, 6.5.5.

6.2.7.1. The explanation of the long grade must therefore start from the lengthening in the nom. s. m. f. of certain stem classes. This is found quite regularly in nasal and liquid stems and in *s*-stems, e.g.

**ghiyōm* 'winter' (Gr. *χιών*, Lat. *hiems*), **k(u)wōn* 'dog' (Gr. *κύων*), **ghm̥ōn* 'man' (Lat. *homō*, Goth. *guma*), **mātēr*, **bhrātēr*, **swesōr*, **(a)usōs* 'dawn' (Skt. *uṣās*, Aeol. *αὔως*, Lat. *aurōr-a*), comparatives such as **meg-yōs* 'bigger', **sen-yōs* 'older' (Lat. *maiōr, seniōr*). In contrast to these, stems in vowels and stops have *-s* without long grade in the nominative, e.g. **ekwos* 'horse', **owis* 'sheep', **sūnus* 'son', **nok^{w}ts* 'night'. From the functional standpoint it is clear that all animate (m. f.) stems must formerly have had *-s* as the sign of the nominative, as Martinet has also pointed out. If the stem classes mentioned above show lengthening but no *-s*, the conclusion must be that this is a case of compensatory lengthening, i.e. the normal nominative endings *-ers -ens -ems* or *-ors -ons -oms* became *-ēr -ēn -ēm* or *-ōr -ōn -ōm.*[1] Similarly in *s*-stems *-es-s* or *-os-s* became *-ēs* or *-ōs*, indicating that in nasal and liquid stems also the development of *-ers* to *-ēr* etc. passed through the phase *-err* etc., so that the sequence short vowel+long consonant became the sequence long vowel+short consonant. A fine parallel to this development is provided by Umbrian, with *frateer=frātēr* 'fratres' from *frāter(e)s*.

[1] When I put forward this solution in 1956 and 1957 (see Szemerényi, *KZ* 73, 1956, 190–6=*SM* 804–10; *Trends* 12f., 21; *CTL* ix, 1972, 142, 158), I was not aware that the same explanation had been discovered more than once in the 19th cent.: cf. Pedersen, *The Discovery of Language*, 270; Wackernagel and Debrunner, *Ai. Gr.* iii, 203. Schleicher, Benfey, and Curtius traced OInd. *-ār* to *-ars* (see Schleicher, *Compendium*[4], 1876, 13: *patars, dusmanass, akmans*), and C. Brugman (*sic*) first wished to derive *eugenēs* from *eu-genes-s*, although via *-ehs* (Curtius' *Studien* 4, 1871, 127 n. 52). In our century this explanation has been adopted several times since 1957, under a compulsion, so to speak, of the facts; cf. Szemerényi, *Trends*; Andrejev, *VJ* 1957 (2), 8: *pəters*; Vaillant, *BSL* 56/2, 1961, 191 (*-ers*?), and on my solution also Winter, 'Vocative' 208f.; Szemerényi, *SMEA* 20, 1980, 222f.; *TPS* 1985, 29f. Meid's objection (in Bammesberger 1988, 345 n. 15, and earlier, *Krat* 16, 1971, 44f.) that to postulate a unitary formation for all animate nom. s. is a *petitio principii*, whereas the forms without *-s* represent a 'fundamentally different—and older—type of marking' (happily accepted by Euler, *IF* 96, 1991, 39 n. 13), simply means that a basic principle of comparative philology is abandoned, namely to find a common background for diverging surface phenomena. The same line is adopted by Beekes, *Origins* 151; *Wackernagel Kolloquium*, 1990, 36f., 45. For the old difficulty, the *ā*-stem nom. s., see now Fulk's solution (1986, 142): *-eH-s>-eHH>-ā*. As to the date of my discovery, two letters to Eric Partridge, dated 12 Apr. and 21 June 1955 respectively, state that I had been working 'for some time'/ 'for a long time' on the lengthened grade, and that I now seemed to have reached 'a rational solution'.

6.2.7.2. This explanation is valid also for the dental stems in which, descriptively, both long grade and *-s* occur. Here too it is clear that, for instance, **pod-s* 'foot' gave **poss* by normal assimilation, and this, in accordance with the process described above, had to become **pōs*. In the same way the nominative of **nepot-* 'grandson' became **nepōs*. Cf. Fulk 1986, 62.

6.2.7.3. Among further nominative forms that belong here, only those of the present participle in *-nt-* require a brief discussion. The ending was originally *-ont-s*, which after assimilation to *-onss-* went through the same development as *-ons* in the *n*-stems, i.e. it became *-ōn*. This ending is preserved only in Greek (*φέρων*); in other languages it was reconstituted as *-onts* or a similar form, since *-ōn* would have led to a clash of homonyms. Thus **ferōn* in Latin would have become **ferō* (cf. *homō* from **homōn*), **bharān* in Aryan would have given **bharā*, **bherōn* in Gothic **baira*, all of which would have been identical in form with the 1st s. pres.[1]

[1] But *-ōn* perhaps also survives in East Baltic (see Mažiulis, *Baltų ir kitų ie. kalbų santykiai*, Vilnius 1970, 245; he derives it, however, from *-ōnt*), and in OPers. *tunuvā*. How helplessly one gropes around without the above rules can be seen in Sommerstein, *The Sound Pattern of Ancient Greek*, 77f., and Egli, *Fs. P. Hartmann*, 1983, 337f.

6.2.7.4. Since the lengthening of *u* to *ū* has been mentioned above, it should be remarked that IE **mūs* 'mouse' arose in the way described from **mus-s*; this lengthening has nothing to do with the monosyllabic character of the word.[1] Similarly the nominative of **nas-* 'nose' became **nās*.[2]

[1] So explained by Specht, *KZ* 59, 1932, 280f.

[2] Another possibility is considered by Burrow, *The Problem of Shwa in Sanskrit*, 1979, 67, and Szemerényi, *Gedenkschrift Kronasser*, 1982, 233. Thieme takes a quite different view in *Studia Tovar*, 1984, 369f.

6.2.7.5. That this lengthening has in itself nothing to do with the *-s* but only with the doubling of the consonant is shown by the old word for 'heart'. As a neuter it could, of course, have neither *-s* nor lengthening. Nevertheless, the nominative has in Greek the form *κῆρ*, which is usually regarded as a continuation of IE **kērd*. That this is impossible is shown by the form, since IE **kērd* would have been shortened to **kerd*, from which only Gr. **κερ* could have arisen.[1] The Greek form in fact continues IE **kēr*, which for its part arose from the normal grade **kerd* by assimilation, just as in Latin **kord* became first **korr* and then later *cŏr* (in Latin without lengthening!). Cf. 7.3.3.2.

[1] By Osthoff's Law; see 5.3.7f.

6.2.7.6. It is now also clear why Lat. *uēr*, ON *vār* 'spring' go back to a form **wēr*, while Gr. (ϝ)*ἔαρ* indicates **wesr̥*. The latter form was originally justified only before words beginning with a consonant, whereas it would have been pronounced **wesr* before a vowel. This became by assimilation **werr* (just as *-rs* became *-rr*), whence arose **wēr*.

6.2.7.7. A prevocalic sandhi form lies, moreover, behind the locative ending *-ēi* of the *i*-stems. Originally this case ended in *-ey-i*, but before a vowel it had the variant *-eyy*, which changed to *-ēi* and was generalized in this form.[1] On the analogy of the *i*-stems there arose an ending *-ēu* for the *u*-stems, which replaced the original ending *-ew-i*; similarly *-ōu* took the place of *-ow-i*; see 7.5.1 n. 3 and 7.5.3.

[1] This explanation has been adopted by Schindler, *Sprache* 19, 1973, 153, but not by Beekes (1990, 46 f.). Cf. also Fulk 1986, 96–105.

6.2.8

On the basis of the nominative lengthening which had come about in this way, related *vr̥ddhi* formations were then created (see 6.2.6). In addition to the already mentioned **nēr*, **nēr-ī*, **nēr-o-s* (?), we may refer to the parallel case of **gʷen* (acc.**gʷen-m̥*) 'woman', from which is derived **gʷēn-i-* in Goth. *qēns* (=*kw-*) beside *qinō* from **gʷen-ōn-*. Alongside the hypothetical **nēr-o-s* can be set **sēm-o-s* or **sōm-o-s* 'one, same, like', which is evidenced in Avest. *hāma-*, OCS *samŭ* 'ipse, solus, unus', and which is also the basis of OE *sōm* 'unity, assembly'; from this in turn OE *sēman* 'reconcile' is derived. All these go back in the last resort to the nom. **sēm* or **sōm* of the numeral **sem-* 'one'.

The last-mentioned OE forms also show how the long grade could penetrate verb formations. In this way the type **bhōreyō* arose from **bhōr *bhor-m̥*, while **bhoreyō* remained connected with **bhoros*. From the f. noun type **bhōr-ā*, formed to **bhōr* (or adj.**bhōr-o-s*), was derived **bhōrāyō*.[1]

[1] The first hint of this explanation (6.2.7.1–6.2.8) was given in Szemerényi, *Trends* 12f., 21. Cf. also Martinet, 'Le genre féminin en indo-européen', *BSL* 52, 1957, 83–95; *A Functional View of Language*, 1962, 149–52; *La Linguistique* 8/1, 1972, 12f.; Winter, 'Vocative'; see above, 6.2.7.1 n. 1.

ADDENDUM 1. A further question is whether the long grade in the *s*-aorist should be explained in line with this theory. That the interchange of length from consonant to vowel is not confined to word end can be seen from (*inter alia*) the numerals **wīkm̥t-* 'twenty', **trīkomt-* 'thirty', **kʷetwr̥̄komt-* 'forty', etc., in which *-īk-* *-r̥̄k-* arose from *-ikk-* *-r̥kk-*, which in turn are from *-idk-* *r̥dk-*.[1] If this is the case, then an aorist **bher-s-m̥* could have given rise to **bhērm̥* and later, with restored *s*, to **bhērsm̥*. The development found for the word end is also adequate to explain the 2nd and 3rd s. **bher-s-s*>**bhēr*, **bher-s-t* >**bhēr*, which were later reshaped to **bhēr-s(s)* and **bhēr-s-t* respectively.[2]

[1] In the same way, OIr. *īs* 'under' is not from **pēd-su* (Lewis and Pedersen, *CCCG* § 25. 6) but from **pēsu*, lengthened from **pessu*, i.e. **ped-su*; this modifies Szemerényi 1976, 41 n. 87; a different view is taken in Campanile, *SSL* 13, 1973, 69.

[2] Kuryłowicz, *Categories* 111, and Kortlandt, *Slavic Accentuation*, 1975, 22, give quite different explanations.

ADDENDUM 2. The long grade problem is not in itself directly relevant to perfects such as *ēd- āg- ōd-* from **ed-* 'eat', **ag-* 'lead', **od-* 'smell', which are contracted from *e+e, a, o*. These forms, however, probably played a part in the extension of lengthening to medial position, e.g. in **gʷēm-* (Lat. *uēnī*, Goth. *qēmum*), etc. See 9.4.3 *b, c*.

6.2.9

Since the long grade represents simply a transformation of the normal full grade in particular circumstances, it could have arisen at any time, and therefore its chronology relative to the zero grade cannot be determined. Nevertheless the process, especially the evolution of the various nominal and verbal *vr̥ddhi* formations, must have required a long period.

6.3. *o*-GRADE

In a number of cases, and indeed categories, it is clear that changes of timbre and accentuation are interdependent. The simple πατήρ, ἀνήρ, φρήν contrast with the compounds εὐπάτωρ, δυσάνωρ, ἄ-φρων. Alongside the types δοτήρ, ποιμήν are δώτωρ, δαίμων. To the *s*-stem γένος corresponds the compound εὐγενές. From the verb λείπω is derived the adjective λοιπός as well as the perfect λέλοιπα, from φέρω the abstract noun φορά, etc.

6.3.1

In all these cases an unaccented *o* in the derivative stands in opposition to an accented *e* of the basic word. Hirt concludes from this that *o* arose from *e* 'when this acquired a secondary accent, that is to say, mainly in compounds or in cases of accent shift'. Since the predominantly stress accent which brought about the zero grade could not also have caused a qualitative change of *e* (and *a*) to *o*, it was taken that the change of timbre to *o* was the later effect of a musical low pitch.[1]

[1] Cf. Hirt, *Der idg. Ablaut*, 156; *IG* ii, 172f.; H. Güntert, 'Zur *o*-Abtönung in den idg. Sprachen', *IF* 37, 1916, 1–87; Kuryłowicz, *Études* 97f.; Lehmann, *PIE* 110.

6.3.2

In the 1950s and 1960s Kuryłowicz drew attention to two important points.

1. Since the connection of the zero grade with the accent position is to a great extent still clear, it must be expected that the *o*-grade, if it

really followed the period of the zero grade, would be even clearer in that respect. This is not the case, however. Alongside the instances cited above in favour of an accent connection there were, Kuryłowicz pointed out, many others which ran counter to this explanation, cf., with accented *o*, *φόρος φώρ αἰδώς ἠώς γόνυ* etc. It is in any case clear that the *o*-grade, if it had once really been determined by the accent, had in Indo-European itself already acquired a purely morphological function.

2. It is a fact of experience that the accent does indeed cause vowel weakening and syncope, but not change of timbre; this is determined by the phonetic environment; for example, in Russian *e* has become *o* before a hard consonant, though only when accented.

From these considerations Kuryłowicz first concluded that the period of the *o*-grade did not follow but preceded the zero grade. As regards the conditions of change, he proposed to see these in a phonetic development of early Indo-European. In the weakening of the original sequences *eR oR*, where *R* stands for *r l m n*, the first stage was $_{e}R$ $_{o}R$, which later coalesced in $_{o}R$. For this reason in the perfect tense, for example, s.**wert-* was opposed to pl. *$w_{o}rt$- (not *$w_{e}rt$-). The over-short $_{o}$ was, however, perceived as belonging to the phoneme *o*, with the result that **wort-* arose to replace the singular **wert-*. By the same process in root nouns the original alternance **wert-*/*$w_{e}rt$-, after the falling together of the latter with *$w_{o}rt$-, became **wort-*/*$w_{o}rt$- and finally **wort-*/**wr̥t-*. In this way a starting-point of the *o*-grade is obtained both in the nominal and in the verbal derivation.[1]

[1] Cf. Kuryłowicz, *Apophonie* 36–96; *Categories* 52; but note below, 6.3.4 n. 2. See also Hilmarsson, 'On qualitative apophony in IE', *NTS* 31, 1977, 173–203; Dressler, in Ramat (ed.), *Problemi della ricostruzione in linguistica*, 1977, 108–12.

6.3.3

This novel theory of Kuryłowicz has been sharply attacked by another Polish scholar W. Mańczak, chiefly because of the assumption that full-grade forms could be analogically influenced by weak-grade forms. He also considers the assumption of a falling together of $_{e}r$ and $_{o}r$, which is the starting point of the whole process, to be no less difficult and without foundation. Mańczak proposes two sound laws to account for the origin of the *o*-grade:

(*a*) accented and pre-accentual *e* became *o* before a back vowel (*a*/*o*/*u*);
(*b*) later, post-accentual *e* became *o* before a sonant.

Examples of (*b*): *λέγετε* but *λέγομεν*; *πατήρ πατέρες* but *ἀπάτωρ ἀπάτορες*; *δοτήρ* but *δώτωρ*; *ποιμήν φρήν* but *ἄκμων ἄφρων*. Examples of (*a*): the original perfect **dedérka* 'I have seen' became **dedórka* (Gr. *δέδορκα* with innovated accent), after which also 3rd s. **dedórke*; in thematic nouns the oxytone type (nom. **bhert-é-s*) gen. **bhert-é-syo* became **bhert-ó-syo* with *o* subsequently generalized and extended to other types, but **wérgom* 'work', **sénos* 'old' kept their *e*.[1]

[1] Mańczak, 'Origine de l'apophonie *e/o* en indo-européen', *Lingua* 9, 1960, 277–87. Mańczak concedes that he cannot account for everything, but claims to have explained more than his predecessors and to have assumed only historically attested processes of development. Cf. id., *Fs. Szemerényi*, 1980, 529–35.

6.3.4

Although opinions diverge widely, some points can be regarded as certain.

(*a*) The accent must be excluded as a cause.[1]

(*b*) It is possible that in the case of the *o*-grade different processes have contributed to the final picture. The phonetic environment, however, must have played a decisive part. The effect of the nasal in the change of **(e)bherem* to **ebherom* in the imperfect, or of *-em* to *-om* in the thematic acc., is surely unmistakable, and in general the role of the sonants in post-accentual developments (ἄκμων, δώτωρ) seems certain. The effect of preceding labials, as in **pōs* 'foot', **nepōs* 'grandson', **k^{w}etwores* 'four', is probably to be added. In any case much work still needs to be done in sifting the various factors responsible for the change of timbre.

(*c*) It is not very likely that a change of this kind could have affected the long vowels, which are too stable for it. This means that the change of *e* to *o* preceded the period of vowel lengthening, i.e. *ēr* did not become *ōr*, but *-ers* became *-ors* and this later gave *-ōr*. On the other hand, there are no grounds for supposing that the *o*-grade arose later than the zero grade.[2] [3]

[1] This view goes back to Baudouin de Courtenay, *IF* 4, 1894, 53f.

[2] According to Kuryłowicz, *IG* 257, the *o*-grade is neither later nor earlier than the zero grade.

[3] A quite new theory is proposed by Schmitt-Brandt, 124f. On the theory of Pulleyblank, not discussed here, see Szemerényi, 'New Look' 83f.; Dressler (without realizing it) offers a similar view (above, 6.3.2, n. 1) esp. n. 22. See also Rundgren, *Studia Pagliaro* iii, 1969, 186f.; Kravčuk, in *Tipologija* 12–20, who assumes vowel harmony. Rasmussen 1989, 123–256, and in Vennemann 1989, 156, 251, expects *o* before voiced and *e* before voiceless sounds (and nil).

6.4. THE LARYNGEAL THEORY

In his *Mémoire* (p. 127), the young Saussure put forward the thesis that the vowel of every root was *e*; this root vowel could be followed by a 'coefficient sonantique' (*i u r l m n*), which in the zero grade became the syllabic nucleus: **deik- *kleu- *derk- *bhendh-* became in the zero grade **dik- *klu- *dr̥k- *bhn̥dh-*. To the 'coefficients sonantiques', however, belonged also *A* and *O*; these could appear as *a* and *o*, but only in the zero grade; in the full grade they would be preceded by the universal root vowel *e*, and the resulting sequences *e+A*, *e+O* had given IE *ā* and *ō*.

One looks in vain for a real demonstration of the theory. It is not hard to see, however, how Saussure came to these assumptions. As we have seen (5.3.1 fin.), the great majority of roots have the vowel *e*, and it is certainly very tempting to base a rule of general validity on this empirical fact. It is considerably more speculative to assert that the long vowels are really combinations of this same *e* and modifying elements with which it was contracted. Roots like **stā*- **dhē*- **dō*- certainly give no cause for such an analysis. Saussure could, however (p. 137), point to the parallel between Skt. *ás-mi* 'I am', *s-más* 'we are', Gr. (Dor.) εἶ-μι 'I go', ἴ-μες 'we go' and φᾱ-μί 'I say', φᾰ-μές 'we say'. Just as in the first two instances the full grade of the root (*as*- and ει-) appears in the singular, the zero grade in the plural, so in the third φᾱ is the full grade, φᾰ the zero grade. Put back to front, just as the full grade εἶ- 'arises', as it were, by prefixing *e* to the zero grade *i*-, so φᾱ would arise from φᾰ by prefixing an *e*, i.e. φᾱ is really *phea*- (or *pheA*).[1]

[1] Saussure, *Mémoire*, here quoted from his *Recueil*.

6.4.1

This revolutionary idea, which at a stroke reduced the Indo-European vowel system to a single vowel, could not have come at a worse time. It clashed with another revolution, which in the last few years before Saussure's book had just as fundamentally reshaped the appearance of that same system: the view that Indo-European had possessed not three vowels, like Sanskrit, but five, like Greek, was in process of establishing itself. No wonder that the position won by so much hard work would not be immediately surrendered. Moreover, Saussure's system was not wholly satisfactory.

An obvious defect was that if the long vowels are to be seen as contractions, three coefficients are needed, since there are three long vowels. Saussure indeed saw that the interpretation of στᾱ-/στᾰ- as **stea*-/**sta*- (or **steA*-/**stA*) meant that θη-/θε- would have to be understood as **dhee*-/**dhe*- (*Mémoire* 133), but he allowed himself to be diverted from this conclusion by his inability to discover any difference between *ē* and *ā*, for which reason he traced both to *e+A*. This puzzling error was corrected in the following year by the Danish scholar H. Möller, who assumed three coefficients, so that *ē*=*e+E*, *ā*=*e+A*, *ō*=*e+O*. He also pointed out that Saussure's view that *a* and *o* were always zero grades of *eA* and *eO* was illogical and untenable, since structurally **agō* is to be judged in the same way as **ed-mi*, i.e.

both show the full grade. From here it was but a short step to attribute to these coefficients (which Möller later termed laryngeals under the influence of his own theory of Indo-European and Semitic relationship) the property of changing the timbre not only of preceding but also of following vowels. A root _*ag-_ is thus to be understood not as _Ag-_ (Saussure) but as _Aeg-_, in which the laryngeal itself disappeared after changing the basic vowel to _a_.

If we adopt the now almost universal practice of denoting the laryngeals by H_1 H_2 H_3, the following equivalents result for the IE vowel system:

initial	_e-_=H_1e-	_a-_=H_2e-	_o-_=H_3e-
preconsonantal	_ē_=eH_1	_ā_=eH_2	_ō_=eH_3

Examples:

_*ed-_ 'eat'=*H_1ed-, _*ag-_ 'lead, drive'=*H_2eg-, _*od-_ 'smell'=H_3ed-, _*dhē-_ 'put'=*$dheH_1$-, _*stā-_ 'stand'=*$steH_2$-, _*dō-_ 'give'=*deH_3-.

From these considerations it also follows that _schwa primum_ (see 5.3.4) is simply the syllabic, vocalized manifestation, i.e. the interconsonantal allophone, of the laryngeals: _*stətós_ is *stH_2_tós_, _*dətós_ is dH_3_tós_, etc. It further follows, as Möller's pupil H. Pedersen recognized, that the long syllabic sonants (4.5.3, 5.3.5) are fusions of syllabic sonants with non-syllabic laryngeals: _ī ū r̥̄ l̥̄ m̥̄ n̥̄_ are _iH uH r̥H l̥H m̥H n̥H_.[1]

[1] Information on the literature is given in H. Hendriksen, _Untersuchungen über die Bedeutung des Hethitischen für die Laryngaltheorie_, 1941, 3f., esp. 3 n. 1; Szemerényi 1964, 4f.; 'New Look' 68f.; Polomé in _Evidence_ 11. A detailed history of the initial phase of the laryngeal theory (1878–1935) can be found in Szemerényi, 'La théorie des laryngales de Saussure à Kuryłowicz et à Benveniste: Essai de réévaluation', _BSL_ 68, 1973, 1–25. Cf. also Mayrhofer, 'Zum Weiterwirken von Saussures "Mémoire"', _Krat_ 33, 1988, 1–15.

6.4.2

For nearly half a century the laryngeal theory was regarded as an eccentric fancy of outsiders. The situation changed in 1927, when Hittite provided the long missing 'confirmation'.

The early position was that the laryngeals made their presence known only by their effects, but were not themselves preserved in any language. It is possible to reconstruct words like 'is', 'before', or 'bone' as Proto-IE *H_1esti, *H_2enti, *H_3est-, but in the IE languages there are only reflexes of _*esti *anti *ost-_ (Gr. ἐστί, ἀντί, ὀστ-έον), with no trace of the laryngeals. It therefore came as a surprise when in 1927 the young Polish researcher Jerzy Kuryłowicz announced that, while H_1 had been lost in Hittite also, H_2 and H_3 survived as the spirant _h_. The Proto-IE forms cited above appear in Hittite as _eszi_ (=_es-tsi_ with affrication of _ti_), _hanza_ 'in front' (=_hant-sa_, cf. _hantezzis_ 'first', Lat.

anterior), *hastai* 'bone'. To these can be added further correspondences showing the survival of laryngeals in internal position also; cf. *pahs-* 'protect', OCS *pas-ti* 'to pasture', Lat. *pāscō*.

With this discovery the correctness of the laryngeal theory seemed to be finally proved. As is so often the case, however, the new material not only solved old problems but at the same time brought new ones. There were instances in which Hittite *a* corresponded to IE *a* but with no preceding or following *h*, e.g. Gr ἀπό or ὀπί: Hitt. *appa* 'behind, after'; Hitt. *tāyezzi* 'steals': OCS *tatĭ* 'thief'. To escape this difficulty, Kuryłowicz felt obliged to posit for such cases a fourth laryngeal (H_4), which had the same effect as H_2 in changing *e* to *a*, but unlike H_2 disappeared in Hittite also.[1]

[1] Cf. Kuryłowicz, 'ə indo-européen et *h* hittite', *Symbolae in honorem J. Rozwadowski* i, 1927, 95–104; 'Les effets du ə en indo-iranien', *Prace Filologiczne* 11, 1927, 201–43; *Études* 27–76. Sturtevant, *Lg* 4, 1928, 159–70, discovered independently that Hittite *h* preserved a phoneme which the other IE languages had lost.

6.4.2.1. If we assign to the French scholar Albert Cuny, who has not yet been mentioned, his rightful place in the story, the achievements of the first stage of the theory can be set out as follows (Szemerényi 1973, 22f.). Saussure is the founder of modern views on the IE vowel system and vowel gradation, but the true founder of the laryngeal theory is the Danish scholar Möller. The credit for having first developed and systematized the theory belongs to Cuny. Its final triumph was brought about by Kuryłowicz, who not only supplied the proof by means of the Hittite material but also investigated the many varied consequences of the theory. The theory could then, in spite of the difficulties noted above, celebrate its success in Benveniste's brilliant exposition (*Origines*, 1935, ch. 9).

6.4.3

Despite the difficulties, scholars have in general contented themselves with three laryngeals, e.g. Benveniste in his *Origines* (esp. 147f.), or the Flemish scholar W. Couvreur, who also defined the laryngeals phonetically: H_1 was a glottal stop (Semitic *ālif*), H_2 was an unvoiced, H_3 a voiced laryngeal spirant. The American school, on the other hand, followed Sapir in adopting four laryngeals, of which two, the back velar spirants χ and γ, appear in Hittite as *h*, while the other two, both glottal stops, are lost in Hittite also. As opposed to these varying interpretations, the Danish Nestor of IE and Hittite studies, H. Pedersen, tried to make do with two laryngeals, defined by the equations $eH_1=\bar{e}$, $eH_2=\bar{a}$, while regarding $\bar{o}$ as simply a change of vowel timbre.[1]

[1] Cf. W. Couvreur, *De Hettitische* H, 1937; for the American view, E. H. Sturtevant, *The Indo-Hittite Laryngeals*, 1942, and Lehmann, *PIE* (esp. clear 98, 104f.); H. Pedersen, *Hittitisch und die anderen indoeuropäischen Sprachen*, 1938, 179–90; H. Hendriksen (above, 6.4.1 n. 1); Messing, 'Selected studies in IE phonology', *HSCP* 56/57, 1947, 161–232 (two, perhaps three, laryngeals); the American A. R. Bomhard still hesitates between four (e.g. *Memoriae van Windekens*, 1991, 54f.) and three laryngeals (e.g. 'The Nostratic macrofamily', *Word* 1992, 5); and in general Bomhard 1994.

6.4.4.1. A truly new phase of the laryngeal theory began in the 1950s with the introduction of componential analysis. Starting from the observation that original *ō* (i.e. not the result of vowel gradation) often alternates with *ōw* before a vowel (e.g. **dō-* 'give': Skt. infin. *dāvanē*), Martinet drew the conclusion that *w* must be treated as an 'excretion' of *ō*. This means that *ō* is not adequately defined by the formula $e+H_3$; H_3 must have contained the element *w*, i.e. labial articulation was one of the distinctive features of H_3. If a laryngeal characterized by back tongue position (e.g. H_2 in our interpretation above) is denoted by A, then the labialized H_3 must be denoted by A^{ω}; these two laryngeals were related to one another in the same way as k and k^{ω}. Now it is clear from IE **pibeti* 'drinks', the reduplicated present of the root **pō-* (Lat. *pō-tus*), i.e. *peH_3-, that in the original *pi-pH_3-eti the second *p* became voiced *b* under the influence of H_3. The inference must be that this H_3 had voice as a distinctive feature, since where voice is not distinctive but purely phonetic (as, e.g., usually in *n*) no such assimilation takes place; for example, Russ. *oknó* 'window' does not become *ogno*.[1] If, however, an H_3 with distinctive voice existed, it follows according to the general basic principles of phonology that its partner, a voiceless equivalent to H_3, must also have existed, the two being related in the same way as g^{ω} and k^{ω}. Moreover, since there are grounds for thinking that in certain cases H_2 had voicelessness as a distinctive feature—for instance the reduplicated present of the root **stā* (=*$steH_2$-), *sti-stH_2-eti, gives Skt. *tiṣṭhati*, i.e. tH_2 becomes the voiceless aspirate *th*—one must conclude that there also existed a voiced equivalent to H_2.

By consistent application of these principles Martinet in a later work arrives at a system of ten laryngeals:[2]

		Velar	Pharyngal	Glottal
Without labialization	Open glottis	χ	ḥ	h
	Voice	γ	ϵ	–
	Closed glottis	–	–	ʔ
With labialization	Open glottis	x^{ω}	$ḥ^{\omega}$	–
	Voice	γ^{ω}	ϵ^{ω}	–

[1] On **pibeti*, see Lindeman 1970, 83; id. 1987, 94; *HS* 105, 1993, 166; Winter, *Studies Beeler*, 1980, 487f.; Colarusso, *In Memory of J. A. Kerns*, 1981, 525; Bammesberger, *Studien zur Laryngaltheorie*, 1984, 128f.; Penney, in Bammesberger 1988, 366f.

[2] Martinet, 'Non-apophonic *o* in IE', *Word* 9, 1953, 253–67 (included in *Économie* 212–34);

'Phonologie et laryngales', *Phonetica* 1, 1957, 7–30 (almost identical with the report in *PICL* 8, 1957, 138–55); cf. now his *Steppes*, 1986, 146 (thirteen?), 174. Further possibilities, in particular the setting up of a palatalized series, were exploited by W. Diver and J. Puhvel; the latter first assumed eight laryngeals (see Polomé, in *Evidence* 38), but reduced the number to six (Puhvel, ibid. 92), which is still maintained in his *Hittite Etymological Dictionary* i–ii, 1984. Cf. Adrados 1961; id, 'More on the laryngeals with labial and palatal appendixes', *FoLH* 2, 1981, 191–235; 'Further considerations on . . . H^y and H^w in IE', *Em* 49, 1981, 231–71; he is followed by, among others, J. Gonzáles Fernández, *El perfecto latino en /-ui/*, Seville 1974; A. Bernabé, 'Las raíces con dos laringales', *RSEL* 5, 1975, 345–81. See further Lindeman 1970, 100f.; A. R. Keiler, *A Phonological Study of the IE Laryngeals*, 1970; H. Jonsson, *The Laryngeal Theory*, 1978 (rejected by Lindeman, *IF* 86, 1981, 325; id. 1987, 31–2); Bomhard, *Nostratic* 10–18; Mayrhofer, 'Die Vertretung der idg. Laryngale im Lateinischen', *KZ* 100, 1987, 86–108; Lindeman 1987; id.., 'Tocharian and the Laryngeal Theory', *KZ* 100, 1987, 297–303; 'Phonological reconstruction', *BJL* 3, 1988, 7–183; Bammesberger 1988 (cf. Lindeman, *HS* 102, 1990, 268–97); Rasmussen 1989, 81–109; Kellens 1990; Schrijver 1991; Lindeman, 'Phonology and "Laryngeals" ', *HS* 105, 1993, 161–70.

6.4.4.2. Alternations of the type **kost-/*ost-* 'bone' (see above, 5.4.4) were formerly often explained by assuming prefixes.[1] Recently attempts have been made to account for them as the result of a sandhi development, in which an initial laryngeal following a final laryngeal in the previous word is 'hardened' to a velar stop;[2] conversely it was suggested that the weakening of an initial velar could have given a spirant.[3] It is precisely in the case of OCS *kostĭ*, however, that late origin seems to have been proved.[4]

[1] R. Meringer, *Beiträge zur Geschichte der idg. Deklination*, 1892, 25–54; later Meillet on many occasions, e.g. *MSL* 8, 1893, 291; 23, 1929, 259; also Ernout and Meillet, *Dictionnaire étymologique de la langue latine*⁴, 1959, s.v. *aper*; Pisani, *Miscellanea Galbiati* iii, 1951, 31–3.

[2] Martinet, *BSL* 51, 1956, 56; Lindeman, *SL* 17, 1965, 91–4; *Einführung in die Laryngaltheorie*, 1970, 84f.; id. 1987, 94–8; Dunkel, in *In Memory of W. Cowgill*, 1987, 20; Rousseau, 'k-/Ø-', in Kellens 1990, 149–78. Against: Collinge, *Lingua* 8, 1959, 231; Polomé, in *Evidence* 40.

[3] Schmitt-Brandt, 106f.

[4] Mel'ničuk, *Etimologija*, 1968, 234f.

6.4.4.3. It is, moreover, not very satisfactory to suppose that the *h* preserved in Hittite can be discovered in other languages also, especially in those with a rather obscure history, like Albanian[1] or Armenian.[2]

[1] e.g. Hamp, in *Evidence* 124f., but cf. *CTL* ix, 1972, 1658.

[2] e.g. Greppin, *Handēs Amsorya* 87, 1973, 61–80; against, Considine, *REArm* 13, 1979, 355f., esp. 361f.

6.4.5

Another welcome development of the 1950s was that Russian linguistics after many years of paralysis was able to resume its course, and scholars from the former Soviet Union have become active in this field also. The most important work stems from the Georgian scholar Gamkrelidze, who for Proto-Indo-European posits three pharyngal spirants, which in Indo-European, after timbre change and/or lengthening of the basic vowel, fell together in a single voiced pharyngal spirant *H*, giving rise at that period to the sequences *eH aH oH and He Ha Ho.*[1]

[1] Cf. Th. V. Gamkrelidze, *Hittite and the Laryngeal Theory* (Russ.), Tiflis 1960; brief summary: 'The Anatolian languages and the reconstruction of the IE laryngeal system' (Russ.), in *Problemy sravnitel'noj grammatiki ie. jazykov*, Moscow 1964, 46–50. Other Russian scholars are still more conservative. A. S. Mel'ničuk, *VJ* 1960 (3), 3–16, has two laryngeals: a spirant and a stop. Two laryngeals, not further specified, are assumed by V. V. Ivanov also, most recently in his *Obščeind.*, 1965, 11–18 (with further references); see also G. S. Klyčkov, *VJ* 1963 (5), 3–14, esp. 12f., and the very sceptical attitude of E. Makajev, 'The laryngeal theory and questions of IE linguistics' (Russ.), *Trudy Instituta Jazykoznanija AN Gruzinskoj SSR* 2, 1957, 55–71, who doubts even (the possibility of proving) the existence of the laryngeals.

6.4.6

The laryngeal theory has not been universally accepted. Particularly prominent opponents have been in Germany the Hittitologist H. Kronasser, unfortunately the victim of a car accident, and in Italy the Turin comparatist G. Bonfante. In these countries a general attitude of reserve was noticeable, and was slow to disappear in the post-war period. The American W. F. Wyatt Jr. also takes a negative position.[1]

At the same time it must be remarked that even in Germany and Italy an increasing number of scholars have, since about 1960, been converted to the laryngeal theory, including Mayrhofer, Strunk, Scardigli, and others.[2]

[1] Cf. H. Kronasser, *Vergleichende Laut- und Formenlehre des Hethitischen*, 1956, 79–96, 243–6; *Etymologie der heth. Sprache* i/1, 1962, 94–100; G. Bonfante, first *Em* 4, 1936, 161f., then *Paideia* 12, 1957, 22–8; *AGI* 48, 1963, 57–60; W. F. Wyatt Jr. 'Structural linguistics and the laryngeal theory', *Lg* 40, 1964, 138–52.

[2] Cf. M. Mayrhofer, *Sprache* 10, 1965, 175f., and the paper of 1987 cited above, 6.4.4.1 n. 2; K. Strunk, *Glotta* 43, 1966, 208f.; P. G. Scardigli, 'Osservazioni sulla teoria delle laringali', *Atti e memorie dell' Academia Toscana La Colombaria* 22, 1957, 75–116 (one glottal consonant, several vowels).

6.4.7

We may now turn to the question of the place of schwa in the laryngeal theory. In Saussure's version, the equivalence of **dō-/*də-* with **deO-/*dO-*, or using modern symbols **deH*$_3$*-/*dH*$_3$*-*, entailed the interpretation of schwa as the syllabic form of the 'coefficient sonantique' *H*. How far, however, can this algebraic conception be brought into agreement with linguistic, and in particular phonetic, realities?

6.4.7.1. First, the distributional method can be used to establish the following. Empirically, the following morpheme structures have been found to be relevant to our problem: *TeRT-*, *TeHT-*, *TeRH-*, and *TR̥H*-T-. From *TeHT-* it is evident that *H* has greater sonority than a stop, and from *TeRH-* that it has less sonority than a sonant; this last is also proved directly by the fact that if a sequence *TRHT* occurs in a morpheme combination, the syllabic function is taken over by *R*, not by *H*. This means that in the matter of sonority the laryngeal comes between sonant and stop, in the same way as the spirants, i.e. *the laryngeal is a spirant.*

This conclusion obtained by distributional considerations is combined by many scholars[1] with the phonetic thesis that spirants cannot function as syllabic nuclei. If this is so, then schwa, which is certainly a vowel[2], cannot be equated with a laryngeal. An extreme advocate of this view was the Indologist T. Burrow (d. 1986), who found himself forced to assume different suffixes for every case of schwa, i.e. correspondence of Aryan *i* to non-Aryan *a*. Not only was the equivalence of Lat. *status* and Skt. *sthitas* brought to nothing by analysing the former as *stH₂-etos* and the latter as *stH₂-itos* (from a verb **sth-áyati!*), but even the old and surely securely established word for 'father' was broken up into the variants **pH-i-ter-* (Skt. *pitar-*), **pH-ter-* (alleged Iran. **ptar-*), and **pH-eter-* (Lat. *pater*, etc.).[3] Others simply assume[4] that schwa developed from a 'support vowel' or the *schwa secundum*, the weakening of a short vowel before or after a laryngeal. Only a few[5] see no difficulty in supposing that the laryngeal, even if it is defined as a spirant, could take on a syllabic function.[6]

[1] Kuryłowicz, *Études* 29, 56, 73; K. Ammer, *Sprache* 2, 1952, 212; Lehmann, *PIE* 106f. and 92f.; Martinet, *Phonetica* 1, 1957, 28; Gamkrelidze (works cited above 6.4.5 n. 1), 87 and 47 respectively.

[2] See e.g. Wyatt, *Lg* 40, 1964, 138 f,, against Cuny's consonantal ə; and cf. Lindeman 1987, 30f.

[3] T. Burrow, 'Shwa in Sanskrit', *TPS* 1949, 22–61, esp. 48, 59 and 38, 50; *The Sanskrit Language*, 1955, 88, 104f.

[4] e.g. Adrados 1961, 46f.; Erhart 1970, 25; Lindeman 1970, 88f.; id. 1987, 98f.; Christol, in Kellens 1990, 111f.

[5] More recently Kuryłowicz, e.g. in *Apophonie* 170, also 109[14]; Gamkrelidze (above, 6.4.5 n. 1, 1960), 88; Schindler, *Sprache* 15, 1969, 145; cf. W. Belardi, *Ricerche linguistiche* 4, 1958, 189f. On the zero grade of long vowels, see Kuryłowicz, *Mélanges L. Renou*, 1968, 433f.; Burrow, *Studies Kuiper*, 1969, 251f.; *The Problem of Shwa in Sanskrit*, Oxford 1979 (cf. Szemerényi, *Krat* 28, 1984, 67–77); Tischler, *In Memory of J. A. Kerns*, 1981, 311–23.

[6] Against the often assumed assimilation of *RH* to *RR* see Lindeman, *HS* 102, 1990, 268.

6.4.7.2. Among the problems connected with schwa is the question how many schwas are to be assumed. As we have seen (4.1.11), all IE languages point to one schwa except Greek, which appears to continue three such sounds. In the case of the universally quoted triad *θετός στατός δοτός* it is difficult to avoid the thought that they were or could have been influenced by the full-grade *θη- στᾱ- δω-*. Examples are, however, cited for which no such influence can be proved because of the absence of a related full-grade form, e.g. *ἄνεμος* 'wind' as opposed to *ana- (from *anə-) in W. *anadl*, OIr. *anāl* 'breath', Skt. *ani-ti* 'he breathes'.

If three laryngeals are assumed, the Greek situation can easily be explained: the three vowels α ε ο are the continuations of H_1 H_2 H_3 in their syllabic function.[1] If fewer than three laryngeals are assumed, the Greek plurality cannot be original.

The Greek situation cannot, however, in fact continue an original plurality. There are many instances in which α is found as zero grade of η and ω as well as of ā, e.g. χῆτος: χάτις 'lack', γλῶσσα: γλάσσα 'tongue'. It must therefore be concluded[2] that the weakening of all three long vowels was originally the same, as Brugmann and Hirt had formerly assumed; the few Greek discrepancies must be explained as analogical innovations.

In more recent times, however, Greek negative compounds, which often show νᾱ- νη- νω-, have been brought into the argument. These can be explained theoretically as developed from **n̥H(C)-*, which would prove that the triple representation reflects the diversity of the laryngeals.[3] But this conclusion is firmly rejected by other scholars,[4] and it is in fact hard to see how a difference of the laryngeals could have made itself felt in the environment *R̥H(C)*.

[1] Cuny, *RPhon* 2, 1912, 120f. (following Möller); Kuryłowicz, *Études* 44; Lehmann, *PIE* 92f.; Cowgill, in *Evidence* 153f.; Winter, ibid. 201; Forssman, *Untersuchungen zur Sprache Pindars*, 1966, 145f.; Beekes, *Laryngeals*, 1969; *Francis, *Greek Disyllabic Roots*, Yale Diss. 1970; Rasmussen, 'The case of the IE laryngeals', in *7th Scandinavian Conference of Linguistics* ii, Helsinki 1983, 371–84 (*h*, *x*, γ^{w}); Sihler, 'Greek reflexes of syllabic laryngeals', in Bammesberger 1988, 547–61.

[2] Saussure, *Recueil* 168; Hendriksen (above, 6.4.1 n. 1), 92f.; Kuryłowicz, *Apophonie* 201f.; *IG* 252; *BSL* 72, 1977, 69–72; *Problèmes* 180f.; Wyatt, *IE /a/*, 1970, 72 n. 2, 74 n. 15; Bazell, *CFS* 31, 1978, 37f.; Bammesberger, *KZ* 95, 1982, 290; Lindeman, *The Triple Representation of Shwa in Greek*, Oslo 1982, 36–57; Bammesberger, *Studien zur Laryngaltheorie*, 1984, 62–5; Szemerényi, *Krat* 28, 1984, 56.

[3] First suggested by Sturtevant, *Indo-Hittite Laryngeals*, 1942, 57 (rejected by Zgusta, *AO* 19, 1951, 428f.); later followed by Puhvel, *Lg* 29, 1953, 24f.; Risch, *IF* 66, 1961, 313; Forssman (n.1 above); Beekes, *Laryngeals* 98–113, esp. 103f.

[4] e.g. Kuryłowicz, *Problèmes* 188f.; Lindeman, *Triple Representation* 60f.

6.4.7.3. *Prothesis.* In a number of cases in Greek and Armenian,[1] and before an initial *r* also in Hittite (see 4.4, and cf. Lehmann, 'The distribution of PIE /r/', *Lg* 27 (1951), 13–17), there appears a vowel to which nothing corresponds in the other languages. This phenomenon is known as prothesis (also prosthesis).[2]

Since all the short vowels can occur as protheses (e.g. Gr. ἀμέλγω: Lat. *mulgeō*), the attempt was made, once laryngeals had appeared on the scene, to use them to solve this problem also. The prothetic vowels were thus treated as regular reflexes of earlier laryngeals, e.g. ἀνήρ, ὄνομα from H_2*ner-*, H_3*nom*. An unexplained difficulty lies in the fact that, beside forms with prothesis, forms without prothesis are also found, e.g. ἀμαλδύνω: βλαδαρός, ὀμείχω: μοιχός.[3]

These variations point with certainty to an alternation conditioned by sandhi. This means that initial sonants had to appear as vowels or consonants according to the final sound of the preceding word. A root form **melg-* must thus have alternated with **m̥elg*, giving Gr. ἀμέλγω, etc. Of course before initial *r-* the prothesis was quite regular, and it is likely that there were other causes.

[1] Greppin, *Initial Vowel and Aspiration in Classical Armenian*, Vienna 1973; Olsen, 'IE prothetic vowels in Classical Armenian', *REArm* 19, 1985, 5–17; Bendtsen, 'Prothetic vowel assimilation', *APILKU* 4, 1984, 19–21; Vennemann, 'Syllable based sound changes in Early Armenian', *AAL* 7, 1986, 27–43; M. Picard, 'A reanalysis of Armenian prothesis', *FoLH* 10, 1991, 61–9.

[2] On this subject, see Kuryłowicz (e.g. in Szemerényi 1973, 18f. and *BSL* 72, 1977, 72: prothesis not due to laryngeals; *Problèmes* 179–90); Austin, 'The prothetic vowel in Greek', *Lg* 17, 1941, 83–92; Messing (above, 6.4.3 n. 1), 190f.; Szemerényi, *Syncope* 110f., 152, etc.; Hovdhaugen, *NTS* 22, 1968, 115–32; Beekes, *Laryngeals* 18–126; Makajev, *Struktura* 148, 175; Wyatt, *The Greek Prothetic Vowel*, 1972; Hamp, 'Greek prothetic vowels', *MSS* 37, 1978, 59–64; Mayrhofer, *Fs. Neumann*, 1982, 185–91; Lindeman, *Triple Representation* 57–68; id. 1987, 75–86; *HS* 102, 1990, 286, and 103, 1990, 17–19 (against Lex Rix); Polomé, 'Recent developments in the Laryngeal Theory', *JIES* 15, 1988, 159–67, esp. 165 (also against Lex Rix); Seebold, in Bammesberger 1988, 497f., esp. 498, 512.

[3] In the often quoted forms Hitt. *asanzi* 'are', Gr. ἐενσι, the initial vowels are not from H_1 but analogical; see 9.5.1 below.

6.4.8

As is evident, the laryngeal theory cannot yet be regarded as having reached maturity. It is most interesting that Kuryłowicz, who can truly be said to have rediscovered and confirmed the old laryngeal theory, bases his later work less and less on laryngeals and considers them to be of limited importance for Indo-European and its prehistory,[1] an attitude which stands in sharp contrast to that of the majority of his followers, who multiply laryngeals and find in them the final solution of all mysteries. A critical position, however, will best be taken up below, in relation to the vowel system as a whole (6.6.9–15).

[1] Note also Polomé's statement (above, 6.4.7.3 n. 2), 157: 'the role of the laryngeals . . . has been overstated', and his specific objections to the laryngeal explanation of the Germanic *r*-preterites and the *Verschärfung*.

6.5. MORPHEME STRUCTURE

A first, purely descriptive, analysis of the IE morphemes reveals great variability of structure. Alongside disyllabic roots ending in a long vowel (*TERĀ-*) or long vowel+consonant (*TERĀC-*), in the overwhelming majority of cases monosyllabic roots are found, which in their turn can vary from the fullest form with five consonants (**splend-*) to the simplest with two or even one (**bher-*, **ed-*); see

5.5.1. In many cases, however, root determinatives are recognizable which prove that more complicated structures have often arisen secondarily from simpler ones, e.g. **melp-* **welp-* from **mel-* **wel-* (see 5.5.4).

Even apart from these reduced forms obtained by removal of the root determinatives, it can be empirically established that the majority of the monosyllabic roots contain only two consonants with the basic vowel *e* between them. The number of examples of this *CeC* structure is still further increased if laryngeals are prefixed to roots with initial vowel, so that e.g. **ed-* 'eat' is taken as **H_1ed-* and **ag-* 'lead, drive' as *H_2eg-*.

6.5.1

This fact was interpreted by Möller as indicating that the biconsonantal roots (type *bh-r*, *g-n*) had constituted the earliest stratum. The first, however, to raise the observation to the level of a general theory was Benveniste, in the celebrated chapter on IE root structure in his *Origines*. According to this, every root is monosyllabic and 'trilitère', i.e. it consists of three phonemes, the middle one being always the vowel *e*, while the first and third are any consonants (including laryngeals), subject to the restrictions mentioned above (5.5.2). To explain the longer root forms which are nevertheless present in Indo-European, Benveniste distinguishes suffixes and enlargements ('élargissements'): the suffix has an alternating structure *eC/C*, the enlargement consists of a single consonant. These take the place of the elements generally designated root determinatives.

The two fundamental rules of root extension are as follows: (1) every root can with a suffix produce two 'themes': either the root is accented and keeps its vowel, in which case the suffix occurs without vowel, or the root loses its vowel and the suffix appears with its (accented) vowel; thus the root **pet-* 'fly' with suffix *er* gives the forms (I) **pét-r-* (Skt. *pátra-*) and (II) **pt-ér-* (Gr. πτερόν); (2) a root with suffix can further receive an enlargement, either following Theme I or as an infix preceding the suffix in Theme II; thus **yeu-g-s-* or **yu-n-eg-* (I **yeu-g-*: II **yw-eg-*). Further enlargements or suffixes always produce noun stems.[1]

[1] Cf. H. Möller, *Semitisch und Indogermanisch* i, 1907, p. xiv; É. Benveniste, *Origines de la formation des noms en indo-européen* i, 1935, 147–73: 'Esquisse d'une théorie de la racine'. According to 153 **per-k-s-* is impossible, only **pr-ek-s-* can occur, but this is contradicted by **yeug-s-* (given as example above). For Saussure's opinion, see *Recueil* 9–10 and esp. 172–3. See also Jucquois, 'L'imaginaire en linguistique', *In Memory of J. A. Kerns*, 1981, 159–78; Taillardat, 'La théorie benvenistienne de la racine', in *É. Benveniste aujourd'hui* ii, Paris 1984, 175–82; Jucquois, 'Monosyllabisme originel', *Diachronica* 8, 1991, 17f.

6.5.2

This attractively simple theory was at first received with enthusiasm. With the passage of time, however, it has met with increasing scepticism. And indeed, like every theory of the root, it must satisfy two conditions: it must be in agreement with the empirically established (*a*) size (*b*) structure of the root.

(*a*) First, as regards the size of the root, it is well known that the theory contradicts some obvious facts, since there are certainly longer roots such as **leik*^{w}- 'to leave' ('quadrilitère') and **sneig*^{w}*h*- 'to snow' ('quinquilitère'), and also shorter, e.g. **es*- 'to be' ('bilitère'). Criticisms today are directed almost exclusively against the assumption that all longer roots can be reduced to the norm. In fact the presupposed shorter forms, e.g. in the case of **sneig*^{w}*h*- the forms **snei*- and, as the final unit, **sen*-, for the most part are not found at all.[1]

These objections, however, when looked at from the standpoint of the system, are not decisive: the theory cannot be falsified in this way (see 2.5), since there is no inherent contradiction in supposing that longer root forms must be traced back to shorter ones, even if this entails a high number of homonyms. But there is certainly an inherent contradiction in the assumption that alongside the root forms there also existed suffixes of the form *eC*. For what could have been the source of such forms if in the stock of roots (i.e. in the word stock) only forms with the structure *CeC* were available?[2]

Further, it can be proved that not all IE roots having the structure *eC* go back to a more primitive form **HeC*, i.e. there were not only suffixes but also roots with the structure *eC* (see 6.6.9).

Finally, it must not be overlooked that many clearly archaic roots—deictic particles, pronominal stems—show the structure *CV*.

(*b*) The assumption that all roots contained the basic vowel *e* is a postulate which is refuted by the facts, since there are roots such as **nas*- 'nose', **kas*- 'grey', **sal*- 'salt', **ghans*- 'goose' (see 6.6.4 below).

[1] Cf. T. H. Maurer, 'Unity of the IE ablaut system: the disyllabic roots', *Lg* 23, 1947, 1–22, esp. 22; K. Ammer, 'Studien zur idg. Wurzelstruktur', *Sprache* 2, 1952, 193–214; Kuryłowicz, *Apophonie* 106f.; *IG* 199f.; Schmitt-Brandt, 8f., esp. 12; C. S. Stang, in *To Honor R. Jakobson* iii, 1967, 1890f.; Makajev, *Struktura* 130f., 169–71; Jucquois, 'La théorie de la racine', *La Linguistique* 6/2, 1970, 69–102; 7/1, 1971, 73–91; 8/1, 1972, 73–103; 'La théorie de la racine chez Antoine Meillet', *Muséon* 85, 1972, 281–7; Gercenberg, *Morfologičeskaja struktura slova v drevnix indoiranskix jazykax*, Leningrad 1972, 127–228; Andreev, 'Frühidg. Wurzeln', *VJ* 1978 (5), 46–54, esp. 49f.

[2] Cf. Szemerényi, *PICL* 7, 1956, 481f., 523f.

6.5.3

The opposition of disyllabic and monosyllabic roots is, on the other hand, not primary, as is shown by the frequent alternation of *aniṭ* and *seṭ* roots.

6.5.4

To sum up, it can be said that *the IE root was monosyllabic but of multiple structure*: types *VC, CVC, TRVT, TVRT, Cē, Cā*, etc., existed, and even archaic elements like type *CV*; see also Makajev, *Struktura* 166f., 181.[1]

[1] The root determinatives also belong in general to the type *VC*; thus they never show the form *CV* (so Cuny (above, 5.5.2, n.1, 1943), 162), but usually *VC* (so Cuny, *RPhon.* 2, 1912, 105). On the restrictions affecting the structure of stops in IE roots (above 5.5.2), see also W. L. Magnusson, 'Complementary distributions among the root patterns of Proto-IE', *Lings* 34, 1967, 17–25. G. Jucquois has carried out statistical researches on the frequency of the different consonants in a paper on 'La structure des racines en i-e. envisagée d'un point de vue statistique', in Y. Lebrun (ed.), *Recherches linguistiques en Belgique*, 1966, 57–68. A long-neglected problem, consonant clusters in initial, medial, and final position, has been examined for Latin and Italic by Devine and Stephens (above, 4.7.8 n.1, 107–232.

6.5.5. Secondary ablaut

Alternations of the type **ters-/tres-* (e.g. Lat. *terreō*: Gr. *ἔ-τρεσ-σαν*), usually referred to as *Schwebeablaut*,[1] go back in general to disyllabic basic forms of the type **ter-es-*, which gave **tér-s-* or **tr-és-* according to the position of the accent. In some cases (e.g. with internal *R*) it is possible that metathesis occurred, i.e. **terp-* could have changed directly to **trep-*. In other cases new full-grade forms may have arisen from regularly formed zero grades; in this way **deiwo-* 'the (dweller) in the sky=god' was formed to **diw-*, zero grade of **dyeu-* 'sky', and **gheimo-* (Slav. *zima* 'winter') to **ghim-* from **ghyem-* (Lat. *hiem-s*).[2] Similarly to **dn̥t-* 'tooth' a thematic **dent-ó-* was formed (OE *tind* 'prong, tooth'),[3] and to **widhu-* 'forest' (Eng. *wood*) a form **weidh(w)-o-* 'belonging to the forest, wild', seen (with dissimilatory loss of the second *w*) in Celt. **weido-* (OIr. *fíad*, W. *gŵydd*).[4] The numerals **dwi-* 'two', **tri-* 'three' have the secondary full-grade forms **dwei- *trei-* in compounds in Celtic and Germanic (also in Latin?).[5] On the other hand, Gmc. **hemena-* 'heaven' (Goth. *himins*, etc.) cannot be explained as a *vr̥ddhi* derivative of **akmon-/*kmen-*; it is from IE **kem-* 'to cover'.[6]

[1] The term seems to have been coined by Johansson, *BB* 13, 1888, 115 ('Gleichgewichts- oder Schwebeablaut'); see Mayrhofer, *Krat* 33, 8 n. 23.

[2] Vaillant, *BSL* 38, 1937, 92; Maurer, *Lg* 23, 1947, 1–22; Kuryłowicz, *Apophonie* 130f., 151; *PICL* 9, 1964, 28; *IG* 221, 303; Schütz, *Krat* 11, 1967, 175–7; Anttila, *Proto-IE Schwebeablaut*, Berkeley 1969; V. Kiparsky, *Sbornik v čest' S. B. Bernštejna*, 1971, 416–19; Darms (above, 6.2.6 n.1), 367–443; Nussbaum 1986, 115f., 278, 290f. Schmitt-Brandt, 22f., goes too far.

[3] Anttila, *Sprache* 16, 1970, 172.

[4] Szemerényi, but see also Campanile, *BBCS* 26, 1975, 306, and (somewhat differently) Hamp, *SCelt* 18/19, 1985, 128f. For secondary *au* based on *u*, see Strunk, *Fs. Rix*, 1993, 424–35.

[5] Szemerényi, *Studies O. Skutsch*, 1988, 128–32.

[6] Szemerényi, *Studia Iranica* 9, 1980, 54.

6.6. ORIGIN AND INVENTORY OF THE IE VOWEL SYSTEM

6.6.1

Influenced by the antiquity of Sanskrit, the founders of IE linguistics and their immediate successors assumed that the Old Indic triangular system *i-a-u* represented the original situation. In 1864 G. Curtius drew attention to the fact that in many cases all European languages opposed *e* to the Sanskrit *a*; cf. Gr. δέκα, Lat. *decem*, Goth. *taihun*, Lith. *dešimt*, but Skt. *daśa*. He supposed, however, that in this respect all the European languages had innovated as a closed group, i.e. they had split the original *a* into *e* and *a*. It was not until 1871 that Arthur Amelung came to realize that the European *e* as opposed to Sanskrit *a* represented the original situation, though this view did not win general acceptance until later, with Brugmann's famous article of 1876. The originality of the (European) *e* was then proved within Old Indic also by the discovery of the Aryan law of palatalization (see 4.7.4.7). With this it was demonstrated that the IE vowel system was not like that of Old Indic but showed the five members of the normal vowel triangle, with the addition of schwa:[1]

i				*u*	*ī*				*ū*
	e	*ə*	*o*			*ē*		*ō*	
		a					*ā*		

[1] See A. Amelung, *Die Bildung der Tempusstämme durch Vokalsteigerung im Deutschen*, 1871; K. Brugmann, 'Zur Geschichte der stammabstufenden Declinationen', Curtius' *Studien* 9, 1876, 361f., esp. 367f., 380f. For further literature on this and the following sections, see Szemerényi, 'Structuralism' 3f.; 'New Look' 67f. For the period 1800–70, see W. A. Benware, *The Study of IE Vocalism in the 19th Century*, Amsterdam 1974.

6.6.2

This vowel system had barely been achieved when, in 1878, Saussure's *Mémoire* appeared and dealt with all vowels at a single stroke, deriving them partly from the basic vowel *e* (namely *ē ā ō*), partly as syllabic variants from certain consonantal coefficients (namely *a o i u* from *A O y w*), and adding the syllabic sonants (*r̥ l̥ m̥ n̥* and their long equivalents) likewise to this latter group; see 6.4 above.

Saussure's system, with important modifications by Möller, remained nevertheless only on the fringe of comparative linguistics. In Germany it was totally rejected, and even in France Saussure's pupil Meillet, in his influential *Introduction* (98f., 105f., 154f. of the 8th edn.), gave it only half-hearted support: the vowels *a e o* with the corresponding long vowels were retained as 'voyelles proprement dites', while *i* and *u* with the syllabic nasals and liquids as well as schwa were kept as a separate class of sonants and assigned a middle position between the 'true' vowels and the consonants.

With the discovery of the Hittite correspondences to the IE laryngeals the Saussure–Möller system seemed to have won an unshakeable position, and it is even today supported by the majority of scholars.

6.6.3

In assessing this system the following questions must be raised:

1. How far does the assumption of a single vowel correspond to the facts of the reconstruction process?
2. Can this system be regarded as realistic on general grounds, e.g. of typology?

6.6.4. The status of the phoneme *a*

In the reduction of the IE vowel system to the single vowel *e*, the decisive factor is the observation that, whereas the vowel *e* and its ablaut variant *o* have an extremely important function in all fields of the morphology, the vowel *a* is hardly used at all for such purposes. Added to this is the fact that initial *a*- can be simply replaced by H_2e- and *ā* by eH_2.

In the functional usage of the vowels the importance of the alternation *e/o* is, of course, merely the reverse side of the relatively functionless position of *a*: precisely because *e/o* was employed for all possible functions, *a* was pushed into the background. Yet it was not entirely functionless: it took part in vowel gradation (*a/o* alongside *e/o*) and, as Saussure saw, it was used for semantic purposes in terms denoting various 'weaknesses', e.g **kaikos* 'blind', **laiwos* 'left(-handed)'.[1]

The elimination of *a* by means of a laryngeal[2] is not a complete solution: internal *a* cannot in this way be removed without trace. The attempt has certainly been made to explain various instances of the type *CaT* by assuming CH_2eT and to derive *CaiT* from CeH_2iT. In a considerable number of cases,[3] however, this way of escape is not only without foundation (i.e. invented for the sake of the theory) but also incredible: there is no advantage in deriving **kas-* 'grey', **nas-* 'nose', **sal-* 'salt' etc. from $*kH_2es$- $*nH_2es$- $*sH_2el$-, if the presupposed forms (Theme I) $*keH_2s$- $*neH_2s$- $*seH_2l$- themselves inspire no confidence. In the case of **bhardhā* 'beard', a form $*bhH_2erdh$- can hardly be taken seriously.

Note. If Hoenigswald is right in his view (*Lg* 28 (1952), 182–5; *Fs. Szemerényi*[2] iii, 119–22) that laryngeals following *s* do not cause change of vowel timbre ($*sH_2en$- gives *sen-ex*, not **san-*), this would also refute $*sH_2el$- for **sal-*.

[1] Cf. F. de Saussure, 'Adjectifs indo-européens du type *caecus* "aveugle"', *Fs. V. Thomsen*, 1912, 202f.=*Recueil* 595f.; Meillet, *Introduction* 154, 166, 416; Wyatt, *IE /a/*.
[2] On the elimination of *a*, see Kuryłowicz, *VJ* 1971 (3), 124 (the surely onomatopoeic word **ghans-* 'goose' was in his view originally **ghons-s/*ghn̥s-os* > **ghansos*! Cf. Eichner's curious note in Bammesberger 1988, 132 n. 31); *Studies Palmer*, 1976, 127–133; Mendoza, *Em* 50, 1982, 325–63 (on initial *a-*); Georgiev, *Fs. Knobloch*, 1985, 112 (e.g. **saus-* from **seH-us*, **sāl-* from **seHl-*, **yag-* from **Hi-Heg-*<**agō*!); Lubotsky, *KZ* 98, 1985, 1–10 (*αὖος*<**Hsusos*); 'Against a PIE phoneme *a*', in Vennemann 1989, 53–66 (see Szemerényi, *Diachronica* 6, 1989, 245–8; Lindeman, *Glotta* 70, 1992, 181–96); Eichner, op. cit. 127f., 132f.; Kortlandt, in Beekes, *Origins* 57, who had already expressed the view in *Laryngeals* 133–7.
The vowel *a* is explained as a late fashion by H. Kuhn, *KZ* 71, 1954, 143f.; it appears 'at the end of the Indo-European period' (p. 155) when 'the period of ablaut was past' (p. 159); 'it starts soon after the beginning of the Neolithic Age and extends into the Bronze Age and therewith into the period of the independent individual languages' (p. 161). Scherer on the other hand (*Convegno* 5, 1972, 25f.) thinks that *a* represents a borrowing.
[3] See the lists in Kuryłowicz, *Apophonie* 187–95; Wyatt, *IE/a/* (see Szemerényi, *Lg* 48, 1972, 165–71); Bomhard, *Orbis* 25, 1976, 210–12 (e.g. Lat. *far, dacruma, canere, caper, caput, lacus, scaeuus*, etc.).

6.6.5. The status of the phoneme *o*

In the case of *o* we shall be no more inclined to explain away all the instances (e.g. **bhosos* 'naked', **ghostis* 'stranger', **koksā* 'thigh' etc.) for the sake of the theory.[1]

Note. It is interesting that Kuryłowicz now recognizes *o* as a vowel before the period of ablaut (*Apophonie* 106 n. 10, 392–3).

[1] Mayrhofer, *KZ* 100, 1987, 95, acknowledges the type *CaC* but apparently not the root type *CoC* (without mentioning the clear examples just cited in the text).

6.6.6. The status of the phonemes *i* and *u*

The existence of such sounds in Indo-European is not in dispute, but they are treated as allophones of the consonants *y*, *w*. This position is phonetically untenable, as *i u* and *y w* are fundamentally different sounds, vowels and spirants respectively. But the laryngeal theory also claims that *i u* are always the result of the weakening of *ei eu* or *ye we*, i.e. before the period of the zero grade there was no *i* or *u*. Yet how could e.g. the stressed interrogative pronoun **kʷis *kʷid* be the result of weakening? Clearly the phonemes *i u* existed before the period of weakening, even if many instances were added later through weakening.[1]

[1] See Kuryłowicz (6.6.5 *Note*), and on the phonemic status of *i u*, Szemerényi, 'New Look' 82.

6.6.7

To sum up, we may say that the IE five-vowel system is securely established as a result of reconstruction and cannot be reduced to a one-vowel system.

It is just as questionable whether all long vowels are to be derived from combinations of short vowel with laryngeal. We shall see shortly (6.6.9*a*) that the evidence of Hittite is against this.

6.6.8

The thesis of the laryngeal theory that there was only one vowel must be rejected also on general grounds. No language has so far been found that has only one vowel; the alleged Caucasian parallel has proved on closer examination to be an illusion.[1] It should be taken as axiomatic that Indo-European cannot have had peculiarities that occur in no language on earth.[2] Here the empirical statement of typology is again important: *all languages have* /i a u/.[3]

[1] See Uspenskij, *Strukturnaja tipologija*, 1965, 187 (at least two); Szemerényi, 'New Look' 71f.; Kuryłowicz, *IG* 206; Leroy, *Hommage Buyssens*, 1970, 125–32; Makajev, *Struktura* 146; Halle, *FL* 6, 1970, 95–103; Georgiev, *ZPhon* 22, 1970, 553 (eccentric); Kumaxov, *VJ* 1973 (6), 54–67; 1978 (6), 138–9; Pulleyblank, 'The analysis of vowel systems', *ALHafn* 14, 1973, 39–62; Dressler (above, 6.3.2 n. 1), 108–12; Rasmussen, *Haeretica*, 1974, 5–9 (Sanskrit is a one-vowel language!); Szemerényi, 'Sprachtypologie' (*Acta Iranica* 12, 1977, 339–93), 356 (at least two vowels in every language); D. M. Job, *Probleme eines typologischen Vergleichs iberokaukasischer und indogermanischer Phonemsysteme im Kaukasus*, Berne 1977, 52–7; Crothers in Greenberg (ed.), *Universals of Human Language* ii: *Phonology*, Stanford 1978, 108f.; Hagège and Haudricourt, *La phonologie panchronique*, 1978, 23; Jakobson and Waugh, *The Sound Shape of Language*, 1979, 110, 125; Gamkrelidze, *In Memory of J. A. Kerns*, 1981, 595f. (at least two vocalic elements); Martinet 1986, 137–40 (one vowel). For Abkhaz, see B. G. Hewitt, *Abkhaz*, Amsterdam 1979, 259 (two vowels), and the review of Kumaxov's work (1981) by Zekox in *VJ* 1984 (2), 137f.; cf. also Szemerényi 1985, 4 with n. 6.

[2] Still less acceptable is an early stage of Indo-European in which there were no vowels at all: thus e.g. Lehmann, *PIE*; Mel'ničuk, *VJ* 1979 (5), 3–16; (6), 3–16; *PICL* 12, 1978, 805–8.

[3] So Crothers (n. 1 above), 136. Cf. also Moulton, *Essays Hockett*, 1983, 258f.; I. Maddieson, *Patterns of Sounds*, Cambridge 1984, 126 (the smallest number of phonemic vowels is three).

6.6.9. The laryngeal theory and Hittite

In general Hittite is seen as the chief witness for the truth of the laryngeal theory. This is certainly the case fundamentally, but at the same time Hittite decisively contradicts several aspects of the current laryngeal theory.

(*a*) In a number of cases Hittite presents *vowel+h* where the other languages have a *long vowel*, e.g.

Hitt.	*pahs-*	'protect'	:	Skt. *pā-* 'protect', Lat. *pāscō*
	newah-	'renew'	:	Lat. *nouāre*
	mehur	'time'	:	Goth. *mēl* 'time', Lat. *mē-tior*[1]

In such cases, then, Hittite demonstrates that the long vowel of the other languages has arisen from short vowel+*h*. There are, however, many instances in which a long vowel has no corresponding *h* in Hittite, e.g.

Hitt. *pas-*	'swallow'	:	Lat. *pō-tāre*
hassa-	'hearth'	:	Lat. *āra*, Osc. *aasas* (nom. pl.)
ais, Luw. *assa*	'mouth'	:	Lat. *ōs*
māi-, *miyari*	'thrive, ripen'	:	Lat. *mā-tūrus*

In all these cases *h* would be expected in Hittite. Its absence shows that there were also long vowels which did not go back to vowel+*h*, i.e. *original long vowels*. Especially interesting is the contrast of *pas-*: *pahs-*.

(*b*) The most common form of the laryngeal theory assumes three laryngeals, of which H_2 and H_3 are preserved in Hittite.[2] The following agree with this:

Hitt. *hant-*	'front'	:	Lat. *ante*[3]
hassa-	'hearth'	:	Lat. *āra*
hapin-	'rich'	:	Lat. *op-ulentus*
Luw. *hawi-*	'ram'	:	Lat. *ouis*
Hitt. *happ(a)-*	'river'	:	Skt. *ap-*, Lat. *amnis*<**ap-ni-s*
hara(n)-	'eagle'	:	Gr. ὄρνις, Goth. *ara*
harki-	'white'	:	Gr. ἀργός ἀργι- 'white', Lat. *argentum*, Toch. *ārki*
hartagga-	'bear'	:	Gr. ἄρκτος, Lat. *ursus* (4.6.3 fin.)
hastai-	'bone'	:	Skt. *asthi*, Gr. ὀστέον (6.6.10)
hasterza	'star'	:	Gr. ἀστήρ[4]
hatuka-	'terrible'	:	Gr. ἀτύζομαι 'take fright'
hul-ana-	'wool'	:	Lat. *lāna*, Gmc. **wulla-*[5]

There are, however, correspondences in which Hittite does not oppose *ha-* to an *a-* or *o-* of the other languages:

Hitt. *ais*	'mouth'	:	Lat. *ōs* (Szemerényi, *Studies Hill* iii, 1979, 272f.)
aku(wa)-	'to drink'	:	Lat. *aqua*
appa	'behind, after'	:	Gr. ἀπό or ὀπι-
arkiya-	'testicle'	:	Gr. ὄρχις
arras	'arse'	:	Gr. ὀρρός, IE **orsos*
arsaniya-	'be envious'	:	Skt. *īrṣyati*

With three laryngeals such cases cannot be explained at all. It is then possible—just for such cases—to assume a fourth laryngeal which, like H_2, is *a*-coloured but disappears also in Hittite, and a fifth laryngeal which, like H_3, is *o*-coloured but disappears. But not even this would be enough, for there are also cases in which *h* appears after *e* and therefore cannot be H_1, e.g. *mehur* 'time';[1] it would thus be necessary to posit a sixth laryngeal.

Obviously these attempts to reconcile the Hittite *h* with the laryngeal theory lead nowhere. We must simply accept that a laryngeal cannot be assumed just to match the vowel timbre, but only when it is present in Hittite.[6] Hitt. *es-* 'to be' and *ed-* 'eat' thus indicate IE **es-* **ed-* without laryngeal; Hitt. *henkan* 'fate, plague' attests IE **Henk-* with laryngeal.

From these points it also follows:

1. Only one laryngeal is to be assumed.[7]
2. Indo-European possessed roots of the type *eC* and, in general, *VC*.[8]

[1] Eichner, *MSS* 31, 1973, 54f., escapes the difficulty (*e+h*!) by starting from **mēH₂wr*; accepted by Schindler, *BSL* 70, 1975, 6; Oettinger, *Stammbildung* 547; rejected by Lindeman, in *Hethitisch und Indogermanisch*, 1979, 153.

[2] Kuryłowicz wished to assume the survival of H_2 only (*BSL* 36, 1935, 26). This view is even now represented by Oettinger, *Stammbildung* 546. Eichner, on the other hand, still thinks (n. 1 above) that H_3 was also preserved; cf. Kimball, 'H_3 in Anatolian', *Fs. Hoenigswald*, 1987, 185–92. On Watkins' curious assumption of Palaic *g* from IE H_2, see Szemerényi, *Mélanges Laroche*, 1979, 315–19.

[3] The still widely favoured view that Hitt. *hanti* corresponds to Lat. *ante*, etc., was disproved in 1982 by Szemerényi (see *SM* 1704–6, 1713–16); in spite of my careful demonstration of the contrary, 'other' and 'face, front' continue to be confused by e.g. Bader, in Bammesberger 1988, 34f.; Olsen, *HS* 102, 1990, 228 (Arm. *and* 'there' from *H_2anti*); Puhvel 1991*a*, 89f.

[4] Tischler has pointed out that the uncanny Forrer saw as far back as 1939 that Hittite had a noun *hastera-* 'star' (see Bammesberger, *Das etymologische Wörterbuch*, 1983, 278); it was eventually found by Otten in 1968. The long cherished interpretation of the word for 'star' as derived from **ster-* 'strew' (Grm. *Streusal*!) was therewith finally eliminated and replaced by a derivation from **ās-* 'burn, glow', first by Krogmann, *KZ* 63, 1936, 257, and, independently, by myself in my unpublished 'Studies in the Structure of IE' of 1952 (MS p. 233, see my *Summing Up a Life*, 1992, 24, and cf. *TPS* 1950, 174f.=*SM* 596f.). For the meaning, OIr. *ān* 'fiery, glowing, brilliant, splendid' (from **as-no-*, Pokorny, *IEW*) can be compared, as also Avest. *raoxšna-* 'shining' and OPrus. *lauxnos* 'stars' (above, 4.2.6). For the form, **Hstēr* (*H-*?) is now fairly generally posited (see Szemerényi, *Gn* 43, 1971, 657f.=*SM* 1575f.; Mayrhofer, *Fs. Neumann*, 1982, 187: **H_2ster-* 'fiery one, shiner'; Lindeman, *The Triple Representation of Shwa in Greek*, 1982, 58; id. 1987, 76f.), but on account of the difficulties of the initial syllable it seems to me better to start from **Has-tḗr/*Hs-tr-ós* (or **Hs-ter-s*?), from a normal grade **as-*. In any case there is no justification for Watkins' **H_2ost-ēr* (*Sprache* 20, 1974, 13f.), and less than none for Hamp's interpretation of Hitt. *haster-* as *Ha-ster-* 'one star' (*PICL* 11, 1975, 1050).

[5] Hitt. *hulana-* 'wool' is usually thought to reflect with its *l-n* the sounds of the previously reconstructed IE **wl̥̄nā-*; cf. Carruba, in *Scritti Bonfante*, 1976, 142; Seebold, in Bammesberger 1988, 515; Lindeman, *HS* 103, 1990, 22. But neither is the development of *a* from the long sonant liquid acceptable, nor the Hitt. *hulali-* 'wool bundle' reconcilable with it. The two Hittite forms combine to show that the correspondence to the IE antecedent is just *hula*, not *hulan-*, and this means that the Hittite forms exhibit an assimilated **H(w)ulnā*.

[6] See also Burrow, *The Problem of Shwa in Sanskrit*, 1979, pp. vi, 19, and cf. Szemerényi, *Krat* 28, 1983, 69.

[7] One laryngeal only was recognized by Vaillant (*BSL* 37, 1936, 111f.), when Kuryłowicz and Benveniste had arrived at (at least) three; this was repeated in *Gram. comp.* i, 1950, 241f. So also subsequently Zgusta, *AO* 19, 1951, 428f., esp. 472; Scardigli, *Atti e memorie dell'Accademia Toscana* 22, 1957, 116; Hammerich, *To Honor R. Jakobson*, 1967, 843f.; *Lingua* 22, 1969, 198, 203; Szemerényi, 'New Look' 95; Collinge, *Collectanea Linguistica*, 1971, 97; Gusmani, in *Heth. und Idg.* 63–71; Tischler, *Fachtagung* 6, 1980, 495–522; Bammesberger, *Studien zur Laryngaltheorie*, 1984; id., in Vennemann 1989, 35–41; Seebold, in Bammesberger 1988, 497–525.

'One laryngeal' does not here mean a late development from an earlier situation with several laryngeals, as represented by Gamkrelidze since his dissertation (1960) (see Gamkrelidze–Ivanov, 170f.); Bomhard follows him in this; see his *Nostratic* 11; id., in *Memoriae van Windekens*, 1991, 54 (Kuryłowicz's four laryngeals followed).

[8] See Schindler, *Sprache* 15, 1969, 148 with n. 32; Beekes, *Laryngeals* 90f.; Bammesberger, *GL* 23, 1984, 165f.

6.6.10. The nature of the laryngeal

Indo-European had aspirated as well as plain stops, e.g. the series *bh dh gh*. We know, moreover, that, as R. Jakobson formulated it, 'languages which have the pairs voiced—voiceless, aspirated—unaspirated also have the phoneme /h/'. It seems to follow from this that the laryngeal which we have just accepted was none other than *h*, the normal glottal spirant.[1] With its *h* the IE system was similar to that of Latin.

[1] Cf. Szemerényi, 'New Look' 88f.; Allen, *Vox Graeca*, 51. On *h* in general, see also Grammont, *Traité* 70f.; Hockett 1955, 125f.; for the IE problems, see C. E. Bidwell, 'Aspiration and /h/ in Greek and PIE', *SiL* 22, 1972, 21–4. Note also the direct proof in OInd. *asthi* 'bone' by metathesis from **Hast-* (5.4.5 above).

6.6.11

A further possible means of determining the Proto-IE vowel system would be available, if another language family could be proved to be related to Indo-European. Thus V. M. Illič-Svityč takes it to be related to Ural-Altaic, and since in the latter family the vowels *e a o* are established, he concludes that they existed in Proto-Indo-European also.[1] Others, especially the Finnish scholar Jorma Koivulehto, have produced what looks like conclusive evidence of laryngeals from the Finno-Ugrian languages, and even from Uralic generally.[2]

[1] V. M. Illič-Svityč, 'The origin of the IE guttural series in the light of foreign parallels' (Russ.), in *Problemy sravnitel'noj grammatiki ie. jazykov*, Moscow 1964, 22–6, esp. 26. Since he takes the view that Indo-European had only one vowel, he reckons on a reduction of the original three; see also below, 6.7.2.3 n. 2.

[2] Koivulehto, in Bammesberger 1988, 281–97, 'Idg. Laryngale und die finnisch-ugrische Evidenz' (20 examples); *Uralische Evidenz für die Laryngaltheorie*, Vienna Acad. 1991 (27 examples, see review by Szemerényi, *UAJb* 64, 1994). Cf. also Bańczerowski, 'Die Suche nach den uralischen Laryngalen', *LPosn* 15, 1972, 81–96.

6.6.12

The outcome is that Proto-IE possessed the vowels *i e a o u* and *ī ē ā ō ū*, which persisted into the IE period and in many languages even into historical times.

The long-vowel system was augmented by combinations of vowel+*h*, which were retained only in Hittite and elsewhere fell together with the corresponding long vowel, and by ablaut lengthening.

In the short-vowel system the frequency of the high vowels *i u* was increased by the reduction during the zero-grade period of the diphthongs *ey ay oy* and *ew aw ow* to *i* and *u*; the zero grade of the long-vowel roots brought schwa into the system.[1]

A further augmentation of the vowel system took place in the zero-grade period as a result of the appearance of syllabic nasals and liquids; these short vowels in combination with the laryngeal *h* (and probably with other phonemes; see 6.2.8, Addendum 1) became the corresponding long vowels in preconsonantal position. In the same period the functional co-ordination of *y* and *i*, *w* and *u* was started; formerly they had nothing to do with one another and they continued to be separate phonemes.[2] An IE sequence *ywnkos* can be realized as **yunkos*, **yuwn̥kos*, and theoretically even **iwn̥kos*.

[1] The process of reduction *ey*>*i* looks straightforward on paper but in reality is hard to understand. There can be no question of a simple loss of *e*. H. Sweet (*TPS* 1880–1, 158) therefore supposed the developments *ey*>*ī*>*i* and *ew*>*ow*>*ū*>*u*, while H. Möller (*Englische Studien* 3, 1880, 151 n.) posited *ey*>*ē*>*i* and *ew*>*ō*>*u*; similar ideas are now to be found in Schmitt-Brandt, 22f.

[2] See Straka, *ZPhon* 17, 1964, 314–16; Delattre, *SL* 18, 1965, 14; Voyles, *Lg* 44, 1969, 721; Mel'čuk, *Lings* 109, 1973, 35–60; Ladefoged, *Preliminaries to Linguistic Phonetics*[2], 1973, 81.

6.6.13

The diphthongs, which were discussed in detail above (4.2), have not so far been mentioned. The reason is that the Indo-European diphthongs were not monophonematic but diphonematic. They consisted of a tautosyllabic sequence of a vowel, which formed the syllabic nucleus, and a second element which was either *i u* in non-syllabic function (*ei eu* etc.) or else one of the semivowels *y w*; which of these two possibilities was realized in Indo-European, or in the different periods of Indo-European, cannot be established. The diphthongs, accordingly, have no place in the phoneme inventory. A separate treatment of the diphthongs is nevertheless justifiable from a practical standpoint, as the diphthongal combinations often show a development which could not have been foreseen from their components.[1]

[1] On the general problem of monophonematic or diphonematic valuation, see Trubetzkoy, *Grundzüge der Phonologie*, 1939, 50f.; Martinet, 'Un ou deux phonèmes?' *AL* 1, 1939, 14–24, reprinted with an important addition in *La linguistique synchronique*, 1965, 109–23; Futaky, *Phonetica* 16, 1967, 14–24; Vennemann, ibid. 18, 1968, 65–76; Pilch, *Phonemtheorie* 98f.; Hammarström, 'Monophthongemes and diphthongemes', *Lings* 87, 1972, 50–3. On the IE problem, see Lehmann, *PIE* 11f. (with inadequate arguments); Glušak, in *Tipologija* 21f. (traditional); Allen, *Studies Palmer*, 1976, 9–16.

6.6.14

It is disputed whether Indo-European, and before it Proto-Indo-European, had long diphthongs. The formerly posited roots **pōy-* 'drink', **dhēy-* 'suckle' have become **peH₃y-*, **dheH₁y-* in the laryngeal theory, but neither of these roots had a laryngeal (cf. Hitt. *pas-* 'to swallow', Luw. *titaimi-* 'pupil'), so that on this question also we must probably to some extent return to the old view.[1]

[1] On the long diphthongs, see Kuryłowicz, *Apophonie* 257f.; *IG* 218; Lindeman, *NTS* 22, 1968, 99–114; Glušak (above, 6.6.13 n. 1); Allen (above, 6.6.13 n. 1); Bernabé, *ArchL* NS 7, 1976, 161–190; Cowgill and Mayrhofer 1986, 173f.

6.6.15

The so-called prevocalic syllabic liquids and nasals (4.5.4) can in part be explained as due to the generalization of certain alternations falling under Sievers' Law (5.7.2.1). They can also in part be due to the analogical transfer of certain preconsonantal developments (i.e. occurring before a laryngeal) to prevocalic position. Thus **g*ʷ*l̥H-ē-* could give Gr. βαλ-η-, and as this new form continued alongside the old βλη-, a new μανη- could be formed analogically to the old μνη-.[1]

[1] So Kuryłowicz, *Apophonie* 180, 218f., 394f. A penetrating and original interpretation of the whole development of the IE vowel system is to be found in R. Schmitt-Brandt, *Die Entwicklung des idg. Vokalsystems*, Heidelberg 1967; see Kuryłowicz, *BSL* 63 (2), 1969, 41–9.

6.7. INVENTORY AND DEVELOPMENT OF THE IE CONSONANT SYSTEM

Among the problems of the consonant system, the question most vigorously discussed today is how many kinds of articulation were represented by the stops; concerning the gutturals there is rather less excitement. The laryngeals, of course, properly belong here, but they have already been treated in connection with the vowel system.

6.7.1. The stop series

To start with the number of articulatory types presented by the stops, Old Indic alone attests four different series in a synchronous system. Only three of these, however, have clear correspondences in several languages, while the fourth (the unvoiced aspirates) is supported only by isolated comparisons (see 4.7). The question therefore arises whether this fourth type is to be recognized for Indo-European at all, and if not, how the system is to be interpreted.

6.7.1.1. First, it must be noted that recent research has returned to the view that the *voiced aspirates* known from Indic were present *also in Old Armenian*: the letters generally transcribed *b d g j ǰ* denoted, not voiced stops arising from the IE voiced aspirates, but the IE voiced aspirates themselves preserved without change.[1]

[1] Cf. the mutually independent works of Vogt, *NTS* 18, 1958, 143–61, and Benveniste, *BSL* 54, 1959, 46–56. Pedersen was probably the first to advance this view, *KZ* 39, 1904, 336–7

(cf. Meillet, *Dialectes*², Avant-propos 13), but he abandoned it in 1951 (*Die gemeinie. und die vorie. Verschlusslaute*, 15). See further Szemerényi 1972, 133.

6.7.1.2. Even if Pedersen is right, the determination of the IE series in question as voiced is unaffected. If, however, only this series and those of the voiced and unvoiced stops existed, the question arises what voiced articulatory type lies behind this series, for it seems to be empirically established that voiced aspirates exist only in languages which also have unvoiced aspirates, whereas these latter can occur by themselves.[1]

[1] See the references in Szemerényi, 'New Look' 88; also G. Lakoff, *Studies Presented to R. Jakobson*, 1968, 168–9; Allen, *Studies J. Greenberg* ii, 1976, 237–47. But note that, according to Comrie, *Lg* 67/1, 1991, 200, in some African languages MA are viable without TA.

6.7.1.3. It seems therefore impossible to accept three series of the type *t d dh* for Indo-European. It would, then, be simplest to assume that the voicing was irrelevant in the aspirate series, so that these sounds would be comparable with the emphatic consonants (*emphatica*) of Semitic.[1] On account of the rarity of voiced aspirates in the languages of the world, some would prefer to posit voiced spirants.[2] The assumption of unvoiced spirants[3] must in any case be rejected out of hand, since the sounds in question are voiced in almost all IE languages.[4]

[1] Hammerich, *PBB(T)* 77, 1955, 6f.; *To Honor R. Jakobson*, 1967, 844; Gamkrelidze, ibid. 709; Kuryłowicz, *PICL* 9, 1964, 13; Ivanov, Obščeind. 41f.; Illič-Svityč, *Etimologija* (1966), 1968, 308, 353. See also Szemerényi, 'New Look' 89 n. 76; Rasmussen, *Haeretica*, 1974, 10–15, esp. 11: *t d dh* derive from *Ṭ* (an emphatic stop) *t d*; also (pp. 14–15) Armenian and Germanic did not undergo a sound shift.

[2] Walde, *KZ* 34, 1897, 461; Knobloch, *Convegno* 4, 1965, 153.

[3] Repeatedly made by Prokosch, last in *A Comparative Germanic Grammar*, 1939, 39f.; against, Hammerich (n. 1 above); Galton, *JEGPh* 53, 1954, 589f.

[4] On the subject of the voiced aspirates, see Bomhard, *Nostratic* 31–34; Szemerényi 1985, 11–15.

6.7.1.4. The elimination of the unvoiced aspirates, which is the real reason why the voiced aspirates have become problematical, began with Saussure's discovery in 1891 that some examples of *th* could be traced back to *t*+laryngeal.[1] Thus Skt. *pṛthu-* 'wide' arose from IE **pḷtH-u-*, *tiṣṭhāmi* 'I stand' from **(s)ti-stH-e/o-*. This discovery was extended by Kuryłowicz to all unvoiced aspirates. At the same time he assigned their origin to the Indo-Iranian period, on the grounds that Bartholomae's Law (6.6.2 above) presupposes a situation in which the feature of voicing in the voiced aspirates was not distinctive; otherwise e.g. *bh*+*t* could have given only *pht* or *pth*. The origin of the purely Aryan unvoiced aspirates is, Kuryłowicz holds, the phonological consequence of the falling together of *bh dh gh* after initial *s-*, which phonetically give *sph- sth- skh-* (Siebs' Law, 5.6.4 above), with *p t k* after certain laryngeals.[2]

[1] Saussure, *Recueil* 603; Rasmussen, *Haeretica*, 1974, 10–15, esp. 11: *t, d, dh* derive from *Ṭ, t, d*; 14f.: Armenian and Germanic did not undergo a sound shift.
[2] Kuryłowicz, *Études* 46–54; *Apophonie* 375–82; *Fachtagung* 2, 1962, 107f.; *PICL* 9, 1964, 13; *Problèmes* 197–205; Lehmann, *PIE* 80–4; Szemerényi 1973, 8f., 13, 15f.

6.7.1.5. Against this it can be stated that Bartholomae's Law has nothing to say about the nature of the voiced aspirates—nor, consequently, about the absence of unvoiced aspirates—in Indo-European, since it was clearly an Aryan innovation necessary for the avoidance of homonyms which would otherwise have arisen (e.g. **augh-ta* and **aug-ta* would both have given **aukta*). Siebs' Law is equally untenable. The change from *sbh-* to *sph-* is not only pure invention, it is also contradicted by the retention of the group *-zdh-* in internal position and, according to the evidence of Avest. *zdī* 'be' from IE **s-dhi*, in initial position also.[1]

[1] Kuryłowicz notices this contradiction (*Apophonie* 378–9) but disregards it.

6.7.1.6. Thus it follows that the two necessary supports for the phonological explanation of the origin of the unvoiced aspirates are both unreliable. This means that *the existence of unvoiced aspirates in Indo-European cannot be denied*, even if they do not occur very frequently and their distribution shows some gaps.[1]

[1] Cf. also Makajev, *Struktura* 147f.; Rasmussen, *AL* 18, 1983, 208 n. 13; id., in Vennemann 1989, 154–6.

6.7.1.7. It is often assumed nowadays that the unvoiced aspirates consisted of unvoiced stop+laryngeal, while the voiced aspirates, although in some cases they similarly consisted of voiced stop+laryngeal, were for the most part simply aspirated voiced stops. Since according to our conclusions the 'laryngeal' was the glottal spirant *h*, it is also clear that the unvoiced and voiced aspirates originally represented the combinations *unvoiced stop+h* and *voiced stop+h*, which in Indo-European counted as monophonematic.[1]

[1] Kammenhuber, *MSS* 24, 1968, 76; Hamp, *JAOS* 90, 1970, 228f.; Villar (above 4.8.1 n. 1); Kuryłowicz, *CTL* xi, 1973, 68. See further 4.8.1 and C. E. Bidwell, 'Aspiration and /h/ in Greek and PIE', *SiL* 22, 1972, 21–24; Job (above, 6.6.8 n. 1), 94–105; Mayrhofer 1981, 17. As a rule, *h* is voiceless, and so an unvoiced aspirate would be in order (cf. also Swiss German *phange*, 2.1 above); but could it have been voiced between vowels and between voiced stop and vowel (so that voiced aspirate was also in order)? For *h* and voiced *h*, see Laziczius, *Fonétika*, Budapest 1944, 75–8 (Grm. trans. *Lehrbuch der Phonetik*, Berlin 1961), and the characterization of Hungarian *h* (76) as initially voiceless but between vowels strongly voiced.

6.7.1.8. The phoneme *b* has a peculiar position in the IE system of stops. In all probability it did not exist at all in initial position, whereas in internal position its frequency was normal. Pedersen pointed out that absence of *b*- would have been an oddity, while loss of initial *p*- is found in many languages. He therefore came to the conclusion that IE *b d g* had arisen from earlier *p t k*, and IE *p t k* from *b d g* and IE *bh dh gh* from *ph th kh*, while IE *ph th kh* were secondary combinations of unvoiced stop+laryngeal.

[1] H. Pedersen, *Die gemeinie. und vorie. Verschlusslaute*, 1951, 10f.; Ivanov, *Obščeind.* 41; Shields, 'IE /b/ and the theory of lexical diffusion', *Lings* 17, 1979, 709–14; Džaukjan, 'IE fonema *b*', *VJ* 1982 (5), 59–67; Szemerényi 1985, 11f.; Gamkrelidze–Ivanov, 1317f.; Lühr and Matzel, 'Eine weitere Möglichkeit der Genese von anlautendem germ. *p*-', *KZ* 99, 1986, 254–77; R. W. Westcott, 'Derogatory use of the marginal phoneme /b/ in PIE', *JIES* 16, 1988, 365–9 (most are 'expressive' and 'disparaging in tone', belong to a *paralanguage*, i.e. to 'expressive or emotive speech'); Meid, *Das Problem von idg. /b/*, Innsbruck 1989. Berger's 1987 study on phoneme statistics is of great importance for the whole problem, even if some of the data (see Ternes's review) should not be quite reliable.

The original system with *p b ph* would agree well with typological facts; see Szemerényi, 'New Look' 88. On the other hand it seems also to be a fact that, if *p* is lost in initial position, it does not remain intact in internal position either, which would not be the case in Indo-European. Scherer, *Convegno* 5, 1972, 25, suggests borrowing.

6.7.2. The guttural series

The three series which have been reconstructed for Indo-European (4.7.4) are unfortunately not so cleanly separated from one another as we could have wished.

6.7.2.1.1. The labiovelars can be seen, according to the general view, only in the centum languages; in the satem languages they have fallen together with the pure velars. On the basis of this assumption various attempts have been made to deny altogether the existence of labiovelars in the satem languages and to regard them as an innovation of the centum languages.[1] This view, however, is not only phonetically and phonologically most improbable, it is also positively refuted by the fact that the labiovelars have left clear traces in the satem languages also.[2]

[1] Joh. Schmidt, *KZ* 25, 1881, 134; József Schmidt, *Attempt at a Solution of the IE Guttural Problem* (Hungarian), Budapest 1912, 54; H. Reichelt, 'Die Labiovelare', *IF* 40, 1922, 40–81; Kuryłowicz, *Études* 1–26, 257f., 263f.; *Apophonie* 356–75, 401; *Problèmes* 190–7; Wagner, *TPS* 1969, 212; *Fs. Risch*, 1986, 681–3; Wittmann, *Glossa* 3, 1969, 25. Kuryłowicz is opposed by Bernabé Pajares, 'Estudio fonológico de las guturales ie.', *Em* 39, 1971, 63–107, esp. 77–81; Miller, 'Pure velars and palatals in IE', *Lings* 178, 1976, 47–64.

[2] See above, 4.7.7; cf. further Vaillant, *Gram. comp.* i, 171f.; Pisani, *Sprache* 12, 1967, 227–8; and S. Bendtsen, *APILKU* 5, 1986, 71–9.

6.7.2.1.2. Although the labiovelars are to be posited for the IE period as unitary phonemes (see 4.7.8), they must have arisen from the groups *kw*, *gw*, *ghw*; this is indicated by the fact that beside a full grade k^we a zero grade *ku* is often found.[1]

[1] See Szemerényi, *Syncope* 401, also Hirt, *IG* i, 228f.; E. H. Sturtevant and A. Hahn, *Comparative Grammar of the Hittite Language* i, 1951, 38, 55; Hamp, *BSL* 50, 1955, 45f.; *BBCS* 16, 1956, 282f.; Hooper, *JIES* 5, 1977, 43.

6.7.2.2.1. The sibilants which developed in the satem languages from the IE palatals have in any case arisen from stops. This palatalization is not, however, complete; in a number of instances even some satem languages show a velar stop instead of the expected spirant. So we find:

Skt. *śvaśura-* 'stepfather', Lith. *šešuras*, but OCS *svekrŭ;*
Skt. *paśu* 'cattle' (cf. Lat. *pecu*), but OLith. *pekus*;
Skt. *aśmā* 'stone' (cf. Gr. *ἄκμων*), but Lith. *akmuo*, OCS *kamy*;
Skt. *śru-* 'hear', OCS *sluti* 'be called' (cf. Gr. *κλύω*), but Lith. *klausýti* 'hear'.

This incomplete 'satemization' is especially characteristic of the Baltic and/or Slavic area, less so of the Albanian; examples barely exist for Armenian and Aryan. Nevertheless Skt. *ruk-/ruč-* 'bright, light' (cf. Lat. lūceō, OCS *lučĭ*) is found alongside Skt. *rušant-* 'bright, shining'.[1]

[1] cf. Brugmann, *Grundriss*[2] i, 545f.; H. Sköld, *Beiträge zur allgemeinen und vergleichenden Sprachwissenschaft* i, 1931, 56–79; Bernabé Pajares (above, 7.7.2.1.1. n. 1, 96f. For Albanian, see Ölberg, *Studi V. Pisani*, 1969, 683–90.

6.7.2.2.2. The first attempt to explain these anomalies was to see in them loans from neighbouring centum languages.[1] This could perhaps be accepted for some Balto-Slavic and Albanian instances, although many improbable assumptions would be necessary (e.g. Germanic has no *ahm- 'stone' which would be required for the explanation of Lith. *akmuo*). It could certainly not be accepted for such cases as Skt. *ruk-/rušant-*.[2]

However, the problem is in fact only insuperable—indeed, only exists at all—if the palatals are seen as a series unshakeably established for the whole Indo-European area and so beyond question for the historical linguist, a standpoint few would take today.[3] Most scholars see themselves rather as forced to the conclusion that the palatals arose secondarily from fronted velars, in much the same way as the Romance affricates and, later, spirants (e.g. Fr. *cent*, Ital. *cento*) arose from Latin velars (*cent* from *kentum*). Since on this supposition the development of palatalization depends on certain conditions, especially a following *e i* or *y*, the survival of some non-palatalized forms is in principle to be expected.[4]

Even on this interpretation it would be possible to treat the palatalization itself as a universal Indo-European phenomenon and to ascribe to Indo-European three guttural series, as we did above (4.7.4.3). This would, however, mean that the centum languages subsequently lost this palatalization again (Ascoli's 'healed' type, *tipo risanato*). It would be simpler to see the palatalization (i.e. satemization) as a characteristic of the satem languages; it must then be regarded as having been carried out in each of the satem languages independently,[5] or as having spread in various directions from a centre, losing its effect with distance;[6] in the latter case it would be preferable to think of Iranian[7] or Aryan[8] rather than Slavic[9] as the original centre.

[1] Brugmann, *Grundriss*[2] i, 547, and more recently Bonfante, *Mélanges Fohalle*, 1969, 22 (Lith. *pekus*); Gołąb, '"Kentum" elements in Slavic', *LPosn* 16, 1972, 53–82 (mainly from Venetic).

[2] Kiparsky, *Die gemeinslavischen Lehnwörter aus dem Germanischen*, 1934, 101f.

[3] See Ribezzo, *AGI* 22–3, 1929, 146 (Pan-IE); Karstien, *Fs. Hirt* ii, 1936, 302; Pisani, *Geolinguistica e ie.*, 1940, 292; Kuryłowicz, *Apophonie* 357f., 375; Ivanov, 'Problema jazykov kentum i satem', *VJ* 1958 (4), 12–23.

[4] On the conditions of the palatalization (including the groups *kwe kle kre*, etc.), see Georgiev, *Introduction* 47f.; cf. Hirt, *IG* i, 226f. On the non-palatalized forms, see Georgiev, 50.

[5] Georgiev, op. cit., 61; Abajev, *Skifo-jevropejskije izoglossy*, 1965, 140f.; Campanile, *SSL* 5, 1965, 37–55.

[6] Porzig, *Gliederung* 75–6.

[7] Pisani, *AGI* 46, 1961, 16; *Ricerche slavistiche* 15, 1969, 11; against, Campanile (n. 5 above). On this question it must not be overlooked that the loanword *porśo-* found in many Finno-Ugrian languages (e.g. Finn. *porsas*) from IE **porkos* 'piglet' must be very old—according to Benveniste, *BSL* 45, 1949, 87, 'pré-indo-iranien' or from a 'stade très ancien de l'indo-iranien commun', thus in any case before 1500 BC, and according to Joki, *Uralier und Indogermanen*, 1973, 303, 'pre-Aryan', in any case much earlier than the migration of the 'Iranians' into their historical homeland. Cf. also Minissi, *Studia Pagliaro* iii, 1969, 134f.

[8] Porzig, *Gliederung* 76; W. P. Schmid, *Alteuropa und der Osten im Spiegel der Sprachgeschichte*, Innsbruck 1966, 9f.: but the delabializing of the labiovelars cannot have taken place before the assibilation of the palatals (12).

[9] Senn, *KZ* 71, 1954, 175; Devoto, *Origini indeuropee*, 345, 398. See now also Gamkrelidze and Ivanov, *VJ* 1980 (5), 10–20; (6), 13–22; Shields, 'A new look at the centum–satem isogloss', *KZ* 95, 1982, 203–13; on the gutturals in general, Gamkrelidze–Ivanov, 81–116, 407f.; Bomhard, *Nostratic* 20–6.

6.7.2.2.3. For determining the time of the change of palatals to sibilants the sporadic Aryan, probably Proto-Indic, words in Hittite documents are important. These show that both the Aryan palatalization (4.7.4.7) and the change of IE *e* to *a* were completed by 1500 BC: thus IE **penk^{w}e* 'five' appears as *panza*, cf. Skt. *pañča*. Since the Aryan palatalization presupposes the delabialization of the IE labiovelars, the beginning of the process can hardly be put later than 2000 BC. The whole course of the first palatalization, which changed the IE palatals into sibilants, must lie at least 500 years earlier. That will presumably also fix the area of satemization in southern Russia.[1]

[1] For details, and against a late dating of satemization, see Szemerényi, 'Structuralism' 13; also (for early dating) Georgiev, *Introduction* 49, 53. An unacceptably late date is proposed by Gusmani, *Studia Pagliaro* ii, 1969, 327f., which remains untenable in spite of its reassertion in *InL* 12, 1988, 110 n. 21. Equally untenable is Gusmani's view in 'Forme "satem" nelle lingue anatoliche', op. cit. 105–10, that Luwian (and Lycian?) are satem languages, though Hittite remains firmly anchored in the centum group; cf. A. Morpurgo Davies and J. D. Hawkins, 'A Luwian heart', *Studi G. Pugliese Carratelli*, 1988, 169–82, esp. 179f.; H. C. Melchert, 'PIE velars in Luvian', *In Memory of W. Cowgill*, 1987, 182–204, esp. 204.

6.7.2.2.4. The development itself must have passed through the stages *k>ky>ty>t's'*.[1] Skt. *vaś-mi* 'I wish', *vaṣṭi* 'he wishes' presuppose **vat's'-mi* and **vat's'-ti*, while *vakṣi* 'thou wishest' is from **vat's'-si* by dissimilation (*t's'* to *kṣ*). That Aryan reached the stage *t's'* while still in Europe seems proved by the fact that Finnish *kah-deksan* 'eight', *yh-deksän* 'nine' contain a form of 'ten' (*deksan*) which is the reflex of a Proto-Aryan **det's'an* (with *e* still retained).[2]

[1] Pedersen, *Aspirationen i Irsk*, 1897, 193; Barić, 'Indoeuropski palatali', *Glas Srpske K. Akademije* 124, 1927, 1–57 (German summary 58–72); Leumann, *IF* 58, 1941, 17f. (OInd. *ǰ* from *ź*?); Pinnow, *FoL* 3, 1970, 295; Windfuhr, *JAOS* 92, 1972, 56; Georgiev, *Introduction* 48. The intermediate stage *t'd'*, more often assumed recently (e.g. Morgenstierne, *NTS* 12, 1942, 79; 13, 1945, 227, 231), is unsatisfactory for Aryan.
[2] Szemerényi, *UAJb* 49, 1978, 129f.

6.7.2.2.5. The preconsonantal palatals probably owe their origin, at least in part, to a lost palatal vowel. For example, **ok'tō* can have come by syncope from **okitō*.[1]

[1] See Szemerényi, *Syncope* 399f., and above, 6.1, Addendum 2.

6.7.2.2.6. Traditionally a common palatalization of the IE palatals is assumed for Aryan, though the stage reached shortly before the historical period is variously conceived (*t'* or *t's'*, etc.). Recently, however, following the lead of Morgenstierne, the view has also found support that the *Kafir or Nūristānī* languages of the Pamir region[1] diverge in their representation of the IE palatals and should be taken as forming an independent *third branch of Aryan*.[2] Yet a dialect group known only since the nineteenth century and showing recognizably deep blends of Indic and Iranian can scarcely count as trustworthy witness for a difference which must go back four or five thousand years and in fact rests only on a few examples with a not very clear *c* (=*ts*), e.g. *duc* 'ten': OInd. *daśa*. This sceptical attitude gains some support from a new treatment of the question[3] according to which 'the Nūristānī languages occupy a position significantly nearer to Indic than to Iranian', and it is possible therefore to see in them 'the last remnants of old Indo-Aryan languages which early, in the pre-Vedic period, diverged from the main block of OInd. dialects and retained some few archaic peculiarities which are otherwise no longer to be found in Indic dialects'. A leap over four or five millennia is now more than ever irresponsible, and a third branch of Aryan is left completely in the air.[4]

[1] See Strand, 'Notes on the Nūristānī and Dardic languages', *JAOS* 93, 1973, 297–305. Information on these languages can now be found in Edel'man, *The Dardic and Nuristani Languages*, Moscow 1983; C. F. and F. M. Voegelin, *Classification and Index of the World's Languages*, 1977, 265; *D. N. Nelson, 'The historical development of the Nuristani languages', diss., Univ. Minnesota, 1986, cf. *IC* 32b no. 328: third branch is possible but cannot be ascertained.

[2] G. Morgenstierne (repeatedly since 1926, e.g.), *NTS* 13, 1945, 225f.; *Encyclopaedia of Islam* ii, 1965, 138f. (cf. Redard, *CTL* vi, 1970, 141); *Irano-Dardica*, 1973, 327–43; id., in K. Jettmar (ed.), *Cultures of the Hindukush*, 1974, 1–10, e.g. 9: very difficult to decide whether 'ur-Kafirs separated from Indian in pre-Vedic times or . . . before the final separation of Indian from Iranian'; the latter view is adopted by Edel'man, *Sravnitel'naja grammatika vostočno-iranskix jazykov*, 1986, 42f., and again, *VJ* 1992 (3), 60–5. Cf. also Burrow, *The Sanskrit Language*, 1955, 32.

[3] Budruss, 'Zur Stellung der Nūristān-Sprachen' (*MSS* 36, 1977, 19–38), 28, 33.

[4] See the impressive evaluation of the facts in Campanile (ed.), *Nuovi materiali per la ricerca indoeuropeistica*, Pisa 1981, 36–40; Mayrhofer, 'Lassen sich Vorstufen des Uriranischen nachweisen?' (*Anzeiger, Akad. Wien*, 120, 1983, 249–55), 252–3.

6.7.2.3. If, then, satemization, i.e. the palatalization under certain conditions of original velars, was limited to a part of the Indo-European area, we can accept for PIE only two series of gutturals as original, the velars and the labiovelars.[1] Every other pairing of guttural series, e.g. palatals and velars or palatals and labiovelars, must be considered wholly improbable.

It is, on the other hand, quite possible that even the two-series system goes back to a still earlier situation with a single series. Some hold, indeed, that the triple system $k'/k/k^w$ was differentiated from a single velar series under the influence of the following vowel;[2] but the origin of the labiovelars can certainly not be explained in this way. However, the labiovelars can have arisen from the groups *kw gw ghw*; see 6.7.2.1.2 above. That would mean, of course, that at an earlier time only a single velar series existed.

[1] Hirt, *IG* 227; Bonfante, *Word* 1, 1945, 141f.; Lehmann, *PIE* 8, 100f.; Georgiev, *Introduction* 48; Burlakova, 'Vorgeschichte der slavischen Gutturale', *VSJ* 6, 1962, 46–65; Bernabé Pajares (above, 6.7.2.1.1 n.1); Allen, 'The PIE velar series', *TPS* 1978, 87–110 (e.g. 100f.).

[2] Pedersen, *Aspirationen i Irsk*, 1897, 192; Ribezzo, 'Per la genesi delle tre serie gutturali indoeuropee', *RIGI* 6, 1922, 225–41; 7, 1923, 41–62; cf. also *AGI* 22–23, 1929, 131–51; E. Hermann, *Herkunft unserer Fragefürwörter*, 1943, 16f.; Specht, *Ursprung* 316f.; Otrębski, *LPosn* 9, 1963, 11f.; Illič-Svityč (above, 6.6.11 n. 1) (comparison with Ural-Altaic).

6.7.2.4. At this point it will be useful to recall that a further source of IE *g k* (and Gmc. *kk*?) has been discovered by some in the laryngeals, both in initial position (see 6.4.4.2) and internally.[1] For the latter note such instances as:

OE *naca*, OHG *nacho* 'boat' from **naHw*-;
OE *tācor*, OHG *zeihur* 'brother-in-law': IE **daiwēr* (4.2.1);
OE *cwic* 'alive' from *g$^{\omega}$*Hiw*-<*g$^{\omega}$*Hiw*- (4.1.8, 4.7.5.2; 5.3.5*c*).

In the first example a form **naHu*- is fairly certain (see 7.5.4), and a development to **nakw*- perhaps not impossible. In the second case tortuous assumptions are needed to bring about the desired result, e.g. (according to Kortlandt) Gmc. **taikur* (-*kus*?) from IE **daiHw*- from **daHiw*-, that is, not only the derivation of an uncertain *kw* from *Hw* but also the metathesis of *i*. Lehmann's line from **deXywer*- to the variants I **taiw*-, II **deXyw*->-*aXw*- (and *y* lost?)>-*ak*- is even more incredible.

It is, in conclusion, not very likely that the considerable number of Germanic instances with so far unexplained velars will ever be satisfactorily accounted for with the help of laryngeals.

[1] See Lehmann, *PIE* 47–52; id., in *Evidence* 212–23, esp. 215f.; Winter, ibid. 197f.; Normier, *KZ* 91, 1978, 181f.; Kortlandt, in *Studies E. C. Polomé*, 356. Against the theory, Polomé, in Bammesberger 1988, 401–4; doubtful, Lindeman 1987, 94–8.

6.8. SUMMARY

On the basis of what has been said in the preceding two chapters, a picture can be formed of the phonological system of Indo-European shortly before the break-up of its unity, a picture that should be regarded as established in essentials:[1]

i				*u*	*ī*				*ū*				
	e	*ə*	*o*			*ē*		*ō*		*n̥*	*m̥*	*n̥̄*	*m̥̄*
		a					*ā*			*l̥*	*r̥*	*l̥̄*	*r̥̄*
		y	*w*						*p*	p^h	*b*	b^h	
		m	*n*						*t*	t^h	*d*	d^h	
		l							(*k'*	k'^h	*g'*	g'^h?)	
		r							*k*	k^h	*g*	g^h	
		s	*h*						k^{ω}	$k^{\omega h}$	g^{ω}	$g^{\omega h}$	

A striking feature of the consonant system is the relative poverty in spirants as contrasted with the richly represented system of stops. The proportion of vowels to the total number of phonemes (11:35=31 per cent) is medium; cf. 38 per cent in Finnish, with 8 vowels out of 21 phonemes, and 8 per cent in Bella Coola, an Indian language of Canada with only 3 vowels out of 36 phonemes.[2]

[1] See Szemerényi, 'New Look' 90f.; Hjelmslev, *Le langage*, 1966, 49.
[2] Hockett, *Manual of Phonology*, 138f.; Szemerényi, 'New Look' 85f.; W. Lehfeldt, 'Die Verteilung der Phonemanzahl in den natürlichen Sprachen', *Phonetica* 31, 1975, 274–87. For recent developments, see Bomhard, *In Memory of J. A. Kerns*, 1981, 352–70, diagram 370;

Nostratic 37–59; Martinet 1986, 134f.; Rasmussen 1989, 256–62; Lubotsky, in Kellens 1990, 135 (supporting Kortlandt); Kacnel'son, in Desnickaja (ed.), *Aktual'nyje voprosy sravnitel'nogo jazykoznanija*, 1989, 115–30.

6.9. NEW VIEWS ON THE SUBSYSTEM OF STOPS

In the nineteenth century, as we have seen, a four-member system of stops on the Old Indic model was at first postulated. After the removal of the unvoiced aspirates in the present century this was reduced to a three-member system which, however, provoked doubts on typological grounds; moreover, it was often claimed that in this system neither the rarity of *b* nor the various constraints relating to morpheme structure could be properly understood.

Since the beginning of the 1970s Gamkrelidze and Ivanov in the former Soviet Union and Hopper in the United States have worked out a completely new system,[1] in which the difficulties of the three-member system can be eliminated as follows: the voiced unaspirated stops of the traditional system must be replaced by ejective/glottalized stops, and instead of *t-dh* either *t(h)-d(h)*, with free variation of the aspiration, or (with Hopper) simply *t-d* must be posited. In a glottalized stop the closure of the buccal channel (at the lips, teeth, etc.) is accompanied by an additional closure of the glottis; both closures are released simultaneously, producing a characteristic click in the vocal chords. Such sounds are denoted by *t'*, etc.

The traditional three-member system, which can be represented by

t　　　*d*
　　dh

must accordingly be replaced by

t(h)　　　*t'*　　or　　*t*　　　*t'*
　　d(h)　　　　　　　　*d*

This new doctrine, which is quite in agreement with Thomas S. Kuhn's theory of paradigm change (1970, 43f., 174f.), has already found a considerable body of support,[2] while the opposition is at present fairly muted.[3]

One of the most striking consequences of the new system is that languages which because of their sound shift have hitherto been seen as very far removed from the Indo-European situation (Germanic, Armenian) must now be counted among the most conservative and archaic, because they show in fact no sound shift but preserve the old state of affairs, whereas those languages which according to the traditional view had most faithfully preserved the original Indo-European system (Old Indic, Greek) now find themselves among the foremost innovators.[4]

It is difficult to predict the future, but it will perhaps be useful to draw attention to some doubtful aspects of the new theory.

1. The geographical distribution of glottalized sounds is not particularly favourable to the theory.[5] Of the 317 languages included in the UPSD (=UCLA Phonological Segment Inventory Database), 52 have ejectives. Of these 35 are in America (30 in North America), 14 in Africa, 3 in the Caucasus; among the IE languages only East Armenian has these sounds. The Stanford study of Merritt Ruhlen,[6] based on 693 languages, records ejectives in 129 languages: 75 in America, 11 in Africa, 37 (=all) in the Caucasus and 1 in the IE family (Ossetic, likewise in the Caucasus). The two IE languages (Ossetic and East Armenian) have undoubtedly been influenced by the Caucasian environment. Apart from a few exceptions in Asia and Oceania (Ruhlen, n. 6 below, 146f.) the ejectives thus occur only in America, Africa, and the Caucasus—all regions in which the Indo-Europeans certainly never settled in Proto-IE and earlier times.

2. The ejectives are decidedly unvoiced sounds.[7] How they could have become voiced in so many languages (Old Indic, Greek, Latin, etc.) is and remains a puzzle.

3. If the traditional voiced stops had to be removed and replaced by ejectives, it remains puzzling how they can have been reintroduced in place of the traditional voiced aspirates.

[1] Gamkrelidze and Ivanov, *Konferencija po sravnitel'no-istoričeskoj grammatike ie. jazykov: Predvaritel'nyje materialy*, Moscow 1972, 15–18 (première!); 'Sprachtypologie und die Rekonstruktion der gemein-idg. Verschlüsse', *Phonetica* 27, 1973, 150–56; Gamkrelidze, 'On the correlation of stops and fricatives in a phonological system', *Lingua* 35, 1975, 231–61; 'Linguistic typology and IE reconstruction', *Studies Greenberg* ii, 1976, 399–406; 'Hierarchical relationships of dominance', *Fs. Szemerényi*, 1979, 283–90; Gamkrelidze and Ivanov, 'Drevnjaja Perednjaja Azija i ie. problema', *VDI* 1980 (3), 3–27; 'Rekonstrukcija sistemy smyčnyx obšče-ie. jazyka', *VJ* 1980 (4), 21–35; Gamkrelidze, 'Linguistic typology and language universals', *In Memory of J. A. Kerns*, 1981, 571–609; Gamkrelidze–Ivanov 1984; Gamkrelidze, *JIES* 15, 1988, 47–59; *KZ* 100, 1988, 366–77: 'Neueres zum Problem der idg. Ursprache und der idg. Urheimat' (the Near East); 'The IE glottalic theory in the light of recent critique', *FoLH* 9, 1990, 3–12; Hopper, 'Glottalised and murmured occlusives in IE', *Glossa* 7/2, 1973, 141–66; 'The typology of the PIE segmental inventory', *JIES* 5, 1977, 41–53; '"Decem" and "taihun" languages', *In Memory of J. A. Kerns*, 133–42; 'Areal typology and the Early IE consonant system', in Polomé (ed.), *The Indo-Europeans in the 4th and 3rd Millennia*, 1982, 121–39.

[2] Miller, 'Implications of an IE root structure constraint', *JIES* 5, 1977, 31–40; Normier, 'Indogermanischer Konsonantismus, germanische Lautverschiebung und Vernersches Gesetz', *KZ* 91, 1977, 171–218; Kortlandt, 'PIE obstruents', *IF* 83, 1978, 107–18; 'PIE glottalizovannyje smyčnyje', *VJ* 1985 (4), 43–53; Melikišvili, 'Struktura kornja', *VJ* 1980 (4), 60–70; Gercenberg, *Voprosy . . . prosodiki*, Leningrad 1981, 120f., 157f.; Bomhard, 'IE and Afroasiatic', *In Memory of J. A. Kerns*, 354–474 (469, earlier articles); Colarusso, 'Typological parallels between PIE and the NW Caucasian languages', ibid. 475–557, esp. 546, 560f.; Vennemann, 'Hochgermanisch und Niedergermanisch', *PBB(T)* 106, 1984, 1–45; Bomhard, *Nostratic* 26f.; Cowgill, *Krat* 29, 1985, 6; Suzuki, *KZ* 98, 1985, 285–93; Collinge, *Laws* 259f.; Lehmann, 'Reflexes of PIE *d*<*t*"', *Fs. J. Fisiak*, 1986; Bomhard, 'Recent trends in the reconstruction of the PIE consonant system', *HS* 101, 1988, 2–25. For

an overall appraisal, see also Lehmann, 'The current thrust of IE studies', *GL* 30, 1990, 1–52. A novel variant with two series and *b* mainly from *w* makes its debut with Stanley, *IF* 90, 1985, 50–3.

³ Back, 'Die Rekonstruktion des idg. Verschlusslautsystems', *KZ* 93, 1979, 179–95; Gercenberg: see Szemerényi 1985, 10; D'jakonov, *VDI* 1982 (3), 4–9; Haider, 'Der Fehlschluss der Typologie', in *Philologie und Sprachwissenschaft*, Innsbruck 1983, 79–92; *G. M. Green, 'Against reconstructing glottalized stops', in G. T. Stump (ed.), *Papers in Hist. Linguistics*, 1983, 50–5; Eichner, *BzN* 19, 1984, 450f. (ejectives instead of voiced stops 'from the viewpoint of comparative reconstruction entirely arbitrary'); 'Sprachwandel und Rekonstruktion', in *Akten 13. Österreichische Linguistentagung*, 1988, 10–40 (27: 'the glottalization theory . . . is to be kept away from the reconstruction of the original PIE language'); Szemerényi, *TPS* 1985, 3–15; *Haider, 'The fallacy of typology', *Lingua* 65, 1985, 1–27; Meid, *Fs. Adrados*, 1985, 323f.; Rosén, *BSL* 79/2, 1985, 76–8, 81–2 (sceptical); Meid, 'Germanische oder indogermanische Lautverschiebung', *Fs. R. Schützeichel*, 1987, 3–11; *Das Problem von idg. /b/*, Innsbruck 1989, 5f.; Bernabé, *RSEL* 18, 1989, 357–71; A. Pisowicz, 'Objections d'un arménologue contre la théorie glottale', *Folia Orientalia* 25, 1989, 213–25; Djahukian, 'A variational model of the IE consonant system', *HS* 103, 1990, 1–16. Another rejection, with a new solution based on articulatory force, in Swiggers, 'Towards a characterization of the PIE sound system', in Vennemann 1989, 177–208, 217–19; Ševoroškin, *FoLH* 7, 1988, 227–50, esp. 239f., 245; K. Wedekind, 'Glottalization constraints and Ethiopian counter-evidence', *FoL* 24, 1990, 127f. Some of the objections are answered by Gamkrelidze–Ivanov, 1317f.

⁴ See Szemerényi 1985, 14, and cf. Rasmussen, *Haeretica*, 1974, 14–15; Gamkrelidze, 'The "archaism" of Germanic and Armenian', in Lehmann (ed.), *Language Typology*, 1990, 57–65, esp. 61f.

⁵ For the following data, see Maddieson, *Patterns of Sounds*, 1984, 100f.

⁶ Ruhlen, 'The geographical and genetic distribution of linguistic features', in *Linguistic Studies Offered to J. Greenberg* i, 1977, 137–60.

⁷ Since in the articulation of ejectives the glottis is closed, it is natural that they are almost without exception unvoiced—see Maddieson (n. 5 above), 99f.; Ruhlen, *A Guide to the Languages of the World*, 1976, 40; Swiggers (n. 3 above), 29, 33; Szemerényi 1985, 13f. Cf. also M. E. Huld, 'The unacceptability of the voiced stops as ejectives', *IF* 91, 1986, 67–78.

6.9.1. Addendum: 'Winter's Law'

Werner Winter in 1978 voiced the conjecture that the long vowel which appears in a number of cases in Balto-Slavic in contrast to the short vowel in other languages is conditioned by a following unaspirated voiced stop: cf. Lith. *ė̃du* 'I eat', *sė̃dėti* 'sit', *bė̃gti* 'run': Lat. *edō*, *sedeō*, Gr. *φέβομαι*. This conjecture was immediately welcomed by Kortlandt as Winter's Law and taken as direct proof of the glottal theory: the traditional voiced stop had in fact been a glottalized sound, and was still discernible in the glottalized vowels of Lettish.[1]

It naturally did not escape the author of the new theory that a number of exceptions cannot easily be reconciled with his interpretation. In the case of Lith. *padas* 'sole of foot or shoe', Russ. *pod* 'ground', usually connected with the family of 'foot' (in which case the expected form would be **pōdo-*), he thought that recourse might be had to a new etymology **po+dhē-* (n. 1 below, 439). For Slav. *voda* 'water' he can offer only a borrowing from Gothic (p. 441), which is entirely beyond belief.[2] The weight of exceptions is in any case considerable, and the christening of 'Winter's Law' was perhaps too hasty.[3]

[1] See Winter in Fisiak (ed.), *Recent Developments in Historical Phonology*, 1978, 431–46; Kortlandt, ibid. 447; *IF* 83, 1978, 107–18; 'Long vowels in Balto-Slavic', *Baltistica* 21, 1985, 112–24; Collinge, *Laws* 225f.; Rasmussen, in Vennemann 1989, 160–1; Young, *HS* 103, 1990, 132–4.

[2] Against the law, esp. Strunk, *Fachtagung* 7, 1985, 494, and in *Fs. Hoenigswald*, 1987, 388; Birnbaum, *Fs. Winter*, 41–54; Zimmer, 'Slavisch *ubogъ* und "Winter's Law"', *MSS* 47, 1986, 223–7; W. P. Schmid, 'Zur Dehnstufe im Baltischen und Slavischen', *Fs. H. Bräuer*, 1986, 457–66; Eichner (above, 2.5 fin.); Lindeman, *HS* 102, 1990, 286.

[3] In addition to Winter's Law, the proliferation of various laws in recent years can be seen in the appearance of e.g. (*a*) Lex Stang, (*b*) Lex Rix, (*c*) Lex Eichner, etc. All three have been discussed by Strunk, *HS* 101, 1989, 308f., who also points out that Lex Stang is simply the acceptance of Szemerényi's observations of 1956; cf. below, 7.5.5 n. 4. Against (*b*) see also Lindeman, *The Triple Representation of Shwa in Greek*, 1982, 60f.; *HS* 102, 1990, 271f., 286, 294; 103, 1990, 17–19 (but cf. Rix, *HS* 104, 1991, 186–98, esp. 192; Peters, 'Ein weiterer Fall für das Rixsche Gesetz', *Fs. Rix*, 1993, 373–406): Polomé, *JIES* 15, 1988, 165f.; Meid, in Bammesberger 1988, 345. On (*c*), see Lindeman, *HS* 102, 273f. Both are defended by Mayrhofer, *Krat* 36, 1991, 34 n. 20.

7

Morphology I: Nouns and Adjectives

7.1 PRELIMINARY REMARKS ON NOUN INFLEXION

7.1.1

The only actual distinction between noun and adjective in Indo-European is that the adjective can show different forms according to gender, whereas with the noun this is the case only exceptionally and in a much more limited way (Lat. *equus* : *equa*). The inflexion of the two groups is otherwise identical.

The term *morphology* was coined by Schleicher in 1859; see *Mémoires Acad. Impériale* 7/1/7, 35: 'für die leere von der wortform wäle ich das wort "morphologie"'. For the subject I refer to J. Mugdan, 'Was ist eigentlich ein Morphem?' *ZPSK* 39, 1986, 29–43; H. Bergenholtz and J. Mugdan, *Einführung in die Morphologie*, Stuttgart 1979; J. L. Bybee, *A Study of the Relation between Meaning and Form*, Amsterdam 1985 (also on morphology and morphonology); J. T. Jensen, *Morphology: Word Structure in Generative Grammar*, Amsterdam 1990 (see *Lg* 68, 1992, 413–16); P. H. Matthews, 'Bloomfield's morphology and its successors', *TPS* 90, 1992, 121–86; F. Katamba, *Morphology*, London 1993. On the new *natural morphology*, see e.g. Dressler, 'Typological aspects of Natural Morphology', *ALH* 25, 1985, 51–70; Dressler, W. Mayerthaler, Panagl, W. U. Wurzel, *Leitmotifs in Natural Morphology*, Amsterdam 1987 (see Swiggers, *BSL* 84/2, 1989, 100–3); W. Raible, 'Natürlichkeit in der Sprache', in R. Brinkmann (ed.), *Natur in den Geisteswissenschaften*, Tübingen 1988, 113–18; M. Kilani-Schoch, *Introduction à la morphologie naturelle*, Berne 1988.

7.1.2

Gender is the property of the noun in agreement with which certain words referring to the noun (adjectives and some pronouns) assume different forms. It stands in a certain relationship to natural gender (e.g. words for 'father' and 'son' are masculine, those for 'mother' and 'daughter' feminine), but the latter is not decisive. This is evident from the fact that in Indo-European there were three genders, which are preserved in nearly all the early attested IE languages (Old Indic, Greek, Latin, Celtic, Germanic, Slavic). Later, several languages lost one of the genders, usually the neuter; the original neuter nouns were then assigned to the masculine and feminine. This happened in Lithuanian, and is attested much earlier in the Romance languages. In early attested Hittite, on the other hand, there appear only a common gender (for m. and f.) and a neuter.[1] Further loss leads to one gender, i.e. none, as in English and Persian and, from the beginning of its records, Armenian.

The Indo-European system of three genders must, however, have arisen from a two-class system.[2] This is the only conclusion to be drawn from the fact that in ancient inflexional classes the masculine and feminine do not differ in their inflexion, but together contrast with the neuter: e.g. πατήρ, μήτηρ. It would be wrong, however, to consider the origin of the feminine as a process not yet complete in Indo-European; it is clear that the feminine was fully developed even in the so-called marginal languages.[3]

The question how the early IE two-class system came into being is answered by Meillet by pointing to the fact that for certain concepts two different expressions are found, which apparently differ as *animate* (m. or f.) and *inanimate* (n.), e.g. Lat. *ignis*—Gr. πῦρ, Lat *aqua*—Gr. ὕδωρ (both in Goth. *ahva*—*watō*).[2] The further question how the feminine separated off from the animate class has recently again become the subject of lively discussion, in which there is a predominant tendency to return to the old view that the general development of -*ā*- and -*ī*- as signs of the feminine started from the pronouns (e.g. **sā* and **sī*), which themselves were modelled on certain nouns which happened to have one of these endings (e.g. **g*^{w}*enā* 'woman', see 4.7.5.2).[4]

[1] Loss of the feminine is defended by Pedersen. *Hittitisch* 13f.; Kuryłowicz, *PICL* 8, 1957, 235; *Categories* 211, 217; important observations by Goetze, *RHA* 66, 1960, 49f., and Beekes, *Origins* 26f. Against this, the former existence of the feminine in Hittite is disputed by Neu, *IF* 74, 1970, 235f.; Laroche, *RHA* 28, 1971, 50–7; Carruba, *Convegno* 5, 1972, 175–92; Meid, in *Heth. und Idg.* 165f. On the origin of the classical term *neutrum*, see Strunk, *Fs. Untermann*, 1993, 455–63.

[2] Meillet, *LHLG* i, 199–229, ii, 24–8; *BSL* 32, 1931, 1f.; cf. Létoublon, in S. Auroux 1988, 127–39 (on Meillet's pairs sun/moon, fire/water); K. H. Schmidt, *Fs. Szemerényi*, 1980, 793–800 (animate class from ergative/active); with even greater confidence the duality is traced to an early active structure by Lehmann, e.g. *GL* 31, 1991, 241. The use of *o*-stems also for females (e.g. ἡ ἵππος; θεός m. f., θεά being a later innovation) will reflect this archaic state. A Celtic trace has been found by Meid (above, 3.2 n. 2) 45, in the MIr. name of the great lover of *Medb*, *Fergus mac Roich* 'son of the Great Mare'; *Rōch* is from *ro-ech* with f. *ech* (from **ekwos*), cf. ἡ ἵππος.

The Latin type *lupus fēmina*, long traced to IE usage, was shown by Specht (*KZ* 55, 1928, 13–18) to be a Latin innovation (cf. Schlerath, *KZ* 100, 1987, 215f.); I would even add that it is obviously a calque of the Greek type θήλεια θεός, θήλειαι ἵπποι, frequent in Homer.

[3] In recent times, e.g., Watkins, *AIED* 40; Kammenhuber, *MSS* 24, 1968, 76f.; 'Hethitisch' 253 f,; *Fs. Winter*, 1985, 447f.; Wagner 1985, 81 (two-class system an innovation). For the existence of the *dēvī* type in Anatolian, see Szemerényi 1985, 20; Kammenhuber, *Fs. Winter*, 449f.; Strunk, *InL* 9, 1986, 149; and esp. Starke, *Fs. Neumann*, 1982, 408f. (*i*-feminine was common Luwian); Oettinger, *KZ* 100, 1987, 35–43 (*i*-feminine shows three genders); Szemerényi 1989, 49 (*sollemnis* etc.); Melchert, 'The feminine gender in Anatolian', *Fachtagung* 9, 1992. Against -*i* as feminine, Neu, *HS* 102, 1989, 1–15, esp. 14.

[4] Brugmann, *Grundriss*[2] ii/2, 82–113; Martinet, *BSL* 52, 1957, 83–95; Lehmann, *Lg* 34,

1958, 179–202; Gonzáles Rolán, *Em* 39, 1971, 296f.; Miranda, *JIES* 3, 1976, 199–215; Brosman, *JIES* 10, 1983, 253–72; against, Szemerényi 1985, 19f. Further works on the gender problem: Hirt, *IG* iii, 320–47; G. Royen, *Die nominalen Klassifikationssysteme in den Sprachen der Erde*, 1929 (against Meillet); Fodor, 'The origin of grammatical gender', *Lingua* 8, 1959, 1–41, 186–214; Martinet, *A Functional View of Language*, 1962, 15f., 149–52; Kuryłowicz, *Categories* 207–26; Hofmann–Szantyr 1965, 5f.; Balázs, 'Gli interrogativi slavi e l'origine del genere nell'indeuropeo', *AION-L* 7, 1966, 5–20; Wienold, *Genus und Semantik* 1967; Hovdhaugen, 'Case and gender in PIE', *Fs. Borgstrøm*, 1969, 58–72; R. Lafont, 'Genre et nombre en ie.', *RLaR* 79, 1970, 89–148 (Guillaumian); M. Hassan Ibrahim, *Grammatical Gender: its Origin and Development*, 1973 (see Wienold, *FoL* 14, 1976, 119–25); Villar, *Orígen* 342f.; *Dat. y loc.* 223; Shields, 'Origin of the IE feminine gender', *KZ* 91, 1977, 56–71; 'A theory of gender change', *Glossa* 13, 1979, 27–38; Greenberg, 'How does a language acquire gender markers?' in Greenberg (ed.), *Universals of Human Language* iii, 1978, 47–82; Neu, 'Zum Genus hethitischer *r*-Stamme', *Fs. Ivănescu=Linguistica* (Iaşi) 28–9, 1983, 125–30; Aksenov, 'Aussersprachliche Motivation des Genus', *VJ* 1984 (1), 14–25; Ostrowski, 'Zur Entstehung und Entwicklung des idg. Neutrums', *Fachtagung* 7, 1985, 313–23; H. Rosén, 'Entstehung der nominalen Genus-kategorie im Indogermanischen', ibid. 411–23; Seiller, 'Genus und Pragmatizität', *CFS* 41, 1987, 193–203; Harðarson, *MSS* 48, 1987, 115–37 ($*g^{w}en$-); Euler, 'Entstehung der idg. Genera', *IF* 96, 1991, 36–45; G. G. Corbett, *Gender*, Cambridge Textbooks in Linguistics, 1991 (on 200 languages!), see *Lg* 68, 1992, 605–10; id., 'Typology of the gender systems' (Russ.), *VJ* 1992 (3), 21–30 (note 30: 'in every well investigated language the speakers can with the help of general principles establish the gender in at least 85% of the instances'); Marina Chini, 'Aspetti teorico-descrittivi e tipologici della categoria del genere grammaticale', *LeS* 28, 1993, 455–86; Tichy, 'Kollektiva, Genus femininum und relative Chronologie im Idg.', *HS* 106, 1993, 1–19 (12: saH_2, taH_2m 'prove the formal independence of the IE feminine gender'). On women's and men's speech, see e.g. S. U. Philips, S. Steele, and C. Tanz, *Language, Gender and Sex*, Cambridge 1987 (see Hagège, *BSL* 84/2, 1989, 95–8).

On loss of the neuter in the Baltic noun, see F. Scholz, *KZ* 98, 1985, 269–79; on loss of gender in general, Priestley, *JIES* 11, 1984, 339–63.

7.1.3

Indo-European had three *numbers*: singular, plural, and dual. At the beginning of the tradition the last is still found in many languages, e.g. Old Indic, Greek, Old Irish, Old Church Slavic, Lithuanian, but sooner or later it is lost. Today there are hardly any IE languages that preserve the dual (perhaps Lithuanian); it disappeared earliest in Hittite.[1]

[1] On the category of number in general, see H. Jensen, *Wissenschaftliche Zeitschrift der Univ. Rostock* 1, 1952, 1–23. On plural and dual see Kuryłowicz, *Scientia* 105, 1970, 496, 502; on the dual, J. W. Pauw, *The Dual Number in IE: a Two-stage Development*, 1980, (Ann Arbor, Mich.): 1. duality-unity, 2. numeral/arithmetic; Th. Stolz, *ZPhon* 4, 1988, 476–87. About number in Risch and Gamkrelidze–Ivanov, see Szemerényi 1985, 21. A fourth 'number'—*collective*—is postulated by Neu, *IF* 74, 1969, 239f.; further elaborated as *comprehensive* by Eichner, *Fachtagung* 7, 1985, 134–69, esp. 150, 161; Harðarson, *MSS* 48, 1987, 71–113 (collective=singular neuter); Leukart, *Studies Chadwick*, 1987, 343–66; Neu, 'Zum Kollektivum im Hethitischen', in Carruba (ed.) 1992, 199–212. On the dual, see also Campanile, 'Zum idg. Dual', *TIES* 3, 1989, 121–4 (numerical and natural duality); Tichy, 'Zum homerischen Dual', *Wackernagel Kolloquium*, 1990, 170–87.

7.1.4.1. The *case system*[1] of the different IE languages varies greatly in extent. For example, classical Greek has only five cases, Latin six, Old Church Slavic seven, Old Indic eight. In principle it would be possible for the smaller number of cases to continue the old state of affairs and the greater to represent an innovation of certain languages.[2] That the contrary is the truth is proved by the fact that the languages with a smaller number of cases show a larger number at an earlier stage, or, if that is not so, at least preserve remnants of an earlier richer system. For example, Greek in its Mycenaean stage still has an independent instrumental, remains of which still survive in Homer. Latin has a locative for certain nouns, while Oscan still keeps a fully functional locative in its case system. If, then, the coalescence of formerly independent cases (syncretism)[3] is a historical fact in all IE languages, we must draw the conclusion that Indo-European had at least eight cases, a system best preserved in the satem languages, whereas in the centum languages it has suffered severe losses.[4]

[1] For the term *case* in general, see H.-E. Seidel, *Kasus: Zur Explikation eines sprachwissenschaftlichen Terminus (am Beispiel des Russischen)*, Tübingen 1988; R. D. Brecht and I. S. Levine (eds.), *Case in Slavic*, 1986. For general trends, see Shields, *IE Noun Inflection: A Developmental History*, 1982 (see Bomhard's review in *Diachronica* 1, 1984, 137–41); Bossong, 'Zur Entwicklungsdynamik von Kasussystemen', *FoLH* 6/2, 1987, 285–321; Kazanskij, 'K rekonstrukcii kategorii padež v Pra-IE', in Desnickaja (ed.) 1989, 115–30. On the early adaptation theory of Alfred Ludwig (1832–1912), see Anna de Meo, 'Genesi della flessione dell'ie.', *AIΩN* 9 (1987), 123–31.

For the development of the study of the cases, Hübschmann, *Zur Kasuslehre*, Munich 1875, is still very useful; the first part contains a history of theories of case from antiquity to the author's own time. In recent times the following works have been added: Ana Agud, *Historia y teoría de los casos*, 1980 (very comprehensive), and G. Serbat, *Cas et fonctions*, 1981 (critical). Important for IE but hardly obtainable is *J. A. Booth, *The Evolution of Case in IE Studies*, diss., Univ. Birmingham, 1980.

As regards the various attempts to recognize groups within the case system or more general viewpoints, Hübschmann (131) was of the opinion that nom. acc. gen. were to be assigned to the grammatical group, instr. loc. abl. to the non-grammatical, while the assessment of the dative seemed to him still uncertain. Subsequently the American scholar Whitney (*TAPA* 13, 1882, 88–100: 'General considerations on the IE case system') returned to earlier views and championed the so-called localistic theory: apart from nom. and gen. all the cases were adverbial, i.e. local. This localistic theory was already taught about AD 1300 by the Byzantine grammarian Maximus Planudes, who had perhaps adopted it from the earlier grammarian Priscian: see Robins, 'The case theory of Maximus Planudes', *PICL* 11/1, 1974, 107–11; id. 1993; Calboli, *ANRW* 29/1, 1983, 61f. At all events the doctrine was revived by Bopp at the beginning of the last century and was vigorously supported by Hartung (Hübschmann, 26, 49). About the turn of the century Brugmann (*Griechische Grammatik*[3], 1900, 374) formulated the cautious view that the borderline between local and grammatical cases was vanishing, whereas the Swiss Anton Marty (working in Prague) found the dividing line much clearer (see *Die 'logische', 'lokalistische' und andere Kasustheorien*, 1910, 117f.). In the following period the localistic theory lost this central position; the shift of interest is shown in such works as K. Bühler, 'Das idg. Kasussystem als Beispiel eines Feldgerätes', in his *Sprachtheorie*, 1934 (repr. 1982), 236–51 (mainly on Wundt); Hjelmslev, *La catégorie des cas* i–ii, 1935, 1937; Fillmore 1968 (cf. Heger, *Monem* 113 n.; Feuillet, 'Les fonctions sémantiques profondes', *BSL* 75, 1980, 1–37). But the localistic theory is not dead; it is celebrating a revival in various works of the Edinburgh scholar John M. Anderson, e.g. *The Grammar of Case: Towards a Localistic Theory*, Cambridge 1971; *On Case Grammar: Prolegomena to a Theory of Grammatical Relations*, 1977. In his view case relations are oppositions of the directional notions 'source', 'goal', and 'resting point' (whence–whither–where) (*On Case Grammar* 111), and all cases (including nom. acc. gen.) are to be analysed into local components (Starosta, *Lg* 57, 1981, 722).

To conclude, a few more recent works: G. Calboli, *La linguistica moderna e il latino: i casi*, Bologna 1972; K. H. Schmidt, *Fachtagung* 5, 1975, 268–86; Scherer, *Hb. der lat. Syntax*, 1975, 38–55, 178–206; Kuryłowicz, *Problèmes* 141–56; Mel'čuk, 'Le cas', *RES* 50, 1977, 5–36; S. C. Dik, *Functional Grammar*, 1981, 157–70; Schützeichel, 'Zum Kasusproblem', *Fs. Coseriu* iv, 1981, 339–49; Calboli, *ANRW* 29/1, 1983, 8f., 31f., 64f.; Garde, 'Les cas russes', *BSL* 78, 1983, 337–74.

[2] Cf. Szemerényi, 'Methodology' 19f.; Savčenko, *LPosn* 12/13, 1968, 29f. On the development, see H. van Velten, 'Sur l'évolution du genre, des cas et des parties du discours', *BSL* 33, 1932, 205–23, esp. 216f.; Risch, 'Zur idg. Nominalflexion', *Fs. Seiler*, 1980, 259–67 (deficiencies in case system, no pl. in neuters, etc.). Lehmann writes of a very early phase (4th millennium BC) in Polomé (ed.), *The Indo-Europeans in the 4th and 3rd Millennia*, 1982, 140–55; but cf. also id., *Fs. Meid*, 1989, 124 (the early noun had only active/nominative, inactive/accusative); Gamkrelidze–Ivanov, 267f.; Adrados, 'La flexion nominale . . .', in *É. Benveniste aujourd'hui* ii, 1984, 1–16 (originally five cases only); Tischler, *Fs. Meid*, 1989, 412–14; Ivo Hajnal, *Studien zum mykenischen Kasussystem*, Berlin 1994.

[3] Delbrück, *Synkretismus*, 1907; H. Jacobsohn, 'Kasusflexion und Gliederung der idg. Sprachen', *Fs. Wackernagel*, 1923, 204–16; Risch (n. 2 above); Szemerényi, *Fachtagung* 7, 516f.; Silvia Luraghi, 'Case syncretism in IE languages', *ICHL* 7, 1987, 355–71; G. Meiser, 'Syncretism in IE languages', *TPS* 90, 1992, 187–218.

[4] On the use of the IE cases, see Brugmann, *Grundriss*^{2}, ii/2, 464–651; Meillet, *Introduction* 341–9; Schwyzer, *GG* ii, 52–173; Hofmann–Szantyr 1965, 21–151; Haudry, *L'emploi des cas en védique*, 1977; Hettrich, 'Rektionaler und autonomer Kasusgebrauch', *Wackernagel Kolloquium*, 1990, 82–99, and for the double accusative, id., 'Betrachtungen zum doppelten Akk.', *Fachtagung* 9, 1994, 111–34; Strunk, *Fs. Gamkrelidze*, 1991, 81–91 (instr. as animate associative already in IE).

7.1.4.2. The system, best preserved in Old Indic, consists of the following eight cases: nominative, vocative, accusative, genitive, dative, ablative, locative, instrumental.

The formal differentiation of the cases is complete only in the singular, and even there only in one group, the *o*-stems. In all other declensions the ablative is identical with the genitive in the singular; in the dual and plural it is identical with the dative in all declensions. The vocative is distinct from the nominative only in the singular and not in all declensions; in the dual and plural it is identical with it.[1] The result of the various simplifications is that there are only six separate forms in the plural and only four in the dual. In the neuter, nom. voc. acc. of the same number are not distinguished.[2]

[1] On the vocative in general, see E. Buyssens, 'Étude sémiologique du vocatif', *CFS* 45, 1991, 77–87.

[2] On the newly added *directivus* (discovered by E. Forrer, 'Ein siebenter Kasus im Alt-Kanisischen', *Studien B. Meissner gewidmet*, 1928, 30–5), see Laroche, *RHA* 28, 1971, 22f., 46f.; W. P. Schmid, *Fs. Otten*, 1973, 291–301; Starke 1977; Brixhe, *Mél. Laroche*, 1979, 65–77; Kammenhuber, in *Heth. und Idg.*, 1979, 115–42; Neu, *Studien zum endungslosen 'Lokativ'*, 1980, 12f.; Haudry, *Préhistoire* 22f.; Szemerényi 1985, 22; Villar, *Symbolae Mitxelena*, 1985, 44f.; K. Shields, 'The origins of the old Hittite directive case', *JIES* 10, 1982, 273–82; Dunkel, *Fachtagung* 9, 1992.

The name given by Forrer (*Richtungskasus*) was Latinized as *directivus*. Starke pointed out that the case indicated the goal, not the direction, and suggested *terminative* (1977, 23) but gave this up in 1982 (*BiOr* 39, 358). Now there is a growing consensus in favour of *allative*, introduced in *CHD* iii/1, 1980, p. xvi. On the history of the research, see Starke 1977, 25–8; 1990, 30, 32; Villar 1981, 18f., 124f.

7.1.4.3. The different cases are characterized by *case endings* which are added to the *stem*, the part of the word which carries the meaning and is unchangeable apart from certain ablaut alternations. Thus in the nom. pl. πόδες the case ending -ες is added to the stem πόδ-. If a stem with final vowel took an ending with initial vowel, a contraction already occurred in Indo-European; for example, in *o*-stems the dat. s. ended in *-ōi*, a contraction of the stem vowel *-o-* and the case ending *-ei*, in contrast to the loc. in final *-oi*, consisting of *-o-* and the case ending *-i*.[1]

A comparison of the different IE languages gives the following case endings:

	Sing.	Plur.	Dual
Nom.	*-s, -Ø*[2]	*-es*	
Voc.	Ø	*-es*	*-e, -ī/-i*[6] (Nom., Voc., Acc.)
Acc.	*-m/-m̥*	*-ns/-n̥s*	
Gen.	*-es/-os/-s*[2]	*-om/-ōm*	*-ous? -ōs?*
Abl.	*-es/-os/-s*[3] *-ed/-od*[3]	*-bh(y)os, -mos*	*-bhyō, -mō*
Dat.	*-ei*[4]	*-bh(y)os, -mos*	*-bhyō, -mō*
Loc.	*-i*[4]	*-su*	*-ou*
Instr.	*-e/-o, -bhi/-mi*[5]	*-bhis/-mis, -ōis*	*-bhyō, -mō*

For the neuter, special rules apply in nom., voc., and acc. In the singular the bare stem usually appears, except in the *o*-stems, in which *-m* is added. In the plural the ending is *-ā* or *-ə*, which need not indicate a laryngeal;[7] the ending can also have been uniformly *-ā*.[8] In the dual the ending was *-i* (*-ī*?).

[1] On 'stem', see I. Josch, 'Kritik am Stammbegriff', *Fachtagung* 7, 1985, 229–36; on the structure of the word, see Dunkel, in *In Memory of W. Cowgill*, 1987, 23f. Note John Horne Tooke's early insight (1786, see Arens², 133) that there were originally no abstract 'endings', only independent words which coalesced with others.

On the case endings, see Hirt, *IG* iii, 39f.; Wackernagel and Debrunner, *Ai. Gr.* iii, 28f.; Schwyzer, *GG* i, 547f. There is a bold attempt to determine the prehistory in Kuryłowicz, *Categories* 179f., esp. 196f. See further Ivanov, *Xettskij jazyk*, 1963, 113f., 129–40; Erhart, 'Zur ie. Nominalflexion', *Sbornik Brno* 16, 1967, 7–26; Savčenco, *LPosn* 12/13, 1968, 21–36; C.-J. N. Bailey, *Inflectional Pattern of IE Nouns*, Honolulu 1970, on case endings 17–94; Erhart, *Studien zur ie. Morphologie*, Brno 1970; Fairbanks, *JIES* 5, 1977, 101–31; Palmaitis, *Indojevropejskaja apofonija i razvitije deklinacionnyx modelej*, Tbilisi 1979; Brixhe, *Mélanges Laroche*, 1979, 71f.; Haudry, 'La "syntaxe des désinences"', *BSL* 75, 1980, 131–66 (agglutination); id. (above, 7.1.4.2 n. 1), 20 (postpositional origin of the endings); Villar 1974, 1981; id. 1991, 141f., esp. 207–33; Starke, 'Kasusendungen der luwischen Sprachen, *Fs. G. Neumann*, 1982, 407–25; Meier-Brügger, *Fachtagung* 7, 1985, 271–4; Szemerényi, ibid. 517f.; id. 1985, 21f.; Fulk 1986, 50f.; Erhart, *Die idg. Nominalflexion und ihre Genese*, 1993.

[2] On the alleged identity of nom. and gen., see below, 7.2.1 n. 3; on the gen., see Serbat, 'Zum Ursprung des idg. Genitivs und seiner lat. Verwendung', in Panagl and Krisch 1992, 285–91.

[3] On the abl., see Shields, *Em* 55, 1987, 63–9 (from *dh*!); Kazanskij (above, 7.1.4.1 n. 1), 123f.

[4] On the endings, see Adrados, *Studies Polomé*, 1988, 29–41, and below, 7.2.1 with n. 4.

[5] Cf. Shields, 'Evidence of IE *-bhi* in Tocharian', *FoL* 11, 1977, 281–6; Gamkrelidze–Ivanov, 286–7; eid., *VDI* 1988 (1), 14–39, 19 n. 15; Martinet 1986, 173, and *BSL* 86, 1992, 361f.: *bh* and *m* both from 'pre-nasalized' ^{m}*bh* (?); P. Nieto Hernandez, *Em* 55, 1987, 273–306; Meier-Brügger 1992 ii, 67. See also below, 7.2.1 fin.

[6] Recent research has established (remains of) the dual in Anatolian also, cf. Luw. *pata, issara* '(two) feet, hands', *aruta* 'wings'; cf. Schindler ap. Watkins 1986, 60 n. 33 (*-a*=ε or thematic *-ō*); Starke, *BiOr* 43, 1986, 161 (*-a* from *-H_1e* after consonant); Lindeman, *HS* 102, 1990, 287–8 (good survey); Meier-Brügger 1992 i, 144f. See also below, 7.5.1 n. 6 and 7.6.4.

[7] Recently in favour: Watkins, *Fachtagung* 5, 1975, 362f.; *Gedenkschrift Kronasser*, 1982, 255f.; but against: Lindeman, *Sprache* 29, 1983, 41f. Cf. also Beekes, *Origins* 29f.; Gamkrelidze–Ivanov, 281.

[8] Szemerényi 1985, 20.

7.1.4.4. Originally *ablaut alternations* occurred quite generally in the stem. Basically the full grade had its place in nom. voc. acc. loc. s. and nom. voc. acc. pl. (*strong cases*), often with long grade in the nom. s. of animate stems; in the other cases there appears basically the zero grade (*weak cases*).[1] For example, **dónt-m̥* 'tooth' (acc. s.) but **dn̥t-ós* (gen. s.), **dónt-es* (nom. pl.) but **dn̥t-sú* (loc. pl.). Where the zero grade caused or would have caused difficult consonant groups, the vowel was either not lost at all or soon restored. In the case of **ped-* 'foot', for example, the gen. s. **pd-ós* (i.e. **bdós*) was hardly in use for very long.

It is only in very rare cases that a paradigm 'torn apart' by ablaut is preserved, at least fragmentarily, e.g. Ved. *āyu-/yōḥ* 'life', Avest. *āyu/yaoš* (cf. OInd. *jānu/jñōḥ, dāru/drōḥ*),[2] *ātman-/tan-ā*,[3] **dheghō(m)/* loc. **dhghém-i*.[4]

[1] Kuryłowicz, *Categories* 194 with n. 12, 200f.

[2] Szemerényi, *InL* 4, 1978, 165f.; Beekes, in Bammesberger 1988, 61, 67.

[3] Edgerton, *Lg* 38, 1962, 354; Schindler, *Sprache* 15, 1969, 149.

[4] Szemerényi, *SMEA* 20, 1980, 222f.; cf. above, 4.6.3; and see Fulk 1986, 69f.

7.1.4.4.1. *Accent in noun inflexion*. Accentuation in noun inflexion received no special attention before the twentieth century.[1] It was of considerable significance when in 1926 Pedersen recognized two inflexional and accentual types: the *hysterodynamic* (nom. – –́, gen. – – –́, πατήρ : πατρός) and the *proterodynamic* (nom. –́ –, gen. – –́ –); the distinction was later improved on by Kuiper.[2] Since the 1950s Kuryłowicz has occupied himself very intensively with accent problems,[3] and Kiparsky and Halle,[4] as also Garde,[5] have important achievements to their credit in this field.

Since 1973 the Erlangen school has repeatedly expressed its views on such questions. It has classified the various types of accent with great precision and introduced an impressive terminology, based on suggestions of Karl Hoffmann.[6] Five accent types are distinguished, which are denoted by the terms *static* or *kinetic* depending on whether the accent is fixed or movable; the complete system is as follows:

I	*acrostatic*	accent on first syllable throughout
II	*proterokinetic*	accent on beginning/suffix
III	*amphikinetic*	accent on beginning/end
IV	*hysterokinetic*	accent on final syllable throughout
V	*mesostatic*	accent on suffix

This double-track nomenclature was unified by Rix's introduction of a constant second component *-dynamic*,[7] thus *acrodynamic*, etc.

[1] Cf. however Wackernagel and Debrunner, *Ai. Gr.* iii/1, 1929, 14–28; Hirt, *IG* v, 1929, 214–84 (219: three accent types).

[2] Pedersen, *La cinquième déclinaison latine*, Copenhagen 1926, 24; Kuiper, *Notes on Vedic Noun-inflexion*, Amsterdam 1942, 2f., 30, 36. Cf. also his pupil Beekes, *KZ* 86, 1972, 30–6; *Glotta* 51, 1973, 228–45; *Origins* 1f.

[3] See his *Accentuation*, 1952, 2nd edn. 1958, and the summary of a life's work in his *IG* 1–197, esp. 26f.; 115f.

[4] See above, 5.2.4 n. 1.

[5] Garde, 'Le paradigme accentuel oxyton . . .', *RES* 49, 1973, 159–71, and esp. his *Histoire de l'accentuation slave* I–II, 1976, esp. 318f.; further on this, Kortlandt, *Slavic Accentuation*, 1975, and *KZ* 92, 1979, 269–81. Note also in general Fulk 1986, and Lubotsky's work cited above, 5.2.3 n. 1.

[6] See Eichner, *MSS* 31, 1973, 91; Schindler, *BSL* 70, 1975, 3 n. 2; *Fachtagung* 5, 1975, 262f.; Oettinger, *KZ* 94, 1980, 46.

[7] Rix 1976, 123. Comments on this in Kuryłowicz, *Problèmes* 111; Beekes, *Origins* 1f. On the whole subject, see also Szemerényi 1985, 15f.; Strunk, *Fachtagung* 7, 1985, 490f. For the *holokinetic* type of the earlier systematization, see also Harðarson, *ALHafn* 21, 1989, 80, and on accent in general, id. 1993, 25–37.

7.1.4.5. The case-endings and the principles of their attachment to the stem (including variations of accent and ablaut) were originally the same for all stem classes, i.e. there was only a single declension. Even in Indo-European, however, certain case endings underwent contraction with a final stem vowel and these fusions gave the inflexion in these classes its own particular character. This break-up of the originally unitary declension into a number of more or less different declension classes then became even more marked in the individual languages.

7.1.4.6. As far as can be established, all consonants could take final position in the stem; thus there were *-p-/-t-/-k-* stems, *-s-* stems, and *-m/-n-/-l-/-r-* stems, etc. Of the vowels, on the other hand, only *i*, *u*, *o* and *ī*, *ū*, *ā* could appear in final position, but not *a*, while *e* is combined with *o* in a single class, the so-called thematic or *o*-class. It is also possible that the laryngeal *h* had its place in many of the long-vowel stems, so that these should properly be denoted *-ih*, *-uh*, and *-ah* (or rather *-oh*) stems.[1]

[1] On 'phonological restriction in affixes', see Floyd in *In Memory of J. A. Kerns*, 1981, 87–106; and cf. Rosén, *BSL* 79/2, 1984, 83f.

7.1.4.7. Only a few IE nouns can be designated as root nouns.[1] The great majority are formed by means of various suffixes from simple roots or from already existing derivatives. The study of the intricate rules which thereby come into use, i.e. the study of word formation,[2] is an important part of morphology; see 5.1.1.[3]

[1] See Schindler, *Das Wurzelnomen im Arischen und Griechischen*, Diss. Würzburg 1972; for Latin, see Untermann, in Panagl and Krisch 1992, 137–53.

[2] On general problems, see S. G. Stein, 'The place of word-formation in linguistic description', in H. E. Brekle and D. Kastovsky (eds.), *Perspektiven der Wortbildungsforschung*, Bonn 1977, 219–35; Brekle, 'Wortbildungstheoretische Ansätze in K. Bühlers Sprachtheorie', in *Fs. K. Matzel*, 1984, 189–99; J. Aitchison, *Words in the Mind: An Introduction to the Mental Lexicon*, Oxford 1987.

[3] For the most important IE languages there are excellent treatments of word formation; cf. for Old Indic, Wackernagel and Debrunner, *Ai. Gr.* ii 1–2; for Greek, Schwyzer, *GG* i, 415–544; Risch, *Wortbildung der homerischen Sprache*[2], 1974; for Latin, Leumann, *Lat. Laut- und Formenlehre*[2], 1977, 257–403; for Germanic, F. Kluge, *Nominale Stammbildungslehre der altgermanischen Dialekte*[3], 1926; C. T. Carr, *Nominal Compounds in Germanic*, 1939; H. Krahe and W. Meid, *Germanische Sprachwissenschaft* iii: *Wortbildungslehre*, 1967; A. Bammesberger, *Die Morphologie des urgermanischen Nomens*, Heidelberg 1990; W. Henzen, *Deutsche Wortbildung*[3], 1965; for Slavic, Vaillant, *Gram. comp.* iv, 1974.

Many of these works also deal with the problems of composition; on the fundamental questions of the origin of compound nouns, see e.g. Benveniste, 'Fondements syntaxiques de la composition nominale', *BSL* 62, 1968, 15–31; Lehmann, 'PIE compounds in relation to other PIE syntactic patterns', *AL* 12, 1970, 1–20; Szemerényi, 'Kinship' 26–8. Good examples for Latin (and not only Latin) composition are F. Bader, *La formation des composés nominaux du latin*, Paris 1962; R. Oniga, *I composti nominali latini: una morfologia generativa*, Bologna 1988; Szemerényi 1989.

Many important articles are reprinted in Lipka and Günther, *Wortbildung*, Darmstadt 1981. On one of the basic problems, *agglutination*, esp. in Latin, see Fruyt, *BSL* 85/1, 1990, 173–209.

7.1.4.8. A special class of nouns deserves a brief mention here: names, in particular *personal names*. Under the influence of early heroic literatures, the compound, so-called dithematic, names so frequently found in them (cf. Agamemnon, Menelaos, Patroklos, Kleopatrā) were long held to have been the only type in use in Indo-European. More recently, monothematic names have also had to be acknowledged as part of the IE system (see e.g. Pulgram, *Lg* 36 (1960), 198–202; Campanile, *AION-L* 7 (1966), 21–40), and this claim seemed to gain support from the new Mycenaean evidence. Furthermore, it has become clear in the mean time that the dithematic names were but an offshoot of an IE type of poetic expression (Schramm 1957, 144; Schmitt 1973). We can therefore conclude that in Indo-European, as elsewhere, the first names were monothematic, but later heroic songs made heroic epithets so popular that they were also widely used for name-giving, although they never ousted the earlier type; the two lived side by side, but no doubt with a certain social stratification.[1]

[1] From the immense literature the following may be found especially useful: Schwyzer, *GG* i, 633–8; A. Gardiner, *A Theory of Proper Names*, London 1954; E. Pulgram, 'Theory of names', *BzN* 5, 1954, 149–96; G. Schramm, *Namenschatz und Dichtersprache*, Göttingen 1957; P. Hartmann, *Das Wort als Name*, Cologne 1958; H. S. Sørensen, *The Meaning of Proper Names*, Copenhagen 1963; H. Rix, *Das etruskische Cognomen*, Wiesbaden 1963; E. A. Hahn, *Naming-constructions in some IE Languages*, Ann Arbor. Mich., 1969; Rix, 'Zum Ursprung des römisch-mittelitalischen Gentilnamensystems', *ANRW* 1/2, 1972, 700–58; R. Schmitt, *Idg. Dichtersprache und Namengebung*, Innsbruck 1973; J. Algeo, *On Defining the Proper Name*, 1973; D. R. Shackleton Bailey, *Two Studies in Roman Nomenclature*, New York 1976; G. Koss, *Namenforschung*, Tübingen 1990; R. Schmitt, 'Das idg. und das alte lateinische Personennamensystem', in Panagl and Krisch 1992, 369–93; Meier-Brügger 1992 ii, 39f.

7.1.4.9 Clearly, not all stem classes and declension types can be discussed here. Prominence will be given only to the main classes, which can illustrate facts and methods alike.

7.2 STEMS ENDING IN STOPS

7.2.1

A simple juxtaposition of the paradigms in different languages is sufficient for the most part to demonstrate the original identity and the early state of affairs. Thus, e.g., for the dental stem **ped-/*pod-* 'foot':

		Skt.	Gr.	Lat.	IE
Sing.	Nom.	*pā́d*	πούς (πώς)	*pēs*	**pēs*
	Acc.	*pā́d-am*	πόδ-α	*ped-em*	**péd-m̥*
	Gen.	*pad-ás*	ποδ-ός	*ped-is*	**ped-és/-ós*
	Abl.	*pad-ás*	–	–	**ped-és/-ós*
	Dat.	*pad-ḗ*	–	*ped-ī*	**ped-éi*
	Loc.	*pad-í*	ποδ-ί	*ped-e*	**ped-í*
	Instr.	*pad-ā́*	*pod-e*	*ped-e*	**ped-é*
Plur.	Nom.	*pā́d-as*	πόδ-ες	*ped-ēs*	**péd-es*
	Acc.	*pad-ás*	πόδ-ας	*ped-ēs*	**péd- n̥s*
	Gen.	*pad-ā́m*	ποδ-ῶν	*ped-um*	**ped-óm*
	Abl.-Dat.	*pad-bhyás*	–	*ped-i-bus*	**ped-bh(y)ós*
	Loc.	*pat-sú*	πο(σ)-σί	–	**ped-sú*
	Instr.	*pad-bhís*	*pop-p*^{h}*i*	–	**ped-bhís*

The difference in vowel colouring between πούς and *pēs* is explained by alternation within the paradigm (e.g. nom. **pōs* : gen. **ped-ós*), or between simple and compound (e.g. **pēs* : **su-pōs* 'with good feet'), with subsequent generalizing of one or the other timbre.[1] The long grade in the nom. s. is to be explained as from the assimilated form

**pess* from **ped-s* (see 6.2.7.2); in OInd. the dental was restored and **pāts* gave *pāt* in accordance with the sandhi rule which allows only a single consonant in final position. The acc. s., as indicated by the correspondence *-am*: *-α*: *-em*, had the ending *-m̥*, i.e. the ending *-m* which in final position after a consonant had to become syllabic; similarly, the acc. pl. ending can be reconstructed as *-n̥s*, no doubt assimilated from *-ms*, i.e. *-m* of the singular+pluralizing *-s*.[2] The Germanic correspondence, e.g. OE *fōt* 'foot', shows generalization of the long grade which properly belonged only to the nom. s.; Goth. *fōtus* even shows the formation of a *u*-stem on the basis of the inherited endings acc. s. *-u(n)* from IE *-m̥*, acc. pl. *-uns* from *-n̥s*. The ending of the gen. s. is *-os* in Greek, apparently *-es* in Latin (whence *-is*); *-os* would be simply the *o*-grade of *-es*.[3] It is, however, noteworthy that in the nom. pl. only *-es* is found, never *-os*. The diphthong in the dat. s. is now certainly to be taken as *-ei*;[4] cf. Osc. *paterei* 'patrī', Gr. *Διϝεί-φιλος* 'dear to Zeus', Myc. *tukatere pomene* etc., i.e. *θυγατέρει ποιμένει*. The instr. s. appears to end in *-e/-o* or *-ē/-ō*; the vowel timbre is now decided by Myc. *erepate*=*ἐλέφαντε*; see Brixhe, *Mél. Laroche,* 1979, 73. The gen. pl. has in OInd. the ending *-ām*, in Gr. *-ῶν*, which point to IE *-ōm*. This is consistent with the form in most languages, but hardly with Slavic *-ŭ*, which, like the Old Irish ending, must go back to *-ŏm*. In that case *-om* (a simple adjectival form, cf. *erīlis fīlius*) will have been the original ending, which contracted with a final stem vowel *-ā-* or *-o-* to give *-ōm*; this was later extended to other stems in a number of languages.[5] The loc. pl. has the ending *-su* in the satem languages, but Greek presents *-si*;[6] for the explanation see further below, 7.6.5 n. 23. The abl.-dat. pl. and instr. pl. both have a characteristic *bh*, which was extended in various ways and was no doubt originally a postposition *bhi* (cf. Eng. *by*). In Germanic and Balto-Slavic there appears instead an ending characterized by *m*.[7]

[1] Cf. Schmitt-Brandt, 125 and Schindler, *KZ* 81, 1967, 290f., esp. 303; *BSL* 67, 1973, 31f. (**pōs*/**pedós*—rejected by Kuryłowicz, *Problèmes* 38). The nom. *-s* was in any case adopted from the pronouns (see Bopp, in Arens[2], 226; Kuryłowicz, *Categories* 211), and indeed almost universally; see 6.2.7.1 above. Cf. further Y. M. Biese, *Some Notes on the Origin of the IE Nominative Singular*, Helsinki 1950; Fillmore, in Bach and Harms (eds.), *Universals in Linguistic Theory*, 1968, 13; Villar 1983, 156f.; Martinet 1986, 186f.; Fulk 1986, 60 n. 4; Klingenschmitt, in Panagl and Krisch 1992, 105–18.

[2] See Brandenstein, *Studien zur idg. Grundsprache*, 1952, 10; Luraghi, *JIES* 15, 1988, 366–7: against *-m* as a 'particule latine' (Martinet, Brixhe), she is for *-m* as an 'animacy morpheme' (?). See also 7.6.7 n. 14 below.

[3] On the alternation, see Kuryłowicz, *Apophonie* 76, *Categories* 196 n. 15; Szemerényi, *Fs. Pisani*, 1969, 978 (Latin originally *-os*, but innovated *-is*); Beekes, *Origins* 179; and cf. Coleman, *Proc. Camb. Phil. Soc.* 1991, 8 (accepts *-es*). The attempt to establish an original distinction between gen. in *-os* and abl. in *-ots* (Benveniste, *BSL* 50, 1955, 32) has failed (see Lazzeroni, *SSL* 2, 1962, 12f.; Ivanov, *Obščeind.* 35f.), although the gen. probably arose from an abl., see Kuryłowicz, *Categories* 194, 202. An alternative view, repeatedly advanced since

van Wijk, assumes the original identity of gen. and nom., but is hardly sound; see van Velten, *BSL* 33, 1932, 218; Jespersen, *Language* 383. Nevertheless see Lehmann, *Lg* 34, 1958, 192; H. Amman, *Nachgelassene Schriften*, 1961, 56f.; Schmalstieg, *Fs. Hoenigswald*, 1987, 349–54 (sigmatic nom. from old ergative, asigmatic from old absolutive); Luraghi, *JIES* 15, 1988, 365f.; Lehmann, *Fs. Meid*, 1989, 124: van Wijk's 'identity' points to an early active structure and, according to Klimov's thesis, active languages have no genitive!

[4] The ending *-ai*, once almost universally accepted, was rejected by Beekes, *KZ* 87, 1973, 215f.; *Origins* 125, but defended by Haudry, *BSL* 70, 1975, 115f., esp. 134. On the syncretism of dat. and loc. in Mycenaean, see Panagl, *Myc. Colloquium* 7, 1983, 367–72; Hettrich, *MSS* 46, 1985, 111f.

[5] Meillet, *MSL* 22, 1922, 258 (*-om*); Stang, *Vgl. Gram.* 185 (*-ōm*). In favour of the adjectival interpretation: Petersen, *AJPh* 46, 1925, 159; Vaillant, *RES* 15, 1935, 5; Martinet, *Word* 9, 1953, 258 n. 23; Kortlandt, *Lingua* 45, 1978, 281–300 (without knowledge of the earlier writers); Jasanoff, *JIES* 11, 1983, 187; Fulk 1986, 56.

[6] The idea that the loc. is late IE, that is, not IE, because never developed in the West (Toporov, *Lokativ v slavjanskix jazykax*, 1961, 275f.), or even that it arose only in the period of the individual languages (Ambrosini, *ASNP* 29, 1960, 85), is untenable (so now also Savčenko, *LPosn* 12–13, 1968, 29f.); likewise the supposition that the loc. s. had also a zero ending: in such instances it is a matter of loss of *-i*, see Ferrell, *To Honor R. Jakobson* i, 1967, 656, and cf. Fulk 1986, 96f.

[7] K. H. Schmidt, 'Dativ und Instrumental im Plural', *Glotta* 41, 1963, 1–10. On the 'adverbial' character of these cases, see Meillet, *Introduction* 298f.; Pedersen, *Hittitisch* 30f.; Kuryłowicz, *Études* 168 f.; Categories 201; on Gr. -φι, Lejeune, *BSL* 52, 1956, 187–218; Morpurgo Davies, *Glotta* 47, 1970, 46–54. Cf. further Szemerényi, 'Methodology' 31f.; *Fachtagung* 7, 1985, 519f.; and above, 7.1.4.3 n. 5. On the syncretism in Mycenaean, see Hettrich (n. 4 above).

7.2.2.1. The ablaut alternations and the accent shifts connected with them can be better observed in the *-nt-* stems. The word for 'tooth' shows the following paradigms:

		Skt.	Gr.	Lat.	Goth.	Lith.
Sing.	Nom.	*dán*	ὀδών	*dēns*	**tunþus*	*dantìs*
	Acc.	*d-ánt-am*	ὀδόντα	*dentem*	*tunþu*	*dañtį*
	Gen.	*d-at-ás*	ὀδόντος	*dentis*	–	*dantiẽs*
	Abl.	*d-at-ás*	–	–	–	–
	Dat.	*d-at-é*	–	*dentī*	–	*dañčiui*
	Loc.	*d-at-í*	ὀδόντι	*dente*	*tunþau*	*dantyjè*
	Instr.	*d-at-ā́*	–	–	–	*dantimì*
Plur.	Nom.	*d-ánt-as*	ὀδόντες	*dentēs*	–	*dañtys*
	Acc.	*d-at-ás*	ὀδόντας	*dentēs*	*tunþuns*	*dantìs*
	Gen.	*d-at-ā́m*	ὀδόντων	*dent(i)um*	*tunþiwe*	*dantų̃*
	Abl.-Dat.	*d-ad-bhyás*	–	*dentibus*	–	*dantìms*
	Loc.	*d-at-sú*	ὀδοῦσι	–	–	*dantysè*
	Instr.	*d-ad-bhís*	–	–	–	–

In the Old Indic alternation *d-ant-/d-at-* (*d-ad-* before voiced stops) *-a-* is the zero grade of *-an-*, thus presenting the regular development of *-n̥-*, to which exactly corresponds *-un-* in Goth. *tunþus*, and probably also *-en-* in Lat. *dent-* (see 4.5.1); *-an-* is the full grade of this, corresponding to *-on-* in Gr. ὀδοντ-, *-an-* in Lith. *dant-*, also OHG *zan(d)* (whence NHG *Zahn*), OSax. *tand*, OE *tōþ* (today *tooth*, from **tanþ-*), which all continue IE *-on-*. Clearly the forms **dont-* and **dn̥t-* originally alternated within the paradigm. The distribution of the forms is well preserved in Old Indic, but in the other languages a single grade was generalized; an exception is Greek, where alongside the full grade ὀδοντ- (in which *o-* is a so-called prothetic vowel) the long-grade nominative form ὀδών was originally used, but later similarly replaced by ὀδούς from *ὀδοντ-ς;[1] on *-ōn* from *-onts*, see 6.2.7.3. The IE paradigm was therefore:

Sing. **dōn, *dónt-m̥, *dn̥t-ós, *dn̥t-éi, *dn̥t-í, *dn̥t-ḗ*
Plur. **dónt-es, *dn̥t-n̥s (*dónt-n̥s?), *dn̥t-óm (-ṓm), *dn̥t-bh-, *dn̥t-sú*[2]

This consonant stem was transformed in most languages. In Gothic, on the basis of the accusative forms *tunþu* (s.), *tunþuns* (pl.), it became a *u*-stem. In Lithuanian, on the basis of the accusatives *dañtį*, *dantìs*, it became an *i*-stem. Latin of the classical period normally has an *i*-stem, cf. *dentium*; the archaic *dentum* is found in Varro.[3]

The accent shift is likewise well preserved in Old Indic: full grade (*o*-grade) with accent on the stem, zero grade with accent shifted to the ending.[4]

[1] Cf. Szemerényi, *Syncope* 80f. The zero grade is also attested in Greek: the adverb ὀδάξ is a modification of the old locative form ὀδάσσ(ι) from **dn̥t-si*; see *Krat* 17, 1974, 88; this was already held by Joh. Schmidt, 1889, 427 n. 1

[2] On the vowel grade of the syllable preceding the ending in the acc. pl. of consonant stems, see Hock, *JAOS* 94, 1974, 73–95 (in favour of original full grade as in sing.). On the Greek loc. pl. ending *-essi*, see García-Ramón, *Glotta* 68, 1990, 133–56; Wyatt, in *Fs. Szemerényi*[2] ii, 1992, 85–95.

[3] On the etymology, see Szemerényi, *Fachtagung* 7, 1985, 530; R. Lass, *Studies Fisiak* i, 473–82 (cf. *Krat* 33, 1988, 52): no etymology, certainly not from **ed-*; Seebold, in Bammesberger 1988, 504: from **ed-* if it originally meant 'bite'; Bader, *HS* 101, 1989, 183 n. 42: *tooth* from *mordre*.

[4] On Aryan *-vant-/-mant-* stems, see K. Hoffmann, *Aufsätze* ii, 1976, 555f.

7.2.2.2. The same inflexion was originally used for participles in *-nt-*, and continued to be so used in Old Indic. Thus the participle *s-ant-* of *as-* 'to be' is inflected in the masculine as follows (cf. 9.6.1.1):

Sing. *sán, sántam, satás, saté, satí, satā́*
Plur. *sántas, satás, satā́m, sadbhyás, satsú, sadbhís*

The IE paradigm **sōn, *sónt-m̥, *sn̥t-ós*, etc., was unified in favour of the *o*-grade in Hom. ἐών ἐόντα ἐόντος ἐόντι, etc., but many dialects have directly or indirectly preserved other ablaut grades: Lat. *absens praesens* have in *-sens, -sentis* generalized the zero grade *-sn̥t-*. Behind Lat. *iens euntem euntis* etc. lies an original paradigm **yōn, *yónt-m̥, *yn̥t-ós*, which first gave Lat. **iō, *iontem, *ientis*, etc.; later the nom. **iō* was replaced by *iens*, and *euntem*, an easy modification of **iontem*, provided a model for *eunt-* in the rest of the paradigm.

7.2.2.3. The transformations undergone by the root noun **pont-* 'way' were more radical. The original paradigm was:

Sing. **pōn*, **pónt-m̥*, **pn̥t-ós*, **pn̥t-éi*, **pn̥t-í*, **pn̥t-ḗ*
Plur. **pónt-es*, **pónt-n̥s* (**pn̥t-?*), **pn̥t-óm*, **pn̥t-bh-*, **pn̥t-sú*, **pn̥t-bhí-*

In Slavic **pont-m̥* gave *pontĭ*, which looked like an acc. of an *i*-stem and thus provided the basis for the *i*-stem **ponti-* with generalized *o*-grade (Russ. *put'*, Serb. *put*, etc.); in Old Prussian, on the other hand, the generalized zero grade **pn̥t-* survived in *pintis*. The two grades gave in Greek two nouns, both enlarged to *o*-stems: *πόντος* 'sea' and *πάτος* 'way, path'. Lat. *pons*, inherited as a consonantal stem, was transferred to the *i*-stems, as were almost all stems in *-nt-*.

OInd. *panthās*, acc. *panthām*, gen. *path-as* and Avest. *pantå*, acc. *pantąm*, gen. *paθō*, etc. are transformations of the inherited **pōn*, **pontm̥*, **pn̥tos*, etc., starting with an approximation of nom. **pā* and acc. **pantam* to a unitary **pantā*, **pantām*. At the same time the forms *panthānam*, *panthānas*, Avest. *pantānəm*, *pantānō* arose on the analogy of the *n*-stems (*-ā*, *-ānam*, *-ānas*). The aspirate *th* is perhaps due to the influence of *rath-* 'travel'. The instr. pl. **padbhis*, preserved in Avest. *padəbiš*, was abandoned in OInd. because of homonymy with 'foot' and replaced by a preconsonantal stem *pathi-*.[1]

[1] For the meaning, see Benveniste, *Word* 10, 1954, 256f. On the stem alternation, see also Kuryłowicz, *Apophonie* 377; Kuiper, *IIJ* 1, 1957, 91f. The frequently assumed nom. **ponteH-s* with two full grades is impossible; see Szemerényi, *Fachtagung* 5, 1975, 334f.; laryngeal explanation, Mayrhofer, *Fs. G. Neumann*, 1982, 178; against it, Bammesberger, *Studien zur Laryngaltheorie*, 1984, 137; Fulk 1986, 74–8. For the development proposed above, Leumann's early idea (Leumann[1], 232) that Lat. *sēdēs* arose by contamination of nom. *sēs* and gen. *sēdis* is of interest.

7.3 NASAL AND LIQUID STEMS

It is remarkable that only very few stems in *-m-* and *-l-* are to be found, whereas stems in *-n-* and *-r-* occur in great numbers. In all, the nom. s. of animate (m. and f.) nouns has long grade (see 6.2.7.1); cf. Gr. *φώρ* 'thief'. In Aryan loss of the final consonant can be followed by restoration of *-s* (*kṣās*: *χθων*).[1]

[1] Cf. Rasmussen, *Haeretica Indogermanica*, Copenhagen 1974, 26; Fulk 1986, 70f., 113–20.

7.3.1

For the animate nasal stems we may compare OInd. *rājā* 'king', Gr. *ἄκμων* 'anvil', Lith. *akmuõ* 'stone', Goth. *guma* 'man', Lat. *homō*.

		Skt.	Gr.	Lith.	Goth.	Lat.
Sing.	Nom.	*rāǰā*	ἄκμων	*akmuõ*	*guma*	*homō*
	Voc.	*rāǰan*	ἄκμον	*akmeniẽ*	–	*homō*
	Acc.	*rāǰānam*	ἄκμονα	*ãkmenį*	*guman*	*hominem*
	Gen.	*rāǰñas*	ἄκμονος	*akmeñs*	*gumins*	*hominis*
	Dat.	*rāǰñē*	–	*ãkmeniui*	*gumin*	*hominī*
	Loc.	*rāǰan(i)*	ἄκμονι	*akmenyjè*	–	*homine*
	Instr.	*rāǰñā*	–	*ãkmeniu*	–	*homine*
Plur.	Nom.	*rāǰānas*	ἄκμονες	*ãkmenys*	*gumans*	*hominēs*
	Acc.	*rāǰñas*	ἄκμονας	*ãkmenis*	*gumans*	*hominēs*
	Gen.	*rāǰñām*	ἀκμόνων	*akmenų̃*	*gumane*	*hominum*
	Dat.	*rāǰabhyas*	–	*akmenìms*	*gumam*	*hominibus*
	Loc.	*rāǰasu*	ἄκμοσι	*akmenysè*	–	*hominibus*
	Instr.	*rāǰabhis*	–	*akmenimìs*	–	*hominibus*

Here too, the distribution of strong and weak cases is properly preserved only in Old Indic. In Greek uniformity was introduced by generalizing either the full grade (ἄκμονος after ἄκμονα, etc., ποιμένος after ποιμένα to ποιμήν 'shepherd') or the long grade (ἀγκών, -ῶνα, -ῶνος 'elbow'); remains of the zero grade appear in ἀρνός to ἀρήν 'lamb', κυνός beside κύων 'dog', Pindaric φρασί (from *-n̥si)* beside φρένες.[1] Similar traces of the zero grade are also found in Germanic, cf. Goth. gen. pl. *auhs-n-ē*, dat. pl. *auhsum* (from **uhs-un-miz* from *-n̥-mis*), which deviate from the general type *gumanē gumam* (*-am* from *-an-mis*), but agree very well with the early cognate OInd. *ukṣā* 'ox', the corresponding cases of which are *ukṣ-n̥-ām ukṣ-a-bhis* (from *-n̥-bh-*). In Latin the ablaut variation has been wrecked by the weakening or loss of short vowels in non-initial syllables; in Lithuanian (and Slavic) it is reduced to the alternation *-ōn/-en-*. This alternation of vowel timbre appears also in Germanic, cf. Goth. *guman gumins* from IE *-on-m̥ -en-os*, and certainly goes back to the ancestral language. Thus the following inflexion can be reconstructed for Indo-European:[2]

	Sing.	Plur.
Nom.	*-ōn*	*-en-es*
Acc.	*-en-m̥*	*-(e)n-n̥s*
Gen.	*-(e)n-os*	*-n-om, -n-ōm*
Loc.	*-en-i*	*-n̥-su*

It is possible that in Indo-European there was also *-ēn* beside *-ōn* in the nom. s.,[3] and that acc. s. *-on-m̥* and nom. pl. *-on-es* were already formed after *-ōn*. There are, moreover, indications that (in monosyllables?) a gen. s. in *-en-s -em-s* existed, with zero grade of the ending *-os* and full grade of the preceding part; cf. Avest. *xᵛəng* 'of the sun', *dəng* 'of the house', from IE **swen-s*, **dem-s*. The latter is also to be seen in **dems-potis* 'master of the house' (somewhat modified in Gr. δεσπότης).[4] On the loc. s., see above, 7.2.1 n. 6.

[1] See N. Maurice, 'Le dat.-loc. pl. des thèmes en -N-' (in Mycenaean), *Minos* 23, 1989, 117–46 ('rien des alternances héritées'); on *g^{w}en-*, above, 6.2.8, 7.1.2, and Harðarson, *ALHafn* 21, 1989, 86: PIE proterodynamic *g^{w}en-H_2*, gen. *g^{w}(n̥)n-áH_2-s*. On the transformation in Lat. *canis*, see Szemerényi, *Studi V. Pisani*, 1969, 979–84.

[2] Kuryłowicz, *Apophonie* 62f.; Szemerényi, *Numerals* 158f.; Benediktsson, 'On the inflection of the *n*-stems in Indo-European', *NTS* 22, 1968, 7–31; Euler 1979, 181f.

[3] On the Old Nordic nom. s., see Szemerényi, loc. cit.; Antonsen, in *The Nordic Languages and Modern Linguistics*, 1970, 313f. On the Germanic nom. s., see further Jasanoff, *Essays Beeler*, 1980, 375–82 (*-ē*, *-ō*, and *ō̃* < *-oHō*?).

[4] On this see Szemerényi, *Syncope* 374f. and 410; *SMEA* 20, 1980, 220f.

7.3.2

For the inanimate nasal stems the word for 'name' may be taken as an example; nom. voc. acc. are represented in each number by a single form.

		Skt.	Lat.	Goth.	OCS
Sing.	NVA	*nāma*	*nōmen*	*namō*	*imę*
	Gen.	*nāmnas*	*nōminis*	*namins*	*imene*
	Dat.	*nāmnē*	*nōminī*	–	*imeni*
	Loc.	*nām(a)ni*	*nōmine*	*namin*	*imene*
	Instr.	*nāmna*	*nōmine*	–	*imenĭmĭ*
Plur.	NVA	*nāmā(ni)*	*nōmina*	*namna*	*imena*
	Gen.	*nāmnām*	*nōminum*	*namnē*	*imenŭ*
	Dat.	*nāmabhyas*	*nōminibus*	*namnam*	*imenĭmŭ*
	Loc.	*nāmasu*	–	–	*imenĭxŭ*
	Instr.	*nāmabhis*	*nōminibus*	–	*imeny*

The ending of the nom. s. goes back to *-n̥*, which gave regularly *nāma nōmen* (and Gr. ὄνομα). In Old Church Slavic the result should have been *(im)ĭ* (see 4.5.4), but the stem form *imen-* carried through the whole paradigm[1] was introduced into the nom. also, where it naturally became *imę*. Goth. *namō* is still unexplained; it must somehow be a modification of the expected **namu* (from *-un*<*-n̥*).[2] The nom. pl. shows in most languages the continuation of IE *-ā*, e.g. Lat. *nōmina* etc. Only Aryan departs from this mode of formation, In Indic *nāmā* and *nāmāni* are both found; corresponding to these Avestan has *-ān* (e.g. *nāmąn*) and *-āni* (e.g. *afšmānī* 'verse'), perhaps also *-ā*.[3] It seems clear that *-ā* is the normal Aryan development of *-ān* (cf. 6.2.7.3), while *-āni* is the same form with supporting vowel *-i*; both must have developed from IE *-ōn* as sandhi variants, *-ā* before initial consonant, *-ān* before initial vowel in the following word.[4]

1 On the differences in the root syllable, see Szemerényi, *Syncope* 243f.
2 See Polomé, *RBPh* 45, 1968, 821; Jasanoff (above, 7.3.1 n. 3), 380. Could the ending of **namu* have been changed on the model of *watō* 'water' (IE **wodōr*, see below, 7.3.4)?
3 See Kuiper, *Shortening of Final Vowels in* the RV, 1955, 13f.; against the Avestan hapax *nąma*, see Kuiper, 15: only *-ąn* is real. On the peculiar Avestan type *nāmə̄nīš* (instr. used as nom.-acc. pl.?), see Oettinger, *Fs. Humbach*, 1986, 279–87.
4 The often adduced comparison with Goth. *hairtōna* 'heart' based on IE *-ōn-* (so also Kuiper, 16, 36), is from the structural point of view supported by OInd. *čatvāri* 'four' (nom. pl. n.); cf. 8.5.2, n. 5, and for the lengthening Skt. *(*ǰan*)*-āsi* (7.4.1). See further Kuryłowicz, *Gedenkschrift W. Brandenstein*, 1968, 86; Beekes, *IIJ* 23, 1981, 275f. According to Anttila, *Fs. Winter*, 1985, 17–24, the nom. pl. n. in *-ōn* was the source of the masculine (singular!) type ἀγών in Greek. For *-i* as sign of the plural, see also Melchert, *Hittite Historical Phonology*, 1984, 71.

7.3.3

The liquid stems–in the main, *r*-stems–have basically the same inflexion as the nasal stems (cf. Fulk 1986, 120–36):

		Skt.	Hom.	Lat.	OCS
Sing.	Nom.	*mātā*	μήτηρ	*māter*	*mati*
	Acc.	*mātaram*	μητέρα	*mātrem*	*materĭ*
	Gen.	*mātur*	μητρός	*mātris*	*matere*
	Dat.	*mātrē*	–	*mātrī*	*materi*
	Loc.	*mātari*	μητέρι	*mātre*	*materi*
	Instr.	*mātrā*	–	*mātre*	*materijǫ*
Plur.	Nom.	*mātaras*	μητέρες	*mātrēs*	*materi*
	Acc.	*mātr̥̄s*	μητέρας	*mātrēs*	*materi*
	Gen.	*mātr̥̄ṇām*	μητρῶν	*mātrum*	*materŭ*
	Dat.	*mātr̥bhyas*	–	*mātribus*	*materĭmŭ*
	Loc.	*mātr̥ṣu*	μητράσι	–	*materĭxŭ*
	Instr.	*mātr̥bhis*	–	*mātribus*	*materĭmi*

For these stems too the vowel gradation was in IE:

	Sing.	Plur.
Nom.	*-ēr*[1]	*-er-es*
Acc.	*-er-m̥*	*-r-n̥s*
Gen.	*-r-os*	*-r-om, -r-ōm*
Loc.	*-er-i*	*-r̥-su*

This distribution is, however, preserved only in Old Indic and partially in Greek; elsewhere it has been fairly extensively eliminated by equalization; cf. e.g. the stem *mater-* which is kept throughout in OCS. A remarkable case-ending, not so far satisfactorily explained, is found in the OInd. gen. s. *-ur*, which, though not to be expected from it, no doubt arose from *-r̥s*; this is suggested by Avest. *-ərəš*=*r̥š*, to which ON *-ur* from *-urs* (ON *fǫður* from **patr̥s*) also corresponds; the original formation must have been *-r-os*.[2] The acc. pl. *mātr̥̄s* contrasts with a masculine *pitr̥̄n*; both are innovations for the inherited **mātras* **pitras* (from *-n̥s*) on the model of the *i-* and *u-*stems; the old form is preserved in *usr-ás* 'the dawns', as is the original gen. s. in the identical *usr-ás* and *nár-as* 'of the man' (see 7.3.3.1). The gen. pl. *mātr̥̄ṇām pitr̥̄ṇām* was also innovated in place of **mātrām* (cf. Gr. μητρῶν) **pitrām*; the old formation is still attested in *narām* 'of the men', *svasrām* 'of the sisters'. In OCS the nom. s. **mātēr* has become *mati* with loss of final *-r* and raising of *ē* to *ī*; cf. Lith. *mótė* (now usually *móteris*) 'woman', and see 5.4.5 above. The acc. s. has *-ĭ* from *-im* from *-m̥*, pl. *-i* from *-ins* from *-n̥s*. In the dat. loc. instr. pl. the endings are attached to the stem by means of *-ĭ-*, just as, in Latin, *patribus* shows an *i* before *-bus*; both languages have taken over the *i* from the *i*-stems.

[1] The suggestion of Stiles, *NOWELE* 3, 1984, 3–48, that Older Runic *swestar* cannot with *-ar* reflect an IE nom. *-ēr*, but only a voc. *-ĕr*, is important; the same applies to *brōþar*, see Stiles, *TPS* 86, 1988, 118–43. According to Hamp, *HS* 103, 1991, 102f., the IE nom. s. was **bhrātē*.

[2] See Bammesberger, *JIES* 11, 1983, 105f., but better perhaps is Hollifield, *Sprache* 30, 1984, 39f.: from Proto-Nordic **faðurir*, earlier **faðariz* (*o*-grade?) with raising of *a* to *u* before *i*. Note also Prosdocimi and Marinetti, 'Sulla terza plurale del perfetto latino e indiano antico' (*AGI* 73, 1988, 93–125), 99–101: *-tr̥s* from *-tros*; and Prosdocimi, *AGI* 74, 1989, 160f. For *r*-stems, see also Euler 1979, 198f.

7.3.3.1 Among animate *r*-stems **ner-* 'man' deserves special attention. In Greek it appears with prothetic vowel as ἀνερ-. In Greek, moreover, the vowel gradation is at first fairly well preserved. Homeric ἀνήρ ἀνέρα ἀνδρός ἀνδρί, ἄνερες ἄνδρας ἀνδρῶν ἀνδράσι continues the regular paradigm **nēr* **nér-m̥* **n̥r-ós* **n̥r-í*, **nér-es* **n̥r-n̥s* **n̥r-om* **nr̥-sú*, from which comes Vedic *naram* (acc. s.), *naras* (gen. s.), *narē* (dat. s.), *naras* (nom. pl.), *narām* (gen. pl.). The Greek consonant group -νδρ- rests on a phonetic development of *nr* to *ndr* which has parallels elsewhere (e.g. Flemish *Hendrik* from Henrik), and *ανρ- in place of *αρ- restores the characteristic nasal as in the case of Indic *nar-*. The stem **ner-* also survives in Italy: Oscan has the nom. s. *niir* 'princeps' from **nēr* and gen. pl. *nerum*, while Umbrian has dat. pl. *nerus* 'principibus' and acc. pl. *nerf*; the name *Nero* is a dialect word ('the manly one') formed from the same stem.

7.3.3.2 An archaic neuter is preserved in Hom. κῆρ. It continues IE **kēr*, which was assimilated from **kerd* and then lengthened (6.2.7.5); it is also found in Hitt. *kēr*, written ŠÀ-*ir* and *kir*. The expected forms of gen. and dat., **kr̥d-ós* **kr̥d-í*, were supplanted by Hom. (κῆρος) κῆρι, but survive with changed initial consonant (see 5.4.3) in Skt. *hr̥d-ás hr̥d-í*.[1] In the nom. s. Skt. **hā* (from **hār*) would be expected, but since in this form it would have been well-nigh unrecognizable, the final *-r* and even the stem ending *-d* were restored; **hārd* required a vowel according to the Old Indic rules for final position (see 5.4.5 above) and *hārdi* thus arose. IE **kēr* is also preserved in OPrus. *sīr(an) seyr*, and the acute accent on the long syllable still survives in the acute intonation of Lith. *širdìs šìrdi*.[2] Lat. *cor cordis* must show *o*-grade, cf. the contrary case of *pēs*: *πώς*. In a number of languages the old root noun has been supplanted by a derivative; cf. *καρδία* (from **kr̥d-iyā*), OIr. *cride* (from **kr̥d-iyom*), OCS *srŭdĭce* (from **kr̥d-iko-*), and with a nasal enlargement Goth. *hairtō*, gen. *hairtins*, OHG *herza, herzin*.[1]

[1] See Szemerényi 1970; *Fachtagung* 5, 1975, 335f.; *Studies A. A. Hill* iii, 1979, 270f.; differently Beekes, *Fs. Hoenigswald*, 1987, 51f.

[2] Cf. Szemerényi, *KZ* 75, 1958, 179 n. 1; *SMEA* 3, 1967, 66 n. 74; Stang, *Vgl. Gram.* 158 (unclear on *-d*).

7.3.4

A combination of *r*- and *n*-stems is found in a group of so-called *heteroclite* nouns; the *r*-stem appears only in the nom.-acc. of the singular. Here belong Lat. *femur feminis* 'thigh' and *iecur iocineris* 'liver' (unified from earlier *iecor *iecinis* with metathesis of *iecinoris* to *iocineris*), Skt. *yakr̥t yaknas* 'liver'.[1] To the last corresponds Gr. *ἦπαρ ἥπατος*, so that *-ατος* in the genitive must go back to *-n̥tos*. The same formation is found in Gr. *ὕδωρ ὕδατος* 'water' (cf. Hamp, *HS* 103, 1991) and the corresponding Umbrian nom. *utur*, loc. *une* from *ud-n-i*, Goth. nom. *watō* from **wodōr*, gen. *watins* from **woden(o)s* (cf. OSax. *watar*, OHG *wazzar*). Hittite has well preserved *wadar*, gen. *wedenas*, and has moreover developed the type extensively (see Starke 1990, 433f.), whereas in the other languages it survives only in a few pitiful remnants.[2]

The enlargement of the stem by *-t-* (*-n̥-t-os*), which comes to light in *ἥπατος ὕδατος* etc., is found also in other groups in Greek. The pure *n*-stem of Lat. *nōmen nōminis*, for example, is in Greek transformed into the *t*-stem *ὄνομα ὀνόματος* (from *-mn̥-tos*); this is certainly a Greek innovation.[3]

[1] On Lat. *iecur*, see Szemerényi, *KZ* 73, 1956, 191; *Fachtagung* 5, 1975, 332f. Against IE *ē* in Gr. *ἧπαρ*, see also Beekes, in Bammesberger 1988, 84, and *Wackernagel Kolloquium*, 1990, 41. A different view on the nom. in Schindler, *BSL* 70, 1975, 6; Strunk, *Fachtagung* 7, 1985, 491f., 507f.; Beekes, *Origins* 4f.

[2] The origin of the heteroclite paradigm seems fairly clear in the case of 'water'. The nom.-acc. **wedōr* is a binomial formation from *wed* 'water' and *ōr* 'river, water', while the loc. **uden* represents the syntagm *ud* 'water'+*en* 'in'; see Szemerényi, *PICL* 7, 1956, 524; *CTL* ix, 159; *Richtungen* ii, 125 n. For the whole class see also Pedersen, '*r-n*-Stämme', *KZ* 32, 1893, 240–72 (261f. on the origin); Thurneysen, *IF* 39, 1921, 192–4; H. Petersson 1921, 1922; Schindler, 'L'apophonie des thèmes ie. en *-r/n*', *BSL* 70, 1975, 1–10; Euler 1979, 243f.; Shields, 'The origin of the *-r-/-n-* stems', *JIES* 7, 1979, 213–26; Haudry, *BSL* 75, 1980, 164f.; *Préhistoire* 52f.; Lehmann, in *For G. H. Fairbanks*, Honolulu 1985, 73–4 (?);

Markey, *JIES* 12, 1985, 268f. (270: *-r* grammatical, *-n* concrete); Martinet 1986, 170f.; *BSL* 86, 1992, 361: *-n/-nt>-r/-n* (?).

[3] On these secondary *t*-stems, see the London thesis of my pupil Jennifer Forster, 'The history of *t*-stems in Greek', 1967; Oettinger, *Fs. G. Neumann*, 1982, 233f. Lindeman, *BSL* 81, 1986, 371, suggests that *wodr̥/uden-* was replaced by an animate *ud(e)n-t-s*, where *ud(e)nt-* simply became a variant of **ud-r̥*.

7.4. *S*-STEMS

7.4.1

The inflexion of *s*-stems, for the most part neuter, is well preserved in a number of languages. Cf. **genos* 'kind, family', **nebhos* 'cloud':

		Skt.	Hom.	Lat.	OCS
Sing.	NVA	*janas*	γένος	*genus*	*nebo* 'sky'
	Gen.	*janas-as*	γένεος	*generis*	*nebese*
	Dat.	*janas-ē*	–	*generī*	*nebesi*
	Loc.	*janas-i*	γένεϊ	*genere*	*nebese*
	Instr.	*janas-ā*	–	*genere*	*nebesĭmĭ*
Plur.	NVA	*janāṁsi*	γένεα	*genera*	*nebesa*
	Gen.	*janas-ām*	γενέων	*generum*	*nebesŭ*
	Dat.	*jano-bhyas*	–	*generibus*	*nebesĭmŭ*
	Loc.	*janas-su*	γένεσσι	–	*nebesĭxŭ*
	Instr.	*jano-bhis*	–	*generibus*	*nebesy*

Reconstruction gives:

	Sing.	Plur.
NVA	**genos*, **nebhos*	**genes-ā*, **nebhes-ā*
Gen.	**genes-os*, **nebhes-os*	**genes-om*, **nebhes-om*
Loc.	**genes-i*, **nebhes-i*	**genes-su*, **nebhes-su*

The difference in qualitative ablaut between nom.-acc. s. and all other cases is especially clear in Greek and Old Church Slavic, but is also unmistakable in Latin.[1] In Gothic, *-es-* has been analogically extended to the nom.-acc.: *riqiz*, gen. *riqizis* 'darkness';[2] so also in Hittite.

In the nom. pl. IE **genes-ā* above fits only the Gr., Lat., and OCS forms, but not the OInd. To explain OInd. *janāṁsi* the nasalization must first be removed, since it represents an innovation on the analogy of the *-nt-* stems;[3] the remaining **(jan)-āsi* is comparable to the ending *-ās* which survives in Avestan. The relationship of these endings is the same as between OInd. *-āni*, Avest. *-ān* in the *n*-stems (see 7.3.2), i.e. the ending was *-ās*, probably from *-ōs*.[4]

[1] Schindler, *Fachtagung* 5, 1975, 259–67, esp. 266, thinks that *-os* in the nom.-acc. is a late

innovation; originally there was only *-s*, as can still be seen in Aryan *mans dhā-* (later *manas-*) and *yauš dhā-*; further examples in Meier-Brügger, *HS* 102, 1989, 58–61. On the *o*-grade, see Kuryłowicz, *Apophonie* 67f.; Hamp, 'On the *-o-* in *tempus*, *-oris*', *FoLH* 8, 1989, 507. On *yauš*, see Szemerényi (above, 7.1.4.4 n. 2).

[2] But the class as a whole has been absorbed into the *a*-stems: Schenker, *PBB(T)* 93, 1971, 46–58; see also Unwerth, *PBB* 36, 1910, 1–42.

[3] See Wackernagel and Debrunner, *Ai. Gr.* iii, 288; Hoffmann, *Aufsätze* ii, 1976, 556; G. Schmidt, *Fs. W. Thomas*, 1988, 65.

[4] See Kuiper (above, 7.3.2 n. 3). On the whole class, see further Euler 1979, 208f.; Fulk 1986, 151f., 159f.; on the Greek neuters, Ruijgh, *Myc. Colloquium* 7, 1983, 391–407; on Latin and Greek abstracts in *-es/-os*, see R. Höfer (1984), quoted by Meier-Brügger (n. 1 above), 58 n. 1.

7.4.2

Alongside the neuters there is a smaller group of animate *s*-stems in *-ōs*, e.g. Gr. *αἰδώς*, *αὔως ἠώς ἕως*, Lat. *honōs, flōs*. Their inflexion is identical with that of the neuters except that as animate nouns they have a formal distinction between nom. and acc. (also voc.). The long grade of the nom. s. arose from *-os-s* (see 6.2.7.1). In Greek, in contrast to the neuter, the *o*-grade is carried through, e.g. acc. s. *αἰδῶ* from *-os-m̥*, gen. s. *αἰδοῦς* from *-os-os*, dat. s. *αἰδοῖ* from *-os-i*; only occasionally in isolated forms is the *e*-grade still found.[1] In Latin in general not only the *o*-grade but also the lengthening of the nominative is carried through; the single exception is *arbōs* (Virgil, *Georgics*, ii. 66), *arbŏris*. To this is added the early intrusion into the nom. s. of the *r* developed from intervocalic *s*, so that *honōs honōrem* was replaced by *honōr honōrem*. Furthermore from Plautus on *-ōr* was increasingly shortened to *-ŏr*, and this led to a relationship *-ŏr -ōrem* which was the reverse of the IE situation.[2]

[1] e.g. *αἰεί*, see Hoenigswald, in *In Memory of W. Cowgill*, 1987, 51f.; *ICHL* 7, 1987, 283; Hamp, *Glotta* 67, 1989, 41.

[2] On the comparatives in *-yōs* and the perfect active participles, see Szemerényi, 'The Mycenaean and historical Greek comparative', *Studia Mycenaea*, Brno 1968, 25–36; 'The perfect participle active in Mycenaean and IE', *SMEA* 2, 1967, 7–26; and below 7.8.4, 9.6.1.2.

7.5. *i*- AND *u*-STEMS, DIPHTHONG STEMS

The *i* and *u*-stems are inflected, especially in Old Indic, according to two models, which can be distinguished as the main and subsidiary type[1] or as closed and open inflexion.[2]

[1] Wackernagel and Debrunner, *Ai. Gr.* iii, 138.

[2] Kuryłowicz, *Études* 137f.; *Apophonie* 132; *Categories* 220; *Problèmes* 111. On both stem classes, see further Beekes, *Glotta* 51, 1973, 228–45; *Origins* 78f., 85, 92; Euler 1979, 130f., 143f.; Fulk 1986, 78f.; Klingenschmitt, in Panagl and Krisch 1992, 113–27.

7.5.1

The main type can be illustrated by OInd. *agnis* 'fire'=Lat. *ignis*, Gr. πόλις, OCS *gostĭ* 'guest', Goth. *qēns* 'woman', and OInd. *bāhus* 'arm'=Gr. πῆχυς, Lat. *manus*, Goth. *sunus* 'son' ~ OCS *synŭ*.

(*a*)		Skt.	Gr.	Lat.	Goth.	OCS
Sing.	Nom.	*agnis*[1]	πόλις	*ignis*[1]	*qēns*	*gostĭ*
	Voc.	*agnē*	πόλι	–	–	*gosti*
	Acc.	*agnim*	πόλιν	*ignem*	*qēn*	*gostĭ*
	Gen.	*agnēs*	πόλεως	*ignis*	*qēnais*	*gosti*
	Dat.	*agnayē*	πόλει	*ignī*	–	*gosti*
	Loc.	*agnā(u)*	πόληι	–	*qēnai*	*gosti*
	Instr.	(*agninā*)	–	–	–	*gostĭmĭ*
Plur.	Nom.	*agnayas*	τρεῖς	*ignēs*	*qēneis*	*gostĭje*
	Acc.	*agnīn*	τρίνς	*ignīs*	*qēnins*	*gosti*
	Gen.	*agnīnām*	τριῶν	*ignium*	*qēnē*	*gostĭjĭ*
	Dat.	*agnibhyas*	–	*ignibus*	*qēnim*	*gostĭmŭ*
	Loc.	*agniṣu*	τρισί	–	–	*gostĭxŭ*
	Instr.	*agnibhis*	–	*ignibus*	–	*gostĭmi*

(*b*)						
Sing.	Nom.	*bāhus*	πῆχυς	*manus*	*sunus*	*synŭ*
	Voc.	*bāhō*	πῆχυ	–	*sunau*	*synu*
	Acc.	*bāhum*	πῆχυν	*manum*	*sunu*	*synŭ*
	Gen.	*bāhōs*	πήχεος	*manūs*	*sunaus*	*synu*
	Dat.	*bāhavē*	πήχει	*manuī*	–	*synovi*
	Loc.	*bāhā(u)*	–	–	*sunau*	*synu*
	Instr.	(*bāhunā*)	–	–	–	*synŭmĭ*
Plur.	Nom.	*bāhavas*	πήχεες	*manūs*	*sunjus*	*synove*
	Acc.	*bāhūn*	πήχεας	*manūs*	*sununs*	*syny*
	Gen.	*bāhūnām*	πήχεων	*manuum*	*suniwē*	*synovŭ*
	Dat.	*bahubhyas*	–	*manibus*	*sunum*	*synŭmŭ*
	Loc.	*bāhuṣu*	πήχεσι	–	–	*synŭxŭ*
	Instr.	*bāhubhis*	–	*manibus*	–	*synŭmi*

These paradigms show a large measure of agreement in the main type of *i*- and *u*-stems. In nom. and acc. s. the stem vowel *i* or *u* appears with the case endings *s* and *m* respectively: *-is -im*, *-us -um*.[2] In Latin *-im* became *-em* either phonetically or by analogy with the consonant stems; in OCS it became *-ĭ*, as *-um* became *-ŭ*; in Gothic *-im* disappeared, *-um* became *-u*. The voc. ends in *-ei -ou*, the latter being especially clear in Goth. *sunau*, Lith. *sūnau*, while *-ei* is preserved in Ποσει(-δάον) 'O lord'=OInd. *patē*; the simple *-i -u* in Greek and to some extent in Gothic have followed the nom.[3] The gen. s. shows a diphthong *-eis* or *-ois* (on πόλεως see 7.5.3, on *ignis* see below) and *-ous* (on πήχεος see 7.5.3).

The dat. s. ended, on the evidence of Old Indic, in *-eyei*, i.e. the ending *-ei* added to the full grade of the stem vowel *i*, or in the case of the *u*-stems *-owei* (required by OCS) or *-ewei* (Greek), which has the same structure as *-eyei*. Latin, OCS (and Lith.) require *-ei* in *i*-stems, which presumably arose from *-eyei* (=double *-ei*) by haplology; in the *u*-stems *-owei* developed regularly in Latin to *-uwī*, *-uī*. The loc. s., as shown by Old Indic, had a long diphthong or long vowel. In the *i*-stems the ending is determined by the Greek evidence as *-ē*, which can be reconciled with the stem vowel *i* only on the assumption that it goes back to *-ēi*; Gothic also agrees with *-ēi*. For the *u*-stems OCS (with Lith.) and West Germanic (OE and OSax.) agree on *-ōu*, which may also underlie Goth. *-au*, although this, together with Proto-Nordic *-iu*, could go back to *-ēu*.[4]

The nom. pl. ended in (*a*) *-ey-es* and (*b*) *-ew-es* or (*c*) *-ow-es*. From (*a*) after the loss of intervocalic *y* arose Lat. *-ēs*, which displaced the inherited ending *-ĕs* in the consonant stems, and Greek *-ēs*, written -εις in Att.-Ion.; *-eyes* gave Goth. *-ijis*>*-īs* (written *-eis*), while OCS *-ĭje* from *-iyes* received *-i-* on the analogy of the other plural cases. In the *u*-stems Greek and Gothic (*-jus* from *-iwis* from *-ewes*) point to (*b*), whereas (*c*) is required by OCS and perhaps by one Lithuanian dialect[5] and OE. The acc. pl. had the structurally clear endings *-i-ns* *-u-ns*. The gen. pl. ended in *-i(y)om*, *-ōm* and *-u-(w)om*, *-ōm*; the latter was reshaped to *-ew-om*, *-ōm* or *-ow-om*, *-ōm*. The remaining plural cases added the usual endings to the stems in *-i* and *-u*.[6]

On the basis of these observations the following paradigms can be established for Indo-European:[7]

	Sing.		Plur.	
Nom.	*-is*	*-us*	*-eyes*	*-owes/-ewes*
Voc.	*-ei*	*-ou*	*-eyes*	*-owes/-ewes*
Acc.	*-im*	*-um*	*-ins*	*-uns*
Gen.	*-eis/-ois*	*-ous/-eus*	*-iyom*	*-uwom*
Dat.	*-eyei*	*-owei/-ewei*	*-i-bh-*	*-u-bh-*
Loc.	*-ēi*	*-ōu/-ēu*	*-isu*	*-usu*

1 The original form of 'fire' was **n̥gni-*; see Szemerényi 1978, 30f. The same analysis was later made by Kortlandt; see Beekes, *Origins* 3.

2 In the neuter, of course, nom.-acc. had no ending, e.g. Lat. *mare*<**mari-*. Cf. also Beekes, 'IE neuters in *-i*', *Fs. Hoenigswald*, 1987, 45–56.

3 Kuryłowicz, *Categories* 198f.: *-ei -ou* were innovated from *-i -u*; cf. further Watkins, *Trivium* 1, 1966, 113f.; Winter, 'Vocative' 210f. A different view on Gothic in Ebbinghaus, *GL* 11, 1971, 100f.

4 See 6.2.7.7. But Antonsen, *Diachronica* 6/2, 1989, 288, would prefer *-ew-i/-ow-i*. For the

instr. in *-ī -ū*, Kretschmer, *KZ* 31, 1891, 381f., had already assumed contraction from *-i+e*, *-u+e*.

[5] Stang, *Vgl. Gram.* 216; Kazlauskas, *Lietuvių kalbos istorinė gramatika*, 1968, 224; Mažiulis, *Baltų ir kitų ie. kalbų santykiai*, 1970, 297f. Less probable is Bammesberger, *Anglia* 103, 1985, 365–70.

[6] For *-ī -ū* of the n. pl. Kretschmer (n. 1 above), again assumed contraction of *-i+a*, *-u+a*; see Szemerényi 1985, 20. Watkins, *Gedenkschrift Kronasser*, 1982, 255f., starts for the n. pl. from *-iH -uH*, which he claims still appear as *-ī -ū* in Old Hittite, but according to Lindeman, *Sprache* 29, 1983, 41f., the OHitt. spelling *a-as-su-u* denotes not *-ū* but the accent. For *-ī -ū* in the dual Kretschmer, loc. cit., supposes contraction as for the instr. s.; Risch, *Fachtagung* 5, 1975, 253 n. 15, posits a (first) laryngeal as the ending.

[7] The explanation of the Greek type *polis polēos* as a continuation of a hysterodynamic type *-ēis/-yos* (Beekes, *Glotta* 51, 1973, 241–5) is unconvincing, especially in the case of a word for which the evidence of other languages (Lith., OInd.) guarantees only *pol-*. The correct explanation is given below, 7.5.3 fin.

7.5.2

The subsidiary type[1] differs in that the stem vowel *i* or *u* shows no ablaut variation but remains unchanged before the endings, becoming of course *y* or *w* before vowels. This type is best preserved in Old Indic, but remnants of it are found in Avestan, Greek, and even Germanic.

Vedic has this type of inflexion in four *i*-stems (*ari-* 'stranger',[2] *avi-* 'sheep, *pati-* 'husband', *sakhi-* 'friend') and seven *u*-stems (e.g. *kratu-* 'understanding', *madhu-* 'honey', *pašu-* 'cattle'):

	Sing.	Plur.
Nom.	*aris, kratus*	*aryas*
Voc.	*arē*[2]	
Acc.	*arim, kratum*	*aryas, pašvas*, Avest. *pasvō*
Gen.	*aryas, avyas, kratvas, pašvas*	Avest. *pasvąm*
Dat.	*patyē, kratvē, pašvē*	
Loc.	*kratau*	
Instr.	*patyā, kratvā, madhvā, pašvā*	*kratubhis*

This type is to be seen in Gr. ὄ(ϝ)ις 'sheep'. gen. s. οἰός, nom. pl. οἶες, gen. pl. οἰῶν, from **owis* **owyos* **owyes* **owyōm*. To this can be added Hom. γόνυ 'knee', γουνός γοῦνα γούνων, and δόρυ 'spear', δουρός δουρί δοῦρα δούρων, from **gonu* **gonwos* **gonwa* **gonwōm*, etc. Lat. *ouis* must have had the same inflexion, e.g. gen. s. *ouis* from **owyos* (like nom. s. *alis* from **alyos* beside the usual *alius*); this will also have contributed to the spread of the gen. ending *-is* in the *i*-stems. In Germanic, 'chin' and 'man' owe their form to this inflexion. The former is *kinnus* in Gothic, in which *-nn-* comes from *-nw-* in gen. s. **kenwos*, dat. s. **kenwei*, etc., from IE **genus* **genw-os* (cf. γένυς); the latter is similarly modified from **manus* **manw-os*; cf. Goth. gen. s. *mans*, dat. s. *mann*, nom. pl. *mans*.[3]

1 Wackernagel and Debrunner, *Ai. Gr.* iii, 138; Hock, *JAOS* 94, 1974, 89f.
2 Thieme, *Der Fremdling im Rgveda*, 1938; Szemerényi 1978, 125f.
3 On **doru*, **gonu*, and **owis* see Kuryłowicz, *Apophonie* 58, 336; *IG* 287; *Problèmes* 170f.; Nagy 1970, 153–66; Hamp, *Glotta* 48, 1970, 72–5; Lindeman, *NTS* 26, 1972, 217–31; Hock (n. 1 above), 90; Schindler, *BSL* 70, 1975, 7; Bailey, in Lüdtke 1980, 180; Oettinger, *Fs. Neumann*, 1982, 240 (CLuw. *darw-an-assi*).

7·5·3

In reconstructing the *prehistory* of these two kinds of declension it must first be stated that today, under the influence of the alternations *ei/i eu/u*, it is generally assumed that the suffix was *-ei- -eu-* or *-tei- -teu-*, etc.[1] Since, however, *i* and *u* are now again recognized as full members of the IE vowel system in their own right, there are no grounds for supposing that the stem in the subsidiary type **owi-s* **owy-os* had once had the form **owei-*; the word must always have been **owis*, as also 'cattle' **peku(s)*, not **pekeus*. It must even be asked whether the main types *-is/-eis, -us/-ous* did not also have *-i-* and *-u-* as basic vowels, so that *-ei-* and *-ou-* are of secondary origin.

At this point it is important to observe that in the subsidiary type the nominative *-is/-us* is always preceded by a single consonant, whereas in the main type it is preceded by at least two consonants (e.g. *ignis*), or had at one time been so preceded (e.g. OInd. *mati-* 'thought' from **mn̥-ti* from **men-ti*), or it is preceded by a heavy syllable with a long vowel (e.g. **bhāghus* 'arm'). For this suggests that the difference *-yos/-eis, -wos/-ous* is connected with these facts.

If we think this through, we obtain the following two original types:

		I		II	
Sing.	Nom.	**pot-i-s*	**kret-u-s*	**men-ti-s*	**bhāgh-u-s*
	Acc.	**pot-i-m*	**kret-u-m*	**men-ti-m*	**bhāgh-u-m*
	Gen.	**pot-i-os*	**kret-u-os*	**men-ti-os*	**bhāgh-u-os*
	Dat.	**pot-i-ei*	**kret-u-ei*	**men-ti-ei*	**bhāgh-u-ei*
Plur.	Nom.	**pot-i-es*	**kret-u-es*	**men-ti-es*	**bhāgh-u-es*
	Acc.	**pot-i-ns*	**kret-u-ns*	**men-ti-ns*	**bhāgh-u-ns*
	Gen.	**pot-i-om*	**kret-u-om*	**men-ti-om*	**bhāgh-u-om*

From I arose, of course, with the simple change of *-i-os* to *-y-os*, etc., the subsidiary types of the early historical period. The early IE syllabic structure did not, however, permit the corresponding change in II: **men-ti-os* could not become **mentyos* but only **mentiyos*, and **bhāgh-u-os* could only become **bhāghuwos*. Since the forms corresponding to these in the historical period are **mn̥teis* and **bhāghous*, we must conclude that **mentíyos* became **mentéyos* and after the zero-grade law came into effect **m(e)ntéy(o)s*, i.e. **mn̥téis*, and **bhāghuwos* similarly became **bhāghow(o)s*, i.e. **bhāghous*.[2]

This theory also explains why *ei* appears in *i*-stems and *ou* in *u*-stems. At first a 'phonetic' justification accounted for gen. *-eis/-ous*, dat. *-eyei/-owei*, nom. pl. *-eyes/-owes*. The parallelism of the structurally related paradigms led, however, to analogical equalizations, so that *-eis/-eus* and *-ous/-ois*, *-eyei/-ewei*, *-eyes/-ewes* also made their appearance.

In the loc. s., *-ey-i* and *-ow-i* led to *-ēi* and *-ōu* (see 6.2.7.7), later also to *-ēi/-ēu*. The Greek gen. ending (πήχ)εος is from -ευς reshaped after -ος; (πόλ)εως is from (πόλ)ηος, modified from (πόλ)εος on the analogy of loc. πόλη-ι; see 7.5.1 n. 7.

[1] See Meillet, *Introduction*[8] 253, 261, 273–4; Fulk 1986, 82f.

[2] Cf. **tū* 'thou': **tu-o-*>**towos* 'thy', **sū-*>**sowos* 'his, etc.', **nū*>**nowos* 'new'>**newos* (?). Somewhat differently Kiparsky, *Lg* 49, 1973, 817f.

ADDENDUM. The Greek type in -ευς (e.g. βασιλεύς 'king') is an early Greek innovation from IE material and neither an inherited IE type nor a borrowing from the Mediterranean area; cf. Szemerényi, *Gedenkschrift Kretschmer* ii, 1957, 159f.; *Atti e memorie del 1° Congresso di Micenologia*, 1968, 720f.; *SMEA* 6, 1968, 7–13; *Krat* 18, 1974, 43–53 (on Perpillou). Differing recent treatments include Schindler, *Studies Palmer*, 1976, 349–52; Leukart, *Myc. Colloquium* 7, 1983, 234f.; Beekes, *Origins* 94f.; Rasmussen 1989, 273f.: starts from Schindler's laryngeal variant **ekwe-H*₁ *u-s*, gen. **ekwe-H*₁ *w-os*. Bader, in *Fs. Szemerényi*[2] iii, 1993, 47 n. 54 (substantivized from *-u-*?). On the Arcado-Cypriot innovated type with nom. *-ēs*, see Masson, *BSL* 73, 1978, 287–91 (and Perpillou, ibid. 293–9); *Kadmos* 19, 1980, 75. Risch, *Myc. Colloquium* 8, Skopje 1987, 281–98, thinks that the type *-eus/-ēn*, formed on the model of Ζεύς/Ζῆν, had already led in Mycenaean to a nom. *-ēs*, seen in many names in *-e*=*-ēs*.

7.5.4

Special circumstances led to a peculiar declension for **reh-i-* 'possession, thing' and **nah-u-* 'what floats, ship'. They followed the subsidiary type, so that the forms were:

	Sing.		Plur.	
Nom.	**reh-i-s*	**nah-u-s*	**reh-y-es*	**nah-w-es*
Acc.	**reh-i-m*	**nah-u-m*	**reh-i-ns*	**nah-u-ns*
Gen.	**reh-y-os*	**nah-w-os*	**reh-y-om*	**nah-w-om*
Dat.	**reh-y-ei*	**nah-w-ei*	**reh-ibh(y)os*	**nah-u-bh(y)os*

In Vedic the paradigms *rayis rāyas* and *naus nāvas* are still found; they arose regularly by loss of the *h* (before consonants with lengthening of the preceding vowel). The second noun also has a correspondence in Hom. *νηῦς νη(ϝ)ός*, Att. *ναῦς νεώς*, which in Latin became an *i*-stem.[1] IE **rehis *rehyos* led to Lat. *rēs*.[2]

[1] Szemerényi, 'Latin *rēs* and the IE long-diphthong stem nouns', *KZ* 73, 1956, 185f.; Fulk 1986, 96.

[2] Szemerényi, op. cit., 167f.; see also Schindler, *Sprache* 19, 1973, 148f. (against Georgiev, cf. *BalkE* 17/2, 1974, 5–8); Schmalstieg, *KZ* 87, 1973, 111–13, and in Vennemann 1989, 68f.; Beekes, *Origins* 80, 83; Fulk 1986, 90.

7·5·5

True diphthong stems are the important words **dyeu-* 'daylight, sky, sky god' and **gʷou-* 'ox, cow'. The complicated inflexion can be restored from a simple comparison of the paradigms:

(*a*)	Skt.	Gr.	Lat.
Nom.	*dyaus*	*Ζεύς*	*diūs*[1]
Voc.	(*dyaus*)	*Ζεῦ*	*Iū(piter)*
Acc.	*dyām*	*Ζῆν*	*diem*
Gen.	*divas*	*Δι(ϝ)ός*	*Iouis*
Dat.	*divē*	*Δι(ϝ)εί-φιλος*	*Iouī*
Loc.	*diví/dyávi*	*Δι(ϝ)ί*	*Ioue*
Instr.	*divā*		*Ioue*

In the nom. s. OInd. *dyaus* points to a long-grade IE *dyēus*, while the voc. had full grade; **dyeu* gave *Ζεῦ* and Lat. *Iū-* (*dy->y* and *eu>ou*), which was always combined with *pater* (cf. *Ζεῦ πάτερ*) to give *Iūpiter* (and with expressive lengthening *Iuppiter*).[2] The acc. is in the highest degree peculiar: *dyām=Ζῆν=diem* (shortened from *diēm*) leads to IE **dyēm/*diyēm* (see 5.7.2.2). The weak cases are formed from the zero grade of **dyeu*, i.e. **diw-*: gen. **diw-os*, dat. **diw-ei*. In the loc. both full grade and zero grade of the stem occur: Skt. *dyav-i* and *div-i*. The full grade gave Lat. *Ioue* (from **dyewi*), *Iouī* (from **dyew-ei*), on the pattern of which *Iouem* and *Iouis* were also formed, while the acc. *diēm* generated on the one hand a nom. *diēs* and *Diēs-piter*, on the other the oblique cases *diēī diē*, etc. As a result, the originally single word was split into two paradigms.

The view that the nom. s. was formed with long grade and final *-s*, i.e. as **dyēus*, while the acc., originally **dyeum*, was lengthened to **dyēum* on the analogy of the nom., with subsequent loss of the second element of the long diphthong, contradicts the structural principles of the IE inflexion.[3] The original forms must rather have been **dyeus *dyeum*;[4] the acc. then became **dyēm* by absorption of *u* and compensatory lengthening,[5] and the long vowel was in Aryan carried over into the nom. also.[6]

[1] In the expression *nu-diūs tertius* 'now (is) the third day=the day before yesterday'.

Somewhat differently, Watkins, *Celtica* 6, 1962, 17f.: 'and (*nu*=Hitt. connective *nu*) it is the third day'.
[2] On 'sky father', see Strunk, *Fs. Neumann*, 1982, 427–38.
[3] The view is still found in Lindeman, *NTS* 21, 1967, 133f.; Lane, *KZ* 81, 1968, 200f.
[4] Szemerényi, *KZ* 73, 1956, 186f.; accepted by Stang, *Symbolae Kuryłowicz*, 1965, 292f., and by Kuryłowicz himself, *IG* 220. Note also Dunkel, *Sprache* 34, 1992, 2. As to an alleged Lex Stang, see Strunk, *HS* 101, 1989, 308f.
[5] Schindler's *dyeum*>*dyemm* (*Sprache* 19, 1973, 154) is phonetically incredible.
[6] A nom. _*dyēu_, which then with the addition of *-s* became _*dyēus_, is wholly without foundation. Beekes's treatment, *Origins* 83f., and 1990, 42, is quite unsatisfactory. Cf. also Fulk 1986, 94f. For a loc. _*diw-en_ see Haudry, *LALIES* 5, 1987, 31–46.

(*b*)		Skt.	Gr.	Lat.	Umbr.
Sing.	Nom.	*gaus*	βοῦς	*bōs*	–
	Acc.	*gām*	βῶν (Dor.)	*bouem*	*bum*
	Gen.	*gōs*	βο(ϝ)ός	*bouis*	–
	Dat.	*gávē*	–	*bouī*	–
	Loc.	*gávi*	βο(ϝ)ί	*boue*	–
	Instr.	*gávā*	–	*boue*	*bue*
Plur.	Nom.	*gāvas*	βό(ϝ)ες	*bouēs*	–
	Acc.	*gās*	βῶς (Dor.)	*bouēs*	*buf*
	Gen.	*gávām*	βοῶν	*boum*	*buo*
	Loc.	*góṣu*	βουσί	–	–

The agreement of OInd. *gām*=βῶν=Umbr. *bum*, *gās*=βῶς=*buf* (for the initial consonant, see 4.7.5.2) again guarantees _*g^{w}ōm_ and _*g^{w}ō(n)s_ as the acc. s. and pl., similarly formed from _*g^{w}oum_ and _*g^{w}ouns_ (see n. 4 above); the nom. s. _*g^{w}ous_ was correspondingly modified, at least in Aryan, to _*g^{w}ōus_. The gen. is _*g^{w}owos_ where nom. _*g^{w}ous_ is kept, but _*g^{w}ous_ in Aryan, where the nom. had become _*g^{w}ōus_.

The following IE paradigms can thus be reconstructed for these nouns:

	Sing.	Sing.	Plur.
Nom.	_*dyeus_	_*g^{w}ous_, _*g^{w}ōus_	_*g^{w}owes_
Voc.	_*dyeu_	_*g^{w}ou_	_*g^{w}owes_
Acc.	_*dyēm_	_*g^{w}ōm_	_*g^{w}ōs_
Gen.	_*diwós_	_*g^{w}owós_, _*g^{w}ous_	_*g^{w}owom_
Loc.	_*dyéwi_	_*g^{w}owi_	_*g^{w}ousu_[1]

[1] Schindler (n. 5 above), 157, posits gen. s. _*g^{w}ewos_, loc. s. _*g^{w}ewi_, gen. pl. _*g^{w}ewom_, loc. pl. _*g^{w}eusi_; see also Schmalstieg, *KZ* 87, 1973, 114; Fulk 1986, 92f.; Lubotsky, in Kellens 1990, 133f.: _*$g^{w}eH_3$-u-_.

7.6. THEMATIC STEMS

The term 'thematic' is used for those stems which end in a distinguishing vowel, mostly *o* but in some of the cases also *e*; hence they are also known as *o*-stems or more precisely *e/o* stems.[1] The material for reconstructing their inflexion, illustrated by words for 'wolf' and the neuter 'yoke', is essentially as follows:

Sing.	Skt.	Gr.	Lat	Lith.	OCS	Goth.
Nom.	*vr̥kas*	λύκος	*lupus*	*vilkas*	*vlĭkŭ*	*wulfs*
Voc.	*vr̥ka*	λύκε	*lupe*	*vilke*[1]	*vlĭče*	*wulf*
Acc.	*vr̥kam*	λύκον	*lupum*	*vilką*	*vlĭkŭ*	*wulf*
Gen.	*vr̥kasya*	λύκοιο	*lupī*	–	–	*wulfis*
Abl.	*vr̥kād*	–	*lupō(d)*	*vilko*	*vlĭka*	–
Dat.	*vr̥kāya*	λύκῳ	*lupō(i)*	*vilkui*	*vlĭku*	–
Loc.	*vr̥kē*	(οἴκοι)	*domī*	*vilke*	*vlĭcē*	*wulfa?*
Instr.	*vr̥kā, -ēṇa*	–	–	*vilku*	*vlĭkomĭ*	*wulfa*
Dual						
Nom.	*vr̥kā*	λύκω	–	*vilku*	*vlĭka*	–
Gen.-Loc.	*vr̥kayōs*	λύκοιιν	–	–	*vlĭku*	–
Dat.-Abl.	*vr̥kābhyām*	–	–	*vilkam*	*vlĭkoma*	–
Plur.						
Nom.	*vr̥kās*	λύκοι	*lupī*	*vilkai*	*vlĭci*	*wulfōs*
Acc.	*vr̥kān(s)*	λύκους	*lupōs*	*vilkus*	*vlĭky*	*wulfans*
Gen.	*vr̥kānām*	λύκων	*lupōrum*	*vilkų*	*vlĭkŭ*	*wulfē*
Dat.-Abl.	*vr̥kēbhyas*	–	–	*vilkams*	*vlĭkomŭ*	*wulfam*
Loc.	*vr̥kēṣu*	λύκοισι	*lupīs*	*vilkuose*	*vlĭcēxŭ*	–
Instr.	*vr̥kais*	λύκοις	*lupīs*	*vilkais*	*vlĭky*	–
Sing. Nom.	*yugam*	ζυγόν	*iugum*	–	*igo*	*juk*
Dual Nom.	*yugē*	ζυγώ	–	–	*i(d)zē*	–
Plur. Nom.	*yugā(ni)*	ζυγά	*iuga*	–	*iga*	*juka*

7.6.1

These stems were either masculine or neuter, nom. s. *-os* or *-om* respectively. Feminine nouns in *-os* appear to be an innovation of the classical languages (cf. f. ἵππος 7.1.2 n. 2), neuters in *-os* (*-us*) an innovation of Latin.[2] The masculine forms will be discussed first.

7.6.2

The nom. and acc. s. present everywhere the endings *-os* and *-om* or their further developments, e.g. *-us -um* in classical Latin. The voc., on the other hand, shows *-e* as the characteristic vowel; this led to the distinction in OCS between palatalized *vlĭče* and nom. *vlĭkŭ*. This is the only declension class in which gen. and abl. s. are formally differentiated. The abl. has the ending *-ōd* in early Latin (*-d* was lost *c.*200 BC), and OInd. *-ād* is identical with this (see Porzio Gernia 1974; Prat 1975). The Balto-Slavic gen. in Lith. *-o*, Slav. *-a* points in the first instance to *-ād*, of which *-ā-* is unexplained.[3] The ending *-ōd* is in any case a contraction of the thematic vowel *o* and an ending *-ed*, which survives possibly in the Hitt. instr. *-ed* and certainly in pronominal ablatives such as Lat. *mēd*, OInd. *mad*, and was no doubt the source of the noun ending.[4] The gen. at first glance shows very heterogeneous formations. OInd. *-asya* and early Greek *-οιο* (together with Arm. *-oy*) point to *-osyo*. Behind the Goth. ending *-is* lies IE *-eso*, in other Gmc. dialects also *-oso*, to which the OCS pronominal gen. *česo* 'of which?' and perhaps the OPrus. gen. *deiwas* 'God's' (*-oso*) correspond.[5] The Lat. gen. *-ī* was for a long time equated with the Celt. *-ī* (Ogam *maqī* 'son's', OIr. *maicc*), but the Faliscan forms in *-osio* (*Kaisiosio* 'Caesii', etc.) and the new genitives *Popliosio Valesiosio* on the Latin inscription from Satricum (see *Lapis Satricanus*, The Hague, 1980) prove that Latin too at one time possessed the forms in *-osyo*;[6] the Proto-Irish *-ī* can also go back to *-esyo*. Hittite *-as* appears at first sight to show that the *o*-stems had originally the same gen. ending as the athematic stems, namely *-os*.[7] The Hieroglyphic Hittite gen. in *-asi*, however, with the adjectival stem (cf. Lat. *erīlis*) in *-asi-*, Luw. *-assi-*,[8] indicates rather that inherited *-osyo* by apocope of the final vowel became *-asi*, which then acquired an inflexion (adj. *-asi-*): Hitt. *-as* may show a further apocope. Since *-osyo* (*-esyo*) seems to have been present in so many languages, it is possible that Gmc. *-esa* also arose from *-esyo* by dissimilation,[9] and is not a different ending. Whether this ending *-osyo* is to be analysed further as *-os-yo*, in which *-os* would be the consonant stem ending and *-yo* the (undifferentiated?) relative pronoun,[10] remains for the time being disputable; see further 8.3.2. There are, however, no grounds for asserting that the multiplicity of genitive formations indicates that IE did not possess a genitive.[11] The dat. s. had quite unequivocally the ending *-ōi*, which was a contraction of *-o+ei*,[12] while the loc. ending *-ei* or *-oi* coalesced from the stem vowel *e* or *o+i*. The instr. s. had, as shown by Lith. *vilku*, an *-ō*, which was also the basis of OHG *wolfu*; Goth. *wulfa*, as also the pronominal *þamma* 'to this', must on the evidence of *hvamme-h* 'to each' go back to *ē*. Both show lengthening of the stem vowel *e/o*, i.e. contraction with an ending *e/o* (or with the laryngeal *h*?).[13]

7.6.3

In the neuter, in contrast to all other declension classes, the form of the nom. voc. acc. singular was not the plain stem, but was characterized by the ending *-om*.[14]

7.6.4

In the dual the ending of the nom. voc. acc. masculine was unequivocally *-ō*, i.e. as in the *i-* and *u*-stems (*-ī -ū*) it was characterized by lengthening of the stem vowel. Since the ending in consonant stems was *-e* (e.g. Gr. *πατέρ-ε*), the lengthening seems to rest on contraction with this *e*, i.e. *-ō -ī -ū* arose from *-o+e*, *-i+e*, *-u+e*.[15] In the neuter the ending was *-oi*, i.e. *-o+ī*.[16] Gen. and loc. have only one ending in OInd. and OCS, of which OCS (*vlĭk*)u from *-ous* as opposed to OInd. *(vṛk)ayōs* from *-oyous* represents the original state of affairs; *-ay-* comes from the numeral 'two' and the pronouns. Lith. *pusiau* 'broken in two' ('in two halves' from *pùsė* 'half') and *dviejau* 'in twos, as a pair' point to a form of the locative without *-s*; Avestan appears even to distinguish loc. *zastayō* (*-ou*) from gen. *vīrayå* (*-ōs*). We can thus perhaps posit loc. *-ou*, gen. *-ōs*.[17] For instr., dat., and abl. a single form is used, which ends in *-bhyō(m)* or *-mō*.

7.6.5

The nom. pl. masculine in Aryan and Gothic ends in *-ōs*, with which Oscan-Umbrian agrees (not cited above, e.g. Osc. *Núvlanús* 'Nolani', Umbr. *prinuvatus* 'ministri'); to these can be added the OIr. voc. in *-u* (e.g. *firu* 'men') from *-ōs*, which continues the old nom., while for the nom. an innovated form in *-oi* (e.g. *fir* from **wiroi* 'men') is used; cf. K. H. Schmidt, *I Coloquio sobre lenguas . . . de la peninsula iberica* (Salamanca, 1976), 335. The same innovation is shown by a number of other languages, including Greek, Latin, Baltic, and Slavic; cf. Gr. *λύκοι*, Lat. *lupī*, OCS *vlĭci* (*c* from *k* before *i* from *oi*), Lith. *vilkai*. The innovation started from the pronouns and proceeded via the adjectives; it is interesting that in Oscan-Umbrian the pronouns succumbed to the pressure of the noun group and adopted *-ōs*, e.g. Osc. *pús* 'qui'. The noun ending *-ōs* is, of course, a contraction of the stem vowel *o* and the ending *-es*.[18] For the acc. Gothic and Greek require an ending *-ons*; Gr. *-ους* is from *-ονς*, attested in some dialects. On the other hand OInd., Lith.,[19] and perhaps Lat. point to *-ōns*. The original form must have been *-on-s*; this, however, should have given *-ōn* (6.2.7.1). The form *-ōns* can thus be understood as the phonologically regular *-ōn+s* from the consonant stems (*-n̥s*); in many languages *-ōns* was shortened again to *-ons* or simplified to *-ōs*. The gen. pl. ending was *-ōm*, still kept in Greek and Lith.; shortened to *-ŏm* it appears also in Old Latin and in some instances even in classical Latin (*deum* etc.), but in general it was replaced by *-ōrum* on the analogy of the *ā*-stems. In OInd. the original ending *-ām* is still found in *dēvāñ ǰanma* 'race of gods', but is otherwise replaced by *-ānām*, introduced from the *n*-stems. A still unsolved problem is Goth. *-ē*,[20] which must have arisen by analogy. For the dat.-abl. OInd. uses *-bhyas*, to which Lat. *-bus* in the other declensions corresponds, thus *-bhyos* and *-bhos*. To this *-bh-* suffix[21] corresponds a suffix with *-m-* in Gmc. and Balt.-Slav., probably *-mos*, although OLith. shows *-mus*, from which modern *-ms* comes by syncope.[22] The loc. pl. ends in *-si/-su* preceded not by the stem vowel *-o-* but by the diphthong *-oi-*; the original ending was certainly *-ois*, from the s. *-o-i* with pluralizing *-s*, which was then extended by means of the particle *i* 'here' (Gr.) or *u* 'there' (OInd., Slav.). The ending *-oisi* is still attested in Mycenaean as *-oi(h)i*.[23] Lat. *(lup)īs* originated from instr. *-ōis* and at least in part from loc. *-oisi* or *-oisu*; for the apocope, cf. *mox* from **moksu*. Lith. *-uose* was also reshaped from *-oisu*.[22] The instr. had in this class a quite isolated ending *-ōis*, which can be seen in OInd. and Lith.[22] and is certainly present in OCS *-y*; this ending has now come to light in Mycenaean also.[24] Lat. *-īs* may in part go back to this formation.

7.6.6

In the nom. voc. acc. pl. of the neuter an ending *-ā* appears in OInd., OCS, Goth., *-ă* in Greek; Latin has *-ă*, but this must go back to *-ā*; see 7.1.4.3. The rule prevailing in Attic, OInd., OIran. (Gathic), Hittite, and perhaps British,[25] that with a neuter pl. subject the verb is in the singular, is connected with the original collective function of these forms.[26]

7.6.7

The *o*-declension[27] can therefore be reconstructed as follows:

	Sing.	Plur.	Dual
Nom.	*-os,-om*	*-ōs,-ā*	*-ō,-oi*
Voc.	*-e,-om*	*-ōs,-ā*	*-ō,-oi*
Acc.	*-om,-om*	*-ōns,-ā*	*-ō,-oi*
Gen.	*-es(y)o/-os(y)o*	*-ōm*	*-ōs*
Abl.	*-ōd*	*-bh(y)os,-mos*	*-bhyō(m), -mō*
Dat.	*-ōi*	*-bh(y)os,-mos*	*-bhyō(m),-mō*
Loc.	*-ei/-oi*	*-oisi/-oisu*	*-ou*
Instr.	*-ē/-ō*	*-ōis*	*-bhyō(m),-mō*

[1] On the alternation *e/o* and the inflexion, see Benveniste, *Origines* 172; Kuryłowicz, *Apophonie* 74f.; *IG* 271f.; Schmitt-Brandt, 128; Hilmarsson, *NTS* 31, 1977, 189f.; Fulk 1986, 136f.; Klingenschmitt, in Panagl and Krisch 1992, 93–104; and see further below, n. 27. As noted by Meillet, *Introduction*[8], 139, the Lith. voc. in *-e* may have to be derived from *-ē*; if so, it might have arisen by the secondary addition of the vocatival ending *-e*, i.e. from *-e+e*. For the function of the thematic vowel, note A. W. Grundt, 'The functional role of the IE theme vowel', *Pacific Coast Philology* 13, 1978, 29–35: *e* forms a 'definite inflectional stem' in contrast to the 'indeterminate stem' without it. Winter, 'Vocative' 219, is hardly correct on the voc. *-e*; cf. Shields, *GL* 25, 1985, 1–3.

[2] See provisionally Szemerényi, *Syncope* 319f.; and for *uīrus*, Szemerényi 1989, 87–94; for East Baltic, Ikuo, *JIES* 14, 1986, 273–88.

[3] Szemerényi, *Krat* 2, 1957, 101f.; Stang, *Vgl. Gram.* 181 (unlikely).

[4] Szemerényi *KZ* 73, 1955, 68; on contraction of *-o-ed*, Kuryłowicz, *Études* 154f.; *Apophonie*

75f.; and more recently L. C. Prat, *Morphosyntaxe de l'ablatif en latin archaique*, 1975 (*-ō* and *-ōd*; on this cf. Calboli, *ANRW* 29/1, 1983, 36f.); Starke, *Fs. Neumann*, 1982, 416f. For the abl., *-d* is posited by Laroche, *BSL* 55, 1960, 170; Starke, *ZA* 70, 1980, 157; *-t* (*-oti*) by Neu, in *Heth. und Idg.* 186. Dunkel's derivation of *-ōd* from *-o+ad* 'toward' (!), in Bammesberger 1988, 115, is very unlikely.

[5] Szemerényi, *Krat* 2, 102f.; Stang (n. 3 above); Miller, in *Fs. Kahane*, 1973, 335. According to de Hoz, in Villar (ed.), *Studia Indogermanica et Palaeohispanica in honorem A. Tovar et L. Michelena*, 1990, 315–29, esp. 325, Celtic had in the *o*-stem singular two forms for the abl. and gen. (*-ī* and *-o*); traces of both survive in Lepontic, elsewhere only of one.

[6] Pisani, *Rheinisches Museum* 98, 1956, 315–24; *Storia della lingua latina* i/1, 1962, 82; but the derivation of a form **lupeyye* from **lupoyyo* is impossible, we must start from *-io-* stems, in which the development was *-iosyo*>*-ioyyo*>*-iy(y)o*>*-ī* (as is well known, the *-io-* stems form their gen. in *-ī*, not *-iī*, down to Lucretius); this *-ī* was then carried over to the *o*-stems (instead of *-ei*). The comparison of Lat. *-ī* with OInd. adverbial formations in *-ī* (still made by Rundgren, *Eranos* 58, 1960, 51f., and again by J. Gil, *Em* 36, 1968, 25f.) was shown to be impossible by Bloch, *KZ* 76, 1960, 182f. (*pace* Schlerath, in *Fs. Thomas*, 1988, 37–47); see also Prat, *Latomus* 38, 1979, 862–76; Schindler, *Fachtagung* 6, 1980, 386–93; Bader, *É. Benveniste aujourd'hui* ii, 1984, 32f.; 'Génitif thématique', *Myc. Colloquium* 9, 1992, 1–17; and cf. Gamkrelidze—Ivanov, 375f.; Dunkel, in *In Memory of W. Cowgill*, 1987, 34; Prosdocimi, *AGI* 74, 1989, 158–9; Lejeune, *REL* 69, 1990, 63–77. According to Prosdocimi, op. cit. 162–74 and *AGI* 75, 1990, 56-64, Messapic *-ihi* is not to be equated with *-ī* but derives from *-isi*, original *-esie/o*; he also discusses (62-4) further possible reflexes of gen. *-esiie* in Italic. S. Mariotti (*Studies O. Skutsch*, 1988, 82–5) thinks that OLat. *Mett(i)oio Fufetioio* is not a Graecism but an archaic gen. like *Titoio* (from Ardea). A new explanation of the *cvi*-formation has been presented by E. Tichy, *WJA* 16, 1990, 11f.; *Wackernagel Kolloquium*, 1990, 11f. On the phonetic development, see Szemerényi, *Glotta* 38, 1959, 117. That *-osyo* would have given Lat. *-orio* (Bonfante, *AGI* 51, 1966, 8) has long been refuted by *eius cuius*. To ascribe *Popliosio* to the Volscan dialect (Coleman, *TPS* 1986, 120f.) is unjustifiable.

[7] Borgstrøm, *NTS* 7, 1934, 121–8; Kuryłowicz, *Études* 146f., 155, 260; Berg, *NTS* 18, 1958, 224.

[8] Mittelberger, *Krat* 11, 1967, 99–106; Georgiev, *RHA* 81, 1967, 157–65. Cf. also Neumann, *Sprache* 16, 1969, 61–2.

[9] Cf. Must, *Lg* 29, 1953, 301–5; Szemerényi, *Krat* 2, 1957, 102; Markey, *ICHL* 3, 1977; Roberge, *IF* 88, 1984, 143f.

[10] Knobloch, *Sprache* 2, 1951, 131–49; Watkins, *Celtica* 6, 1962, 16, 28; Poultney, *Lg* 43, 1968, 871–2, 877, 880; Bader, *BSL* 68, 1973, 41; 70, 1975, 28; G. Schmidt, *IF* 82, 1979, 70–3 (gen. *-s*+uninflected relative **yo*); Lehmann, *In Memory of J. A. Kerns*, 1981, 179–88 (*-osyo* only where *yo-* occurs as relative, i.e. Aryan, Greek, Armenian—he overlooks Faliscan and Latin, which have *-osyo* without rel. *yo-*); Haudry, *BSL* 76, 1982, 198; Bader, *BSL* 86, 1991, 89–157 (*-os-*=nom. s. *-os*); Beekes, 'The genitive in *-osyo*', *FoLH* 11, 1992, 21–25 (=*-o-sio*).

[11] Watkins, in *AIED*, 38. A gen. s. in *-ŏ* is proposed for Hispano-Celtic by Untermann, *Fs. Pokorny*, 1967, 281–8; cf. K. H. Schmidt, in Panagl and Krisch 1992, 42; McCone, *Fachtagung* 8, 1992, 17.

[12] A different view in Villar, *Symbolae Mitxelena*, 1985, 31–48, esp. 44f.

[13] Kuryłowicz, *Categories* 196.

[14] Cf. 7.1.4.3, but note that *-om* has also been explained differently: not as thematic *o*+ending *m*, but as an enlargement unconnected with the (later) stem vowel *-o*; see Szemerényi 1985, n. 58 on Burrow, Villar.

[15] Specht, *Ursprung* 311; a laryngeal explanation in Erhart, 'Die ie. Dualendung *-ō(u)* und die Zahlwörter', *Sbornik Brno* 1965/A-13, 11–32. See also Forssman, *MSS* 25, 1969, 39–50; Beekes, *Laryngeals* 158; Peters 1980, 128f.; Shields, *ŽA* 32, 1982, 27–32; *JIES* 15, 1988, 341–52; Oettinger, in Bammesberger 1988, 355–9.

[16] Szemerényi, 'Development' 220; in spite of Watkins, *Fachtagung* 5, 1975, 368–70; Strunk, *PBB* 114, 1992, 188.

[17] Benveniste, *BSL* 34, 1933, 26; Anttila (above, 6.5.5 n. 2), 59–60; Risch, *SMEA* 1, 1966,

56–8. K. Hoffmann, *Aufsätze* ii, 1976, 561 n. 2, postulates *-Hou-*, not *-ou-*; cf. also Dubois, *BSL* 72, 1977, 169–86; Lindeman 1982, 31. Shields, *JIES* 15, 1988, 346, is unacceptable.

[18] Eichner (*Fachtagung* 7, 1985, 157f.) again argues for the derivation of Lith. *-ai* from the neuter *-ā-i*. The explanation of *-ōs* as from *-o-es* goes back to the founding father Bopp; see Wackernagel and Debrunner, *Ai. Gr.* iii, 101, and cf. K. H. Schmidt, *ZCP* 45, 1992, 278. The Aryan material for nom. pl. m. *-āsas* (collected by R. Schmitt, *Fs. Eilers*, 1967, 265–77) has been explained as showing the original ending *-ōs* expanded with the normal ending *-es*. The recent attempt by Beekes, *Fs. Meid*, 1989, 29–44, to explain the phenomenon (and the more doubtful Germanic material) as based on Brugmann's Law (see above, 4.1 n. 2) stands or falls with the acceptability or otherwise of this much disputed law.

[19] Stang, *Vgl. Gram.* 186; a different view in Schmalstieg, *Lingua* 16, 1966, 377f. On Slavic *-ōn*, see Vaillant, *Gram. comp.* ii/1, 256.

[20] Cf. W. Morgenroth, *PBB(H)* 87, 1965, 328–36; Lehmann, *Papers in Honor of L. Dostert*, 1967, 108–11; Kuryłowicz, *Gedenkschrift W. Brandenstein*, 1968, 87 n. 8; Bech, *Lingua* 23, 1969, 55–64; Kortlandt, *Lingua* 45, 1978, 291; Shields, *LB* 68, 1979, 257–68; Jasanoff, *JIES* 11, 1983, 188 (against Kortlandt: remains a riddle); Kortlandt, ibid. 170f.; J. F. Eska, *IF* 93, 1988, 186f.

[21] K. H. Schmidt, 'Dativ und Instr. im Plural', *Glotta* 41, 1963, 1–10.

[22] Stang, *Vgl. Gram.* 185f.; Gamkrelidze–Ivanov, 379f.

[23] Szemerényi, 'Development' 222f.; Lazzeroni, *SSL* 8, 1968, 173–97; Szemerényi, *Fachtagung* 7, 1985, 518; Moralejo, '"Dativo" de plural en griego antiguo', *Fs. Adrados*, 1984, 339–64; Dunkel, in Bammesberger 1988, 111; Beekes, *Fs. Meid*, 1989, 35 (*-si* Greek innovation); Wathelet, *REG* 104, 1991, 1–14. Quite differently Kortlandt, *Fs. Hoenigswald*, 1987, 222; *-oisu* contains the plural ending *-i* (an Indo-Uralic morph?), seen in the pronominal nom. pl. **to-i* (see below, 8.2.1 fin.), but that would imply two pluralizing elements in the same form.

[24] On this case, see Szemerényi, *Fachtagung* 7, 517f.

[25] See Hamp, *SCelt* 10/11, 1977, 58f. The rule seems to be still valid in New Persian; see Minovi, *JRAS* 1942, 41–7; Hincha, *Islam* 37, 1961, 151. For Hittite, see also Eichner, in *IC* 34, 1992, 375 fin. B 180.

[26] On this, see Lehmann, *Lg* 34, 1958, 179f.; Kuryłowicz, *Categories* 205f.

[27] The *o*-stems started from the adjectives according to Scherer, *PICL* 7, 1956, 177, 536; A. García Calvo, *Congreso Español de Estúdios Clásicos* 2, 1964, 111f. (really inflected genitives in *-os*; 109: *-e* of the vocative can be a particle, *-ei* of the locative likewise); Haudry, *Préhistoire* 36 (*e/o* 'article défini postposé'); but according to Beekes, *Origins* 192, the nom. in *-os*, an ergative, is the foundation of the whole inflexion; cf. also *Fs. Meid*, 1989, 34f.

7.7. *ā*- AND *ī*-STEMS

7.7.1

The declension of the *ā*-stems can be illustrated by the paradigms of the following words: OInd. *sēnā* 'army', Gr. *θεά* 'goddess', Lat. *dea* 'goddess', Lith. *galvà* 'head', OCS *noga* 'foot', Goth. *giba* 'gift'.

	Skt.	Gr.	Lat.	Lith.	OCS	Goth.
Sing.						
Nom.	*sēnā*	*θεά*	*dea*	*galvà*	*noga*	*giba*
Voc.	*sēnē*	*θεά*	*dea*	*gálva*	*nogo*	*giba*
Acc.	*sēnām*	*θεάν*	*deam*	*galvą*	*nogǫ*	*giba*
Gen.	*sēnāyās*	*θεᾶς*	*deae*	*galvos*	*nogy*	*gibōs*
Dat.	*sēnāyai*	*θεᾶι*	*deae*	*galvai*	*no(d)zē*	*gibai*

	Skt.	Gr.	Lat.	Lith.	OCS	Goth.
Loc.	*sēnāyām*	–	–	*galvoje*	*no(d)zē*	–
Instr.	*sēn(ay)ā*		*deā (Abl.)*	*galva*	*nogojǫ*	–
Dual						
Nom.	*sēnē*	θεά	–	*galvi*	*no(d)zē*	–
Gen.-Loc.	*sēnayōs*	θεαῖν	–	–	*nogu*	–
Dat.-Abl.	*sēnābhyām*	θεαῖν	–	*galvom*	*nogama*	–
Plur.						
Nom.	*sēnās*	θεαί	*deae*	*galvos*	*nogy*	*gibōs*
Acc.	*sēnās*	θεάς	*deās*	*galvas*	*nogy*	*gibōs*
Gen.	*sēnānām*	θε(ά)ῶν	*deārum*	*galvų*	*nogŭ*	*gibō*
Dat.-Abl.	*sēnābhyas*	–	*deīs*	*galvoms*	*nogamŭ*	*gibōm*
Loc.	*sēnāsu*	θεαῖς	*(deābus)*	*galvose*	*nogaxŭ*	–
Instr.	*sēnābhis*	*anijapi*	–	*galvomis*	*nogami*	–

The nom. s. is the bare stem in *-ā* (but see Fulk, 6.2.7.1, n. 1 fin.), shortened in several languages. The acc. s. has with the suffix the ending *-ā-m*; cf. Lindeman, *IF* 94 (1989), 5f. The voc. s. is originally distinct from the nom., cf. Hom. νύμφᾰ, Sappho's Δίκᾰ Ἔλενᾰ, OCS *nogo*; there is also Umbr. *Tursa* in contrast to the nom. in *-o* and the difference of intonation in Lith. All this points to voc. *-ă* as opposed to nom. *-ā*. The Aryan voc. in *-ai* (OInd. *-ē*) falls quite outside the scheme. It is by no means, however, the 'pure stem form' in *-ai*, comparable with Gr. γύναι,[1] but a reshaping of the inherited *-ă* on the model of the *ī*-stems (e.g. *dēvi* 'O goddess'), which have strongly influenced the OInd. *-ā* paradigm in other respects also. The innovation started from the thematic adjectives, where it was very important to distinguish masculine and feminine, both of which had *-ă* in the voc.; the old **priya* 'dear' and the new **priyi* gave **priyai*, OInd. *priyē*. The shortening of the original IE ending *-ā* to *-ă* is regular, as the voc., if used at the beginning of a sentence or alone, was accented on the first syllable but was otherwise enclitic and unaccented; a derivation from *-ah* with the assumption of a prevocalic sandhi variant in *-a*[2] fails, therefore, to explain the shortening. The gen. in *-ās* is contracted from *-ā+os*, the dat. in *-āi* from *-ā+ei*, the loc. in *-āi* from *-ā+i*. The Aryan forms in *-āyās -āyāi -āyām* were transformed under the influence of the *ī*-stems.[3] The OCS gen. in *-y* (=nom. and acc. pl.) appears to rest on *-ans* transformed from *-ās*.[4] The Lith. loc. in *-oje* is from *-oj* (IE-*āi*) enlarged by the postposition *-e(n)*.[5] The instr. had originally the ending *-ā* (from *-ā+e*), and to avoid homonymy with the nom. the form was reshaped in OInd. on the model of the pronouns and *ī*-stems.[6] Lith. had *-ān* which agrees with Slav. *-ǫ* (pronominal *-ojǫ*).[5]

In the dual Skt. *-ē* was for a long time taken as continuing IE *-ai*, but Mycenaean has shown that the ending was *-oi*.[7] Clearly this form is also the basis of the gen.-loc. *sēnayōs* (IE *-oy-ous*), while OCS *nogu* was reshaped on the analogy of the *o*-stems.

The nom. pl. has *-ās* from *-ā+es*; the acc. pl. should properly have had *-ān(s)* from *-ā+ns*, but appears either as *-ās* or as *-ăns*. The gen. was originally *-ōm* from *-ā+om*, preserved in Lith. and Goth.,[8] but shortened to *-om* in OCS. Lat. *-ārum* and Hom. ᾱων, both from *-āsōm*, have the pronominal ending; in these languages the nom. pl. was also modified to *-ai* on the analogy of the pronominal *-oi* of the (masculine) *o*-stems. The OInd. gen. ending *-ānām*, as in the case of the *o*-stems, was taken over from the *n*-stems.[9] The dat.-abl. has the already familiar ending, the loc. has *-ā-su*. The instr. pl. is now represented by Mycenaean *-pi*, perhaps to be taken as *-φις* and equivalent to OInd. *-bhis*.[10]

[1] Ahrens, *KZ* 3, 1854, 86f.; Collitz, 'The origin of the *ā*-declension', *BB* 29, 1905, 81–114 (*-ā* from *-āy*, voc. shortened to *-ăi*, Ind. gen. *-āy-ās*); revived by Georgiev, *Symbolae Kuryłowicz*, 1965, 81, 83; *KZ* 88, 1974, 117f.; Watkins, *Trivium* 1, 1967, 119 n. 37; Rasmussen, *SL* 27, 1973, 90f. (but cf. Pokorny, *KZ* 46, 1914. 284!). A different view in Brosman, *JIES* 5, 1981, 255–73 (from neuter abstracts in *-ahh*=Harðarson, *MSS* 48, 1987, 126); Beekes, *Origins* 20–37. Note also Pirart, *MSS* 47, 1986, 159–91: *-H_2ē*, *-H_2ēm*, voc. *-H_2ei*, etc.; Klingenschmitt, in Panagl and Krisch 1992, 89–93.

[2] Lehmann, *Lg* 34, 1958, 191 (with a remarkable contradiction between the text and n. 21); Winter, 'Vocative' 218f.; Hock, *International Journal of Dravidian Studies* 4, 1975, 29–43; Beekes, *Origins* 102f.

[3] Wackernagel and Debrunner, *Ai. Gr.* iii, 119f.; Kuryłowicz, *Categories* 219; Hock (n. 2 above). For Celtic, see Szemerényi, *ZCP* 44, 1991, 308f.; F. Motta, *SCO* 38, 1991, 1–12, and *Fs. Untermann*, 1993, 269–74.

[4] Schmalstieg, *SEEJ* 12, 1968, 44f.; on the nom.-acc. pl., also *Word* 21, 1966, 238f.; G. Schmidt, *Fs. Knobloch*, 1985, 396. According to Schelesniker, *Fs. Issatschenko*, 1976, 383–91, the f. gen. in *-y/-ę* is originally a loc. in *-(y)ām*.

[5] Stang, *Vgl. Gram.* 199.

[6] Kuryłowicz, *Categories* 219f.

[7] Szemerényi, 'Development' 217f. For that reason Risch, *Fachtagung* 5, 1975, 253 (*-ai* is from $ə_2+ə_1$) and Watkins, ibid. 368 (from *-eH_2-ī*) are unacceptable; the ending is *-oi* from *-o+ī* like masc. *-ō* from *-o+e*.

[8] A different account in Kortlandt, *Lingua* 45, 1978, 293: *-ō* not from *-ōm*, but from *-ōan*< *-ā+om*(?).

[9] Disputed by G. Schmidt (n. 4 above), 393f.

[10] On the Greek inflexion as a whole, see Morpurgo Davies, *TPS* 1968, 12f.; on the dat. s. in *-āi*, see Villar, *IF* 92, 1987, 135–67.

7.7.2

The *ā*-stems are principally feminine, but in several languages masculines also appear in this class. Their inflexion is usually the same, but in Greek the masculines are differentiated[1] in the nom. and gen. s. (nom. ᾱς, gen. ᾱο) in most dialects, and indeed, as we now know, as early as the Mycenaean period.[2]

[1] According to T. Gonzáles Rolán, *Em* 39, 1971, 291–304, in Latin also, cf. f. nom. *-ā*, gen. *-ās*: m. nom. *-ā/-ās*, gen. *-āi*.

[2] Szemerényi, *Atti e memorie del 1º Congresso di Micenologia*, 1968, 720; Risch, *BSL* 69, 1974, 109–19; Méndez Dosuna, *Glotta* 60, 1982, 65–79; Masson, *Myc. Colloquium* 7, 1983, 256; A. Lillo, *KZ* 98, 1985, 250–6 (against Lillo, Szemerényi 1989, 40 n.). On the Hom. nom. in -τᾰ, see Hooker, *Glotta* 45, 1968, 14f.; Gil, *Em* 37, 1969, 372f.; Wathelet, *Les traits éoliens*, 1970, 229f.; A. Quattordio Moreschini, *SMEA* 25, 1985, 337f., esp. 346; Lillo, op. cit., 255f.

7.7.3

Closely connected with the *ā*-stems is another class, also basically feminine, which is still represented in Vedic by two subclasses. These can be illustrated by *dēvī* 'goddess' and *vṛkīs* 'she-wolf'.[1]

	Sing.		Dual		Plur.	
Nom.	*dēvī*	*vṛkī́s*	*dēvī*	*vṛkyā̀*	*dēvīs*	*vṛkyàs*
Voc.	*dēvi*	*vṛ́ki*	*dēvī*	*vṛkyā̀*	*dēvīs*	*vṛkyàs*
Acc.	*dēvīm*	*vṛkyàm*	*dēvī*	*vṛkyā̀*	*dēvīs*	*vṛkyàs*
Gen.	*dēvyās*	*vṛkyàs*	*dēvyōs*	*vṛkyṑs*	*dēvīnām*	*vṛkī́nām*
Dat.	*dēvyāi*	*vṛkyḕ*	*dēvībhyām*	*vṛkī́bhyām*	*dēvībhyas*	*vṛkī́bhyas*
Loc.	*dēvyām*	*vṛkī́*	*dēvyōs*	*vṛkyṑs*	*dēvīṣu*	*vṛkī́ṣu*
Instr.	*dēvyā*	*vṛkyā́*	*dēvībhyām*	*vṛkī́bhyām*	*dēvībhis*	*vṛkī́bhis*

The *vṛkī-* type is limited to nouns with accented *-ī* and shows a consonant-stem inflexion, in which *ī* is kept before endings beginning with a consonant but becomes *iy* before those beginning with a vowel; this is, however, concealed by the spelling (*vṛkyàm* instead of *vṛkíyam*, etc.).[2] The equivalence of *vṛkīs* and ON *ylgr* (from Gmc. **wulgīz*) is enough in itself to establish the IE age of this inflexion, but it has left many traces in other languages also.[3] The IE inflexion **wḷkʷī́s* **wḷkʷíy-m̥* **wḷkʷíy-os* **wḷkʷíy-ei*, etc., is thus very ancient, although it was preserved as such only in Vedic and soon coalesced with the *dēvī*-type.[4]

The *dēvī-* type, on the other hand, is preserved in many languages. It is well represented in Gothic, e.g. *mawi* 'girl' (from **magw-i*, a feminine formed to *magus* 'boy'), acc. *mauja*, gen. *maujōs*, dat. *maujai*, etc. (like *giba*, 7.7.1); *frijōndi* 'friend' (f.), formed to *frijōnd-s* (m.), properly participial derivatives (with IE *-nt-* and *-nt-ī*) from the verb *frijōn* 'to love'. Lith. *martì* 'daughter-in-law', acc. *marčią*, gen. *marčios* from *-tī*, *-tyām*, *-tyās* belongs to the same type, as do the feminine participles, e.g. *duodanti* 'giving', gen. *duodančios*, etc.; similarly in Slavic, OCS *nesǫšti* 'carrying', acc. *nesǫštǫ*, etc. The type is best known, however, from the Greek stems with *alpha impurum*, e.g. μοῦσα μοῦσαν μούσης μούσῃ, which goes back to **montyă*, *-tyăm*, *-tyās*, *-tyāi*.

The *dēvī-* type is thus really an *-ā-* type, but the *ā* is always preceded by *y* and in the nom. s. there appears not *-yā* but *-ī*, or in Greek

-ya. In the acc. s. *-īm* occurs in Old Indic, but *-yām* in most other languages except Greek, which has *-yăn*. It seems fairly certain[5] that the acc. originally ended in *-iyṃ*, which gave Gr. *-ια*, later *-ιαν* and transformed the nom. also to *-ια*, while elsewhere either *-yā-* or *-ī-* were introduced. The old inflexion was thus nom. *-ī*, acc. *-iyṃ*, gen. *-yās*, dat. *-yāi*, etc., to which corresponded the inflexion *-ī(s)*, *-iy-ṃ*, *-iy-os*, *-iy-ei*, etc., in the *vṛkī-* type.[6]

For the explanation of the *dēvī-* type it is often supposed[7] that a complex suffix *-y-eH₂-* gave the form *-yā-* of the oblique cases, while in the nom. s. the zero grade *-i-H₂* gave *-ī*. Since, however, no ground for the zero grade can be suggested (indeed the *ā*-stems have *-ā* in the nom. s.), it would be better to assume that an original nominative in *-iyeh* had contracted to *-īh*; the dual ending *-ī* from *-i-e* (7.6.4) would provide a good parallel to this. Nevertheless it is to be noted that clearly an originally open *i*-inflexion (7.5.1) came in the course of time more and more under the influence of the *ā*-stems. This supports the view that the original type was formed with *-i-h-*[8] and inflected as a consonant stem: *-ih-s*, *-ih-ṃ*, *-ih-os*, *-ih-ei*, etc., type *wḷkʷīs*. Later under the influence of the *ā*-stems this inflexion was reshaped to *-ih*, *-ih-ṃ*, *-ih-ās*, *-ih-āi*, and later still, probably in the period of the individual languages, became in the northern languages *-ī*, *-yām*, *-yās*, *-yāi*.[9]

[1] Wackernagel and Debrunner, *Ai. Gr.* iii, 163f.; Fulk 1986, 142–9; Klingenschmitt (above, 7.7.1 n. 1). On the Latin type *māteriēs*, *-iam*, see Steinbauer, ap. Mayrhofer 1986, 133: *-yeH₂-s*: *-yeH₂-m* > *-iēs*: *-iam*.

[2] Wackernagel and Debrunner, *Ai. Gr.* iii, 170f.

[3] Lohmann, *Genus und Sexus*, 1932, 63f., 68, 79. For Celtic, see Szemerényi, *KZ* 88, 1975, 279f.; *ZCP* 36, 1979, 297; Lindeman, *EC* 19, 1982, 160; for Iranian, Mayrhofer, *Hommages M. Leroy*, 1980, 130–52.

[4] Thumb and Hauschild, *Handbuch des Sanskrit* i 2, 1959, 62f.; Prosdocimi, *AGI* 74, 1989, 156–7.

[5] Brugmann, *Grundriss*², ii/2, 124.

[6] A different account, with many laryngeal laws, in Peters, *Untersuchungen zur Vertretung der idg. Laryngale im Griechischen*, 1980, 127f.; Gamkrelidze–Ivanov, 284f.

[7] e.g. Martinet, *BSL* 52, 1957, 87.

[8] Lehmann, *Lg* 34, 1958, 184 n. 11, 191. But the 'collective' meaning of this formation (ibid. 188f.) is hardly tenable; see Kuryłowicz, *Apophonie* 132 (collectives from abstracts). On *-ī-*, see also *Apophonie* 129; *Accentuation*² 31f.; *Categories* 199, 220f. On the Gothic types *bandi/wrakja*, see Beekes, in Kellens 1990, 49–58.

[9] Cf. Szemerényi, *Syncope* 305 n. 1, 309 n. 2 (here also on alleged *-ū/-wā-*); Joffe, *LPosn* 17, 1973, 9–19; Prosdocimi, *AGI* 74, 1989, 154–6.

7.8. ADJECTIVES AND DEGREES OF COMPARISON

7.8.1

The chief characteristic of the adjective as opposed to the noun is variation according to gender. The majority of adjectives can indicate the three genders by their form.[1] The *o*-stems have the nominative in the masculine in *-os*, in the neuter in *-om*; the feminine has mostly *-ā* but can also, especially in Old Indic, have *-ī*. For example:

IE **newos*, **newom*, **newā* 'new': OInd. *navas*, *navam*, *navā*; Gr. νέ(ϝ)ος, νέ(ϝ)ον, νέ(ϝ)ᾱ; Lat. *nouos*, *nouom*, *noua*; OCS *novŭ*, *novo*, *nova*.

All other stems have a separate form for the neuter, but the feminine is either identical with the masculine or, if different, is formed with *-ī-/-yā-*, not *-ā-*. For example:

IE **swādus*, **swādu*, **swādw-ī-* 'sweet': OInd. *svādus*, *svādu*, *svādvī*; Gr. ἡδύς, ἡδύ, ἡδεῖα, (from -εϝyα, modified from *-wī-* on the analogy of ἡδέϝος etc., or *-duwī-* > *-dewī*);

IE **bheront-ī* 'carrying' (f.): OInd. *bharant-ī*, Gr. φέρουσα (from *-ontya*); Goth. *bairandei* (enlarged to an *n*-stem); OIr. *birit* 'pig' (from *-n̥tī*).

In the corresponding Latin adjectives the feminine in *-ī*, modified to *-is*, has in part become the sole form (**swādus* and **swādwis* both continue as *suāuis*), in part by a secondary development fallen together with the masculine (**ferentis* > *ferens* by syncope). The more recent theory[2] that *-is* is an additional suffix *-i-*, not a development of the feminine *-ī*, or that the type *ferens* never had an *i*, is refuted *inter alia* by *fertilis* (from **fertr-ī* 'bringer', f.) and *neptis*[3]; cf. also[4] the form *Laurentis* (*terra*) in Ennius.[5]

[1] Brugmann, *Grundriss*², ii/2, 105f.; Sommer, *Zum attributiven Adjectivum*, 1928; Schwyzer, *GG* ii, 173–85; Untermann, 'L'aggettivo', *QPL* 7, 1988, 3–31.

[2] Hirt, *IG* iii, 1927, 272–6; Sturtevant, *Lg* 10, 1934, 266–73; Specht, *KZ* 65, 1938, 201f.; Burrow, *TPS* 1949, 31; Benveniste, *Fs. F. Sommer*, 1955, 3; Kastner, *Die griechischen Adjektive zweier Endungen auf* -os, 1967, 16; Laroche, *RHA* 28, 1971, 52f.

[3] Szemerényi, *Studi V. Pisani*, 1969, 987f.; *Studies Palmer*, 1976, 401f.; see also Stang, *NTS* 17, 1956, 142; Watkins, in *AIED* 40. The forms *fertilis*, *neptis* (and *peluis*? cf. OInd. *pālavī*) from IE *-ī(s)* show also that Specht's view, according to which *-ī* became *-īx* in Latin (loc. cit. n. 2 above; cf. *fēlīx* from **dhēlw-ī*), cannot be right. On the other hand, it becomes ever clearer that what can be established for Latin applies also to Hittite: cf. *parku-nu-* 'make clean', *parkw-i-s* 'clean', and Luwian formations such as *-ant-i-*, *assi-*; see above, 7.1.2 n. 3, and esp. the work of Kammenhuber cited there.

[4] See Nussbaum, *HSCP* 77, 1973, 207–15 (*-ī-* f. to the *-nt-* stem), and cf. O. Skutsch, *The Annals of Q. Ennius*, Oxford 1985, 189.

[5] For Greek, see *A. Blanc, *Les adjectifs sigmatiques en grec*, 1987; C. de Lamberterie, *Les adjectifs grecs en* -us, i–ii, Louvain, 1990 (reviewed *BSL* 86/2, 1992, 145–9). For Germanic, cf. F. Heidermanns, 'Zur primitiven Wortbildung im germ. Adjectivsystem', *KZ* 99, 1986, 279–307; Bammesberger 1990, 217–63 (declension and material).

7.8.2

A peculiarity of certain adjectives in composition was first observed by the Dutch Indologist W. Caland (*KZ* 31 (1889), 267f.; 32 (1892), 592). According to 'Caland's Law', adjectives in *-ro-* (*-no-* etc.) replace this suffix with *-i-* when they occur as first members of a compound; cf. OInd. *dabhīti-* 'injurer, deceiver' from **dabhi-iti* 'with hurtful going': *dabhra-*; *śiti-pad-* 'white-footed' from **śviti-pad-*: *śvitra* 'bright'; Avest. *tiži-aršti* (from *tigi-*) 'with sharp spear': *tiγra-* 'sharp'; Gr. *κυδι-άνειρα* 'bringing renown to men': *κυδρός* 'renowned', etc. This synchronically interesting exchange rests on the fact that at the time when this type of compound was formed the adjectives constituting the first members had only *-i-*; later they were enlarged with *-ro-* (and similar) and in *-i-ro-* the *i* was lost by syncope, so that the clear opposition *-i-*: *-iro-* was replaced by *-i-*: *-ro-*.[1]

[1] Szemerényi, *Syncope* 395–8. Cf. Hirt, *IG* iii, 1927, 274f.; Kuryłowicz, *Categories* 232; Chantraine, *Fs. Pokorny*, 1967, 21f.; Bader, *Mél. Benveniste*, 1975, 19–32; *RPh* 49, 1975, 19, 48; Nussbaum, *Caland's Law and the Caland System*, diss., Harvard, 1976; Collinge, *Laws* 23f.; Fulk 1986, 154; Oettinger, *KZ* 100, 1987, 35–43; Tucker 1990 ·of.

7.8.2.1 In some languages the adjectives are not merely considerably influenced by the pronominal inflexion, but even develop two types of inflexion, known as *strong* and *weak* or indefinite and definite. This is especially familiar in the Germanic and Balto-Slavic groups.[1] The Gothic adjective of the first type, for example, has a pronominal form in place of the inherited nominal form in the m. acc. dat. s. and nom. gen. dat. pl. The general principle of the restructuring of the inherited inflexion is fairly clear, but the line of development cannot always be fully explained in detail.[2]

[1] See the account of Kuryłowicz, *CTL* xi, 1973, 79–82.

[2] On Germanic, see Curme, 'The origin and growth of the adjective declension in Germanic', *JEGPh* 9, 1910, 439–82; Haudry, 'Les deux flexions de l'adjectif germanique', *BSL* 76, 1981, 191–200; Harðarson, *ALHafn* 21, 1989, 81f. The Balto-Slavic adjective seems to attract less interest; see e.g. Birnbaum, *Common Slavic*, 1979, 158; reference may nevertheless be made to Seiler, *Relativsatz* 102, 169f.

7.8.3

From the standpoint of Latin or English, it seems natural that an adjective should have two degrees of comparison, a *comparative* and a *superlative*. The IE languages, however, present several kinds of formation, so that one must ask what the system was like in which they had their place. First it is necessary to set out the facts.

7.8.4

A *comparative* with the suffix *-yes-*/*-yos-* appears in Aryan, Latin, and Celtic; of. OInd. *san-yas-* 'older' = Lat. *seniōr-* = OIr. *siniu*, all from IE **sen-yos-*/**sen-yōs-*, formed to **seno-* 'old' in Lat. *senex*, etc. (see 4.4.2). The same suffix is concealed in OCS *bolje* (n.) 'bigger' from *-yos*; *-yes-* is preserved in the Lith. comparative *saldesnis* 'sweeter' from *-yes-nis*, an *n*-enlargement as in the Germanic comparative, e.g. Goth. *bat-iz-in* 'better',[1] whereas the old comparative without nasal enlargement is used in Lith. as comparative adverb (e.g. *geriaũs* 'better') and, inflected, as superlative (e.g. *geriáus-yas* 'the best', from **ger-ē-yōs*); without the help of the related languages it would be impossible to recognize IE *-yos-* in the short forms of the Greek comparative βελτίω (acc. s. m. f. and nom. acc. pl. n.) from *-yosm̥* and *-yosa* and βελτίους (nom. acc. pl. m. f.) from *-yos-es*.[2]

The original inflexion of the comparative made full use of the ablaut possibilities of the suffix *-yes-/-yos-*; only *-yēs-* is unattested. The distribution was in late IE approximately as in the *n*-stems, see Szemerényi, n. 2 below, p. 27; Kuryłowicz, n. 3 below, 229; also nn. 4 and 5.

	Sing.		Plur.	
Nom.	m. f. *-yōs*	n. *-yos*	m. f. *-yos-es*	n. *-yos-a* (*-ah*?)
Acc.	*-yos-m̥*	*-yos*	*-yos-n̥s*	*-yos-a* (*-ah*?)
Gen.	*-yes-os*			
Loc.	*-yes-i*			

At an earlier stage even the zero grade *-is-* may have had its place in the weak cases (e.g. gen. s. *-is-os*, pl. *-is-om*); its presence in the nom.-acc. s. n. is in any case guaranteed by the fact that an adverb in *-is* exists in Latin (*magis* as opposed to *maius* from **mag-yos*) and Germanic (Goth. *mais* 'more' from **ma-is*, *mins* 'less' from **minn-is*, etc.), and *-is-* as the weak form of the suffix is also shown by Gmc. *-iz-in*, Slav. *-ĭš-* (from *-is-y-*) and the IE superlative suffix *-is-to-* (see 7.8.5); cf. Kuryłowicz, n. 3 below, 228f.

The full inflexion of *-yos-* is preserved only in Latin and Aryan. In Celtic the inflexion was lost, and the uninflected comparative (and superlative) can be used only as a predicate, e.g. 'he is older'. In Germanic and Greek an *n*-inflexion is found (Goth. *batizin-* like Gr. βελτιον-), from which the existence of an IE *-is-on-* had been inferred; but Mycenaean has shown that the Greek development is late and can therefore have nothing to do with the similar Gmc. innovation, though this has possibly influenced Lithuanian; see Szemerényi, n. 2 below, pp. 27f.

The variation between *-yos-* and *-iyos-*, which is especially well attested in Old Indic and in Greek (OInd. *san-yas* 'older', *svād-īyas* 'sweeter'; Gr. μείζων 'greater' (-ζ- from *-gy-*), but ἡδίων 'sweeter'; is obviously due to Sievers' Law (5.7.2.1).[6] The Germanic type in *-ōzan-*, e.g. Goth. *frōdōzan-* 'wiser', which is formed only from stems in *-a-* (IE *-o-*), and the Slavic type in *-ēji*, e.g. OCS *novēji* 'newer', are, on the other hand, innovations. They have been explained as derived from, or influenced by, adverbs (Goth. *-ō-*, Slav. *-ē-*); see Kuryłowicz, n. 3 below, 233, and n. 7.

[1] Stang, *Vgl. Gram.* 260, 267f. According to W. P. Schmid, *Fs. Meid*, 1989, 241–50, the Gmc., Lith., and OPrus. formations are based on an adverb *-is*.

[2] Güntert, 'Zur Geschichte der griechischen Gradationsbildungen', *IF* 27, 1909, 1–72; Szemerényi, 'Comparative', 1968. A different view in Palmer, *The Greek Language*, 1980, 47: not clear whether *-jōs* or *-jōn* is meant (in Mycenaean), but *-jōs* being more remote from alphabetic Greek, '*-jōn* should perhaps be preferred'.

[3] Kuryłowicz, *Categories* 227f.

[4] Id., *Apophonie* 70.

[5] Brugmann, *Grundriss*², ii/1, 548f.; K. Hoffmann, *Aufsätze* ii, 556.

[6] Szemerényi (n. 2 above), 31. Against, Seiler, *Steigerung* 18. According to Cowgill, in Cardona (ed.), *IE and IEs*, 1971, 136, *-ī(yas-)* continues a laryngeal.

[7] See further Euler 1979, 245f.

7.8.5

A superlative with the suffix *-isto-* appears in Greek (*βέλτ-ιστος*), Aryan (*náv-iṣṭha-* 'newest'), and Germanic (Goth. *bat-ista-* 'best'); *-isto-* seems to be a combination of *-is-*, the zero grade of the comparative suffix, and the suffix *-to-* (see 7.8.8).[1]

[1] Traces of *-isto-* are perhaps to be found in Celtic also (see Szemerényi 1978, 128 f.), and even in Venetic if KTVLISTOI, etc., are rightly interpreted as *Klut-isto-*, etc. (*Gn* 51, 1979, 13), but certainly not in Lat. *iouiste*, see Szemerényi, *Studies Palmer*, 1976, 408. Furthermore (see ibid. 410), formations in *-isteros* and (Lat.) *-istumus* could be extensions of superlatives in *-isto-*; see also Szemerényi 1989, 43–6.

7.8.5.1. The vowel grade of the root before the comparative and superlative suffixes is clear only in Indo-Iranian and Greek, and even there it is not wholly straightforward. According to Meillet, full grade was the norm in both language groups, e.g. OInd. *uru-* 'wide': *var-īyas-*, *-iṣṭha-*; *pr̥thu-* 'wide': *prath-īyas-*, *-iṣṭha-*; *guru-* 'heavy': *gar-īyas-*; Gr. *πολύς* 'much, many': *πλείων*, *πλεῖστος* (cf. OInd. *prāyas-*) from **pleH-?*.[1] On the other hand Osthoff was of the view [2] that only the comparative showed full grade, as opposed to zero grade in the superlative. However, forms like *πλεῖστος*, *μήκιστος*, *ἥκιστα* perhaps support rather the former opinion.[3]

[1] Meillet, *MSL* 11, 1899, 6f. (it is from the outset unlikely that *κρέσσων/κράτιστος* represents anything old), but *Introduction* 270f. (*κρεσσ-/κρατ-* may be old); so also Brugmann, *Grundriss*², ii/1, 392f., 557f.; Wackernagel and Debrunner, *Ai. Gr.* ii/2, 455f.; more recently Cowgill (above, 7.8.4. n. 6), 126.

[2] Osthoff, in *MU* 6, 1910, 70–157; so also Seiler, *Steigerung* 20f., 122, who attaches particular importance to the accent difference between comparative and superlative in Germanic.

[3] See further Euler 1979, 246.

7.8.6

Whereas *-yes-* and *-isto-* have the same functions in all languages in which they occur, namely to form comparatives and superlatives, there are two further groups of formations which in some languages are used as true degrees of comparison but also, alongside this, and in other languages exclusively, for other purposes.

In Aryan *-tara-* and *-tama-* are used in concurrence with *-yas-* and *-iṣṭha-*, e.g. *tavas-tara-* 'stronger', *puru-tama-* 'very many'. The corresponding Greek forms are *-τερος* and *-τατος*, the latter clearly reshaped from *-ταμος* on the analogy of the ordinal numerals, in which *-ατος* had likewise gained ground at the expense of *-ταμος*.[1]

In Greek *o*-stem adjectives the stem vowel is lengthened to *ω* before these suffixes if otherwise a sequence of four short vowels would arise, e.g. *σοφώτερος* (not *σοφο-τερος*). Saussure saw the lengthening as required by rhythmical needs;[2] today its origin is sought in adverbs in *-ω*;[3] Schwyzer's suggestion [4] of *πρότερος* and *ἀνώτερος* as models for the alternation *o*/*ω* deserves attention.

The basic suffixes *-tero-* and *-tm̥o-* appear in forms derived not only from adjectives but also from adverbs; e.g. **ud-* 'up', Vedic *ut-tara-* 'upper, higher, later', *ut-tama* 'uppermost, highest, last' and Gr. *ὕστερος*, *ὕστατος*; Lat. *ex-terus*, *ex-timus*; *in-terus*, *in-timus*. Here it can also be seen that most adverbs show an earlier form of these suffixes, namely *-ero-* and *-m̥o-*:[5] e.g. **upo*, **upero-*, **upm̥o-/*upmo-* in OInd. *upa*, *upara-*, *upama-*, Lat. *s-ub*, *s-uperus*, *s-ummus*, Gr. *ὑπό*, *ὕπερος*, *ὕπατος* (from *ὕπαμο-*); IE **n̥dher*, **n̥dhero-*, **n̥dhm̥o-* in OInd. *adhaḥ*, *adhara-*, *adhama-*, Lat. *inferus*, *infimus*. In Germanic likewise both modes of formation occur; cf. Goth. *hindar* 'behind', *hindumists* 'hindmost' from *-ter-*, *-tm̥o-* and *uf*, *ufar*, *auhuma* from **upo*, **uper*, **upm̥o*;[6] the widespread view that formations in *-uma-* are comparative is false.[5] In Celtic we similarly find partly *-tamo-*, e.g. in Gaul. *Ver-tamo-corī*, name of a tribe in Upper Italy, 'the highest army' (*vertamo-* from **uper-tm̥o-*), partly *-amo-*, e.g. in Hispano-Celtic *veramos* 'supremus' (from **uper-tm̥o-*); a modification of *-tero-* must be present in the Old Irish equative, e.g. *déinithir* 'as swift as' (from **deinitri-*?).[7]

A peculiar variant is found in the superlative of the Italic and Celtic languages. Neither the old *-isto-*[8] nor the possible *-(t)amo-* is used in this function, but an innovation *-samo-* or *-isamo-*.[9] This form is especially clear in Celtic; cf. Gaul. *Οὐξισάμη* 'very high', (*Marti*) *Rigisamo* 'most kingly'. Since *Οὐξάμη*, which also occurs, is clearly shortened from *Οὐξισάμη*, it is probable that forms such as OIr. *tressam* 'strongest', *nessam* 'nearest' have arisen from **treg(si-)samo-* **nes(si-)samo-*, and thus have the same suffix as OIr. *sinem*, OW *hinham* 'oldest', both from **senisamo-* (not **sen-samo-*). In Latin the usual suffix is certainly *-issimus*, but the type *facillimus pigerrimus* in any case points, in agreement with Celtic, to **faklisamos* **pigrisamos*, so that *-issimus* will have arisen from *-isamos* on the analogy of *-errimus* *-illimus*;[10] *maximus* too must have come by syncope from **mag-is-*

amos,[11] as do *ōximē proximus* from **ōk-isamo- *prop-isamo-* (with *ps*> *ks*), while *ōc-issimus* reflects the new type.

Since *-isamo-* is confined to the Italic and Celtic languages, whereas *-isto-*, occurring in the south-east (Indic and Greek) and north-west (Germanic), must according to the principles of linguistic geography have at one time existed in the intervening area and so in Indo-European as a whole, it seems clear that *-isamo-* has displaced an earlier *-isto-*. The innovation *-isamo-*, more precisely *-i-somo*, finds a correspondence in the Germanic type present e.g. in Goth. *lustu-sama* 'longed for', OHG *lust-sam* 'lovely, pleasant'. Semantically these formations corresponded to the English type *godlike*, *ladylike*, etc., and as emphatic forms they came into competition with the old superlative, which they finally ousted.[12]

[1] Kuryłowicz, *Categories* 238. Did the suffix *-tero-* also exist in Hittite? In favour would be Kronasser's interpretation of *kattera-* 'lower' as *katta-tera-* (*Etymologie* 187).

[2] Saussure, *Recueil* 465; cf. Schwyzer, *GG* i, 239; Szemerényi, *Syncope* 272f.

[3] Kuryłowicz, *Categories* 234.

[4] Schwyzer, *GG* i, 535.

[5] Szemerényi, '*Auhuma*' 3f., in spite of Trutmann, *Studien zum Adjectiv im Gotischen*, 1972, 44f.

[6] Szemerényi, op. cit., 25.

[7] Meid, 'Zum Aequativ der Keltischen Sprachen', *Fs. Pokorny*, 1967, 223–42; but see Campanile, *Studi Pisani*, 1969, 195 (*-teroi*); Charles-Edwards, *Ériu* 22, 1971, 188f.; Lambert, *EC* 14, 1976, 479f.; Jasanoff, *Sprache* 34, 1992, 186–8.

[8] Lat. *iuxta* is hardly evidence for *-isto-*.

[9] On *-isamo-*, cf. Kuryłowicz, *Categories* 238; Cowgill (above, 7.8.4 n. 6), 125, 129–31; Faust and Tovar, *BzN* 6, 1971, 347f. (names), and more examples further in the text. See also Jasanoff (n. 7 above), 171–89. Hispano-Celtic coins have *Letaišama* (=*Letisama*?) from **pletism̥ā* 'very wide (plain)', and Celtic (?) place-name *Ledesma* (near Salamanca), pre-Celtic *Bletisama*, see K. H. Schmidt, *I Coloquio sobre lenguas . . . de la peninsula iberica* (1974), 1976, 333.

Note that *-tamo-* in Italo-Celtic forms derivatives not only from adverbs but also from nouns, cf. Lat. *fini-*, *mari-timus*, *aestumō*, and Celtic *Cuno-*, *Rigo-tamo-*, which certainly do not, as Hamp thinks (*EC* 14, 1976, 188f.), contain **(s)tə-mo* 'standing'.

[10] Bartoněk, 'K problematice latinského superlativu na *-issimus*', *Listy Filologické* 78, 1955, 1–8 (9–10 French summary).

[11] F. Skutsch, *Vollmöllers Romanische Jahresberichte* 7, 1905, i 49; Haudry, *Hommage R. Schilling*, 1983, 485: from *mag(i)s-m̥mo-*, not from *-issimus*.

[12] Szemerényi, *Studies Palmer*, 1976, 407–18, esp. 413f.

7.8.7

From these facts it follows that Indo-European, or at all events late Indo-European, had a system of comparison in which *-yes-* and *-isto-* were used to form comparatives and superlatives in the familiar sense. Alongside these, however, was a group of formations in *-(t)ero-* and *-(t)m̥o-*, which in contrast to the adjectival group were based mainly on adverbs. While *-tero-* still showed no trace of a comparative use, *-(t)m̥o-*, used as an elative, came very close to the superlative, cf. *summus* and (*uir*) *clārissimus*.

On the basis of pairs such as *exterus–interus*, *dexter–sinister*, *δεξιτερός–ἀριστερός*, *ἡμέτερος–ὑμέτερος*, it has long been supposed that the suffix *-tero-* was used to mark the opposition of contrasting concepts.[1] Against this Benveniste put forward the opinion[2] that the opposition was not between two forms in *-tero-* but between one form in *-tero-* and another in the positive; the contrasting pairs were thus *δεξιός–ἀριστερός*, *σκαιός–δεξιτερός*, or *ὑμός–ἡμέτερος*. Moreover a noun like Lat. *mātertera* did not stand in opposition to *māter*, as 'la presque mère', but to *amita* as the 'real' aunt from whom the 'maternal' aunt was to be distinguished. Similarly, Aryan names for animals like OInd. *ašva-tara-* 'mule' (NPers. *astar*) or NPers. *kabōtar* 'dove' (from **kapauta-tara-*) were to be understood not comparatively, as 'nearly horse' etc., but as differentiating the mule, 'of the horse kind', from the ass, etc. Thus a 'differentiating value' or 'separative function' is ascribed to *-tero-*; it 'qualifie surtout des notions de caractère spatial (positions dans l'espace et dans le temps)' (n. 2 below, 121).

The suffix *-yes-* was formerly thought to have been used to form verbal adjectives, serving 'to intensify a verbal notion' but, in contrast to *-tero-*, 'without special regard to another'.[1] In Benveniste's view[2] formations in *-yes-* display 'une qualité intrinsèque' in its clearest aspect; they are adjectives 'de sens dimensionnel': **mag-no-* is 'positivement grand' and **mag-yes-* 'mesurablement grand' (pp. 121–4).

Parallel to this semantic difference, Benveniste maintained (pp. 140f.), runs a syntactical difference which can be illustrated by Lat. *maior mē* and *maior quam ego*. The use of the case was normal with *-yes-*, and it served as an equative: *lūce clārior* meant properly 'clair *comme* le jour', *melle dulcius* 'sweet *as* honey'. The construction with the particle, originally normal with *-tero-*, had a disjunctive function, expressing a choice between two alternatives: *plūs mihi dedit quam tibi*.[3]

This elegant theory is attractive especially because it ties together three properties—form, function, and construction. It does not, however, do justice to the facts. The expressions *melle dulcius*, *lūce clārior* simply do not mean 'sweet as', 'clear as' (there were ways of saying this), but just 'sweeter than', 'clearer than'.[4] The attempt to connect *-tero-* with the particle construction is made merely for the sake of symmetry; in fact *-τερο-* is found also with the genitive, e.g. (*ἵπποι*) *λευκότεροι χιόνος*, and *-ίων* also with *ἤ*, e.g. *πλέονες σόοι ἠέ πέφανται* 'more are unharmed than killed'.[5]

[1] Schwyzer, *GG* ii, 183f.

[2] Benveniste, *Noms d'agent et noms d'action en indo-européen*, 1948, 115f.; cf. Szemerényi, *ArchL* 1, 1950, 187–91; Euler 1979, 251f. A noteworthy parallel to *-tero-/zero* is provided by the opposition between *-yes-* and a positive in the Gathic pair *spanyå–angra* (Y. 45, 2), see Schaeder, *ZDMG* 94, 1940, 401; Humbach, *Gathas* i, 34b *a* and ii, 62 ('wholesome–

pernicious'). With this can be compared Hungarian *jobb* 'right' (a comparative, properly 'better')–*bal* 'left'.

[3] Latin usages have been studied in the light of this theory by A. Ghiselli, *Grammatica e filologia*, 1961, 23–67, and Witwer, *Glotta* 47, 1970, 54–110 (with many idiosyncrasies of interpretation).

[4] Cf. also H. Thesleff, *Studies on Intensification in Early and Classical Greek*, 1954, 127f.; Risch, *Glotta* 33, 1954, 215f.; Belardi, *AGI* 65, 1981, 1–13; *In memoria A. Pagliaro*, Rome 1984, 77.

[5] N. Berg, 'Einige Betrachtungen über den idg. Komparationskasus', *NTS* 18, 1958, 202–30, esp. 212f. On comparison, see further V. Skard, *Dativstudien*, 1952, 72f.; Puhvel, 'Nature and means of comparison in PIE grammar', *JIES* 1, 1973, 145–54; Panagl, 'Präsuppositionen und die Syntax der lateinischen Komparation', in G. Drachman (ed.), *Salzburger Beiträge zur Linguistik* i, Tübingen 1975, 361–75; N. Reiter, *Komparative*, 1979; P. K. Andersen, in Ramat (ed.), *Linguistic Reconstruction and IE Syntax*, 1980, 225–36; *Word Order Typology and Comparative Constructions*, Amsterdam 1983; R. Stefanelli, *SSL* 24, 1984, 187–225; Krisch, 'Presupposition in Old Norse comparative constructions', *TPS* 86, 1988, 44–62; Rivara 1990.

7.8.8

The fact remains that *-yes-* and *-tero-*, although in Aryan and Greek they show the same constructions, had certainly at one time expressed something different, since even formally they are different. It is also certain that the comparative use of *-tero-* is an innovation of those languages and not of IE date, whereas the comparative use of *-yes-* and the superlative use of *-isto-* must be ascribed to Indo-European.

At an earlier stage things must have looked somewhat different. Thus it has recently been conjectured by various authors that *-yes-* originally formed not a comparative adjective but an intensive noun, which through being used as predicate was early transformed into an adjective and, coupled with positives, acquired an elative and subsequently comparative meaning.[1] This would also provide a good explanation for the superlative. For if *-yes-* was adjectival from the beginning, it is impossible to explain how *-isto-* acquired its form and function. The view that *-isto-* arose from comparative *-is-* and demonstrative *to-*[2] has against it that we should then have expected comparative *-yōs-* and *so*, i.e. *-yōsso(s)*, while the idea that it combines adverbial *-is* (cf. *magis*) and the *-to-* of the ordinal numerals[3] leaves the formation wholly unexplained. From a noun in *-is-*, on the other hand, we obtain with the usual suffix *-to-* (cf. Lat. *cēnātus barbātus*) a formation[4] which completely explains the basic elative meaning of the superlative.

In the case of *-tero-* it is first to be noted that beside it stands *-ero-*. The *-t-* has been explained as a connecting consonant, occurring originally only after sonants like the suffix *-t-* in root nouns (e.g. OInd. *kr̥-t-* 'maker'), and later used to eliminate hiatus; this accounted for OInd. *ni-t-ara- vi-t-ara-*, from which *-tara-* was also extended to *ka-tara-* (Gr. πότερος), etc.[5] On the other hand it has also been held that *-ero-/-tero-* were *o*-stem derivatives from neuters in *-er-/-ter-*:[6] πρότερος would then be from **pro-ter* 'front', OInd. *antara-* 'interior' from **antar* 'inside', IE **en-ter* (Lat. *inter*), and even OInd. *aśvatara-* 'mule' from **aśva-tar-* 'horse-nature'. Since, however, this type of formation certainly started from adverbs of place, it seems clear that **up-er* 'above', **en-er* 'within', etc., are compounds of **er-* 'earth' (Gr. ἔρα, Goth. *airþa*, etc.); IE **ant-* 'front, face (Lat. *ante*) gave **ant-ar-o-* (Lat. *anterior*), and from this *-tero-* may have been carried over to **pos-tero-*, etc.[7]

The suffix *-m-*, which appears in the forms *-mo- -m̥o- -tm̥o-* (Lat. *summus* from **s-up-mo-s*; *infimus* from **n̥dh-m̥o-s*=OInd. *adhama-*; *postumus*), is firmly anchored in the IE system as the elative counterpart of *-ero-/-tero-*. Whether it is identical with the similar suffix of the ordinals[8] and in the last resort originates from them,[9] remains uncertain.

[1] Friš, *AO* 21, 1953, 101–13; Erhart, *AO* 24, 1956, 432f.; Berg (above, 7.8.7 n. 5), 225f.; Kuryłowicz, *Categories* 227f.

[2] e.g. Aitzetmüller, *Sprache* 3, 1957, 132.

[3] Schwyzer, *GG* i, 537.

[4] So also Friš (n. 1 above), 109, who refers to Lat. *iūstus*, and (?) Kuryłowicz, *Categories* 230; cf. Benveniste (above, 7.8.7 n. 2), 161f.; Szemerényi, *Numerals* 91 and *Studies Palmer*, 1976, 411f.

[5] Kuryłowicz, *Categories* 235f.

[6] Burrow, *The Sanskrit Language*, 1955, 147, 149.

[7] Szemerényi, *PICL* 7, 1956, 483; a different view in Reiter (above, 7.8.7 n. 5), 88.

[8] Szemerényi, *Numerals* 86f.

[9] Kuryłowicz, *Categories* 236f.

7.8.9. Suppletivism

A peculiarity which can be observed in English or Latin adjectives, and is denoted by the comprehensive term *suppletivism*,[1] is that forms expressing the different degrees of comparison do not always come from the same root (*good–better–best*, *bonus–melior–optimus*). This peculiarity was obviously more widespread in the earlier stages of the IE languages. Since it particularly affects value concepts like 'great–small', 'good–bad', 'many–few', etc., and in spite of equalizing trends can be repeatedly reintroduced, it is impossible to reconstruct common IE expressions for such concepts. Compare, for instance, the terms for 'good': OInd. *vasu-*, Gr. ἀγαθός, Lat. *bonus*, Gmc. **gōđaz*, etc. In these circumstances it is interesting that as first members of compounds **su-* 'good' and **dus-* 'bad' can be reconstructed for Indo-European; cf. OInd. *su-/duṣ-*, Gr. εὐ-/δυσ-, OIr. *su-/du-*, Gmc. *Su(gambri)/tuz-*, OCS *sŭ(dravŭ)/dŭždĭ* 'rain' (from **dus-dyus* 'bad sky').[2]

According to Humboldt, this peculiarity of language is undesirable, and uniformity in speech symbolism is, on the other hand, to be desired: both roots and grammatical features should be uniform and stable.[3] The ever-self-renewing process of suppletivism shows, however, that from a historical viewpoint the uniformity and stability of paradigms do not always appear as the highest aim.

[1] Osthoff, *Vom Suppletivwesen der idg. Sprachen*, 1899; Seiler, *Steigerung* 27f.; Jaberg, 'Suppletività', in *Raccolta in onore di G. D. Serra*, 1959, 27–38 (reprinted in Jaberg, *Sprachwissenschaftliche Forschungen und Erlebnisse*, NS 1965, 223–32); Mańczak, 'La nature du supplétivisme', *Lings* 28, 1967, 82–9; *Sprache* 15, 1969, 8–13; Levin, 'Non-paradigmatic forms: suppletion or preemption', *FL* 8, 1972, 346–59; Strunk, 'Überlegungen zur Defektivität und Suppletion im Griechischen und Indogermanischen', *Glotta* 55, 1977, 2–29, esp. 10f.; Werner, 'Suppletivwesen durch Lautwandel', in G. Drachmaṇ (ed.), *Akten der 2. Salzburger Frühlingstagung für Linguistik*, Tübingen 1977, 269–83.

[2] Cf. Friš, *AO* 21, 1953, 175–8; Schlerath, 'Some remarks on I-I **dus*- and **su*-', *Cama Oriental Institute Golden Jubilee Volume*, Bombay 1969, 113–20; Mayrhofer, *KEWA* iii, 478f.; Szemerényi 1978, 46; Klein, *Sprache* 28, 1982, 24; Gamkrelidze–Ivanov, 780; Catsanicos, *BSL* 81, 1986, 169f.: IE **(H)su*- 'bien' in Hitt. *su-hmili*-; Meier-Brügger, *HS* 102/1, 1989, 60 and n. 17; *G. Costa, *I composti ie. con* dus- *e* su-, Pisa 1990. On suppletivism in the verb, see below, 9.4.4.3.

[3] See T. Vennemann and T. H. Wilbur, *Schuchardt*, 1972, 184.

8

Morphology II: Pronouns and Numerals

8.1. PRELIMINARY REMARKS ON THE PRONOUNS

Although the inflexion of the pronoun is not in principle different from that of the noun and adjective, there are nevertheless some peculiarities which separate the pronoun from them.

(*a*) Different stems are used for case forms which, we feel, ought to be based on one single stem. Thus the nom. of the personal pronoun 'I' is **egō* (and similar), but the acc. is **me*; the animate nom. s. of the main demonstrative pronoun is **so*/**sā*, but all other cases are formed from a stem **to*-.

(*b*) Pronouns do not always use the case-endings of the noun. Sometimes there are no endings at all; sometimes endings are found that are unknown in noun inflexion. Further, certain insertions often appear between stem and ending. Cf. e.g. acc. **me*, **t(w)e* 'me, thee' as opposed to **ekwo-m* 'horse', and OInd. dat. s. *ta-sm-ai* 'this', not **tāi* or **tāya*.

(*c*) Pronouns are very often strengthened by means of various deictic particles, as in the French series *ce*, *celui*, *celui-ci*. Cf. e.g. Lat. *ego-met nōs-met*.

(*d*) The personal pronouns show no difference of gender. The demonstratives and interrogatives distinguish gender, but some make no difference between masculine and feminine.

The pronouns which distinguish gender resemble nouns closely in inflexion, and are treated here before those which do not distinguish gender, i.e. the personal pronouns.[1]

[1] For detailed information on 49 non-European languages, see U. Wiesemann (ed.), *Pronominal Systems*, 1986. Cf. also F. Corblin, *Indéfini, défini et démonstratif*, Geneva 1987; Serbat, 'Le signifié pronominal', in *Convegno* 7, 1987, 517–26.

8.2. DEMONSTRATIVE PRONOUNS

Since the function of demonstrative pronouns—*deixis*—includes an indication of position in relation to the person speaking, corresponding to different degrees of distance there are a number of demonstratives. In the IE languages the maximum appears to be a system of four: (*a*) *I-deixis* (here, near the speaker), (*b*) *thou-deixis* (there, near the person addressed), (*c*) *that-deixis* (there, without a particular spatial reference), (*d*) *yonder-deixis* (yonder, over there).[1] More frequent is the ternary system of Latin with *hic*, *iste*, *ille*, to which of course the neutral *is* must be added. The most important, or at least the most amply represented, of the demonstrative pronouns are the antecedents of *the*, *that*, and *it*, IE **so*, **sā*, **tod* and **is*, **ī*, **id*.

[1] Brugmann, *Die Demonstrativa der idg. Sprachen*, 1904; *Grundriss*[2] ii 2, 302f.; Wackernagel, *Vorlesungen über Syntax*[2], ii, 1928, 103 (*hic, iste, ille, to-*); Frei, 'Systèmes déictiques', *AL* 4, 1944, 111–29; the most widespread systems are the *binary*, *here-there*, and *ternary*, *hic-iste-ille*; the complex is older; Mendoza, 'La organización de las deixis', *RSEL* 6, 1976, 89–111; Biraud, 'L'évolution des systèmes démonstratifs en grec ancien', *Document* 8 (Univ. Nice), 1983, 2–28. In general: J. Lyons, *Introduction to Theoretical Linguistics*, 1968, 275f.; R. Harweg, *Pronomina und Textkonstitution*, 1968; 'Formen des Zeigens und ihr Verhältnis zur Deixis', *ZDL* 43, 1976, 317–37, esp. 328f.; Milewski, *Lings* 59, 1970, 94f.; Fillmore, *Santa Cruz Lectures on Deixis*, IULC 1975; J. Weissenborn and W. Klein (eds.), *Here and There: Cross-linguistic Studies on Deixis and Demonstration*, Amsterdam 1982 (cf. *LeS* 19, 1984, 639f.); G. Rauh, *IF* 87, 1982, 26f. (on the deixis system of W. P. Schmid); G. F. Meier, 'Funktionalgrammatische Studie zur Deixis', *ZPhon* 37, 1984, 143–52; P. Auer, 'On Deixis and Displacement', *FoL* 22, 1988, 263–92; P. de Carvalho, *BSL* 86, 1991, 211–44 (on Latin demonstratives); M.-A. Morel and L. Danon-Boileau (eds.), *La deixis: Colloque en Sorbonne*, Paris 1992; G. M. Diewald, *Deixis und Textsorten im Deutschen*, Tübingen 1991.

8.2.1

The best-attested demonstrative, as has been said, used the stems **so-*/**sā-* and **to-*/**tā-*. For the paradigm OInd. (*a*), OCS (*b*), Lith. (*c*), Goth. (*d*), and Gr. (Doric) (*e*) are of decisive importance.

(*a*)	Sing.			Plur.			Dual		
	M.	N.	F.	M.	N.	F.	M.	N.	F.
Nom.	*sa*	*tad*	*sā*	*tē*	*tā(ni)*	*tās*	*tā(u)*	*tē*	*tē*
Acc.	*tam*	*tad*	*tām*	*tān*	*tā(ni)*	*tās*	*tā(u)*	*tē*	*tē*
Gen.	*tásya*		*tásyās*	*tḗṣām*		*tā́sām*	*táyōs*		
Abl.	*tásmād*		*tásyās*	*tḗbhyas*		*tā́bhyas*	*tā́bhyām*		
Dat.	*tásmai*		*tásyai*	*tḗbhyas*		*tā́bhyas*	*tā́bhyām*		
Loc.	*tásmin*		*tásyām*	*tḗṣu*		*tā́su*	*táyōs*		
Instr.	*tḗna*		*táyā*	*tḗbhis (tais)*		*tā́bhis*	*tā́bhyām*		

(*b*)	Sing.			Plur.			Dual			(*c*) Sing.		Plur.	
	M.	N.	F.	M.	N.	F.	M.	N.	F.	M.	F.	M.	F.
N.	*tŭ*	*to*	*ta*	*ti*	*ta*	*ty*	*ta*	*tē*	*tē*	*tas*	*ta*	*tiẽ*	*tõs*
A.	*tŭ*	*to*	*tǫ*	*ty*	*ta*	*ty*	*ta*	*tē*	*tē*	*tą*	*tą*	*túos*	*tás*
G.	*togo*		*toję*	*tēxŭ*			*toju*			*to*	*tos*	*tų̃*	*tų̃*
D.	*tomu*		*toji*	*tēmŭ*				*tēma*		*tám*	*tai*	*tíems*	*tóms*
L.	*tomĭ*		*toji*	*tēxŭ*				*toju*		*tamè*	*tojè*	*tuosè*	*tosè*
I.	*tēmĭ*		*tojǫ*	*tēmi*				*tēma*		*tuomì*	*tą*	*taĩs*	*tomìs*

	(*d*) Sing.			Plur.			(*e*) Sing.			Plur.			Dual
	M.	N.	F.	M.	N.	F.	M.	N.	F.	M.	N.	F.	
N.	*sa*	*þata*	*sō*	*þai*	*þō*	*þōs*	ὁ	τό	ἁ̄	τοί	τά	ταί	τώ
A.	*þana*	*þata*	*þō*	*þans*	*þō*	*þōs*	τόν	τό	τᾱ́ν	τούς	τά	τᾱ́ς	τώ
G.	*þis*		*þizōs*	*þizē*		*þizō*	τοῦ		τᾶς	τῶν		τᾶν	τοῖν
D.	*þamma*		*þizai*	*þaim*			τῶι		τᾶι	τοῖς		ταῖς	τοῖν

Without Old Indic, the relationships would be hard to recognize. OInd. *tasmai* shows, however, that in Goth. *þamma -mm-* is assimilated from *-sm-*, which is confirmed also by Umbrian *esmei* 'huic', *pusme* 'cui', and OPrus. *stesmu* (dat. s. m. n.) 'the, this'. Similarly *tasya tasyās* etc. indicate *-sy-* in these cases, which is supported by Hom. τοῖο, Lat. *eius cuius* from **esyo(s)* *k^w*esyo(s)*. The difference between *tēṣām* and *tāsām* etc. in the plural is blurred in OCS and Gothic, but is proved to be original (**toisōm*, **tāsōm*) by Gr. τᾶν, earlier τᾱ́ων, Lat. *(is)tārum* from **tāsōm*. Possibly the Greek pronoun τοῖος was based on the inherited gen. pl. τοίων from **toisōm*, which in any case is presupposed by OCS and Germanic (cf. the adjectival gen. pl. Goth. *blindaizē*, *-aizō*).

Not all cases can be restored with certainty, but in essentials the following paradigm correctly reproduces the late IE situation (cf. also Beekes, in *Studies Polomé* (1988), 83; Dunkel, in *Wackernagel Kolloquium*, 1990, 107):

	Sing.			Plur.			Dual		
	M.	N.	F.	M.	N.	F.	M.	N.	F.
Nom.	**so*	**tod*	**sā*	**toi*	**tā*	**tās*	**tō*	**toi*	**toi*
Acc.	**tom*	**tod*	**tām*	**tōn(s)*	**tā*	**tā(n)s*	**tō*	**toi*	**toi*
Gen.	**tosyo*		**tosyās*	**toisōm*		**tāsōm*			
Abl.	**tosmōd*		**tosyās*	**toibh(y)os*		**tābh(y)os*			
Dat.	**tosmōi*		**tosyāi*	**toibh(y)os*		**tābh(y)os*			
Loc.	**tosmi(n)*			**toisu*		**tāsu*			

The suppletive relationship of **so-*/**to-* can hardly be traced back to a single stem by way of an IE sound law (e.g. **to-tò*>**tto* and then *tt*>*ss*;[1] it is more probable that the duality continues an archaic separation of animate and inanimate (cf. Hungarian *ki* 'who?', *mi* 'what?'). The neuter **tod*, on the other hand, must represent an earlier **tot*, i.e. a repetition **to-t(o)* for the purpose of emphasis; see 5.4.5 n. 3, and Szemerényi, *SM* ii. 930, n. 24. On the gen. **tosyo*, see 8.3.2 below. In regard to the *-sm-* forms it is interesting that, alongside these 'pronominal' forms, substantivally used forms without *-sm-* also occur in various languages,[2] e.g. *tād* beside *tasmād*, etc. It is therefore likely that *-sm-* serves the purpose of emphasis, and is thus either the pronoun stem for 'same'[3] or rather the later numeral **sem-*'one'. The original 'endings' were thus dat. *-sm-ei* (cf. Umbr. *esmei*), abl. *-sm-ed*, which later became *-smōi*, *-smōd* by analogy with the *o*-stems, while the loc. *-sm-i(n)* remained unchanged. For the feminine forms dat. **tosyāi*, abl. **tosyās* one would correspondingly think of feminine 'endings' *-sm-yāi*, *-sm-yās*, i.e. assume simplification of *-smy-* to *-sy-*, in spite of Edgerton's Law.[4] In nom. acc. pl. all forms are identical with those of nouns apart from **toi*, which shows *i* as a mark of the plural; this *i* seems also to occur in the other oblique cases of the masculine and neuter, although for **toisōm* a different explanation is preferable (see below). Like m. **toisōm* the gen. pl. f. **tāsōm* seems to contain an ending *-sōm*, preceded by the feminine stem *-ā*. It is possible that **tāsōm* was innovated in order to avoid the unclear **tōm* (from **tāōm*); the starting-point may have been the loc. pl. **tāsu* which, understood as **tās-su*, led to **tās-ōm*, on the analogy of which a gen. **toi-sōm* was also formed to the nom. pl. m. **toi*;[5] see also below, 8.3.2.

[1] So Heller, *Word* 12, 1956, 7f.; cf. also Hirt, *IF* 2, 1893, 131: nom. **sī* from **t(e)-sī*.
[2] Dal, 'Ein archaischer Zug der germanischen Pronominalflexion', *NTS* 9, 1938, 186–218.
[3] Lane, 'On the formation of the IE demonstrative', *Lg* 37, 1961, 469–75, esp. 471; Anttila, *Introduction* 369; G. L. Cohen, 'On the origin of *-sm-* in IE pronouns', *IF* 81, 1977, 18–24.
[4] On *-sm-*, *-sy-* see also Villar, *RSEL* 2, 1972, 357f.; G. Schmidt, *IF* 82, 1979, 73 (**tosyās* after **tosyo*); Beekes, *Studies Polomé*, 1988, 78–81. See also below, 8.2.2 n. 3. On the development *smy*>*sy*, cf. further δέσποινα<*-ponya* from *-potnya* formed to δεσπότης.
[5] Hermann, 'Der Diphthong *-oi-* im Stamm der geschlechtigen Fürwörter und die Genitivendung *-sōm*', *Fs. Wackernagel*, 1923, 217–19. Conversely, Laroche, *RHA* 76, 1966, 41, seeks to explain **tāsōm* as formed with *-ōm* from the nom. pl. **tās*, which runs counter to the principles of IE case formation. Cf. also Villar, 'El plural de los demonstrativos ie.', *RSEL* 5, 1975, 433–50; Kortlandt, *Fs. Hoenigswald*, 1987, 222 (*-i* plural sign in pronouns and the verbal ending *-nt-i*).

8.2.2

No less widely represented is the anaphoric pronoun **i-*, though its details are not so well preserved. The nom s. m. and n. are well attested as **is *id* by Lat. *is id*, Goth. *is it-a* (OInd. n. *id-am*); similarly the acc. as **im* (**id*) by OLat. *im* (also *em*), Goth. *in-a*, OInd. *im-am*. The *i*-declension is also clear for the nom. acc. pl. m. in Goth. *eis* (from **ey-es* like *gasteis* from **ghostey-es*), *ins*. An alternative stem **e-* appears in other cases. A comparison of Lat. *eius* with OInd. *asya* (m. n.) leads to the gen. s. m. n. IE **esyo*; the dat. s. m. n., as shown by Umbr. *esmei* and OInd. *asmai*,[1] was IE **esmei*, and similar forms with *-sm-* are attested for the abl. and loc. s. m. n. by OInd. *asmād* and *asmin*, while for the corresponding forms of the feminine an element *-sy-* is certain (cf. **to-sm-ei*: **to-sy-āi*, etc.). By a 'coincidence' which is repeated again and again in the Indo-European field, the OInd. gen. pl. m. n. *ēṣām* finds an exact correspondence in Oscan *eisun-k*, both from IE *eisōm (cf. *toisōm), with which Goth. *ize* (from *isōm), with the usual modification of the stem (cf. *þize*), and OCS *ixŭ* agree. The loc. and dat.-abl. pl. can also be determined as **ei-su* (OInd. *ēṣu*, OCS *ixŭ*) and **ei-bh(y)os* (OInd. *ēbhyas*, OLat. *ībus*).

Since the only stems to appear up to this point are **i-*, **e-*, and **ei-*, the Latinist is justified in asking how the Lat. *eo-/eā-* fits into this system. The answer usually given is that these stems have been 'thematicized' from **ei-/*i-*.[2] Such a procedure is not, however, found in any of the other pronouns (not even in **yo-*; see 8.3.3) and must be rejected. A comparison with Oscan-Umbrian shows that *eo-/eā-* was originally confined to the acc. s. m. f. and nom. acc. pl.; Gothic shows further that of these cases only the acc. s.f. and nom. acc. pl. f. n. were originally formed from this stem, and Aryan demonstrates that the original form of the nom. s. f.=nom.-acc. pl. n. was **ī*, to which acc. s. f. **īm/*iyṃ*, nom. acc. pl. f. **iyās* and **iyā(n)s* also belong. We know, however, that *-ī* in the nom.-acc. pl. n. of *i*-stems in the classical languages and Germanic was in general modified to *-i-ā* (cf. OInd. *trī*: Gr. *τρία*, Lat. *tria*, Goth. *þrija*); in Latin accordingly the nom.-acc. pl. n. must also have become **iā*. The forms with prevocalic *i-* (**iā*, **iās*) were then changed to *ea* etc. by analogy with the initial *e-* of *eius* etc., and these forms with **ea-* finally led to the creation of 'thematic' forms like *eum*, *eōrum*, etc.[3]

The IE inflexion of the anaphoric pronoun can accordingly be established as follows:[4]

	Sing. M.	N.	F.	Plur. M.	N.	F.
Nom.	*is	*id	*ī	*eyes	*ī	*iyās
Acc.	*im	*id	*iyṃ	*ins	*ī	*iyā(n)s
Gen.	*esyo		*esyās	*eisōm		
Abl.	*esmōd			*esyās		*eibh(y)os
Dat.	*esmōi			*esyāi		*eibh(y)os
Loc.	*esmi(n)			*eisu		

[1] Dat. **esmei* was modified to **esmōi*, as was **tosmei* to **tosmōi*. In several languages *-m-*, not *-sm-*, appears, but the Gothic *-mm-* shows that here assimilation has taken place and perhaps similarly in Hittite, see Puhvel, *KZ* 92, 1979, 104. The Hispano-Celtic of the Botorrita inscription seems likewise to show *-m-*, cf. dat. *somui* (l.7), loc. *somei* (l.8). According to Rasmussen ('IE ablaut *i~e/o*', '*APILKU* 7, 1988, 125–42) *i* was clitic, *e* accentable, e.g. *im/ésyo*.

[2] Krahe, *Idg. Sprw.* ii, 45. See also Otrębski, 'Die lat. Demonstrativpronomina', *Sprache* 12, 1966, 16f.; J. Molina Yébenes, 'Los pronombres latinos', *Em* 34, 1966, 87f.

[3] Provisionally Szemerényi, *Thes. Ling. Lat.* s.v. *is*. It is strange that for this pronoun Beekes (and Kortlandt), *KZ* 96, 1983, 208f., cite Blümel and not this *Introduction*.

[4] On some forms of the paradigm there is a different view in Hamp, *SCelt* 10/11, 1976, 68f.

8.3. INTERROGATIVE AND RELATIVE PRONOUNS

8.3.1

The _interrogative_ pronoun, which also served as _indefinite_ and in this function was enclitic,[1] is attested in all IE languages. The stem _*k$^{\omega}$i-_ had the same inflexion as the anaphoric _*i-_. The _i_-stem is clearest in the nom. s. m. f. n., e.g. Lat. _quis quid_, Hitt. _kwis kwid_, Gr. _τίς, τί_, and in the acc. s. m.f. Lat. _quem_, Hitt. _kwin_, Gr. _τίν-α_; also Avest. instr. _čī_ 'by what'=Lat. _quī_ 'how' (IE _*k$^{\omega}$ī_), nom. pl. m. OLat. _quēs_=Avest. _čayas(-ča)_ (IE _*k$^{\omega}$eyes_),[2] nom. pl. n. Avest. _čī(-čā)_=Lat. _quia_, preserved only as a conjunction, but still interrogative in _quianam_ 'why then?', and dat.-abl. pl. _quibus_. Beside this there also appears an _e/o_-stem, for certain cases the only stem. Thus the gen. s. m. n. is OInd. _kasya_=Avest. _kahyā_ and _čahyā_, Hom. _τέο_, Att. _τοῦ_, Lat. _cuius_ (early _quoius_), Goth. _hwis_, OHG _hwes_, OCS _česo_, i.e. IE _*k$^{\omega}$es(y)o_.[3] The dat. s. m. n. is OInd. _kasmāi_=Avest. _kahmāi_ and _čahmāi_, i.e. IE _*k$^{\omega}$esmōi_ (_-mei_?) etc. This stem _*k$^{\omega}$e-_ or _*k$^{\omega}$o-_ also invaded other cases which were the domain of _*k$^{\omega}$i-_; cf. OInd. _kas_ 'who', _kam_ 'whom', but in Vedic still also _kis_ 'who', _na-kis_ 'no one'; _kad_ 'what', but IE _*k$^{\omega}$id_ survives in the particle _čid_ 'even, at least'.[4] By using all sources the IE paradigm can be restored as follows (cf. Beekes, in _Studies Polomé_ (1988), 73–87):

	Sing. M. F.	N.	Plur. M. F.	N.
Nom.	_*k$^{\omega}$is_	_*k$^{\omega}$id_	_*k$^{\omega}$eyes_	_*k$^{\omega}$ī_
Acc.	_*k$^{\omega}$im_	_*k$^{\omega}$id_	_*k$^{\omega}$ins_	_*k$^{\omega}$ī_
Gen.	_*k$^{\omega}$esyo_		_*k$^{\omega}$eisōm_	
Dat.	_*k$^{\omega}$esm-ei, -ōi_		_*k$^{\omega}$eibh(y)os_	
Loc.	_*k$^{\omega}$esmi_		_*k$^{\omega}$eisu_	
Instr.	_*k$^{\omega}$ī_			

[1] On the question whether the indefinite pronoun arose from the interrogative or vice versa, and also whether the question has any meaning at all, see the references in _Glotta_ 35, 1956, 99 n. 4, and in addition Nehring, _Sprachzeichen und Sprechakte_, 1963, 204f.; Monteil, _La phrase relative en grec ancien_, 1963, 129; Hofmann—Szantyr, 457. Note Orlandini's view, quoted by Serbat, _BSL_ 81, 1986, 311, that 'un _quid_ interrogatif présuppose un _quid_ indéfini'. On the indefinite pronoun, see also N. Danielsen, _ZDS_ 24, 1968, 92–117, esp. 109f.

[2] The Avestan hapax is not certain: according to Andreas it is an _s_-stem from _či-_ 'to note'; according to Oettinger, _MSS_ 42, 1983, 184 n. 12, in any case not a pronoun.

[3] Szemerényi, _Glotta_ 35, 1956, 197f. On the stems, see further Vaillant, _BSL_ 37, 1936, 103f.; Tedesco, _Lg_ 21, 1943, 133; Rasmussen (above, 8.2.2 n. 1).

[4] See further Hamp, 'The British interrogative pronoun', _SCelt_ 10/11, 1976, 56–69.

8.3.2

An interesting feature of this paradigm is the _e_ vocalism of the gen. s. etc., which agrees with the anaphoric _*is_ (gen. s. _*esyo_) but stands in contrast to the _o_ vocalism of _*tosyo_. The _e_ vocalism explains the palatalization by which k^{w}- becomes _č_- in the main satem languages. Beside these, however, there were also adverbial forms with _ku_-, which kept the velar, and _*k^{w}osyo_, analogous to _*tosyo_, was probably also formed. These circumstances explain the fact that in Avestan, alongside the expected _ča-/či-_, _ka-_ is also found, and the latter has even obliterated almost every trace of the palatalized form in Old Indic. In OCS the pair _ko-/či-_ was used to indicate the opposition of animate/inanimate: _kŭ-to_ 'who', _čĭ-to_ 'what'.

It is of course even more interesting that in the inflexion of the _i_-stem _*k^{w}i_ a stem _*k^{w}e-/*k^{w}o-_ appears in the genitive and some other cases, and is then also used in derivatives like _*k^{w}oti_ 'how many' (OInd. _kati_, Lat. _quot_), _*k^{w}oteros_ 'which of two' (OInd. _kataras_, Gr. _πότερος_). Here it would be possible simply to take note of the fact that various enlargements could be formed from the interrogative stem (but from which?), and that these were even combined in a single paradigm. But here again, as in the case of Lat. _eo-/eā-_, we can ask whether the _e-/o-_ stem is not of secondary origin. For this we must examine more closely the pronominal genitive in _-syo_.

It is generally assumed that the pronominal gen. in _-syo_ is an extension of an original gen. in _-es/-os_, i.e. that in the case of _*tosyo_ the gen. was at first simply _*tos_. The element _-yo_ is viewed in different ways, e.g. as identical with the 'suffix of belonging' _-yo-_[1] or with the relative pronoun _*yo-_.[2] But in that case how is the remaining part _*k^{w}es- *es-_ to be assessed, if it is already a gen. s. in itself? Correctly put the question must be: how can _*k^{w}es *es_ represent the genitive of _*$k^{w}$is *is_? Since the gen. s. of these _i_-stems was _*k^{w}eis *eis_, the conclusion inevitably follows that the extended forms _*k^{w}eis-yo *eis-yo_ became _*k^{w}esyo *esyo_ by dissimilation. In the same way the dat. s. was originally _*k^{w}eyei-smei_, which became _*k^{w}eismei_ by haplology and then _*k^{w}esmei_ by dissimilation. The gen. pl. _*k^{w}eisōm_ is from original _*k^{w}eisyo_ extended with _-om_, giving _*k^{w}eisyōm_ which became _*k^{w}eisōm_ by dissimilation. The direction of dissimilation in the plural was doubtless determined by the nom. pl. _*k^{w}ey-es_; the new _*k^{w}eisōm_ must have been responsible for the variant _-so_ of the gen. s. (OCS _česo_, Goth. _hwis_ from _*hwesa_).[3]

The new stems _*k^{w}e-/*k^{w}o-_, _*e-/*o-_, which had thus arisen through purely phonetic processes, were then introduced into cases in which originally _i_ was in place, e.g. acc. s. _*k^{w}om_ beside or instead of _*k^{w}im_. In this the demonstrative _*to-_, an _o_-stem from the beginning, must have served as model.

[1] Brugmann, *Grundriss*², ii/2, 121; Knobloch, *Sprache* 2, 1950, 143 (*-s* is ergative!); Bader, *HS* 101, 1989, 209 n. 133 (**kʷoy-yo-*).
[2] Since Schleicher, see Wackernagel and Debrunner, *Ai. Gr.* iii, 96; Watkins, *Celtica* 6, 1962, 16 n. 1, 28 n. 2. The idea that the combination of two pronominal stems (*e+syo*, *to+syo*) produced a gen. (Specht, *Ursprung* 363f.) can only be described as bizarre.
[3] Brugmann (n. 1 above), 161, 361. Cf. also above, 7.6.2 and 8.6.7 n. 6.

8.3.3

The interrogative pronoun, as has been said, is also used as an indefinite in all IE languages. In some, however, it is used additionally as *relative*, either without (Hittite) or with formal differentiation (Lat. *quo-* as opposed to *quis*). To the group which uses **kʷi-/*kʷo-* as a relative belong Anatolian, Tocharian, Italic, later also Celtic and Germanic. Another group comprising Aryan, Greek, Phrygian, and Slavic uses **yos*, **yā*, **yod* as the relative:[1] OInd. *yas*, *yā*, *yad*; Gr. *ὅς*, *ἥ*, *ὅ*; Phryg. *ιος*, Slav. *i-že*. This state of affairs gives rise to several questions.

In the first place, as regards the origin of these relative pronouns, it is clear that **kʷi-* is identical with the interrogative-indefinite already discussed. One must ask, however, how the relative developed on this basis. Some think that it arose from the indefinite,[2] but probably the interrogative also played a part in its development; cf. *pecuniam quis nancitor, habeto*, originally 'Someone finds money? Then let him keep it', and 'Do what he orders' from 'What does he order? Do it'.[3] On the other hand, the origin of **yos* from a demonstrative, namely the anaphoric **i-*, is certain[4] and can be compared to English 'that'; cf. 8.2.2 n. 2.

The second problem is concerned with area and period: were both relatives already present in Indo-European, and if so, what was their distribution? Since no IE language uses both pronouns as relatives, the point of the first question can only be whether all IE languages retained, alongside the relative, traces of the other pronoun also in that function. Thus **yo-* certainly does not exist in Hittite or Tocharian, but Hitt. *ya* and Toch. A *yo* 'and' have been derived from a relative *yo-*;[5] this is in no way conclusive, since a demonstrative 'so, then' would be sufficient, and the same applies also to Goth. *jabai* 'if, when', and similar. The theories that IE had possessed **yo-* as relative,[6] or that **kʷi-* was used as a generalizing relative and **yo-* as a definite relative[7] are therefore untenable. On the contrary, the common IE validity of **kʷi-* as relative seems to be proved by the fact that **kʷe* 'and', which is derived from this stem and was originally a modal adverb meaning 'as, like' (**pətēr mātērkʷe* 'father like mother'), is common Indo-European.[8] The relative use of **kʷi-* is therefore not an innovation of Hittite, etc.,[9] but an archaic feature of these languages, in contrast to which the relative **yos* represents an innovation of the satem languages and Greek.[10, 11]

[1] Gonda, 'The original character of the IE relative pronoun *yo-*', *Lingua* 4, 1954, 1–41; *Old Indian*, 1971, 138–41; Benveniste, *BSL* 53, 1958, 49; Seiler, *Relativsatz, Attribut und Apposition*, 1960 (cf. *Krat* 12, 1968, 41–52); *Relative Clause Festival*, 1972; Brunel, 'La relative grecque', *BSL* 72, 1977, 211–40; Chr. Lehmann, 'Der idg. *kwi-/kwo-* Relativsatz im typologischen Vergleich', in P. Ramat (ed.), *Linguistic Reconstruction and IE Syntax*, 1980, 155–69; Kurzová, *Der Relativsatz in den ie. Sprachen*, 1981; Touratier, 'Genèse de la relative dans les langues ie.', in *Travaux* 4, *Univ. de Provence*, 1986, 61–79. On the relative used in a conditional sense (*qui=si quis*), see R. Iordache, *ŽA* 39, 1990, 17–30. According to Lehmann, *Lg* 49, 1973, 56, OV languages have no relatives: 'in keeping with this observation, early IE had no relative pronouns'; *In Memory of J. A. Kerns*, 1981, 187: relative *yo-* did not exist in IE.

In connection with relative *yo-*, it must still be asked whether Armenian with *or* belongs to the *yo-* group (so Bonfante, *JAOS* 64, 1944, 183; Pisani, *Sprache* 12, 1967, 229). On the other hand *yo-* in Hispano-Celtic and in Celtic generally (*pace* K. H. Schmidt, *BBCS* 26, 1976, 385; *KZ* 100, 1987, 113; *ZDL* 53, 1989, 345) must be seen as an independent innovation; see the next paragraph in the text.

[2] e.g. A. Hahn, *TAPA* 95, 1964, 115; *JAOS* 85, 1965, 49 n. 9; Haudry, *BSL* 68, 1973, 147f., esp. 165f.; *La Linguistique* 15/1, 1979, 106f.; Kurzová (n. 1 above), 24; A. Rousseau, *BSL* 79, 1984, 107; Hettrich, *Krat* 50, 1985, 46.

[3] See Delbrück, *Grundfragen der Sprachforschung*, 1901, 135f. (rel. 'who' from the interrog. *and* indef.); Hofmann–Szantyr, 555; K. H. Schmidt, 'Der Relativsatz im Südkaukasischen', *REGC* 6–7, 1990–1, 63–79. On the Latin relative, see also Serbat in *É. Benveniste aujourd'hui* i, 1984, 177–85.

[4] Brugmann, *Grundriss*², ii/2, 347; Ivanov, *VJ* 1958 (5), 41; Monteil (above, 8.3.1 n. 1), 12f.; Hahn, *JAOS* 85, 49.

[5] Ivanov, loc. cit.; Watkins, *Celtica* 6, 1962, 16. Hitt. *ya* is rightly compared to Goth. *ja-h* by Neumann, *IF* 67, 1962, 200; Rosenkranz, *AION-L* 7, 1966, 172.

[6] Brugmann (n. 4 above); Hofmann–Szantyr 555.

[7] Sturtevant, *Curme Volume*, 1930, 141–9; Hahn, *TAPA* 95, 113f.; of. Monteil (above, 8.3.1 n. 1).

[8] See Watkins, *Fs. Knobloch*, 1985, 491f.; Szemerényi, 'Syntax, meaning and origin of the IE particle **kʷe*', in *Fs. H. Gipper* ii, 1985, 747–75; Migron, *MSS* 51, 1990, 129–45. Hettrich, *Krat* 33, 1988, 77–8, argues for single *ca* being original and double being later (cf. Szemerényi, op. cit. 762f., and Dunkel, *Sprache* 28, 1983, 140). Kurzová (n. 1 above) 64, has clearly not understood the argument in the text above. A. Rousseau's analysis, op. cit. 126 (négation *-k-* + particule *we* 'ou'), is quite impossible.

[9] Kammenhuber, *KZ* 77, 1961, 45; *MSS* 24, 1968, 88.

[10] On this cf. Porzig, *Gliederung* 173, 191, 198; Kammenhuber, *KZ* 77, 1961, 41; Meier-Brügger 1992, ii, 87. On the (Hispano-)Celtic *yo-* see n. 1 above.

[11] On the relative clause, see also the monographs of Touratier, *La relative: essai de théorie syntaxique*, 1980, and Chr. Lehmann, *Der Relativsatz*, 1984 (on this Hettrich, *Krat* 30, 1985, 42–52); on the typology of relative clauses, *Lings* 24, 1986; G. D. Prideaux and W. J. Baker, *The Processing of Relative Clauses*, Amsterdam 1986.

8.4 PERSONAL PRONOUNS

In contrast to the pronouns so far discussed, the personal pronouns show no gender differences; the pronoun of the 3rd person, which distinguishes gender, is of course not a personal but an anaphoric pronoun. There is also a reflexive pronoun, the inflexion of which is identical with that of the 2nd person singular. In addition there is a series of possessive pronouns.[1]

[1] General literature: P. Forchheimer, *The Category of Person in Language*, Berlin 1953 (in all languages of the world:); Benveniste, *BSL* 43, 1946, 1–12; 'La nature des pronoms', *For R. Jakobson*, 1956, 34–7; Heger, 'Personale Deixis und grammatische Person', *ZRP* 81, 1965, 76–97; *Flexionsformen, Vokabeln und Wortarten*, Abh. Heidelberger Akad., 1985, 35f. For the IE material, see Brugmann, *Grundriss*[2], ii/2, 378–427; Schwyzer, *GG* i, 599–609; G. Schmidt 1978 (no system, only stems and inflexional forms); Seebold 1984 (see Szemerényi 1985, 59 n. 53); Savčenko, 'System der Personalpronomina in verschiedenen Sprachfamilien', *IANOLJ* 43/6, 1984, 483–91. Concerning the observation that the plurals of personal pronouns are pluralized forms of the singular, see Wunderli, *ZFSL* 99, 1989, 130–41, esp. 134, and cf. 8.4.4*c* below.

8.4.1

First the inflexion of the personal pronouns in the more important languages is given: (*a*) 'I, we', (*b*) 'thou, you'. The enclitic forms are enclosed in brackets.

(*a*)	Ved.	OCS	Gr.	OLat.	Goth.	Hitt.
Sing.						
Nom.	*ahám*	*azŭ*	ἐγώ	*ego*	*ik*	*ug*
Acc.	*mām* (*mā*)	*mene* (*mę*)	ἐμέ (με)	*mēd*	*mik*	*amug*
Gen.	*máma* (*mē*)	*mene*	ἐμεῖο (μευ)	*meī*, *mīs*	*meina*	*amel*
Abl.	*mad*	–	–	*mēd*	-	*amedats*
Dat.	*máhya(m)* (*mē*)	*mĭnē* (*mi*)	ἐμοί (μοι)	*mihī*	*mis*	*amug*
Loc.	*máyi*	*mĭnē*	–	–	–	*amug*
Instr.	*máyā*	*mŭnoją*	–	–	–	–
Plur.						
Nom.	*vayám*	*my* (*ny*)[1]	ἡμεῖς/ ἄμμες	*nōs*	*weis*	*wēs*
Acc.	*asmā́n* (*nas*)	*nasŭ* (*ny*)	ἡμέας/ ἄμμε	*nōs*	*un(sis)*	*antsas* (*nas*)
Gen.	*asmā́kam* (*nas*)	*nasŭ*	ἡμέων	*nostrī*, *-rum*	*unsara*	*antsel*
Abl.	*asmád*	–	–	*nōbīs*	–	*antsedats*
Dat.	*asm-ḗ*, *-ábhya(m)*	*namŭ* (*ny*)	ἡμῖν/ ἄμμι(ν)	*nōbīs*	*un(sis)*	*antsas* (*nas*)
Loc.	*asm-ḗ*, *-ā́su*	*nasŭ*	–	–	–	*antsas*
Instr.	*asmā́-bhis*	*nami*	–	–	–	–
(*b*)						
Sing.						
Nom.	*tvam*	*ty*	σύ	*tū*	*þu*	*tsig*
Acc.	*tvām* (*tvā*)[2]	*tebe* (*tę*)	σέ (σε)	*tēd*	*þuk*	*tug*
Gen.	*táva* (*tē*)	*tebe*	σεῖο (σευ)	*tuī*, *tīs*	*þeina*	*twel*

	Ved.	OCS	Gr.	OLat.	Goth.	Hitt.
Abl.	*tvad*	–	–	*tēd*	–	*twedats*
Dat.	*tubhya(m)*	*tebē*	σοί (σοι)	*tibī*	*þus*	*tug*
	(tē)	*(ti)*				
Loc.	*tvē, tváyi*	*tebē*	–	–	–	*tug*
Instr.	*tvā, tváyā*	*tobojǫ*	–	–	–	–
Plur.						
Nom.	*yūyám*	*vy*	ὑμεῖς/	*uōs*	*jūs*	*sumes*
			ὕμμες			
Acc.	*yuṣmā́n*	*vasŭ (vy)*	ὑμέας/	*uōs*	*izwis*	*sumas*
	(vas)		ὕμμε			*(-smas)*
Gen.	*yuṣmā́kam*	*vasŭ*	ὑμέων	*uostrī*	*izwara*	*sumel*
	(vas)			*-rum*		
Abl.	*yuṣmád*	–	–	*uōbīs*	–	*sumedats*
Dat.	*yuṣm-ḗ,*	*vamŭ (vy)*	ὑμῖν/	*uobīs*	*izwis*	*sumas*
	-abhya(m)		ὕμμι(ν)			*(-smas)*
Loc.	*yuṣm-ḗ*	*vasŭ*	–	–	–	*sumas*
	-āsu					
Instr.	*yuṣmā-bhis*	*vami*	–[3]	–	–	—

8.4.2

A first glance reveals only a great variety of forms. On closer inspection the distance between the different languages decreases and at the same time the structure becomes more apparent.

Nominative. For the 1st person *singular* the form is **egō* (the classical languages) and **eg(h)om*; for the 2nd person **tū/*tu*, which in Aryan with a particle *-am* (probably taken over from *ah-am* and appearing in other persons also) gave *tuv-am* (Vedic *tvam* is often disyllabic), later monosyllabic *tvam*.[4] The *plural* is formed from another stem; for the 1st person **wei* is used, from which with *-am* came OInd. *vayam*, and in Gothic and Hittite, with the noun ending of the nom. pl., **wey-es*, which developed further to Goth. *weis* (cf. *þreis*), Hitt. *wēs* (with loss of *-y-* and contraction). For the 2nd person we find **yūs* in Goth. *jūs*, Avest. *yūš* and *yūž-əm*, and the latter shows that OInd. *yūyam* was modified from **yūš-am* on the analogy of *vay-am*. The Greek, Latin, and OCS forms will be discussed presently.

Accusative. In the *singular* an ending *-e* seems to be added: **(e)m-e*, **tu-e=*twe*, which then became also **te* (see 5.4.2); alongside these apparently **mē *twē* in Aryan and, with a nasal, also **mēm *t(w)ēm* in Aryan and Slavic; since the particle *-am*, so common in Aryan (*ah-am tuv-am*), is unknown in Slavic, these forms must contain not *-am* but the *m* of the accusative. Hitt. *amug tug*, Goth. *mik þuk* (the latter for **þik* from **teg*, cf. OHG *dih*) and Venetic *mego* are all modified on the analogy of the nom. **egō*, and the analogical processes led in Hittite even to nom. **teg*, acc. *tug*, with later palatalization of **teg* to *tsig*[5]. OLat. *mēd tēd* have of course nothing to do with the abl.; the repetition common in personal pronouns led to **tē–te*, which became by apocope **tēt* and then *tēd*; by analogy also *mēd*.[6]

In the *plural* OInd. *asmān yuṣmān* and Gr. ἡμέας/ἄμμε, ὑμέας/ὔμμε belong closely together. Avest. *ahma* 'us' shows that the OInd. forms arose secondarily, by addition of the acc. pl. ending, from **asma* **yuṣma*, which are identical with Aeolic ἄμμε ὔμμε. The fact that *nas vas* are the enclitic forms in Aryan and have clearly a common basis with Lat. *nōs uōs*, OCS *nasŭ/ny vasŭ/vy*, Hitt. *nas*, and Goth. *uns* (from **n̥s*) leads to the conclusion that the Aryan and Greek forms arose from **n̥sme* **usme*, in which *n̥s* and *us* are the zero grades of **nos* and **wos*; Hitt. *sumes* comes by metathesis from **usme(s)*;[7] OInd. *yuṣm-* has its *y-* from the nom.; Goth. *izwis* is from **uswes*.

Genitive. In the *singular* the 1st person **mene* is represented in OCS *mene* (and Lith. *manęs*), Avestan (*mana*) and Welsh;[8] OInd. *mama* certainly comes from it by assimilation, while Hitt. *amel* must be from **amen(e)* by dissimilation.[9] Gr. ἐμεῖο is from **emesyo* with the pronominal ending. Lat. *meī* can be the same form or the gen. of the possessive pronoun *meus*, as also *tuī*, *nostrī uestrī* and *nostrum uestrum*. In the 2nd person s. **tewe* or **tewo* is attested in Aryan and (modified on the analogy of the dat.) in OCS, as also in Celtic. Gr. σεῖο is from **twesyo*. Alongside these accented forms there are the enclitic **mei*/**moi*, **t(w)ei*/**t(w)oi*, which also serve as dative, in Aryan, Greek (dat. only), OCS (dat. only), and OLat. (gen. *mīs tīs* extended with *-s*). Goth. *meina þeina* are usually regarded as possessive forms, but are more probably a cross between **mei* and **mene*. In the *plural*, OInd. *asmākam yuṣmākam* are clearly the neuters of the possessive pronouns, and the same applies to the Latin and Germanic forms. On the other hand, Gr. -έων has been extended on the analogy of the nouns, and OCS *nasŭ vasŭ* from **nōsom* **wōsom* are genitives of **nōs* **wōs*.

Ablative. The Aryan formation in *-ad* has now an exact counterpart not only in Lat. *mēd tēd* but also in Hitt. *amed- twed- antsed- sumed-*, which were all extended with the noun ending *-ats*.[10] In Latin the plural forms have been replaced.

Dative. The simple forms of the singular in OInd., Greek, and OCS have already been treated in connection with the genitive; the OInd. plurals *asmē yuṣmē* clearly belong to the same type: **n̥smei* **usmei*. A quite different formation is presented by OInd. *mahya(m) tubhya(m) asmabhya(m) yuṣmabhya(m)*, in which *-m* is a secondary addition on the analogy of *-am*; cf. Avest. *maibyā taibyā ahmaibyā yušmaibyā* (*xšmaibyā*). The formation is clearly identical with that in OCS *tebē* (*sebē*) and Lat. *tibī* (*sibī*), which have, however, been modified on the analogy of the noun dative from *bhi*, which in OInd. is found extended with *-a* (from *-ā*?).[11] The IE forms were **mebhi *tebhi* (see 8.4.4*d*).

Lat. *mihi* and OInd. *mahyam*, which appear to correspond in respect of *h*, both represent a late dissimilation of IE *m-bh-*. OCS *mĭnē* replaces **mebē* under the influence of gen. *mene*. Lat. *nōbīs uōbīs* (like OCS *namu vamu*) are late innovations on the basis of 'stems' *nō- uō-* abstracted from *nōs uōs*. Goth. *mis þus* seem to have taken their *-s* from *uns izwis*.

Locative. OInd. *tváyi* is from **twoi*, found in *tvē*, with loc. *i* added a second time for clarity; similarly *máyi*. In the plural we would have expected **asmi *yuṣmi*, attested by Aeolic ἄμμι ὔμμι. With OInd. *asmē* homonymy was clearly avoided between **asmi* 'in us' and *asmi-n* 'in this' (with secondary *-n*); *asmē yuṣmē* are no doubt from **asmayi *yuṣmayi*.[12]

Instrumental. The old instr. is present in OInd. *tvā*, formed simply from *tu*+*ā*. The type is also found in the plural, in which *asmā yuṣmā* are authenticated partly by *yuṣmā-datta* 'given by you', partly by Iranian.[13] The innovation *tváyā máyā* came about on the analogy of the *ā*-stems,[14] and the same process also accounts for OCS *mŭnojǫ tobojǫ*.[15]

[1] Against *ny* as nom., see Strunk, *Fachtagung* 5, 1975, 313 n. 39.

[2] On *tuvam/tvam*, see Sihler, *Lg* 47, 1971, 67; Horowitz, *Sievers' Law and the Evidence of the RV*, 1974, 59, 63, and above, 5.7.2.2. On Hittite, see Melchert, *MSS* 42, 1983, 151–65, and (on IE also) Villar, *JIES* 16, 1988, 1–8 (but note *IC* 33, 1989, A 290: 'worthless').

[3] An alleged IE pronoun of polite address is reconstructed by Seebold, *Sprache* 29, 1983, 27–36, cf. also below 8.4.6 n. 2; on the forms in question, see G. Schmidt 1978, 218–28.

[4] See Sommer, *IF* 30, 1912, 398f.; Normier, *KZ* 91, 1978, 210; Hamp, *BBCS* 29, 1980, 84 (*em* 'indeed'); Kuiper, *IIJ* 30, 1987, 1–8: nom. *tuHám*, acc. *twaHám*. Avest. *yūṣ* and *yūž-əm*, mentioned further on, show according to Brugmann, *Grundriss*² i, 866, voicing in front of sonorants, but the change is obviously due to the environment *VšV*, cf. *Sūša*>OPers. *Hūža*; see Szemerényi, *Sprache* 12, 1967, 191 (=*SM* 1856). Gathic *tu* as a variant of the normal *tuvəm* was called in question by Strunk (n. 1 above), 320f.

[5] See Szemerényi, *BSOAS* 27, 1964, 160, and cf. also Kammenhuber, 'Hethitisch' 209, 250 n. 308; Normier (n. 4 above). On Palaic nom. *ti* 'thou', acc.-dat. *tu*, see Melchert (n. 2 above); a different view in Eichner, *KZ* 96, 1983, 237 n. 25 fin.

[6] Szemerényi, *TPS* 1973, 55–74. Although this explanation had been advanced in 1973, Calboli did not see even ten years later how the acc. and abl. of *ego* could have the same form (see *ANRW* 29/1, 1983, 37).

[7] Schwyzer, *GG* i, 601; Benveniste, *HIE* 76. On Goth. *izwis*, see Shields, *NOWELE* 10, 1987, 95–108.

[8] On the early apocopated Welsh gen. *men(e)*, see Thurneysen, *GOI* 281.

[9] So also Georgiev, *RHA* 28, 1971, 18f.; Shields, 'Hittite pronominal suffixes in *-l*', *IF* 88, 1984, 191–201; Swiggers, '*-ēl* en hittite', *Hethitica* 6, Louvain 1985, 199–204. On the other hand a (foreign?) suffix is still favoured by Lazzeroni, *ASNP* 29, 1960, 120 (Hattic?); Kammenhuber, 'Hethitisch' 270; G. Schmidt 1978, 91f., 162f.

[10] Szemerényi, *KZ* 73, 1955, 59f., 67.

[11] Insler, *IF* 71, 1967, 232 n. 15; Poultney, *Lg* 43, 1968, 877, 880. The alleged Avest. *ahmāi* 'us' does not exist (see Humbach, *Gathas* i, 29f.), in spite of Gershevitch, *BSOAS* 25, 1962, 368f.

[12] Insler (above, n. 11), n. 16.
[13] On Gathic *əhmā*, see Hoffmann, *Aufsätze* ii, 376 (first in *MSS* 4, 1954).
[14] Insler (above, n. 11), 231.
[15] Vaillant, *Gram. comp.* ii, 449f.

8.4.3

On the basis of the preceding analysis we can reconstruct the essential components of the IE paradigms as follows:

Nom.	**eg(h)om*, **egō*	**tū*, **tu*
Acc.	**(e)me*, **mē*, **mēm*	**twe/*te*, **twē/*tē*, **twēm/*tēm*
Gen.	**mene*, encl. **mei/*moi*	**tewe/*tewo*, encl. **t(w)ei/*t(w) oi*
Abl.	**med*	**twed*
Dat.	**mei/*moi*, **mebhi*	**t(w)ei/*t(w)oi*, **tebhi*
Nom.	**wei*, **n̥smés*	**yūs*, **usmés* (*uswes*?)
Acc.	**nes/*nos*, **nēs/*nōs*, **n̥sme*	**wes/*wos*, **wēs/*wōs*, **usme*, **uswes*
Gen.	**nosom/*nōsom*	**wosom/*wōsom*
Abl.	**n̥sed/*n̥smed*	(**used*?)/**usmed*
Dat.	**n̥smei*	**usmei*

8.4.4

The explanation of these paradigms[1] can now be carried somewhat further.

(*a*) The relationship of **egō/*eg(h)om* to **em-/m-* of the other cases is in general seen as a phenomenon of great antiquity; see Kuryłowicz, *Categories* 183. It would then, however, be impossible to understand why the verbal ending of the 1st person s. is not **eg-*. The conclusion is unavoidable that the verbal ending is *-mi* because at the time when it was formed there was no **eg(h)ō*, only *m*.[2] The element which carries the meaning in the nom. is therefore not **eg(h)* but *-om*; **eg(h)* is a particle which was prefixed to the pronoun **em*. The original form is thus **eg(h)om*, which is preserved in Aryan and also underlies the Germanic form. The form **egō*, which occurs especially in the classical languages, is secondary, probably an innovation on the analogy of the verbal *-om/-ō*.[3]

(*b*) In the acc. s. an ending *-ĕ* appears to be present in **mĕ* from **em-é*, **twé* from **tu-é*.[4] The alternative forms **mē *t(w)ē* would be emphatic variants with lengthening,[5] and **mēm *t(w)ēm* would contain the familiar acc. ending *-m* (see 8.4.2). But *-e* as acc. ending would be odd, whereas **m-em *tw-em* would be correctly formed. One may perhaps suppose that the acc. forms characterized by *-em* could have lost the nasal[6] with subsequent lengthening of the final vowel; a cross between e.g. **mē* and **mem* gave **mēm*. In the same way the acc. pl. **n̥sme* arose from **n̥smēn*, itself from **n̥smens* (see 6.2.7.1).

(*c*) A suppletive relationship seems to exist in the 1st pl., in fact twice over: nom. **wei* is in opposition to an 'oblique' **n̥s*, extended to **n̥sme*, and both are in contrast to **eg(h)om*/**em*-. For the difference **eg(h)om*:**wei* a rationalized explanation is even given: '*nōs* signifie "moi et d'autres", et non plusieurs "moi" '; '*we* is not "I and I" but "I and you", and *you* (pl.) can be "you and he" '.[7] Against this it has rightly been emphasized that the plurals of pronouns are true plurals, that 'we' includes 'I', and that this connection of 1st s. and 1st pl. finds linguistic expression in very many languages;[8] cf. Lith. *mes*, OCS *my*, Arm. *mekh*, etc.

It is usually supposed that Lat. *nōs* is not in its proper place in the nominative, that only **wei* has a right there. Since, however, all the oblique cases are formed from the stem **nos*, this conclusion is clearly wrong; **wei* is a substitute form, not anything original. Similarly, Greek is enough to prove that **n̥smes* has just as much right in the nominative, obviously as an emphatic variant of **nōs*, and since repetition is a favoured means of expressing emphasis, **n̥smes* seems to be simply **n̥smés*,[9] i.e. **mes-més* with weakening to **m̥s* in the unaccented part; for **n̥s* from **m̥s* cf. the ending -*n̥s* of the acc. pl. For the 1st pl. the nom. **mes* is proved also by its identity with the verbal 1st pl. ending -*mes*; it is, of course, the regular plural **(e)m-es* of **em* 'I'.[10]

This settles the question, long fiercely debated, whether **n̥s-me* or **n̥s-sme* is the form to be interpreted, and whether -*sm*- in **n̥s-sme* is related to -*sm*- in **tosmei* etc., which is in any case ruled out by the fact that -*sm*- occurs in demonstrative pronouns only in the singular, in personal pronouns only in the plural; an analysis as **n̥-s-me* 'that one plus him plus me=us' is equally out of the question.[11]

The influence of the 1st pl. **n̥s-mes* on the 2nd pl. explains why we find Gr. *ὔμμες*, OInd. *yuṣma*-; for we should properly expect **us-wes* from **wes-wes*, which is in fact present in Goth. *izwis*.[12]

The nominatives of the 1st and 2nd pl. were thus originally **mes* **wes* or **mos* **wos*, to which **n̥s-mes* **us-wes* (or **us-mes*) were later added; **mos* was then modified to **nos* under the influence of **n̥s*. From **nōs* the dual **nō* (OInd. *nā*, Gr. *νώ*) arose by back-formation; cf. thematic pl. -*ōs*, dual -*ō*.

The secondary and non-pronominal character of **wei* is, moreover, shown by the fact that its nucleus **we*- (*i* is merely the pronominal sign of the plural) is used also for other persons. Thus we find in the dual Ved. *vām* (from *vā-am*), *āvam*[13] 'we two', OCS *vě* 'we two', *va* 'you two'. This makes it clear that **we*- in this function is simply the numeral 'two'; **wei* is formed from the dual **we* with the plural ending -*i*.[14]

The position of the 2nd pl. nom. **yus* is more problematical. A direct connection with **wes*, for instance by making **wes* a simplified form of **ywes/*yus*,[15] is impossible. Nevertheless, it remains an attractive idea that *us* in **yus* is the zero grade of **wes*, while *y*- could be a pronominal element *i* prefixed to it.[16] On the other hand, it seems clear that **wes* is itself simplified from **twes*, the regular plural of **tu* (cf. **mes* from **em-es*); this is confirmed by the verbal ending *-tes*, which represents a simplification in internal position of **twes*.[17]

(*d*) The dat. s. **mei *t(w)ei* is quite obviously the stems **em- *tu-* with the dative ending *-ei*. The *o*-grade forms **moi *t(w)oi* are certainly due to the preceding labial (see 6.3.4*b*). The 'fuller' forms **mebhi *tebhi* are similarly to be analysed as **(e)m-ebhi *t(w)-ebhi* and contain the postposition **ebhi* 'to', which (or its *o*-grade **obhi*) is present in OInd. *abhi*, OPers. *abiy*, and OCS *obŭ*.[18] The original meaning thus anticipated the Romance developments *ad me*, *ad te*, in contrast to the purely datival **moi *t(w)oi*, which being shorter soon became enclitics. The dat. *-ebhi* has, of course, nothing to do with the instr. *-bhi*.

The *locative* function of **mei *t(w)ei* simply goes back to the period in which dat. (*-ei*) and loc. (*-i*) were not yet separate. The use of **mei *t(w)ei* as *genitives*, on the other hand, rests on the syntactical possibilities of the *dativus sympatheticus*, found in ὦ τέκνον μοι, *gnāte mī* (in which *mī* arose from **moi*);[19] **mei/*moi* is perhaps also the starting point of the Hittite possessive *mi*-; see Eichner, *KZ* 96 (1983), 236f.

(*e*) The case ending *-os* of the gen. s. would have given **(e)m-ós *tw-ós*, and these forms, reinterpreted as possessives and inflected as *o*-stems, are indeed found in Gr. ἐμός σός. The gen. **mene* is obviously an innovation, and is in fact an ablatival form: **(e)m-enē* 'from me', 'de moi' (like Lat. *supernē* 'from above', Goth. *utana* 'from outside'), which was shortened to **menĕ*.[20] The form **meinē* in Goth. *meina* arose from a cross between **menē* and enclitic **mei*. From gen. **tu-ós* came not only **twós* but also, as in *u*-stem nouns, **towós*, then from this the possessives Lat. *tuus* and with secondary ablaut **tewos* in Gr. τε(ϝ)ός; from this again by back-formation the gen. **tewo* or **tewe*.[21]

(*f*) The abl. is constructed with *-ed*, as the forms show: **twed* must be divided as **tu-ed*; **ed* is a postposition which still survives in OCS *otŭ* 'away from'.[22]

[1] Of modern works I mention the following: Schwyzer, *GG* i, 599f. (outstanding survey and bibliography); H.-F. Rosenfeld, *ZMf* 23, 1955, 59f.; *FF* 29, 1955, 150–6 (esp. on Germanic); Szemerényi, 'Hittite pronominal inflection', *KZ* 73, 1955, 57–80; G. Liebert, *Die ieur. Personalpronomina und die Laryngaltheorie*, 1957, esp. 55f. (excessive use of laryngeals); Savčenko, 'Das Problem der Entstehung der Verbalendungen im Idg.', *LPosn* 8, 1960, 44f.; A. Nehring, *Sprachzeichen und Sprechakte*, 1963 (ch. 6, 111–21: 'Pronomina'); C. Hauri, *Zur Vorgeschichte des Ausgangs '-Ena'*, 1963; *KZ* 78, 1963, 115–25; Myrkin, 'Typologie des Personalpronomens und Probleme seiner Rekonstruktion im Idg.', *VJ* 1964 (5), 78–86; 'Entstehung der germ. Personalpronomina vom Gesichtspunkt der Sprachgeographie', *VJ*

1966 (6), 71–5; Erhart, 'Die ieur. Dualendung *-ō(u)* und die Zahlwörter', *Sbornik Brno*, 1965/A-13, 11–23; Cowgill, in *Evidence* 169–70; Majtinskaja, 'Zur Entstehung pronominaler Wörter in Sprachen verschiedener Systeme', *VJ* 1966 (1), 15–25; also 'Zur Typologie der genetischen Verbindung der Personal- und Demonstrativpronomina', *VJ* 1968 (3), 31–40; Brandenstein, *Fs. Pokorny*, 1967, 17–19; further, Houwink Ten Cate, *RHA* 79, 1967, 123–32; Josephson, ibid. 133–54; Friedrich, *Fs. Eilers*, 1967, 72–3 (all three esp. on Hittite problems); Erhart 1970, 34–67, 151–61; Leumann², 461f.

The distinction between *inclusive* and *exclusive* pronouns (e.g. Bloomfield, *Language*, 1935, 255–7) has no significance for IE, but may have played a part in the prehistoric period—cf. Watkins, *Verb* 47; A. Quattordio Moreschini, 'L'inclusivo e l'esclusivo', *SSL* 10, 1971, 119–37; Ivanov, *Glagol* 20f.; Gamkrelidze and Ivanov, *IANOLJ* 60, 1982, 30; and for other language families: Hymes, *Studies Traeger*, 1972, 100–21; Jacobsen Jr., *PCLSP* 16, 1980, 204–30; Gamkrelidze–Ivanov, 291f.

2 So Myrkin (n. 1 above, 1964), 79; Savčenko, (n. 1 above) 49. Cf. also Dolgopolsky, in *Gedenkschrift B. Collinder*, 1984, 90; Vallini, *AIΩN* 9, 1987, 65. The segmentation of **egHom* as *e-* stem, *g* particle, *H* nom. ending, *om* particle, by G. Schmidt 1978, 45, 117f., should have been kept secret, although Bader, *BSL* 84/2, 1989, 239, also favours a segmentation **e-g(h)om* with particle *g(h)e*, as was suggested by Brugmann in 1904 (n. 3 below), 72f.

3 J. Schmidt, *KZ* 36, 1900, 405f. (411: interprets **eghom* as a neuter abstract meaning 'breath, soul'); Brugmann, 'Die Demonstrativpronomina der idg. Sprachen' (*Sächs. Abh.* 22, 1904, 1–150), 71, prefers *Hierheit* 'the being here'; cf. also Majtinskaja (n. 1 above, 1968), 33f. On Balt. *ež*, see Stang, *Vgl. Gram.* 247.

4 It is hardly feasible to derive **twé* from **t-wé* (Cowgill) and not, as is clearly indicated by the meaning, from **tu-é* (*pace* Cardona, in *In Memory of W. Cowgill*, 1987, 4 with n. 8). An acc. ending *-me* (s. and pl.!) assumed by G. Schmidt 1978, 177, 217, and *MSS* 49, 1988, 123 with n. 11, is quite unacceptable.

5 Schwyzer, *GG* i, 600.

6 On this supposition, see Meillet, *Introduction* 173.

7 Meillet, 333; Hirt, *IG* iii, 21. Cf. also Prokosch 1939, 282: 'A real plural of "I" cannot exist, of course—there is no "I plus I plus I"'.

8 Isačenko, *VJ* 1961 (1), 41; Myrkin (n. 1 above, 1964), 78. See also Benveniste's '*je* dilaté', *BSL* 43, 1946, 10f.; Hattori, *CFS* 25, 1970, 143f.; Prieto, 'Una nota de gramática: "nosotros", ?plural de "yo"?' *Estudios a E. Alarcos Llorach* i, 1976, 209–16; Wunderli (above, 8.4 n. 1).

9 Myrkin (n. 1 above, 1964), 80; cf. Prokosch 1939, 282f.

10 For **(e)m/mes*, see also Illič-Svityč, *Sbornik Bernštejn*, 1971, 396–406.

11 Schwyzer, *GG* i, 601 (*-sm-=to-sm-*), against which Lane, *Lg* 37, 1961, 471 n. 8; Erhart (n. 1 above, 1965), 14. Benveniste, *HIE* 76, assumes a pluralizing *-m-*; on this, see Szemerényi, *KZ* 73, 1955, 70. On **n̥-s-me*, see Liebert (n. 1 above), 101.

12 IE **us-wes* must also be the basis of Celtic **swe-* in OIr. *si*<**swēs*, W. *chwi*, etc.; cf. Lewis and Pedersen, *CCCG* 215; Cowgill, in Cardona et al. (eds.), *IE and IEs*, 1971, 115; Lindeman, *EC* 14, 1976, 567–70.

13 OInd. *vām* and OCS *vě* prove that *ā* in OInd. *āvam* does not go back to **n̥H-* (Erhart, Cowgill) but is a prefixed particle; for the same reason Gmc. *unk-* cannot be traced back to **n̥Hw-*, as held by Erhart (1970, 88), Normier (*KZ* 91, 1978, 182), Seebold (1984, 37), and Rasmussen (in Vennemann 1989, 158). For Gmc. *unkw-* 'we two' one would properly have to start from **n̥s-dwo-*, and as has recently been shown (see *Symbolae Mitxelena*, 1985, 268) this would have given **untw-*; *unkw-* would thus be a modification of that form. The 2nd dual *inkw-* must have been formed to *unkw-* on the basis of the plural *uns-/izw-*; it cannot in any case rest on an unfounded **i-wə-we-* (Seebold 1984, 38); cf. further Prokosch 1939, 284f.; Lindeman 1987, 97f.

14 Cf. Brugmann, *Grundriss*², ii/2, 380, 455; Liebert (n. 1 above), 94f.

15 Vaillant, *Gram. comp.* ii, 543; earlier Pedersen, *Symbolae Danielsson*, 1932, 264f.; *Hittitisch* 75f.

16 Cf. also Brugmann (n. 14 above), 380: **yu-* is *i+we* 'he and you'; Liebert (n. 1 above), 104: **yu-=i+u* 'I plus thou' and **wi-* 'we'=*u+i* 'thou plus I'.

17 **wes* is thus not to be assigned with **te-we* to Avest. *ava-*, etc. (Brugmann, 381f.); see also above, 5.4.2 and below, 9.7.1.2 n. 9.

[18] Brugmann, 820f.; Pokorny, *IEW* i, 287. Hamp is too fanciful in *PCLSP* 16, 1980, 147–9; *BSL* 77, 1982, 260. Cf. also Serbat, *Hommages à J. Cousin*, 1983, 61–7 (*me+ghei* 'hic').
[19] Schwyzer, *GG* ii, 189, and (against n. 3) esp. Havers, *Untersuchungen zur Kasussyntax der idg. Sprachen*, 1911, 62f.
[20] This explanation (already given in the 1st edn. of this book in 1970) was also discovered by G. Schmidt; see his *Studien zum germ. Adverb*, Diss. Berlin 1962, 107 (made available to me by the kindness of the author 6 Jan. 1971), and *Stammbildung und Flexion der idg. Personalpronomina*, 1978, 92f. In any case *ne* is not related to *nōs* (Brugmann, 382), nor is it from **meme* (Schwyzer, *GG* i, 601); according to Cowgill it is from **me-me* with suffix *-me*.
[21] For the development **tu-os*>**towos*, see above, 7.5.3 n. 2. The gen. **tewe* is certainly not from **t(w)e(t)we* (Schwyzer, n. 20 above) or with a suffix *-we* from **te* (Cowgill, n. 4 above). On the genitives, see also G. Schmidt, *KZ* 82, 1969, 227–50; id. 1978, 87f., 136f.
[22] Szemerényi, *KZ* 73, 1955, 59f., 67f., and above, 7.6.7 n. 4.

8.4.5

From the personal pronouns *possessives* were also formed.[1] The earliest forms seem to have been **(e)mos* **twos* **n̥smos* **usmos* (*-sw-*), e.g. in Gr. ἐμός σός ἄμμος ὔμμος; Avest. *ma-* 'meus', *θwa-* 'tuus',[2] OInd. *tva-* 'tuus'. Alongside **twos* there was also **tewos*/**towos* (see 8.4.4*e*), e.g. Gr. τε(ϝ)ός.[3] Enclitic **mei*/**moi* is the basis of Lat. *meus*, OCS *moji*, as also of Goth. *meina-* etc. (see 8.4.4*e*), while in OInd. the classical *madīya- tvadīya* etc. were formed from the ablatives *mad tvad* etc. serving as stems for the personal pronouns, and still in the Vedic period the possessives *mamaka- asmāka- yuṣmāka-* from the genitives of the personal pronouns. In the plural, forms with the contrastive suffix *-(t)ero-* also occur in several languages; cf. Gr. ἡμέτερος ὑμέτερος, OLat. *noster uoster*, Goth. *unsara- izwara-*.[4]

[1] Cf. Brugmann, *Grundriss*² ii/2, 403f.; Schwyzer, *GG* i, 608; G. Schmidt 1978. On the Gmc. possessives, see also T. Frings and E. Linke, *Fs. F. Maurer*, 1963, 91–117; Bader, 'Pronoms ie.: *mō* unité/dualité', *Verbum* 2/2, 1980, 137–52.
[2] The Avestan form *ahma-* 'noster' cited by Schwyzer (following Brugmann?) does not exist.
[3] If the Cypr. ἐμεϝός is correctly read by Masson, it must be formed after τεϝός; see Heubeck's note *HS* 102, 1990, 310.
[4] On Hittite, see Eichner, *Untersuchungen zur heth. Deklination*, diss., Erlangen, 1974, 30f., 67f., and on *mi-*, above, 8.4.4*d* fin.

8.4.6

Beside the personal pronouns there is a reflexive pronoun, which survives in Lat. *sē*, *suī*, *sibī*, Gr. ἕ, οὗ, οἷ, etc. It has no nominative; of the other cases it is possible to reconstruct e.g. acc. **s(w)e*, dat. **s(w)oi* and **sebhi*, forms which correspond to those of the 2nd s. pronoun. This is no accident, since they are formed from the anaphoric pronoun **se* on the model of **t(w)e*, etc.[1]

The reflexive possessive, which survives in Lat. *suus* and Gr. ἑ(ϝ)ός, ὅς (from **sewos*, **swos*), had the peculiarity of referring to all persons, just as e.g. in modern Russian it is used in sentences such as 'I go to my house', 'you go to your house', etc., instead of 'my', 'your', etc. This usage has its explanation in the social system of the extended family: in regard to any external possessions (in contrast to 'my foot', etc.) there was of course no personal ownership; everything belonged to the extended family. This was called *swe-/*swo- 'family, kin' (from *sū- 'be born'), and the adjectival form *swo-s meant 'belonging to the family'='own'.[2]

[1] Benveniste, *BSL* 50, 1955, 36; Szemerényi, *Syncope* 314f.; Beekes (and Kortlandt), *KZ* 96, 1983, 212. The reflexive **swe-* is interpreted (?) by Cardona, in *In Memory of W. Cowgill*, 1987, 4, as the pronoun *s*+the oppositive *we/wo*; differently Bader, in Bammesberger 1988, 19. On the whole class, see E. Geniušienė, *The Typology of Reflexives*, Berlin 1987.

[2] Szemerényi, *Syncope* 314f., 334f.; somewhat differently id. 1978, 42f. On the background, see also H. B. Rosén, 'Veräusserlicher—nicht veräusserlicher Besitz', *Lingua* 8, 1959, 264–93; W. Diem, 'Alienable and inalienable possession in Semitic', *ZDMG* 136, 1986, 227–91; B. Jacquinod, 'Une expression de la possession inaliénable en grec homérique', *LALIES* 1, 1980 (cf. *IC* 27, 201). Gr. σφ- is derived from IE **sghuwent-* 'powerful' by Seebold (above, 8.4.3. n. 3); cf. id. 1984, 88–90.

8.5. NUMERALS

The IE numerals had a highly developed system of cardinals and ordinals, in which the decimal system was consistently carried through; influences of a duodecimal system have often been conjectured but must be rejected. In addition a smaller stock of multiplicatives can be established.[1]

[1] An almost complete bibliography up to *c*.1960 can be found in my *Numerals*. To this should be added: Gonda, 'Observations on ordinal numbers', *Fs. P. S. van Ronkel*, 1950, 135–45; A. Suprun, *Slavjanskije čislitel'nyje*, Minsk 1969; Risch, 'Das idg. Wort für 100', *IF* 67, 1962, 129–41; Benveniste, *Hittite et indo-européen*, 1962, 78–87; Kuryłowicz, *Categories* 236f.; Watkins, 'On the syntax of the ordinal', *Lochlann* 3, 1965, 287–97; K. Hoffmann, 'Zu den altiranischen Bruchzahlen', *KZ* 79, 1965, 247–54; Erhart, 'Die ieur. Dualendung -*ō(u)* und die Zahlwörter', *Sbornik Brno*, 1965/A-13; Henning, *In Memoriam P. Kahle*, 1968, 144; J. R. Hurford, *The Linguistic Theory of Numerals*, 1975; Greenberg, 'Generalizations about numeral systems', in Greenberg et al. (eds.), *Universals of Human Language* iii, 1978, 249–95; Solari, 'Sulla posizione del gotico: i numerali', *RIL* 116, 1982, 181–93; Gamkrelidze–Ivanov, 842f.; Hurford, *Language and Number: the Emergence of a Cognitive System*, 1987; C. Justus, 'IE numerals', in Arbeitmann 1988, 521–41; H.-J. Seiler, *Numeral Systems*, AKUP 1989; W. P. Schmid, *Wort und Zahl: Sprachwissenschaftliche Betrachtungen der Kardinalzahlwörter*, Akad. Mainz 1989; A. Lillo, *The Ancient Greek Numeral System*, 1990; J. Gvozdanovič, *IE Numerals*, 1992.

8.5.1

In respect of the numerals 1–10, the tens (20, 30, etc.), and 100, the agreement between the most diverse IE languages, often down to the finest details, is proverbial. Of these only 1–4 and 100 had inflexion; the great majority were uninflected.[1] The IE forms that can be reconstructed are set out below.

[1] The whole IE system is considered late by Lehmann (*GL* 31, 1991, 131–40), and 1, 2, 3 are traced to the demonstratives 'this one here, that one there, that one yonder' (135f.), although this could at most explain the ordinals only, not the cardinals; e.g. how could 'that yonder' denote three persons/things? For a more rational approach, see e.g. Carruba, in *Fs. Szemerényi*, 1979, 198f., on 2, 3, 4, and Benveniste (below, 8.5.2 n. 3).

8.5.2

**oinos* 'one', inflected like a thematic adjective: OLat. *oinos*, class. Lat. *ūnus*, Goth. *ains*, OIr. *oin*, OPrus. *ains*, Gr. οἰνή 'the one on a dice'. 'One' was here regarded as 'single, alone'; cf. Gr. οἶ(ϝ)ος 'alone', to which the Iranian *aiva-* 'one' exactly corresponds; a further variant is **oikos* in OInd. *ēka-* 'one'.[1] In contrast 'one' is denoted in its aspect of togetherness, unity, in:

**sem-*: Gr. εἷς ἕν μία from **sem-s* **sem* **smiya*; **sems* is an innovation for earlier **sēm* (see 6.2.7.1); also Lat. *semel*, *semper*, *simplex*; Goth. *simlē* 'once, formerly'.[2]

duwō*/dwō* m., **duwoi*/**dwoi* f. n. 'two': OInd. *d(u)vā*, *d(u)vē*; Gr. δύω, later only δύο; Lat. *duo*; Goth. *twai*; OCS *dŭva*, *dŭvē*; Lith. *dù* m., *dvì* f. On the alternation *duw-*/*dw-*, see 5.7.2.2; the variant *dw-* has become fixed in Goth. *twai*, OE *twā*, etc., and in the odd-looking Arm. *erku*, in which only *ku* (with *k* from *dw*) continues the old form **dwō*.[2] On the inflexion, see 7.6.4.

**treyes* m., **t(r)isres* f., **trī* n. 'three':[3] OInd. *trayas*, *tisras*, *trī*; OIr. *tri* m. n., *teoir* f.;[4] elsewhere two forms (no separate feminine): Gr. τρεῖς, τρία; Lat. *trēs*, *tria*: Goth. *þreis*, *þrija*; OCS *trĭje*, *tri*. The inflexion was nom. **treyes*, acc. **trins*, gen. **triyom*, loc. **trisu*, etc. (see 7.5.1), whence e.g. Lat. *trēs*, *trīs*, *trium*.

**k^{w}etwores* m., **k^{w}etesres* f., **k^{w}etwōr* n. 'four': OInd. *čatvāras*, *čatasras*, *čatvāri*; OIr. *ceth(a)ir* m. n., *cethéoir* f.; otherwise no separate feminine form: Gr. τέτταρες, -ρα; OCS *četyre* m., *četyri* n. f.; or one form only: Lat. *quattuor*, Goth. *fidwōr*. The -*ō*-, originally justified only in the neuter (see 7.3.2 n. 4),[5] was in some languages extended to the masculine also, e.g. OInd. *čatvāras*, Goth. *fidwōr* from **fedwores*,[6] and certainly in Proto-Slavic, where its former presence explains the long vowel *y* from *ū*, instead of *ŭ*.[7] The paradigm was nom. **k^{w}etwores*, acc. **k^{w}eturn̥s*, gen. **k^{w}eturom*, loc. **k^{w}etwr̥su*.[8]

**penk^we* 'five': OInd. *pañča*, Gr. πέντε/πέμπε,[9] Lat. *quīnque*,[10] Goth. *fimf*, OCS *pętĭ*,[10] Lith. *penkì*.

**s(w)eks* 'six': OInd. *ṣaṣ-*, Lat. *sex*, Goth. *saihs*, OCS *šestĭ*,[11] and Lith. *šešì* show **seks*; Gr. ἕξ (Delph. ϝέξ), Avest. *xšvaš*, Gaul. *suexos*, and W. *chwech* show **sweks*. OPrus. *uschts* 'sixth' and Lith. *ušēs* 'the six weeks of a woman in childbed' (cf. also Arm. *vech*) point to a form without initial *s-*, which could have been the original; in that case *s-* may have been adopted from 'seven'.[12]

**septm̥* 'seven': OInd. *saptá*=Gr. ἑπτά=Lat. *septem*, one of the finest IE word equations; Goth. *sibun*, OCS *sedmĭ* show modifications.[13]

**oktō* 'eight': Gr. ὀκτώ, Lat. *octō*, OInd. *aṣṭā* (see 5.6.1), Goth. *ahtau*, OCS *osmĭ*, Lith. *aštuonì*.[14]

*newn̥ 'nine': OInd. *náva*, Lat. *nouem*, Goth. *niun*, Gr. ἐννέ(ϝ)α, OCS *devętĭ*, Lith. *devynì*.[15]

*dekm̥t/*dekm̥ 'ten':[16] OInd. *dáša*, Gr. δέκα, Lat. *decem*, Goth. *taihun*, OCS *desętĭ*, Lith. *dešimt*.[17]

1 On Hitt, *eka*-(?), see Carruba, *Fs. Szemerényi*, 1979, 197. Beekes, *KZ* 96, 1983, 225, wishes to reconstruct a paradigm for *sem- with nom. s. *sōm-s*. On PIE *smH-, allegedly 'pair', see Sihler, *JIES* 1, 1973, 111–13.

2 On *d(u)woi, see Szemerényi, 'Development' 220; a different view in Watkins, *Fachtagung* 5, 1975, 368f. On further questions, see Benveniste, *HIE* 86; Hiersche, *KZ* 78, 1963, 159 (incorrect); Erhart (above, 8.5 n. 1), 20; Schindler, *IF* 71, 1967, 236; Olzscha, *IF* 73, 1968, 146f.; Erhart 1970, 90f.; Carruba (n. 1 above), 198f.; Rasmussen 1989, 269; Villar, in Polomé 1991, 136-54; Strunk, *PBB* 114, 1992, 194–200; Mayrhofer, *EWA* i/10, 1992, 761–3. Note also Merkelbach, 'Die Gliederung des Volkes in Zweier- und Dreiergruppen', *Fs. F. Vittinghoff*, 1980, 87–99. On Celtic, see Thurneysen, *GOI* 182; Jackson, *Language and History in Early Britain*, 1954, 371, 374; Cowgill, *Lg* 43, 1968, 134; *MSS* 46, 1985, 24f.; Hamp, *BBCS* 26, 1975, 97. On the alternation *duw-/dw-*, see Sihler, *Lg* 47, 1971, 67f.; Horowitz, *Sievers' Law and the Evidence of the RV*, 1974, 37, 66. On Arm. *erku*, see Szemerényi, *Numerals* 96; *Syncope* 295[7]; *Fs. Winter*, 1985, 790f., and above, 2.9, as against Meillet and, more recently, Vennemann, *AArmL* 7, 1986, 27f. (cf. *BSL* 86/2, 1992, 26, and Swiggers, *Orbis* 34, 1991, 280).

3 Benveniste, *HIE* 86f.: *ter- 'dépassement'; Carruba, loc. cit.

4 Cowgill, *Lg* 33, 1957, 341–5, considered that Celtic, like Aryan, requires only *tisres, *k^{w}etesres (not *-sor-*), but Hamp, *Ériu* 24, 1973, 177f., rightly emphasizes that the disyllabic *teüir* demands a *tisores, and 4 as well would then have been *k^{w}etesores. On the origin of the element *-sr-*, see Szemerényi, *Syncope* 313 n. 1, 335; *Krat* 11, 1967, 206f., esp. 220f.; id. 1978, 39f. Normier, *IF* 85, 1981, 47, is wrong on this point.

5 Szemerényi, *Numerals* 15 (on this also Meillet, *BSL* 29/2, 1929, 171), and for OInd. *-i* 133 n. 64 (as against J. Schmidt 1889, 191, 235). The Aryan form *čatvā expected from IE *k^{w}etwōr seems to be attested in Ashkun *ċatā* (Morgenstierne, *NTS* 15, 1949, 203). Schmitt-Brandt, 24 n., is wrong on *k^{w}etwor-.

6 Cf. Krahe, *IF* 66, 1961, 36f.; but *-ō-* is not Indo-European.

7 Vaillant, *Gram. comp.* ii, 628; a different explanation in Schmalstieg, *AION-L* 4, 1962, 59f.

8 Szemerényi, *Syncope* 288; *SMEA* 1, 1966, 34; on Gr. τ-/π- and Gmc. *f-* ibid., 40; *Studies T. B. L. Webster*, 1986, 226 (πίσυρες from *k^{w}etur-*, *pace* Cowgill and Mayrhofer 1986, 176); van Windekens, *IF* 87, 1983, 8f.; García-Ramón, 'Lesbio *pessures*', *Fs. Adrados* i, 1984, 179–89. Rix, *Fs. Knobloch*, 1985, 348, accepts the view that, being trisyllabic, *k^{w}étwores changed its accent to *k^{w}etwóres. On the etymology see Erhart, (above, 8.5 n. 1), 23f.; id. 1970, 95 (*k^{w}et- 'pair'!); Čop, *UAJb* 44, 1972, 170, thinks that *k^{w}et-wor-es contains *wer- 'man' (cf. *dai-wer- 'husband's brother') as *k^{w}ete-sor-es contains *sor- 'woman', but the correct form is *esor-; see my 'Kinship' 34f., esp. 40, and cf. Oettinger, in Meid (ed.), *Zum idg. Wortschatz*, 1987, 190. On the paradigm, see also Hamp, *Ériu* 24, 1973, 177, but certainly the oblique cases already had *k^{w}et-, not *k^{w}t-, in Indo-European; also Beekes, *JIES* 15, 1988, 215–19. For further details, see P. Stiles, 'The fate of the numeral 4 in Germanic', *NOWELE* 6, 1985, 81–104; 7, 3–27; 8, 3–25; A. Lillo, *MSS* 49, 1988, 71–3 (on Dor. τέτορες); Stiles, *TPS* 86, 1988, 115 (*-ōr* n. pl.); Shields, in *Memoriae van Windekens*, 1991, 265–72 (new etymon).

9 Szemerényi, *SMEA* 1, 1966, 40f. On the etymology, see Polomé, *Fs. Kuiper*, 1969, 99–101; van Brock, *Mél. Chantraine*, 1973, 266f.; Crevatin, *InL* 4, 1978, 7–11, but also Mayrhofer, *Mél. Renou*, 1968, 513; van Windekens, *IF* 87, 1983, 8f. Yet Saussure had already anticipated the correct view in his *Mémoire* (117), namely that *penk^{w}e contains the connective particle *k^{w}e 'and'; the first part is not, however, *pen- 'one' or 'thumb' (Pedersen, *KZ* 32, 1893, 272), but *penk- 'fist' (='five'), attested in Gmc. *fūhsti- (<*funh-sti-) and Slav. *pensti-, Russ. *pjast'*, as no doubt also in Ved. *paṅkti* (see my *Numerals* 113f.); *penk^{w}e was thus the completion of the first pentad: 1, 2, 3, 4, *and* 5. Carruba (n. 1 above), 196, similarly sees *k^{w}e at the end, but at the beginning he (with Polomé) looks for *penk(u)- 'community'.

[10] On *qu-* (cross between **penkʷe* and **kʷetwores*) see Szemerényi, *Lg* 46, 1970, 142f. (=*SM* 474f.); on *ī* see Eichner, in Panagl and Krisch 1992, 70f. On Slavic, see Szemerényi, *Numerals* 107f.: in place of *penče* on the analogy of *pentŭ*, not IE **penkʷti-* (favoured again by Hoffmann, *KZ* 79, 1966, 253; Eichner, *Fachtagung* 7, 1985, 166).

[11] On the Slavic forms of 6–10, see Szemerényi, *Numerals* 109f.

[12] Ibid. 78f.; cf. also Nehring, *Sprache* 8, 1962, 129f.; Stang, *Vgl. Gram.* 279. Hamp, *Studies A. A. Hill* iii, 1978, 81–90, reconstructs an all-inclusive **ksweks*, whereas Erhart (1970, 97–100) proposes a **(s)Hʷeks*, allegedly **Hʷe-k(e)s*=2×3. Does the difficult Arm. *vech* come from a Sievers' Law variant **suweks*? See *Fachtagung* 6, 1980, 419 n. 25a; Hamp, op. cit. 85; Bolognesi, in *Saggi in onore di L. Heilmann*, 1984, 5. The IE numerals 6 and 9 are compared with Hamito-Semitic and Old Egyptian forms by Dunant, *AO* 56, 1988, 352–6 (cf. *IC* 33, 1989, A 276).

[13] Szemerényi, *Numerals* 35, 109f. On East Slavic, also Liewehr, *Zeitschrift für Slawistik* 12, 1967, 726.

[14] On the palatal *k*, Szemerényi, *Syncope* 399f.; on the etymology, Erhart 1970, 96; Olzscha (n. 2 above), 152; Pisani, *Paideia* 35, 1980, 47 (from Caucasian). Since **oktō* looks like a dual (see Rasmussen 1989, 126f.), it has often been seen as proof of an original quaternary system (alongside and before the decimal system); cf. Erhart 1970, 94f.: the basis was **Hʷo-kʷete* 'two double pairs'; Strunk, *PBB* 114, 1992, 192f.

[15] On the Greek form, see Szemerény, *Syncope* 107–18 (not IE **enwn̥!*); *KZ* 88, 1974, 25f. (=*SM* 1434f.). Wackernagel's **en newm* (*KZ* 28, 132f.=*KSchr.* i, 1953, 614 f: *en* 'denoting the full number'?) is accepted by Schwyzer, *GG* i, 591; Dunkel, *MH* 47, 1990, 28 n. 17; differently, Beekes 1969, 45f. On 9 see also Dunant (above, n. 12 fin.).

[16] Szemerényi, *Numerals* 68f.; Erhart 1970, 93 (**de-km̥t* 'one decad'); Olzscha (n. 2 above), 146f.; Shields, 'A new etymology', *BalkE* 27/4, 1984, 75–80; Eichner (n. 10 above); Markey, *JIES* 12, 1985, 284 (**de-km̥t* 'two hands full'); F. Motta, in *Fs. Szemerényi*[2] iii, 1993, 293–303.

[17] In some languages subtractive terms are used for certain numbers, e.g. Lat. *un-*, *duo-dē-uīgintī*, which are perhaps due to Etruscan influence (so Lejeune, *BSL* 76, 1981, 248); on this cf. also Hamp, *Ériu* 33, 1982, 179 n. 1a. Lehmann, *JIES* 5, 1978, 26, connects the difference in, for instance, 12 (*ten-two* or *two-ten*) with difference of word order, i.e. OV and VO.

8.5.3

For the *multiples of ten* compounds of the so-called *dvigu* type can be established for Indo-European. The first element in these is the stem of the unit, while the second is **(d)komt*, an ablaut variant of **dekm̥t* 'ten'; the initial consonant group of the second component was simplified, with compensatory lengthening of a short final vowel or sonant in the first component.[1] The IE forms were:

**wīkm̥t*, **trīkomt*, **kʷetwr̥̄komt*, **penkʷēkomt*, **s(w)ekskomt*, **septm̥̄komt*, **oktōkomt*, **newn̥̄komt*.

The development of *r̥̄ m̥̄ n̥̄* to *rā mā nā* gave in Latin the 'connecting vowel' *ā* characteristic of all the tens except 80: *quadrāgintā*, *septu(m)āgintā*, *nōnāgintā* changed also **quinquē-*, **sex-* to *quinquāgintā*, *sexāgintā*. In Greek, on the other hand, the inherited 'connecting vowel' of πεντήκοντα was generalized from 60 upwards: *τρῑκοντα became τρι-ᾱ-κοντα on the analogy of *τετϝρᾱκοντα, which was itself later modified to τετταρᾰκοντα. The ending *-ā* or α was introduced as a supporting vowel to avoid the reduction of *-komt* to *-kon*.[2] In the case of 20, early **wīkomt* became **wīkm̥t* on the analogy of

**dekm̥t*, and because of its meaning underwent a formal adaptation to the duals: **wīkm̥tī* gave West Greek (see Lillo, *MSS* 48 (1987), 175–8), Boeot., Thessal. ϝίκατι (with final vowel shortened as in the case of δύο); in the East Greek dialects it gave ἐ(ϝ)ῑκοσι, εἴκοσι under the influence of -κοντ- and with a prothetic vowel of obscure origin. In Latin **uīcentī* became **uīcintī* by assimilation of the middle vowel, and then *uīgintī* by extension of the *g* voiced from *k* after *r̥̄ m̥̄ n̥̄*.[3]

It is not necessary here to give a detailed account of the forms in all other languages; this is provided in my *Numerals*. The development in Germanic, however, may be of special interest, and shall be briefly treated.[4] The IE system survives in 70–90, e.g. in Goth. *sibuntēhund*, *ahtautēhund*, *niuntēhund*. These continue the old **septm̥̄komt*, **oktōkomt*, **newn̥̄komt*, from which first arose **seftunhand*, **ahtōhand*, **newunhand*, preceded in the series by **fimfēhand* and **sehskand*; this original ending *-hand* was later adapted to conform with 20 and 100, thus becoming *-hund* in 30–90 also. Among these tens 60 stood out from the rest and was modified to **sehsēhund* by analogy with 50. The influence of 50 and 60 led to **seftunēhund*, but since in 50, 60, and 80 the principle of formation was unmistakably unit + *-(ē)hund*, and 7 already had the form **sefun*, **seftunēhund* became **sefuntēhund*, **seƀuntēhund*. The metathesis thus led to a formation which synchronically could only be taken as 'seven' + *-tēhund*, and so led to the Gothic series

ahtau-tēhund—niun-tēhund—taihun-tēhund.

In West Germanic, on the other had, the early series

**seftunhund—*ahtōhund—*ne(w)unhund*

became under the influence of 80

**seƀuntōhund—*ahtōhund—*niuntōhund*

from which came in OHG, with omission of the 'superfluous' ending,

sibunzo—ahtozo—niunzo,

and from the ninth century, under the influence of 20–60,

sibunzug—ahtozug—niunzug.[5]

[1] Szemerényi, *Numerals* 5f., 115f.; see also above, 6.2.8 Addendum 1. A different view in Eichner, *Fachtagung* 7, 1985, 166. On Arm. *yisun* 'fifty' (from *hinis-*), see Olsen, *HS* 102, 1990, 234.

[2] *Numerals* 133f.

[3] On **wi-*, see *Numerals* 131, 134; Risch, *IF* 67, 1962, 134; Lejeune, *RPh* 36, 1962, 276; Erhart 1970, 100.

[4] In detail, *Numerals* 27–44. A different account in G. Schmidt, 'Zum Problem der germ. Dekadenbildungen', *KZ* 84, 1970, 98–136 (118f. **sibūn-tēhund*>**sibŭn-tēhund*); G. Porru Mazuoli, 'I nomi dei numerali da 70 a 100 in gotico', in *Mille: I dibattiti del circolo linguistico fiorentino 1945–1970*, Florence 1970, 173–83 (176: abstract nouns *sebm̥t* etc. +*dkm̥t*); Lühr, 'Die Dekaden im Germanischen', *MSS* 36, 1977, 59–71 (69: in **sibuntēhund*, *tē*=Lat. *dē*); Bammesberger, 'Germanic decads 20–60', in Brogyanyi and Krömmelbein (eds.), *Germanic*

Dialects, 1986, 3–8; Darms (above, 6.2.6 n. 1), 34–48 (*-tēhund* is vrddhi); Kortlandt, 'Greek numerals and PIE glottalic consonants', *MSS* 42, 1983, 97–104: *d* can become *H* and thus (97) *dkm̥tom>H̦k->*ἐκ × ἕν>ἑκ-; (98) *penk^{w}wedkomt>-eHk->-ēk-*; (99) ἑβδμηκ->ἕβδομος> ογδοϝος>ογδϝηκ, ενεϝνη-κ-; (100) *dwi-dk->Hwīk-/wīk-*: all a meaningless play. For these problems, see also Peters, in Bammesberger 1988, 377 n. 16 (*dk* by irregular development gave *Hk*); Swiggers, in Vennemann 1989, 79 (glottalic explanation does not account for ϝίκατι); Rasmussen 1989, 126f. with n. 4; Nielsen, 'OE and Gmc. decades', *IC* 34, 878, 105–17.

[5] As is well known, J. Schmidt (*Urheimath der Indogermanen und das europäische Zahlsystem*, Abh. Akad. Berlin, 1891, 41–56) connected the 'break' in the system of tens with the Babylonian sexagesimal system; see against this my *Numerals* 2f., and more recently Mańczak, 'IE numerals and the sexagesimal system', in *ICHL* 6, 1985, 347–52. On the numerals, see further Szemerényi 1985, 34.

8.5.4

For 100 the IE languages unanimously give a neuter noun **km̥tóm*: Lat. *centum*, Goth. *hund*, OIr. *cēt* (i.e. *k^{j}ēd*), Gr. ἑ-κατόν (probably *one-hundred*), OInd. *šatam*, Avest. *satəm*, Lith. *šimtas*,[1] OCS *sŭto*, Toch. *känt(e)*.

It is beyond all doubt that **km̥tóm* arose from **dkm̥tom*, i.e. it is formed from **dekm̥t* 'ten'. The only question is, *how* was it formed? Since all the multiples of ten are formed of unit + *(d)komt*, it would be most natural to start from **dekm̥̄kómt* or **(d)km̥̄kómt*. I am now inclined to think[2] that this form was shortened to **km̥̄kómt* and then with loss of *-t* (cf. **dekm̥* from **dekm̥t*) to **km̥kóm*, from which **km̥tóm* arose by dissimilation,[3] and was soon taken as a neuter *o*-stem. Others suppose that **(d)km̥tóm* was the ordinal of 10 and its meaning 'the tenth (ten)';[4] this overlooks the fact that, with groups of men for instance, the 'tenth ten' is still 10 and does not mean 100, and also that the other tens are not formed in this way.

[1] Lithuanian has lost the neuter and transferred its former neuter nouns to the masculine.

[2] As opposed to *Numerals* 140.

[3] Cf. Grm. *Kartoffel* from Ital. *tartuffolo* (and similar).

[4] Lohmann, *Genus und Sexus*, 1932, 13; Risch, *IF* 67, 1962, 135f., 140f.; cf. Erhart 1970, 94 (haplology from *kom km̥-t-om* 'decad of the decads'); also Olzscha, *IF* 73, 1968, 149; Kortlandt (above, 8.5.3 n. 4), 97.

8.5.5

There is no common IE method of denoting the *hundreds*. In OInd. e.g. 300 can be expressed in three ways:[1] (*a*) with 100 as noun; thus *trī šatā(ni) (gavām)* 'three hundreds (of oxen, gen.)'; (*b*) from the two numerals a *bahuvrīhi* is formed with the meaning 'numbering so many hundreds': *trišatās . . . šaṅkavas* 'three hundred spokes'; (*c*) the compound becomes a collective noun, either a neuter in *-a-* or a feminine in *-ī-*, e.g. *trišatam pašūnām* 'a three-hundred of cattle'. The first possibility (as though, e.g., Lat. *tria *centa*) is unknown in the classical languages,[2] but is common in Gothic: *þrija hunda*. Of the other two, (*b*) is the rule in Latin (*trecentī*) and, with an extension in *-io-*, in Greek (*τριακόσιοι*); in Old Latin (*c*) was also in use: *argenti sescentum et mille* (Lucilius 1053).

Again, there is no general IE expression for 1,000. Nevertheless it is noteworthy that Aryan and Greek, and perhaps Latin, shared a common term: an IE **gheslo-*[3] underlies OInd. *sa-hasra-m* (*sa-* from **sm̥-* 'one', cf. Gr. *εἷς*), OIran. *hazahra-* (NPers. *hazār*), Gr. *χέλλιοι χῑλιοι*; Lat. *mīlle*[4] possibly goes back to **mī(hī)lī* from **(s)mī *hēlī*, in which **hēlī* from **gheslī* was an abstract noun in *-ī*; see under (*c*) above. It is no less interesting that Germanic and Balto-Slavic have a common expression: Goth. *þūsundi* and OCS *tysęšti* (also *tysǫšti*). These forms cannot go back to a common IE **tūsn̥tī*, as in Slavic *s* after *u* would have to appear as *š* or *x*.[5] Since, on the other hand, the meaning 'thousand' must somehow be based on 100, we have to postulate an IE **tūso-km̥t-ī*, as an original **tūs-k-* would have kept the group *-sk-* in Germanic; **tūso-* must thus be an adjective 'strong'; cf. **tū-mo-* 'strong' (OHG *dūmo* 'thumb'), **tū-ro-* 'swollen' (Lat. *obtūrō*). After the sound shift the 'connecting vowel' in **þūsa-* disappeared, and *-sh-* was simplified to *-s-*.[6] The Germanic form is also the source of the Slavic and not vice versa;[7] Lith. *tūkstantis* is modified from **tūsant-*.[8]

1 Wackernagel and Debrunner, *Ai. Gr.* iii, 390f.
2 See, however, Szemerényi, *Syncope* 287.
3 At long last an ingenious explanation has been advanced by Rix for this word ('Uridg. **gʰeslo-* in den südidg. Ausdrücken für 1000', in *Memoriae van Windekens*, 1991, 225–31): **gheslo-* 'hand', **ghesliyo-* 'amount of corn that can be held in one hand'. See also Szemerényi, *TPS* 92/2, 1944.
4 Szemerényi, *ArchL* 6, 1954, 38f., and Hamp, *Glotta* 46, 1969, 274f.
5 See Shevelov, *A Prehistory of Slavic*, 1964, 130. A proto-form **tūt-sn̥t-ī* 'forming a great quantity' is posited by Pijnenburg, *HS* 102, 1989, 99–105.
6 For the loss of the compositional or stem-final *a* in disyllabic first members of compounds, cf. Goth. *gud-hūs* 'temple', *laus-handus* 'with empty hands'; see Kieckers, *Hb. der vgl. got. Gram.*, 1960, 97f.; C. T. Carr, *Nominal Compounds in Germanic*, 1939, 277; Krahe and Meid, *Germanische Sprachwissenschaft* iii, 1967, 21.
7 Hamp, *PCLS* 9, 1973, 172f.
8 Vaillant, *Gram. comp.* ii, 647f.; but cf. Stang, *Vgl. Gram.* 282.

8.5.6

The *ordinals* were originally simply thematic adjectives formed with *-o-* from the cardinals, with zero grade of the preceding syllable;[1] cf. OInd. *saptama-*=OLat. *septumus*, both from IE **septm̥-o-s*, Lat. *nōnus* (from **nouenos*), etc. This principle was later obscured by the fact that in the case of **dekm̥t*: **dekm̥t-o-s* the loss of final *-t* in 10 gave rise to the pair **dekm̥*: **dekm̥tos*; from this a new suffix *-to-* was abstracted, which, because of the importance of 10, extended its range further and further, first to 5th, from there to 4th and 6th, from 4th to 3rd and similarly upwards to 20th, etc.[2] A table shows this:[3]

Proto-IE	IE	Late and Post-IE
**triy-o-*	**tri-yo-*	**tri-to-*, **tri-tiyo-*
**kʷtur-o-*	**kʷtur(i)yo-*	**kʷetur-to-*, **kʷetwr̥-to-*
**pn̥kʷ-o-*	**penkʷ-to-*	**penkʷ-to-*
**(s)uks-o-*		**sweks-to-*
**septm̥-o-*		**septm̥-o-*
**oktuw-o-*		**oktuw-o-*, **oktōw-o-*
**newn̥-o-*		**newn̥-o-*
**dekm̥t-o-*	**dekm̥-to-*	**dekm̥-to*, **dekm̥-o-*
**wīkm̥t-o-*	**wīkm̥t-to-*	**wīkm̥tto-*, **wīkm̥tt-m̥o-*
**trīkm̥t-o-*	**trīkm̥t-to-*	**trīkm̥tto-*, **trīkm̥tt-m̥o-*

IE **kʷtur-(i)yo-*, from **kʷetwor-* with zero grade of both vowels, is continued in OInd. *turīya*, **wīkʷm̥tto-* in Boeot. ϝικαστός and, modified on the analogy of the cardinal εἴκοσι, in εἰκοστός, while the extended formation in *-m̥o-* is represented by Lat. *uīcenss-imus*, OInd. *viṁśat-i-t-ama-*. In Latin the old situation was long retained in 7th–9th, and even extended to 10th; in Greek, on the other hand, 9th came early under the influence of 10th and instead of **(e)newn̥os* an extended **enewn̥tos* came into use, giving *ενεϝατος and later, with syncope, *ἔν(ϝ)ατος.[4] This process went even further in Germanic, where IE *-to-* was also extended to 7th–9th, so that the whole series 3rd–10th shows this suffix either with *t* (after spirants) or with ð (*d* after *n*) which developed from it: Goth. *þridja*, **fidurda*, *fimfta*, *saihsta*, **sibunda*, *ahtuda*, *niunda*, *taihunda*.

In all languages 'first' and, to begin with, 'second' stand apart. The latter was originally expressed by 'the other' (Goth. *anþar*, Lat. *alter*, later replaced by *secundus* 'the following'), the former by an adjective which meant roughly 'in front, foremost' and had in most IE languages the form **pr̥wo-* or **pr̥mo-* (from **pro* 'before'); compare on the one hand OInd. *pūrva-*, *pūrvyá-* 'prior', OCS *prŭvŭ*, and perhaps Gr. πρῶτος, Dor. πρᾶτος from **prāwo-to-s*,[5] on the other hand Lith. *pìrmas*, OE *forma* from **furmo-*, while Goth. *fruma* has been modified on the pattern of the 'superlatives' in *-uma*. Lat. *prīmus*, as Paelignian *prismu* shows, arose from **prīsamos*, i.e. **pri-isamos*, the superlative corresponding to *prior*; see 7.8.6 and n. 6 below.[7]

[1] Benveniste, *Noms d'agent et noms d'action*, 1948, 144f.; Szemerényi, *ArchL* 1, 1950, 191; *Numerals* 67f.; Kuryłowicz, *Categories* 236f.; Cowgill, in Cardona et al. (eds.), *IE and IEs*, 1971, 117f.; Rasmussen 1989, 123–30. On the Balto-Slavic ordinals see Szemerényi, *Numerals* 109f.; W. Smoczyński, *Studia Balto-Słowiańskie* i, 1989, 61–108.

[2] Szemerényi, *Numerals* 92. On Gaulish *dekanto-*, Hispano-Celtic *dekamet-ino-* and Oscan *dekento-*, *dekmā*, see Prosdocimi, *SE* 48, 1980, 437f., 619; Szemerényi 1985, 35f.; *ZCP* 44, 1991, 303–10; Motta, *Fs. Szemerényi*², iii, 1993, 293–303.

[3] *Numerals* 92; G. Schmidt, 'Idg. Ordinalzahlen', *IF* 97, 1993, 197–235.

[4] Szemerényi, *Numerals* 89; *Syncope* 115f.; *KZ* 88, 1974, 25f.; Rix, *MSS* 27, 1970, 101. For

ἕβδομος, ὄγδοος, see also Cuny, *BSL* 32, 1931, 42f.; Comrie, *SEER* 53, 1975, 323–9; Winter, in *In Honor of M. S. Beeler*, 1980, 487–90; Kortlandt (above, 8.5.3 n. 4), 99.—Is Lat. *octāuos* in reality simply **oktō-os*, i.e. the normal thematic derivative with a hiatus filler?

5 Cowgill (n. 1 above), 123 (**pro-atos*, as also Deroy, *AC* 39, 1971, 375f.); Bonfante, *Mél. Fohalle*, 1969, 30f. (**p̥̄tos* with *rā* and *rō*); Bammesberger, *Studien zur Laryngaltheorie*, 1984, 60f.

6 Szemerényi, *Studi V. Pisani*, 1969, 985f.; *Studies Palmer*, 1976, 416 n. 84; id. 1989, 43f. The form **prīsamos* is supported by OIr. *riam, remi*, see Thurneysen, *GOI* 528; Guyonvarc'h, *Celticum* 18, 1970, 303f.

7 An Anatolian ordinal suffix *-anna-* (IE *-ono-*?) has been assumed by Watkins, *Fachtagung* 5, 1975, 376, but according to Melchert, *HS* 102, 1989, 26 n. 7, 'evidence . . . is false': *-anna* is acc. *-an*+geminating *-a* 'and'.

8.5.7

A limited range of numeral adverbs was already formed in the IE period.[1] Certainly **dwis* and **tris*, which are found in many languages, go back to Indo-European: OInd. *dviṣ triṣ*, Avest. *biš θriš*, Gr. δίς τρίς, Lat. *bis ter* (still also *terr* in Plautus), OIce. *tvis-var* 'twice', *þris-var* 'thrice', OHG *zwiro (-ror, -n)* and *driror*.[2] To these may be added IE **kʷetrus* 'four times', formed in the same way as **dwis *tris*, therefore from **kʷetwr̥-s*, in Avest. *čaθruš*, OInd. *čatuḥ* (from *-ur-s*) and Lat. *quater*.[3] For 'once' no common IE term can be shown, and no doubt it was continually renewed; cf. OInd. *sakr̥t*, Gr. ἅπαξ (both with **sm̥-* 'one' and a word meaning 'blow'), Lat. *semel*, etc.

1 Wackernagel and Debrunner, *Ai. Gr.* iii, 423f.

2 On this, see G. Schmidt, *Studien zum germ. Adverb*, diss., Berlin, 1962, 356f. (**dwi-*, **tri-zwōs*); also Hollifield, *Sprache* 30, 1985, 50.

3 Early **quatrus* became **quatr̥s* by syncope and then developed to **quaters*; it was followed by **tris*>**tr̥s*>**ters*. Dunkel, in *In Memory of W. Cowgill*, 1987, 28, suggests, no doubt rightly, that **dwis* is formed on the model of **tris*. But is **tris* then a loc. **tri-si/-su*?

9

Morphology III: Verbs

9.1. PRELIMINARY REMARKS ON THE IE VERBAL SYSTEM

The verbal systems of the various IE languages differ from one another in important ways. Some languages have extremely complicated, others quite simple systems, and this situation causes great difficulties for the comparatist.

Thus the Greek verb has a system which is organized as follows:

voices: three (active, middle, and, in aorist and future, passive);
moods: four (indicative, subjunctive, optative, imperative);
tenses: seven (present, imperfect, future, aorist, perfect, pluperfect, future perfect).

The tense forms themselves have three numbers, of which the singular and plural have three persons, the dual only two. To these personal forms, the finite verb, are added the forms of the non-finite verb, the various infinitives and participles.

The structure of the Old Indic verb system in its oldest, Vedic, phase is very similar:

voices: three (active, middle, passive);
moods: four (as in Greek) or, with the injunctive, five;
tenses: seven (present, imperfect, aorist, perfect, pluperfect, future, conditional).

On the other hand, we find in Gothic:

voices: two (active and passive);
moods: three (indicative, subjunctive, imperative);
tenses: two (present and perfect).

Lithuanian is similar:

voices: one;
moods: three (indicative, optative, imperative);
tenses: four (present, preterite, future, imperfect).

Hittite at an early period shows a 'minimal' system:

voices: two (active and medio-passive);
moods: two (indicative, imperative);
tenses: two (present, preterite).

Thus the question of what can and should be considered as belonging to the IE system arises even more urgently for the verb than for the noun. Can we simply take it that the 'maximal' system of Aryan and Greek was that of Indo-European, from which all the others came through gradual impoverishment, or is the maximal system a special development in a particular area of the Indo-European domain, which never took place in the other regions? In that case, should the 'minimal' system be recognized as that of Indo-European or late Indo-European?

That the second alternative cannot be correct follows from a number of observations which, as for the noun, reveal the remnants of an earlier, richer system. Thus Aryan and Greek distinguish a perfect and an aorist, but not so Latin, Germanic, Celtic, etc. Nevertheless the evidence of the south-eastern group must be acknowledged as decisive on this point at least, since the Latin perfect combines forms from the old perfect and the old aorist, those from the *s*-aorist being particularly clear; the same is true of Celtic, while Slavic still has an aorist, which in the main continues the old aorist.

As opposed to the four moods of Greek, Latin has only three: indicative, subjunctive, imperative. This says nothing, however, against the Indo-European character of the optative, for some of the most important Latin verbs still use the old optative: *sim* and *uelim* are such forms. The former existence of the subjunctive is equally certain: Lat. *erō*, though a future, was once the subjunctive, as is shown by its agreement with Greek and Aryan. The situation in Hittite must therefore be seen as an impoverishment; cf. 9.7.3.

On the basis of such considerations we may provisionally recognize *the following categories for the IE verb*:

two *voices*: active and middle;
four *moods*: indicative, subjunctive, optative, imperative;
three to six *tenses*: present, aorist, perfect; perhaps also future, imperfect, pluperfect.

Of the tenses the systems of the present and aorist belong closely together, whereas the perfect stands more apart and occupies a place of its own.

For the expression of these varied relations different means are used. The distinction between λούει 'he washes (someone/something else)' and λούεται 'he washes (himself)', i.e. the distinction of voice, is carried solely by the personal ending. In the case of *λούεις—λούῃς—λούοις—λοῦε* the ending of the last form is enough to distinguish it from the rest and characterize it as imperative. In the first three forms, on the other hand, the ending is the same; they are distinguished by the element between the stem *λου-* and the ending *-ς*, and characterized as indicative, subjunctive, and optative respectively. In the pair *λούεις—λούσεις* the *-σ-* alone is sufficient to establish the tense difference between present and future.

In general the tense stem (St) is followed by the element showing mood (M), and this by the personal ending (E). The ending may or may not be preceded by a so-called thematic vowel (Th), and the corresponding types of inflexion are called respectively *thematic* and *athematic*.

This can be represented by the following formulae:

thematic	athematic
St+M+Th+E	St+M+E

In the indicative M usually=zero, so that the formula is reduced to St +(Th+) E.

In accordance with this structure the problems of the verb will be discussed as follows:

Personal endings and thematic vowel; voices
Formation of moods
Tense stems:
  Present stem
  Aorist and future stem
  Perfect stem
  Augment, polymorphism, suppletivism, system, aspect, accent
Synthesis: paradigms with comments
The non-finite verb
Prehistory [1]

[1] For further study: Brugmann, *Grundriss*², ii/3; Meillet, *Introduction* 195f.; Hirt, *IG* iv, 83f.; Pedersen, *Hittitisch* 79f.; Savčenko, 'Drevnejšije gram. kategorii glagola v ie. jazyke', *VJ* 1954 (4), 111–20; Ambrosini, 'Concordanze nella struttura formale delle categorie verbali indo-europee', *SSL* 2, 1962, 33–97; Kuryłowicz, *Categories* (almost the whole book deals with the verb); Adrados, *Verbo* (cf. Cardona, *Lg* 41, 1965, 105–14); Ivanov, *Obščeind.* 55f.; Watkins, *Verb*; K. Hoffmann, *MSS* 28, 1970, 19–41; F. R. Palmer 1986. The whole IE field is surveyed in Schwyzer, *GG* i, 639f. (for early Greek, see also Chantraine, *Grammaire homérique* i², 1948, 282f.; Duhoux 1992); Leumann², 505f.; also of interest, though in general without bibliographical references, are Vaillant, *Gram. comp.* iii (*Le verbe*), and Stang, *Vgl. Gram.* 308f. See also Meid, 'Keltisches und idg. Verbalsystem', in K. H. Schmidt (ed.), *Indogermanisch und Keltisch*, 1977, 108–31; Rix, 'Das keltische Verbalsystem', ibid. 132–58 (favours the Aryan-Greek model); Erhart, *Das ie. Verbalsystem*, 1989.

9.2. PERSONAL ENDINGS, THEMATIC VOWEL, VOICES

Most IE languages use different verbal endings for the active and middle voices, for present and past within these voices, and yet others for the perfect or imperative. The endings, of course, differ according to number and person as well: three for the three persons of the singular (1–3) and three for the three persons of the plural (4–6) are the rule, but in Indo-European there were in addition three forms for the three persons of the dual (7–9). The complete set can be grouped as follows:

Active endings of the present-aorist system
Middle endings of the present-aorist system
Endings of the perfect
The Anatolian system
Endings of the imperative

The endings of the present and aorist are also used in the moods properly so-called, the subjunctive and optative; only the imperative has endings of its own.

9.2.1. Active endings in the present and aorist system

These endings are attested basically in double form for persons 1–3 and 6: one set, the *primary endings* (PE), has final *-i*, the other, the *secondary endings* (SE), is without *-i*: thus *-mi/-m*, *-si/-s*, etc. The PE are used in the present, the SE in the aorist, but, as indicated above, not only in these forms; thus the SE are also used in the optative.

These endings can be joined to the stem either directly or with the help of a thematic vowel (see above); accordingly *athematic* and *thematic* formations are distinguished, e.g. **es-ti* 'is' but **bher-e-ti* 'carries'. Both types of formation use the same endings with the exception of the 1st singular.

9.2.1.1

The primary endings in the languages which are most important for reconstruction are as follows:

	Ved.	Avest.	Hitt.	Greek	OLat.	Goth.	OCS	Lith.
1	*mi*	*mi*	*mi*	μι	*m*	*m*	*mĭ*	*mi*
2	*si*	*si*	*si*	σι	*s*	*s*	*si*	*si*
3	*ti*	*ti*	*tsi*	τι	*t*	*t/þ*	*tĭ*	*ti*
4	*mas(i)*	*mahi*	*weni*	μεν/μες	*mus*	*m*	*mŭ*	*me*
5	*tha(na)*	*θa*	*teni*	τε	*tis*	*þ*	*te*	*te*
6	*nti*	*nti*	*ntsi*	ντι	*nt*	*nd*	*ntĭ*	–
7	*vas*	*vahi*	–	–	–	*(ō)s*	*vē*	*va*

	Ved.	Avest.	Hitt.	Greek	OLat.	Goth.	OCS	Lith.
8	*thas*	?	–	τον	–	*ts*	*ta*	*ta*
9	*tas*	**tas*	–	τον	–	–	*te, ta*	–

The secondary endings are:

	Ved.	Avest.	Hitt.	Greek	OLat.	Goth.	OCS	Lith.
1	*m*	*m*	*n*	ν	*m*	Ø	(*n*)	?
2	*s*	*s*	*s*	ς	*s*	*s*	Ø	?
3	*t*	*t*	*t*	Ø	*d*	Ø	Ø	Ø
4	*ma*	*ma*	*wen*	μεν/μες	*mus*	*m(a)*	*mŭ*	*me*
5	*ta(na)*	*ta*	*ten*	τε	*tis*	þ	*te*	*te*
6	*n*[*t*], *ur*[1]	*n, at*	*ir*	ν[τ]	*nt*	*n(a)*	*n*	–
7	*va*	*va*	–	–	–	*u, wa*	*vē*	*va*
8	*tam*	–	–	τον	–	*ts*	*ta*	*ta*
9	*tām*	*təm*	–	τᾱν	–	–	*te, ta*	–

From the unanimous testimony of Aryan, Hittite, and Greek it can first of all be inferred that in Indo-European the following endings were in use:

	PE	SE
1	*-mi*	*-m*
2	*-si*	*-s*
3	*-ti*	*-t*
6	*-nti*	*-nt*

Although the other languages would not give this result by themselves, they confirm the endings reconstructed above.

It is true, for example, that classical Latin has only the ending *-t* for the 3rd s., but in Old Latin from the earliest inscriptions down to the beginning of the literary period we find a distinction between FECED, KAPIAD, SIED (the later *fēcit*, *capiat*, *siet*=*sit*) and IOVESAT (=*iurat*), which is explained by the fact that original final *-t* became at first *-d*, whereas *-ti* remained unvoiced *-t*; at the beginning of the literary period the double ending *-t*/*-d* was given up in favour of *-t*.[2]

Similarly, Gothic -þ (e.g. *bairiþ* 'carries') presupposes a final vowel (which can with the help of the more archaic languages be determined as *i*), since final *-t* was lost; cf. *wili* 'he will' as opposed to *wileiþ* 'you will' from **welīt* (=Lat. *uelit*, both originally optative) and **welīte* (=Lat. *uelītis*).

Old Irish, not included in the table above, confirms these results in another way. The 3rd s. and 3rd pl. of *ber-* 'carry' are *berid* /b′er′ið′/ and *berait* /b′erid′/ in the simple, so-called absolute form, but *as-beir*

/b'er'/ 'says' ('brings forth', from **eks-bher-*) and *as-berat* /b'erad/ in the compositional, so-called conjunct form. The palatalization of the final consonant in the absolute form and the *i* in *berid* (from *e* by umlaut) point to a final *-ti*, thus to **bhereti* and **bheronti*, whereas *-beir* and *-berat* go back to forms without *-i*, i.e. **bheret* and **bheront*.[3] See further 9.2.1.2, n.7.

The prehistory of the other personal endings is less clear.[4] In the 1st pl. a PE *-mesi* (or *-mosi*?) is indicated by Iranian, in part by Old Indic and Old Irish, but *-mes* by Doric and *-mos* by Latin;[5] *-mēs*, which appears in OHG, cannot go back to IE *-mēs(i)*.[6] A nasal variant is present in East Greek -μεν, to which Hitt. *-weni* (with primary *-i*) is close.[7] The SE differs for certain from the PE only in Aryan and Hittite, though not in the same way. It seems reasonable to posit *-mes*, extended to *-mes-i* in Aryan and Old Irish, as the original PE, to which *-me(m)* with a variant *-me* or *mē* belonged as SE; cf. 8.4.4*b*.

We find a similar situation in the 1st dual, except that here the PE *-wes/-wos* is supported by Goth. *-ōs* (contracted from *o-wos* or *-ōwos*), and the SE had the form *-we/-wē*.[8]

In the 2nd pl. the PE seems to have been *-te(s)*, the SE *-te*; Aryan *-th-* is an innovation,[9] and the vowel was in any case short.[10] For the 2nd dual the agreement between Aryan and Gothic is noteworthy, as Goth. *-ts* is certainly the result of dissimilation of the two spirants *-þs* (from *-tes*).[11] It is nevertheless impossible to recover any IE form for the 2nd and 3rd dual, although the SE of the 3rd dual was presumably *-tā(m)*.[12]

1 Lazzeroni, *SSL* 27, 1987, 145: *-ur* in impf. and aor. from plupf.

2 Szemerényi, 'Marked–unmarked' (*TPS* 1973, 55–74) 55–6.

3 On the absolute and conjunct endings, see Meid, *Die idg. Grundlagen der air. abs. und konj. Verbalflexion*, 1963; Kuryłowicz, *Categories* 132 is decisive for our problem. Cf. also Rix, *Fs. Pokorny*, 1967, 267–75; Campanile, *AION-L* 8, 1968, 41f.; Cowgill, *Fachtagung* 5, 1975, 40–70; *Ériu* 26, 1975, 27–32 (both represent the PE); McCone, *Ériu* 30, 1979, 1–34, esp. 24f.; 33, 1982, 1–29; Kortlandt, *Ériu* 30, 35–53; P. Sims-Williams, *TPS* 1984, 138–201; Cowgill, *Fachtagung* 7, 1985, 109–18; McCone, ibid. 261–70. Watkins, *Ériu* 21, 1969, 1f., is strange, esp. 6 (IE *-ti* 'a mirage'); *Verb*, 164f.

4 Nevertheless, in view of the facts marshalled in the text further on, it is impossible to agree with Lehmann, *PIE Syntax*, 1974, 201–2, that: 'The system of verb endings clearly points to an earlier period in which there was no verbal inflection for number'; this is quite untrue of any IE reconstructed on the evidence of the member languages. No more acceptable is the further statement: 'For the dual and plural endings are obviously defective. We cannot reconstruct endings in these two numbers which are as well supported as are those of the singular, except for the third plural.' The truth is that the dual and plural do not present simple blanks but systems which may differ in detail but nonetheless show that there was a system.

5 Meid (n. 3 above), 57f. Watkins, *Verb* 146–7, posits for 1st and 2nd pl. *-mo*, *-te*, both extended with *-s(i)* in the Italic period. On the 1st and 2nd pl. see further Villar, *RSEL* 4, 1974, 391–409.

6 See Bech, *Studia Neophilologica* 34, 1962, 195f.; Polomé, *RBPh* 45, 1968, 821 (*-mēs* a cross between *-mes* and SE *-mē*, reviving Brugmann, *KVG* 591; Petersen, *Lg* 12, 1936, 173 n.); Hollifield, *Sprache* 26, 1980, 149f.: *bheromo weis*>*-mo(w)is*>*-mais*>*-mēs*.

[7] Wyatt, 'Prehistory of the Greek dialects' (*TAPA* 101, 1971, 557–632), 605: -μεν an innovation for the general -μες, cf. -μεσθα; Negri, *Acme* 27, 1974, 377 (-*men* for -*wen*); Cohen, *IF* 84, 1980, 107–12; Shields, *Glotta* 60, 1983, 197–204.
[8] Kuryłowicz, *Categories* 152; Bammesberger, *PBB(T)* 105, 1983, 169–76; *Studien zur Laryngaltheorie*, 1984, 99f.; *Der Aufbau des germanischen Verbalsystems*, 1986, 159.
[9] Kuryłowicz (n. 8 above).
[10] OIr. *beirthe* cannot be taken back to **bheretēs* (as e.g. Meid, n. 3 above, 58f.); this would be unexampled, and receives no support from OHG -*mēs*—see n. 6 above. Cowgill's solution (*Fachtagung* 7, 113) would perhaps be possible: **beretes-es*>**berete(h)es*>-*tēs*.
[11] Dissimilation suggested as early as Brugmann, *Grundriss*[2], ii/3, 641. Cf. also Dal, *NTS* 16, 1952, 331f.; a different explanation in K. H. Schmidt, *Lings* 130, 1974, 83–6; Shields, *IF* 84, 1980, 216f., 221 (?). Stang, *NTS* 15, 1949, 335f.; proposes -*t*H_1 *es*.
[12] Kuryłowicz, *Categories* 153–6.

9.2.1.2

The endings just discussed can be designated the *mi*-endings, as they are shown especially clearly in the *athematic* (so-called *mi*-) inflexion. There is also, however, the *thematic* or so-called ō-inflexion which differs at least in the 1st s. from the *mi*-inflexion, in that the PE is -ō; cf. Gr. φέρω, Lat. *ferō*, Goth. *baira*, OIr. (abs.) *biru* and (conj.) -*biur* from **berū*, Gath. *spasyā* '*speciō*' (becoming -*āmi* in Avest. and OInd. through contamination with *mi*), Lith. *nešù* 'I carry'.[1]

Apart from this the thematic inflexion has the same endings as the athematic—certainly in the SE and most probably in the PE also, although for some members of the latter series other views have recently been put forward, which are based on a small number of languages and concern mainly the 2nd singular.

In the 2nd s. of the thematic inflexion Lithuanian has the ending -*ì* (e.g. *neši* 'carriest'), which because of the reflexive form -*íes(i)* must go back to -*ei(si)*. This ending -*ei* can be compared with Gr. -εις: in Greek an original -*ei* would have been extended to -*ei-s* and a new 3rd s. in -*ei* formed to it. Furthermore OIr. (conj.) -*bir* can also go back to **bherei*, so that all three languages, it is argued, would point to -*ei* and not -*esi*. Finally in the 3rd s. Lith. *veda* 'leads', like OIr. (conj.) -*feid*, appears to go back to IE **wedhe-t*, and this is also possible for Gr. -ει (with loss of -*t* and modification of -ε to -ει). Thus the endings of the singular of the thematic inflexion would be -ō, -*ei*, -*et*, all different from the PE of the athematic inflexion.[2] A slight variation of this view is to take 3rd s. -ει as -*e*+Ø+*i*, in which *e* is the thematic vowel and *i* the mark of the PE, while the ending itself is zero;[3] this analysis would even be applicable to Hitt. -*ai* (e.g. *da-i* 'he takes').[4] Others would prefer to equate the 3rd s. -ει with Hitt. -*ah-i*, while tracing the Lith. ending -*ì* back to -*ēi*, which together with Gr. -ει-ς would point to an ending earlier than *e-si*.[5] Finally, it has also been suggested[6] that Gr. -ει might correspond to the OInd. -*ē* of the middle *śay-ē* 'lies', *bruv-ē* 'says' (-εις would then be formed to this on the model of the impf.

ἔφερε : ἔφερες); but this is decisively contradicted by the difference of voice.

Not one of these interpretations will bear scrutiny. OIr. (abs.) 2nd s. *biri* 'can incontestably be traced back to **bheresi*', and for (conj.) *-bir* a start must be made from **bheres*, not **bher-ei*.[7] That Lith. *-(s)ì* in athematic verbs (*esì* 'thou art': OInd. *asi*) goes back not to *-s-ie* from *-sei* but to simple *-si* has in the mean time become as clear as the origin of thematic *-i* from athematic *-(s)i*.[8] It is therefore no surprise that reminders have come from several quarters that for Greek a start can be made only from the universally attested *-si*, *-ti*.[9] Whether we should go to the trouble of a special sound law[10], rather than thinking in terms of an analogical process,[11] seems doubtful; the second alternative seems to be supported by developments such as produced 2nd s. διδοῖς, 3rd s. διδοῖ, starting from **didōsi*, which became *διδωι and then διδωις and, with shortening, διδοις.[12]

There are thus no grounds for supposing that the thematic inflexion diverged from the athematic beyond the 1st singular. For the plural and dual the identity of the two inflexions is generally recognized. As a further point of contact between the two systems the 3rd pl. may be mentioned, which has a vowel before *-nti* not only in thematic but often also in athematic verbs, cf. **s-enti* 'are'; this vowel is as a rule *e*.[13]

[1] On a third type, the so-called semi-thematic inflexion, see Vendryes, *IF* 26, 1909, 134f.; Meillet, *MSL* 17, 1911, 197f.; *BSL* 32, 1931, 197f.; Bonfante, *BSL* 33, 1932, 111f.; 34, 1933, 133–9; see further below, 9.2.6 n. 4, and Leumann², 519, 567f. On Nagy, see Szemerényi, *SM* iii, 1609.

[2] Meillet, *RC* 28, 1907, 369–73, and finally *Introduction*⁸, 227f. (see Meid's criticism, above, 8.2.1.1 n. 3, 19f.). He is followed by Pedersen, *Hittitisch* 87f., 93f.; Watkins, *Origins* 140 n. 16; *Ériu* 21, 1969, 6; *Verb* 121f.; Adrados, *Fachtagung* 2, 1962, 149; not wholly decided Stang, *Vgl. Gram.* 407f. Cf. in addition Risch, *Symbolae Kuryłowicz*, 1965, 235–42; Negri, *Acme* 27, 1974, 359–79, esp. 370; Kortlandt, *Ériu* 30, 1979, 36–8; *Lingua* 44, 1979, 67; *JIES* 11, 1984, 312; Ivanov, *Glagol* 56f.

[3] So Watkins, *Origins* 103, without saying how this explanation is compatible with that of the 2nd s. Cf. also *Ériu* 21, 6; *Verb* 52, 122f.; and almost a century ago Jacobi, *Composition und Nebensatz*, 1897, 61f. On this, see also Kuryłowicz, *Categories* 153, 156; S. Levin, *The IE and Semitic Languages*, Albany, NY, 1971, 379f.; Hilmarsson, *NTS* 31, 1977, 195f. But if the 'ending' really is *-e*, it must, like athematic *-t*, be the demonstrative!

[4] Pedersen, *Hittitisch* 88, 93; Watkins, *Origins* 103; Evangelisti, *Acme* 18, 1965, 3 (as a Gr.-Hitt. innovation in Asia Minor!); Untermann, *Gedenkschrift Brandenstein*, 1968, 166 with n. 3; Bader, *Word* 24, 1970, 25; Negri (n. 2 above).

[5] Hirt, *IG* iv, 151; Vaillant, *BSL* 37, 1936, 112; 40, 1939, 17f., 30; *Gram. comp.* iii, 9, 20.

[6] Birwé, *Griech.-arische Sprachbeziehungen im Verbalsystem*, 1955, 10–11. Against, Watkins, *Verb* 123.

[7] Meid (above, 9.2.1.1, n. 3) 56; Campanile, *AION-L* 8, 1968, 59f., in spite of Watkins, *Ériu* 21, 1969, 5; *Verb* 165. A different view in Kuryłowicz, *BPTJ* 27, 1970, 13; and again supporting **bheresi* Cowgill, *Fachtagung* 7, 1985, 104. Note also K. H. Schmidt's conclusion (*KZ* 94, 1980, 190): 'the distinction between absolute and conjunct endings cannot be traced back to the IE dichotomy but is . . . a Celtic innovation' caused by an affix, in compounds after the preverb, in simple verbs after the verb, e.g. OIr. *berid* from **bheret-id* as against *dobeir* from **to-(i)d-bheret*.

[8] Kazlauskas, *Lietuvių kalbos istorinė gramatika*, 1968, 293f., 299; Schmalstieg, *Lingua* 10,

1961, 369–74; *Fs. Stang*, 1970, 467f.; Kuryłowicz, *BPTJ* 27, 13f. Cowgill, *Fachtagung* 7, 107, thinks that Slav. *-si* and the East Baltic 2nd s. *-(s)ie* are both reflexes of the IE middle ending *-soi*.

[9] Poldauf, *ZPhon* 9, 1956, 160; Kiparsky, *Glotta* 44, 1967, 112; Kuryłowicz, in *Phonologie der Gegenwart*, 1967, 166, and *BPTJ* 27, 12f.; Mańczak, *Fs. Szemerényi*², ii, 1992, 67–75.

[10] Kiparsky's solution (*-esi*, *-eti* first became *-eis*, *-eit*) had already been considered by Schulze; see Schwyzer, *GG* i, 842 on 661; cf. also the modification of the rule in Cowgill, *Fachtagung* 7, 100f.

[11] Kuryłowicz, *Phonologie der Gegenwart* 166, and later in *Directions* 77.

[12] A different account in Schwyzer, *GG* i, 687; cf. Strunk, *Glotta* 39, 1960, 114–23; Negri, *Acme* 27, 1974, 372.

[13] For this Narten, *Fs. Kuiper*, 1969, 13f.; Watkins, *Verb* 41; Francis, *Glotta* 52, 1974, 22 n. 27; Kortlandt, 'The Greek 3rd pl. endings', *MSS* 49, 1988, 63–9: on *-n̥t* and *-ent* (and *-ur*). On the thematic 1st s. *-ō*, see below, 9.7.1.3 fin. Lazzeroni, *Scritti in onore di T. Bolelli*, 1985, 165f., 178, derives the indicative endings from the subjunctive, i.e. 1, 2, 3 from *-ō*, *-e*, *-e*.

9.2.2.1. *Middle endings of the present and aorist system.* In the tense forms in which the active endings discussed above appear, the following middle endings are attested. First the primary endings:

	Ved.	Avest.	Hitt.	Greek	Goth.
1	*ē*	*ē*	*ha(ha)ri*	μαι	*da*
2	*sē*	*sē*	*ta(ti)*	σοι	*za*
3	*tē*, *ē*[1]	*tē*	*ta(ri)*	τοι	*da*
4	*mahē*	*madē*	*wasta(ri)*	μεθα	*nda*
5	*dhvē*	*dvē*	*duma(ri)*	(σ)θε	*nda*
6	*ntē*	*ntē*	*nta(ri)*	ντοι	*nda*
7	*vahē*	–	–	–	
8	*āthē*	–	–	(σ)θον	
	ithē	–	–		
9	*ātē*	–	–	(σ)θον	
	itē[2]	*tē*	–		

The secondary endings are:

	Ved.	Avest.	Hitt.	Greek
1	*i*	*i*	*ha(ha)t(i)*	μᾱν
2	*thās*	*sa*	*tat(i)*	σο
3	*ta*	*ta*	*tat(i)*	το
4	*mahi*	*madi*	*wastat*	μεθα
5	*dhvam*	*δwəm*	*dumat*	(σ)θε
6	*nta*	*nta*	*ntat(i)*	ντο
7	*vahi*	*vadi*	–	–
8	*āthām*	–	–	(σ)θον
	ithām	–	–	
9	*ātām*	*ātəm*	–	(σ)θᾱν
	itām	*itəm*	–	

In the first place, it should be noted as an important point of agreement that in the PE 1, 2, 3, and 6 an *i*-diphthong is indicated by Aryan and Greek. This was for a long time reconstructed as *-ai* on the basis of the forms as they are in almost all Greek dialects. At the beginning of the 1950s the Spanish Hellenist M. S. Ruipérez pointed out that this reconstruction does not account for the situation in Arcado-Cyprian (2 -σοι, 3 -τοι, 6 -ντοι), nor is it properly intelligible at the IE stage, for which the SE are established as *-so*, *-to*, *-nto*. His convincing conclusion that 1, 2, 3, and 6 must be reconstructed as *-ai*, *-soi*, *-toi*, *-ntoi* was shown to be correct scarcely a year later by the recently deciphered Mycenaean texts.[3] It is possible, though not certain, that Gr. -μαι instead of -αι acquired its *m* from the active ending *m(i)*. Of the SE, 2, 3, and 6 are certainly to be reconstructed as *-so*, *-to*, *-nto*; OInd. *-thās* was 'adopted' from the perfect ending (see 9.7.1.3); the original *-so* was preserved not only in Iranian (see Dunkel, in *In Memory of W. Cowgill* (1987), 18) but also in the OInd. imperative 2nd s. ending *-sva*, a modification of *-sa* on the analogy of the 2nd pl. *-dhva*. In the 1st s. Aryan *-i* and Greek -μᾱν are seemingly irreconcilable. The Aryan *-i* could, of course, be the zero grade of PE *-ē* (IE *ai*: *-i*), but this would agree neither with the other SE nor with the optative ending *-a* (e.g. OInd. *īś-īy-a* 'I should possess'); on the other hand, this *-a* would not only suit the PE *-ai* and explain the SE *-i* as a secondary formation to this *-ai*, but also allow a connection to be established with Gr. -μᾱν. Compared with -μαι, -μᾱν has in any case a secondary -ν (which could be either the -ν of the 1st s. of the active or the widespread final nasal; see 8.4.4*b*), and -μᾱ or, without the *m*, -ᾱ could have been shortened in final position (hence -ă) and with the primary *i* have given **-ā-i*, i.e. *-ai*;[4] cf. further 9.7.1.3, n. 13.

The Aryan PE of the 1st pl. was *-madhai*, which at any rate belongs with Gr. -μεθα, again on the basis of an IE *-medha* or *-medhā* to which with primary *i* Aryan *-madhai* from **-medhā-i* was formed; the Aryan SE *-madhi* is obviously formed to this by analogy. The 2nd pl. must in the first place be reconstructed as *-dhwe* on the basis of *-dhva(m)* and -(σ)θε; to this in Aryan the PE **-dhwai* was formed and the SE modified to **-dhwam*.

On the basis of Aryan and Greek the following endings can therefore be reconstructed:[5]

	PE	SE
1	*-ai/-mai*	*-ā/-mā*
2	*-soi*	*-so*
3	*-toi*	*-to*
4	*-medha* (*-ā*?)	*-medha* (*-ā*?)
5	*-dhwe*	*-dhwe*
6	*-ntoi*	*-nto*

This picture can be in part modified, in part confirmed with the help of the other languages.

The Hitt. 1st s. *-ha* shows that for Indo-European *-ha* should be posited in preference to *-ā*; *-ha* and *-hai* are satisfactory for Aryan, while for Greek *-μᾱ* metathesis of *-ha* to *-ah* could perhaps be assumed.[6] The 2nd s. *-ta* obviously belongs together with OInd. *-thās*; see 9.7.1.3. 2nd pl. *-duma* from *-duwa* is modified from *-dhwe* by analogy with the remaining endings with final *-a*. The 1st pl. *-wasta* is particularly interesting, for though it diverges from the reconstructed *-medha*, it has an almost exact correspondence to Hom. *-μεσθα*. Perhaps, corresponding to the active endings, a PE *-mes-dha* and SE *-me-dha* must be posited for the middle also,[7] though it is not clear why the PE was lost in Aryan, especially Iranian.

Confirmation rather than modification comes from Germanic. The passive endings in Gothic clearly correspond to the IE endings in *-ai/-oi*, not to some alleged and otherwise unknown endings in *-ō*.[8] In the present they are as follows (*haitan* 'be called'):

1	*haitada*	4	*haitanda*
2	*haitaza*	5	*haitanda*
3	*haitada*	6	*haitanda*

Obviously 2, 3, and 6 with *-za*, *-da*, *-nda* correspond to the IE endings *-soi*, *-toi*, *-ntoi*. It is, however, remarkable that all three persons of the plural have the same form and that the 1st and 3rd s. are identical. The last is shown to be a Gothic innovation by OIce. *heite* 'I am called', which goes back to **haitai* with the ending of the 1st s. known from Aryan. It is also clear that the similarity in the plural is a secondary development, but certainly not through simple transference of the 3rd pl. ending to the 1st and 2nd pl.[9] We must rather suppose that the inherited ending of the 1st pl. *-omedha* or, as in Aryan, *-omedhai* gave in the first place *-amida*, which then became *-anda* by syncope, obviously in order to reduce the length of the ending and bring it into line with the other persons.[10] At this stage it was also possible for the 1st s. to be replaced by the 3rd s., especially as the phonetic development of *-ai* to *-a* gave a form resembling the 1st s. of the active. In the 2nd pl. the ending *-edhwe* first became phonetically *-edu*, then analogically *-eda*, *-ada* and finally, through assimilation to 4 and 6, *-anda*.

The 2nd pl. *-dhwe* is also present in Celtic; OIr. *-id* in the deponent verbs is not due to adoption of the active ending (IE *-ete*), but a regular development from *-edhwe*;[11] cf. OIr. *ardd* 'high' from **ardwo-* (Lat. *arduus*).

[1] See below, 9.7.1.3 n. 1; G. Schmidt, *KZ* 85, 1972, 256f.

[2] K. T. Schmidt, *Fachtagung* 5, 1975, 289: 3rd dual pres. mid. Toch. B *tasaitär* 'resemble' from *-a-itai* ~ Ar. *-a-itai*; further Hollifield, *KZ* 92, 1979, 225, and (against) van Windekens,

Le tokharien ii/2, 1982, 277f. Against a sole thematic vowel *o* in the Tocharian middle see Ringe, *Tocharian and IE Studies* i, 1987, 98–138, esp. 118f.

3 Ruipérez, *Em* 20, 1952, 8f. (but he posits *-əi*, not like myself *-ai*, for the 1st s.), and then *Minos* 9, 1968, 156–60 (against which Neu, *IF* 73, 1969, 347–54); see also Szemerényi, *1° Congresso di micenologia*, 1968, 717 and n. 10. On the origin of Gr. *-σαι* etc. see Kuryłowicz, *Categories* 59. The old view (*-tai*, not *-toi*) is again supported by Cowgill, *AIED* 1966, 80f.; Wyatt, *SMEA* 13, 1971, 120; F. W. Schwink, *JIES* 17, 1990, 127–54 (Myc. *-tai* and *-to*); but against, Watkins, *Verb* 130.

4 Cf. Kuryłowicz, *Categories* 60; Cowgill, *Fs. Kuiper*, 1969, 24–31. Watkins, *Verb* 138f., thinks that the *-i* of the 1st s. is identical with the *-i* of the 3rd s. of the aorist passive! A different view is taken by Schmalstieg, *FoL* 12, 1980, 360 (**bheroi* is a noun form). See also García-Ramón, *Fachtagung* 7, 1985, 202–17 (SE 1st s. mid. *-H_2*). According to Georgiev, ibid. 220, the s. *-moi*, *-soi*, *-toi* were datives of pronouns.

5 See also Petersen, *Lg* 12, 1936, 157–74, esp. 167; Erhart, 'Die griech. Personalendung *-μην*', *Sbornik Brno* 14, 1966, 21–28; G. R. Hart, 'The Greek secondary ending of the first singular middle', *Studies Chadwick*, 1987, 221–6 (cf. Perpillou, *Krat* 34, 1989, 83). Further IE reconstructions in Neu (2), 131, 139, 154; Kortlandt, *Ériu* 32, 1981, 16 (with fanciful constructions of a trans. and intrans. middle); *IF* 86, 1982, 123–36. According to Yoshida 1990, 117, the PE in *-oi* were innovated from the SE in *-o* on the analogy of the active *-mi*/*-m*, etc. Lehmann (*Fs. O. Hietsch*, 1992, 141) thinks that the middle expressed by *-o* indicated both reflexive and reciprocal meanings.

6 See Kortlandt, *IF* 86, 130; G. Schmidt, *Fs. G. Neumann*, 1982, 345f.

7 See Pedersen, *Hittitisch* 102; Lazzeroni, *SSL* 7, 1967, 56; also Watkins, *Verb* 128f. (1st and 2nd pl.=active!); Wyatt, *IE/a/*, 1970, 43f. (*-mahi* from *-medha* with *-a* to *-i*). On *-μεσθα*/*-wasta*, see Seebold, *KZ* 85, 1972, 194; Negri, *Acme* 27, 378f.; Georgiev, *Fachtagung* 7, 222: *-wasta* from *-wesd(u)wo*. On *s* in Gr. *-σθε*, see also Risch, *Fachtagung* 5, 1975, 258.

8 Postulated by Meillet, *BSL* 23, 1922, 68; Petersen (n. 5 above), 162f.; Kuryłowicz, *Apophonie* 353; Savčenko, *LPosn* 12/13, 1968, 28 n. 23. Goth. *-(d)a* from IE *-(t)o* (Kuryłowicz, *BPTJ* 28, 1970, 24f.; Watkins, *Verb* 213; Markey, *SL* 26, 1972, 45; Kortlandt, *IF* 86, 1982, 131f.) is impossible. In favour of *-ai*, also Guxman, 'Schicksal des idg. Mediums in den germ. Sprachen', *Trudy Instituta Jazykoznanija* 9, 1959, 52–91, esp. 80; Lindeman, *NTS* 21, 1967, 137f.

9 So e.g. Krause, *Hb. des Gotischen*, 1953, 247. Cf. also Cowgill, *Fs. Winter*, 147f.

10 On this, see also van Helten, *IF* 14, 1903, 88; against, Brugmann, *IF* 39, 1921, 46–9; Lindeman (n. 8 above) n. 3. On *-anda* see also Lühr, *MSS* 37, 1978, 113f. (*-o-medhai*, *-edhwoi*); G. Schmidt, *KZ* 90, 1976, 263f.; *Fs. Neumann*, 1982, 346. On Gothic *-a* see n. 8 above.

11 Already in Brugmann, *Grundriss*[2], ii/3, 651 (in spite of Schwyzer, *GG* i, 671[1]; Watkins, *AIED* 40), and more recently Kortlandt, *Ériu* 32, 1981, 18; Cowgill, *Ériu* 34, 1983, 80. The IE ending was not *-dhum* (so Petersen (n. 5 above), 165; Savčenko, *BPTJ* 20, 1961, 115). Toch. B (2nd pl. pret.) *-t* is perhaps from *-dhu*, zero grade of *-dhwe*, see Pedersen, *Zur toch. Sprachgeschichte*, 1944, 6f.; van Windekens (n. 1 above), 292f. According to Neu (2), 131 n. 50, the IE ending was *-dhwa*; according to Georgiev (n. 7 above), Hitt. *-duma* comes from **duwo* 'two'.

ADDENDUM. Lat. *-minī* is traditionally equated with the Homeric infinitive in *-μέναι* or the masculine plural (!) of the participle in *-menos*;[1] both suppositions are highly suspect on syntactical grounds. It would surely be logical to connect *-minī* with the established IE ending. This is possible if we start from an extended form *-dhwe-noi* (modified on the pattern of the PE from a particle *-ne*, cf. Ved. *-thana*, *-tana* alongside *-tha*, *-ta*), which gave *-b(e)nei* and *-mnei*, and finally with anaptyxis *-minī*. A somewhat different explanation is given by Hendriksen, *AO* 17, 1949, 313. Cf. also Forssman (below, 9.2.5,

n. 10); Georgiev's idea (*Fachtagung* 7, 1985, 224) that *b-n* arose from **dwinoi* 'both' is impossible.

[1] So again Watkins, *Verb* 177 (from *-mnos*).

9.2.2.2. r-*endings*. In contrast to the endings of the *-to/toi* type worked out above there appear in certain languages and to a certain extent endings characterized by *r*. These are no doubt best known from Latin, but they are also characteristic of Italic, Venetic, Celtic, Hittite, Tocharian, and Phrygian.[1]

A simple *r* appears in the West as a passive-impersonal form in Old Irish (*berair* 'is brought'), Welsh (*cerir* 'one loves', *dywedir* 'on dit'),[2] Umbrian (*ferar* 'feratur', *ier* 'itum sit'?) and Oscan (*loufir* 'libet' ='uel'); in the East in Hittite (*haltsiyari* from *haltsāi-* 'call'); as a personal form in Hittite (*es-ari* 'he sits') and perhaps in Venetic (*tolar* 'brings', **didōr* 'gives'?).[3] In Aryan *r*-endings occur only in the 3rd pl., e.g. *duhrē* 'they milk', *śērē*=Avest. *sōire* 'they lie'.[4]

Better known are the *r*-endings which occur in combination with the *mi*-endings discussed above and are used in middle and/or passive verbs:[5]

	Lat.	Osc.-Umbr.	OIr.	Phryg.	Hitt.	Toch. A/B
1	*-(ō)r*		*-ur*		*-ha(ha)ri*	*-mār/mar*
2	*-re/-ris*		*-ther*		*-tati, -tari*	*-tār/tar*
3	*-tur*	*-ter*	*-thir*	*-tor*	*-ta(ri)*	*-tär/tär*
4	*-mur*		*-mir*		*-wasta-ri, -ti*	*-mtär/mtär*
5	*-minī*		*-the*		*-duma(ri)*	*-cär/tär*
6	*-ntur*	*-nter*	*-tir*		*-nta(ri)*	*-ntär/ntär*

It is clear, especially in Hittite and Tocharian, that the *r*-endings were originally used only in the PE. In these languages they are found in all persons, even if in Hittite they were originally only optional, whereas in Latin and Old Irish they were originally missing from the 2nd persons: Lat. *-re* continues IE *-so*, OIr. *-ther* is probably from *-thēs* subsequently extended by *r*,[6] but the 2nd pl. is without *r* in both languages. In the 1st s. Hittite and Tocharian diverge widely, which shows that their forms were late and independent creations. Latin and Old Irish, on the other hand, agree so well in the 1st s. and pl. that *-ōr* and *-mor* must no doubt be seen as a common innovation, all the more so because *-mor* in both is presumably a modification of inherited *-mod(a)*, the *o*-grade form of IE *-medha*.[7]

It follows that the *r*-forms were originally limited to the primary endings and, there, to the 3rd persons. The early forms were for Latin

-tor/-ntor, for Hittite *-tori/-ntori*, for Old Irish (giving conjunct endings *-ethar/-etar*) *-tro/-ntro*.[8] See also 9.7.1.3, nn. 12–16.

[1] For the *r*-endings in general, see the ample bibliography in Porzig, *Gliederung* 83, with brief discussion 84f.; in addition: Pisani, 'Uxor', in *Miscellanea Galbiati* iii, 1951, 1–38; Leumann, *Morphologische Neuerungen im aind. Verbalsystem*, 1952; H. Hartmann, *Das Passiv*, 1954: Calbioli, *Studi grammaticali*, 1962, 56f. (history of the research); K. H. Schmidt, 'Präteritum und Medio-Passiv', *Sprache* 9, 1963, 14–20; 'Venetische Medialformen', *IF* 68, 1963, 160–9; 'Zum altirischen Passiv', ibid. 257–75 (against: Pokorny, *IF* 70, 1966, 316–21); Neu (1) and (2); Campanile, *SSL* 8, 1968, 64f.; Watkins, *Verb* 174f.; H. Jankuhn, *Die passive Bedeutung medialer Formen*, 1969, 30f.; Lane, in *IE and IEs*, 1971, 77f.; Cowgill, ibid. 142; *Ériu* 34, 1983, 73–111, esp. 75f.; Gonda, *Old Indian*, 1971, 107; Jasanoff, 'The *r*-endings of the IE middle', *Sprache* 23, 1977, 159–70; Cowgill, *Fachtagung* 7, 1985, 116; H. Katz, 'Zu den *r*-Endungen des idg. Verbs', *HS* 101, 1988, 26–52; K. Yoshida, *The Hittite Mediopassive Endings in* -ri, 1990 (see Pinault, *BSL* 86/2, 1992, 134–41; Garett, *Lg* 69, 1993, 226–7; and note also Melchert, *HS* 102, 1989, 26, claiming that the middle existed in Lycian also.

[2] On their origin, Martinet, *Word* 11, 1955, 130f.; K. H. Schmidt, *IF* 68, 1963, 270f. (**bheror* 'passive verbal noun'); Meid, in *Indogermanisch und Keltisch*, 1977, 118f. (verbal form in *-r* an impersonal, cf. *-r* in 3rd pl. perf.); Hartmann, ibid. 171, 198f.; Rosén, *KZ* 92, 1979, 143–78; Schmalstieg, *FoL* 12, 1980, 360f., and in *Studies Polomé*, 1988, 594f.; Lehmann, *GL* 29, 1989, 241: 'the function of *-r* was to indicate the affective meaning'.

[3] See Pellegrini and Prosdocimi, *La lingua venetica* ii, 1967, 122f. (where *kvidor* is still read), 175; as also Pellegrini, *Fs. Meriggi*, 1969, 241f. Lejeune, *Manuel de la langue vénète*, 1974, 279, reads *didōr*; cf. Prosdocimi and Marinetti, *AGI* 73, 1988, 114f. (on *toler/-ar, kvidor*).

[4] See esp. Leumann (n. 1 above), 11f.; Narten, *Fs. Kuiper*, 1969, 9.

[5] Armenian is not treated here, as its *r*-endings are not connected with those we are discussing; see Pedersen, *Hittitisch* 104f.; *Banaţeanu, 'L'élément *r* médio-passive en arménien classique', *Revue Roumaine de Linguistique* 10, 1965, 509–25; Watkins, *Verb* 175, but against, R. Schmitt, *Grammatik des Klassisch-Armenischen*, 1981, 141.

[6] Watkins, *Verb* 188: IE *-tha+i>the*, to which *-r* is added. For OInd. *-thās* see 9.7.1.3, n. 3.

[7] Watkins (*Verb* 179, cf. 146) wrongly supposes that IE *-medha* need not have been present (and later modified); the ending is in fact guaranteed by first-class evidence. Cf. also Hollifield, *KZ* 92, 1979, 221.

[8] On Celtic, Italic, and Hittite, see also Kuryłowicz, *EC* 12, 1969, 14f.; on Hittite, esp. Yoshida 1990, and, less convincingly, Katz (n. 1 above).

9.2.3. Endings of the perfect

The perfect originally showed special endings. These are well preserved in Aryan and Greek, and to some extent in Old Irish, but they have been overlaid in Latin and OCS. The endings can be most simply read off in the paradigms of the verb 'know':[1]

	OInd.	Greek	Goth.	IE
1	*véd-a*	ϝοῖδ-α	*wait*	*-a*
2	*vét-tha*	ϝοῖσ-θα	*waist*	*-tha*
3	*véd-a*	ϝοῖδ-ε	*wait*	*-e*
4	*vid-má*	ϝίδ-μεν	*wit-um*	*-me*
5	*vid-á*	ϝίσ-τε	*wit-uþ*	?
6	*vid-úr*	ϝίσ-ᾱσι	*wit-un*	*-r(o)*
7	*vid-vá*		*wit-u*	*-we*
8	*vid-áthur*		*wit-uts*	
9	*vid-átur*			

The endings 1–3 can, on the evidence of OInd. and Greek, be determined as *-a*, *-tha*, *-e*; for 4 we have *-me* and for 7 *-we*. Of the other persons it can only be said with certainty that for 6 the ending was *-r* or *r̥*; Gr. *-ᾱσι* from *-αντι* and Goth. *-un* from *-n̥t* show the invasion of more frequent forms. See further 9.4.3*a* and 9.7.1.3.[2]

These endings are also the basis of the Latin forms, which, as the early inscriptions show, were in the singular *-ai*, *-tai*, *-eit*, clearly variants of the above forms extended with a primary *i*.[3] The Latin 3rd pl. *-ēre* is important; it goes back to *-ēro* (cf. 2nd s. pass. *-re* from *-so*), and together with Toch. B *-āre/are*, Hitt. *-ir* (e.g. *es-ir* 'they were'), and OInd. *-ur* proves an IE *-r*/-ro for the 3rd pl.[4]

[1] On the endings, see Belardi, *Ricerche Linguistiche* i, 1950, 98f.; Watkins, *Origins* 102; *Verb* 51 (*-Ho/-tHo/-Ø*)=Neu (2), 138; Kuryłowicz, *BPTJ* 31, 1973, 8 (Aryan *-tha* from *-ta*, Gr. -*θα* by Bartholomae's Law, thus no laryngeal); Eichner, *Fachtagung* 5, 1975, 86; Dunkel, *AJPh* 98, 1977, 141–9; Cowgill, in *Heth. und Idg.*, 1979, 25–39: from a thematic adjective—but if a nominal form at all then (in my view) an athematic root noun (of the agent) with demonstrative *e* in the 3rd s. Note also K. H. Schmidt, *ZCP* 41, 1986, 163, 176: Gaul. *dede* 3rd s. from *-e-i*; *ieuri* 1st s. from H_2*e-i* (but see Szemerényi, *ZCP* 44, 1991, 303–6); Hisanosuke, 'IE perfect and Hitt. verbal system', *JIES* 14, 1986, 195–204. According to Schmalstieg (*FoL* 12, 1980, 354), personal endings cannot be constructed for the perfect voice 'which was completely a nominal form', and Lehmann holds much the same view (*Fs. Meid*, 1989, 121): it is 'well known that the IE perfect is defective . . . the singular has specific endings only in the first and second persons; the plural has adopted endings from the *mi* inflection. Such a pattern is characteristic of inactive inflection.'

[2] On the 2nd s. in Germanic, see Rosenfeld, *ZPhon* 8, 1955, 377f.; L. Rösel, *Gliederung der germ. Sprachen*, 1962, 39–44; Bech, *Studia Neophilologica* 41, 1969, 75–92 (adopted by Bammesberger, *Anglia* 100, 1982, 416 n. 15; *Studien zur Laryngaltheorie*, 1984, 96–8); Meid, *Das germ. Präteritum*, 1971, 12f.; Barnes, *Studia Neophilologica* 47, 1975, 275–84; Markey, *Germanic Dialect Geography and the Position of Ingvaeonic*, 1976, 13f.; Feuillet, *BSL* 76, 1981, 220f.; Wagner, *ZCP* 42, 1987, 27–8. See also below, 9.4.2.1.1 n. 6.

The 2nd s. is determined as *-sta* by Bonfante, *Lg* 17, 1941, 205f.; Cowgill, in *Evidence* 172f.; Risch, *Fachtagung* 5, 1975, 258; Jasanoff, *Fs. Hoenigswald*, 1987, 179; but still as *-ta* by Kuryłowicz, *IG* 341. According to Antonsen, *NTS* 29, 1975, 237, 242f., the 1st s. pret. *wraita* on the runic inscription of Reistad (5th cent.?) proves that the IE ending was still preserved.

[3] See Vendryes, *REIE* 1, 1938, 3–5; Watkins, *Verb* 80; Untermann, 'Zwei Bemerkungen zur lat. Perfektflexion', in *Gedenkschrift Brandenstein*, 1968, 165–71; G. Schmidt, *KZ* 85, 1972, 262.

[4] See Leumann, *Morphologische Neuerungen im aind. Verbalsystem*, 1952, 40; Bader, 'Le système des désinences de 3. personne du pluriel du perfectum latin', *BSL* 62, 1968, 87–105; de Simone, *Lapis Satricanus* (quoted above, 7.6.2), 1980, 74–80: *steterai* 'steterunt, set up'; Prosdocimi and Marinetti, 'Sulla terza plurale del perfetto latino e indiano antico', *AGI* 73, 1988, 93–125 (114: *teuters* 3rd pl.; 103: *-ēr* from *-ers*); Eichner, *Untersuchungen zur heth. Deklination*, 1974, 17: Hitt. 3rd pl. *-er* from *-ēre*; on the three forms with *-ar* see Neu, *HS* 102, 1989, 16–20; K. Hoffmann ap. Eichner, *Fachtagung* 5, 1975, 87: Aryan *-r̥* is a secondary contrast formation to middle *-ro*. On the Germanic *r*-preterites (3rd pl. *-run*) see Shields, *ABäG* 24, 1986, 1–10; Polomé, 'Recent developments in the laryngeal theory', *JIES* 15, 1988, 159–67 (157: 'I do not think a convincing case can be made out for the so-called *r*-preterites').

9.2.4. The Anatolian system

What we have so far seen of the Hittite system of verbal endings is only a part of the total picture. Alongside the *mi*-conjugation characterized by the endings discussed above, there is also the so-called *hi*-conjugation. The two systems differ in the active only in the three persons of the singular present and preterite and in the 3rd s. imperative, in the middle only in the 3rd s. of these tenses and moods. It will be useful to set out the endings here in a complete scheme:[1]

Active

	Present		Preterite		Imperative	
	mi-conj.	*hi*-conj.	*mi*-conj.	*hi*-conj.	*mi*-conj.	*hi*-conj.
1	*mi*	*(ah)hi)*	*(n)un*	*hun*	*(a)llu*	
2	*si*	*ti*	*s, t(a)*	*s, ta, sta*	*Ø, i, t*	*Ø, i*
3	*tsi*	*i*	*t, ta*	*s, ta, sta*	*tu*	*u*
4	*weni*		*wen*		*weni*	
5	*teni*		*ten*		*ten*	
6	*ntsi*		*ir*		*ntu*	

Medio-passive

	Present		Preterite		Imperative	
	mi-conj.	*hi*-conj.	*mi*-conj.	*hi*-conj.	*mi*-conj.	*hi*-conj.
1	*ha(ha)ri, ha*	*ha(ha)ri*	*ha(ha)t(i)*	*ha(ha)t(i)*	*ha(ha)ru*	
2	*ta(ti/ri)*	*ta(ti)*	*tat(i), ta*	*at(i), tat*	*hut(i)*	
3	*ta(ri)*	*a(ri)*	*tat(i), ta*	*at(i)*	*taru*	*aru*
4	*wasta(ti/ri)*	*wasta(ti)*	*wastat*	–	–	
5	*duma(ri)*	*duma*	*dumat*	*dumat*	*dumat(i)*	
6	*nta(ri)*	*nta(ri)*	*ntat(i)*	*ntat(i)*	*ntaru*	

It is important that, whereas in Greek, for example, *-mi* signifies an athematic and *-ō* a thematic inflexion, both types of Hittite inflexion are compatible with consonant stems as well as vowel stems; e.g. *es-mi* 'I am', *ija-mi* 'I do', *ar-hi* 'I reach', *da-hi* 'I take'.

Even more important for the Indo-Europeanist is the fact that the Hittite system of two conjugations stands in contrast to a quite different system in the other ancient Anatolian languages. The characteristic endings in Luwian are as follows:[2]

	Active			Medio-passive	
	Pres.	Pret.	Impv.	Pres.	Impv.
1	*mi/wi*	*ha*	*allu*		
2	*si/tis?*	*s/ta*	*Ø*		
3	*ti/i(a)*	*t*	*tu*	*(ta)ri*	*(ta)ru*
4	*min*	*han?*			
5	*tani*		*ranu*	*duwar(i)*	
6	*nti*	*nta*	*ntu*	*ntari*	*ntaru*

As can be seen, Luwian has nothing to correspond with the Hittite *hi*-conjugation;[3] on the other hand, the 1st s. of the so-called *mi*-conjugation (3rd s. *-ti*) appears in double form, with *-mi* and with *-ui*, e.g. *aw-i-mi* 'I come',[4] *aw-i-si* 'comest', *aw-i-ti* 'comes', exactly corresponding to Gr. εἶ-μι, εἶ (from **ei-si*), εἶ-σι (from **ei-ti*), but *tiyanesui* 'I fill', *hapusui* 'I mend'. It seems clear that *-ui* is an extension with primary *i* of *-u*, and this comes from IE *-ō*; the original *-ō-i* was shortened to *-ŏ-i* and, before the change of *o* to *a*, *-o-i* was assimilated to *-u-i*.[5] Thus Luwian would retain traces of both IE conjugations (*-mi*/*-ō*), whereas of these only the *mi*-conjugation remained in Hittite.

Luwian, on the other hand, together with the other Anatolian languages, has in the preterite a 1st s. ending *-ha*, which in Hittite appears in this function only in the modified form *-hun* (a crossing of *-ha* with *-un*), apart from its obvious presence in *-hi* (a crossing of *-ha* with primary *i*). The *hi*-conjugation is thus not inherited but a Hittite innovation, which is not shared even by the other Anatolian languages.[6]

[1] Friedrich, *Heth. Elementarbuch* i², 1960, 77; Pedersen, *Hittitisch*, 79f.; Sturtevant and Hahn, *A Comparative Grammar of the Hittite Language*, 1951, 139f.; Kronasser, *Etymologie*, 1965, 369; Kammenhuber, *MSS* 24, 1968, 73f.; Eichner, *Fachtagung* 5, 1975, 75f.

[2] Here account is taken of Cuneiform Luwian as well as Hieroglyphic Luwian, but they are not precisely distinguished. For the facts, see Friedrich (n. 1 above), 191; Laroche, *Dictionnaire de la langue louvite*, 1959, 142; Kammenhuber, 'Hethitisch' 251; Eichner, *Fachtagung* 5, 77f.; Oettinger, *Stammbildung* 561, 565; Morpurgo Davies, *KZ* 94, 1980, 86–108, esp. 108. A different view of *-han* in Carruba, *SMEA* 24, 1985, 57–69: in reality it is 1st s. *-ha* with optional nasalization, not 1st pl. For 4 and 5 Carruba (*Sprache* 14, 1968, 21) posited pres. *-unni* (earlier *-wani?*), *-tani*, pret. *-man*, *-tan*.

[3] So Laroche, see Puhvel, *AIED* 243, but cf. Morpurgo Davies, *Fs. Szemerényi*, 1979, 577–610; *KZ* 94, 108.

[4] According to Kronasser, *Etymologie* 86, 377, n. 1, and Eichner, *Fachtagung* 5, 79, with original *-mi*. On the other hand Laroche (n. 2 above) 36, and Oettinger, *KZ* 92, 1978, 84, think that *awimi* is from **awiwi* by dissimilation (?); still more difficult is Neu's view, *E. Benveniste aujourd'hui* ii, 1984, 102, that *awimi* represents a lenition of **awiwi*.

[5] Formulated somewhat differently in Szemerényi, *BSOAS* 27, 1964, 159. The ending is usually associated with Hitt. *-u-n* (1st s. pret.), to which should be added Lycian (Milyan) *-u*, Lydian *-u*, West Toch. *-w-a*, and Lat. *-u-ī*; see Benveniste, *HIE* 18; Watkins, *Origins* 105; Gusmani, *AION-L* 6, 1965, 80f.; Kronasser, *Etymologie* 371f.; Ivanov, in *Slavjanskoje Jazykoznanije*, 1968, 226; Watkins, *Verb* 53, 207; against, again Kammenhuber, 'Hethitisch' 322; Viredaz, *BSL* 71, 1976, 171 n. 25 (not *-u-n*, but *-m̥*). Toch. *-wa* is not entirely clear (see Winter, *KZ* 79, 1966, 206–9, and Thomas, *Erforschung des Tocharischen*, 1985, 84, 86f.), but Lat. *-u-* is certainly not a personal ending.

[6] More on this below, 9.7.1.3. On the origin of the *hi*-conjugation, see Rosenkranz, *Jarhbuch für Kleinasiatische Forschungen* 2, 1953, 339–49 (347: *ī/tī/īt*); *KZ* 75, 1958, 215–21; Georgiev, *ZPhon* 22, 1970, 556; G. Schmidt, *KZ* 85, 1972, 261; Beekes, *IF* 76, 1972, 72–6; Eichner, *Fachtagung* 5, 85f.; Risch, ibid. 247f.; Neu (2), 125f.; *Studies Palmer*, 1976, 239–54; Bader, *RHA* 33, 1977, 5–29; Cowgill, in *Heth. und Idg.*, 1979, 25–39; Jasanoff, ibid. 79–90 (and cf. Bammesberger 1988, 236 n. 21); Kuryłowicz, ibid. 143–6; Tischler, in *Gedenkschrift Kronasser*, 1982, 235–49, esp. 249; Kammenhuber, *Fs. Winter*, 1985, 437; *Heth. Wb. i²*, fasc. 8, 1984, 579: only Hittite has *-hi* in 3rd s. present of active and middle; cf. Rosenkranz, *Krat* 31, 1986, 92. See also the monograph study by Rikov, cf. *IC* 34, B 130 (8), and against its

being an innovation, see Catsanicos, *BSL* 78/2, 1983, 86. According to Lehmann, *Fs. Meid*, 1989, 120, 'the *mi* inflection reflects an earlier active paradigm . . ., the *hi* an inactive paradigm of the verb'. How can this be asserted if *hi* was not IE?

9.2.5. Imperative endings[1]

(*a*) *The simple imperative.* For the 2nd s. active the thematic verb uses the stem, i.e. the root with the thematic vowel, e.g. Lat. *age*=Gr. ἄγε, while the athematic verb uses either the bare stem, e.g. Lat. *ī* from **ei*, or the stem reinforced with a particle; in the latter case the stem may have full grade (e.g. Lith. *ei-k* 'go') or zero grade (Gr. ἴ-θι=OInd. *i-hi*, Gr. ϝίσ-θι 'know'=OInd. *vid-dhi*).

For the 2nd pl. of both types the indicative with secondary endings but without augment (the so-called injunctive) is used; cf. φέρετε as opposed to ἐ-φέρετε, OInd. *bhárata*: *ábharata*. In the case of athematic verbs the 2nd pl. also shows both full grade and zero grade: OInd. *stó-ta* and *stu-tá* 'praise'; perhaps both forms were originally represented in Indo-European.[2]

Injunctive forms are also used in the medio-passive. Cf. **sekʷeso* 'follow' in Gr. ἕπου, Lat. *sequere*; **sekʷedhwe* in Gr. ἕπεσθε, Lat. *sequiminī* (9.2.2.1 fin.); similarly in Aryan, except that here, no doubt under the influence of the 2nd pl. *-dhwe(m)*, **sekʷeso* was modified to **sekʷeswo*:[3] OInd. *sačasva* (9.2.2.1). The Aryan imperative forms for the 3rd s. and pl. in *-tām* and *-ntām* (e.g. OInd. *bharatām* 'let it be carried') are of course not accusatives of abstract nouns in *-tā*,[4] but the injunctives *bharata*, *bharanta* (=φέρετο, φέροντο), extended with the particle *-am*.[5]

Such injunctive forms were also used in the 3rd s. and pl. of the active; they occur extended by the particle *u* in OInd. *bharatu*, *bharantu*, IE **bheret*, **bheront*, athematic *astu*, *santu* 'let it/them be', IE **est*, **sent*. The same kind of formation is found also in Hittite: *estu*, *asandu* 'let it/them be', *eptu*, *appandu* 'let him/them take', *kwendu*, *kunandu* 'let him/them kill', *aku*, *akkandu* 'let him/them die'; this element *u* was used almost universally in Hittite even in the medio-passive; see 9.2.4.

For the imperative, therefore, the following endings were available:

	Active		Medio-passive
	Athematic	Thematic	
2	*-Ø, -dhi*	*-e*	*-so*
3	*-t(+u)*	*-et(+u)*	*-to*
5	*-te*	*-ete*	*-dhwe*
6	*-ent(+u)*	*-ont(+u)*	*-nto*

(*b*) *The future imperative.*[6] Alongside the 'simple imperative', Old Indic, Greek, and Latin have formations which can be called the future imperative. Its main characteristic is the ending *tōd*, which is still preserved in this form in Old Latin, but from 200 BC appears as -*tō*, as in Greek from the earliest records; the corresponding form in OInd. is, of course, *tād*. Furthermore, it is interesting that the same form is used for more than one person, e.g. Lat. *agitō*, 2nd and 3rd s., OInd. *gacchatād* 'you (s.)/he shall go'. Old Indic even shows that the same form was used for the 2nd pl.; not, however, for the 3rd pl., so that the widespread view that it was in use for all persons and numbers is wrong. This negative conclusion is confirmed by the fact that in the classical languages there is a special form for the 3rd pl.: cf. Gr. φερόντω, Lat. *ferunto*.

Thus for Indo-European the following paradigms can be reconstructed:

	Athematic	Thematic
2	**estōd*	**bheretōd*
3	**estōd*	**bheretōd*
5	**estōd*	**bheretōd*
6	**sentōd*	**bherontōd*

As opposed to this wide use of **bheretōd*, the classical languages show significant restrictions. In Latin the 2nd pl. was more clearly marked by the addition of -*te*, thus replacing **datō(d)* by *datōte*. In Greek the form was restricted to the 3rd s.: φερέτω. In Old Latin, on the other hand, these forms were also used for deponent verbs, e.g. *ūtitō ūtuntō*, but they were early replaced by *ūtitōr ūtuntōr*. In Greek new mediopassive forms arose through crossing with the infinitive in -σθαι, also used as an imperative: 3rd s. and pl. φερέσθω, later also 3rd pl. φερό(ν)σθω.[7] In Latin the 2nd and 3rd s. *(frui)minō* was the product of a similar innovation; but on this see also Watkins, *Verb* 177f.

With regard to the formation itself it follows in the first place that, as Gaedicke noticed in 1882, its future reference is due to the ending -*tōd*, which was properly the abl. s. of the pronoun **to-* (see 8.2.1) and meant 'from there, thereafter'. The difference from the simple imperative emerges clearly from examples such as Plautus, *Pseudolus*, 647: *tu epistulam hanc a me accipe atque illi dato* ('take now, give later').[8]

As to the part of these forms preceding *tōd*, it was long maintained that *es*, *bhere*, etc., continued to attest an archaic use for all persons and numbers.[9] This view is already undermined by the objection stated above, that a different form is in fact used for the 3rd pl.; it is further proved untenable by the consideration that the ablative *tōd* presupposes a period in which persons and numbers had long been fully developed. Since, then, it is clear that the 2nd s. **bheretōd* arose from the 2nd s. **bhere* plus *tōd*, the same must be assumed for the other persons also. It follows therefore that

2	*bheretōd is from	*bhere-tōd
3	*bheretōd	*bheret-tōd
5	*bheretōd	*bherete-tōd
6	*bherontōd	*bheront-tōd[10]

i.e. the 2nd persons contain the simple imperative forms and the 3rd persons the injunctive forms. The reduction of the 3rd pl. **bheront-tōd* to **bherontōd* is clear, as is the haplological shortening of the 2nd pl. **bherete-tōd* to **bheretōd*. The consequent identity of the 2nd s. and 2nd pl. must have contributed to the simplification of the 3rd s. **bheret-tōd* to **bheretōd*.[11]

[1] Cf. Brugmann, *Grundriss*² ii/3, 563f.; Schwyzer, *GG* i, 797f.; Winter, 'Vocative' 221f.; for the Anatolian endings, see 9.2.4, for the Greek forms Bammesberger, *Fs. Szemerényi*², ii, 1992, 41–5, and Strunk, *Fs. A. Dihle*, 1993, 468–72. On the difference between imperative and prohibitive in Hittite, see Wagner 1985, 96f.

[2] Cf. Watkins, *Verb* 32f.; Lindeman, *BSL* 71, 1976, 113–21; Bammesberger, *JIES* 10, 1982, 45; and especially clear Oettinger, *Stammbildung* 97 n. 24: in contrast to the indic. the 2nd pl. impv. had full grade. On the OInd. 'imperative' type *stōṣi, darṣi*, see Szemerényi, *Lg* 42, 1966, 1–6; Rasmussen, *Fachtagung* 7, 1985, 384–99; Jasanoff, in *In Memory of W. Cowgill*, 1987, 92–112 (assumes a *-si* impv. for IE).

[3] Watkins, *Verb* 52f.; Hollifield, *EC* 20, 1983, 96 n. 4; another view in Shields, in *Hethitica* 5, Louvain 1983, 124. The impv. form *päklyossu* of Toch. A cannot be treated as evidence for IE *-swe* (so Watkins, 193) as long as it is uncertain which person it expresses; cf. K. T. Schmidt, *Die Gebrauchsweisen des Mediums im Toch.*, 1974, 237f.; van Windekens, *Le tokharien* ii/2, 1982, 296f.; Jasanoff (n. 2 above). On the other hand, it is not impossible that MW *ker-ych* (from the 2nd s. impv. mid.) showed an ending *-swo* (following Loth, Pedersen, *VKG* ii, 356, and Hollifield, loc. cit.), which, however, in that case arose in the manner indicated in the text. It is also probable that, alongside the source indicated (inj. *-so*; see above, 9.2.2.1), there was another, namely an active impv. with the acc. of the reflexive pronoun **swe*; see below, 9.7.1.3 n. 12, and Szemerényi, *Studies Hill* iii, 1978, 279.

[4] So Brugmann, *IF* 39, 1920, 56.

[5] Of course this form cannot be compared to the Greek (active!) φερόντων (as by Hirt, e.g. *IG* iv, 141, and again by Pisani, *AGI* 41, 1957, 152; Thumb and Hauschild, i/2, 212f.), since this was surely from *φεροντωδ, nor to the 3rd s. ending *-ām* (e.g. *duhām*, so Schwyzer, *GG* i, 803), as this was obviously formed after *-tām*. The explanation given in the text is also presented by Watkins, *Verb* 94; G. Schmidt, *Glotta* 63, 1985, 76; it was first proposed in 1885 by Thurneysen, *KZ* 27, 175. Neu, in *Studies Polomé*, 1988, 462, stresses that the 2nd s. impv. (e.g. παῦε) was originally voice-indifferent, and thus the middle forms are shown to be later formations.

[6] See Brugmann, *MU* 1, 1878, 163–73: only one form *bheretōd*, the abl. of a noun in *-to-*; Hirt, *IG* iv, 112f.; Szemerényi, 'The future imperative of IE', *RBPh* 31, 1953, 937–54, with bibliography; and more recently Forssman, *Fachtagung* 7, 1985, 181–97.

[7] See also Risch, *MH* 21, 1964, 8f.

[8] See also Strunk, *IF* 73, 1969, 285f.

[9] A view still found in Watkins, *Verb* 121; K. Hoffmann, *MSS* 28, 1970, 37.

[10] The interpretation proposed here has been adopted, with a few modifications, by Forssman (n. 6 above). He reconstructs even more consistently, e.g. 3rd s. **age(tu)tōd*, 3rd pl. **agon(tu)tōd*; 3rd s. **sekʷe(to)tōd*, 3rd pl. **sekʷon(to)tōd*; he is in difficulty with the 2nd s. mid., in which **sekʷeso-tōd* cannot well be reduced to the authenticated **sekʷetōd*. Cf. also his explanation (195f.) of the 2nd pl. mid. *-minī* and the weakly based starting-point of *-mV-* for Hitt. *-dumat*, which has clearly arisen from *-dhwe* (or *-dhwo*?); see above, 9.2.2.1.

[11] The Gothic imperatives in *-(n)dau* are often, but still unconvincingly, compared to the impv. forms in *-(n)tod* and *-(n)tu*; cf. in more recent times Markey, *SL* 26, 1972, 46f.; Cowgill, *Fachtagung* 5, 1975, 65; Shields, *JIES* 5, 1978, 133f.; also Suzuki, *IF* 89, 1985, 169–78; G. Schmidt (n. 5 above).

9.2.6. Thematic vowel and ablaut: verbal accent

The verbal endings, as we have seen, are attached to the relevant verb stem or tense stem either with or without the so-called thematic vowel. The thematic vowel is either *e* or *o*, the latter before a nasal (*m*, but also *n*) and *w*; *a* from *o* in the 2nd pl. is found only in West Germanic and Lithuanian (see Brugmann, *Grundriss*², ii/3, 59). It is obvious that the thematic vowel was originally *e* everywhere and underwent phonetic change to *ō* only before labials.[1] The distribution of *e* and *o* can be illustrated by the following paradigms (pres. indic. act.):

	Greek	Goth.	OCS	Lith.
1	φέρω	*baira*	*berǫ*	*vedu*
2	φέρεις	*bairis*	*bereši*	*vedi*
3	φέρει	*bairiþ*	*beretŭ*	*veda*
4	φέρομεν	*bairam*	*beremŭ*	*vedame*
5	φέρετε	*bairiþ*	*berete*	*vedate*
6	φέροντι	*bairand*	*berǫtŭ*	*veda*
7	—	*bairōs*	*berevē*	*vedava*
8	φέρετον	*bairats*	*bereta*	*vedata*
9	φέρετον	—	*berete, -ta*	*veda*

The Gothic paradigm with *a* (from *o*), *ō*, and *i* (from *e*) has, with one exception, the same distribution of *e*/*o* as the Greek; this is confirmed by Old Irish and Latin (*quaesō quaesumus*, *legunt*), although in general the alternation is almost completely eliminated by the phonetic developments. On the other hand, Baltic and Slavic show a morphologically, not phonetically conditioned assimilation: in Lithuanian *e* is ousted by *a* (from *o*), while in Slavic *e* gains the upper hand except in 1 and 6; in the aorist and imperfect, however, the old distribution is kept.

With regard to the origin of the thematic vowel two opposed standpoints have been taken: that it was part of the stem,[2] or that it was a 'formative element'.[3] On the former view, it would be possible to make the presence or absence of thematic vowel dependent on certain phonetic or accentual factors, on the latter the formative element should properly appear in all persons, as it would have to characterize the stem, not individual persons. From this point of view the *semi-thematic* type postulated by some scholars is highly improbable; that Lat. *ferō fers fert ferimus fertis ferunt* represents an IE type **bherō *bhersi *bherti *bheromos *bherte(s) *bheronti*[4] remains unproved and irreconcilable with the verbal accent (on the stem in the singular, on the ending in the plural); see 9.2.1.2 n. 1.

In athematic verbs the *full grade* of the root is usual in the *singular*, the *zero grade* in the *dual and plural*, and correspondingly the accent is on the root vowel in the singular, on the ending in the other numbers, e.g. **éimi* 'I go', **i-més* 'we go'. The presence of the thematic vowel in all persons and numbers of thematic verbs should properly mean that the accent was fixed on this vowel, requiring the root syllable itself to have zero grade. This happens, however, in only a small number of instances, which possibly have no claim to belong to the Indo-European period. In the majority of cases we find an accented full-grade vowel in the root syllable, e.g. **bhérō*, **bhéromos*, **bhéronti*. It follows that in this type considerable equalization has taken place. It has been conjectured that the thematic vowel first established itself in the zero-grade strong aorist (e.g. **luk-ó-m*, **luk-é-s*, **luk-é-t*) and from there was extended to the present and imperfect,[5] or that the oxytone type of present (with accent in the singular on the thematic vowel) was unified from an alternating inflexion *TR̥T-óm/-és/-ét*: *TR̥T-*$_e$*mé/-té/-ént* to an inflexion with fixed thematic vowel *TR̥T-óm/-és/-ét/-óme/-éte/-ónt*, thus providing a model for *TéRT-om/-es/-et*, etc., instead of the earlier and regular *TéRT-*$_e$*m/-s/-t*, etc.[6] The thematic vowel must have arisen, even if not exactly as described, at all events in a very similar way. It is, however, certain that it was universally established with the alternation set out at the beginning of this section in the Indo-European or late Indo-European period. The individual languages did not consolidate in different ways a state of affairs that was still fluid, but inherited a fixed situation which in the course of time they modified according to the demands of their own rules.

1 See above, 6.3.4*b*. Cf. also Couvreur, *Mélanges Boisacq* i, 1937, 207 (originally only *o*; forms with *e*, i.e. 2, 3, and 5, secondary and late); Poldauf, *ZPhon* 9, 1956, 165 (*o* before labials); Kuryłowicz, *Apophonie* 72; Watkins, *Verb* 64, 70, 106, 108; Jasanoff, *Stative* 47f.; Hilmarsson (above, 6.3.2 n. 1), 193–8; Ivanov, *Glagol* 56f.; Rasmussen 1989, 136f. and in Vennemann 1989, 156f., 170 n. 10. According to Oettinger, *Fachtagung* 7, 1985, 298, *a* becomes *e* by umlaut after *y*, but (311) *o* throughout in the middle. On the origin of the thematic inflexion, see L. Dubois, *Recherches sur le dialecte arcadien* i–iii, Louvain 1986, and cf. García-Ramón, *HS* 102, 1990, 313.

2 Fick, *BB* 1, 1877, 1f.; Hirt, *IG* ii, 167; iv, 159f.

3 e.g. Meillet, *Introduction* 174; Specht, *Ursprung* 103f., 245f., 309f. (pronoun *e/o*); Knobloch, 'La voyelle thématique *e/o* serait-elle un indice d'object indo-européen?', *Lingua* 3, 1953, 407–20, rejected by Kuryłowicz, *Apophonie* 74 n. 47; Kortlandt, *JIES* 11, 1984, 310f. Eichner, *Fachtagung* 5, 1975, 77 n. 3, thinks that 'the original function of the thematic vowel, to change the aspect of the verb', is kept in one (solitary!) known instance, that of the pair **Heit-t-* 'goes' (non-specific): **Hei-e-to* 'keeps on going, strides along'.

4 Szemerényi, *Syncope* 189f., 195f. On this, see Elfenbein, *Ricerche Linguistiche* 2, 1951, 180f., and Stang, *Vgl. Gram.* 319; Schmalstieg, *La Linguistique* 8/1, 1972, 123–6 (in favour); Vaillant, *BSL* 38, 1937, 97f.; *Gram. comp.* iii, 365f., 438; Cowgill, *Lg* 31, 1963, 263; Kuryłowicz, *Categories* 79f. (against). Cf. also W. P. Schmid, *Studien zum baltischen und idg. Verbum*, 1963, 97, 101; Nagy 1970, 20–6, 31; Strunk, *KZ* 83, 1970, 220f.; Ringe, *Sprache* 34, 1992, 87 n. 74.

5 Kuryłowicz, *Apophonie* 72; against, Watkins, *Lg* 34, 1958, 384.

6 Kuryłowicz, *Categories* 116f. Cf. also Adrados, *Verbo* 601f.; Risch, *Symbolae Kuryłowicz*,

1965, 239 (against Risch's uniform *-ske-* inflexion, see Hitt. *-skami*; cf. Neu (2), 43; Eichner, *MSS* 28, 1970, 13 n. 2); Schmitt-Brandt, 128f.; Kuryłowicz, *IG* 271f.; Kerns and Schwartz, *Lg* 44, 1969, 717–9; M. García Teijeiro, *Los presentes ie. con infijo nasal*, Salamanca 1970, 99f.

9.2.6.1. *Proterodynamic verbs.* On the basis of certain full-grade middle forms (e.g. OInd. *śayē*=Gr. κεῖμαι 'I lie') and a few long-grade active forms occurring almost exclusively in Aryan (OInd. *tāṣṭi* 'works in wood' from *takṣ-*), Prof. Johanna Narten (*Fs. Kuiper*, 1969, 9f.) concluded that alongside the types already discussed Indo-European also had a 'proterodynamic' root present, i.e. with fixed accent on the root;[1] cf. from **steu-*'solemnly proclaim': act. 1st s. **stḗu-mi*, 1st pl. **stéu-mes*, mid. 1st s. **stéw-ai*, 1st pl. **stéu-medha*. In the new terminology (see above, 7.1.4.4.1 and below, 9.4.4.6) these verbs are now called *acrostatic*.

According to Insler (*MSS* 30, 1972, 55–64), there is a parallel, not noticed by Narten, between the proterodynamic (or acrostatic) presents and the sigmatic aorist, especially in the active participles and in the middle; only the indicative active diverges in that the sigmatic aorist has the long grade throughout, and this must be ancient, since there was no model for long grade in the 3rd pl. (see below, 9.4.2.1 fin.). Forms like *śāsati* show that the earlier form must have been **tākṣati*, which was replaced by *takṣati* on the analogy of *dádat/dádati*. This could mean that the active proterodynamic present originally, like the sigmatic aorist, had long grade throughout.[2]

[1] Already noted by Brugmann, *KVG* § 638, § 647; Meillet, *MSL* 13, 1905, 110–15. Cf. further Lindeman, *NTS* 26, 1972, 65–79; Insler, *Lg* 48, 1972, 557f.; G. Schmidt, *KZ* 85, 1972, 264; Beekes, *KZ* 87, 1973, 86–98; Tichy, *Glotta* 54, 1976, 71–84; Harðarson 1993, 58f. Mayrhofer wishes (most recently *VJ* 1985 (3), 28f.) to add as a (single!) example from Old Persian the 1st s. mid. *āxšnavaiy* 'I hear', but (*pace* Harðarson, 124 n. 107) the reading is uncertain, see *Krat* 24, 1980, 57.

[2] Against Insler, see Strunk, *Fachtagung* 7, 1985, 498f., 506f., 511f.; *Fs. Hoenigswald*, 1987, 388; Kortlandt, ibid. 219.

9.2.7. Voices[1]

Two voices are sharply distinguished by the personal endings: active and middle. Sometimes an active was paired with a middle, e.g. Gr. λούω 'I wash (someone/thing)', λούομαι 'I wash (myself)'. Sometimes no active was possible from a verbal stem, only a middle (*media tantum*); this is the case with e.g. IE **sekʷetoi* 'follows', which appears in OInd. *sačatē*, Gr. ἕπεται, Lat. *sequitur*, OIr. *sechithir*. Naturally a middle could not be formed to every active (*activa tantum*), e.g. Gr. ἀποθνήσκει 'dies'.

To grasp the full meaning of these voices is extremely difficult. It would, of course, be possible to dispense with any such definition and limit oneself to determining the difference in purely formal terms, but this would surely be intolerable in the long run. The active is less of a problem than the middle. Since the middle is predominantly used for the expression of bodily functions such as sitting, lying, jumping, etc. (Gr. *ἧσται, κεῖται, ἅλλεται*), and in particular with verbs of feeling such as to be afraid, to be ashamed, pleased, etc. (Gr. *φοβέομαι, αἰδέομαι, ἥδομαι*), its main function could be seen in the latter sphere: 'in the middle it is expressed that the subject accompanies the action (taken in the widest sense) with a mood, an emotion';[2] the definition is not, however, adequate for the verbs of bodily function cited above. It might be better to hold, with Brugmann, that the *media* (*tantum*) predominantly 'denoted actions, processes, or states which have their scene essentially in the subject and within the scope of the subject, in which the subject is wholly and solely interested, and similar'.[3] To this Benveniste's definition, which quite rightly attempts to grasp the opposition of middle to active, comes very close: 'Dans l'actif, les verbes dénotent un procès qui s'accomplit à partir du sujet et hors de lui. Dans le moyen, qui est la diathèse à définir par opposition, le verbe indique un procès dont le sujet est le siège; le sujet est intérieur au procès';[4] cf. also the definition that the middle expresses 'that a process is taking place with regard to, or is affecting, happening to, a person or a thing'.[5] In conformity with this the middle could be described as the *subjective* voice,[6] which accords well with its name in Old Indic grammar, *ātmanē-padam* 'word for oneself'.[7]

The boundary between active and middle is not sharp. Sometimes there is no difference in meaning between the two (*σπέρχω=σπέρχομαι* 'I hasten'), or the reason for choosing one or the other voice is incomprehensible to us in semantic terms: *εἰμί* 'I am' is active, *ἔσομαι* 'I shall be' is middle. It is especially common to find an active perfect beside a *medium tantum* in the other tenses; e.g. *γίγνομαι* 'become': *γέγονα*, *δέρκομαι* 'see': *δέδορκα*; Lat. *reuertor* 'return': *reuertī*; OInd. *vártē* 'become': *vavárta*, *mr̥̥ṣyatē* 'forgets': *mamarṣa*. The reason must of course be that originally the perfect denoted only states, not actions or processes;[8] see below, 9.7.4.

Meillet's view that the present active can stand in contrast to an imperfect middle has often been repeated, especially in the French school, but Debrunner has shown that in the case of *φημί/φάτο, φάμενος* the middle forms are aorist. In this connection Jamison made the important observation that in the Rigveda a middle form in an otherwise active paradigm occurs almost without exception only in the 3rd pl. (*-anta*), and only from present stems of the form ⏑⏑⏑ (many of them in *-aya-*).[9]

The subjective character of the middle, to which attention was drawn above, is well shown in pairs like Gr. *θύει*, OInd. *yajati* 'he sacrifices' (of the priest) as opposed to Gr. *θύεται*, OInd. *yajatē* 'he sacrifices' (of the one who ordered the sacrifice, or who sacrifices for himself). To this use is linked the *reflexive* middle, e.g. *τρέπομαι* 'I turn (myself)', the *reciprocal* middle, e.g. *μάχεσθαι* 'to fight', and the *intensive* or *dynamic* middle, e.g. *πολιτεύω* 'I am a citizen': *πολιτεύομαι* 'I engage in the activities of a citizen'.[10]

Only two voices can be formally distinguished for Indo-European (cf. below, 9.7.4). Since the non-active voice in early Indic and Greek had predominantly, if not exclusively, a middle function, the second IE voice is usually defined as middle (as it was above). The *passive*, which cannot be entirely dismissed even at the beginning of the history of Indic and Greek, is then treated as having arisen secondarily from the middle, and in fact from its reflexive use.[11] This explanation seems today hard to understand. For the past three decades Chomsky's transformational grammar has been for many *the* new grammar, and the *passive transformation*[12] has quite rightly been taken as the prototype of transformational relationships.[13] No wonder that Kuryłowicz felt himself obliged to declare the transformational opposition of active : passive to be hierarchically higher than the purely semantic contrast of active : middle. Even if at the beginning of the tradition in Indic the old situation seems to be represented by *bharati* : *bharatē* (act. : mid.), this, he holds, is false, since the basic opposition active: passive is found in *bharati* : *bhriyatē*; the innovation *bhriyatē* took over the fundamental function of the passive, leaving *bharatē* confined to the secondary, intransitive and middle, function.[14] Also in Greek the passive function of the old -*τοι* inflexion was transferred to innovated forms, at least in the aorist (and future); the old forms were restricted to the secondary (middle) function, although even here both coexist, e.g. *τιμήσομαι* 'I shall assess'/'I shall be honoured'.[15]

It seems to contradict this interpretation of the facts that in the passive the agent is very often not mentioned, that the passive is used in particular where the agent is not known, and that the passive appears mostly in the 3rd person.[16] The explanation is very simple.[17] The three-part passive construction of the type *discipulus laudātur ā magistrō* is a transformation of *magister discipulum laudat* and as such differs from the active construction only in its 'expressive' function, not in the 'symbolic', representational function; it is thus simply a stylistic variant of the active construction. The two-part construction, on the other hand, in which the agent is suppressed, can be used even when the agent is in fact unknown or is merely not to be mentioned,[18] thus in cases where Indo-European had no equivalent active expression, since sentences with indefinite subject such as Fr. *on* did not exist. The two-part *discipulus laudātur* is thus necessary and for that reason statistically commoner than the three-part type, which is merely a stylistic variant and therefore less important.[19]

ADDENDUM: the stative. On the basis of certain formal and semantic peculiarities, in recent times a further voice, the *stative*, has been postulated, for which there is provisional evidence only (or primarily) in the 3rd person; compare, for instance, OInd. *bruvē* 'is called, named' (stative) with *(upa)brūtē* 'calls on, invokes (for himself)'.[20] Rix thinks that the distinction is also demonstrable in the 2nd person and reconstructs the following parallel systems:[21]

Middle	2	*-so*	3	*-to*	6	*-nto*
Stative	2	*-tha*	3	*-o*	6	*-ro*

All this is for the present fairly uncertain, and dissent ranges from mild doubt[22] to emphatic rejection.[23]

[1] An introduction to the problems involved and further literature in Schwyzer, *GG* ii, 222f.; W. Boeder, *Studien zum gr. Medium*, Diss. Freiburg i. Br. 1961; Hofmann–Szantyr, 287f. (291 bibliography). To these can be added: S. Szlifersztejnowa, *Kategoria strony*, Wrocław 1969 (history of the voices from antiquity to the present day); C. García Gual, *El sistema diatético en el verbo griego*, Madrid 1970; G. Calboli, *La linguistica moderna e il latino*, Bologna 1972, 196f.; Harweg, 'Zur Definition von Aktiv und Passiv', *Lings* 97, 1973, 46–71; Anziferowa, 'Wortbildende Struktur des lat. Deponens', *AAntHung* 21, 1973, 161–83; Flobert, *Les verbes deponents latins*, 1975; Szemerényi, *Studies Hill* iii, 1978, 277f.; Meid, *InL* 4, 1978, 39; Strunk, 'Zum idg. Medium', *Fs. Seiler*, 1980, 321–37; **Actants, voix et aspects verbaux*, Angers 1981; Flobert, 'Benveniste et le problème de la diathèse', in *É. Benveniste aujourd'hui* ii, 1984, 51–61; Perel'muter, 'Ie. medij i refleksiv', *VJ* 1984 (1), 3–13; 'Le passif', *Cercle Linguistique d'Aix-en-Provence, Travaux* 2, 1984; P. Trost, 'Medium und Reflexiv', *Fs. Winter*, 1985, 825–7; Gamkrelidze—Ivanov, 330 f.; I. Werlen, 'Das Passiv als Verfahren der Fokussierung', *CFS* 41, 1987, 205–16; Schmalstieg, 'The intransitive nature of the IE verb', in *Convegno* 7, 1987, 511–16; M. Shibatani (ed.), *Passive and Voice*, Amsterdam 1988 (see *Lg* 67, 1991, 141f.); Perel'muter, 'K istoričeskoj tipologii zalogovyx struktur', in Desnickaja (ed.) 1989, 82–95; P. K. Andersen, *Passive*, 1990; *A New Look at the Passive*, 1991; 'Zur Diathese', *HS* 106, 1994, 177–231; M. H. Klaiman, *Grammatical Voice*, Cambridge 1992; Duhoux 1992, 100f.; S. Kemmer, *The Middle Voice*, 1993; B. A. Fox and P. J. Hopper (eds.), *Voice: Form and Function*, 1993. Cf. also below, 9.4.4.4 n. 1. According to Koller, *Glotta* 37, 1958, 31, the opposition active—passive was first discovered by Greek grammarians.

[2] O. Hoffmann, *BB* 25, 1899, 178 (quoted with approval by Schwyzer, *GG* ii, 223 n. 2).

[3] Brugmann, *Grundriss*² ii/3, 685.

[4] Benveniste, 'Actif et moyen dans le verbe', first published 1950, now included in his *Problèmes de linguistique générale*, 1966, 168–75 (quotation from 174). Cf. also Strunk (n. 1 above, 1980) 322: 'A general function of the middle . . . [is] to set behaviour denoted by the verb in essential relationship with the subject'; and see Ruipérez, quoted by Hettrich, *Krat* 35, 1990, 125.

[5] Gonda, 'Reflections on the IE medium', *Lingua* 9, 1960, 30–67 (quotation from 66) and 175–93; *Old Indian*, 1971, 133f.; *The Medium in the Ṛgveda*, Leiden 1979; cf. Lehmann, *Fs. O. Hietsch*, 1992, 140.

[6] Bechert, *Krat* 10, 1967, 170; cf. also Hermodsson, *Reflexive und intransitive Verba im älteren Westgermanischen*, 1952, 28f.; Guxman, see above 9.2.2.1 n. 8; K. H. Schmidt, *ZDMG* 116, 1966, 18f.; Rosén, *Lingua* 17, 1967, 324f.; Savčenko, 'Kategorija mediuma v ie. jazyke', *BPTJ* 20, 1961, 99–119.

[7] See Croft, Shyldkrot, and Kemmer, *ICHL* 7, 1987, 179–92 (simple or direct reflexive); A. M. Schenker, 'Slavic reflexive and IE middle: a typological study', in *American Contributions, 10th Congress of Slavists*, 1988, 363–83.

[8] According to Neu, *Fachtagung* 7, 1985, 281f., the perfect is a voice; cf. also Schulze, *FoLH* 10, 1991, 10f.; Perel'muter (below, 9.7.1.3, n. 15), 60f.; and again Neu, in *Fachtagung* 7, 288; *Studies Polomé*, 1988, 462 (middle a kind of contamination of active and old perfect of state), rejected by Lazzeroni, 'Studio sul medio', *SSL* 30, 1991, 1–22, esp. 18f. (middle endings connected but not identical with perfect endings). See also below, 9.7.4 n. 5).

[9] Cf. Meillet, *BSL* 23, 1922, 64f.; Chantraine, *RPh* 53, 1927, 153f.; Debrunner, *Glotta* 25, 1936, 73; Schwyzer, *GG* i, 673 n. 1; Jamison, *IIJ* 21, 1979, 149–69. In the replacement of 3rd pl. *-an(t)* by *-anta* it seems to be clear that when *-ant* was in process of change to *-ann* a more careful pronunciation led to *-antə* and finally to *-anta*, since *-ti* and *-tu* had to be avoided. Similarly *-οντο* arose in Greek (e.g. *στενάχοντο*) because *-ον-τα* would have fallen together with the participle.

[10] Cf. Schwyzer, *GG* ii, 229f.; Burrow, *The Sanskrit Language*, 1955, 293f.; Thumb and Hauschild, i/2, 185f. For classification of the middle, see Neu (2), 92f.; García Gual (n. 1 above), 21f.; Justus (n. 11 below), 301f.

[11] P. Diels, 'Über das idg. Passivum', *Jahrbuch der schlesischen Gesellschaft für vaterländische Kultur*, 1913, 1–8; Meyer-Lübke, *Vom Wesen des Passivums*, 1926; Schwyzer, *GG* ii, 224, 236, 238; on this, cf. esp. E. Wistrand, *Über das Passivum*, 1941, 5f.: the development of middle to passive is almost a natural law. See also Hendriksen, *The Active and the Passive*, 1948; Gonda, *Remarks on the Sanskrit Passive*, 1951; Hermodsson (n. 6 above), 19–25; H. Hartmann, *Das Passiv*, 1954, 8, 13f. (passive late and not universal); Zsilka, 'Das Passiv in Homers Heldengesängen', *AAntHung* 12, 1964, 277–310.

On the origin of the passive, see also Neu (2), 1f., 5; Jankuhn, *Die passive Bedeutung medialer Formen*, 1969; Schmalstieg, *FoL* 12, 1980, 358f. (from the middle); Statha and Halikas, *PCLS* 13, 1977, 578–89 (from the impersonal); G. Schmidt, *Em* 46, 1978, 383f., esp. 409 (from infinitive constructions!); G. Stein, *Studies in the Function of the Passive*, 1979 (133: a new proposal); C. Justus, 'IE etymology with special reference to grammatical category' (in Lehmann and Malkiel 1982, 291–328), 306f.; Lehmann, *Fs. Meid*, 1989, 122 ('In Hittite there is no passive . . . We cannot therefore reconstruct a passive for PIE'); id., *GL* 29, 1989, 237 (the passive was developed in the individual languages); Schulze, above n. 8: the passive is not a voice. According to Pulgram, 'IE passive paradigm', *Forum Linguisticum* 2/2, 1979, 95–106, the passive was a universal. On this question, see E. Keenan, *Passive in the World's Languages*, Trier 1981; Michelini, *Il passivo*, 1981, 27f., 54; A. Siewierska, *The Passive: A Comparative Linguistic Analysis*, London 1984; Gamkrelidze–Ivanov, 336f.; P. K. Andersen, 'On passive morphology', in *Fs. Szemerényi*[2], i, 207–39; 'Eine alternative Sprachtypologie für das Reflexiv', *FoL* 27, 1993, 107–46; 'Zur Diathese' (see n. 1 above, end).

[12] Chomsky, *Syntactic Structures*, 1957, 42f., 112; *Aspects of the Theory of Syntax*, 1965, 103f. Cf. Lyons, *Introduction to Theoretical Linguistics*, 1968, 257f., 261f., 373; J. Svartvik, *On Voice in the English Verb*, 1966, 1f., 164; Brekle, *Lings* 49, 1969, 84; Abraham, *FoL* 4, 1970, 38–52; but against, Langacker, *Lg* 58, 1982, 22.

[13] A. Bach, *An Introduction to Transformational Grammar*, 1966, 62f.; Williams, *LIn* 13, 1982, 160–3. Against the passive transformation, see L. F. Bouton, *Fs. R. and H. Kahane*, 1973, 70–84.

[14] The passive use of the type *bharatē* is found not only in Vedic (see Delbrück, *Ai. Syntax*, 1888, new edn. 1976, 263f.) but also in Avestan (see Reichelt, *Aw. Elementarbuch*, 1909, new edn. 1967, 298). Against Goto's denial of a passive sense see Hettrich, *HS* 102, 1990, 304.

[15] Kuryłowicz, *Categories* 72–85. In his article of 1929 'Le genre verbal en indo-iranien' (*RO* 6, 199–209), K. had already voiced the opinion that the intransitive-passive use of the 'middle' was older than the reciprocal or reflexive, and Marguliés as early as 1924 (see *Die Verba reflexiva in den slav. Sprachen*, and *KZ* 58, 1931, 116, 120) had derived the middle from the passive, a view still noted as incorrect in Hofmann–Szantyr, 287. See also Flobert, *Les verbes déponents des origines à Charlemagne*, 1975.

[16] See Schwyzer, *Zum persönlichen Agens beim Passiv*, 1943; *GG* ii, 238f.; K. H. Schmidt, 'Zum Agens beim Passiv', *IF* 68, 1963, 1–12, 269, 274f.; Jamison, *KZ* 93, 1980, 196–219; *Sprache* 25, 1980, 129–43: in Vedic and earlier in Indo-European the agent was mostly

expressed by the instrumental, but other cases were also possible, the genitive, to be sure, only late (although Schmalstieg, *Studies Polomé*, 1988, 591–600, puts it at the very beginning); cf. S. Luraghi, 'Distribution of instrumental and agentive markers for human and non-human agents of passive verbs', *IF* 91, 1986, 48–66; Calboli, 'Das lat. Passiv', *IF* 95, 1991, 104–60. See also H. Amman, 'Das Passivum als Leideform' and 'Probleme der verbalen Diathese' (1952, 1955), in *Nachgelassene Schriften*, 1961, 95–111.

[17] Kuryłowicz, *Categories* 72f.

[18] See Shibatani (*Lg* 61, 1985, 821–48), 837: 'the main pragmatic function of passives' is 'agent defocussing'; cf. also Michelini, *Il passivo*, 1981, 71; P. K. Andersen, *Fachtagung* 7, 1985, 47–57; id., *A New Look at the Passive*, 1991.

[19] See further Schauwecker, 'Genera verbi im Deutschen', *Muttersprache* 78, 1968, 366–70; Brinker, *Das Passiv im heutigen Deutsch*, 1971. Jankuhn (n. 11 above), disputes that the passive goes back to IE; N. La Fauci, 'Passivi', *Scritti T. Bolelli*, 1985, 137–64.

[20] See Oettinger, 'Der idg. Stativ', *MSS* 34, 1976, 109–49; *Stammbildung* 514f.; Eichner, *Fachtagung* 5, 1975, 99; Rix, in *Idg. und Keltisch*, 135f.; Lehmann repeatedly, e.g. *GL* 29, 1989, 228f.; Oettinger, 'Function des idg. Stativs', *Fs. Rix*, 1993, 347–61. Jasanoff, *Stative*, deals not with the new stative but with ē-verbs.

[21] Rix (n. 20 above) 136, 145f.

[22] Cowgill, in *Heth. und Idg.*, 28 n. 9.

[23] Neu, *Studies Palmer*, 1976, 253 n. 57; *Fachtagung* 7, 1985, 292f.; *Fs. Meid*, 1989, 169 n. 36. Cf. also Szemerényi 1985, 24.

9.3. MOOD FORMATIONS

9.3.1

Of the four moods (see 9.1 and 9.7.3) only three are indicated by special modal signs or personal endings. The *indicative* is opposed as the unmarked mood to the other three marked moods; it is indicated by, at most, the tense signs and thematic vowel. Only the 2nd s. of the imperative is an exception: this is usually the bare stem.[1]

[1] See the research reports by Calboli, 'I modi del verbo greco e latino 1903–1966', *Lustrum* 11, 1966, 173–349; 13, 1969, 405–511; 'Sintassi latina e linguistica moderna', *LeS* 3, 1968, 307–17; *ANRW* 29/1, 1983, 80–109; Erhart 1985; Rix 1986; Neu, 'Person und Modus im Idg.', *Studies Polomé*, 1988, 461–73 (six moods). See also F. Kieper, 'On defining modality', *FL* 21/1, 1987, 67–102; A. Maniet, 'Le système des modes en latin classique', *Studies Polomé*, 1988, 439–48; G. Michelini, 'Va postulata per l'ie. la classe del congiuntivo?', *ASGM* 23, 1988, 58–62.

9.3.1.1

The *subjunctive*[1] stands out clearly from the other moods and is in particular opposition to the indicative: if the indicative is athematic, the subjunctive is its thematic counterpart; if the indicative is thematic, the subjunctive is characterized by the connecting vowel *ē/ō*. Thus the subjunctive to athematic **eimi*, **eisi*, **eiti* 'go, goest, goes' is **ey-ō*, **ey-e-s(i)*, **ey-e-t(i)*, but to **bherō*, **bheresi*, **bhereti* it is **bherō*, **bherēs(i)*, **bherēt(i)*; in the latter *ē* and *ō* clearly represent the sequences *e+e* and *o+o* respectively, i.e. the thematic vowel (of the indicative)+the subjunctive sign. See further 9.7.2, and on the thematic vowels *e/o* Rasmussen, works cited in 9.2.6, n. 1.

The thematic subjunctive of athematic verbs is clear in certain Greek forms, e.g. *ἴομεν* 'let us go' as opposed to the indicative *ἴμεν*; similarly the long-vowel subjunctive of thematic verbs, e.g. *φέρωμεν*, *φέρητε*.

The latter type does not exist in Latin, at least not in this form. Since, however, the subjunctive of **es-mi* (in Latin modified to *sum*), i.e. IE **esō*, **eses(i)*, **eset(i)*, etc., certainly survives in Lat. *erō*, *eris*, *erit*, i.e. has become future, it is certain that a correspondence to the Gr. subj. *φέρω φέρης* (or -*ῃς*) is to be found in the Lat. future *agēs*, *aget*, *agētis*, where the forms originally with -*ō*- have been unified to *ē*, thus *agēmus*, *agent*; the 1st. s. *agam* is borrowed from the new *ā*-subjunctive.[2]

It is probable that originally there was only one form of subjunctive for each verb. This is indicated by the fact that in old Latin the subj. of *tangō* was *tagam* (*nē attigās*) and of *aduenio*, *aduenat*, etc.; only later were these assimilated to the present stem, thus *tangam*, *aduениam*, etc.[3] Similarly in early Indic the opposition was between *kr̥nōti* 'he makes' (present stem characterized by -*nō*-) and *karat(i)* 'let him make' (from the verb root); not till later was a present subj. formed as *kr̥nav-at*.[4]

In general the subjunctive stem takes SE, cf. OLat. *kapiad* 'capiat', Arc. *ἔχη* (from -*ē*-*t*), Thess. *θέλη*; in Attic-Ionic the original -*ης*, -*η* were modified to -*ηις*, -*ηι* on the analogy of the indicative. In OInd., however, a mixture of SE and PE is found, or an apparently free choice between both. The OInd. personal endings are:

1	-*ā*, -*āni*	4	-*ma*	7	-*va*
2	-*s*, -*si*	5	-*tha*	8	-*thas*
3	-*t*, -*ti*	6	-*n(t)*	9	-*tas*

That is, only PE are used in the 1st s., 2nd and 3rd dual, 2nd pl., only SE in the 1st dual, 1st and 3rd pl.; free variation is allowed in the 2nd s. between -*si* and -*s*, in the 3rd s. between -*ti* and -*t*; in the 1st s., as has been said, -*ā* is the primary ending (=Gr. *ω*, Lat. -*ō*), while the variant -*āni* shows this -*ā* extended by the particle -*ni*, or even -*ā*-*na* modified to -*ā*-*ni* under the influence of primary *i*. In the middle, on the other hand, the PE in -*ē* or variants in -*ai* are used almost exclusively; only in the 3rd pl. is the SE also admitted. Cf. *bharāsi/bharās*, *bharāti/bharāt*; from *i*- 'go': 1 *ay-ā(ni)*, 2 *ay-a-s(i)*, 3 *ay-a-t(i)*; from *as*- 'be': 1 *as-āni*, 2 *as-a-s(i)*, 3 *as-a-t(i)*, 5 *as-a-tha*, 6 *as-a-n*, etc.[5]

A more detailed examination of these variations[6] seems to show that the SE were the original but the PE continued to gain ground,[7] probably in connection with an ongoing process of approximation in content to the indicative. From a historical point of view this interpretation seems better founded than the supposition that this very limited variation (properly only in the 2nd and 3rd s.) is to be attributed to differences in content[8] or to the former existence of two 'tenses', present and imperfect subjunctive.[9]

[1] See Schwyzer, *GG* i, 790f.; Leumann², 573f.; Hahn, *Subjunctive* 59; D. Lightfoot, *Natural Logic and the Greek Moods*, 1975; Scherer, *Fachtagung* 4, 1973, 99–106.

[2] A different view in Lazzeroni (below, 9.3.1.3 n. 8).

[3] See Lazzeroni, 'Gli ottativi vedici del tipo *gamema*', *SSL* 27, 1987, 123–50 (146, 149: *aduenat* is old injunctive of *ā*-verbs). So also in Celtic, see Marstrander, *SO* 37, 1962, 147f. (OIr. *gaibid/gabaid*); McCone 1991, chs. 4–5.

[4] Renou, *BSL* 33, 1932, 15f.; Kuryłowicz, *Apophonie* 28; *Categories* 139.

[5] Renou, op. cit. 5f.; Kuryłowicz, *RO* 3, 1927, 173f.

[6] Gonda, *Moods* 110f.

[7] See Lazzeroni, in *Scritti in onore di R. Ambrosini*, 1985, 129–33.

[8] K. Hoffmann, *Injunktiv* 268 n. 4, 276.

[9] Kuryłowicz, *Categories* 139. See also Watkins, *Verb* 133; Beekes, *IIJ* 23, 1981, 21–7: rejects Hoffmann and Kuryłowicz (22), explanation possible (24) with Kortlandt's endings (*Lingua* 44, 1979, 67) (?). Cf. also Kellens, *Krat* 36, 1991, 22.

ADDENDUM 1. Some scholars dispute the existence of a subjunctive in IE (e.g. Pedersen, *Tocharisch* 191f.; Lane, *Lg* 35, 1959, 157, and op. cit. below, 9.3.1.3 n. 8). Since, however, the short-vowel subjunctive of athematic verbs is attested for Aryan, Greek, Latin, and Celtic (see Kuryłowicz, *Categories* 113f.), there can be no doubt that it was already present in IE; cf. K. Hoffmann (1970), now *Aufsätze* ii, 538.

ADDENDUM 2. The view of the variation *e/o*, *ē/ō* proposed here is probably held by the majority of scholars, but there are some who see at least *ē/ō* as a secondary variation which has taken the place of *ē*, formerly the only valid sign; so first O. Schrader, Curtius' *Studien* 10, 1878, 306, followed by Brugmann, *MU* 3, 1880, 30f.; Hirt, *IG* iv, 296; Pedersen, *Tocharisch* 192; Watkins, in *AIED* 42f.; Lazzeroni (below, 9.3.1.3 n. 8), 182f. On the subjunctive of 'to be', see below 9.5.1.

9.3.1.2

The *optative* has in athematic verbs an unmistakable formation: a suffix *-yē-* in the singular, *-ī-* in the other numbers, is attached to the zero grade of the stem; to this the SE are then added.[1] This formation can be most neatly reconstructed for **es-* 'to be' (see 9.5.1):

1	**s-yē-m*	4	**s-ī-me*
2	**s-yē-s*	5	**s-ī-te*
3	**s-yē-t*	6	**s-iy-ent*

This paradigm is perhaps retained most clearly in Old Latin: *siem*, *siēs*, *siet*, *sīmus*, *sītis*, *sient*; somewhat modified, with **es-* restored but with loss of intervocalic *-s-*, in Gr. *εἴην*, *-ης*, *-η*, *-εῖμεν* (< **es-ī-m-*), *εἶτε*, *εἶεν*. In OInd. *-yā-* is carried through the whole paradigm: *syām*, *syās*, *syāt*, *syāma*, *syāta*, *syur*. Gothic, on the other hand, shows generalization of the zero grade *-ī-* in (*wiljau*), *wileis*, *wili*, *wileima*, *wileiþ*, *wileina* 'I will' etc. from **wel-ī-*; similarly in Latin: *uelim*, *uelīs*, etc.

In thematic verbs there appears before the SE an element *-oi-*, which seems to consist of the thematic vowel *-o-* and the zero grade of the athematic *yē/ī*.[2] The formation can be reconstructed on the basis of Greek, Gothic, and Old Indic:

	Greek	Goth.	OInd.	IE
1	*φέροιμι*	*bairau*	*bharēyam*	**bheroy-m̥*
2	*φέροις*	*bairais*	*bharēs*	**bheroi-s*
3	*φέροι*	*bairai*	*bharēt*	**bheroi-t*
4	*φέροιμεν*	*bairaima*	*bharēma*	**bheroi-me*
5	*φέροιτε*	*bairaiþ*	*bharēta*	**bheroi-te*
6	*φέροιεν*	*bairaina*	*bharēyur*	**bheroy-n̥t*

Forms 2–5 are unanimously attested; 1 and 6 should have given Gr. **φέροια*, which is possibly attested by Arcadian 1st s. *ἐξελαύνοια*.[3] In Gothic we would have expected **bairaju* and **bairajun*, and it seems clear that *bairau* developed regularly through loss of intervocalic *-j-*, whereas the 3rd pl. was remodelled on the analogy of the other persons of the plural.[4] In OInd. **bharaya* was made clearer by the addition of *-m*, the 3rd pl. **bharayat* was provided with the SE *-ur*, and both forms introduced the characteristic *ē* of the other persons.

If, as is highly probable, *o* in *-oi-* is the thematic vowel,[5] it is not entirely easy to understand why *e* does not appear in combination with the true suffix *-ī-*. The explanation that the *o* of the optative is 'founded on' the indicative[6] is by no means obvious. One could rather suppose that at first, as in the indicative and subjunctive, *o* appeared in only some of the persons: thus 1 *-oy-m̥*, 4 *-oi-m-*, 6 *-oy-n̥t* and 2 *-ei-s*, 3 *-ei-t*, 5 *-ei-te* stood in opposition to one another, with *-oi-/-ei-* reproducing purely analogically the alternation *-o-/-e-* of the indicative and subjunctive; then later a generalization of *-oi-* took place.[7] This explanation could find support in Baltic, if its imperatives formed with *-ei-* (originally optatives), such as OPrus. *weddeis*, really go back to IE *-ei-*, not *-oi-*.[8]

[1] Schwyzer, *GG* i, 793; Leumann[2], 573; Stang, *Vgl. Gram.* 421f.; Vaillant, *Gram. comp.* iii, 29f.; Benediktsson, 'The Germanic subjunctive', *NOWELE* 1, 1983, 31–60. Following Kuryłowicz, *Categories* 136f., 140f., Neu, *Studies Polomé*, 1988, 465, analyses *yē* as *y* + *ē*, first in 1st s., before it was carried into the pl.; in 2nd and 3rd persons it was also secondary. Meid, in *Heth. und Idg.*, 167f., thinks that Hittite has not lost an optative; against, see Cowgill, ibid. 33; Strunk (below, 9.7.3).

[2] So first J. Schmidt, *KZ* 24, 1879, 303; 26, 1883, 12; cf. Kuryłowicz, *Categories* 141f.

[3] Meillet, *IF* 45, 1927, 45, ascribes this explanation to Wackernagel (*Vermischte Beiträge*, 1897, 45), but in fact (see Kretschmer, *Glotta* 18, 1930, 228f.) it goes back to Brugmann, see Curtius' *Studien* 9, 1876, 309f.; *BB* 2, 1878, 245f.; Paul, *PBB* 4, 1877, 378; Osthoff, *MU* 4, 1881, 302f. (**bheroi̯m̥*), and finally Benediktsson (n. 1 above), 38f., 51f.; on Dubois (-*οια* from *-oi-ə₂o*, after Watkins), see *HS* 102, 1990, 313. Concerning the so-called 'Aeolic optative' (*δείξειας*, *-ειε*, *-ειαν*), see K. Forbes, *Glotta* 37, 1958, 165–79; Kortlandt, *Fachtagung* 8, 1992, 235–9.

[4] Benediktsson (n. 1 above) 38: 1st s.; Bammesberger, *Studien zur Laryngaltheorie*, 1984, 115f.; cf. G. Schmidt, *Glotta* 63, 1985, 76f., 90.

[5] Meillet, *BSL* 32, 1931, 199, joined *oi* and *yē* in an original *-oyē-*, but Watkins (*Verb* 226f., esp. 234) has rejected this: according to him the element *-oi-* is not *-o + ī-*, but ultimately the 3rd s. (middle!) PE *-oi* of the indicative. The chief support of this view, however, the optative type *gamēma*, is not something old but a late innovation, see Insler, *Sprache* 21, 1975, 6–12; Lazzeroni (above, 9.3.1.1 n. 3), agrees with Insler that the type is an innovation (p. 131) and thinks (p. 136) that *dr̥šan*, interpreted as *dr̥š-a-n*, gave rise to *dr̥š-ē-t* on the analogy of *bhar-a-n*: *bhar-ē-t*. Cf. also Kuryłowicz, *Problèmes* 98; Bammesberger, *IIJ* 24, 1982, 283–7. Gunnarson, *NTS* 27, 1973, 44f., stresses that the *-oi* optative is limited to the eastern languages, but his attempt to explain away the Goth. optative with *-ai-* as a subjunctive in *-ē-* is unacceptable.

[6] Kuryłowicz, *Categories* 142f.

[7] See Hilmarsson, *NTS* 31, 1977, 198f.

[8] See Schmid, *IF* 68, 1963, 60f.; Stang, *Vgl. Gram.* 439; also Watkins, *Verb* 230 (but against, Kuryłowicz, *Problèmes* 98); Ivanov, *Glagol* 193f.; Bammesberger (n. 5 above).

9.3.1.3

An *ā-subjunctive* appears in Latin, Old Irish,[1] and Tocharian. To Lat. *feram*, *ferās*, *ferat* correspond OIr. *bera*, *berae*, *beraid*, both from **bher-ā-m*, *-ā-s(i)*, *-ā-t(i)*, etc., and Toch. A *-am*, *-at*, *-aṣ*, etc., e.g. *kalkam* 'eam'.[2]

The *ā*-subjunctive was long considered to be a past tense with modal use, cf. Lat. *eram*, *amā-bā-s*.[3] Trubetzkoy then pointed out that in Latin all IE subjunctives became futures (*eris*, *agēs*), and all Latin subjunctives, as far as their source can be established, come from IE optatives. From this he drew the conclusion that the *ā*-subjunctive also represents an original optative: in IE there would have been the optative in *-yē-*/*-ī-* for athematic verbs, for thematic verbs an optative in *-oi-* or *-ā-*, but hardly both in one and the same individual language.[4] A quarter of a century later Benveniste took up this idea and made the attempt to establish a connection with other formations in *-ā-*, especially past-tense forms like Lat. *erās*, *-bās*, by deriving the past formations from the original optative; examples of this can be found, cf. Eng. *he would get up early=he used to . . .*[5]

Against this it has rightly been pointed out that the *ā*-formations of Italic and Celtic cannot be separated from those of Balto-Slavic, nor the Latin *ē*-formations in the imperfect (and pluperfect) of the subjunctive (*es-s-ē-s*, *fuis-s-ē-s*) from the *ē*-formations of Balto-Slavic; then if all forms of the Latin subjunctive were old optatives, this would have to apply also to the *ē*-formations, but *ē*-optatives are not known in any language. From this it follows that the Latin formations in -*ā*- and -*ē*- (and the *a*-formations of Celtic), which must be equated with the Balto-Slavic formations in -*ā*- and -*ē*-, were, like them, formerly past tenses.[6] To use Kuryłowicz's formulation: the Latin *ā*-subjunctive, earlier optative, goes back to an aorist which is well attested in Balto-Slavic; the subjunctive use is the modal residue of this old aorist, whose characteristic sign, *ā* or *ē*, comes from old *sēṭ*-roots, and survives also in the Greek aorist in -*ην*.[7] If, however, the long vowel comes from the *sēṭ*-roots, then it can also have existed in the present and in the verb stem generally, as is shown by Tocharian, in which, as in Italic and Celtic, *ā*-subjunctive, *ā*-preterite, and *ā*-present are found side by side in the same system; Lat. *secās* (pres. indic.) and *tegās* (pres. subj.) are originally the same formation, and the same applies to -*bām*, the old preterite (**bhwā-m*) of 'to be'.[8]

The following picture therefore emerges for Latin. The IE subjunctive (*e*/*o* and *ē*/*ō*) became a future. Before this change, however, *s*-formations had given rise to thematic subjunctives, which provided the basis for the impf. and plupf. subj. The new pres. subj. was constructed partly from the IE optatives, partly from modally used *ā*-formations.[9] No evidence can be produced for an IE *ā*-optative.

Contrary to the efforts sketched above to bring various *ā*-forms together, in more recent times there have again been attempts to keep the different *ā*-formations separate from one another. Thus it is maintained that the Tocharian *ā*-formations are quite independent of the European, and that in Europe the Balto-Slavic preterite forms have nothing to do with the Italo-Celtic modal formations.[10]

1 Over a century ago Thurneysen (*BB* 8, 1884, 269–88) connected the *a*-subj. of Old Irish with the Lat. *ā*-subj. This old comparison has recently been rejected by Rix (*Idg. und Keltisch*, 151f.): the OIr. and Brit. *a*-subj. goes back to a desiderative in -*ase*- (<-*Hse*-), whereas the Lat. *ā*-subj. is derived from an aor. subj., e.g. *fuat* from **bhuwā-e*-. This explanation, according to McCone ('From IE to Old Irish', *PICCS* 7, 1986, 222–66) 'one of the most important insights of recent years into Celtic verbal morphology', must in his view also mean that the Irish *a*- and British *h*-subjunctive derive from a common source -*āse*- (rather than -*asā*-, 247f.), to the exclusion of Italic, and not the other way round, from agreement between Irish and Italic to the exclusion of British. Rix was partly supported by Kortlandt, *Ériu* 35, 1985, 182 f., but K. H. Schmidt, *ZCP* 41, 1986, 174 n. 40, pointed out that *Hse*>*ā* was in Celtic impossible since intervocalic *s* was still preserved in Gaulish (*lubias*). Bammesberger (*Ériu* 33, 1982, 65–72, and *Studien zur Laryngaltheorie*, 1984, 77–9) explained both the Latin and Old Irish formations as thematic subjunctives from *ā*-aorists, while Sandoz, *Latomus* 41, 1982, 766–70, equated the type *tulat* with Gr. *ἔτλāν*. For the remains in British, see Watkins, *Origins* 149f.; on Messapic *beran* (from -*ā-nt*), see Milewski, *Symbolae Kuryłowicz*, 1965, 209.

2 Krause and Thomas, *Tocharisches Elementarbuch* i, 1960, 226f.; K. T. Schmidt, *Fs. Neumann*, 1982, 366.

3 Leumann², 575.

4 Trubetzkoy, 'Gedanken über den lat. *ā*-Konj.', *Fs. Kretschmer*, 1926, 267–74.

5 Benveniste, 'Prétérit et optatif en indo-européen', *BSL* 47, 1951, 11–20; accepted by Watkins, *Origins* 118f. (cf. 151); *AIED* 41. On the use of the optative to express a repeated action in the past, see W. Neisser, *ZII* 5, 1927, 281–3; Pisani, *IF* 50, 1932, 21f.; Couvreur,

BSL 39, 1938, 247f.; Hoffmann, *Aufsätze* ii, 1976, 605–19; Lazard, 'La catégorie de l'éventuel', *Mél. Benveniste*, 1975, 347–58; Szemerényi, *Krat* 28, 1984, 76.

[6] Safarewicz, *Eos* 46, 1954, 102–5 (*ā*-aorist>plupf.>impf.; pret. often unreal).

[7] Kuryłowicz, *Apophonie* 35, 131 with n. 35; *Categories* 115, 137, 142. Cf. also Vaillant, *RES* 29, 1952, 120; Hahn, *Subunctive* 34–51; Stang, *Vgl. Gram.* 374f.; Rundgren, *Sprache* 12, 1967, 138f.

[8] See the important article by G. S. Lane, 'Tocharian evidence and the Trubetzkoy–Benveniste hypothesis', *Lg* 38, 1962, 245–53, now reprinted in *Studies in Honor of G. S. Lane*, 1967, 61–75 (but n. 27 he wrongly denies the existence of the subj. in IE); see further 82f., and cf. Thomas, *RPh* 82, 1956, 212; Ambrosini, *SSL* 2, 1962, 37f., 60f.; K. H. Schmidt, *SCelt* 1, 1966, 25; Negri, *Acme* 37/2, 1984, 31–9; Lazzeroni, *SSL* 24, 1984, 171–86: when the old *-t* was differentiated as *-ti/-t*, *-āti* became the pres, indic., *-āt* the pret. + inj.; the same happened with *-ēti/-ēt*, and the subj. *-ē-* is not from an IE subj. but belongs with the aoristic *-ē-*.

[9] For the unreal use (Plautus, *Miles* 1371: *si honeste censeam te facere posse, suadeam*) Romance provides good parallels; cf. Fr. *si j'avais faim* (see Lausberg, *Romanische Sprachwissenschaft* iii/2, 1962, 194f.); for wishes and commands, e.g. *eāmus*, cf. the Russian perfects used as imperatives: *pošli, pojexali* 'let us go/drive', *načali* 'let us start'; see Gvozdev, *Sovremennyj russkij literaturnij jazyk* i, 1958, 310; and for similar German usage (e.g. *aufgepasst!*); see Karin Donhauser, *Fs. K. Matzel*, 1984, 367–74.

[10] See Rix (n. 1 above), and again recently Jasanoff, *IF* 88, 1984, 75–82; K. T. Schmidt (n. 2 above), 362f., 366 (Toch. *ā*-subj. and *ā*-pret. to be kept apart); Oettinger, 'Zur Diskussion um den Lat. *ā*-Konj.', *Glotta* 62, 1985, 187–201, esp. 200f.: Tocharian is separate; between Italo-Celtic and Balto-Slavic the 'strong divergence in function and stem formation' cannot be overcome (modal pret.); for Italo-Celtic the theory that the *ā*-subj. had a common origin from the inj. or subj. of root aorists in *-ā* is again somewhat more plausible; Kortlandt, *Ériu* 35, 1985, 184: the comparison of the Old Irish *a*-subj. with the Latin *ā*-subj. is fallacious; similarly McCone (n. 1 above).

9.3.1.4

The *imperative* with its two forms, present imperative and future imperative, has already been dealt with in 9.2.5.

9.3.1.5

The *injunctive*,[1] which has already been mentioned a number of times, is a highly controversial subject. It is customary to use this term for the unaugmented imperfect or aorist indicative of Old Indic or Aryan when they have a modal function. This means that the injunctive is not formally independent, since the past tenses can also appear as such without augment, i.e. they are not necessarily to be taken as true injunctives even when they lack an augment. Because of this ambiguity of form and content the injunctive has often been rejected,[2] but in more recent times it has been taken up again by several scholars,[3] and K. Hoffmann has made a thorough investigation of it in a monograph.[4]

In the other IE languages there is nothing that corresponds to this mood; admittedly, it must be kept in mind that on this problem only Greek has any contribution to make, since it is in Greek alone that the augment (and the impf.) is preserved in a relevant form. If in the 2nd pl. of the pres. impv. a form in *-te* is used which is identical (in Aryan and Greek) with the unaugmented form of the 2nd pl. impf., we can speak at most of an IE, not of a Greek 'injunctive', since the imperative has become quite independent in Greek and the unaugmented form (when it really functions as such) can only be an imperfect. Against the view that the injunctive is a grammatical category like the indic., subj., etc.,[5] it cannot be emphasized too often that in the Indic system the injunctive is not an independent category;[6] one can at most bring together under this name certain uses of the old unaugmented preterite forms.

9.3.1.5.1

One of the best-known uses of the injunctive in Old Indic is with *mā* in prohibitions.[7] As A. Hahn recognized,[8] this usage rests on the modal, prohibitive force of the *particle*. The injunctive is not, however, used because something should be 'mentioned',[9] but because, in contrast to the use of the imperative in commands, prohibition is properly expressed by the particle *mā* alone, so that in the verb the zero mood, i.e. just the injunctive, is sufficient.[10] The Hittite prohibition with *lē* and indic. (not impv.) is comparable, e.g. *lē istamasti* 'hear not' in contrast to the command *istamas* 'hear', or the Accadian *lā taqabbi* 'do not say' with the present, thus an emphatic 'you do not say';[11] OInd. *mā tiṣṭhas* 'do not stay' may then have retained an old present form: 'you do not stay'. Since, however, prohibitions can also be expressed with past tense forms, as in the older Accadian usage *ā taqbi* 'do not say',[11] the injunctive may also have preserved an original past tense.

Attention should be paid, however, to Hoffmann's thesis that the meaning of a prohibitive sentence differs fundamentally according to the tense of the injunctive: *mā* with the present or perfect is 'inhibitive', i.e. the action is interrupted, *mā* with the aorist is 'preventive', i.e. an action 'already in preparation' is not to be permitted, is to be avoided. According to Hoffmann, the tenses also express aspect—the aor. inj. the perfective, the pres. inj. the imperfective. According to Meid, the Vedic distinction, inherited from IE, is reflected in Old Irish also: *na* with impv. is inhibitive, *ni* with pres. subj. is preventive.[12]

9.3.1.5.2

In this connection it is a particularly important feature of the injunctive that it can take over and replace any mood. Cf., for instance, from the Rigveda:

(*a*) x.80, 1: *dadāti . . . čarat* '(Agni) gives . . . wanders (pres.).
(*b*) i.42, 7: *kṛṇu . . . vidas* 'make . . . find' (impv.).
(*c*) vi.40, 4: *śṛṇava(s) . . . dhāt* 'thou shalt hear . . . it shall give' (subj.).

(*d*) ii.33, 14: *parivṛ̥jyās . . . parigāt* 'may it pass by . . . may it avoid us' (prec.).

As Kiparsky has seen, such cases exemplify a 'conjunction-reduction', which he was the first to observe: verbal marks can be replaced by neutral forms when they have already been precisely expressed, and the neutral form is in fact the injunctive.[13] In descriptive terms this meant originally that a sequence of present indicatives *-ti . . . -ti . . . -ti* could become *-ti . . . -t . . . -t* and imperatives *-tu . . . -tu . . . -tu* could become *-tu . . . -t . . . -t*, etc., whereby a residual form arose which permitted the most varied uses. The important point is that after prohibitive sentences with *mā* this use takes in the second largest group of injunctives.

The third group is motivated by the subject matter—its mythological or ritual content.[14]

Thus the injunctive cannot be recognized as a special mood for Indo-European, still less for an individual language.[15] Even in late IE the 'injunctive' was something left over from a period in which the form **bheret* still existed as an indefinite variant alongside the more definite **bhereti*. Imperative forms like OInd. *bharat-u bharant-u* are likewise remnants; see 9.2.5 above.[16]

[1] See above 9.2.5.The term was coined by Brugmann, *MU* 3, 1880, 2; cf. Herbig, *IF* 6, 1896, 247.

[2] Esp. forcefully by A. Hahn, *Subjunctive* 38f., 44f. ('fantastic concept . . . should be definitely discarded'); cf. also Benveniste, *BSL* 51/2, 1956, 26.

[3] Kuryłowicz, *RO* 3, 1927, 164–79; Renou, 'Les formes dites d'injonctif', *Étrennes Benveniste*, 1928, 63–80; Burrow, *The Sanskrit Language*, 1955, 298; Gonda, *Moods* 33f.; Thomas, *RPh* 82, 1956, 216f.; *REA* 63, 1961, 91f.; Watkins, *Celtica* 6, 1962, 45f.; *Origins* 111f.; Meid, *Die idg. Grundlagen der air. abs. und conj. Verbalflexion*, 1963, 89f.; Kuryłowicz, *Categories* 145, 152; see also Campanile, *AION-L* 8, 1968, 41f.; Meid, *Scottish Studies* 12, 1968, 53f.; Ivanov, *Glagol* 34f.

[4] K. Hoffmann, *Der Inj. im Veda*, 1967 (see the reviews by Cardona, *Krat* 15, 1972, 47–51, and W. Thomas, *OLZ* 68, 1973, 75–84); *MSS* 28, 1970, 32f. On his suggestions, see Dressler, *KZ* 85, 1971, 7: 'K. H. reconstructs as basic function . . . "mention" in contrast to "report". His thesis would have been still more convincing, if he had adduced a parallel from a living language'. Cf. further Kuryłowicz, *Problèmes* 107f.

[5] Hoffmann, *Injunktiv* 35; Gonda, *Old Indian*, 1971, 103f., esp. 105 (old and inherited formations); Lazzeroni, *SSL* 17, 1977, 20f. (le forme micenee ed omeriche senza aumento sono degli ingiuntivi), 28f. (line of development); *SSL* 20, 1980, 29f.

[6] Cf. C. D. Buck, *Comparative Grammar of Greek and Latin*, 1933, 238: 'one must guard against supposing that this is a distinct formal category, coordinate with the other moods'.

[7] On this, see V. Georgiev, *Das Verbot im Gr., Lat., Bulg., Ai. und der Inj.*, Sofia 1935; Schwyzer, *GG* ii, 343; Gonda, *Moods* 44f., 197f.; *The Aspectual Functions of the Rgvedic Present and Aorist*, 1962, 184f.; Moorhouse, *Studies in the Greek Negative*, 1959, 12f.; Rundgren, *Erneuerung des Verbalaspekts im Semitischen*, 1963, 92f.; Kuryłowicz, *Categories* 146f.; Hoffmann, *Injunktiv*, 43f.; M. L. West, 'An unrecognized injunctive usage in Greek', *Glotta* 67, 1989, 135–8. This is the only use that Meillet mentions, *Introduction* 247. On the disputed connection with the prohibitive constructions of the classical languages, see Hofmann—Szantyr 337, 456.

[8] Hahn, *Subjunctive* 41f., 54f.; *Lg* 29, 1953, 252f.

[9] Hoffmann, *Injunktiv* 106.

[10] P. Kiparsky, 'Tense and Mood in IE syntax' (*FL* 4, 1968, 30–57), 48. Against: W. Thomas, *Hist. Präs. oder Konjunktionsreduktion*, Wiesbaden 1974, 21f., 62; Lazzeroni, *SSL* 17, 1–30, esp. 12 (ingiuntivo non sempre in 2. o ulteriore sede); and Tristram, *Tense and Time in Early Irish Narrative*, Innsbruck 1983, 8f., 31f.

[11] A somewhat different account in Rundgren (n. 7 above), 96.

[12] See Hoffmann, *Injunktiv* 43f.; Meid, *ZCP* 1962, 155–72, and *CTL* ix, 1972, 1196. On this, see further W. Thomas, 'Zum Problem des Prohibitivsatzes im Indogermanischen', *Fs. H. Patzer*, 1975, 307–23; 'Indogermanisches in der Syntax des Tocharischen: Zum Ausdruck eines Gebotes und Verbotes', in *Fs. der Wissenschaftlichen Gesellschaft an der J. W. Goethe-Universität*, 1981, 481–97; *Krat* 28, 1984, 59–60.

[13] Kiparsky (n. 10 above), 34f.

[14] Ibid. 37.

[15] According to Watkins, *Verb* 45, it is 'not an Indo-European but an Indo-Iranian category'. Similarly Kammenhuber, *Fs. Winter*, 1985, 444f., esp. 447: 'hardly a fully developed PIE inj. category . . . The inj. has accordingly expanded in Vedic'. An injunctive is still accepted for IE by Neu, in *Studies Polomé*, 1988, 466f.

[16] This conclusion now appears also in Lazzeroni, *SSL* 17, 28f. On the views of Wright ('The so-called injunctive', *BSOAS* 33, 1970, 184–99), see Gonda, *Old Indian*, 103 n. 6.

9.4. TENSE STEMS

All IE languages show in the indicative, and for the most part also in the other moods, a variety of formations which are usually referred to as *tenses*. Thus Latin distinguishes six tenses in the indicative, four in the subjunctive; only two in the imperative, though a perfect impv. form still survives in *mementō(te)*. In Latin all tenses fall into two main divisions, those of incomplete and those of completed action (*actio infecta/actio perfecta*); the latter usually and the former very often are characterized by special features; cf. *amā– amā–u-*, *pungō pupugī* etc. On the basis of such formal criteria at least three tense stems can be distinguished, from which additional indicative tenses and also modal forms can be constructed.

9.4.1. Present formations

The IE languages show a number of present formations[1] which for the most part can be clearly understood only in their formal aspect. They can have athematic or thematic inflexion and admit either a single voice (*activa tantum*, *media tantum*) or both. They can consist of the root without further addition or derive new present stems from verbal stems (*deverbatives*) or nominal stems (*denominatives*) by means of formative elements, e.g. Lat. deverb. *spec-iō* and denom. *custōd-iō*;[2] to these in recent times have been added *delocutives*, i.e. derivatives from verbal expressions, such as *salutāre* from *salūtem dīcō*.[3] The varied origin of verbs plays no part in their use.

[1] Cf. Brugmann, *Grundriss*², ii/3, 86f.; Meillet, *Introduction* 195: Meillet–Vendryes, 173f.; Leumann², 521f.; Schwyzer, *GG* i, 672f.; Bader, 'Hittite duratives and the problem of IE present formations with infix and suffix', *JIES* 15, 1987, 121–56.

[2] Schwyzer, *GG* i, 717f., 722f.

[3] Debrunner, *Fs. Vasmer*, 1956, 113–23; Benveniste, *Fs. Spitzer*, 1958, 57–63; Colaclidès, *Glotta* 49, 1971, 93; Rey-Debove, 'Les verbes délocutifs', *TLL* 13/1, 1975, 245–51 ('dénominatifs', non 'délocutifs'); Brekle, *Sprachwissenschaft* 1, 1976, 357–78; 'Delokutive Verben', in *10. Ling. Kolloquium (Tübingen)* ii, 1975, 69–76; Leumann², 547; Dixon, *Fs. Lehmann*, 1977, 21–38; Szemerényi, '*šam* . . .', *InL* 4, 1978, 171 (on *iūrāre*), 182 n. 78; Darms, 'Problèmes de la formation *délocutive*', *MH* 37, 1980, 201–11; Mignot, *BSL* 76, 1982, 327–44 (on *salutāre*); 'Y a-t-il des verbes délocutives en latin?' in Touratier (ed.), *Syntaxe et latin*, 1985, 505–12; M.-E. Conte, in *É. Benveniste aujourd'hui* i, 1984, 65–7; an especially fine example is Goth. *waifairhvjan* 'lament' (=OHG *wēferhen*) from *wai fairhvau* 'woe to the world', see Meid, *Fs. K. Oberhuber*, Innsbruck 1986, 168. Note also Dunkel, in *In Memory of W. Cowgill*, 1987, 32: *negō* not from *nec* (Benveniste), but *ne ego*.

9.4.1.1. *Root formations.* Root formations can also function as present stems, both (*a*) athematic and (*b*) thematic. Examples for (*a*):

**es-mi* 'I am': OInd. *asmi*, Gr. εἰμί, Goth. *im*, etc.;
**ei-mi* 'I go': OInd. *ēmi*, Gr. εἶμι, Lat. *īmus* from **ei-mos*, etc.;
**kei-* 'lie': Gr. κεῖ-μαι, Hitt. 3rd s. *kita(ri)*, OInd. *śē-tē*;
**ēs-* 'sit': Gr. ἧσ-ται, OInd. *ās-tē*, Hitt. 3rd s. *es-a(ri)*.

The root can, of course, be disyllabic (5.3.5). In that case it usually takes the form *CeCə-* in the present stem, cf. OInd. *vámi-ti* 'vomits', *áni-ti* 'breathes'. While this type does not survive in other languages in the active (cf. the thematic modifications of **wemə-* in Gr. (ϝ)εμέω and Lat. *uomō*), it is still represented in the Greek middle, cf. ἔρα-μαι 'I love', κρέμα-μαι 'I hang', etc.[1]

Examples for (*b*) are, first, those with accented and consequently full-grade root syllable:

**bhérō*: Gr. φέρω, Lat. *ferō*, OInd. *bharāmi*, etc.;[2]
**sérpō* 'I creep': Gr. ἕρπω, Lat. *serpō*, OInd. *sarpāmi*;

secondly, those with accent on the thematic vowel and consequently zero grade in the root syllable:

**glubhō* in γλύφω 'carve, hollow out' beside **gléubhō* in Lat. *glūbō* 'pare', OHG *klioban* 'split', Eng. *cleave*;
**gr̥bhō* in γράφω 'write' (orig. 'scratch') beside **gerbhō* in MHG *kerben*, OE *ceorfan*, NE *carve*.

This type, usually called the *tudáti* type (OInd. *tudáti* 'strikes' cf. Lat. *tundō tutudī*) is very rare, as it is generally used for the thematic aorist, e.g. Gr. ἔφυγον 'I fled'.[3]

[1] Cf. Schwyzer, *GG* i, 680f.; Szemerényi, *SMEA* 3, 1967, 82f., and *Fs. Risch*, 1986, 441 (ἐρέω 'I row'). The ablaut *e/a* in the Hitt. present (e.g. *epp-/app-* 'seize') is according to Kammenhuber (*KZ* 94, 1980, 36) IE *ē/ə*; see further below, 9.4.3 n. 28. On Slav. *damĭ*, see Kořínek, *Listy filologické* 65, 1938, 445f.; Szemerényi, *Études Slaves et Roumaines (Budapest)* 1, 1948, 7–12 (IE **dō-mi*, not reduplicated **di-dō-*); Kuryłowicz, *To Honor R. Jakobson*, 1967, 1127f.; Bammesberger, *IF* 87, 1983, 239f.; Smoczyński, 'On the Balto-Slavic present stems in *-dō*', *MSS* 48, 1987, 197–212; *Studia balto-słowiańskie* i, Wrocław 1989, 16–18.

[2] On the IE age of this form, see Szemerényi, *Syncope* 189f.; note also Lazzeroni, *SSL* 27,

1987, 147 (old subjunctives 'passati a significare l'indicativo'); and esp. A. Lehrman, *Simple Thematic Imperfectives in Anatolian and IE*, diss., Yale, 1985, with the conclusion (pp. 232–65) that Anatolian has no simple thematic stems, this class is an IE (=extra-Anatolian) innovation, an argument (p. 264) in favour of the Indo-Hittite hypothesis.

[3] Schwyzer, *GG* i, 683; Kuryłowicz, *Categories* 116; Watkins, *Verb* 63; Lazzeroni, *SSL* 18, 1978, 129–48; 27, 1987, 136. On this type in OE, see Seebold, *Anglia* 84, 1966, 1–26; Bammesberger, *KZ* 87, 1973, 272f., and for Proto-Germanic in J. Untermann and B. Brogyanyi (eds.), *Das Germanische und die Rekonstruktion der idg. Grundsprache*, 1984, 1–24. According to Benveniste, *Origines* 167, this type is always derived from nouns.

ADDENDUM. In some cases the *o*-grade seems to occur, cf. Goth. *mala*, Lith. *malù* 'grind'; from this the existence of *o*-grade thematic and even athematic IE presents has been inferred; see Meillet, *Introduction* 203; Hiersche, *IF* 68 (1963), 149–59. It is striking, however, that in several such cases other grades appear alongside the *o*-grade (cf. OIr. *melim*, OCS *meljǫ*), and in particular that in most cases a labial precedes or follows; see Szemerényi, *SMEA* 1 (1966), 45f., esp. n. 74.[1]

[1] See further Meillet, *MSL* 19, 1916, 181–92; Beekes, *Laryngeals* 131, and also 28f., 40f., 58f.; Jasanoff, in *Heth. und Idg.*, 84f.; Lindeman, *HS* 102, 1990, 277 (references to Meid, Hiersche, Stang). Meid, *Präteritum* 65f., thinks that the *o*-grade presents have been remodelled from perfects; on this cf. Vaillant's explanation of *bojati* (below, 9.4.3. n. 18).

9.4.1.2. *Reduplicated formations.* The main characteristic of this kind of formation is the repetition of the root, which may be *total* or *symbolic*.[1] In total reduplication the whole root is repeated, e.g. OInd. *dar-dar-ti* 'bursts, splits', Gr. μαρμαίρω 'gleam' from **mar-mar-yō*, πορφύρω 'surge, be in turmoil' from φυρ-φυρ- with dissimilation, OCS *glagolati* 'speak' from **gal-gal*; sometimes an *i* is inserted: OInd. 3rd s. *bhar-ī-bhar-ti*, 3rd pl. *bhar-i-bhr-ati* 'carry continually', where the interchange of *ī* and *i* is clearly determined by rhythmic factors.[2] In symbolic reduplication, on the other hand, only part of the root is repeated; for the different possibilities cf. OInd. *var-vart-(t)i* 'turns', *dē-diš-* 'show' from **dei-dik-*, *rō-ruč-āna-* 'shining' from **leu-luk-*.

The most common form of symbolic reduplication is the repetition of the initial phoneme(s). Only this type of reduplication seems to have been 'grammaticized' in IE, and it will be referred to here simply as reduplication.

In reduplication as a rule the initial consonant appears with *i* before the root:[3] OInd. *bi-bhar-* 'carry', Lat. *gi-gnō*. In the case of an initial consonant group the first consonant only is usually repeated: Gr. ἀπο-δι-δρά-σκω 'run away'. However, in the case of initial *s*+stop the whole group seems originally to have been repeated, but this led in most languages to dissimilation; cf. **stā-*, reduplicated **sti-st-*: Lat. *sistō*, Gr. ἵστᾱμι (from **si-st-*), but OInd. *tiṣṭh-*.[4] For initial vowel cf. Gr. ἰ-άλλω 'send', OInd. *iy-ar-ti* 'sets in motion'; with this type *total* (*intensive*) reduplication often occurs, in which the vowel and first consonant are repeated, e.g. *ἀρ-αρ-ίσκω* 'join', OInd. *ar-ar-ti* 'moves'.[5]

On the semantic side, a sense of repetition or intensity was doubtless connected originally with reduplication in general. In the historical languages, however, this is so only in the case of total or almost total reduplication, as in the OInd. intensives; in grammatical reduplication this shade of meaning is not observable.[6]

Reduplicated present formations can again be athematic or thematic. Examples of the first type:

**dhi-dhē-mi* 'I put': Gr. *τίθημι*, Lat. *crēdō* from **kret-dhidhō*;[7]
**di-dō-mi* 'I give': Gr. *δίδωμι*, Vestinian *didet* 'dat', presumably also Lat. *reddō* from **re(d)didō*;
**sti-stā-mi* 'I set up': Gr. *ἵστᾱμι*; cf. Bader, *BSL* 81/2, 1986, 129–32.
**ghi-ghē-ti* 'leaves, goes': Gr. **κίχημι*, OInd. *ji-hī-tē*, cf. OHG *gān*;
**bhi-bher-ti* 'carries': OInd. *bi-bhar-ti*.

Examples of thematic forms:

**sti-st-ō*: Lat. *sistō*, OInd. *tiṣṭhāmi*;
**pi-b-e-ti* 'drinks': OInd. *pibati*, Lat. *bibit*, OIr. *ibid* (6.4.4.1 above);
**si-zd-ō* 'I set down, sit': Lat. *sīdō*, OInd. *sīdati*, Gr. *ἵζω*;
**si-s-ō* 'I throw, sow': Lat. *serō*, perhaps Hitt. *sissa-*.[8]
**i-aw-ō* 'I help': Lat. **i-ewo*, *iouō*, *iuuō*; see Szemerényi, *TPS* 1950, 178 (=*SM* 600), citing Specht, cf. Schlerath, *KZ* 100, 1987, 216.
**H_2i-H_2g-ō* 'I drive': OInd. *īǰatē*; Strunk, in Bammesberger 1988, 565f.

1 On reduplication in general: Brugmann, *Grundriss*², ii/3, 20f.; Vendryes, *MSL* 20, 1916, 117–23; Meillet–Vendryes, 235; Pisani, 'Sul raddoppiamento indoeuropeo', *RAL* 6/2, 1926, 321–37; Hirt, *IG* iv, 1928, 6–15; Meillet, *Introduction* 179–82; Schwyzer, *GG* i, 646f.; ii, 260; Ambrosini, 'Ricerche ittite', *ASNP* 28, 1959, 285–92; N. van Brock, 'Les thèmes verbaux à redoublement du hittite et le verbe i-e.', *RHA* 75, 1964, 119–65; Kronasser, *Etymologie* 569; L. Herlands Hornstein, *Studies J. A. Kerns*, 1970, 59–64; Dressler, *KZ* 85, 1971, 14f.; Heller, *Word* 22, 1973, 303–9; Tischler, *Zur Reduplikation im Idg.*, Innsbruck 1976; Strunk, 'Einige reduplizierte Verbalstämme', in Bammesberger 1988, 563–82; Meier-Brügger, *KZ* 100, 1988, 313–22; Giannakis, *Glotta* 69, 1991, 48–76 (*μίμνω* etc.).

2 Beekes, 'The disyllabic reduplication of Skt. intensives', *MSS* 40, 1981, 19–25 (from roots with initial group *HC-*); but cf. also Hitt. *takku-takkuwa-*.

3 Original *i*-vocalism for presents is accepted by Leumann (above, 9.2.2.2, n. 1), 27, 44f., as earlier by Brugmann, *Grundriss*², ii/3, 104. That IE had only **didōmi* is disputed by Schwyzer, *GG* i, 648; Emeneau, *Lg* 34, 1958, 409f.; Cowgill, *Lg* 40, 1964, 346 n. 21; Insler, *IF* 73, 1968, 64 n. 8. Nevertheless *i*-reduplication must already have been established for presents in IE; the *e*-reduplication was confined to the aorist (Kuryłowicz, *Categories* 119) and perfect. But *e*-reduplication is proved for an earlier period by OInd. *ǰagat* 'world' (later pres. *ǰigāti*); see Narten, in *India Maior: Congrat. Vol. Gonda*, 1972, 161–6; and Bech, *Idg. Verbalmorphologie*, 1972, 52, 63. Cf. also Rasmussen, *APILKU* 7, 1988, 125–42 (on *i/e*); Melchert, *HS* 101, 1989, 220 (*i*-redupl. 'probably old', *e*-redupl. 'may be as well'; *a*-redupl. must be an innovation).

4 See Meillet, 'Sur des formes à redoublement', *Mél. Havet*, 1909, 263–78; Brugmann, *IF* 31, 1913, 89–94.

[5] This should not be called *Attic reduplication* (so e.g. Schwyzer, *GG* i, 647, for ὀρορ-, ἀγαγ-); the term should remain confined to the perfect type ἔδηδα, ἐλήλουθα (so also Rix 1976, 204), on which see further below, 9.4.3 *b* with n. 11.

For intensive reduplication (cf. Rix 1976, 205) Anatolian provides interesting parallels, e.g. 3rd s. pres. *el-elhaiti*, but 3rd s. impv. *elhadu*; see Watkins, *Fachtagung* 5, 1975, 372, and much earlier Forrer, *SPAW* 1919, 1035; *ZDMG* 76, 1922, 221; also Laroche, *Dict. de la langue louvite*, 1959, 36; we can now add *as-es-* 'settle', *hul-huliya-* 'fight', Risch, 'Die Ausbildung des Griechischen im 2. Jahrtausend', in *Reinisch-Westfäl. Akad. Abh.* 72, 1984, 183 n. 36 (thus perhaps not a Greek innovation).

[6] Vendryes, *MSL* 20, 1916, 117f., ascribed an 'aspect déterminé' to the reduplicated presents; see Schwyzer, *GG* i, 690, where the suggestion of a causative meaning is also discussed (more recently Kronasser, *Etymologie* 571–2); for this the examples are insufficient. Brock (n. 1 above), 147f., returns to an iterative meaning.

[7] Szemerényi, *ArchL* 4, 1952, 49; Serbat, *RPh* 42, 1968, 86. OIr. *íad-* 'shut' represents an IE **epi-dhi-dhə-* 'put on/to'—see Hamp, *Ériu* 24, 1973, 163; for a Gmc. **dedō*, see Lühr, in Untermann and Brogyanyi (above, 9.4.1.1 n. 3), 39f.

[8] See Laroche, *BSL* 58, 1963, 75; K. H. Schmidt, *BBCS* 26, 1976, 388: Hispano-Celtic *sisonti* 'they send off'.

9.4.1.3. *Nasal formations.* Most IE languages have a formation in which a nasal, at first only 'infixed' in the root but later also suffixed, serves to form a present from the verbal stem. The earliest types are best preserved in Old Indic, and in examining the types in the other languages the situation in Old Indic must be taken as guide.[1]

In their ten-class system of present formations, the Old Indic grammarians assigned a class each to the three nasal formations. The seventh class is illustrated by the present formation of the root *yuǰ-* 'join', which shows ablaut:

1 **yunáǰ-mi*, 2 *yunák-ṣi*, 3 *yunák-ti*—4 *yuñǰ-más*, 5 *yuṅk-thá*, 6 *yuñǰ-ánti*. Cf. also *bhid-* 'split': 3 *bhinát-ti*—6 *bhind-ánti*; *čhid-* 'cut off': 3 *čhinát-ti*—6 *čhind-ánti*.

In all these forms it looks as if the element *na*[2] had been infixed in the zero-grade root (*yuǰ-*, *bhid-*, etc.), giving *yu-na-ǰ-*, *bhi-na-d-*, and outside the singular this had become *n* (*yu-ñ-ǰ-*, *bhi-n-d-*). The resulting present stem has athematic inflexion.

A similar structure is to be observed in the OInd. fifth class:

šru- 'hear': 3 *šr̥ṇōti*—4 *šr̥ṇumás*, 6 *šr̥ṇuvánti*;

and in the ninth class:

krī- 'buy': 3 *krīṇāti*—4 *krīṇīmás*, 6 *krīṇánti*.

We owe to Saussure the recognition that *šr̥ṇō-* arose from *šru-* in the same way as *bhinad-* from *bhid-*, namely as *šr̥-ṇa-u-*. The situation is somewhat more complicated in the ninth class, but here too he suggests that *punāmi* 'I clean' and *pavatē* 'he cleans', *pūta-* 'clean' (adj.), from **pew(ə)-etoi* and **puə-to-* respectively (see 5.3.5), show the same relation in that *punā-* arose from **pu-na-ə*, with *a-ə* becoming *ā*. The three kinds of formation are thus completely parallel; transformed into Indo-European we have:

**yeug-/yug-*	**kleu-/klu-*	**pewə-/puə-*
**yuneg-/yung-*	**kl̥neu-/kl̥nu-*	**puneə-/punə-*.

Of these three types, only one is preserved without change in Greek, that of the OInd. ninth class.[3] Cf.

1 δάμνᾱμι, 3 δάμνᾱσι—4 δάμνᾰμεν, 5 δάμνᾰτε;

in Homer (with ᾱ>η) δάμνημι δάμνησι

The type of the OInd. fifth class was to some extent refashioned:

1 δείκνῡμι	4 δείκνῠμεν
2 δείκνῡς	5 δείκνῠτε
3 δείκνῡσι	6 δεικνύᾱσι;

the ablaut νῡ/νῠ was modified from *neu*/*nu* on the analogy of νᾱ/νᾰ.

The type of the OInd. seventh class is nowhere preserved with certainty outside Aryan; one possible exception is Hittite.[4]

Alongside these three athematic types there are the corresponding thematic variants. Skt. *bhinatti* becomes in Pāli the thematic *bhindati*, and only *findō* is found in Latin; to OInd. *yunakti* corresponds Lat. *iungit*, to athem. *riṇakti* 'leaves, gives up', Lat. *linquit*. Often in Aryan quite early only the thematic formation is in use, cf. OInd. *siñčati*, Avest, *hinčaiti* 'pours out', as opposed to OInd. them. *vindati*, Avest. athem. *vinasti* (from *-ad-ti*) 'finds'. The transfer to thematic inflexion presumably started from the 3rd pl. in *-onti*, which though athematic could also be seen as thematic, and in some cases as early as the IE period, cf. Lat. *rumpō*=OInd. *lumpāmi* 'break'[5].

The clearly characterized final parts *-nā-* and *-neu-*, in which originally only *n* or *ne* was the formative element, came increasingly to be used as unitary suffixes[6], as in Lat. *asper-nā-ri conster-nā-ri*,[7] OInd. *badh-nā-ti* 'binds', or Lat. *sternuō*, Gr. ζεύγνῡμι.[8] The thematized forms *-n(ə)-o-* and *-nw-o-* also gained ground; cf. Gr. τίνω 'pay' from *τινϝω; to *-n(ə)o-* were added suffixal *-no-* and *-n̥o-*, e.g. θηγάνω 'whet'.[9] In all IE languages the originally athematic formations with nasal infix[10] were gradually replaced by thematic (often suffixed) nasal formations.[11]

[1] Cf. Schwyzer, *GG* i, 690f.; Specht, *Ursprung* 283f.; Kronasser, *Die Nasalpräsentia und Kretschmers objective Konjugation im Idg.*, 1960; Puhvel, *Laryngeals and the IE Verb*, 1960, 14f.; Erhart, 'Bemerkungen zum Nasalinfix im Slavischen', *Sbornik Brno* A/12, 1964, 59f.; Ivanov, *Obščeind.* 175f.; Kronasser, *Etymologie* 432f.; Strunk, *Nasalpräsentien und Aoriste*, 1967, and the works cited in n. 3 below; Otkupščikov, *Iz istorii ie. slovoobrazovanija*, 1967, 96–106 (all *n*-formations are denominative); Lindeman, 'Bemerkungen zu den germ. Nasalverben', *NTS* 22, 1968, 83–90; M. García Teijeiro, *Los presentes ie. con infijo nasal y su evolución*, Salamanca 1970; Jasanoff, *Lg* 49, 1973, 866 (on the Gmc. variants *-nō-*, *-ni-*, *-nai-*); Rix 1976, 209f.; Bader, *BSL* 74, 1979, 191–235 (*nu*-verbs); Strunk, *InL* 5, 1980, 85–102;

'Réflexions sur l'infixe nasal', in *É. Benveniste aujourd'hui* ii, 1984, 151–60; Rasmussen, 'The IE background of the Slavic nasal-infix presents', *APILKU* 7, 1988, 185–94; on Old Irish, McCone 1991; G. Meiser, 'Funktion des Nasalpräsens im Uridg.', *Fs. Rix*, 1993, 280–314.

On the origin of the infixes, see R. Ultan, 'Infixes and their origins', in Seiler (ed.), *Linguistic Workshop* iii, 1975, 157–205. Since only *n* appears as an infix (*m* only before labials), it is not impossible that it arose through the resolution of an emphatic consonant in certain common verbs, for instance **yungō*, **rumpō* from **yuggō*, **ruppō*, then spread further and even produced a secondary full grade *VneH* to *VnH*; Lat. *iungō* certainly cannot be traced with Bader (*Word* 24, 1970, 29 n. 69) to an impossible IE **yunegō*. On the infix, see further n. 10 below.

[2] IE *ne/n* is assumed by Saussure, *Recueil* 224; Specht, *KZ* 59, 1932, 82; Cowgill, *Lg* 39, 1963, 252. Simple *n*, on the other hand, is supported by Hirt, *Die idg. Ablaut*, 1900, 46, 138f.; *IG* iv, 1928, 198f.; Benveniste, *Origines* 159f.; Strunk, *Nas.* 26. Benveniste supposes that the nasal is infixed in his 'thème II', i.e. not in **yug-*, but in **yweg-*; against this Cowgill, loc. cit. Rasmussen, *Wackernagel Kolloquium*, 1990, 188–201, derives the infix from a suffix by metathesis (e.g. the various stages of the way from **leik^{w}-n-* to **linek^{w}-*, 194), and discusses some changes in the nasal formants.

[3] On the OInd. seventh class, see Brugmann, *MU* 3, 1880; 143–58, and now also Strunk, *KZ* 83, 1970, 216–26 (cf. Szemerényi, *Gn* 44, 1972, 507); *IF* 78, 1973, 51–74; against, Lazzeroni, *SSL* 20, 1980, 47, and Viredaz, Hart (n. 4 below). On the OInd. eighth class (*tanoti*), see Strunk, *Nas.* 72f.; against, Beekes, *Laryngeals* 279.

[4] On Hittite, see N. van Brock, 'Thèmes verbaux à nasale infixée en hittite', *RHA* 70, 1962, 31–6; Kronasser, *Etymologie* 432f.; Lindeman, *BSL* 71, 1976, 114f.; Viredaz, ibid. 165–73; Hart, *ArchL* 8, 133–41; Oettinger, *Stammbildung* 135–41; Strunk, in *Heth. und Idg.*, 237–56 (Hitt. *hunek* ~ *OInd. yunaǰ-*); Puhvel, *KZ* 100, 1987, 238–42.

[5] So Strunk, *Nas.* 32f.

[6] Kuryłowicz, *Categories* 107f.

[7] Against Meillet's thesis (e.g. *Mél. Vendryes*, 1925, 275–85; *Introduction* 217; still accepted by Stang, *Vgl. Gram.* 323) that only *-nā-* existed in IE, more recent research has shown that there were also presents in *-nē-* and *-nō*: see Cowgill, *Lg* 39, 251; Strunk, *Nas.* 53f.; Beekes, *Laryngeals* 250f.; Rix, *MSS* 27, 1970, 94; Campanile, *SCO* 32, 1982, 285–9 (against Wackernagel's **βάλλημι* **ὄμνωμι*, but in favour of a new equation: *εἰλέω* 'turn' ~ OIr. *fillim*, both from **wel-nē-*); Bammesberger 1984, 20–6, 87–90; Lindeman, *SCelt* 26–7, 1993, 1–2, 5 n. 3.

Sandoz, *BSL* 69, 1974, 55–61, even supposes a type in *-nei-/-ni-*, with which he thinks he can throw light on the still unclear ablaut of OInd. *nā/nī*, but on this a quite different opinion is held by e.g. Kuryłowicz, *Apophonie* 259; *BPTJ* 21, 1962, 97 n. 3; *IG* 230; or Schmalstieg, *KZ* 85, 1973, 127f., and Rasmussen (n. 1 above). On the root formation of Greek verbs like *κίρνᾱμι*, see Szemerényi, *Webster Memorial*, Bristol 1986, 225–30 (=*SM* 1524–29). On the difficulties presented by *πίνω*, Lat. *bibō*, *pōtāre*, OInd. *pibati*, Slav. *piti*, etc., see Szemerényi, *Krat* 28, 1984, 74f. (=*SM* 569).

[8] The supposition that *nu* also arose from *nA^{w}* (so e.g. Martinet, Puhvel, and García Teijeiro, n. 1 above, 84) seems to me unfounded; so also Cowgill, *Lg* 39, 249f., esp. 253f.; Strunk, *Nas.* 112. On the other hand, it has also been supposed that in some cases *-νυ-* arose in Greek from *-νο-* and an original alternation *-νω-/-νο-* led to *-νω-/-νυ-* and finally to *-νῡ-/-νῠ-*; cf. Cowgill, op. cit. 256; Rix 1976, 210. Merlingen, *Laryngaltheorie und Laryngale*, Vienna 1983, 119, thinks that the infix *-nu-* was really identical with the adverb **nu* 'now', so that for instance **su-nu-mes* meant nothing else than 'we *now* press out'.

[9] On *-ano-* see Kuryłowicz, *Apophonie* 173; Watkins, *Fachtagung* 5, 1975, 377f.

[10] The nasal infixes were originally (in part? see n. 1 above) nasal suffixes; a root **yeu-* had an extension **yeu-n-* and both of these could be extended with a determinative *-eg-*: the forms **yéu-eg-* and **yeu-n-ég-* gave **yeug-* and **yunég-* respectively. Cf. Brugmann, *Grundriss*[2], ii/3, 274; Schwyzer, *GG* i, 691;; Kuryłowicz, *Categories* 106. Watkins, *Verb* 24, thinks that the problem can be solved with a *transform rule*, *CCeCn->CCneC-*.

[11] For the deverbative type OInd. *gṛbhāyati*, see further below, 9.4.1.5 n. 3.

9.4.1.4. -sk- *formations*. A well-characterized suffix *-sk-* is common Indo-European.[1] In many languages it continues to be productive, while in others only traces of it remain. It is found only in the thematic form and consequently with zero grade of the root,[2] e.g.:

**pr̥k-sk-ō* 'ask': OInd. *pr̥ččhāmi*, Lat. *poscō* (from **porskō*), OIr. *arco*, OHG *forscōn* 'search' (from the noun *forsca*);

**gʷm̥-sk-ō* 'go': OInd. *gaččhāmi*, Gr. *βάσκω*.

Other grades were introduced presumably by analogy from other forms, e.g.:

**gnō-sk-ō* 'know': Lat. *(g)nōscō*, Gr. (Epirote) *γνώσκω*, OPers. *xšnā-s-ātiy* 'noscat'.

Likewise, only one formative process can originally have been applicable; a formation like Gr. *γιγ-νώ-σκω*, with reduplication and *-sk-*, must be a contamination of **γί-γνω-μι and γνώ-σκω*.[3]

In form *-sk-* would seem to be a combination of two suffixes, *s+k*,[4] rather than an independent word, e.g. Toch. A *skē-* 'strive'.[5] In meaning the various languages show very different kinds of development. The inchoative function so important in Latin is scarcely known in the other languages, and is certainly a secondary extension from cases in which the stem suggested the inchoative meaning, such as *crēscō*. In Hittite, where this formation is very productive, an iterative, durative, or distributive meaning can be established, cf. *walliskitsi* 'he praises repeatedly', *atskantsi* 'they eat (all through the night)'.[6] It is interesting that in Tocharian B *-sk-* usually develops a causative sense: *rittäskau* 'I bind'; there are, however, still traces of an iterative or durative meaning.[7] It is therefore probable that all later shades of meaning have arisen from a basic iterative-durative sense,[8] which still survives in Homeric usage.[9]

[1] The sole exception is Baltic, but the suffix *-st-* commonly used in this function perhaps arose from *-sk-*; see Leumann, *IF* 58, 1942, 128f.; Hamp, *PCLS* 9, 1973, 173f. In Germanic only isolated remnants are preserved, e.g. OHG *wascan*, OE *wasćan* 'wash' from **wod-sk-* to (Goth.) *watō* 'water'; OHG *eiscōn*, OE *āscian* 'ask' (cf. Lat. *quaerō* from **co-ais-ō*, see Szemerényi, *Glotta* 38, 1960, 232–8), from Gmc. **ais-sk-*. On the *-sk-* formation in general, see Vendryes, *Mél. Lévi*, 1911, 173–82; Schwyzer, *GG* i, 706f.; Couvreur, 'Les dérivés verbaux en *-ske/o-* du hittite et du tokharien', *REIE* 1, 1938, 89–101; Ruipérez, *Aspectos y tiempos del verbo griego antiguo*, 1954, 130f.; Hiersche, *Sprache* 6, 1960, 33–8; Kuryłowicz, *Categories* 106f.; Szemerényi, *Syncope* 5, 67f.; Risch, in *Symbolae Kuryłowicz*, 1965, 239f.; Ivanov, *Obščeind.* 139f.; Kronasser, *Etymologie* 575f.; A. G. Ramat, *AGI* 52, 1968, 105–23; Watkins, *Verb* 56f., 70f., 111; Mignot, *Les verbes dénominatifs latins*, 1969, 145f.; Berretoni, 'Considerazioni sui verbi latini in *-scō*', *SSL* 11, 1971, 89–169; Lehmann, *PIE Syntax*, 1974, 147f.; Rix 1976, 213; Leumann², 535f.; Ivanov, *Glagol* 205f.; Shields, *Em* 52, 1984, 117–23.

[2] Szemerényi, *Syncope* 5; Kronasser, *Etymologie* 581f. But the OPers. verb meaning 'go' is not **r̥satiy* (R. Schmitt, *IIJ* 8, 1965, 275f.) but *rasatiy* (Weber, *Inchoativa im Mitteliranischen*, diss., Göttingen 1970, 109, *pace* Schmitt, *Krat* 20, 1976, 47), which had been modified on the analogy of *ǰasatiy* (attested in Avestan). In Hittite the inflexion is thematic but follows the *-mi* class: see Pedersen, *Hittitisch* 82.

[3] Leumann[2], 537, and op. cit. (above, 9.2.2.2 n. 1), 45; R. Schmitt, *IIJ* 8, 279f. Cf. further Schwyzer, *GG* i, 710; Forssman, *MSS* 23, 1968, 14–20.

[4] Ivanov, *Obščeind.* 139f.; *Glagol* 207–11 (Toch. B *pāsk-*: A *pās-*, etc.); Kronasser, *Etymologie* 581; Adrados, *IF* 86, 1982, 96f.

[5] A unitary *-sk-* is demanded by Porzig, *IF* 45, 1927, 166; a second member is considered by Schwyzer, *GG* i, 707 n. 1; Georgiev, *KZ* 97, 1984, 233f. (as in the text).

[6] Kronasser, *Etymologie* 575, and esp. clear Friedrich, *Heth. Elementarbuch* i[2], 1960, 140f.; see also Dressler, *Studien zur verbalen Pluralität*, 1968, 159–236. Von Soden, *Fs. Otten*, 1973, 311–19, leans towards assuming an Accadian influence (*-tan-* iterative!) via the scribal schools, so also H. Wagner 1985, 82–92. A closer connection between Homeric preterital *-ske-* and Hittite *-ske-* is postulated by Puhvel 1991*b*, 13–20.

[7] Krause, *Westtoch. Gram.* i, 1952, 82f.

[8] Kuryłowicz, *Categories* 107; Ramat (iterative-intensive); Couvreur, less correctly, causative-intensive. 'Iteration proceeding by fits and starts or act by act' was proposed by Porzig (*IF* 45, 152–67), whereas Meillet (*Introduction* 221) ascribed an 'aspect déterminé' to this formation, 'indiquant un procès dont le terme est envisagé' (204). See also Leumann[2], 536f.

[9] See Wathelet, 'Études de linguistique homérique', *AC* 42, 1973, 379–405 (apparently an archaic formation, kept and further developed in the Ionic of Asia Minor); Rix 1976, 229; Kimball, 'A Homeric note', *Glotta* 58, 1980, 44–6 (iteratives).

9.4.1.5. -yo- *formations.* Undoubtedly the most important and productive present suffix of late Indo-European is *-yo-*, which served for the formation of both deverbative and denominative presents. The inflexion was thematic, but in Hittite, as with the *-sk-* verbs, it followed the *-mi* class.[1] The formation was clear in IE, but in various individual languages it has been obscured by loss of *-y-* between vowels or by change after consonants; Lat. *moneō*, Gr. δοκέω ended originally in *-eyō*; the sequences *-gy- -dy-* and *-ky- -ty-* gave in Greek -ζ- and -σσ-/-ττ- respectively, cf. ἅζομαι 'worship' (ἅγιος 'holy'), ἐρίζω 'dispute', φυλάσσω 'guard', λίσσομαι 'beseech' (from ἐριδ-, φυλακ-, λιτ-). Through later contractions the original state of affairs became almost unrecognizable: Lat. *dōnās* 'you (s.) give' comes from **dōnāyesi*, *monēs* 'you (s.) warn' from **moneyesi*, etc.

In the case of derivatives from verbs, *-yo-* can be used for the purpose of forming a present stem to a verbal root or a true deverbative from a verb. Thus from the root **spek-* 'look at' the present was formed not as **spek-mi* or **spek-ō* but as **spekyō*: Lat. *speciō*, *conspiciō*, OInd. *paśyāmi*; Gr. σκέπτομαι arose by metathesis. On the other hand φοβέομαι 'flee, fear' stands beside the simple φέβομαι 'flee'. Among the deverbatives two types in particular are widespread, in which the 3rd s. ends in *-ā-ye-ti* and *-eye-ti* respectively, the latter with *o*-grade of the root when the basic vowel is *e*; the meaning is iterative-intensive or causative; cf. Lat. *domāre*=OHG *zamōn*, IE **domāyō*,[2] and *moneō* from **moneyō* 'remind' formed to **men-* 'remember' in *meminī*. Beside these there are long-grade formations with *ē* such as Gr. ληκάω 'dance', Lettish *lēkāju* 'hop', Gr. πηδάω 'leap', Lat. *cēlāre* 'hide' to **kelō* in *occulō*, *sēdāre* 'calm' to *sedeō* 'sit';

with *ō* such as τρωπάω 'turn this way and that', πωτάομαι 'fly about'; and zero-grade forms such as OHG *borōn* 'bore', Gr. σφριγάω 'teem, abound'. Long-grade formations are found also in the *-eye-* group, e.g. Gr. πωλέομαι 'versor' to πέλομαι, OInd. *svāpayati* 'lulls to sleep' to *svap-* 'fall asleep', OHG *fuoren* 'cause to travel, lead' to *faran*.

Denominatives can be formed with *-yo-* from all stem classes; cf. OInd. *namas-* 'reverence': *namas-yáti* 'reveres', *šatru-* 'enemy': *šatru-yáti* 'acts as an enemy', Hitt. *laman-* 'name' : *lamniya-* 'to name',=Gr. ὄνομα : ὀνομαίνω=Goth. *namō*: *namnjan*. In the case of *o*-stems the verb ends in *-e-yō*: δῶρον 'gift': δωρέομαι 'give', πόλεμος 'war': πολεμέω 'make war'; later *-o-yō* was also introduced in some languages, as in Greek (e.g. ἐλευθερόω as early as Mycenaean), perhaps in Phrygian (in *kakoioi*?—see Brixhe and Lejeune, *Inscriptions paléo-phrygiennes*, 1984, 87; Neumann, *ÖAW Sb.* 499 (1988), 13), and in Germanic (see Dishington (n. 3 below, 859–63). The ending *-āyō*, which of course originally had a place only in *ā*-stems (e.g. OInd. *pr̥tanā* 'fight': *pr̥tanāyáti* 'fights', Gr. τιμάω 'I honour', Lat. *cūrā-re*, Russ. *rabota* 'work': *rabotaju* 'I work'), extended its range and in Latin can form verbs from all stems (cf. *gener-āre*, *laud-āre*, etc.); as a replacement for *-eyō* in *o*-stems its use goes back, as it seems, to late Indo-European, cf. Lat. *dōnāre* from *dōnum*, Gr. *ὑπνάω in Hom. ὑπνώοντας from ὕπνος.[3]

This interpretation[4] is not universally accepted, especially as regards the deverbatives. The types **moneyō *domāyō* were formerly considered to be denominatives,[5] and these *o*-grade forms certainly suggest derivation from nouns: φορέω ποτάομαι seem at first sight to belong with φόρος ποτή.[6] Chronologically the zero-grade **lukéye-* from a verbal adjective **luké-/*lukó-* (cf. Vedic *ručayanta* 'let them shine' from *ruča-* 'bright') should then represent the earliest stage: the next was presumably the formation of the type **louké-ye* from the newly introduced verbal adjective **loukó-* (cf. Vedic **rōčayati* from *rōča-* 'shining'), and this acquired a partly iterative-intensive, partly causative meaning, the latter especially in contrast to a medio-passive, cf. φοβέομαι 'flee, fear': φοβέω 'put to flight, frighten'.[7]

Most individual languages show thematic inflexion. This is particularly clear for the deverbative type **spekyō*, but for the most part also for the deverbatives and denominatives of the types **moneyō *dōnāyō*. Chiefly on the basis of Greek dialects (Aeolic and Arcado-Cyprian; see Tucker 1990, 73, n. 83) in which athematic τίμᾱμι φίλημι ἀξίωμι are used instead of τιμάω φιλέω ἀξιόω, the assumption is of course repeatedly made that *-ᾱμι* at least is just as old as *-άω*, perhaps even older, i.e. it goes back to Indo-European,[8] but it is precisely for this class that the idea of an IE athematic *-āmi* must be vigorously resisted. In the Greek dialects in question traces of the thematic inflexion still survive (e.g. Aeol. 3rd s. *τίμαι* from -*ā*-*ει*), in Germanic Goth. *salbōs* (2nd s.) and *salbōþ* (3rd s. and 2nd pl.) point to -*āyesi* -*āyeti* -*āyete*, etc.;[9] the Hittite formations in -*ah*-*mi*, which at first glance appear to be related, do not belong here, as they are in principle derived from adjectives, e.g. *newahmi* 'I renew' from **newa*- 'new', whereas the verbs under discussion are derived from nouns.[10]

For the verbs in -*eyō*, comparison leads to no uniform result. Aryan and Greek (e.g. *φοβέω*) point to a regular thematic inflexion -*eyō* -*eyesi* -*eyeti* -*eyomos*, etc., with which the Latin paradigm (e.g. *moneō*, -*es*) and the Germanic (e.g. Goth. *nasja*, -*jis* 'save' from **noseyō* **noseyesi*) agree. Slavic, on the other hand, offers as corresponding forms *nositi* 'carry' or *saditi* 'set down, plant', with presents in -*jǫ* -*iši* -*itŭ* -*imŭ* -*ite* -*ętŭ* (from -*int*-); the 1st s. thus shows -*yō*, not -*eyō*, and in the other persons -*i*- appears throughout, which goes back to *ī* or *ei*, but apparently not to -*eye*-/-*eyo*-. To this type corresponds in Baltic the Lithuanian type with infinitive in -*īti* but present (modified) in -*ō*-, e.g. *prašýti* 'ask', pres. *prašaũ, prašaĩ, prãšo, prãšome, prãšote, prãšo*.

In contrast to this *iterative-causative* type Balto-Slavic has another group of verbs, which in meaning can be described as *stative* and in form are characterized by the fact that, alongside the present in *j*/*i* (this time so formed not only in Slavic but also in Lithuanian, with -*i*- not -*ō*-), the infinitive ends in -*ēti* and this -*ē*- occurs also in the preterite; cf. OCS *mĭnēti* 'think', *po-mĭnēti* 'remember', Lith. *minēti* 'remember, mention', with the present OCS *mĭnjǫ mĭni-ši mĭni-tŭ* etc., Lith. *miniù minì mìni mìnime mìnite mìni*, and the preterites OCS 3rd s. aor. *mĭnē*, Lith. 3rd s. pret. *minē-jo*. This group is clearly connected with certain formations in Germanic and Latin.[11] In Germanic the third class of weak verbs shows, in the first place, striking lexical agreements with Latin: cf. Goth. *haban* 'have', *þahan* 'be silent', *ana-silan* 'become quiet' with the corresponding Lat. *habēre*,[12] *tacēre, silēre*. Furthermore, the agreement of the OHG present inflexion (*habēm* -*ēs* -*ēt* -*ēmes* -*ēt* -*ēnt*) with the Latin can hardly be ascribed to coincidence. A detailed examination of the material shows[13] that Proto-Germanic had the present inflexion -*yō*, -*ēyis*, -*ēyiþ*, -*yam*, -*ēyiþ*, -*yanþ*, which was developed and unified in various ways in the individual languages; in Gothic, for instance, -*ēyi*- led via -*ēi*- to -*ai*- (2 *habais*, 3 and 5 *habaiþ*), while the forms with bare -*y*- became 1 *haba*, 4 *habam*, 6 *haband*, obviously by contraction of -*aya*- to -*a*-. The inflexion of Latin *habēre* could agree with this if the forms with -*ē*- came from -*ēye*/-*ēyo*. The Baltic and Slavic stative verbs would not agree with this inflexion; the denominatives on the other hand, such as OCS *o-slabēti* 'languish, grow weak' (from *slabŭ* 'weak'), with their inflexion -*ējǫ* -*ēješi* -*ējetŭ*, etc., could correspond to the Italo-Germanic type.

Instead of a single class we have thus on closer inspection at least three, which for the most part were again mixed in the individual languages:

(*a*) Iterative-causatives, type **moneyō*, *-eyesi*: Lat. *monēo*, Goth. *nasjan*, Gr. *φοβέω*, etc.; with modification of the present inflexion in Balto-Slavic to OCS *-ją -iši* etc., inf. *-iti*.[14]

(*b*) Statives, type Lat. *tacēre*: pres. *taceō tacēs* etc., Goth. *þaha þahais* etc.; in Balto-Slavic inf. in *-ēti*, but pres. as in (*a*) (even in Baltic!).

(*c*) Denominatives, type Lat. *albēre* 'be white': *albeō albēs* etc., Goth. *leikan* 'please'; in Balto-Slavic inf. in *-ēti*, pres. OCS *-ēją -ēješi* etc.[15]

There are, however, differences not only in the form of the stem but also in the inflexion and especially in the form of the suffix which so far we have hardly touched on.

In the first place it must be noted that even in its simplest form, *-ye-/-yo-*, the suffix is split into the allomorphs *-ye-* and *-iye-* according to Sievers' Law (5.7.2.1). In formation IE **spek-yō* 'I look at' and **sāg-iyō* 'I track' are thus identical. The 2nd s. **spekyesi* and **sāgiyesi* then give in Latin *specis* (cf. *alis alid* from **alyos* **alyod*) and *sāgīs* (*ī* contracted from *iye*); to Lat. *capis* from **kap-ye-si* corresponds OHG *hevis* as opposed to Goth. *hafjis* with restored *j*, while Lat. *sāgīs* corresponds exactly to Goth. *sōkeis* 'thou seekest' from **sōkiyisi*.[16] The converse of Sievers' Law (5.7.2.3 above) explains how IE **logheyō* 'lay' became Goth. *lagja*, or **noseyō*, Goth. *nasja*.[17]

It is often supposed that beside the 'fixed' suffix *-ye-/-yo* there was also a suffix with ablaut *-yo-/-i-* or *-yo-/-ī-*. The main support for this supposition is Balto-Slavic where, as we have seen, the iterative-causatives show in Slavic, alongside the infinitive in *-iti*, the present endings *-ją*, *-i-ši*, *-i-tŭ*, and the statives, alongside the infinitive in *-ēti*, have the same present endings in Slavic, *-jo-/-i-* in Baltic (Lith.). That the iterative-causative type, which from Indic and Greek in the East to Germanic, Celtic, and Italic in the West displays everywhere the same form (**moneyō*), should show an IE dialect feature in Balto-Slavic is impossible; it must be a matter of post-IE transformation, in which *-eye-* was replaced by *-ei-*.[18] As regards the stative verbs, we have in their case no general grounds for or against; moreover, the analysis given above for Germanic is not the only one possible. Thus it was assumed *inter alia* that Goth. *-ai-* continued IE *-əi*[19] or that the IE athematic (!) paradigm was based on accented *-ēi-* in the singular and on unaccented *-əi-* in the other numbers, whereby *ē*, *ei* (thence Slav. *ī*), *i* (from plural *-əi* with loss of *ə*), and *y* (3rd pl. *-əy-énti* gave *-y-énti*) are all explained,[20] but not the structure of the paradigm. Still more improbable was the attempt to introduce palatalized laryngeals on the pattern of the labiovelar laryngeals (4.4.4.1), so that *eH*^{y} would have given *ē* and *H*^{y} in certain conditions would have become *i* or *y*.[21] The latest explanation is clearer, which takes the divergence in vowel length between Slavic and Lithuanian as the starting-point: since Slav. *i* and Lith. *i* can be equated only in final position, it is supposed that the whole present inflexion was built on the forms Lith. *mìni*=Slav. *mĭni-(tŭ)*, which for their part represent the 3rd s. of the perfect (ending -*e*+present -*i*); thus the stative meaning is given a reason and a link between -*i*- and -*ē*- is established by way of the aorist (cf. Gr. -*η*-*ν*).[22]

Finally, with regard to the origin of the formation it can first be stated from a purely formal point of view that the suffix -*yo*- arose at least in part from the thematizing of *i*-stems. The stem **poti*- 'master' became by thematization a verb **potyetoi* 'possess' (from 'be master of'), which survives in Lat. *potitur*, OInd. *patyatē*.[23] It is, however, not impossible that composition played a part in the spread of this formation, both with **ei*- 'go'[24] and, especially in the case of factitives, with **yo*- 'make', for which we may refer to Hitt. *iyami* 'make, do'.[25]

1 Cf. Brugmann, *Grundriss*², ii/3, 178f.; Meillet, *Introduction* 217–20; Schwyzer, *GG* i, 712–37; Ivanov, *Obščeind.* 181–4; Bammesberger, *Deverbative* jan-*Verba des Altenglischen*, Diss. Munich 1965; Stang, *Vgl. Gram.* 354f.; Vaillant, *Gram. comp.* iii, 261f.; Kronasser, *Etymologie* 467; Mignot, *Les verbes dénominatifs latins*, 1969, 17f., 81f., 245f.; 'La conjugaison "faible" en latin', in Isebaert (ed.) 1993, 167–81; E. Tucker, *TPS* 86, 1988, 93–114 (early OInd. denominatives are a disparate class; no basis for reconstructing **deiweyeti*, **wosneyeti*); id. 1990, esp. 73 n. 83.

2 Cf. Benveniste, *BSL* 51, 1965, 15f.

3 Szemerényi, *SMEA* 3, 1967, 78. But alongside denominative -*āyō*- verbs there are perhaps also deverbatives which go back to a nasal formation, e.g. OInd. *gr̥bhāyati*, if this is from **ghr̥bh-n̥-ye-ti* (or -*n̥H-ye*-); see Saussure, *Recueil* 235; Jasanoff, *IF* 88, 1984, 72.

4 See esp. Schwyzer (n. 1 above).

5 Brugmann, *Grundriss*², ii/3, 162, 245 (-*eyō* from *i*-stems!); cf. Specht, *Ursprung* 329.

6 Vaillant, *BSL* 38, 1937, 98.

7 Cf. Kuryłowicz, *Apophonie* 86f.; *Categories* 84f., 105. Further on this, Rundgren, *Orientalia Suecana* 12, 1964, 104f.; *Sprache* 12, 1967, 133f.

8 So e.g. Schwyzer, *GG* i, 729; cf. also Stang, *Vgl. Gram.* 330; Polomé, *Orbis* 15, 1966, 197–8; Lindeman, *NTS* 22, 1968, 88; Watkins, *TPS* 1971, 91.

9 For Greek preliminarily Cowgill, in *AIED* 81f.; Wyatt, *TAPA* 101, 1971, 606f.; *H. H. Hock, *Aeolic Inflection of the Greek Contract Verbs*, Yale diss. 1971; W. P. Schmid, 'The Aeolic conjugation of the contract verbs', *Fs. Risch*, 1986, 245–52 (against, Hettrich, *Krat* 34, 1989, 36f.); for Germanic, Wissmann, *Nomina postverbalia* i, 1932, 199f.; Cowgill, *Lg* 35, 1959, 1–15; Kortlandt, 'The Germanic first class of weak verbs', *NOWELE* 8, 1986, 27–31; Bammesberger, 'The paradigm of *jan*-verbs in Germanic', *JIES* 16, 1989, 233–9; for Balto-Slavic, Vaillant, *Gram. comp.* iii, 365f.

10 See Kronasser, *Etymologie* 422f. Pedersen's attempt, *Hittitisch* 126, has no justification.

11 Cf. H. Wagner, *Zur Herkunft der* ē-*Verba in den idg. Sprachen*, diss., Zürich 1950; *ZCP* 25, 1956, 161–73; Schmalstieg, 'The Slavic stative verbs in -*i*-', *International Journal of Slavic Linguistics and Poetics* 1–2, 1959, 177–83; W. H. Bennett, 'The parent suffix in Germanic weak verbs of class III', *Lg* 38, 1962, 135–41; Cowgill, *Lg* 39, 1963, 264f.; W. P. Schmid, *Studien zum baltischen und idg. Verbum*, 1963, esp. 83, 94f.; Kuryłowicz, *Categories*

76–84; Stepanova, 'The geographical distribution of the ē-verbs in the IE languages' (Russ.), *VJ* 1965 (4), 110–18; K. H. Schmidt, *Ériu* 20, 1966, 202–7; *SGGJ* iv, 1966, 385f.; Polomé, *Fs. Pokorny*, 1967, 83–92; Perel'muter, *VJ* 1969 (5), 15f.; Jasanoff, *Stative* 56f., 94f.; *IF* 88, 1984, 65.

12 Goth. *haban* goes back to **kapē-* and is cognate with Lat. *capiō*, not *habēre*, but morphologically they both represent the same type. Cf. Ringe, *TIES* 1, 1987, 130f.; Kortlandt, 'The Germanic third class of weak verbs', *NOWELE* 15, 1990, 3–10.

13 Wagner (n. 11 above), 4, 49f.; *SGGJ* iv, 389. Cf. also Sehrt, *Festgabe Frings*, 1956, 6; Krahe, *IF* 66, 1961, 37–9; Watkins, *TPS* 1971, 51–93; Hock, *Fs. Kahane*, 1973, 333; Gunarsson, *NTS* 27, 1973, 42f.; Jasanoff, *Lg* 49, 1973, 866f.; Dishington, *Lg* 52, 1976, 851–65 (see also Hollifield, *Sprache* 26, 1980, 50); Feuillet, *BSL* 76, 1982, 219f.

14 Cf. Bammesberger, *KZ* 94, 1980, 4–9; Jamison 1983.

15 Not only this class but also class (*a*) is seen by many as denominative: cf. Hirt, *IG* iv, 1928, 227f.; Kuryłowicz, *Apophonie* 86; Redard, *Mél. Chantraine*, 1972, 183–9.

16 Niedermann, *Mél. de Saussure*, 1908, 43–57; Graur, *BSL* 40, 1939, 127–50; Pariente, *Em* 14, 1946, 1–81; Collinge, *Laws* 283f.; Ringe, *Diachronica* 3, 1986, 107f.

17 J. W. Marchand, *Lg* 32, 1956, 285–7.

18 Cf. preliminarily Kuryłowicz, *Categories* 84; see also Vaillant, *Gram. comp.* iii, 438–9; Cowgill, *Lg* 39, 263.

19 Bennett (n. 11 above); against, *SGGJ* iv, 387.

20 W. P. Schmid (n. 11 above; n. 9 above (athem.)); Bammesberger, *PBB(T)* 109, 1987, 346f. (same forms but interpreted as thematic).

21 Diver, 'Palatal quality and vocalic length in IE', *Word* 15, 1959, 110–22; Cowgill, *Lg* 39, 264f. (on Puhvel). An alternation *-ey-/-yo-* is postulated by Schmalstieg, *La Linguistique* 8/1, 1972, 8.

22 Kuryłowicz, *Categories* 81, 83; Watkins, *Verb* 222; Schmalstieg, *KZ* 87, 1973, 137; Jasanoff, *Stative* 94f.

23 Szemerényi, *Syncope* 378.

24 Hirt, *IG*, iv, 226.

25 Vaillant, *BSL* 38, 1937, 98; Schwyzer, *GG* i, 714; Georgiev, *PICL* 9, 1964, 741; Schmitt-Brandt, 129.

9.4.1.6. *Further formations.* In addition to these main present formations there are also smaller groups, which were formed with less productive suffixes.[1]

Among the stops the dentals are used relatively often for such formations; cf. Lat. *pectō plectō flectō nectō* with *t*;[2] *sallō* (cf. *salsus* from **sald-tos*) *cūdō tendō* with *d*;[3] Gr. *πλήθω* 'am full', *πύθεται* 'rots' with *dh*.[4] The spirant *s* is used to form the present in Hitt. *ar-s-tsi* 'flows'=OInd. *arṣati*; OInd. *śrō-ṣ-ati* 'hears' (from *śru-*); Gr. *αὐξάνω*: Lat. *augeō*; *ἀλέξω* 'defend': aor. *ἀλ-αλκ-εῖν*, etc.[5]

For most of these less productive suffixes the function can hardly be determined; in this they come close to the root determinatives discussed above (5.5.4).

1 In general, see Brugmann, *Grundriss*², ii/3, 336f., 362f.; Schwyzer, *GG* i, 701–6.

2 Cf. Lommel, *KZ* 53, 1925, 309f.; Szemerényi, 'The IE cluster *-sl-* in Latin', *ArchL* 6, 1954, 31–45 (=*SM* 711–25), esp. 33f. (=713f.); Vaillant, *BSL* 56, 1961, 15–20; Peruzzi, *Rivista di Filologia ed Istruzione Classica* 40, 1962, 394–408. The coherence of the group was emphasized by M. Bloomfield in 1894 (*IF* 4, 69f.): 'a number of verbs meaning "binding, twisting" have *-t-*: *plecto, pecto, necto, flecto*'.

3 For *d* laryngeals were brought into play by Rosén, *Lingua* 10, 1961, 199f., whereas it was explained by Thibau, *Rapports entre le latin et le grec*, 1964, 7, as a 'strengthening' of *y* after *l*

or *n*; neither supposition is very clear. Cf. *B. H. Vine, *IE Verbal Formations in* -d-, diss., Harvard 1982; Smoczyński (works cited above, 9.4.1.1, n. 1).

4 Benveniste, *Origines* 188f.; cf. 189: '*-dh-* exprime l'état, spécialement l'état achevé'.

5 Schwyzer, *GG* i, 706; Kronasser, *Etymologie* 394f.; according to Gonda, *Four Studies in the Language of the Veda*, 1959, ch. 2, *-s-* also formed causatives. On the *s*-formations, see in addition Ivanov, *Obščeind.* 139f.; Adrados, 'IE *-s*-stems', *IF* 86, 1982, 96–122; Shields, 'IE sigmatic verbal formations', in *In Memory of J. A. Kerns*, 1981, 263–79; Jasanoff, 'Some irregular imperatives in Tocharian', in *In Memory of W. Cowgill*, 1987, 92–112 (esp. 98f. on OInd. *śrōṣa-*, cf. Rix, *Krat* 35, 1990, 42f.).

9.4.2. Aorist and future

9.4.2.1.

For the aorist stem there are two sharply distinguished possibilities of formation: derivation from the verb stem either by means of *-s-* (sigmatic type) or without *-s-* (asigmatic type). In the case of the latter type there are two subdivisions: the endings (SE) are added to the aorist stem either with or without a thematic vowel.[1]

(*a*) *Athematic asigmatic aorist stem.* This is best represented in Greek and Aryan; cf. Gr. ἔ-γνω-ν 'I recognized', OInd. *a-dā-m* 'I gave'.[2]

That this type originally had full grade in the singular of the active, zero grade in the other numbers and throughout the middle is shown by the inflexion of certain long-vowel roots in Greek, e.g. ἔ-θη-κα 'I placed': ἔ-θε-μεν, ἔ-δω-κα 'I gave': ἔ-δο-μεν, Hom. ἕ-η-κα 'I threw, sent': 1st pl. -ἕμεν, and the corresponding middle forms ἐ-θέ-μην, ἐ-δό-μην, ἕ-ντο. Even in Homer this alternation is limited to the verbs already mentioned and perhaps Hom. ἔ-βη-ν: βά-την, and in general it has been replaced by an opposition between full-grade active and zero-grade middle, e.g. ἔφθην 'I anticipated', 1st pl. ἔφθημεν: mid. φθάμενος. The same situation is found in Old Indic from the beginning of its recorded tradition, e.g. *a-dā-m* 'I gave': 3rd s. mid. *a-di-ta*=Gr. ἔ-δο-το: *a-sthā-m* 'I stood'= Gr. ἔ-στη-ν: 3rd s. mid. *a-sthi-ta*.

In the case of diphthong stems or stems in (IE) *e*+*R* the same ablaut is found, but the zero grade is often retained in the active, especially in the 3rd plural. Cf., e.g., *a-śrav-am* 'I heard', 3rd s. *a-śrō-t* (IE **klew-m̥*, **kleu-t*); *śri-* 'make for', 2nd s. *a-śrē-s*, 3rd s. *a-śrē-t*, 3rd pl. *a-śriy-an* (IE **klei-s*, **klei-t*, **kliy-ent*); *gam-* 'go', 1st s. *a-gam-am*, 2nd and 3rd s. *agan*, 3rd pl. *a-gm-an* (IE **gʷem-m̥*, **gʷem-s*, **gʷem-t*, **e-gʷm-ent*); similarly *a-kr-an* 'they made' as in the middle 1st-3rd s. *a-kr-i*, *a-kr̥-thās*, *a-kr̥-ta*, etc. In Greek also there are still traces of this old kind of formation, cf. from κτείνω 'kill' (stem κτεν-) aor. act. 1st pl. ἔ-κτα-μεν (**kt*n̥*-m-*), 3rd s. mid. ἀπ-έκτατο (**ktn̥-to*), to which the 1st s. act. must at one time have been *ἔκτενα (**kten-m̥*).[3] To σεύω 'chase', χεύω χέ(ϝ)ω 'pour' belong the archaic 3rd s. mid. ἔσσυτο, ἔχυτο, 3rd pl. ἔχυντο; it is therefore possible that the aor. act. 1st s. ἔχε(ϝ)α belongs to this type and the singular originally had the form **ghew-m̥ *gheu-s *gheu-t*, from which 1st s. ἔχεα and by analogy 2nd s. ἔχεας, 3rd s. ἔχεε arose.[4]

(*b*) *Thematic asigmatic aorist stem.* This is distinguished from the foregoing type by the presence of the thematic vowel between verb stem and ending; the verb stem appears mostly in the zero grade. This type is used in Vedic in nearly sixty verbs and is widespread in Greek;[5] cf. OInd. *a-vid-a-m* 'I found', *a-čchid-a-t* 'he cut off', *a-vr̥ǰ-a-n* 'they turned'; Gr. εἶδον (ἔ-ϝιδ-ο-ν) 'I saw', ἔφυγον 'I fled', ἔδρακον 'they saw'. This type is likewise found in other languages, e.g. in Celtic: cf. OIr. *lod* 'I went', *luid* 'he went' from **ludh-o-m*, **ludh-e-t*, to be equated with Gr. ἤλυθον, ἤλυθε.[6] In these circumstances it is surprising that so few word correspondences extending over a number of languages are to be found; it has even been asserted that at most the aorist **wid-o-m* 'I found, saw' (Old Indic and Greek, see above) has any claim to be of IE date,[7] while others would perhaps add **ludh-o-m* 'I went' (Greek and Old Irish, see above).[8]

Nevertheless there can be hardly any doubt that the type reaches back as far as the late IE period. It is interesting, however, that this kind of formation, which fairly soon became extinct everywhere, still had at first a capacity for expansion in Aryan and Greek, in that verbs of type (*a*) were transferred to it, sometimes even the same verbs in both languages. Thus the OInd. 3rd pl. *adr̥šan*, equivalent to Gr. ἔδρακον, has led to the assumption of an IE type (*b*) **e-dr̥k-ont*.[9] At the beginning of the Indic tradition, however, there is an athematic aorist: 1st s. *dáršam*, 1st. pl. *ádaršma*, and it is beyond doubt that *(a)dr̥šan* is just the zero-grade form belonging to it; cf. above *akaram*: *akran*, etc.;[10] see Lazzeroni, *SSL* 27, 1987, 131–8.

A subdivision of this type is formed by the reduplicated aorists, which are mostly (in Greek always) thematic; they are especially frequent in early Greek and Old Indic,[11] cf. πείθω 'persuade': πεπιθεῖν, φεν- 'kill': ἔπεφνε, κέλομαι 'call': ἐκέκλετο, χαίρω 'rejoice': κεχάροντο, etc. In some verbs these aorists have a causative meaning, e.g. ἐλάθετο 'forgot': ἐκ-λέλαθον 'made (him) forget', λαγχάνω 'obtain by lot': λελάχωσι '(that) they may allot (me) a share'. In forms with initial vowel intensive reduplication occurs, e.g. ἀρ-αρ-εῖν 'fit together'; cf. 9.4.1.2 n. 5, and 9.4.3*b* with n. 11. The reduplicated aorists of Old Indic are basically always causative, e.g. *a-vī-vr̥dh-at* 'caused to grow'.

An individual example which certainly goes back to the IE period is the fine equation OInd. *avōčam* 'I said'=Gr. ἔ(ϝ)ειπον from IE **e-we-wkʷ-om* to **wekʷ-* 'say'; in Greek *-weukʷ-* was dissimilated to *-weikʷ-*.

(*c*) *Sigmatic aorist stem.* This type was the most productive mode of formation in late Indo-European. In the prehistoric period of a number of languages it was combined with the perfect into a unified system, as for example in Celtic and Latin, but it remained independent in Aryan, Greek, and Slavic. The type is athematic, i.e. the SE are added directly to the aorist stem formed with *s*;[12] cf. e.g. Gr. ἔδειξα 'I showed' from **e-deik-s-m̥* as opposed to εἶδον from **e-wid-o-m*.

The stem showed ablaut in the root syllable, but the evidence of the principal witnesses is not in agreement. Old Indic has long grade in the active, and zero grade, or for roots in *i* or *u* full grade, in the middle; the subjunctive has full grade in both active and middle. For example, *nī-* 'lead' has in the active singular 1 *a-naiṣ-am*, 2–3 *a-nai-ṣ* (for **a-nai-ṣ-s* and **a-nai-ṣ-t*), in the middle 1 *a-ne-ṣ-i*, 2 *a-ne-ṣ-ṭhās*, 3 *a-ne-ṣ-ṭa*, in the active subjunctive 1 *ne-ṣ-āṇi*, 2 *ne-ṣ-as(i)*, 3 *ne-ṣ-at(i)*, while from *rudh-* 'obstruct' the corresponding forms in the 1st s. are *a-raut-s-am*, *a-rut-si*, *rot-s-āni*. In Greek, on the other hand, the verb stem usually appears in the same form as in the present, e.g. δείκνυμι:ἔδειξα, γράφω:ἔγραψα, but also τίνω:ἔτεισα. Further witnesses to long grade in the active are apparently Latin and OCS, cf. Lat. *uehō*:*uēxī* and OCS *vezǫ*:*vēsŭ*, both from IE **weghō*:**wēh-s-*. Consequently the conclusion formerly seemed self-evident that in Indo-European the *s*-aorist had long grade in the active.[13] Today the tendency is rather to see Greek as representing the original situation.[14] But in Greek itself traces of the old long grade still remain which have not so far been recognized as such. Thus ἔρρηξα 'I broke' is not simply the *s*-aorist of ῥήγνυμι: a root *ϝρηγ- could not have produced the zero grade ῥαγῆναι,[15] and conversely this zero grade requires a full grade *ϝρεγ- of which *ϝρῆξα is the long grade. Similarly γηρά(σκ)ω is based on the aorist *ἔγηρα—cf. γηραντ-[16]—which arose from **gēr-s-m̥*.[17] Long grade can also perhaps be claimed for Celtic, cf. the OIr. subjunctive *ro-bria* from **bhrēusāt*,[18] and even for Tocharian, if Toch. B *preksa* and Toch. A *prakäs* (3rd s.) really go back to **prēks-*.[19] In any event, we have to acknowledge the long grade for the active of the *s*-aorist.[20] Of course the long grade will have had its original place, again, not in the whole of the active but, as in the case of the present formation (e.g. OInd. *mārṣṭi* 'wipes'), in the singular of the indicative;[21] on its origins, see 6.2.8, Addendum 1.

The wide extent of the sigmatic aorist shows that it does at any rate belong to the Indo-European period,[22] although it is perhaps the latest of the IE aorist formations.[23] On its origin there is only one probable suggestion, namely that it is the preterite of an *s*-present.[24] The idea that it was a kind of objective conjugation in which the *s* was a pronominal element[25] has nothing in its favour, nor has the supposition that the *s* was originally the 3rd s. ending or else an extension of nominal origin: thus **prek-s-* 'asking (occurred)'.[26]

9.4.2.1.1. *The 'aorist passive'*. The Aryan 'aorist of the 3rd person singular with predominantly passive meaning' (Thumb and Hauschild, *Handbuch des Sanskrit*, i/2, 298), thus the type OInd. *(a)jani* 'was born', has in recent times been variously explained. According to Watkins it represents the stem followed by a particle *-i*; according to Insler it developed from a 3rd s. mid. in *-o* (e.g. **key-o* 'lies'), while Kortlandt (as formerly Osthoff, and Burrow, *The Sanskrit Language*, 340) sees in it a neuter in *-i*, and Hollifield a formation with laryngeal suffix and zero ending.[27]

The function, moreover, is not entirely unambiguous; at all events the formation does not seem to have been purely passive. According to Jelizarenkova it is most frequently intransitive middle or impersonal, whereas Migron prefers to see it as a true passive.[28]

The Greek aorist passive in *-θην* also represents an innovation. It is still not completely clear whether the starting-point is in a correspondence of *-θης* to the OInd. mid. 2nd s. SE *-thās*, or in the root *θη-*, or still to be sought elsewhere.[29]

[1] For introduction and further literature, see Schwyzer, *GG* i, 739f.; Thumb and Hauschild, i/2, 296f.; Jelizarenkova, *Aorist v Rigvede*, Moscow 1960 (on all kinds); Chantraine, *Morph.* 161 f.; Kuryłowicz, *Categories* 109; Kortlandt, 'Sigmatic or root aorist?' *AArmL* 8, 1987, 49–52; Harðarson 1993. For the Greek views of the aorist, see P. Berrettoni, 'La definizione stoica dell' aoristo', *SSL* 28, 1989, 57–79.

[2] Cf. L. Gil, 'Sobre la historia del aoristo atemático griego', *Em* 32, 1964, 163–83; for the ablaut, Kuryłowicz, *Categories* 119f. For epigraphic examples of ἀν-εθε̄ etc., see Masson, *Krat* 31, 1986, 185–6; on origin and inflexion of ἔθηκα, etc., Harðarson 1993, 146f.

[3] Against Hoffmann's view (*Fs. Kuiper*, 1969, 7, accepted by Rix 1976, 214), see Francis, *Glotta* 52, 1974, 26; Bammesberger, *GL* 21, 1982, 233f.; *JIES* 10, 1982, 47f. In favour of Hoffmann's view, and even its extension to the root present **esmi* (**esmes*, **este*, **senti*), again Campanile, *SCO* 37, 1987, 373–83 (see below, 9.5.1).

[4] Cf. Schwyzer, *GG* i, 745; also Pariente, *Em* 31, 1963, 79; Strunk, *Nas.* 89; Hettrich, *MSS* 35, 1976, 47–61; Peters, *Sprache* 23, 1977, 329.

[5] See MacDonell, *Vedic Grammar*, 1910, 371; Schwyzer, *GG* i, 746f. (in 120 verbs!).

[6] It is often supposed that the 2nd s. of the preterite of strong verbs in West Germanic, e.g. OHG *zugi*, *nāmi*, goes back to the 2nd s. of an IE them. aorist (so still H. Wagner, *ZCP* 42, 1987, 27–8), but it is now again traced back to the perfect optative by Polomé, *PICL* 9, 1964, 879; Makajev, *Lings* 10, 1964, 35; Hiersche, *Fs. Matzel*, 1984, 94f.; Bammesberger, *Germanisches Verbalsystem*, 1986, 47f.; id., *Studies Polomé*, 1988, 59. Bech derives it from an analogical innovation on the model of the present; see above, 9.2.3 n. 2 where further references are given. On Slavic, see Vaillant, *Gram. comp.* iii, 45f.

[7] Thurneysen, *IF* 4, 1894, 84; *KZ* 63, 1936, 116 n. 1; Schwyzer, *GG* i, 746 n. 2. Cf. also Watkins, *Verb* 63, 100f.; Strunk, *Nas.* 97f.

[8] Cardona following Anttila, *PIE Schwebeablaut*, 1966, 35; rejected by Watkins, *Verb* 64.

[9] See Schwyzer, *GG* i, 747, and Frisk, *Griechisches etymologisches Wörterbuch* i, 368.

[10] Strunk, *Nas.* 97; cf. Narten, *Sprache* 14, 1968, 113f., esp. 117; Lazzeroni, *SSL* 18, 1978, 129f.; 20, 1980, 34; 27, 1987, 135 (the them. aorist is built on the athem. 3rd pl. *-ont*). Bammesberger, *Fachtagung* 7, 1985, 71–4, thinks that the them. root aorist did not exist at all in Proto-IE.

[11] Schwyzer, *GG* i, 748; Thumb and Hauschild, 300f., also (302) on the athem. forms of OInd.

[12] On the OInd. *s*-aorists, see Narten, *Die sigmatischen Aoriste im Veda*, 1964, esp. the summaries 17–23, 50–59, 80f. On this, cf. Meid, *Krat* 10, 1967, 59f.; Gonda, *Old Indian*,

1971, 97f.; and see also Adrados, 'On IE sigmatic verbal stems', *ArchL* 2, 1971, 95–116. Since Watkins, *Verb* 44f., thinks that *-s-n̥t* with zero-grade ending is not attested in any languages which have a sigmatic aorist, we may here refer to Venetic, where *donasan* 'donauerunt' certainly continues *-sn̥t-*.

[13] See Schwyzer, *GG* i, 751; Kuryłowicz, *Apophonie* 159f., 272f.; W. P. Schmid, *IF* 68, 1963, 226; Strunk, *Fachtagung* 7, 1985, 499. Beekes (1990, 42–3) would trace the lengthened grade to monosyllabic injunctive forms. Wagner, *ZCP* 30, 1967, 4, would also like to consider Celtic long grades like *sāss-* to *saigid* 'seeks' as Indo-European.

[14] Watkins, *Origins* 18f., esp. 41, 49f. (against, Wagner, loc. cit.); Meid, *Sprache* 12, 1966, 105; Otkupščikov (above, 9.4.1.3 n. 1), 47f. As *vēsŭ* is not attested in OCS literature (see Watkins, op. cit., 35f., 41), reference should be made to Kölln, *ScSl* 7, 1961, 265f., who proves it from Serbian Church Slavic; see also Mathiassen, *ScSl* 15, 1969, 201–14.

[15] *Rē-* should give zero grade *R̥ə*, i.e. *R̥̄*. Cf. Meillet, *Introduction* 160; Kuryłowicz, *Apophonie* 170 n. 9, 175, 205.

[16] Schwyzer, *GG* i, 682 and (incorrect) 708; Gil, *Em* 32, 1964, 169, 176; Strunk, *Fachtagung* 7, 1985, 495 (also on Barton, see below); Peters 1980, 314f., but see Jasanoff, in Bammesberger 1988, 231f.; Harðarson 1993, 72f.

[17] Risch, *Wortbildung der homerischen Sprache*², 1974, 234, has given a similar explanation for *ἔσβης* (from **e-sgʷēs-s*); but cf. also Barton, *Glotta* 60, 1982, 31.

[18] See Lewis and Pedersen, *CCCG* 8, and for the phonetic development Hamp, *JIES* 1, 1973, 221; *EC* 19, 1982, 140; but Campanile, ibid. 151–3, would start from **bhreyHāt*!

[19] See Lindeman, *Sprache* 18, 1972, 44–8, and cf. van Windekens, *Le tokharien* ii/2, 1982, 158; Strunk, *Fachtagung* 7, 504f.; Thomas, *Erforschung des Tocharischen*, 1985, 43, 76f.

[20] The extent remains to be determined; cf. Strunk, *Fachtagung* 7, 495: the long grade must be recognized for IE 'within a certain range'.

[21] Cf. Thumb and Hauschild, 306. On the Greek elimination of the long grade, see Kuryłowicz, *Apophonie* 272f.; and on the structure of the *s*-paradigm Risch, *Fs. Vasmer*, 1956, 424–31; also Lejeune, *Parola del Passato* 98, 1964, 326, on Mycenaean *qejameno*. It must be mentioned here that, according to K. Hoffmann, alongside some *s*-aorists there was a root aorist optative which showed full grade of the root and zero grade of the suffix, e.g. Avest. *varəzimā*; on the ensuing controversy, see the report of Kellens, *Verbe* 362f., 390, and cf. also Narten, *Sprache* 30, 1985, 96f.

[22] See Insler (above 9.2.6.1); Schlerath, *KZ* 95, 1982, 182f.; Strunk, *Fachtagung* 7, 495 (earlier than the individual languages). Otkupščikov's idea (op. cit. above, 9.4.1.3 n. 1), 49, that the *s*-aorist was first developed in the individual languages, e.g. in Latin after the break-up of the Italic unity (!), is quite impossible; cf. also Watkins, *Origins* 101f.

[23] So Meillet, *Mél. Saussure*, 1908, 79f.; cf. Schwyzer, *GG* i, 749 n. 2; Kuryłowicz, *Categories* 109.

[24] e.g. Schwyzer, loc. cit.; Kuryłowicz, *Apophonie* 33, *Categories* 104 n. 1, 110; Ivanov, *Obščeind.* 173f.; G. Schmidt, 'Zum idg. *s*-Futur', *Fs. Risch*, 1986, 33–59. Bammesberger, *Fachtagung* 7, 1985, 74–8, has the quite different view that the starting-points were 2nd s. **yeug-s* taken as **yeuks-s* and mid. **də-so* interpreted as **də-s-so*, but this represents all too narrow a basis and especially in the middle is hardly a real possibility.

[25] Kretschmer, *Objective Konjugation im Idg.*, 1947, 11f.; Kronasser, *Die Nasalpräsentia und Kretschmers objective Konjugation im Idg.*, 1960, 21.

[26] Watkins, *Origins* 68f., 97f., 99, 105f.; Jasanoff, in Bammesberger 1988, 230. For Lat. *-is-/ -er-*, see G. Schmidt, 'Lat. *amāuī*', Glotta 63, 1985, 52–92 (with references); Rasmussen 1989, 46 (*-is-* from long-diphthong *s*-aorists).

[27] See Watkins, *Origins* 103; *Verb* 52, 138; cf. above, 9.2.2.1 n. 4; Insler, *IF* 73, 1968, 312–46; *Lg* 48, 1972, 562; Kortlandt, *IF* 86, 1982, 121, 127, and earlier Osthoff, cited by Streitberg, *IF* 3, 1894, 390: an *i*-stem verbal abstract; Hollifield ap. Jasanoff, *IF* 88, 1984, 82.

[28] Jelizarenkova (n. 1 above), 119; Migron, *FoL* 8, 1975, 271–310.

[29] Earlier attempts at a solution (but only up to 1949) are listed by Jankuhn, *Die passive Bedeutung medialer Formen*, 1969, 40; in addition see Kuryłowicz, *Categories* 76f. (-θω×-ην); Pisani, *Paideia* 19, 1964, 245 (θη=pass. *-fē-* in Osc. *sakra-fī-r* 'sacrator'); Bech, *Beiträge zur genetischen idg. Verbalmorphologie*, Acad. Copenhagen 1971, 49–60 (impf. **ἐθεθην* reinterpreted).

9.4.2.2.

A *future* does not appear in all IE languages. Thus Hittite and Germanic have no special form for the future. Other languages have forms which certainly represent fairly late innovations, e.g. the *b*-future of Latin.[1] Finally there are a number of languages which show a mode of formation for the future so similar, even identical, that it seems justifiable to ask whether they have not indeed preserved an IE future form.[2]

The futures in question are:

(i) the Greek future in -*σω* -*σεις* -*σει*, etc., i.e. a tense formed with suffix -*s*- and thematic inflexion; beside this stands the so-called *Doric future* in *σέω*. e.g. *παιδεύ-σ-ω* 'I shall educate', in Doric areas *παιδευσέω* (or -*σίω*);

(ii) the Latin type *faxō*, e.g. Plautus, *Truculentus* 643: *ego faxo* (=*faciam*) *dicat*;

(iii) the Old Irish type in -*s*- formed from the verb stem by six verbs only,[3] e.g. *seiss* 'will sit' from **sed-s-ti*, *reiss* 'will run' from **ret-s-ti* (with the stem of Lat. *rota*);

(iv) the Aryan future with suffix -*sy*-, e.g. OInd. *dā-sy-āmi* 'I shall give';

(v) the Baltic future (Stang 1966, 397f.), e.g. Lith. *duo-siu* 'I shall give', 2nd s. *duo-si*, 3rd s. and pl. *duo-s*, 1st pl. *duo-si-me*, 2nd pl. *duo-si-te*;

(vi) The Old Irish *ē*-future, type *génaid* 'will wound', is equated with the OInd. desiderative;[4] *génaid* (pres. *gonaid* 'wounds') is first taken back to **gignāti* and this, together with OInd. *jighāṁsati* 'wishes to injure' to IE **g^ω^hi-g^ω^hn̥̄-seti*,[5] Proto-Irish **gignāseti*. Apart from this type, which is properly limited to verbs with final sonant, the reduplication is usually kept, e.g. *gigis* 'will ask for' from **gi-ged-s-ti*, IE **g^ω^hi-g^ω^hedh-s-ti* (see 4.7.5.3).

It follows in the first place that there are *three* types of *s*-future.

(a) The Latin future *faxō* is clear in its structure: since beside the future *faxō* there is a subjunctive *faxim*,[6] we have to do with the same relation as that of *erō* to *sim*, IE **esō* to **syēm* (see 9.3.1.1–2), i.e. *faxō* was originally a subjunctive to the aorist stem **fak-s-*; the fact that in Latin the old aorist stem survives only in these modal forms, which has sometimes been made an objection,[7] does not affect the issue, since the aorist stem *fak-s-* is attested in the indicative form *faχs-θo* in closely related Venetic.[8] The Old Irish type *seiss*, (iii) above, then agrees with this type of future from an aorist subjunctive, as does the usual Greek future with -*s*-, (i) above.[9] On the formal side, an objection frequently brought against this explanation[10] is that the future

stem is often different from the aorist stem, especially in Greek, cf. *ἔπαθον* : *πείσομαι* 'suffer', *ἤλυθον* : *ἐλεύσομαι* 'come', *ἔσχον* : *ἕξω* 'have, acquire'. This overlooks the fact, which is also clearly shown in Old Indic, that a verb could have several aorist formations and that the *s*-subjunctive had full grade, as is the case with *πείσομαι* from **πενθ-σ-* and *ἐλεύσομαι* from **leudh-s-* etc. From a syntactical viewpoint it can be mentioned that the subjunctive is often used as prospective, which is virtually equivalent to a future; cf. *ἴδωμαι*, *γένηται*,[11] and n. 1 fin.

(*b*) A second and (at first glance) unitary type seems to be present in the satem languages: the apparent equivalence of OInd. *dā-sy-āmi* and Lith. *duo-si-u*, both from IE **dō-sy-ō*, has even led to the supposition that here, in contrast to the multiplicity of future formations in the western languages, we have a common eastern innovation.[12] But in the first place it must be pointed out that the solitary participle *byšęšt-*, hitherto almost universally regarded as evidence for the former existence of the *sy*-future in Slavic (cf. Vaillant, *Gram. comp.* iii, 104), must now definitively be left out of account, since it is a fairly late innovation formed from the aorist *byšę*, and in accordance with its origin has not only a future but also a past meaning ('having become').[13] If, then, the Baltic future is to be equated with the Aryan, this can only be understood as a contact phenomenon from the period when Balts lived in the Dnieper region in the immediate vicinity of the Iranians.[14] Further, in more recent times the athematic character of the Baltic future has been repeatedly stressed: the Lithuanian paradigm (e.g. 1 *dúosiu*, 2 *dúosi*, 3 and 6 *duõs*, 4 *dúosime*, 5 *dúosite*) shows in the 3rd person an athematic form **dō-s(-t)*—although alongside it in Daukša *duosi* from **do-s-i(-t)* also occurs—and the plural forms with *-i-me* and *-i-te* diverge from the *-yo-me-* *-ye-te-* of Aryan;[15] it is therefore argued that even the convincing equation OInd. *dāsyā(mi)*=Lith. *dúosiu* must be given up.[16] This is altogether untenable; the two inflexions differ from one another in the same way as Lith. *mìni*: OInd. *manyatē* 'thinks', and the discrepancy is due in both cases to a secondary development that took place in Baltic.[17] We should thus hold to the view that Aryan and Baltic, at an earlier stage possibly even Balto-Slavic, had in common a future formation with the thematic suffix *-syo-*, which must have come from the Aryan domain.

(*c*) The third future type would, as we have seen, be confined to Aryan and Old Irish, and its structure would be reduplication + root (full or zero grade) + *s* + thematic vowel[17] + ending. The usual equation of OIr. *génaid* with OInd. *jighāṁsati* on the basis of **gʷhi-gʷhn̥-seti* is, however, suspect because the OIr. *-ā-* can hardly be separated from the *-ā-* of the subjunctive; cf. from *ernaid* 'grants' 3rd s. subj. *-era*: fut. *ebra* (**perā-*: **piprā-*), which must presumably be based on an extension of the *-ā-* of *sēṭ* roots.[18] The Aryan form is in any case a clear *s*-formation with desiderative meaning.

We can accordingly recognize:

1. *s*-futures, which continue subjunctives of *s*-aorists, limited to Greek, Latin, Celtic.
2. *sy*-futures, which probably arose in Aryan and did not spread beyond the satem area; but see n. 12;
3. *s*-desideratives, limited to Aryan.

As to the mutual relationship of these formations, the futures in *-s-* seem, as aorist subjunctives, quite clear both in form and in function, while those in *-sy-* are hard to connect with the *s*-aorist. From a purely formal standpoint an *s*-present could provide a basis (9.4.1.6), of which *-so-* would be the subjunctive or the thematized form, *-syo-* an extension, and even the Doric future could be regarded as a different kind of extension (*-se-yo-*); the *s*-aorist would be the preterite form to this present.[19] However, in view of the clear connection of the western formations with the subjunctive of the *s*-aorist, we must hold to this explanation of them, while the eastern *-sy-* formations will have another independent starting-point in the desideratives.[20] Whether *-sy-* with its *-y-* belongs with **ei-* 'go'[21] is a question that cannot be decided.[22]

[1] The Lat. *b*-future together with the OIr. *f*-future was for a long time traced back to an Italo-Celtic formation with *-bh(w)ō*, as still by Campanile, *Studi sulla posizione dialettale latino*, Pisa 1968, 55–8; Kuryłowicz, *TCLP* 4, 1971, 67–73 (also in *Esquisses* ii, 323–9); Wagner, *ZCP* 32, 1972, 278; Rasmussen, *Haeretica indogermanica*, 1974, 41–52; 'Herkunft der lat. *b*-Tempora und des air. *f*-Futurums', *Fs. Rix*, 1993, 406–12; Quinn, *Ériu* 29, 1978, 13–25; Bammesberger, *BBCS* 28, 1979, 395–8; Kortlandt, *Ériu* 35, 1985, 185f.; Pohl, 'Herkunft des lat. Imperfekts und *b*-Futurums', in *Latein und Indogermanisch*, 1992, 207–220. But in recent times the OIr. suffix has more often been derived from *-sw-* and the formation itself from a desiderative in *-su-* (and the future from *-su-ā-*). This was first put forward by Pisani, 'Studi sulla preistoria delle lingue ie.', *Memorie RAL* 6/4/6, 1933, 631 (*sw* > Lat. *b*!), and later *Paideia* 10, 1955, 276f.; *Storia della lingua latina*, 1962, 108; Thurneysen, *GOI* 398; and in more recent times Watkins, 'The origin of the *f*-future', *Ériu* 20, 1966, 67–81 (78: *-swā-* derived from desiderative *-su-* by his pupil Goddard); Giacomelli, *RAL* 33, 1978, 57–65; Hollifield (following Watkins), *KZ* 92, 1979, 229f.; *IF* 86, 1982, 187 n. 35.

Rasmussen, *Fachtagung* 7, 1985, 384–99, discovers a 'prospective'; cf. G. Schmidt (above, 9.4.2.1 n. 24); Bybee and Pagliuca, *ICHL* 7, 1987, 109–22 (all uses from prediction!).

[2] Cf. Schwyzer, *GG* i, 779f.; *G. d'Elia, *Origine e sviluppo del futuro nell'ie.*, Lecce 1942; Thumb and Hauschild, 325f.; Strunk, *IF* 73, 1969, 298f., against an IE future, as also Rix, in *Idg. und Keltisch*, 140.

[3] Thurneysen, *GOI* 410; K. H. Schmidt, *SCelt* 1, 1966, 19–26.

[4] Thurneysen, *GOI* 404, 414; Puhvel, *Lg* 29, 1953, 454–6; Kuryłowicz, *Apophonie* 254; Emeneau, *Lg* 34, 1958, 410; Cowgill, *Lg* 39, 1963, 262; K. H. Schmidt, *SCelt* 1, 21; McCone 1991, ch. 7, esp. 165f. On the origin of the Aryan desiderative formations, see Leumann (above 9.2.2.2 n. 1), 45–7; Thumb and Hauschild, 352f.; Insler, *IF* 73, 1968, 57–66.

[5] Against this, no word correspondences and parallels are found by Leumann, op. cit. 45; Thumb and Hauschild, 351, 353.

[6] J. St. John, *KZ* 88, 1974, 147–53, is mistaken on *faxim*; also Xodorkovskaja, *ŽA* 25, 1976, 31–7.

[7] Thomas, *Latomus* 15, 1956, 11; *RPh* 82, 1956, 207f. (but see 210f.); cf. also Watkins, in *AIED* 41.

[8] Leumann², 573f., 621f.; Hahn, *Subjunctive* 61; Cowgill, *Lg* 39, 263.

[9] Hahn, loc. cit. n. 115; Pariente, *Em* 31, 1963, 59f.; 33, 1965, 23f.

[10] Schwyzer, *GG* i, 787; Householder, *Lg* 30, 1954, 398; W. P. Schmid, *Studien zum baltischen und idg. Verbum*, 1963, 43 n. 163; K. H. Schmidt, *SCelt* 1, 23.

[11] Schwyzer, *GG* ii, 309f.; Kuryłowicz, *Categories* 140.

[12] Porzig, *Gliederung* 88; also Savčenko, *LPosn* 12–13, 1968, 34–5. The new Gaulish future forms in *-syo-* (e.g. *bissiet* 'will strike') could, as K. H. Schmidt says (in *Le lingue ie. di frammentaria attestazione*, Pisa 1983, 78), lead to a revival of the old theory that this formation was common IE. So also Hollifield, *IF* 86, 1981, 161–89, and *EC* 20, 1983, 91–9.

[13] Aitzetmüller, *Gedenkschrift W. Brandenstein*, 1968, 11–16; but see Jasanoff, in Bammesberger 1988, 232 n. 13 (against).

[14] On the spread of the Balts in the south-east as far as the Desna-Sejm line and on Iranian influence, see V. N. Toporov and O. N. Trubačev, *Lingvističeskij analiz gidronimov verxnego Podneprov'ja*, 1962 (esp. 231 and map 2 with the geographical distribution); M. Gimbutas, 'Ancient Baltic lands', *International Journal of Slavic Linguistics and Poetics* 6, 1963, 69–102; Pauls, 'River names in the Pripet Basin', *Names* 12, 1964, 185–96; Filin, *VJ* 1967 (3), 28–41; on the region south of the Pripet and Desna, O. N. Trubačev, *Nazvanija rek pravoberežnoj Ukrainy*, Moscow 1968, esp. 5–14 (research report) and 269–89 (evaluation of the various language elements, with maps). Against, Arumaa, 'Baltes et iraniens', *Studi Pisani*, 1969, 73–90. See also Sulimirski, 'Neighbours of the Baltic tribes', *Acta Balto-Slavica* 5, 1968, 1–17.

[15] W. P. Schmid (n. 10 above), 55f.; Stang, *Vgl. Gram.* 397; Kazlauskas, *Lietuvių kalbos istorinė gramatika*, 1968, 365f., is particularly thorough. See also Watkins, *Verb* 216; Jasanoff, *Stative* 106, and the review in Klein, *Lg* 60, 1984, 136.

[16] W. P. Schmid (n. 10 above), 78.

[17] See 9.4.1.5 n. 11 above and Cowgill, *Lg* 39, 264. That the athem. 3rd s. of Old Irish (*gigis* 'will ask' from **gi-ged-s-ti*) is also secondary is clear from *-lili* 'will follow' from **li-li-s-e-t* (Thurneysen, *GOI* 414).

[18] Cf. Watkins, *Origins* 161.

[19] Schwyzer, *GG* i, 787; Kuryłowicz, *Apophonie* 33 n. and 34; cf. W. P. Schmid (n. 10 above), 43f.; Poultney, *Lg* 43, 1968, 873, 878–9. Yet Kuryłowicz, *Categories* 115, again starts from the *s*-aorist.

[20] H. Smith, *JA* 240, 1952, 169–83, esp. 182, started from an athematic *-s-ti*, which appears variously reshaped as *-s-t-ti* in Proto-Prakrit, as *-s-ya-ti* in Aryan, as *-siu* in Baltic, as *-σ-ε-ται* in Proto-Greek. But Proto-Prakrit was not different from Aryan; see Berger, *MSS* 4, 1954, 25; Alsdorf, *Studies W. N. Brown*, 1962, 4.

[21] e.g. Hirt, *IG* iv, 176; cf. Hahn, *Subjunctive* 71 n.

[22] For periphrases of the future, cf. Pinkster, 'The development of future tense auxiliaries in Latin', *Glotta* 63, 1985, 186–208 (*uelle, debēre, posse, habēre, īre*).

9.4.3. Perfect

A perfect with a clearly defined place in the system is found only in Aryan and Greek. But if the distinctive characteristics of this formation are examined, it can easily be recognized that the old perfect is preserved in Germanic almost intact, in Old Irish with some mixing, while in Latin perfect and aorist have fused into a new perfect.[1]

As we have already seen, the perfect has special personal endings. These are added without connecting vowel to the perfect stem, which in verb roots with *e* as basic vowel has *o*-grade in the active singular, zero grade elsewhere; cf. from γίγνομαι 'become, am born' Hom. 3rd s. γέ-γον-ε 'is': 3rd dual (ἐκ)γε-γά-την, where γα represents the zero grade *gn̥*. These forms at the same time show a further characteristic of the perfect, reduplication.

(*a*) The *personal endings* of the singular (see 9.2.3) were *-a -tha -e*. The reconstruction of the 3rd s. as *-e* is based not only on Greek but also on Celtic, for the opposition of OIr. 1st s. *gád*: 3rd s. *gáid* points to IE *-a*: *-e*;[2] in any case, Greek and Celtic contradict the assumption[3] that the 3rd s., and with it the whole of the singular, had *a*-timbre. The 2nd s. is especially prone to innovation. In Greek from the beginning of its tradition the old ending is properly preserved only in the verb οἶδα (οἶσθα from **woid-tha*); in general it is replaced by -ας, as also in Old Irish; on the other hand it is preserved in Lat. *-(s)tī* and Goth. *-t*, the development after a spirant, e.g. *gaf-t* 'gavest'.[4]

Originally the perfect had only 'active' endings. This can be seen at once from the fact that many middle verbs have only active inflexion in the perfect; cf. γίγνομαι: γέγονα, μαίνομαι: μέμηνα 'rave'. Later under the influence of the basic middle form the perfect also acquired middle inflexion, and there arose γεγένημαι alongside and in place of γέγονα, πέπεισμαι 'trust' in place of the old πέποιθα from πείθομαι, etc. (see Chantraine 1927, 21f.); in Old Indic, to the active *tu-tōd-a* (from *tudati* 'strikes', Lat. *tu-n-d-ō*), the only form (3rd s.) in Vedic literature, was later added the middle *tu-tud-ē*. The Latin endings (9.2.3) can be seen as variants of the active endings extended with *i*, the sign of the 'here and now'.[5] The difficulty is that the root form of perfects like *de-d-ī*, i.e. their zero grade, does not agree at all with the active forms of the perfect, while on the other hand the full grade of forms like *uīdī fūgī* (from **woid- *bhoug-*), etc. does not suit middle endings; it is therefore possible that in Latin too a middle was formed to the active perfect. The form **woidai* just mentioned is also the basis for the only clear trace of the perfect in Slavic, *vēdē* 'I know'; it is by no means admissible to derive the paradigm athematically constructed on *vēd-* (1 *vēdē*, 2 *vēsi*, 3 *vēstŭ*, etc.) from an *ē*-perfect **woid-ē-m*, the *-ē-* of which could not have been lost.[6] The perfect endings are further discussed below, 9.7.1.3.

(*b*) *Reduplication* in the symbolic form (9.4.1.2) had become in late IE a purely grammatical expedient. In roots beginning with a consonant the initial consonant, or in the case of *s*+stop the whole group, was repeated with *e* before the root; cf. Gr. δέ-δορκ-α 'I have seen', Goth. *stai-staut* 'struck', etc. In various languages the vowel of the reduplication was assimilated to the root vowel in the course of their history or even in their prehistory; cf. e.g. Lat. *momordī spopondī poposcī pupugī cucurrrī*, which in early Latin still began with *mem-*

spep- pep- pep- cec-, or OIr. *-cuála* 'I heard' from **kuklowa*, IE **kek-low-a*, OInd. *bubudhē* 'I was awake' from IE **bhe-bhudh-*.[7] From IE **bheu-* 'become', on the basis of an IE 3rd s. **bhe-bhow-e*, 3rd pl. **bhe-bhuw-r̥*, in the first place OInd. **babhāva*, **babhūvur* were to be expected; the latter is in fact the normal form, but the former was reshaped according to the general rule to **bubhāva* and finally became *babhūva* by metathesis, just as **su-sāv-a* 'gave birth to' became *sasūva*. In Avestan, on the other hand, the 3rd pl. was kept as *babuvar* (written *bābvarə*), the 3rd s. as *bubāva* (written *bvāva*).[8] In some cases the reduplication vowel is lengthened in Aryan and Greek (?), e.g. OInd. *dādhāra* to *dhar-* 'hold'; the lengthening is presumably of rhythmic origin.[9]

In roots beginning with a vowel, lengthening of the vowel takes place, e.g. Lat. *ēdī ōdī*, Goth. *uz-ōn* 'breathed out' (IE **ān-*, cf. Lat. *animus*), OIce. *ōl* 'grew', *ōk* 'travelled' (IE **āl- *āg-*, cf. Lat. *alō agō*); it must have been caused by contraction of the reduplication vowel *e* with *a e o* to *ā ē ō*.[10] Lat. *ēdī* and (perhaps) *ōdī* have their equivalents in Gr. ἔδηδα and ὄδωδα. This *Attic reduplication* is based on the *ἦδα *ὦδα which correspond to the Latin forms, but were liable to marked changes in different environments (e.g. 2nd s. *ἦσθα=ἦσθα 'you were (s.)', 2nd pl. *ἦστε=ἦστε 'you were (pl.)'), and were therefore morphologically filled out, just as *ἐστός from **ed-to-s* was filled out to ἐδ-εστός 'edible'; see Wackernagel, *KSchr.* 717, and more recently Szemerényi, *Minos* 12 (1972), 309f.

From these and other forms from monosyllabic roots such as ἄρηρα ὄλολα ὄπωπα ὄρωρα the rule was extended to disyllabic roots: thus from **ākowa *ēgora *ēnoka* (from ἀκούω, ἐγείρω, ἐνεκ- 'carry') arose **ak-ākowa *eg-ēgora *en-ēnoka*, Att. ἀκήκοα ἐγ-ρ-ήγορα ἐνήνοχα.[11] The Attic reduplication in the perfect is thus fundamentally different from the similarly named reduplication in the present or aorist; see 9.4.1.2 n. 5.

In so far as they have a perfect, reduplication is the general rule in the historical languages.[12] An exception, probably the only exception, in late or common Indo-European must be reckoned the perfect **woida* 'I know', which from **wewoida* led by assimilation to **wowoida* and then, owing to frequent use, to the simplification **woida* (see 9.2.3); a trace of the old reduplication still survives in the participle **weid-wōs*, the vocalism of which can be explained only from **we-wid-*, since original **weid-* would have had to give the zero-grade form **wid-wōs*.[13] Of course, further instances and even classes of perfects without reduplication arose secondarily in the individual languages. Thus reduplicated perfects in Latin lost their reduplication in compounds (e.g. OLat. *tetulī*, but *contulī*, etc.), and the shorter forms could then make their way into the simple verb, e.g. classical *tulī*. In Greek the shortening of a long vowel before the group liquid or nasal+stop or *s* (Osthoff's Law) led to forms without reduplication, especially in Ionic, cf. ὄργυια 'fathom' from *ωρ(ο)γυια (see 5.3.7f, and *Syncope* 209, 229f.). Old Indic also has sporadic losses to record, namely finite forms from half a dozen roots and three participles, e.g. *takṣur* 'they made', *dāś-vas-* 'paying homage'.[14] A more systematic elimination of reduplication took place in Germanic: removed from the first six classes of strong verbs, it now survives only in the seventh, and even there really only in Gothic; in the other Germanic languages apart from a few remnants it has been entirely given up; nevertheless cf. Goth. *saisō* 'sowed'=OIce. *sera*, Goth. *haihait*=OE (Anglian) *heht*, etc.[15] The loss of reduplication is difficult to explain in detail,[16] but it cannot in any case be done by supposing that reduplication was only used in IE if the root vowel could not show *o*-grade;[17] such an assumption is at once contradicted by the Gothic type *lailōt* with reduplication and *o*-grade (pres. *lētan* 'let'), and by the Italic perfects **fēked*, **făked*, **fefēked*, *fefăked*, all from *faciō*, etc. (see Lejeune, *Fs. Sommer* (1955), 145–53).

(*c*) The *root syllable* shows as far as possible *o*-grade in the singular (active), elsewhere the zero grade. A good example of this is the IE paradigm **woid-a *woid-tha *woid-e*, but pl. **wid-me* etc., and the change to *o*-grade is especially clear in early Greek, Germanic, and Celtic, cf. Gr. λείπω:λέλοιπα 'leave', Goth. *niman*: *nam*, etc., OIr. *gegon* 'I have wounded'. It is probable that in Slavic some presents with *o*-grade, e.g. OCS *bojati sę* 'be afraid', go back to IE perfects.[18] There are, however, some deviations from this basic rule.

In Old Indic, where the contrast between *e* in the reduplication and *o* in the root is indicated by the palatal law (*kar-* 'make': perf. *ča-kar-a*), we find that the 3rd s. of roots with single final consonant has in Vedic *ā* in contrast to *a* in the 1st s. (see MacDonell, *Vedic Grammar*, 353f., 356); cf. 1 *ča-kar-a*: 3 *ča-kār-a*, 1 *ǰa-gam-a*: 3 *ǰa-gām-a* 'went', 1 *bi-bhay-a*: 3 *bi-bhāy-a* 'feared'. At first it was thought that this distinction could be explained with the help of the so-called Brugmann's Law, IE *o*>*ā*; see 4.1, n. 2; thus 3rd s. *ǰa-gām-a* would have come regularly from IE **g^{w}e-g^{w}om-e*. The consequence of this would, of course, have been that 1st s. *ǰagama* could not be derived from **g^{w}eg^w-oma*, but the form **g^{w}eg^{w}ema* proposed as a solution[19] finds no support anywhere and in Aryan itself is in conflict with the palatal law. Laryngeals came to the rescue: Brugmann's Law was, it was claimed, correct, since the difference between 1st and 3rd s. stemmed from the fact that the forms were **g^{w}e-g^{w}om-Ha* and **g^{w}e-g^{w}om-e*, and only the latter had *o* in an open syllable.[20] But this leaves the *sēṭ* roots still unexplained: if 1st s. *ǰaǰana* (and causative *ǰanayati*) has *ă* because the root is **ǰanH-*, then the 3rd s. from **ǰa-ǰanH-a* would have to give OInd. **ǰaǰana* and not the actually attested *ǰaǰāna*. This difference definitely proves that the long vowel of the 3rd s. (later optionally of the 1st s. also) is not phonetically based (*pace* Adrados, *FoLH* 2 (1981) 193). It was perhaps introduced on the analogy of morphological parallels such as OInd. zero-grade *tud-* 'strike' and *sad-* 'sit', where in the *o*-grade *taud*: *sad* was modified to *taud*: *sād*,[21] but even so it remains puzzling why the two persons, which have the same structure, should have been treated differently.[22]

Long-grade forms are also found in other languages, but not restricted to a single person. An example occurs in Gr. *γέγωνε* 'he is audible' from **gen-* 'recognize', and perhaps in *εἴωθα* 'I am accustomed': *ἔθων* 'according to his wont'.[23] Much more important, however, is the role of the long grade in the perfect system of the other European languages, especially those of the West.

Here we must first call to mind the Latin perfects with long grade throughout: *clēpit* 'stole', *ēdī*, *ēmī*, *(co-)ēpī*, *frēgī*, *lēgī*, *sēdī*, *uēnī*; *scābī*; *fōdī*, *ōdī*. The perfects of roots with initial vowel are in any case inherited: *ēdī*, together with Gr. *ἔδ-ηδ-α* (see above under *b*) and Goth. *frēt* 'ate', goes back to an IE **ēd-*, and probably the OCS present *ēmi* 'I eat' also belongs here, just as Lat. *ōdī* with Gr. *ὄδ-ωδ-α* and Lith. *uodžiu* 'I smell' (**ōdyō*) leads back to IE **ōd-*.[24] As regards form, *ēdī* and *ōdī* can be derived from IE **H_1e-H_1d-ai* and **H_3e-H_3d-ai*,[25] but, quite apart from the unfounded laryngeal in **ed-* (6.6.9), the middle in the system of these verbs would also be unfounded and their clear relationship with forms in other languages would have to be abandoned; the old explanation from **e-ed-* and **e-od-* is preferable.[26]

In roots with initial consonant the Latin forms find direct correspondences in Germanic; cf. *clēpit frēgimus sēdimus uēnimus* and Goth. *hlēfum brēkum sētum qēmum*. Against these obvious comparisons the objection is often brought that in Germanic the long grade is found only in the plural, whereas in the singular the IE *o*-grade had its place, cf. *hlaf brak sat qam*. On the other hand, it has been rightly pointed out that *ēt* in Goth. *frēt* and *sēt* in OHG *gi-saaz* (Weissenburg Catechism) are in agreement with Latin in showing long grade also in the singular, so that in the fifth class of strong verbs the *o*-grade must have been introduced only analogically.[27] Since in the OInd. inflexion type 3rd s. *sasāda*/1st pl. *sēdima* the latter certainly arose from the regular zero-grade form IE **se-sd-*, it is very tempting to trace back the type **sēd-* in roots with initial consonant to a similar phonetic development **sezd-*>**sēd-* in Indo-European, although the conditions are not clear.[28]

A Greek peculiarity is the *aspirated perfect*: in the strong perfect of verb stems with final guttural or labial this consonant is aspirated in Attic-Ionic, e.g. φυλακ-: πεφύλαχα, κόπ-τω: κέκοφα.[29]

(*d*) The perfect originally denoted a *state in the present* arising from an action in the past; cf. IE **woida* 'I have found it (out) and now have it, know it',[30] Lat. *(g)nōuī* 'I have recognized and now I know', Gr. τέθνηκε 'he is dead', ἕστηκε 'he has taken up his position and is now standing'. This also explains the Germanic preterite-presents.[31] At an early date, however, the perfect came to be used not only intransitively but also transitively, of an action continuing in its subject: λαγχάνω 'I obtain by lot': λέλογχα 'I have as my portion'; naturally also in passive transformations: γοῦνα λέλυνται 'their knees are loosened, weakened'. Only after Homer does the perfect denote an action continuing up to the present in the object (*resultative perfect*): δέδωκε 'he has given', τετίμηκε 'he has honoured'. This perfect then developed (in the third century BC) into a *narrative* tense: πέφευγε 'he fled',[32] and this has even been seen as embodying a general law of development.[33]

In addition to state the perfect also expresses elementary actions[32] such as 'he shouts', 'roars', 'smells', 'is joyful' (κέκρᾱγε, βέβρῡχε, ὄδωδε, γέγηθε), which cannot be derived from 'resulting state' but on the other hand can very well be understood as intensives. Both the intensive and the resulting state are consistent with reduplication, which gives expression to just these meanings.[34]

Since the perfect is so easily transferred to a narrative use,[33] the attrition of perfect forms is very great and they must continually be replaced. This accounts for the large number of innovations in this area of the verbal system. In classical Latin the *ui*-perfect, which is still not fully explained,[35] is of the highest importance, in Greek the *k*-perfect[36] continually extends its range, in Germanic the still obscure weak preterite is already complete at the outset;[37] in Italic new creations are the *f*-perfect of Oscan-Umbrian, the *tt*-perfect of Oscan and the *nś*-perfect of Umbrian.[38] A dental preterite appears in Continental Celtic also.[39]

At the end of the IE period the fully developed perfect had as characteristics, first, special endings, secondly, reduplication, and thirdly, when possible, *o*-grade and zero grade.

[1] Brugmann, *Grundriss*², ii/3, 427f.; Schwyzer, *GG* i, 764f.; Belardi, 'La formazione del perfetto nell'ie.', *Ricerche Linguistiche* 1, 1950, 93–131; K. H. Schmidt, 'Das Perfekt in idg. Sprachen', *Glotta* 42, 1964, 1–18; K. Hoffmann, *MSS* 28, 1970, 39–41; Meid, 'Osservazioni sul perfetto', *InL* 4, 1978, 31–41; P. di Giovine, *Studi sul perfetto ie.* i: *La funzione originaria del perfetto*, Rome 1990 (cf. *IC* 34, 331f.); Lazzeroni (above, 9.2.7 n. 8); Rix, *Fs. Untermann*, 1993, 329–48; Prosdocimi and Marinetti, ibid. 297–328.

[2] Thurneysen, *GOI* 433.

[3] Pisani, *KZ* 60, 1933, 221f.; Belardi (n. 1 above), 101; Neu, *IF* 72, 1968, 225.

[4] See G. Schmidt, *Glotta* 63, 1985, 90f.; Sihler, *MSS* 47, 1986, 193–222 (Gmc. 2nd s. *-st*); Jasanoff, *Fs. Hoenigswald*, 1987, 179 (Lat. *-i-stī*); Nielsen, *NOWELE* 14, 1990, 74–6 (Gmc. *-st*).

[5] See further Bader (above, 9.2.3 n. 4), 97 n. 36; Untermann, *Gedenkschrift Brandenstein*, 1968, 165–71.

[6] Vaillant, 'Le parfait ie. en balto-slave', *BSL* 57, 1962, 52–6; *Gram. comp.* iii, 76, 448; Aitzetmüller, *Slawistische Studien zum 5. Kongress*, 1963, 209f.

[7] Leumann, *Fs. Kuiper*, 1968, 54; McCone, *PICCS* 7, 1986, 233: Indo-Iranian reduplication more conservative than Greek, in general *e*, but in roots with *i/u*, assimilated. On the difference in the reduplication of πέπτηκα:ἔπταικα, see Gunnarson, *NTS* 24, 1971, 81, and (against) Kuryłowicz, *BSL* 68, 1973, 95.

[8] A somewhat different account in Brugmann, *Grundriss*², ii/3, 25, 441, 454; Benveniste, *Symbolae Kuryłowicz*, 1965, 25f.; Strunk, *KZ* 86, 1972, 21–7; Rasmussen, *Haeretica*, 1974, 36f.; Pisani, *Sodalizio Milanese* 19, 1978, 26; Jasanoff, in *Studies Polomé*, 1988, 299–308; also Bammesberger, *GL* 21, 1982, 231–5; Kellens, *Verbe* 404, is uncertain.

[9] Schwyzer, *GG* i, 648; cf. also Kuryłowicz, *Apophonie* 342f.; Benveniste (n. 8 above); Lindeman, *NTS* 23, 1969, 20; but see again Kuryłowicz, *IG* 312.

[10] See above, 6.2.8, Addendum 2. Benveniste, *ArchL* 1, 1949, 17, uses laryngeals.

[11] Wackernagel, *KSchr.* 901, is not entirely clear, while Schwyzer, *GG* i, 276 has two different views: in the text the view represented here (ἐνήνοχα<*ἤνοχα), but in n. 8 a quite different one. Solta, *InL* 5, 1979, 82 n. 59, thinks that the archaic character of ἐγρήγορα was proved by Avest. *fra-γrā-γrā*.

For the explanation of *Attic reduplication* the laryngeal theory was first brought into play by Kuryłowicz in 1927: thus e.g. ἐληλουθ- was derived by purely phonetic processes from **Hle-Hloudh-*, see his *Études* 31–33; subsequently maintained by Chantraine, *SMEA* 3, 1967, 26; Beekes, *Laryngeals* 113–24; Ruijgh, *Mél. Chantraine*, 1972, 216f.; Rix 1976, 204. This hypothesis was later abandoned by its author and an internal Greek development suggested: **lel-loudh-e*>ἐλ-έλουθε>ἐλ-ήλουθε (with compositional lengthening!), see *Apophonie* 269f.; *Fs. Safarewicz*, 1974, 111–15; *Metrik und Sprachgeschichte*, 1975, 19; and cf. Cowgill, in *Evidence* 153; Schmeja, *Studies Palmer*, 1976, 353f.; Lindeman, *The Triple Representation of Shwa in Greek*, 1982, 59; and above, 9.4.1.2 n. 5 and 9.4.2.1*b*. The young Kuryłowicz is defended (against himself!) by Mayrhofer, e.g. *Krat* 33, 1988, 11. For the prothesis, see 6.4.7.3.

[12] On this fairly controversial question, see K. Hoffmann, *Aufsätze* 539; Bader, *BSL* 64, 1970, 57–100; Meid 1971, 53f., 68f., 78; Kammenhuber, *KZ* 94, 1980, 36; Bammesberger, *Fachtagung* 6, 1980, 1f.

[13] Szemerényi, 'The PPA in Mycenaean and IE', *SMEA* 2, 1967, 25; Ruijgh, *Lingua* 26, 1971, 191 (εἰδώς replaced ϝιδϝως); now again Rasmussen, *Fs. Rix*, 1993, 411 n. 4; Winter, ibid. 479–84.

[14] MacDonell, *Vedic Grammar*, 1910, 353; Wackernagel and Debrunner, *Ai. Gr.* ii/2, 1954, 910; cf. also Thumb and Hauschild, i/2, 277; Leumann (n. 7 above).

[15] Cf. Prokosch 1939, 176f.; Hirt, *Urgerm. Gram.* ii, 1932, 142f.; *SGGJ* iv, 1966, 248f., as also Kuryłowicz, *Apophonie* 312 n.; Feuillet, *BSL* 76, 1981, 209f.

[16] Kuryłowicz, *BPTJ* 10, 1950, 29–31; Rosenkranz, *KZ* 75, 1958, 221; Bech, *Das germ. reduplizierte Präteritum*, 1969; *Idg. Verbalmorphologie*, 1971, 70; Meid 1971, 53; Höfler, *FoL* 4, 1971, 110–20; Rasmussen, *Haeretica*, 1974, 33–40 (against reduplication); Kuryłowicz, *Metrik und Sprachgeschichte*, 1975, 155f.

[17] Cf. Meillet, *Introduction* 206; Kuryłowicz, *Categories* 70f.; Bader (above, 9.2.3 n. 4), 98; also Belardi (n. 1 above), 95; Brock, *RHA* 75, 1964, 149f.; Lindeman, *Fs. Knobloch*, 1985, 237 (reduplication given up in general, retained only where without it a monosyllabic form would have arisen).

[18] Vaillant, *BSL* 57, 1962, 53; *Gram. comp.* iii, 77. On the *o*-grade, see above 6.3 and Kuryłowicz, *Categories* 70.

[19] First presumably by Saussure, *Mémoire* 72f. A more complicated (and unique) system with *e* in 3rd pl., *o* in 2nd and 3rd s., and zero grade in 1st s. was proposed by G. Schmidt, *KZ* 85, 1972, 249f., 254f., 263f.

[20] So first Kuryłowicz, *Prace filologiczne* 11, 1927, 206f., and still found in Mayrhofer, *Sanskrit-Grammatik*², 1965, 18; *Sprache* 10, 1965, 178; Insler, *IF* 73, 1969, 332.

[21] See Kuryłowicz, *BSL* 45, 1949, 57–60; *Apophonie* 321f., 332 (causatives), and esp. 337. This view has been represented by Pisani since the 1930s: *RAL* 6/10, 1934, 401–3; *AGI* 34,

1942, 21; Pisani and Pokorny, *Allgem. und vergl. Sprachwissenschaft*, 1953, 48.

[22] See further Belardi, (n. 1 above), 95f.; Thumb and Hauschild i/2, 278.

[23] Cf. Schwyzer, *GG* i, 770, 703[4]. But ἔωθα (later spelt εἴωθα) is perhaps simply from **ēotha*, the regular development from **swe-swoth-a*, by metathesis.

[24] Vaillant, n. 18 above. A different view in Kuryłowicz, *Apophonie* 306f. Cf. also Bammesberger, *Germ. Verbalsystem*, 1986, 57 (*ēt* from impf. **e-ed-*).

[25] Benveniste, *ArchL* 1, 1949, 16f. Cf. also Cowgill, *Lg* 36, 1960, 491f.; Makajev, *Lings* 10, 1964, 42 n.; Polomé, *PICL* 9, 1964, 873; Lindeman, *IF* 72, 1968, 275f.; *NTS* 22, 1968, 76; Bader, *BSL* 63, 1969, 160f.

[26] For laryngeals, Leumann[2], 589f.; but see Feuillet, *BSL* 76, 1981, 207. A different view in Leumann[1], 332.

[27] Fourquet, *Festgabe Hammerich*, 1962, 61–8; Makajev, *Lings* 10, 41, in spite of Polomé (n. 25 above).

[28] Kuryłowicz, *Categories* 71. On the long-grade perfects in Celtic, see Meid, in *Idg. und Keltisch*, 1977, 124f. Hittite has an ablaut *a/e* (e.g. *sak-/sek-* 'know'), which has been connected by Kammenhuber, *KZ* 94, 1980, 36, with the Germanic ablaut *a/ē*; Lindeman's view on this ablaut, *Fs. Knobloch*, 1985, 239, is improbable.

[29] See Christol, *BSL* 67, 1973, 69–83, and (especially attractive) Ringe, 'εἴληφα and the aspirated perfect', *Glotta* 62, 1984, 125–41: he suggests (136–7) that εἴληφα as perfect to λαμβάνω is a cross between **labh-* and **lab-* from **slag*^{w}*-* in λάζομαι; cf. also Slings, *Glotta* 64, 1986, 9–14.

[30] So e.g. Oertel, *KZ* 63, 1936, 260f.; Schwyzer, *GG* ii, 263; Seebold, *Sprache* 19, 1973, 20–38, 158–79, esp. 176. Taken differently (from **wid-* 'observe'), e.g. Leumann, *Morphologische Neuerungen im ai. Verbalsystem*, 1952, 77; K. Hoffmann, *Aufsätze* 539; Meid, *InL* 4, 1978, 33; Cowgill, in *Heth. und Idg.*, 1979, 36.

[31] Meid (n. 1 above); Th. Birkmann, *Präterito-Präsentia*, Tübingen, 1985; Ruipérez, *É. Benveniste aujourd'hui* ii, 1984, 137–41; Euler, *Moduskategorien der Perfektopräsentien im Indogermanischen*, 1993.

[32] Cf. Wackernagel, *Vorlesungen über Syntax* i[2], 1950, 166f.; Schwyzer, *GG* i, 768; ii 263f., 286f.; Hofmann–Szantyr, 317f.; MacDonell, *A Vedic Grammar for Students*, 1955, 341f. On the Greek perfect: McKay, 'The use of the Ancient Greek perfect down to the 2nd cent. AD', *Bulletin of the Institute of Classical Studies* 12, London 1965, 1–21; on the resultative perfect: Keil, *Glotta* 41, 1963, 29–41; Meid 1971, 41; Kuryłowicz, *BPTJ* 29, 1972, 24–8. On the perfect and possessive relationship see Lohmann, *KZ* 64, 1937, 42–61; Vendryes, *Mél. van Ginneken*, 1937, 85f.; Benveniste, *BSL* 48, 1952, 52–62; Allen, *Lg* 40, 1964, 337–43. The perfect originally denoted states of mind, not a resultative state, according to Perel'muter, *VJ* 1967 (1), 92–102 (coincides with Schwyzer, *GG* ii, 263!).

[33] Grünenthal, *KZ* 63, 1933, 135–40, esp. 136; Kuryłowicz, *Apophonie* 29; *Categories* 25f., 56f.

[34] On these problems, see Meid 1971, 34f.; Berrettoni, 'L'uso del perfetto nel greco omerico', *SSL* 12, 1972, 25–170 (conclusion 150); 16, 1976, 207.

[35] Szemerényi, *KZ* 70, 1951, 72–6; Lindeman, *IF* 71, 1967, 280 n. 11; *NTS* 22, 1968, 48–67; Wagner, *TPS* 1969, 218f.; Watkins, *Verb* 151; Meid 1971, 81, 131; Lejeune, *Lepontica*, 1971, 94 (*dedū* from *dedō-u*); Wyatt, *Lg* 48, 1972, 691; Parlangèli, *RIL* 100, 1972, 236–41; Narten, *MSS* 31, 1973, 136f.; J. Gonzáles Fernández, *El perfecto latino en /-ui/*, Seville 1974; Bammesberger, *Lg* 50, 1974, 689f.; Markey, *Germanic Dialect Grouping*, 1976, 53f. (OE *sǣwan* an innovation); *JIES* 7, 1979, 65–75; *Krat* 27, 1983, 134–6; *KZ* 98, 1985, 266; Bammesberger, *Fachtagung* 6, 1980, 14f.; id. 1986, 60f.; Lindeman, *Fs. Knobloch*, 1985, 238f. (on OE *sēow* etc.); G. Schmidt, *Glotta* 63, 1985, 52–92 (*-u-* 'there, then'); Matzel, *KZ* 100, 1987, 175f.; Shields, *ŽA* 41–2, 1992, 15–19; Rix, 'Entstehung des lateinischen Perfektparadigmas', in *Fachtagung* 9, 1992, 221–40 (part. *-wos*); Prosdocimi and Marinetti, 'Appunti sul verbo latino', in *Fs. Untermann*, 1993, 297–308. Schmitt-Brandt, 123 is quite improbable.

[36] Cf. Kronasser, *AO* 25, 1957, 518f.; Pisani, *Krat* 3, 1958, 19; Lazzeroni, *ASNP* 29, 1960, 120f. (all in favour of a connection – by borrowing? – with the Anatolian preterite in *-ha*); Markey, *IF* 85, 1981, 279–97; Dunkel, in *In Memory of W. Cowgill*, 1987, 25f.; Kimball, 'Origin of the Greek *k*-perfect', *Glotta* 69, 1991, 141–53; Untermann, *Fs. Rix*, 1993, 461–9; Harðarson 1993, 146–50.

37 Among more recent attempts at explanation: Watkins, *Ériu* 19, 1962, 45; Kuryłowicz, *Categories* 126f.; Polomé, *PICL* 9, 878; Hiersche, *Zeitschrift für deutsche Philologie* 87, 1968, 391–404 (on Wisniewski, Hammerich, Bech); Knapp, *Fs. Höfler*, 1968, 301–14; Ball, *TPS* 1968, 162–88; Meid 1971, 107–17; Bech, *Idg. Verbalmorphologie*, 1971, 68f.; Migačev, *VJ* 1972 (4), 80–9; Rasmussen, *Haeretica*, 1974, 51 n. 14; G. Schmidt, *KZ* 90, 1977, 262–70; Jasanoff 1978, 91 (**mn̥-to>munda-ï*); Birkhan, *Das Zipfsche Gesetz*, Vienna Acad. 1979, 55–80; Pohl, in *Fs. Vernay*, 1979, 354–8; Hollifield, *Sprache* 26, 1980, 150–60; Kortlandt, *IF* 86, 1982, 128; Feuillet, *BSL* 76, 1982, 210–17; Lühr, in Untermann and Brogyanyi (eds.), *Das Germanische und die Rekonstruktion der idg. Grundsprache*, 1984, 41–51; Mańczak, *KZ* 97, 1984, 99–112; Bammesberger 1986, 69f.; id., *PBB* 109, 1987, 344; Matzel (n. 35 above), 187–203 (188: dental pret. *sēðē* from verbal adj. -*ða*-; 199: Goth. -*dēdum*); *Krat* 34, 1989, 139; Pohl, *Fs. Meid*, 1989, 193–207 (-*to*- part.); Kortlandt, 'The Germanic weak preterit', *ABäG* 28, 1989, 101–9; Bammesberger, *PBB(T)* 113, 1991, 22–7 (pret. of *arjan* transformed to *ēr-/eur-*, but cf. Lindeman, *NTS* 22, 1968, 74f.); L. Melazzo, *On the Germanic Weak Preterite*, Palermo 1991 (worthless). For the history of the research, see Tops, *The Origin of the Germanic Dental Preterit: a Critical Research History since 1912*, Ithaca, NY, 1972.

38 See e.g. Osc. *fufens, fufans* 'fuerunt', *dadikatted* 'dedicauit', Paelignian *coisatens* 'curauerunt', Umbr. (fut. perf.) *purdinšiust* 'porrexerit' (from -*nky*-), and cf. (for *f*) Poultney, *The Bronze Tables of Iguvium*, 1959, 134; Olzscha, *Glotta* 41, 1963, 290–9; Negri, 'I perfetti osco-umbri in -*f*-', *RIL* 110, 1977, 3–10 (from -*dh*- ~ θω); Rix, in *Le lingue ie. di frammentaria attestazione*, 1983, 101; (for *tt*) G. Schmidt, *KZ* 90, 1977, 269; Xodorkovskaja, *VJ* 1979 (3), 106–18 (-*t*- ~ -*dh*-); (for *nš*) Poultney, op. cit. 135; Jerrett, *TAPA* 104, 1974, 169–78; Pisani, *AGI* 60, 1975, 220–22; Markey, *KZ* 98, 1985, 260–8 (**enek*- 'carry'); Shields, *HS* 102, 1989, 74–83 (79: -*N*+*ki*). On all Osc.-Umbr. formations, see Rix, in *Fachtagung* 9, 1992, 238–40.

There is apparently also an Osc. *k*-perfect, e.g. *kellaked* 'concamerauit (?)' to Lat. *cella* (?) on an inscription from Bovianum Vetus, see Lejeune, *Mél. Heurgon*, 1976, 553f.; Poccetti, *Nuovi documenti italici*, 1979, 33f.; cf. Pisani, *Le lingue dell'Italia antica oltre il latino*[2], 1964, 52. On the Slavic imperfect, see Rasmussen, *IC* 33, A 261 (9).

39 See Eska, *HS* 103, 1990, 81f.

9.4.4. Augment, polymorphism, suppletivism, system, aspect, accent

9.4.4.1

In the south-east of the Indo-European area, an additional sign characterizes not only the aorist but also certain formations from the present and perfect stems which, like the aorist, do not take primary endings. This element, called the *augment*, is especially well known from Greek and Aryan, where the formations marked by the augment from the present and perfect stems, the *imperfect* and *pluperfect*, have a place clearly assigned to them in the verbal system.

(*a*) The augment[1] in verb stems beginning with a consonant is *e*-, the *syllabic augment*. In stems beginning with a vowel this *e*- contracted with the initial vowel in the IE period[2] to give the corresponding long vowel (*temporal augment*), thus *e*+*e*=*ē*, *e*+*o*=*ō*, *e*+*a*=*ā*. Cf. Gr. ἔ-φερε-ς=OInd. *a-bhara-s* 'you (s.) carried', IE **ebheres*; Gr. ἦα=OInd. *āsam* 'I was', IE **ēsm̥* from **e-es-m̥*; Gr. ἆγες (Att. ἦγες)=OInd. *āǰas* 'you (s.) led', IE **āges* from **e-ag-e-s*.

Outside Greek and Aryan, traces of the augment remain in Phrygian (εδαες 'statuit', cf. Hitt. *dais* 'he set'), and in a particularly interesting way in Armenian (Meillet 1936, 123f.): the augment is kept in the 3rd

s. aorist, but only when a verb with initial consonant would be monosyllabic without it, cf. 1 *beri*, 2 *berer*, 3 *eber* from **ebheret*, or 1 *lkhi*, 2 *lkher*, 3 *elikh* 'left' from **elik*^{w}et=Gr. ἔλιπε.

This rule is certainly connected with the well-known tendency not to allow word length to fall below a certain minimum, and is also to be observed in Greek: omission of the augment is not permitted if thereby a short monosyllable would have resulted; στῆ γνῶ are allowed, but only ἔκτα ἔσχε, not *κτα *σχε (see Schwyzer, *GG* i, 651).

In the early writings of Greek and Aryan, which are all verse, the use of the augment is optional; in prose, on the other hand, it is compulsory from the beginning. From this and from its geographical spread the conclusion is usually drawn that the augment was an innovation in a limited area within Indo-European, and one which, moreover, had not fully established itself.[3] In principle, of course, its absence from other languages could have been 'due to subsequent loss' (Porzig 1954, 87); it would nevertheless be welcome if its former area could be enlarged, just as its earlier existence in Slavic has already been postulated on the strength of certain accentual peculiarities of the aorist.[4] The attempt has been made to discover it in Hittite,[5] and perhaps it can also be demonstrated for Germanic.[6] The Mycenaean documents, in which except for a single form the augment is unknown,[7] certainly seem to support its optional use, but in reality they face us with a dilemma, since the temporal augment of the historical period presupposes a pre-Mycenaean contraction of *e*+*e* to *ē*.[8] On the other hand, a linguistic explanation has recently been given for the use and non-use of the augment, namely that there is a functional difference between the augmented and the unaugmented forms, with the consequence that the function of the augmented indicative is 'to report', that of the unaugmented injunctive 'to mention'.[9]

That the augment was originally an independent word, presumably an adverb, can among other indications be inferred from the fact that it carries the accent and consequently the verb is treated as an enclitic; its meaning was perhaps 'really'[10] or 'formerly, once'[11] or local, 'there'[12] or both together 'illic et tunc';[13] at any rate it was not a conjunctive particle.[14] Beside *e*, especially before sonants, *ē* also occurs as syllabic augment, e.g. OInd. *āyunak āyukta* from *yuǰ*- 'to yoke', *āriṇak* from *rič*- 'to set free', Gr. ἠ-ϝείδη 'knew' to ϝοῖδα.[15] An initial laryngeal could be postulated in such cases,[16] but examples are few, and reference may rather be made to the reduplication syllable with *e*/*ē* or alternations such as *ne*/*nē*, *pro*/*prō*.[17]

The general tendency is for the augment to be abandoned in the course of time. It is therefore the more remarkable that it survives even today at two points in its former area: in Greek and in Yaghnōbi, the descendant of the east Iranian language of Sogdiana; cf. mod. Gr. *ἔφυγα* 'I departed' and Yaghn. *akúnim* 'I made', *ašávim* 'I went'.

(*b*) The augment characterizes the indicative of the past tenses, i.e. the aorist, imperfect, and pluperfect; see Euler 1990.

The *imperfect* is the present stem supplied with augment and secondary endings; it is thus in opposition to the present, which is characterized by primary endings, cf. **ebheret*: **bhereti* in Gr. *ἔφερε*: *φέρει*, OInd. *ábharat*: *bharati*. The imperfect is at first glance restricted to the same area of Indo-European as the augment. The Lat. impf. in *-bā-* is in any case a young innovation.[18]. But the OCS aorist seems to have absorbed many of the old imperfect forms: the 2nd and 3rd s. aor. of thematic verbs, e.g. *vede* to 1st s. *vēsu* 'led', and of verbs in *-nǫ* such as *minǫ* 'go past', 2nd and 3rd s. aor. *minǫ*, must surely go back to IE imperfects such as **wedhes*, **wedhet* and *-*neus*, *-*neut*,[19], just as the Armenian aorist *eber* continues an imperfect form **ebheret*, which can never have been an aorist; the Old Irish imperfect[20] and the Baltic preterite in *-ē-* have also been traced back to the IE imperfect.[21] Slavic has formed a new imperfect in *-axŭ*, cf. *nesti* 'carry': *nesēaxŭ*[22], while Lithuanian has introduced a new formation with *-dava-*.[23]

The *pluperfect*[24] seems to be a much younger creation, but since the perfect—a present tense—is old, its past tense must be at least as old as the imperfect. In Greek beside *οἶδα* the preterite *ἠϝειδη-* (2nd s. *ἠείδης*, 3rd s. *ἠείδη* with variants) is widespread; its *-η-* occurs also in the future *εἰδήσω*. Slavic offers for comparison the aorist stem **vědě* and infinitive *věděti*, which prove a past-tense form in *-ē-* from the perfect *vědě* 'I know';[25] the attempt to connect *ᾔδεα* with Lat. *uīderam*,[26] by supposing *-ε(σ)α* to correspond with Lat. *-eram* on the basis of IE -*es-*, breaks down because the Greek form goes back to *-ē-*, which occurs readily in other verbs, especially the participle, cf. *κεχαρηότα*.

An older type, in which the SE were added directly to the stem, is preserved in dual and plural forms;[2] cf. *ἤιστην* 'both knew', *ἕστασαν* 'they stood', *ἐπέπιθμεν* 'we trusted'. This formation has parallels in Old Indic, e.g. *a-bi-bhē-t* 'was afraid', *ajāgar* 'was awake', *avēdam* 'I knew' to the present perfects *bibhāya*, *jāgāra*, *vēda*.[27]

[1] Schwyzer, *GG* i, 650f.; Meillet, *Introduction* 242; Chantraine, *Morph.* 309f.; Kuryłowicz, *Categories* 131; L. Bottin, 'L'aumento in Omero', *SMEA* 10, 1969, 69–145; Wright, *BSOAS* 33, 1970, 187, 199.

[2] But not with high vowels; in a number of cases forms such as *a-icchas* (RV x 108, 5) have to be restored: see Gonda, *Old Indian*, 1971, 9 n.

[3] Schwyzer, *GG* i, 56. Cf. Wackernagel, *Philologus* 95, 1942, 1f.; Pisani, *AGI* 51, 1967, 110f.; Ambrosini, *SSL* 2, 1962, 66f.; Blumenthal, *IF* 79, 1975, 67–77 (with the comments of Lehmann, *SLang* 3, 1979, 86); Lazzeroni, *SSL* 17, 1977, 29f.

[4] Vaillant, *Gram. comp.* iii, 17, 551; against, Durante, *Sulla preistoria della tradizione poetica greca*, 1976, 24 n. 25. On Lithuanian, see Hamp, *Baltistica* 12, 1976, 25f.

[5] See Eichner, *Fachtagung* 5, 1975, 78 (*ēsun* 'was' from **e-Hes-m̥*); against, Kammenhuber, *Fs. Winter*, 1985, 459 n. 7, but again defended by Eichner, in Bammesberger 1988, 125 n. 13.

[6] For Germanic the still puzzling Goth. *iddja* would be important; it could continue the reduplicated imperfect of the root *yā* 'go' (OInd. *yāmi*), i.e. **e-ye-yā-m*; other more recent but unacceptable suggestions in Cowgill, *Lg* 36, 1960, 483f. (on which see Makajev, *Lings* 10, 1964, 42 n. 49); Lindeman, *IF* 72, 1968, 275–86; Jasanoff, *MSS* 37, 1978, 86–7; Bammesberger, *Beiträge zu einem etym. Wb. des Altenglischen*, 1979, 44; Hollifield, *Sprache* 26, 1980, 162f.

[7] On this, see Duhoux, *Minos* 9, 1968, 92; Negri, *Convegno* 8, 1991, 50f.

[8] Szemerényi, *Atti e memorie del 1° Congresso di micenologia* ii, 1969, 724.

[9] R. Schmitt, *KZ* 81, 1967, 65–7, following Hoffmann, *Injunktiv* 145f.; against, Ferrari, *SSL* 9, 1969, 231f. On another possibility of augment loss, see Kiparsky, *FL* 4, 1968, 39.

[10] Schwyzer, *GG* i, 652 ('gewiss, sicherlich'); Cowgill, in J. H. Greenberg (ed.), *Universals of Language*, 1963, 108f. ('really'); Mayrhofer, *EWA* i, 36.

[11] Brugmann, *Grundriss*², ii/3, 11; Erhart, *Sbornik Brno* A/14, 1966, 17; Neumann, *Phrygisch* (above, 1.6 n. 7), 9; see also Kiparsky (n. 9 above), 45.

[12] E. Hermann, *GGN* 1943, 638 (demonstrative *e-/ē-*).

[13] Lazzeroni, *SSL* 17, 22f.; *Scritti in onore di R. Ambrosini*, 1985, 130f.

[14] So Watkins, *Celtica* 6, 1963, 15: *e-*=Luwian *a* 'and'; against, Friedrich, *Heth. Wb. Suppl.* 3, 49. Cf. further Bader, *BSL* 68, 1973, 60f.; Ivanov, *Obščeind.* 245f., and in *Slavjanskoje Jazykoznanije*, 1968, 230 n. 20; Ambrosini, *SSL* 2, 63, has a quite different view.

[15] Debrunner, 'Das Augment *ē*', *Fs. Fr. Zucker*, 1954, 85f.; Wyatt, *The Greek Prothetic Vowel*, 1972, 74–9.

[16] Kuryłowicz, *Études* 31, *Apophonie* 268, 339; Lehmann, *PIE* 77; also Cowgill, in *Evidence* 163, 169. The dreadful article of J. Daugmann, 'Long vowel augments in Sanskrit and Greek', *Lings* 35, 1968, 7–27, should never have been printed.

[17] Brugmann (n. 11 above); Schwyzer, *GG* i, 653.

[18] See Leumann², 579f. (bibliography); Baldi, *Lg* 52, 1976, 839–50: *amans-bhwām* (?); G. Schmidt, *KZ* 90, 1977, 265f.; Xodorkovskaja, *VJ* 1979 (3), 113f. (*-b-*<*-dh-*; cf. Machek, *Charisteria F. Novotný*, 1962, 102f., and esp. Thibau, *Rapports entre le latin et le grec*, 1964, 10f., for the same solution); *Pariente, 'Las formas verbales lat. en *-bam, -bo*', *Univ. Barcelona, Anuario do filosofía* 5, 1979, 19–71; Rix, in Vineis 1983, 101; Pohl, in *Latein und Indogermanisch*, 1992, 207f.

[19] Vaillant, *Gram. comp.* iii, 51, 54, 230.

[20] See e.g. K. H. Schmidt, 'Zum altirischen Imperfekt', *SCelt* 1968; Campanile, *AION-L* 8, 1968, 51; Rix, *Idg. und Keltisch*, 1977, 157.

[21] Kuryłowicz, *Categories* 135; Schmalstieg, *AION-L* 6, 1965, 123; Barton, *IF* 85, 1981, 246–78.

[22] On this see Hermann, *KZ* 69, 1948, 68f.; Karstien, *Fs. Vasmer*, 1956, 224f.: *-āskom* (~*-σκον*)>*-ks-*>*-x-*; Sadnik, *Welt der Slaven* 5, 1960, 19–30; Vaillant, *Gram. comp.* iii, 66f.; Bech, *Idg. Verbalmorphologie*, 1972, 5–29; Georgiev, *BalkE* 13/3, 1975, 28–30; Pohl, *ZSP* 38, 1975, 349–60; *Fs. H. Vernay*, 1979, 358–9, and in *Philologie und Sprachwissenschaft*, Innsbruck 1983, 203–10 (basically the same as Sadnik); Kortlandt, 'The origin of the Slavic imperfect', *Fs. Bräuer*, 1986, 253–8; cf. K. H. Schmidt, 'The imperfect in IE and the Kartwel languages', *VJ* 1992 (5), 34–9.

[23] Hermann, *KZ* 69, 67 (*-davau* ~ Goth. *tau-jan*); Machek (n. 18 above); Vaillant, *Gram. comp.* iii, 66 (?); Bech (n. 22 above), 29–37.

[24] Schwyzer, *GG* i, 776; Kuryłowicz, *Categories* 91; Berg, 'Ursprung des altgriech. aktiven Plusquamperfekts', *NTS* 31, 1977, 205–63; Perel'muter, *Obščeie. i grečeskij glagol*, 1977, 78 (*IC* 24 b, no. 376).

[25] On the *ē*-extension in Greek, see Chantraine, *BSL* 38, 1937, 9–39; on Slavic, Vaillant, *BSL* 40, 1939, 5–30, esp. 14f.; 57, 1962, 52; *Gram. comp.* iii, 47, 77, 452.

[26] Pedersen, *Formes sigmatiques du verbe latin*, 1921, 15, and again Pisani, *AGI* 41, 1957, 158. On the other hand the Lat. plupf. is taken back to *-is-ā-* by Leumann², 608; Safarewicz, *Eos* 46, 1954, 100f.; Kuryłowicz, *Categories* 125; Watkins, in *AIED* 43. Different again, but hardly correct, Ruijgh, *Mél. Chantraine*, 1972, 223.

[27] Thieme, *Das Plupf. im Veda*, 1929, 35f.; Schwyzer, *GG* i, 777f.; Leumann (above, 9.4.3 n. 30), 32.

9.4.4.2.

The IE verb could show different formations both in the present stem and in the aorist stem. This *polymorphism* is developed especially in Aryan[1] and, to a lesser extent, in Greek.[2] Cf. e.g. OInd. *bharati* 'carries': *bibharti* 'carries around'; also, with no change of meaning, *sačatē* and *siṣakti* 'follows'; *stavatē* 'praises' : *stumási* 'we praise'; *bhayatē* : *bibhēti* 'fears'; *tudati* : *tundatē* 'strikes'; *dabhanti* : *dabhnuvanti* 'they deceive'. The root *hū-* 'call' shows the greatest variability, with five different present formations, which of course are not all equally common; in order of frequency they are *havatē*, *hvayati*, *huvé* (1st s.), *hūtē*, *juhūmas(i)*. Well-known examples in Greek are πυνθάνομαι: πεύθομαι 'inquire', λήθω : λανθάνω 'escape notice', μένω : μίμνω 'wait', and an extreme case κεράννυμι : κίρνημι:[3] κιρνάω : κεραίω : κεράω 'mix'. To a different problem area belongs the universal tendency to replace old athematic forms by thematic; only in Baltic did the old type enjoy a late flowering (see Stang 1966, 310), although today it has come to an end; thus from the athematic IE **sti-stā-mi*, which is preserved in Gr. ἵστημι, Latin has the thematic *sistō*, Old Indic the similarly thematic *tiṣṭhāmi*, and to the athematic OInd. *mārǰ-mi* 'I rub' corresponds in Greek the thematic ἀμέλγω 'milk', etc.

With regard to the different present formations, it would be natural to think that each of them brought with it a special shade of meaning; thus an 'aspect déterminé' has been inferred for the reduplicated formations,[4] and for the *-sk-* formations a basic iterative-durative meaning is probable,[5] etc. It has been rightly pointed out, however,[6] that this view would only be justified if all these formations had been present and productive in the same synchronic system, which is demonstrably not the case. Thus the suffix *-ye-/-yo-*, which in the historical period was increasingly productive everywhere (9.4.1.5), is certainly late in reaching this rich development. It is said to be much more important that all secondary present formations served to build up the ever diminishing stock with new durative forms. For this, the normal course would be from a basic verb by way of a deverbative noun to a (denominative) verb derived from this noun; the denominative verb is then brought into relation with the basic verb and reinterpreted as derived from the basic verb; e.g.:

Basic verb	Deverbative noun	Denominative verb	Deverbative verb
**wegheti* 'uehit'	**wogho-* 'carrying'	**woghe-ye-* from **wogho-*	**wogh-eye* from **wegheti*.

This means also that the question whether, for instance, Lat. *dō* should be traced back to IE **di-dō-mi*, the formation attested in

Greek, Aryan, and Italic, or rather to **dō-mi*, which is found in Balto-Slavic,[7] has from this point of view no interest: both forms once existed in Indo-European. The same applies to West Germanic **dōn* 'do', a transformation of IE **dhē-mi*, and IE **dhi-dhē-mi* in Gr. τίθημι. The reduplicated formation was in these cases the iterative variant, which often supplanted the basic verb and allowed it to survive only as an aorist, cf. OInd. *dadāmi* 'give' : *adām* 'I gave'.[8]

In the aorist polymorphism is similarly a well-known phenomenon of late Indo-European, so far as relates to the presence together of asigmatic and sigmatic forms. Here too it finally comes back to the coexistence of different present stems, one of which was diverted to the purely aoristic function.[9] Functionally, however, no difference can be shown between the two basic types.

[1] On this, see Vekerdi, 'On polymorphic presents in the Rgveda', *Acta Orient. Acad. Hung.* 12, 1961, 249–87; Jelizarenkova, 'The meaning of present stems in the Rigveda' (Russ.), in *Jazyki Indii*, Moscow 1961, 91–165; U. Joachim, *Mehrfachpräsentien im Ṛgveda*, Frankfurt a. M. 1978; Lazzeroni, *SSL* 20, 1980, 43.

[2] On this, see the London thesis of my pupil O. Kujore, *Greek Polymorphic Presents*, Amsterdam 1973.

[3] On the formation, see Szemerényi, in *Studies T. B. L. Webster* i, 1986, 225–30.

[4] See above, 9.4.1.2 n. 6.

[5] See above, 9.4.1.4 n. 8.

[6] See esp. Velten, 'Studien zu einer historischen Tempustheorie des Idg.', *KZ* 60, 1933, 185f.; Kuryłowicz, *Apophonie* 32; *Categories* 105, 109; *Problèmes* 99.

[7] Szemerényi, 'Zwei Fragen des urslavischen Verbums', *Études Slaves et Roumaines (Budapest)* 1, 1948, 7f.; Kuryłowicz, 'Slavic *damĭ*', in *To Honor R. Jakobson* ii, 1967, 1127–31; a different view in Otrębski, *LPosn* 9, 1963, 24; Georgiev, *Krat* 10, 1967, 216; Tedesco, *Lg* 44, 1968, 11.

[8] Campanile, *Scritti in onore di R. Ambrosini*, 1985, 65–7, rightly sets alongside the presents **steH-ti*, **bhuH-ti* the preterite forms **steH-t*, **bhuH-t*, of which only the latter survive as aorists. The same will apply to the relation between *-neu-* present and *-eu-* aorist: at first *-eu-* present and *-neu-* present existed side by side, then the former was displaced from the present, so that only the preterite form, i.e. the aorist, remained; cf. Strunk, *Nas.* 128.

[9] See above, 9.4.2.1 n. 24.

9.4.4.3.

The combination of different stem formations into a single paradigm, known as *suppletivism*, which is prevalent in nouns and particularly in adjectives (see 7.8.9), can also be observed in verbs. There is no need to point out that the perfect of the Latin verb *ferō* is not, for instance, **ferī* or **feruī*, but from a quite different stem, *tulī*, OLat. *tetulī*; furthermore, the verbal adjective of this same verb is not formed as **fertus* but, regarded synchronically, from a third stem, *lā-tus*, although diachronically it can be established that this arose from **tlātos* and is thus cognate with *tulī*. In Greek etymologically unrelated stems form a single paradigm for 'see': ὁρῶ, ὄψομαι, εἶδον; 'say': λέγω, ἐρῶ, εἶπον; 'go': ἔρχομαι, εἶμι, ἦλθον, etc.

The opinion is often encountered that suppletivism is something primitive. This is at once contradicted by the fact that there are fairly recent cases of it: e.g. Eng. *went* is not found as the preterite of *go* before the fifteenth century.[1] A good post-Latin example is provided by Ital. *vado*: *andiamo*, Fr. *je vais*: *nous allons*. Clearly suppletivism is only an aspect of the never-ending process of renewal in the life of language, to which the frequently used elements, whether of vocabulary or of grammatical system, are especially exposed.[2]

It is often maintained that some verb stems had particular meanings which made it impossible for them to occur in certain formal categories. Thus it is alleged that the meaning of the stem **dō*- was momentary, and therefore a present **dō-ti* was impossible.[3] On the other hand, it is supposed that the root **bher*- formed neither an aorist nor a perfect in Indo-European, and for this reason the corresponding forms in Greek are ἤνεγκον, ἐνήνοχα, in Old Irish *ro-uic*, in Latin *tetulī*;[4] but it is certainly a fact that Old Irish formed the aorist from this stem (*birt* 'carried'), and in Old Indic from the Vedic period there are the root aorist (precative *bhriyāsam*, imperative *bhr̥tam*), the *s*-aorist *abhārṣam*, and the *iṣ*-aorist *abhāriṣam*. Similarly, the verbal adjective from this root is supposed to be impossible—and for this they refer to Lat. *lātus*, Gr. οἰστός—but it exists in Ved. *bhr̥tá*- and OIr. *brithe* represents an extension of it, while the original form is kept in the function of a preterite passive. It is obviously impossible to infer from suppletive relationships that restrictions of meaning are to be placed on certain verbal roots.[5]

[1] It is perhaps worth recalling that some transformationalists have tried to derive *went* from *go* through a series of transformations; see H. Penzl, 'Positivism and "hocus-pocus"', *AJGLL* 1, 1989, 1–16.

[2] See Mańczak, 'La nature du supplétivisme', *Lings* 28, 1967, 86f.; Strunk (above, 7.8.9 n. 1), 12f.; Ivanov, *Glagol* 177 f.

[3] Tedesco (above, 9.4.4.2 n. 7); and again F. Létoublon, *Les verbes de mouvement en grec: supplétisme et aspect verbal*, Paris 1985 (fc. *JHS* 107, 1987, 211–12).

[4] e.g. Pokorny, *IEW* 128; Meillet, *Fs. Kretschmer*, 1926, 140–1; Watkins, *Ériu* 21, 1969, 7.

[5] Dressler, *KZ* 85, 1971, 14, also thinks there is a confusion of ideas here.

9.4.4.4.

From the material so far discussed we can infer for the late IE *system* an opposition between active and passive-middle, and within these an opposition between present and aorist.[1] The first opposition rested on the form of the personal endings, e.g. **bhereti* 'carries' : **bheretoi* 'is carried, carries for himself', the second primarily on the form of the stem and only secondarily on the endings and where possible the augment, of. **bhéugeti* 'flees': **(é)bhugét* 'fled' (Gr. φεύγει : ἔφυγε), **yunégti* 'yokes' : **(e)yēuk-s-t ekwō* 'yoked the two horses' (OInd. *yanákti* : *áyaukṣ-īt*. Beside these there existed the perfect, which was really a present, of which as a stative verb only an active was possible;

not until the end of the IE period could corresponding forms be constructed in the passive-middle and, perhaps earlier, a corresponding preterite. The opposition of present to aorist, at first simply an opposition of present to non-present (directed towards the past), had to change fundamentally as and when a second past tense, formed directly from the present stem, was created; the binary opposition **bhéugeti* : **(é)bhugét* was transformed to a ternary **bhéugeti* : **(é)bhéuget* : **(é)bhugét*, whereby the old preterite became for the first time properly the aorist, while the new preterite, identical with the present in its stem, i.e. the imperfect of the south-east area, simply transferred the durative action to the past. This expansion in the direction of the past must have brought with it the creation of the future tense to complete the system with regard to the future; this process, as we have seen, in part spread from Aryan to Baltic (and perhaps Slavic), in part gave rise to a different innovation in Greek.

In late Indo-European the moods were also firmly established: the subjunctive, optative, and no doubt much earlier the basic mood of command, the imperative. It is less clear how far these moods had already developed in late IE in the direction of their historical position in the individual languages. The Latin subjunctive has four 'tenses', Greek has three subjunctive forms, Vedic similarly has three, Gothic, with only two tenses overall, has only two. It is usual to infer from the Latin subjunctives *aduenat*, *tagās*, etc. (see 9.3.1.1) that the IE subjunctive was not yet correlated with the tense stems and that therefore there could be only one subjunctive form. This conclusion can be confirmed by the following observation. The individual languages, e.g. Greek or Old Indic, have an aorist subjunctive the meaning of which bears no relation to the past meaning of the indicative. This fact is not explained by assuming for the aorist a momentary, punctual aspect, since if the aorist subjunctive were really derived from the aorist, it would similarly have had to show a past meaning. The explanation of the facts is simply that the subjunctive of the *s*-aorist was formed at a time when the *s*-aorist was still just the preterite of an *s*-present and the *s*-subjunctive was a present subjunctive. When the related *s*-present disappeared as a category, the *s*-subjunctive was assigned to the *s*-aorist, and on the analogy of its relationship with the indicative a new subjunctive was added to the asigmatic aorist, with a stem to match the indicative, although the subjunctive actually required by the system already existed in the present subjunctive. The peculiar syntactical behaviour of the aorist subjunctive is thus not the consequence of a peculiar semantic aspect of the aorist, but a feature inherited virtually unchanged from an earlier period; only the aorist indicative was changed, and that as a result of the disappearance of its present-tense counterpart.

It follows that the aorist must, or at least could, have had an optative and imperative, both without any reference to past time. The same is true in principle for the perfect, except that in the description of a state the moods originally could surely not have been meaningful. But with the development of perfects denoting an action, moods also became possible; cf. Lat. *mementō* from **me-mn̥-tōd* to the indicative **me-mon-a(i)*, or even OInd. opt. *ba-bhū-yā-s* 'be'.

The development of this part of the system can be illustrated in the active as follows:

	Present formations without -*s*-		*s*-formations
Stage 1			
Pres. Ind.	**bhéug-e-ti*	**yuneg-ti*	**yeug-s-ti*
Pret. Ind.	**bhug-é-t*	**yuneg-t*	**yeug-s-t*
Pres. Subj.	**bhéug-ē-ti*	**yuneg-e-ti*	**yeug-s-e-ti*
Stage 2			
Pres. Ind.	**bhéug-e-ti*	**yuneg-ti*	
Impf. Ind.	**bhéug-e-t*	**yuneg-t*	
Pres. Subj.	**bhéug-ēti*	**yuneg-e-ti*	
Aor. Ind.	**bhug-é-t*	**yeug-s-t*	
Aor. Subj.	**bhug-ē-ti*	**yeug-s-e-ti*	

In Stage 1 **bhéugeti* and **bhugét* stand in opposition to one another, with the subjunctive **bhéugēti* alongside. At this time **yunegti* and **yeugsti* with three forms each are on the same level. Subsequently the relations are shifted, in that the present **yeugsti* is displaced by **yunegti*, while the preterite **yeugst* is assigned to the present system **yunegti*/**yunegt*, and this puts **yeugst* into opposition with **yunegt*. Imperfect and aorist are thereby differentiated. Elsewhere only the opposition **yunegti* : **yeugst* is continued.

If we include the perfect and for the south-east area of Indo-European the future also, and ignore the optative and imperative, the following general picture is obtained for the Late-IE period:[2]

General IE	South-East IE
Pres.Ind.-Pres.Subj. Perf.Ind.-Perf.Subj.	Pres.Ind.-Pres.Subj.
–	Impf.Ind.
Pret.Ind.	Aor.Ind.-Aor.Subj.
Fut.Ind. (orig. Pret.Subj.)	Fut.Ind. (orig. Desid.)

[1] On general problems of the verbal system, see Velten (above, 9.4.4.2 n.6), esp. 195f., 198f., 211; Schwyzer, 'Zum persönlichen Agens beim Passiv', *Abh. Preuss. Akad.* 1942/10, 1943, 11f. (verb stems are *energetic—anenergetic*, i.e. transitive/intransitive—static/metastatic); K. Hoffmann, 'Das Kategoriensystem des idg. Verbums', *MSS* 28, 1970, 19–41 (=*Aufsätze* ii,

323–40); Bader, *RPh* 45, 1971, 311–17 (criticizes Watkins's *Verb* for its neglect of the system, which Kiparsky, *FL* 9, 1972, 283, also censures); 'Parfait et moyen en grec', *Mél. Chantraine*, 1972, 1–21 (21 diagram); Eichner, 'Die Vorgeschichte des hethitischen Verbalsystems', *Fachtagung* 5, 1975, 71–103; Meid, 'Raümliche und zeitliche Gliederung des Indogermanischen', ibid. 204–19, esp. 213f.; Neu, 'Rekonstruktion des idg. Verbalsystems', *Studies Palmer*, 1976, 239–54, esp. 252; *Fachtagung* 7, 1985, 281 (dynamic—static=active—perfect), 294; 'Dichotomie im grundsprachlichen Verbalsystem', *Fs. Meid*, 1989, 153–76; Rix, in *Idg. und Keltisch*, 1977, 132–58, esp. 141f., 155f.; Szemerényi, *Studies A. A. Hill* iii, 1978, 277–9 (action>active—passive, non-action=state> middle—perfect); *TPS* 1985, 24f., 45–50; Meid, *InL* 4, 1978, 39 (active—stative, the latter>medio-passive—perfect); *Heth. und Idg.*, 1979, 159–76, esp. 167f.; Schlerath, 'Ist ein Raum/Zeit-Modell für eine rekonstruierte Sprache möglich?', *KZ* 95, 1981, 175–202, esp. 183, 187f.; Gamkrelidze–Ivanov, 293f., 300f., 333f., 336.

[2] The important problem, how far individual formations determine others and give them mutual support, seems hardly to have received attention. Particular areas have been treated, e.g. the connection of *neu*-present and *eu*-aorist by Strunk (above, 9.4.4.2 n.8); Bader, *BSL* 68/2, 1973, 124–30; Lazzeroni, *SSL* 20, 1980, 23–53, esp. 39f. (present classes and aorists assigned to them).

9.4.4.5. *Aspect.*[1] As a rule, the verb of a Slavic language is really a pair of verbs: two verbs are needed to describe the same action, process, or state according to whether the action, etc., is treated in regard to its duration or its completion. 'Yesterday I read a novel' is expressed in modern Russian either as (*a*) *včerá ja čitál román* or (*b*) *včerá ja pročitál román*; (*b*) gives the information that the novel was read to the end, (*a*) does not.[2] Two *vidy* are therefore distinguished, which today are incorrectly referred to in the western languages as *aspects*, although originally two species, two kinds, two classes were meant;[3] these are the *completed* aspect, *vid soveršénnyj*, (*b*) above, and the *incomplete* aspect, *vid nesoveršénnyj*, (*a*) above, which are usually also called *perfective* and *imperfective aspects* (earlier, *action types*).[4] A further peculiarity of the Russian system is that the present of a perfective verb, because it emphasizes completion, cannot be a true present, but is a future: 'I shall write' is *ja na-pišú* when the end of the writing, e.g. the completion of a letter, is envisaged, but *ja búdu pisát'* when it is merely stated on what task I shall be engaged.

These facts were observed in Czech in 1603, in Polish in 1778, but in Russian not until 1805.[5] Shortly after 1850 they became known to Georg Curtius, who taught in Prague 1849–54, from the work of Czech scholars. He then discovered the Slavic opposition in the relation of the imperfect to the aorist in Ancient Greek, and finally to these two *time types* was added a third, the perfect.[6] The term *action type* ('Aktionsart', still often used by German linguists) was introduced by Brugmann in 1885 as a substitute for *time type* ('Zeitart'), and Curtius' three classes, *continuing*, *occurring*, *completed* ('dauernde', 'eintretende', 'vollendete'), were replaced by the terms still in use, *imperfective*, *perfective*, *perfect*; see Szemerényi (n. 6 below).

A decisive influence was now exerted on the development of the theory by Streitberg's article (*PBB* 15, 1889, 70–177), in which he discovered an aspect corresponding to that of Slavic in Germanic, more precisely in Gothic. He found *inter alia* that compound verbs with the most varied prepositions acquired perfective meaning, but that 'compounds with *ga*- play the most prominent part in respect of both quantity and quality' (102); he further thought he could show that 'the present of a perfective verb represents the future' (126f.), and that the indicatives of the Greek aorist and the Gothic preterite, though they do not entirely coincide, are nevertheless closely related to one another (142).

In these and similar ways the aspects were now discovered in almost all IE languages and correspondingly postulated for Indo-European as their common source. This was, however, quite clearly a wholly unjustifiable transference of the Slavic situation to other IE languages and then to the original language. For, in the first place, neither in Greek nor in any other ancient IE language is there a system which could reflect the thoroughgoing dualism of the Slavic verb. The Slavic verb differs from the verb of all other IE languages in being organized in pairs in all its tenses, a feature quite unknown in the verb of all other languages. The distinction of the two aspects can be realized in Slavic for the most part only by means of morphologically differentiated variants (i.e. either by preverbs or suffixes, rarely by different stems), whereas in the other languages, e.g. in Greek, a certain distinction is expressed by *different tenses*, namely imperfect and aorist, *of the same verb*. Compare, for example, on the one hand the Russian pairs *stróit'* (ipf.) : *postróit'* (pf.) 'build', *ubít'* (pf.) : *ubivát'* (ipf.) 'kill', *govorít'* (ipf.) : *skazát'* (pf.) 'speak, say', and on the other hand the absence of one of the aspects in the Greek present (e.g. ποιεῖ is only imperfective), as well as the absence of different verbs in the pair for the past: ἐποίησε (pf.) : ἐποίει (ipf.).

Since mention was made above of Streitberg's view that in Gothic the preverb *ga*- played a prominent part in the expression of the perfective aspect, this question must be briefly discussed. According to Streitberg (82f.), in contrast e.g. to the durative, i.e. imperfective, verbs *saihwan* 'see', *hausjan* 'hear', the *ga*-compounds *ga-saihwan*, *ga-hausjan* have the perfective meaning 'catch sight of', 'perceive by hearing'.[7] Since this has been regularly repeated even in more recent times (e.g. W. Krause, *Handbuch des Gotischen* (1953), 200), it must be clearly stated that the theory has long since been proved false and untenable: *ga*- alters not the aspect but the meaning of the basic verb. Thus *sitan* means 'sit', but *ga-sitan* 'sit down'; *bairan* is 'carry', but *ga-bairan* 'give birth'; *standan* is 'stand', *ga-standan* 'stand fast, remain'.[8]

Aspect was in any case 'not a morphological category in Gothic',[9] and there is no doubt that Streitberg's theory cannot be maintained.[10] This negative judgement is also valid for the other Germanic languages.[11]

For many other languages it has been shown in more recent times that aspect, which was formerly taken for granted, does not really exist at all. The often repeated view that in Middle Persian the particle *bē* has a perfective function has been proved to be untenable by no less an expert than G. Lazard: for the most part the particle clearly indicates 'out, away', i.e. it modifies the meaning, but even where this is not the case it does not introduce a different aspect.[12] The latest research has shown that Lettish, which is related to Lithuanian and somewhat less closely to Slavic, has likewise no aspect.[13] Latin is no exception. The view of the aspectual nature of Varro's oppositional pair *infectum—perfectum*, so vigorously advocated by Meillet especially, has recently been refuted actually on its home ground; there remains, if anything at all, at most an (aspectual?) opposition between *perfectum* and *imperfectum*.[14] In Old Indic the position is so unclear that many scholars do not mention aspect at all (Burrow; Renou, *Grammaire védique*); others deny its existence.[15] Only a few give a positive answer to the question. But Gonda's assertion, 'the tendency [*sic!*] to distinguish between an "aoristic" and an "imperfectic" aspect though often completely absent . . . is indeed unmistakable',[16] is hardly sufficient to confirm such a belief, especially as an aspect which can often be entirely imperceptible would be a very odd aspect. Even a more thorough investigation must admit at every step how unsafe the ground is.[17] In addition, there is the surprising way in which aorist and imperfect are turned, so to speak, into their opposites: the aorist can express what lies within the speaker's experience, what is near him in the passage of time, thus the recent past, whereas the imperfect indicates what has not 'happened today', thus the more distant past.[18]

To sum up, it can therefore be said that aspect is firmly attested for two areas only, Slavic and Greek.[19] But the difference between the two is very great: Slavic has a thoroughgoing paired system, extending to all tenses, while in Greek there is a distinction only in the past tenses of the same verb.

Before we can proceed further, another question must be clarified.[20] As previously mentioned, Curtius wished to recognize *three aspects* ('time types'), continuing, occurring, and completed, represented by the imperfect, aorist, and perfect. With Brugmann's change of terminology this doctrine held its position for a long time, and was vigorously defended by Kuryłowicz throughout his life; only shortly before the end did he change his opinion: 'la distinction traditionnelle de *trois* aspects correspondant au système ie. présent-aorist-parfait est évidemment fausse'.[21] It is simply impossible to conceive of aspect as other than an opposition of contradictory terms, or, more sharply formulated, 'einen dritten Aspekt kann es gar nicht geben' [22]—a third aspect is impossible.

How then is the bipolar opposition of aspect and the difference between its two representatives, Slavic and Greek, to be understood? As we have already seen, the (alleged) facts of the individual languages led more than a century ago to the assumption that aspect was already present in Indo-European. This view is still repeated; cf. for example the assertion:[23] 'such a contrast [=aspect] is certain for Proto-IE, and in my opinion has to be posited for a prehistoric stage of Anatolian'—for which, however, no proof is offered. And since in Greek there is clearly no opposition of aspect in the present, this is also explained:[24]

The opposition aorist-imperfect expresses in Greek as in Slavic a difference of aspect. The difference of meaning finds expression only in the time stage of the past; it is cancelled in the time stage of the present.

The same result can be reached in another way:[25]

The category of verbal aspect . . . consisting in the opposition *imperfective*: *perfective* implies the existence of tense differences, since this contrast is neutralized under the dominance of the present tense.

The fact is, however, that aspect is absent in the present; 'cancelled' and 'neutralized' are wholly unjustified labels.

It has been clear for some considerable time that aspect in Slavic is not something archaic but represents an innovation [26] which is still in its early stages in Old Church Slavic. For us it is only important that the Slavic aspect is not inherited from Indo-European and cannot prove an Indo-European aspect. How the development took place is less important here, although there is much to be said for the view that the starting-point was the derivation of durative verbs by means of suffixes; these provided imperfectives, as a counterpart to which the perfective aspect arose. Much more important, if it should prove to be true, would be Galton's theory (*The Slavic Verbal Aspect*, 299f.) that aspect in Slavic developed between 700 BC and AD 300 in southern Russia under Iranian and Greek influence.

If, then, only Greek remains as the sole language which could have inherited aspect and would even have to prove aspect for Indo-European, a conclusion of this kind will not be accepted lightly. The origin of aspect will rather be seen in connection with the fact that the Greek aspect is limited to the past tenses.[27] The evidence of many modern languages shows that

the tense that most often evinces aspectual differences is the past tense . . . It may well be a general characteristic of human languages to resort to greater aspectual differentiation in the past than in other tenses. (Comrie, *Aspect*, 71f.)

Thus in the Romance languages, for example, an 'aspect' is found only in the past tenses,[28] as in French in the pair *imparfait—passé simple*.

Here a further fact must be taken into account. As we have seen (9.4.4.4), the ternary system present—imperfect—aorist is only secondary, and perhaps did not arise at all over the whole Indo-European area; it was in any case preceded by a simpler binary system present—preterite. This must, of course, mean that at that point in time an opposition limited to the past was impossible; aspect could have arisen only after that period, and we have no right to presuppose it for languages which do not possess it in the historical period.

If, then, the Slavic system, as indicated above, in fact started from the opposition durative—punctual in the present system, its development was quite different from that of the Greek system. For the latter, the leading role of the past tenses is a vivid reminder of Weinrich's theory. Even if one is not prepared to agree that there are 'no linguistic aspects at all' and therefore 'aspect theory must be expelled entirely from linguistics',[29] this is far from meaning that his further theses are also to be rejected, namely that 'the key to the problem of the tense pair *imparfait—passé simple*' must lie 'in distinctions of narrative and narrative technique' (*Tempus*, 157), and further that: 'The *imparfait* is in narrative the tense of the background, the *passé simple* is the tense of the foreground' (159).[30] Without accepting the unqualified claim that provision of 'relief' is the one and only function of these tenses, this theory is so self-evident that it can be applied without hesitation to the Indo-European situation. It also means that Slavic, in which the development of aspect did not remain confined to the past tenses but actually started from the present, took a quite different course from Greek.

To sum up, we can therefore say that the two languages for which aspect can be recognized in the early IE group show two rather different types of the category.[31] In any case, aspect as an early category, and one that even preceded tense, must be firmly rejected.[32] The Greek variety presupposes first the existence of the opposition present—past and then the division of the past into two tenses as the foundation for the contrast of aspect.[33] In the Slavic variety, which is based on the prominence of iterative verbs, the priority of the past tenses cannot be asserted with the same certainty; it remains a possibility nevertheless.[34]

[1] The following is a selection of fairly recent works from the enormous literature: E.

Koschmieder, *Zeitbezug und Sprache: Ein Beitrag zur Aspekt- und Tempusfrage*, 1929, cf. Bondarko, *VJ* 1992 (4), 131–42; Schwyzer, *GG* ii, 246f.; Ruipérez, *Sistema de aspectos*, 1954 (French translation, *Structure du système des aspects et des temps du verbe en grec ancien*, Paris 1982); W. Pollak, *Studien zum Verbalaspekt im Französischen*, 1960, 47f.; Pisani, *Glottologia indeuropea*³, 1961, 262 n. (bibliography); J. Perrot, 'Les faits d'aspect dans les langues classiques', *L'information littéraire* 1961, 109–18, 154–63; Gonda, *The Aspectual Function of the Rgvedic Present and Aorist*, 1962; Heger, *Die Bezeichnung temporaldeiktischer Kategorien*, 1963, esp. 49f.; M. Joos, *The English Verb*, 1964, 101f.; Kuryłowicz, *Categories* 19f., 25f., ch. 3; H. Weinrich, *Tempus*, 1964; Safarewicz, *Symbolae Kuryłowicz*, 1965, 246–54; W.F. Bakker, *The Greek Imperative: the Aspectual Differences between the Present and Aorist Imperatives in Greek Prayer*, 1966; Kölln, 'Aspekt und Diathese im Slavischen', *ScSl* 12, 1966, 57–79; Vaillant. *Gram. comp.* iii, 460f.; Panzer, 'Die Begriffe "Aktualität" und "Nichtaktualität" in der Aspekt- und Tempustheorie des Slavischen', *Dankesgabe an E. Koschmieder*, 1967, 68–81; Haltof, 'Die Aspekte des modernen Russischen', *ZfSlawistik* 12, 1967, 735–43; Heger, 'Temporale Deixis und Vorgangsquantität ("Aspekt" und "Aktionsart")', *ZRP* 83, 1967, 512–82; *V. Crisafulli, 'Aspect and tense distribution in Homeric Greek', diss., North Carolina 1967; Lyons, *Introduction to Theoretical Linguistics*, 1968, 313f., 397f.; Dressler, *Studien zur verbalen Pluralität*, 1968, 39f.; H. Stobitzer, *Aspekt und Aktionsart im Vergleich des Französischen mit dem Deutschen, Englischen und Italienischen*, diss., Tübingen 1968; H. G. Klein, *Das Verhalten der telischen Verben in den romanischen Sprachen (Interferenz von Aspekt und Aktionsart)*, diss., Frankfurt a. M. 1969; Seiler, 'Zur Problematik des Verbalaspekts', *CFS* 26, 1969, 119–35; Strunk, *Gymnasium* 76, 1969, 289–310; Szemerényi, 'Unorthodox views of tense and aspect', *ArchL* 17, 1969, 161–71 (bibliography), esp. on Galton, MacLennan, Weinrich; J. Forsyth, *A Grammar of Aspect: Usage and Meaning in the Russian Verb*, Cambridge 1970; R. Martin, *Temps et aspect*, Paris 1971; Verkuyl, *On the Compositional Nature of the Aspects*, Dordrecht 1972; Kuryłowicz, *Studies in Semitic Grammar and Metrics*, 1972 (83: aspect as a grammatical category does not exist in Semitic!); 'Verbal aspect in Semitic', *Orientalia* 42, 1973, 114–20; T. H. Amse-de Jong, *The Meaning of the Finite Verb Forms in the Old Church Slavonic Codex Suprasliensis*, 1974; A. Schopf (ed.), *Der englische Aspekt*, Darmstadt 1974; H. G. Klein, *Tempus, Aspekt, Aktionsart*, Tübingen 1974; Lehmann, *PIE Syntax*, 1974, 139–48, 186–90; P. Friedrich, *On Aspect Theory and Homeric Aspect*, 1974; H. Gross, *Der Ausdruck des 'Verbalaspekts' in der deutschen Gegenwartssprache*, 1974; W. H. Hirtle, *Time, Aspect, and the Verb*, Quebec 1975; Coseriu, 'Der periphrastische Verbalaspekt im Altgriechischen', *Glotta* 53, 1975, 1–25 (first in Spanish, 1968); *Das romanische Verbalsystem*, Tübingen 1976, 81f.; Comrie, *Aspect*, Cambridge 1976; Galton, *The Slavic Verbal Aspect*, Skopje 1976; M. Markus, *Tempus und Aspekt*, 1977; Lyons, *Semantics*, 1977, 703–18; M. Bennett and B. Partee, *Toward the Logic of Tense and Aspect in English*, IULC 1978; N. B. Thelin, *Towards a Theory of Aspect*, Uppsala 1978; Szemerényi, *Studies A. A. Hill* iii, 1978, 273f., 277f.; Perrot, 'Aspects de l'aspect', *Étrennes M. Lejeune*, 1978, 183–97; C. Fuchs and A. M. Léonard, *Vers une théorie des aspects*, Paris 1979 (all languages have aspect!); A. L. Lloyd, *Anatomy of the Verb*, Amsterdam 1979; B. Newton, 'Scenario, modality, and verbal aspect in Modern Greek', *Lg* 55, 1979, 139–67 (165: against the view that 'aspectual distinctions reflect . . . some sort of vague, inchoate mode in which events are viewed. Aspect reflects logical form; the choice in Greek is determined by time adverbials: always/usually/every time'); J. David and R. Martin (eds.), *La notion d'aspect*, Paris 1980 (includes 13–25 Coseriu, 'Aspect verbal ou aspects verbaux?'); G. Serbat (ed.), *Le sens du parfait en latin*, 1980 (cf. Hiersche, *Krat* 29, 1985, 120–5); K. Trost, 'Verbale Zeitstruktur v. Handlungsstruktur und die paarigen Fortbewegungsverba im Russischen', *FoL* 12, 1980, 385–404 (aspect not only *Zeit* but also *Handlung*); P. J. Tedeschi and A. Zaenen (eds.), *Tense and Aspect*, New York 1981; **Actants, voix et aspects verbaux*, Univ. Angers 1981; Hopper (ed.), *Tense–Aspect*, Amsterdam 1982; P. Stork, *The Aspectual Usage of the Dynamic Infinitive in Herodotus*, Groningen 1982 (cf. García-Ramón, *Krat* 29, 1985, 104–16); Pinkster, 'Tempus, Aspect and *Aktionsart* in Latin', *ANRW* 29/1, 1983, 270–319; Schopf, *SLang* 7, 1983, 283–304 (review of M. Ljung, *Reflections on the English Progressive*, 1980); Perrot, *Le problème de l'aspect verbal*, 1983, 98 n. 9; Niculescu, 'Ot bezvidovogo jazyka k vidovomu', *VJ* 1984 (2), 115–21; Pulgram, 'The functions of past tenses: Greek, Latin, Italian, French', *LSci* 6, 1984, 239–69;

A. Galton, *The Logic of Aspect: an Axiomatic Approach*, Oxford 1984; W. Saurer, *A Formal Semantics of Tense, Aspect and Aktionsarten*, IULC 1984; Ö. Dahl, *Tense and Aspect Systems*, 1985; Comrie, *Tense*, Cambridge 1985; Szemerényi, *Fachtagung* 7, 1985, 521f.; Edgren, 'The progressive in English', *SL* 39, 1985, 67–83; Windfuhr, 'A spatial model for tense, aspect, and mood', *FoL* 19, 1985, 415–61; R. Quirk et al. (eds.), *A Comprehensive Grammar of the English Language*, 1985, 188f.; U. Stephany, *Aspekt, Tempus und Modalität*, 1985; Szemerényi, 'The origin of aspect in the IE languages', *Glotta* 65, 1987, 1–18; *Aspects, modalité: problèmes de catégorisation grammaticale*, Univ. Paris VII, 1987; Pulgram, *FoLH* 7, 1987, 381–97; Comrie, *The World's Major Languages*, 1987, 57, 193, 429; Schmitt-Brandt, 'Aspektkategorien im PIE?' *JIES* 15, 1988, 81–92; L. J. Brinton, *The Development of English Aspectual Systems*, Cambridge 1988; R. Chatterjee, *Aspect and Meaning in Slavic and Indic*, 1988; J. L. Bybee and Ö. Dahl, 'The creation of tense and aspect systems', *SLang* 13, 1989, 51–103; D. Cohen, *L'aspect*, 1989; W. Abraham and T. Janssen (eds.), *Tempus–Aspect–Modus*, 1989; Wunderli, 'Aspect verbal en français', *TL* 18, 1989, 73–94; Comrie, 'The typology of tense–aspect systems in European languages', *LeS* 25, 1990, 259–72; Raible, 'Types of tense and aspect systems', in *Toward a Typology of European Languages*, 1991; Rundgren, *Krat* 36, 1991, 180 ('aspect is a textual category'); C. S. Smith, *The Parameter of Aspect*, 1991; M. J. Sicking, 'The distribution of aorist and present', *Glotta* 69, 1992, 14–43, 154–70; Duhoux 1992, 136f.; S. Mellet, 'Temps, aspect et Aktionsart', in Isebaert (ed.), *Miscellanea linguistica*, 1993, 183–93; Y. Tobin, *Aspect in the English Verb*, London 1993.

[2] On aspect in Russian, see e.g. J. Forsyth (n. 1 above, 1970), esp. 8 and 29f.; J. Fontaine, *Grammaire du texte et aspect verbal en russe contemporain*, 1983 (cf. *BSL* 80/2, 1986, 155f.); M. S. Flier and A. Timberlake (eds.), *The Scope of Slavic Aspect*, 1985; C. Mouton, *Aspects grecs, aspects russes*, 1986 (cf. *BSL* 83/2, 1988, 162f.); M. Guiraud-Weber, *L'accent du verbe russe*, 1988 (see Hagège, *BSL* 85/2, 1990, 143–50); R. Schuyt, *The Morphology of Slavic Verbal Aspect*, 1990; Bondarko, 'The meanings of aspect in Russian', *VJ* 1990 (4), 5–24; P. Durst-Andersen, *Mental Grammar: Russian Aspect and Related Issues*, 1992.

[3] This is well explained by Mazon, 'L'aspect des verbes chez les grammairiens russes' (*Mélanges É. Picoti*, 1913, 343–67), 360; cf. G. MacLennan, *El problema del aspecto verbal*, 1969, 69 n. 42.

[4] In recent times instead of these terms Eng. *telic–atelic*, Grm. *telisch–atelisch* have been preferred; these are intended to convey that the telic verb is directed towards a completion and the atelic verb implies no completion; see Garey, *Lg* 33, 1957, 106, and again Dahl, in Tedeschi and Zaenen, *Tense and Aspect*, 79–90.

[5] On this, cf. Mazon (n. 3 above), 349–54; C. G. Regnéll, *Ursprung des slavischen Verbalaspektes*, Lund 1944, 5–11; W. Pollak (n. 1 above, 1960), 30f.; H. Wissemann, 'Der Verbalaspekt in den älteren Darstellungen der russischen Grammatik', *ZSP* 26, 1958, 351–75.

[6] See Schwyzer, *GG* ii, 251f., esp. n. 1 and 250 n. 8; Serbat, *REL* 54, 1977, 325; Szemerényi, *Fachtagung* 7, 521. The long-prevalent view that aspect was discovered by the Stoics has now in my opinion been decisively refuted by Hiersche, *KZ* 91, 1978, 275–87; cf. also Berrettoni, 'An idol of the school: the aspectual theory of the Stoics', *RivLing* 1, 1989, 33–68.

[7] Cf. H. Wagner, *ZCP* 42, 1987, 29–36, with the conclusion: 'almost undeniable that there are historical connections between the verbal-prefix systems of Celtic-Germanic-Slavic, Germanic-Slavic-Ossetic, Ossetic-Kartwelian.'

[8] See the excellent articles by A. M. Lorusso, 'Aspetto e modo dell'azione nella struttura funzionale del verbo gotico' (*Annali, Facoltà di Lettere, Univ. Perugia*, 4, 1966/7, 559–83), esp. 568–70 on pairs with and without *ga-* (576: preverb modifies not aspect but Aktionsart), and A. Martellotti, 'Osservazioni sul gotico *wisan* "essere" e il presente *wisa*' (*RAL* 27, 1973, 207–48), 222–30. Cf. also H. Rosén, *Gedenkschrift Collinder*, 1984, 378–87 (*s.f.* 'essen' now established!).

[9] J. W. Marchand, 'Gotisch', in L. E. Schmidt (ed.), *Kurzer Grundriss der germanischen Philologie bis 1500* i, 1970, 118; cf. also Mirowicz (n. 10 below), and Lloyd, *Glotta* 68, 1990, 129–31 (defends aspect in Gothic).

[10] A. R. Wedel's concluding sentence (*Lings* 123, 1974, 45–58) is comical: 'Streitberg's aspectual theory is basically correct, at least when applied to the OHG Isidor'. See also

LACUS 15, 1988, 424f. (on Germanic aspect). On this, cf. further A. Mirowicz, *Die Aspektfrage im Gotischen*, Wilno 1935, 16 and 48 with the quotation from Trnka: the aspect theory in Germanic is 'the greatest scientific fiction'; Goedsche, *JEGP* 39, 1940, 189–96; A. L. Lloyd (n. 1 above, 1979); and note Zandvoort's terse judgement that 'the attempts to transfer the category of aspect from Slavonic to Germanic have been futile' (1962), quoted by Diensberg (n. 19, below), 189. See also n. 9 above.

[11] For Germanic in general cf. *SGGJ* iv, 1966, 252, 270; for Old English Pilch, 'Das ae. Präverb *ge-*', *Anglia* 71, 1953, 129–39; Lindeman, 'OE preverbal *ge-*', *JEGP* 64, 1965, 65–83; and for German, Marchand (n. 9 above); W. Pollak, 'Aspekt und Aktionsart', *Linguistik und Didaktik* 1970/2, 163: 'it would be wholly misleading to speak of a "verbal aspect" in German'.

[12] See G. Lazard, *Monumentum H. S. Nyberg* ii, 1975, 1–13; *CFS* 41, 1987, 109–16; and cf. R. L. Fisher, *KZ* 91, 1978, 219–30, on *pa-*.

[13] See Hauzenberga and Šturma, *KZ* 93, 1980, 279–316, esp. 313.

[14] See Serbat (ed.), *Le sens du parfait en latin*, 32f., where Meillet's view is discussed. On this cf. the early article of P. Hartmann, 'Die Verbalsysteme der Schulsprachen' (*KZ* 59, 1932, 145–78), 166, and more recently Kravar's numerous contributions, e.g. 'L'aspect verbal en latin', *ŽA* 25, 1976, 52–61. Note also B. García-Hernandez, 'Le système de l'aspect verbal en latin', in Touratier (ed.), *Syntaxe et latin*, 1985, 516–36 (for aspect=Aktionsart, etc.), and earlier Grassi, *Problemi di sintassi latina*, 1967, 105 (Latin aspect can be established with the help of Italian!); F. Palmer, *Grammar*, 1972, 93 (aspect only 'where a language has two separate verbal categories', but Latin has it all the same); Pinkster 1988, 336–9 (against aspect in Latin and Greek); Duhoux, 'La dynamique des choix aspectuels en grec ancien', *CILL* 18/3–4, 1992, 45–66. On Old Irish, see Sjoestedt-Jonval, 'Le temps et l'aspect en vieil-irlandais', *EC* 3, 1938, 219–63; McCone, *The Early Irish Verb*, 1987, 119f.; K. H. Schmidt, 'Aspect and tense in Old Irish', *Celtica* 21, 1990, 593–603. On modern Irish, see Wigger, *Ériu* 23, 1972.

[15] Vekerdi, 'On past tense and verbal aspect in the Rgveda' (*Acta Orient. Acad. Hung.* 5, 1955, 75–100), 99: 'in the Rgveda there is no semantic difference between the forms derived from the present system and those belonging to the aorist system either in respect of *Zeitart (Aktionsart, aspect)* or in respect of *Zeitstufe* (recent past and remote past)'.

[16] See Gonda, *Old Indian*, 1971, 129, and cf. also *The Aspectual Function of the Rgvedic Present and Aorist*, 1962, 259f.

[17] See Hoffmann, *Der Injunktiv im Veda*, 1967, 270–4, e.g. 274: 'the question of Aktionsart and aspect is often insoluble'.

[18] See Gonda, *Aspectual Function* 50, 272f.; and cf. Hoffmann, *Injunktiv* 151, 153f., and above, 9.3.1.5 with n. 12.

[19] A modern system like e.g. that of English (*I write–I am writing*) is of course irrelevant to the diachronic problem of Indo-European linguistics. Cf. P. Fenn, *A Semantic and Pragmatic Examination of the English Perfect*, 1987; L. J. Brinton, *The Development of English Aspectual Systems*, Cambridge 1988 (see B. Diensberg, *FoLH* 11, 1992, 187–197).

[20] On what follows, see Szemerényi, *Fachtagung* 7, 521f.; also *TPS* 1985, 25f.

[21] Kuryłowicz, *Problèmes* 60.

[22] So Rix, in *Idg. und Keltisch*, 137. For other opinions, see Szemerényi, *Fachtagung* 7, 522f.

[23] See Cowgill, *Heth. und Idg.*, 34.

[24] Schelesniker, *Welt der Slaven* 4, 1959, 402.

[25] Kuryłowicz, *Scientia* 105, 1970, 499.

[26] See e.g. Maslov, 'Zur Entstehungsgeschichte des slavischen Verbalaspektes', *ZfSlawistik* 4, 1959, 560–8, esp. 566, and *VJ* 1959 (2), 153; Vaillant, *Gram. comp.* iii, 462; Galton (n. 1 above, 1976), 46, 300.

[27] See Rix 1986, 12: 'introduction and implementation of the opposition of aspect in phase B'; 16: 'The creation of the sigmatic aorist was the first and decisive step on the way to an opposition of aspect'.

[28] See Garey, *Lg* 33, 1957, 110; Christmann, *Romanische Forschungen* 71, 1959, 6; Pollak (n. 1 above, 1960), 205: in French 'in contrast to Russian, the indication of aspect remains limited to the past'; Stobitzer (n. 1 above, 1968), 2: 'To speak of aspect is thus to speak of the past tenses, since . . . only at this point of the tense system does the French language have at

its disposal two simple formal categories [*passé simple–imparfait*], which agree also in mood' (cf. 34); Pulgram, *LSci* 6, 1984. Coseriu's view (*Das romanische Verbalsystem*, 1976, 157) that in the Romance languages the imperfect is a member of a ternary opposition together with the pluperfect and conditional present is not applicable to our problem.

29 Weinrich, *Tempus*, 1964, 155. Even the concept of aspect is eliminated by Rothstein, 'Temps, aspect et modalité', *Sigma* 1976 (1), 8–94.

30 Of course it cannot also be accepted that (*Tempus*, 162) 'the contrast in prominence of background and foreground is *the one and only function* that the *imparfait* and *passé simple* have in the sphere of narrative'.

31 The accounts of G. Raugh, *IF* 87, 1982, 43f., and 88, 1984, 33f., are irrelevant to our problem.

32 Cf. Pedersen, 'Zur Lehre von den Aktionsarten', *KZ* 37, 1904, 219–50, esp. 219f.; Meltzer, 'Zur Lehre von den Aktionen besonders im Griechischen', *IF* 17, 1905, 186–277; Vaillant, *BSL* 40, 1939, 30: 'La flexion du hittito-indoeuropéen est bâtie essentiellement sur une opposition du présent et du prétérit: il n'y a pas de raison de supposer en indo-européen une antériorité de la catégorie de l'aspect sur la catégorie du temps'; Maslov (n. 26 above), 560f. According to Schwyzer, *GG* ii, 253, aspect is not as old as Indo-European; so also Szemerényi 1985, 25, and Galton, *ICHL* 7, 1987, 251–65 (258: the Anatolian group never lost aspect because IE did not have it). The view is already found in van Wijk, 'Sur l'origine des aspects slaves', *RES* 9, 1929, 237–53.

33 The observations of Strunk, *Glotta* 49, 1971, 198f., can easily be combined with this view; see also in Bammesberger 1988, 575f.

34 Duhoux, *L'information grammaticale (Paris)* 56, 1993, 3–5, also rejects an IE aspect, and shows convincingly that Mycenaean played an important role in preparing the development of aspect in the first millennium. On aspect and the perfect, see also Isebaert, in *Actes du 1. Collogue de la syntaxe du grec classique*, Nice 1992, 99–112.

9.4.4.6. *Accent in verbs.* The accent classes newly established for the noun (see 7.1.4.4.1) have in more recent times been gradually discovered or introduced for the verb also. Of the five new accent types, two have so far emerged particularly clearly, mainly through the work of K. Strunk.[1]

The *acrostatic* type was first recognized in the present type formerly called *proterodynamic* (see 9.2.6.1 above), e.g. OInd. *stáuti*, *stávē* 'he praises', Lith. *bė̃gu*, Gr. *φέβομαι* 'I run away'. The sigmatic aorist, however, with a long grade due to 'secondary gradation' (9.4.2.1*c* above), no doubt also belongs to this type. The *amphikinetic* (or *amphidynamic*) type is represented by instances such as:

**stér-nH-x-* (Lat. *sternit*): **str̥-nH-x́-* (OInd. *str̥ṇánti*)
Lat. *spernit*: Gmc. **spurna-* 'spur'
**pstér-nu-x-* (Lat. *sternuō*): **p(s)tr̥-nu-x́-* (Gr. *πτάρνυμαι*).

1 See Strunk, 'Flexionskategorien mit akrostatischen Akzent und die sigmatischen Aoriste', *Fachtagung* 7, 1985, 490–514, esp. 493, 495; 'Zum Verhältnis zwischen gr. *πτάρνυμαι* und lat. *sternuo*', in *Festgabe für K. Hoffmann* iii (=*MSS* 46), 1985, 221–42. Cf. also Eichner, *MSS* 31, 1973, 91, note 33; Oettinger, *Stammbildung* 96f., 99f.; Rasmussen 1989, 247–62; Isebaert, 'Spuren akrostatischer Präsens-flexion im Latein', in *Latein und Indogermanisch*, 1992, 193f.; Harðarson 1993, 25–37. On the verbal accent see also above, 9.2.6.1.

9.5. SYNTHESIS: PARADIGMS WITH COMMENTS

The results so far obtained analytically can, for a clearer overall view, be represented synthetically in the form of reconstructed paradigms.

9.5.1

The present system of the verb **es-* 'be' can be reconstructed almost completely.[1]

(*a*) Pres.	OInd.	Greek	Lat.
1 **ésmi*	*ásmi*	εἰμί[2]	*sum*[3]
2 **és(s)i*	*ási*	εἶ, εἶς, ἐσσί	*ess, es*
3 **ésti*	*ásti*	ἐστί	*est*
4 **smés(i)/smós(i)*	*smás*	εἰμές, Ion. εἰμέν	*sumus*
5 **sté(s)*	*sthá*	ἐστέ	*estis*
6 **sénti*	*sánti*	εἰσί	*sunt*, Osc. *sent*

Note. The principle of formation—full grade of the root in the singular, zero grade in the other numbers—is most clearly preserved in Old Indic. Campanile, *SCO* 37, 1987, 373–83, interprets differently, but see Lindeman, *EC* 26, 1989, 76[2]. In the 2nd s. *-ss-* seems to have been shortened to *-s-*; in Hom. ἐσσί, OLat. *ess*, *-ss-* has been restored; see Szemerényi, 'Etyma Graeca VIII', *TPS* 92 (1994), n. 4. On the Latin paradigm see my *Syncope* 190f.; on ἐς- from H_1s- Catzanikos, *BSL* 81 (1986), 171f.; Cowgill and Mayrhofer 1986, 120f.; Kimball, in *In Memory of W. Cowgill*, (1987), 181.

(*b*) Impf.	OInd.	Greek
1 **ēsm̥*	*āsam*	ἦα, Att. ἦ, ἦν
2 **ēss*	*ās, āsīs*	ἦσθα
3 **ēst*	*ās, āsīt*	Dor. ἦς, Hom. ἦεν, Att. ἦν
4 **ēsme*	*āsma*	ἦμεν
5 **ēste*	*āsta*	ἦστε, ἦτε
6 **ēsent*	*āsan*	Dor. ἦεν, Hom. Att. ἦσαν

Note. The singular is **e-es-m̥*, **e-es-s*, **e-es-t*;[4] in the plural **e-s-me* etc. would be expected, but the long vowel of the singular is extended to the plural by analogy. OInd. 2nd and 3rd s. *ās* come from **ās-s*, **ās-t*, as in final position only a single consonant is allowed; for the same reason *āsan* is from *-nt*. In Greek the 1st s. ἦα is the regular form, which contracted to ἦ, and this with the almost universal SE -ν became ἦ-ν. The 2nd s. ἦσθα took over the perfect ending -θα. In the 3rd s. Doric ἦς is the continuation of IE **ēst*.[5] Hom. ἦεν, Att. ἦν were originally the 3rd pl., which is preserved as a plural in Doric; the Homeric and Attic use as a 3rd s. started from sentences in which the

3rd pl. had a neuter plural subject; see Schwyzer, *GG* i, 677[6]. The 1st pl. ἦμεν shows regular loss of σ before μ, then by analogy with ἦ-μεν the 2nd pl. became ἦ-τε; the 3rd pl. ἦσαν was necessitated by the shift to singular of the original ἦεν.

(*c*) Subj.[6]	OInd.	Greek	Att.	Lat.
1 **esō*[7]	*asā-ni*	ἔω	ὦ	*erō*
2 **eses(i)*[8]	*asas(i)*	ἔῃς	ᾖς	*eris*
3 **eset(i)*[8]	*asat(i)*	ἔῃ	ᾖ	*erit*
4 **esome*	*asāma*	ἔωμεν	ὦμεν	*erimus*
5 **esete*	*asatha*	ἔητε	ἦτε	*eritis*
6 **esont*	*asan*	ἔωσι	ὦσι	*erunt*

(*d*) Opt.[9]	OInd.	Greek	Lat.	OHG
1 **syēm*	*syām*	εἴην	*siem, sim*	*sī*
2 **syēs*	*syās*	εἴης	*siēs, sīs*	*sīs*
3 **syēt*	*syāt*	εἴη	*siet, sit*	*sī*
4 **sīme*	*syāma*	εἶμεν	*sīmus*	*sīn*
5 **sīte*	*syāta*	εἶτε	*sītis*	*sīt*
6 **siyent*	*syur*	εἶεν	*sient, sint*	*sīn*

9.5.2

The verb **ei-* 'go' has a very similar inflexion.[10]

(*a*) Pres.	OInd.	Greek	Lat.
1 **éimi*	*ēmi*	εἶμι	*eō*
2 **éisi*	*ēṣi*	εἶ	*īs*
3 **éiti*	*ēti*	Dor. εἶτι, Att. εἶσι	*it*
4 **imés(i)*	*imás*	ἴμεν	*īmus*
5 **ité(s)*	*ithá*	ἴτε	*ītis*
6 **yénti*	*yánti*	ἴᾱσι	*eunt*

Note. The OInd. paradigm continues the Indo-European almost without change. In Greek, ἴᾱσι is modified from *ἴενσι on the analogy of the verbal ending -αντι, and *ἴενσι itself is from *ἕνσι with the addition of the zero-grade stem ἰ-. Latin *eō* is from **eimi* transferred to thematic inflexion: **ey-ō* lost intervocalic *y*; similarly *eunt* is from **eyonti*, this extended from **yonti* on the analogy of the full-grade stem *ei-*; 1st and 2nd pl. are from **ei-mos*, **eit-es*, in which *ei-* has been introduced in place of *i-*. For further details see Schwyzer, *GG* i, 674; on the subjunctive, see 9.3.1.1.

9.5.3

For *bher- 'carry' the following thematic inflexion can be reconstructed:

	Pres.	Impf.	Subj.	Opt.
1	**bherō*	**(e)bherom*	**bherō*	**bheroym̥*
2	**bheresi*	**(e)bheres*	**bherēs(i)*	**bherois*
3	**bhereti*	**(e)bheret*	**bherēt(i)*	**bheroit*
4	**bheromes*	**(e)bherome*	**bherōme*	**bheroime*
5	**bherete(s)*	**(e)bherete*	**bherēte*	**bheroite*
6	**bheronti*	**(e)bheront*	**bherōnt*	**bheroyn̥t*

Note. On the present, see 9.2.6, on the subjunctive, 9.3.1.1, on the optative, 9.3.1.2.

9.5.4

The *s*-aorist with its subjunctive of **yeug-* 'joke' was inflected as follows:[11]

	Ind.		Subj.
1	**(e)yēug-s-m̥*	ἔζευξ-α	**yeug-s-ō*
2	**(e)yēug-s-s*	ἔζευξ-ας	**yeug-s-es(i)*
3	**(e)yēug-s-t*	ἔζευξ-ε	**yeug-s-et(i)*
4	**(e)yug-s-mé*	ἐζεύξ-α-μεν	**yeug-s-ome*
5	**(e)yug-s-té*	ἐζεύξ-α-τε	**yeug-s-ete*
6	**(e)yug-s-n̥t*	ἔζευξ-α-ν	**yeug-s-ont*

9.5.5

The corresponding forms of the thematic aorist of **bheug-* 'flee' are as follows:[12]

	Ind.		Subj.
1	**(e)bhug-o-m*	ἔφυγον	**bhug-ō*
2	**(e)bhug-e-s*	ἔφυγες	**bhug-ēs*
3	**(e)bhug-e-t*	ἔφυγε	**bhug-ēt*
4	**(e)bhug-o-me*	ἐφύγομεν	**bhug-ōme*
5	**(e)bhug-e-te*	ἐφύγετε	**bhug-ēte*
6	**(e)bhug-o-nt*	ἔφυγον	**bhug-ōnt*

9.5.6

For the inflexion of the perfect **woida*, see 9.2.3 and 9.4.3.

9.5.7

For the two imperatives, see 9.2.5 above.

9.5.8

Following these models the passive-middle forms can easily be reconstructed, e.g. **sek^{w}etoi*, **sek^{w}ontoi*.

[1] See Watkins, *Verb* 25f.; Bader, *BSL* 68/2, 1973, 125–30, and 71, 1976, 27–111; Ivanov, *Glagol*, 1981, 73–92; Lühr, in Untermann and Brogyanyi (above 9.4.1.1 n. 3), 27–38; Hamp, *Symbolae Mitxelena*, 1985, 224f. (indulges in fantasies).
[2] The Attic diphthong is a pre-Doric innovation; see Arena, *IC* 32/2, 93 (3).
[3] On Lat. *sum*, Osc. *sim*, see *IC* 30/1, 105; *AJPh* 108, 1987, 675–93.
[4] On Hitt. *esun* see 9.4.4.1 n. 5. As do others, Watkins, *Verb* 40, posits **es-m̥, -s, -t*, regarding the argument as dialectal.
[5] All the Greek dialect forms are now collected by O. Masson, *Étrennes Lejeune*, 1978, 123–8.
[6] See above, 9.3.1.1.
[7] Eichner, *Fachtagung* 5, 1975, 80f., wished to recognize in Hitt. *asallu/eslit* 'sim' an IE **H_1esoH_2*; against, Neu, *Studies Palmer*, 1976, 245 n. 23; Meid, in *Heth. und Idg.*, 172f. On the Hittite forms, see most recently Neu, in *É. Benveniste aujourd'hui* ii, 1984, 102; Kammenhuber, *Fs. Winter*, 1985, 459.
[8] Watkins, *Verb* 61, recognizes only **eses*, **eset*.
[9] See above, 9.3.1.2.
[10] See Ivanov, *Glagol* 97–102; Hamp (n. 1 above), 223f.
[11] See above, 9.4.2.1*c*.
[12] See above, 9.4.2.1*b*.

9.6. THE NON-FINITE VERB

The non-finite verb included in Indo-European a number of adjectival forms firmly anchored in the system, namely the participles and verbal adjectives; nouns, on the other hand, appear not yet to have become a fixed part of the verbal paradigm: the later infinitives existed, if at all, only as independent nominal forms.

9.6.1.1

An *-nt-* participle is found in all IE languages, although in some it is no longer a living category.[1] The most archaic inflexion is preserved in Old Indic, and with its help the IE paradigm can be reconstructed with a fair degree of certainty. Cf. **sont-* from **es-* 'be', **yont-* from **ei-* 'go' (9.5.1, 9.5.2), **bheront-* from **bher-* 'carry' (see also 7.1.4.4, 7.2.2.2):

Sing.	Nom.	**sōn*	**yōn*	**bhérōn*
	Acc.	**sónt-m̥*	**yónt-m̥*	**bhéront-m̥*
	Gen.	**sn̥t-ós*	**yn̥t-ós*	**bhérn̥t-os*[2]
	Loc.	**sn̥t-í*	**yn̥t-í*	**bhérn̥t-i*
Plur.	Nom.	**sónt-es*	**yónt-es*	**bhéront-es*
	Acc.	**sónt-n̥s*	**yónt-n̥s*	**bhéront-n̥s*
	Gen.	**sn̥t-óm*	**yn̥t-óm*	**bhérn̥t-om*
	Loc.	**sn̥t-sú*	**yn̥t-sú*	**bhérn̥t-su*

The long-grade nom. s. (see 6.2.7.3) is kept only in Greek: ἐών (in Attic contracted to ὤν), ἰών, φέρων.[3] In the other languages the nom. in *-ont-s* is for the most part restored: OInd. *bharan* from **bharant-s*, Goth. *bairands*, Lith. *vedąs*, and OCS *vedy* 'leading'.[4] In Latin the *o*-grade is kept only in *sōns* 'guilty' ('he who it is'), *insōns* 'innocent',[5] partly in *iens*, *euntis*,[6] and in the derived noun *uoluntās*; otherwise the zero-grade *-ent-* from *-n̥t-* is generalized, even in the early isolated noun *dēns* 'tooth' (7.2.2.1). The neuter is similarly from the *-nt-* stem, but the feminine has the further suffix *-ī* (type *dēvī*; 7.7.3 and 7.8.1):

**sn̥t-ī* in OInd. *satī*, Gr. Arc. ἔασσα from **e-sn̥t-ya*;
**bheront-ī* in OInd. *bharantī*, Gr. φέρουσα.[7]

A peculiarity of Anatolian in contrast to all other IE languages is that in transitive verbs this participle has passive meaning; thus e.g. Hitt. *asant-*, like OInd. *sant-* etc., means 'being', but from *kwen-* 'kill', IE **gʷhen-* (see 4.7.4.7, 4.7.5.3), the participle *kunant-* is not, like OInd. *ghn-ant-*, 'killing' but 'killed'. The view that this indifference to voice is original[8] is continually gaining ground.[9] It may be further supported by the fact that *-nt-* is also used to form noun derivatives,[10] particularly in Hittite but also in other IE languages.

As regards the origin of the suffix, it is to be noted that it has the form *-ont-* even in athematic verbs (e.g. **s-ont-*, **y-ont-*, etc.); *-nt-* is thus secondary, e.g. *-ānt-* from *-ā-* + *-ont-* and similar. This alone invalidates the explanation of it as from the pronouns **n(o)- *t(o)-*,[11] which is surely in any case inapplicable to names of peoples: Ἄβαντες are naturally 'those who possess Ἄβα', as it were Ἄβαν ἔχοντες.[12] It would thus be possible for *-ont-* to be formed from **em-* 'take' with the suffix *-t-* of nouns of agent/action and to have been originally compounded with nouns: **bher-om-t-* 'taking the carrying'; this would agree with the fact that the *-nt-* formation did not originally belong to the verb.[13]

[1] Traces are found even in Armenian: see Szemerényi, *Fachtagung* 5, 1975, 329; cf. Olsen, *HS* 102, 1990, 226, 233.

[2] On the ablaut even in thematic verbs, see J. Schmidt 1889, 187f., 422f.; Szemerényi, *SMEA* 2, 1962, 23–4; against, Rix 1976, 144; Oettinger, *Fs. G. Neumann*, 1982, 241. On the athematic verbs, see Bammesberger, *KZ* 95, 1982, 286–92.

[3] For the Greek nom. Collings, *Glotta* 49, 1972, 221, supposes the influence of the type λέων; Oettinger (n. 2 above, 245) thinks of δράκων (?).

[4] For one or two other languages with *-ōn*, see 6.2.7.3 n. 1. See also Schindler, *Gedenkschrift für H. Kronasser*, 1982 (three types of nom. s. in Avestan); cf. Kellens, *Krat* 36, 1991, 18.

[5] On the Latin words, see Watkins, *Studies G. S. Lane*, 1967, 186f.; Seebold, *Sprache* 15, 1969, 26f. But the nom. s. **sēnt(s)* required by the latter is unacceptable; see Anttila, *Sprache* 16, 1970, 171f.

[6] Cf. Meillet, *MSL* 13, 1905, 354f. Beekes, *Origins* 70, and Hamp, *Symbolae Mitxelena*, 1985, 223f., can hardly be right.

[7] On this, see above, 7.8.1, and cf. K. H. Schmidt, *BalkE* 31, 1988, 25–7 (the Gaulish inscription of Larzac has four forms in *-ontias*, being gen. s. or nom. acc. pl.). On the

problem of participles without gender distinction in Greek, see Petersmann, *Sprache* 25, 1979, 144–66.

[8] Cf. Sommer, *Hethiter und Hethitisch*, 1947, 67; Jacobsson, *ScSl* 9, 1963, 123–38; Schmidt, *IF* 69, 1964, 6; Evangelisti, 'Ricerche sul suffisso -NT- di participio', *Acme* 18, 1965, 3–19; Watkins, *Verb* 142–5.

[9] A different view in Schwyzer, *GG* ii, 241 n. 1; Kuryłowicz, *PICL* 8, 1958, 239, but willing to compromise *Categories* 167. Cf. also Wagner 1985, 73f.

[10] Szemerényi, *KZ* 71, 1954, 208f.; *Glotta* 33, 1954, 275f. (277 n. 1 bibliography); Kammenhuber, *MSS* 8, 1956, 43–57; Pokorny, *MSS* 15, 1959, 5–16; Kronasser, *Sprache* 8, 1962, 213f.; Laroche, *BSL* 57, 1962, 23–43; Benveniste, ibid. 44–51; Georgiev, *AO* 33, 1965, 175f.; 36, 1968, 189f.; Neu, *HS* 102, 1989, 1–15, esp. 12–15.

[11] Kretschmer, *Glotta* 32, 1953, 192.

[12] On this, cf. Brandenstein, *AO* 17, 1949, 74.

[13] On the formation, see further Wackernagel and Debrunner, *Ai. Gr.* ii/2, 160f., 417f.

9.6.1.2

Obviously the *-nt-* suffix is closely connected with the present system of the active, and its extension to the aorist and later the future, as subsystems secondarily separated from this system, is therefore not surprising; for the perfect system, on the other hand, also characterized as independent by its endings, an entirely different suffix established itself: *-wos-* and *-wōs-* in the full and long grades, *-us-* in the zero grade; the feminine is formed with *-ī-* (Gr. *-ya*) from the zero grade and, like the feminine of the *-nt-* participle, follows the *dēvī* type of inflexion.[1]

The best known example of this formation is the participle of **woida* 'I know'. It appears in Old Indic as m. s. nom. *vidvān*, gen. *viduṣ-as*, f. s. nom. *viduṣ-ī;* corresponding Greek forms are in Homer *(ϝ)εἰδ(ϝ)ώς*, *(ϝ)εἰδ(ϝ)ότος*, *(ϝ)ἰδυ(σ)ῖα*. Greek has thus an *-s-*/*-t-*stem, and the OInd. paradigm similarly shows case forms with *-t-*, e.g. n. s. nom. *vidvat*, instr. pl. *vidvadbhis*. From this the conclusion was drawn that Indo-European had a heteroclite paradigm in *-wos-*/*-wot-*, although the distribution of the two forms could not be determined (no case shows the *-t-* form in both Greek and Old Indic), and it should not have been overlooked that the feminine in *-us-ī* speaks for the unity of the suffix in the form *-wos-*/*-us-*. This has now been made a certainty by Mycenaean, which knows a *-t-* as little as does Iranian; its introduction in Greek and Old Indic is an innovation carried out independently in the two languages, as it was for this word in Gothic also. Mycenaean further shows that **wid-* also occurred as a weak stem in the masculine. The original paradigm was thus as follows:

	Masc.	Neut.	Fem.
Sing. Nom.	**weid-wōs*	**weid-wos*	**wid-us-ī*
Acc.	**weid-wos-m̥*	**weid-wos*	**wid-us-īm*
Gen.	**wid-us-os*	**wid-us-os*	**wid-us-yās*
Dat.	**wid-us-ei*	**wid-us-ei*	**wid-us-yāi*

This complicated alternation was generalized in Old Indic in favour of the zero-grade root form **wid-*, which in early Greek was retained in the feminine but elsewhere gave way to the full-grade **weid-*, later even in the feminine: cf. Att. *εἰδώς, εἰδυῖα*.[2]

As regards the origin of the suffix, the *e*-grade *-wes-* has on purely formal grounds been considered as formed with *-es-* from roots in *-u-* [3] or been divided as *we+s*[4]. In view of the meaning of 'state' it would be possible that it contains the root **wes-* 'stay'.[5]

[1] On the Old Indic nasalization, see K. Hoffmann, *Aufsätze* ii, 555f.

[2] All relevant problems are discussed in Szemerényi, 'The perfect participle active in Mycenaean and IE', *SMEA* 2, 1967, 7–26. On the stem ablaut, see Bader, *BSL* 64, 1970, 57f.; in favour of a generalized zero grade (also in **widwos*) are Anttila, *Proto-IE Schwebeablaut*, 1969, 74; Kellens 1984, 424f. On the Greek *-t* inflexion, see also Ruijgh, *Études sur la grammaire et le vocabulaire du grec mycénien*, 1967, 90; Beekes, *KZ* 86, 1972, 33 (also against Ruijgh), and *JIES* 10, 1982, 58–63 (unacceptable); Hamp, *JIES* 11, 1984, 379–82 (also unacceptable); G. Schmidt, *Fs. W. Thomas*, 1988, 66 (in favour of IE *-wot-*). On Tocharian, see Lane, in *AIED* 218; on Balto-Slavic Bammesberger, *Lg* 50, 1974, 690–2.

[3] Adrados, *Hommages Niedermann*, 1956, 25.

[4] Erhart, *Charisteria Novotný*, 1962, 71f.

[5] On the whole group, see further Euler 1979, 242f.

9.6.1.3

In the passive-middle, as in the active, there was likewise a suffix which was assigned to the present system but later, like *-nt-* in the active, extended to the aorist and future and, after the creation of the perfect passive, even to the perfect.[1] The form of the suffix was *-meno-* or *-mno-*, cf. Gr. *ἑπόμενος* 'following', OInd. *sača-māna-*, but Avest. *barəmna-*. Traces of this formation are Lat. *fēmina*, properly 'one giving suck' from **dhē(yo)-menā* (cf. *θήσατο* 'suckled'), *alumnus* 'nursling, pupil' from **alo-menos*, passive participle of *alō* 'feed', and *ignōminia* 'shame', which is not (as Walde-Hofmann and Forssman, *KZ* 81 (1967), 97f.) from *nōmen*, but from **in-gnōmenos* 'one who is not recognized'.[2]

The suffix *-mo-* of the Balto-Slavic present participle passive (cf. Russ. *iskómyj* 'sought', *vídimyj* 'visible', Lith. *nešamas* 'carried'), which was otherwise isolated in Indo-European, has now been associated with the passive participles in *-ma-* found in Luwian and Hieroglyphic Hittite (cf. Luw. *kes-ama-* 'combed', HHitt. *asīma-* 'loved').[3] These Anatolian forms are, however, to be explained as from *-amna-* with assimilation, and belong therefore to the formations in *-meno-/-mno-*. This emerges from the fact that names of 'belonging', which to begin with had the form *-uman-a*, went through the attested stages *-umena-*, *-umna-*, *-umma-*. The earliest Kültepe names (eighteenth century BC) were of the type *Harsumn-uman* 'of Harsumna'; they were successively made thematic (*arun-umana-* 'maritime'), weakened (*Nes-*

umenes 'Nesites'), syncopated (*Nes-umna* 'id.'). Similarly, the inhabitant of *Suppiluli(ya)* was at first *Suppiluliuman-(a)*, from which as early as *c.*1400 BC *Suppilulium(m)a* arose.[4] This means that Anatolian joins the uniform southern zone with *-m(e)no-*,[5] while the Balto-Slavic *-mo-* as a participial formation remains as isolated as before.[6]

For the origin of the suffix a connection with the suffix *-mn̥-* or *-men-/-mon-* has repeatedly been assumed.[7] If, however, the link with the Anatolian ethnic names is correct, it seems preferable to relate these formations to **men-* 'remain'.

Note. In athematic verbs and in the perfect, Aryan has *-āna* instead of *-māna-*, e.g. *dadhāna-* from *dadhāmi* 'put', *duhāna-* from *duh-* 'milk', and in the perfect *tu-tud-āna-*, *da-d-āna-* from *tud-* 'push', *dadāmi* 'give'. The origin of this formation has not been established. If *-āna-* can be equated with the Germanic *-ana-* (e.g. Goth. *baur-ans*) and derived from IE *-ono-*,[8] its *-ā-* must have caused the lengthening of **-mana-* (IE *-meno-*) to *-māna-*; but Saussure had already thought of a metathesis of **bharāmana-* (=φερομενο-) to *-amāna-*.[9]

1 In Greek this participle was also formed from the fut. perf. pass. at a fairly early date, e.g. διαπεπολεμησόμενον (Thucydides), and in late Greek it was even ventured from the fut. perf. mid., cf. τεθνηξόμενος 'moriturus' (Libanios, 4th cent. AD) from τεθνήξομαι (first found in the 2nd cent. BC).

2 See Leumann^2, 322, 583; Schwyzer, *GG* i, 524f.; Brixhe, *RPh* 42, 1968, 319; Flobert, *Les verbes déponents latins*, 1975, 443–8; Klingenschmitt, *Fachtagung* 5, 1975, 159f. (*-mə$_1$no-* or *-mH$_1$ no-*); against, Bammesberger 1984, 118–20 (*-men-/-mn̥-* and with secondary ablaut, see above, 6.5.5, *-meno-*), but in favour, Pinault, in *É. Benveniste aujourd'hui* ii, 1984, 110f.; Euler 1979, 100f.; Mayrhofer, *IC* 32b, 1988, 467 no. 333 (*-mĭna-<-mEno-=μενο?*); Beekes 1988, 191 (*-ámna-<-omH$_1$ no-*, *-āna-<-(C)m̥Hno-*); Bader, *BSL* 85, 1990, 24 n. 39 (against *-mH$_1$ no-*, in favour of *-men-*). The formation is now also attested in Gaulish by the Larzac inscription (K. H. Schmidt, *BalkE* 31, 1988, 27f.), if gen. pl. *barnaunom* 'of those to be sentenced' is from *barnā-mno-*, but it is explained as from *-n-H-uno-* by Hamp, *EC* 26, 1990, 63. Against the continuation of this participle in Armenian see R. Stempel, *Die infiniten Verbalformen des Armenischen*, 1983, 91f. OPrus. *poklausimanas* is, according to Smoczyński, *IC* 32b, 1988, 108–28, to be corrected to *-sīnamas*.

3 Friedrich, *Corolla linguistica: Festschrift Sommer*, 1955, 46; Benveniste, *HIE* 27f.

4 Laroche, *Les noms des hittites*, 1966, 255f., which also deals with the Luwian dissimilation to *-wani-*; on this see further Szemerényi, 'Rückverwandlung' 155f. See also Friedrich, *Heth. Elementarbuch* i^2, 1960, 34; Neumann, *Studi Meriggi*, 1969, 222; against, Kammenhuber, 'Hethitisch' 271 (*-uman-* Anatolian, but taken as acc. s.). For the development of *mn* to *mm*, see Melchert, *HS* 101, 1989, 219f.

5 In spite of Kronasser, *Etymologie* 180; Laroche (above, n. 4), 258 n. 17. So also Polomé, *Oriens* 9, 1956, 108f.

6 But cf. Vaillant, *Gram. comp.* iii, 114 (*-mo-* from *-mno-*). Hamp, *Baltistica* 9, 1973, 45–50, thinks that Albanian also had *-mo-*, cf. *la-m* 'washed'.

7 Cf. Leumann^2, 222; Schwyzer, *GG* i, 524. So also Bammesberger 1984, 120.

8 See Thumb and Hauschild, i/2, 359.

9 See Saussure, *MSL* 3, 1878, now *Recueil* 383; and more recently Bammesberger 1984, 119.

ADDENDUM.

In this connection the Latin gerund and gerundive must be mentioned. Their characteristic *-nd-* appears also in the Italic dialects with assimilation of *-nd-* to *-n(n)-* (cf. Umbr. *popler anferener* 'populi circumferendi = lustrandi', *ocrer pihaner* 'arcis piandae', and Osc. *upsannam deded* 'operandam/faciendam dedit', *sacrannas* 'sacrandae'), but the agreement is so close that it could rather be thought of as a borrowing from Latin.[1] From a purely phonological point of view, a connection with OInd. infinitives such as *pibadhyai* ~ *bibendī* (both from *-n̥dh-*) would be possible,[2] as would a link with Hittite infinitives in *-anna* like *appanna* 'to take' from *-atna*; thus the Lat. *-nd-* could have come from *-tn-*[3] or *-d(h)n-*,[4] a case which once again clearly illustrates the difficulties faced by the student of the individual language when even the comparatist can give no definite answer. For the Latinist there remains the question whether (*a*) the gerund and gerundive are both original, or (*b*) the gerundive arose from the gerund, or (*c*) conversely the gerund from the gerundive. Most scholars opt for (*b*), especially because OLat. idioms such as *lūcis dās tuendī cōpiam* (Plautus), *nāuis incohandī exordium* (Ennius), or *eius* (sc. *fēminae*) *uidendī cupidus* (Terence) seem to support the priority of the gerund:[5] early *lūcis tuendī* would then have been modified to *lūcis tuendae* on the apparent analogy of *lūminis tuendī*.[6] Few are in favour of (*c*).[7] It must not be overlooked, however, that *secundus oriundus* certainly cannot have arisen from gerunds, and therefore presumably support (*a*).[8] It can, on the other hand, be more definitely stated that the meaning of necessity and even the passive value are of secondary origin;[9] cf. e.g. *docendō discimus* or *ad docendum puerum*.[10]

[1] Porzig, *Fs. Krause*, 1960, 184; Porzio Gernia, *AGI* 48, 1963, 13.

[2] Pisani, *KZ* 72, 1955, 217–21; Gernia, op. cit., 20.

[3] Cf. Szemerényi, *TPS* 1950, 169–79.

[4] Risch, *ZRP* 67, 1951, 359.

[5] Cf. Aalto, *Untersuchungen über das lat. Gerundium und Gerundivum*, 1949, 170; Pisani (n. 2 above); Hahn, *TAPA* 74, 1943, 269f.; 96, 1965, 181–207; *Lg* 42, 1966, 393f.; Strunk, *Gymnasium* 69, 1962, 450, 460; Gernia (n. 1 above), 20; Blümel, *Glotta* 57, 1979, 81–95.

[6] Hahn, loc. cit. (1965).

[7] Among these is Sommer, *Handbuch der lat. Laut- und Formenlehre*², 1914, 592.

[8] So Drexler, *Gymnasium* 69, 1962, 429–45.

[9] Hofmann–Szantyr, 370.

[10] Further works: Gray, *BSL* 35, 1934, 76–81 (*-nt-do-*); Godel, *CFS* 12, 1954, 4 (*-en-do-*); Thibau, *Rapports entre le latin et le grec*, 1964, 20 (*regen-yo-s*); Strunk, *Glotta* 52, 1974, 273–87; Hoenigswald, *AGI* 60, 1975, 55–8 (*-ny-*); Leumann², 330f.; G. Schmidt, *Em* 46, 1978, 395f., 400, 405 (*-ndō* and Hitt. *-a-nna* from *-tnōi*; *-ndus*=Lith. *-tinas*); Haudry, *PICL* 12, 1978, 489 (*agrō colom-dō* 'pour le champ, pour le cultiver'); Poultney, *Studies Pulgram*, 1980, 33–41 (*-enyos*); Heberlein, 'Die Diskussion um die *nd*-Formen', *Gymnasium* 88, 1981, 151–72; Pariente, *Em* 49, 1982; Risch, *Gerundivum und Gerundium*, Berlin 1984 (priority of the gerundive; 171–9 *-tno-*; cf. Moussy, *BSL* 80/2, 1986, 198–9); *IC* 30/1, 1984, 116–18 (117 criticized *Krat* 34, 1989, 216 n. 7). See also Stepanov, 'Gerundive and action nouns', *VJ* 1985 (6): *agendum=agen*+particle *dom*=δον; Ambrosini, 'Gerundio e gerundivo in latino', *SSL* 31, 1991, 1–53; Krasuxin, 'Origin of Latin gerund-gerundive', *VJ* 1992 (5), 60–73 (*-nd-*=*-nt*?); Hettrich, 'Nochmals zu Gerundium und Gerundivum', *Fs. Rix*, 1993, 190–209 (against Risch); Meiser, 'Das Gerundivum im Spiegel der Onomastik', *Fs. Untermann*, 1993, 255–68.

9.6.1.4

Whereas the formations in *-nt-*, *-wos-*, and *-meno-/-mno-*, in spite of earlier noun connections, are firmly embedded in the IE verbal system, there are some further formations which were only loosely attached to it. Of especial importance in the history of the individual languages were the suffixes *-to-* and *-no-*, which in so far as they formed verbal adjectives already had a significant role in the late IE period.[1]

The suffix *-to-* is widespread in all IE languages except Anatolian and Tocharian.[2] The earliest mode of formation was from the zero grade of the root. IE **klu-tó-s*, attested by OInd. *śru-ta-*, Gr. κλυτός, Lat. *inclutus*, OHG *Hlot-hari* 'Lothar', OIr. *cloth* (n. noun) 'fame', is not formed from the present **kl̥neumi* (9.4.1.3), but directly from the root, and its meaning is not participial, but simply 'to do with hearing and being heard, famous'. Further examples of this zero-grade formation are IE **gʷm̥-tó-s* in OInd. *gata-*, Gr. -βατός, Lat. *(in)uentus*; **mn̥-tó-s* in OInd. *matá-* 'thought', Lat. *(com)mentus* 'contrived', Goth. *munds* 'thought'; **gn̥̄-tó-s* 'born' in OInd. *jāta-*, Lat. *(g)nātus*, Gaul. *Cintu-gnātus* 'first-born', Goth. *airþa-kunds* 'earth-born, of earthly origin'. In the later history of the languages there is a tendency to restrict the formation to passive use, as in *loved*, *praised*, Lat. *amātus*, *laudātus*. The original lack of voice differentiation is, however, quite clear. OInd. *gatas* very often means 'he went', *prāptas* (*pra-āp-tas*) 'he reached', etc.; in the Latin deponent the *-to-* formation regularly has active meaning, etc.[3]

Alongside *-to-* a suffix *-no-* was employed with apparently the same function. For participial use it was abandoned in Latin and Greek (but cf. *plē-nus*, ἀγ-νός), whereas Aryan, Slavic, and Germanic built it into their verb systems and divided the work between the two suffixes. In Old Indic, for example, almost all roots in *-d-* form their verbal adjectives in *-na-*: *bhid-* 'split' : *bhinna-*; *ad-* 'eat' : *anna-* 'food', etc. In Germanic this formation has been generalized for the past participle of strong verbs, cf. NHG *gestiegen*, *geboren*, *gegangen*, NE *risen*, *born*, *gone*. In Slavic also a distribution took place, by which *-to-* was severely restricted.[4]

The suffix *-to-* is clearly connected with the various *-t-* formations, and must represent a thematic derivative from abstract nouns in *-t-*.[5]

[1] For introduction and bibliography, see Schwyzer, *GG* i, 501f.; Hofmann–Szantyr, 383, 391; further on this: Bernert, *Glotta* 30, 1943, 1–14; Regula, *Glotta* 32, 1953, 89–95; Ammann, *Gedenkschrift Kretschmer* i, 1957, 10–23.

[2] A trace exists even in Anatolian, if for *hastan-uri-* 'grand des princes' my interpretation of *hasta-* as 'born, prince' (*Fachtagung* 5, 1975, 329) is correct.

[3] M.-D. Joffre, 'A propos de l'adjectif en *-to-*: le prétendu passage du passif à l'actif', 5e *Colloque latin*, *CILL* 15, 1989, 197f.

[4] Cf. Vaillant, *Gram. comp.* iii, 116f., and below, 9.6.2 n. 9.
[5] Kuryłowicz, *Apophonie* 77 n. 48. On the south-east, see Euler 1979, 121f.

9.6.2

The category of *infinitive*,[1] which seems so self-evident from the standpoint of the later IE languages, cannot be proved for common Indo-European and should not be ascribed to it. An earlier state of affairs still prevails in Vedic, in which no fewer than sixteen formations can occur with the function of the later infinitive, in case forms determined by the structure of the sentence.[2] As a rule these 'infinitives' are case forms of deverbative abstract nouns, mainly datives and accusatives, only rarely genitives or ablatives, apparently never locatives;[3] in the overwhelming majority of infinitive constructions—more than 600 instances out of about 700 in all—the Rigveda has the dative, only in about 50 the accusative. The dative expresses purpose, the accusative the direct object of transitive verbs and the goal with verbs of motion; cf. *sugān pathō akr̥ṇōn nir-aǰē* (dat.) *gās* 'he made the ways easy to *drive out* the cows (RV iii. 30, 10); *ā gamad . . . barhir āsadē* (dat.) 'let [the host of the Maruts] come *to sit on* the sacrificial grass' (RV v. 46, 5); *šakēma tvā samidham* (acc.) 'may we *kindle* thee [Agni]' (RV i. 94, 3); *iyētha barhir āsadam* (acc.) 'thou [Agni] hast come *to sit on* the sacrificial grass' (RV iv. 9, 1).

The abstract nouns in *-tu-*, *-ti-*, *-(a)s-*, and *-(v)an-* are morphologically of especial importance. Frequent formations from *-tu-* are the dative in *-tavē* or *-tavai* (more than forty), e.g. *dā-tavē* 'give', the gen.-abl. in *-tōs* (ten), e.g. *dā-tōs*, and the acc. in *-tum*, e.g. *dā-tum*. The dative from *-ti-* is used in five verbs, e.g. *pī-tayē* 'for drinking=to drink', *ū-tayē* 'to help'. From *-(a)s-* the dative in *-(a)sē* is frequent (nearly thirty verbs), e.g. *ǰiv-asē* 'to live', *čakṣ-asē* 'to see'. It is interesting that the dative infinitive, which supplies six-sevenths of the instances in the Rigveda, is almost completely extinct in the early post-Vedic period, whereas the acc. *-tum*, corresponding to the Latin (and Slavic) supine, occurs only five times in the Rigveda but is the only infinitive formation in the later language.[4]

The so far unmentioned Vedic formation in *-dhyai* is also of importance for Greek. This form, which dies out after the Rigveda, occurs in thirty-five verbs, e.g. *piba-dhyai* 'to drink', *bhara-dhyai* 'to carry';[5] as it stands completely isolated in the system, it must be inherited from Indo-European. It is in fact preserved in Gr. -*(σ)σαι*, which functions as inf. act. and 2nd s. impv. mid. of the *s*-aorist, e.g. *λοέσσαι/λόεσσαι*, later both *λοῦσαι*.[6] To Vedic *sačadhyai* 'to follow', *bharadhyai* 'to carry' corresponded at first Gr. **ἕπεσσαι* **φέρεσσαι*; but as these could not be assigned to the aorist they were retained in the present system and modified to -εσθαι under the influence of the endings in -σθ-.[7] Aryan and Greek thus guarantee an infinitive formation in -*dhyāi* for at least a part of the Indo-European area.[8]

The Greek infinitive type in -ειν also belongs to the IE period; on the evidence of Mycenaean it goes back to *-e(s)en* and should therefore be connected with the Vedic inf. in *-sani* (e.g. *nēṣani* 'to lead'); the variant -(ε)ναι arose under the influence of -σ(θ)αι. The doublet -μεν/-μεναι in the dialects and Homer is to be explained in the same way.[9]

In the case of the Latin infinitives, the general ending *-re* of the present active, on the evidence of *es-se* (and *uel-le*) and the perfect *-is-se*, goes back to *-se* or *-si* (cf. *ante*: Gr. ἀντί); *agere* as **agesi* would be the locative of an *s*-stem **agos/*ages-* 'the leading', which is semantically not very suitable.[10] There is a striking similarity between OInd. *jīvasē* and Lat. *uīuere*, where Old Indic presents the dative, Latin the locative of an *s*-stem **g*ʷ*īw-es-*.[11] Of the passive infinitives the type of the third conjugation in *-ī* can be taken as the dative (earlier *-ei*) of a root noun; cf. the above-cited OInd. *nir-aǰ-ē* from **agei* and Lat. *agī*. The ending *-rī* of the other conjugations would then be a cross between *-ī* and the active *-re*.[12]

To the OInd. type in *-tayē* from a noun in *-ti-* corresponds the Balto-Slavic infinitive in *-ti* (e.g. OCS *vesti*, Lith. *vesti* 'to lead'), which is traced back to the dative in *-tei* and the locative in *-tēi*. Old Prussian has three endings, *dā-t*, *dā-tun*, *dā-twei* 'to give', of which *-t* goes back to a locative in *-ti*, while the other two represent the accusative and dative of a *-tu* stem.[13] The accusative of a *-tu* stem, *-tum*, exists in OCS and Latin as the supine and is, as we have seen, the only infinitive of classical Sanskrit. The other Latin supine in *-tū* is of unclear origin: alongside the instrumental ablatives *ductū iussū*, etc., and the rare ablative of separation *obsōnātū redīre*, there are many forms which appear to be dative.[14]

Germanic took its own way in using for infinitive the accusative of a neuter in (IE) *-no-*: Goth. *bairan* comes from IE **bheronom*.[15]

[1] In general see Meillet, *BSL* 32, 1931, 188f., 193; Renou, *BSL* 38, 1937, 69–87; Schwyzer, *GG* i, 804f., ii, 358; Kuryłowicz, *Categories*, ch. 6: 'Impersonal verbal forms'; Hofmann–Szantyr, 341f.; E. Seidel, 'Die gram. Kategorie Infinitiv', *PICL* 10/4, 1970, 365–9; Voyles, 'The infinitive and participle in IE: a syntactic reconstruction', *Lings* 58, 1970, 68–91; *Jeffers, 'The infinitives of the IE languages', diss., Cornell Univ. 1972; *Lg* 51, 1975, 133–48; Jeffers and Cantor, *IF* 89, 1985, 91f.; Haudry, 'Sur l'origine des infinitifs en grec ancien', *BSL* 70, 1975, 115–36; Leumann², 580f.; Gippert, *Zur Syntax der infinitivischen Bildungen in den idg. Sprachen*, Frankfurt a. M. 1978; 'Verbum dicendi + Inf. im Indo-Iranischen', *MSS* 44, 1985, 29–57; G. Schmidt, *Em* 46, 1978, 399f.; Disterheft, *The Syntactic Development of the Infinitive in IE*, Columbus, Oh., 1980; S. Rémi-Giraud (ed.), *L'infinitif*, Lyon 1988.

On the problem of the double dative, see Haudry, *BSL* 63, 1968, 141–59; Boeder, in P. Ramat (ed.), *Linguistic Reconstruction and IE Syntax*, 1980, 207–24 (*Vṛtrāya hantavē* 'to kill Vrtra'); Hettrich, *MSS* 43, 1984, 55–106. On an alleged predicative infinitive in Indo-

Iranian, i.e. the use of an inf. instead of a finite verb form, see Disterheft, *KZ* 95, 1981, 110–21, and (against) Gippert, *KZ* 97, 1984, 205–20.

[2] Cf. MacDonell, *Vedic Grammar*, 1910, 407f.; Sgall, 'Die Infinitive im Rgveda', *Acta Univ. Carolinae Philologica* 2, Prague 1958, 135–268; and on the general problem, Gippert, *KZ* 97, 220: 'In the RV as in the Avesta there was no uniform category "infinitive" '.

[3] See Sgall, op. cit. 157, 159, 248. A locative is still assumed for certain Hittite forms: see Eichner, *MSS* 31, 1973, 92; Carruba, *Scritti Bonfante*, 1976, 141.

[4] See M. Deshpande, *Syntax of the Sanskrit Infinitive* -tum, Ann Arbor, Mich., 1980.

[5] See Benveniste, *Les infinitifs avestiques*, Paris 1935, 72f.; Sgall (n. 2 above), 225f. Against Benveniste's view (75) that this inf. is middle or medio-passive, see Gippert, 'Ein indo-iran. Inf. des Mediopassivs?', *MSS* 43, 1984, 25–44. Cf. also Kellens, *Krat* 36, 1991, 21.

[6] Of course with shortening of *-āi* to *-ai*, in spite of Haudry, *BSL* 70, 1975, 118. Berman, *KZ* 91, 1978, 231–9, would like to compare the Hittite suffix *-(a)sha-* to the Greek infinitive.

[7] Haudry, op. cit. 123, is inclined to recognize a development *dhw*>*sth* in Greek, 'since there is no example to the contrary'. See also Cohen, *KZ* 95, 1982, 293–301.

[8] A different view in Benveniste, *Origines* 207f.; cf. Schwyzer, *GG* i, 809; Sgall (n. 2 above), 156 n. 19; Gusmani, *IF* 71, 1966, 64–80; Poultney, *Lg* 43, 1968, 872–3, 876. For *-dhyāi*, see further Jeffers, *Lg* 51, 1975, 134; Rix, *Studies Palmer*, 1976, 328–30 (*-dhyōi*), and in *Le lingue ie. di frammentaria attestazione*, 1983, 94; G. Schmidt, *Em* 46, 1978, 399f.; Gippert (n. 1 above, 1978), 289f.; *MSS* 43, 1984, 25–44; 44, 1985, 45–7.

[9] For the Greek infinitives, see Aalto, *Studien zur Geschichte des Infinitivs im Griechischen*, 1953; Burguière, *Histoire de l'infinitif en grec*, 1960. On *-αι* and the Greek infinitives, see also Wathelet, *Les traits éoliens*, Rome 1970, 315–24; Haudry, *BSL* 70, 1975, 115f.; 75, 1980, 142f.; Rix (n. 8 above, 1976); G. Schmidt, *Em* 46, 1978, 400; Blümel, *Glotta* 57, 1979, 114, 118; Cohen, *KZ* 95, 1982, 293–4; García-Ramón, 'Athematische Infinitivbildungen im Attischen und im Westionischen', *Wackernagel Kolloquium*, 1990, 159–69.

[10] See the text above at n. 3. Blümel (n. 9 above), 78–81, finds in *-s-i* a variant of the dative in *-ei*.

[11] Berman (n. 6 above) also connects *-asē*/*-re* with Hitt. *-(a)sha-*.

[12] Watkins, *Verb* 181, interprets differently: *ag-ī* is to be compared to the Vedic absolutive *-tvī* from *tu*+*ī*; thus the *-ī* in PAKARI of the Duenos inscription (*c*.500 BC) would be in order, and the OLat. infinitives *uortie-r agie-r* etc. could be compared to the absolutives in *-ya*. Also B. Tikkanen, *The Sanskrit Gerund: a Synchronic, Diachronic and Typological Analysis*, 1987 (see *IC* 33 D 35; *BSL* 83/2, 1988, 137f.).

[13] Cf. Vaillant, *Gram. comp.* iii, 126f.; Stang, *Vgl. Gram.* 447f.; Haudry, *BSL* 63, 1968, 144 (*-tei* from *-t-*), cf. *PICL* 12, 1978, 489f.; *BSL* 75, 1980, 143f. Tocharian has an inf. in *-tsi*, which perhaps comes from a *-ti-* stem; see Krause and Thomas, *Toch. Elementarbuch* i, 1960, 261; Winter, *IF* 67, 1962, 21 (~ OInd. *-tayē*). Van Windekens explains differently, positing *-dhyai* in *AION-L* 4, 1962, 17, but *-tyōi* in *Orbis* 21, 1972, 111–13; cf. also *Le tokharien* ii/2, 1982, 250, and the critical review in Thomas, *Die Erforschung des Tocharischen*, 1985, 90, to which Rix (n. 8 above, 1983), 94 n. 5 (*-dhyōi*), should be added. For the Old Prussian forms, reference may be made to Kuiper's reconstruction of a hysterodynamic paradigm *étum*/*itvā̆*; see Beekes, *KZ* 86, 1972, 33.

[14] For an explanation (*-uī*>*-ū*), see Leumann², 354f., 442f.; Haudry, *BSL* 75, 1980, 143, explains differently: short form of **-ew-(ey)* 'où la désinence disparaissait dans un tour double' (?). Cf. Panagl, 'Das lateinische Supinum: Geschichte und Funktion einer grammatischen Kategorie', *Fachtagung* 7, 1985, 324f.

[15] Of course the form is connected with the participle (see above, 9.6.1.4). For *-eno-*/*-ono-*, see Seebold, *Anglia* 85, 1968, 251–69.

9.7. PREHISTORY

The IE verb system, as established by comparison of the systems of the individual languages, must now be investigated in accordance with the principles of internal reconstruction (see 3.1), whereby insight is often gained into the inner relationships of the system and thus into its prehistory.

9.7.1. Personal endings

9.7.1.1.

One of the most striking features of the IE system of personal endings is the distinction between primary and secondary endings, which can be observed throughout the indicative of the present-aorist system both in the active and in the passive-middle. The carrier of this difference in almost all persons (1–3, 6) is the vowel *-i* (cf. 9.2.1.1 and 9.2.2.1):

	Active		Passive-middle	
1	*-mi*	*-m*	*-(m)ai*	*-(m)ā*
2	*-si*	*-s*	*-soi*	*-so*
3	*-ti*	*-t*	*-toi*	*-to*
6	*-nti*	*-nt*	*-ntoi*	*-nto*

These facts suggest the conclusion that the two series of personal endings, and with them the tenses of present and past, were originally one and only later became distinct: to emphasize the *hic et nunc*, the personal endings which were extended with the adverbial element *i* were at first used as a stylistic variant, but this inevitably led to a polarization whereby the unmarked variant was totally excluded from the sphere of the *hic et nunc* and so became the indicator of the past.[1] Thus historically the secondary endings were primary, but to avoid misunderstanding *-m -s -t -nt* should be referred to as the 'primitive' endings.[2]

It is remarkable that the differentiation did not take place in all the persons, and that the 1st and 2nd pl. in particular lack the characteristic of the primary ending. At least it seems unwise to assume for Indo-European as a whole the distinction found in a few individual languages, e.g. Hitt. *-weni -teni*, OIr. *-m(a)i* from *-mosi*, although basically there is no reason to doubt that final *-i* could be lost.[3] On the other hand, attempts to exclude the established primary endings from certain areas, e.g. Old Irish,[4] must be reckoned as methodologically mistaken. Perhaps the selective addition of *-i* to the 1st and 2nd pl. was justified by the consideration that these were in any case well characterized already and the tense was unambiguously determined by the speech situation.[5]

Less attention has hitherto been paid to the difference between active and passive-middle. Yet it also seems fairly certain that at least in some persons the characteristic vowel of the passive SE was original, and that it disappeared in the active as the result of ablaut weakening.[6] The time sequence was, therefore:

		Active	Passive-middle
I	3rd s.	*-to*	*-tó*[7]
II	Vowel loss	*-t*	*-tó*
III	Deictic *-i*	*-ti/-t*	*-tói/-tó*
IV	Recessive accent	*-ti/-t*	*-toi/-to*[8]

[1] Although this idea is fairly generally ascribed to Rudolf Thurneysen (*KZ* 27, 1885, 173), the connection was already recognized in 1857 by the Viennese linguist Friedrich Müller, who is named by Saussure in his *Mémoire* (see *Recueil* 117); Kiparsky's detailed proof is in Watkins, *Verb* 45. On this cf. also Brugmann, *Grundriss*², ii/3, 593; Kieckers, *Sprachwissenschaftliche Miszellen*, 1934, 22; Burrow, *The Sanskrit Language*, 1955, 313; Martinet, *Travaux de l'Institut de Linguistique de Paris* 1, 1956, 17f.; Savčenko, *LPosn* 8, 1960, 47; 12–13, 1968, 32; Kuryłowicz, *Categories* 131 (cf. *Apophonie* 32); Safarewicz, in *Problemy ie. jazykoznanija*, 1964, 14f. (*-i* is IE only in the 3rd person!); Erhart, *Sbornik Brno* A/14, 1966, 17 (*i*='maintenant'); Kiparsky, *FL* 4, 1968, 45; Wright, *BSOAS* 33, 1970, 187–99; Watkins, *Verb* 45. G. Schmidt, *KZ* 85, 1972, 262, thinks that in the perfect the *i* of the *hic et nunc* occurred only in the singular, i.e. it also expressed the singular, so that *-nti* must represent an (IE) innovation on the analogy of *-ti*. But if the SE *-t* could become *-ti*, why could *-nt* not also become *-nti*? Brandenstein, *Fs. Pokorny*, 1967, 18, believes that *i* is the locative ending: **didōmi*='giving (is) with me'.

[2] Against this interpretation Hattori, *CFS* 25, 1970, 145f., thinks that the SE represent the weakened forms of the PE. This was already taught before him by Herbig, *IF* 6, 1896, 247–9, and Kock, *KZ* 34, 1897, 576f., and recently it has again been maintained by Mańczak, in Lüdtke 1980, 45–48. But it is really hard to see pronouns in *-m*, *-s*, *-t* (see further 9.7.1.2); we must no doubt start from *-em*, *-tu*, *-so*, which became by apocope the SE *-m*, *-t*, *-s*, and only then did the PE arise from these with *i*.

[3] Cf. 7.2.1, n. 6, in spite of Brugmann (n. 1 above).

[4] So e.g. Watkins, *Celtica* 6, 1962, 47; *Verb* 46; *Ériu* 21, 1969, 1f. Against, Campanile, *AION-L* 8, 1968, 65. To throw doubt on the general existence of PE and SE, as Watkins does (e.g. *Verb* 46), is in any case quite unjustified; on this see above, 9.2.1.1 n. 3 fin.

[5] It is possible that the middle 1st pl. ending contained a local particle **dhi* or **dha* (so Kuryłowicz, *PICL* 8, 1958, 241; Watkins, *Verb* 78), cf. Gr. *-θι* and *(ἔν)θα*. But the claim that 1st and 2nd pl. mid. had no forms of their own (Watkins, *Verb* 128) must be rejected.

[6] Similarly Meillet, *BSL* 23, 1922, 66, 70, and Savčenko, *BPTJ* 20, 1961, 114. In any case Kiecker's idea (n. 1 above), that *-o* meant 'then', is refuted by the PE *-toi*, which denotes the present in spite of *-o*. It is a sign of the close connection between active and passive (not active and middle) that the noun suffix *-t-* can express both: cf. *ἀγνώς* 'unknown' and 'unknowing'. According to Lehmann, *Glossa* 7, 1973, 81–90, the middle=reflexive-reciprocal in an OV language (like IE) has its characteristic sign in the form of an affix, here *-o*; the change to an SVO type then brought constructions with (reflexive) pronouns, e.g. in Romance or Slavic.

[7] Following Porzig, Kuryłowicz, and others, Watkins (*Verb* 51, 84f., 98) maintains the view that 3rd s. mid. *-to* is a later substitute for earlier *-o*, and this could be right. But when he suggests that Hittite, alongside the usual *kitta(ri)* 'lies', has preserved *in a single instance* the older *kiya* (85f.), this is not only a methodological error (*unus testis nullus testis*) but also factually incorrect, as this form is simply the pronoun *ki* 'this'+*ya* 'and'; see Lindeman, *NTS* 26, 1972, 78 n. 16; Melchert, in *In Memory of W. Cowgill*, 1987, 196 n. 33; Neu, in Kronasser ii, 1987, 409; *Fs. Meid*, 1989, n. 13. Further, since *-o* and *-to* must both be the demonstratives **e-/o-* and **to-* (see above, 9.2.1.2, n. 3), it can at most be said that there may have been a difference in time, but this has not been proved.

[8] In a paper on 'The prehistoric development of the athematic endings in PIE' (*In Memory of Ben Schwartz*, 1988, 475–88), Bomhard reconstructs the set as *m*, *t*, *s/Ø*, *we/me*, *te*, *en/er* (earliest *s-e*?), and refers to Uralic *me*, *te*, *se*, *me*+pl., *te*+pl., *se*+pl.

9.7.1.2

The question of the *origin* of the personal endings has always aroused much greater interest. Since Bopp's earliest writings, indeed since the eighteenth century, it has been usual to find in the personal endings the personal pronouns.[1] In spite of frequent dissent[2] this theory is obvious for the 1st s. *-m*, and for this person is now again almost universally accepted;[3] it is, however, also valid for the 1st pl., where the original form of the pronoun was **mes* (8.4.4*c*), and for the 1st dual, whose ending *-we(s)* similarly contains the pronoun.[4] And if the 1st person is expressed by means of the personal pronoun, the same principle must be expected to operate in the 2nd person also. This is suggested by many other language families. Thus in Finnish the personal endings are 1 *-n* (from *-m*), 2 *-t*, 4 *-mme*, 5 *-tte*, the personal pronouns are 1 *minä*, 2 *sinä* (from *tinä*), 4 *me*, 5 *te*, and the suffixed possessives are 1 *-mi*, 2 *-si* (from *-ti*), 4 *-mme*, 5 *-nne* (from *-nde*).[5] The same connections can be observed in Caucasian and Turkic languages,[6] in Hamito-Semitic,[7] and, not least, also in Basque, where the personal prefixes 1 *n-*, 2 **h-*, 4 *g-*, 5 *z-* stand beside the personal pronouns *ni*, **hi*, *gu*, *zu*.[8]

The principle can without difficulty be recognized in Indo-European for the 2nd pl. also. For the ending *-tes* is simply the plural of the 2nd s. pronoun **tu*: the plural form **twes* (from *tu+es*) was simplified to **tes* just as **twe* and **te* alternate in the singular.[9] The Aryan primary ending *-thas* is according to general opinion modified from *-t-*, probably in connection with the other alternations of the personal endings, especially in the dual.[10]

In the plural the endings *-me(s)dhi* and *-dhwe* are difficult. If, however, it may be assumed that the 1st pl. is to be divided as *-me(s)-dhi* (see Watkins, *Verb* 78) and therefore *-dhwe* is also to be derived from *-dhwe-dhi*, then the latter form can be explained as having arisen from **twe(s)-dhi*, since the sequence *t-dh*, i.e. unvoiced stop–voiced aspirate, was impossible and had to become voiced aspirate–voiced aspirate; the *-dhwedhi* which thus arose was then felt to be over-characterized and *-dhi* was dropped.

On the other hand, the attempt to bring together the 2nd s. ending *-s(i)* and the pronoun **tu* seems hopeless. To suppose that *s* and *t* could be reduced to a common denominator[11]—the pronoun would then be something like **Zwe*—is, for me at least, out of the question. But the problem finds a simple solution if, as has often been assumed in recent research, the 2nd s. ending was originally *-t*, not *-s*. This is indicated in the first place by the fact that among the endings of the perfect the 2nd s. was in any case characterized by *t*,[12] which only secondarily became Aryan *-tha* [13] and is also the basis of the Aryan ending *-thās*.[14] Furthermore, *-t* still appears as the 2nd s. ending in Hittite and Tocharian and correspondingly *-s* in the 3rd s., e.g. Hitt. *dais* 'posuit'.[15] We can therefore suppose that the 2nd s. also was based on the personal pronoun,[16] and was later displaced by the 3rd s. *-s* when *-t* made a breakthrough there.[17]

In the 3rd person we are faced with quite different relationships. The 3rd pl. *-nt-* may indeed be connected with 3rd s. *-t-*, but not in any event as its plural. First as regards the 3rd s. ending *-t-*, it was formerly taken for granted that it contained the demonstrative pronoun **to-*.[18] Then this explanation was called in question, and an attempt was made to identify the *-t-* with the noun suffix which forms both agent nouns (e.g. OInd. *dēva-stu-t-* 'one praising the gods', Lat. *sacer-dō-t-* 'qui sacra facit') and action nouns (e.g. Ved. *stu-t* 'praise'); in the same way the ending *-to(i)* of the passive-middle could be identified with the suffix *-to-* in e.g. verbal adjectives.[19] An ingenious adaptation of this idea seeks to explain the entire verbal inflexion by combining this noun theory with the *ergative construction*.[20] According to this explanation, the agent in the ergative, in the case of personal pronouns in the oblique form of the stem, was added to the abstract noun in *-t-*. Thus a noun **gʷhen-t-* 'stroke, blow' had a series of constructions built from it: **gʷhen(t)-mi* 'blow by me' = 'I strike', **gʷhent-t-i>*gʷhen-si*, **gʷhen(t)-mes*, **gʷhent-wes*; for the 3rd person, on the other hand, simply the noun would have been used: **gʷhen-t-i* 'a blow (comes from someone)' = 'strikes', or with the participle **gʷhn-ont-i* 'strikers' = 'they strike'.[21]

This interpretation would be in agreement with the newly emphasized opposition of 1st and 2nd person to 3rd person, the opposition of 'person' to 'non-person'.[22] But whereas in the 3rd pl. *-nt-* can be connected with the participle, a similar explanation of the 3rd s. is excluded if *-s* as well as *-t* can function as ending. There then remains only the possibility that the *casus rectus* as well as the *casus obliquus* of the demonstrative **so/*to* could be added as subject, probably in a chronological succession; chronological coexistence would mean that **s(o)* or **t(o)* was used according to whether the subject was animate or inanimate.

The endings of the 3rd pl., *-nt* or *-r*, both seem to be of nominal origin:[23] *-nt-* is probably connected with the participial *-nt-*, whereas *-r* has at most a not entirely clear link with the *-r* of the passive-middle formations (9.7.1.3). On the 1st s. ending *-ō*, see 9.7.1.3 fin.

[1] For a short historical survey, see Seebold, 'Versuch über die Herkunft der idg. Personalendungssysteme', *KZ* 85, 1971, 185f. A more detailed account is available in the thesis of W. M. Linker, **IE verb endings from Bopp to Watkins*, diss., North Carolina 1974. Cf. also A. B. Dolgopolskij, 'Personal pronouns in the Nostratic languages', *Gedenkschrift B. Collinder*, 1984, 64–111; Rasmussen, *Wackernagel Kolloquium*, 1990, 193–4: the active is a

periphrasis constituted by an agent noun and a personal pronoun, e.g. *g^{ω}hen- 'killer'+-m 'I', -t (>-s) 'thou', etc., resulting in the nominal sentences 'killer (am) I'='I kill', etc.

[2] Hirt, *IF* 17, 1906, 36f.; Jespersen, *Language*[11], 1959, 383f.; Burrow, *The Sanskrit Language*, 1955, 316.

[3] Brugmann, *Grundriss*[2], ii/3, 5f., 592f. (against Hirt's general rejection); *IF* 39, 1920, 139; Kretschmer, *Sprache*[3], 1923, 35; Savčenko, *LPosn* 8, 1960, 48f.; Ivanov, *Obščeind.* 265; Vaillant, *Gram. comp.* iii, 21; Brandenstein (above, 9.7.1.1 n. 1 fin.); Erhart 1970, 51f., esp. 58.

[4] See 8.4.4*c* above, and cf. Brugmann, *Grundriss*[2], ii/3, 594; *IF* 39, 137: **bherō-wĕ* 'I carry (**bherō*) and the other person (you/he)'. The endings *-mes/-wes* cannot, of course, be treated simply as phonetic variants (so Kuryłowicz, *Categories* 150f.).

[5] Kretschmer (n. 3 above); Szinnyei, *Magyar nyelvhasonlítás*[7], 1927, 120f., 115, 116f.; Hakulinen, *Handbuch der finnischen Sprache* i, 1957, 54, 183; Collinder, *Comparative Grammar of the Uralic Languages*, 1960, 243.

[6] Cf. Savčenko (n. 3 above), 44f.

[7] Moscati, *Comparative Grammar of the Semitic Languages*, 1964, 137f.

[8] Lafon, *BSL* 55, 1960, 216.

[9] See above, 8.4.4*c* and 5.4.2. According to Villar, *RSEL* 4, 1974, 391–409, 1st pl. *-me/-mo*, 2nd pl. *-te* were originally identical with s. *-m*, *-t*, which can at most be correct for a pre-inflexional period, though even then the singular surely could and must have been distinguished from the plural, i.e. other expedients must have been sought.

[10] Kuryłowicz, *Categories* 152f. Vaillant's attempt, *BSL* 38, 1937, 94, to derive *th* from an original group *H-t* is interesting.

[11] Cf. Myrkin, *VJ* 1964 (5), 83f.; Brandenstein (n. 3 above). Similarly Ambrosini, *SSL* 2, 1962, 95. According to Rasmussen, *Wackernagel Kolloquium*, 1990, 194, *-t* 'thou' later became *-s* in final position.

[12] Burrow, *IIJ* 1, 1957, 64, 72; Ambrosini, op. cit. 92f. For Hittite, see Kronasser, *Etymologie* 377f.

[13] Kuryłowicz, *Apophonie* 381; Savčenko, *LPosn* 8, 50 (*-tha* from 1st s. *Ha* and 2nd s. *t*).

[14] Kuryłowicz, *Apophonie* 41, 381; *Categories* 58; Savčenko, *VJ* 1955 (4), 119.

[15] Watkins, *Origins* 74f., 90f., 97f., 102f. (but Old Icelandic has not in any case a 3rd s. *-si* as is stated 86f. and 104). See also Adrados, *Fachtagung* 2, 1962, 150. An entirely different account in Kuryłowicz, *Categories* 156f., and Kammenhuber, 'Hethitisch' 332; against this, Watkins again, *Verb* 53f., and Haudry, *Homage to G. Dumézil*, 1982, 22f.: Ved. *prākṣinās* (RV iv 18, 12) shows IE (3rd s.!) *-s* (?).

[16] The phonetic development was *-tu>-tw>-t* and/or *-tu-i=-twi>-ti*.

[17] At all events a phonetic development *t* to *s*, as in Seebold (n. 1 above), 197f., remains unacceptable (see Szemerényi 1985, 27), whereas Vaillant's supposition of *tt* to *s* (see the text further on) at least represents a rational way and is to be taken seriously.

[18] e.g. Brugmann (n. 4 above).

[19] Cf. Hirt, *IG* iv, 1928, 102, 104; Kieckers (above, 9.7.1.1 n. 1).

[20] On the ergative, see Vaillant, 'L'ergatif ie.', *BSL* 37, 1936, 93–108; Martinet, 'La construction ergative', 1958, reprinted in his *La linguistique synchronique*, 1965, 206–22; Mesčaninov, *Ergativnaja konstrukcija v jazykax različnyx tipov*, 1967 (see Szemerényi 1982, 17f.); Lyons, *Introduction to Theoretical Linguistics*, 1968, 350f.; Aronson, 'Case and subject in Georgian', *Lingua* 25, 1970, 291–301; Seebold (n. 1 above), 203f.; Lafon, 'Ergatif et passif en basque et géorgien', *BSL* 66, 1972, xxii–xxiv, 327–43; Tchekhoff, 'Une langue à construction ergative: l'avar', *La Linguistique* 8/2, 1972, 103–15; Pulgram, *JL* 8, 1972, 164f.; Comrie, 'The ergative', *Lingua* 32, 1973, 239–53; K. H. Schmidt, *Fachtagung* 4, 1973, 114f.; 'Probleme der Ergativkonstruktion', *MSS* 36, 1977, 97–116; Tchekhoff, *Aux fondements de la syntaxe: l'ergatif*, Paris 1978; H. Wagner, 'The typological background of the ergative construction' (*Proc. Royal Irish Acad.* 78C/3, 37–74), 57: 'Uhlenbeck's attempt to reconstruct an ergative construction in PIE . . . I find difficult to accept'; Comrie, 'Ergativity', in W. P. Lehmann (ed.), *Syntactic Typology*, 1978, 329–94; H. Tegey, 'Ergativity in Pushto', *Fs. Penzl*, 1979, 369–418; Dixon, 'Ergativity', *Lg* 55, 1979, 59–138; F. Plank (ed.), *Ergativity*, New York 1979 (contains e.g. K. H. Schmidt, 'Active and ergative stages of Pre-IE', 333–45; W. Boeder, 'Ergative syntax and morphology in language change: the South-

Caucasian languages', 435–80); *Christol, 'L'ergatif ie.: une illusion?', *Actes de la session de linguistique Aussois* (cited *BSL* 75, 1980, 91); Tchekhoff, 'Autour de l'ergatif', *BSL* 75, 1980, 69–93; Sasse, 'Subjekt und Ergativ', *FoL* 12, 1980, 219–52; Givon, 'The drift away from ergativity', *FoLH* 1, 1980, 41–60; S. C. Dik, *Functional Grammar*, 1981, 159f.; Starke, *BiOr* 39, 1982 (on the term *ergative*), see above, 7.1.4.2 n. 2; Bossong, 'Actance ergative et transitivité', *Lingua* 56, 1982, 201–34; Calboli, *ANRW* 29/1, 1983, 14–29; Villar 1983 (cf. Szemerényi 1985, 29f.); Bossong, 'Ergativity in Basque', *Lings* 22, 1984, 341–92; F. Plank (ed.), *Relational Typology*, 1985; Szemerényi 1985, 26–9; Gamkrelidze–Ivanov, 313–19, 1309; Beekes 1985, 172f.; Klimov, 'Über die Grundkasus des ergativischen Systems', *Fachtagung* 7, 1985, 250–6; Kammenhuber, *Fs. Winter*, 1985, 452f.; Modini, *KZ* 98, 1985, 211–13; Nespital, *MSS* 47, 1986, 127–58; Schmalstieg, 'The ergative function of the PIE genitive', *JIES* 14, 1986, 161–72; 'Some of the PIE medio-passive endings', *Studies Polomé*, 1988, 591–600; Vallini, *AIΩN* 9, 1987, 67–74; Zwolanek, *Merkmale der Ergativkonstruktion und die Hypothese eines idg. Ergativs*, 1987; Rumsey, 'The chimaera of PIE ergativity', *Lingua* 71, 1987, 297–318; 'Was PIE an ergative language?', *JIES* 15, 1988, 19–37 (no!); Luraghi, 'PIE as an ergative language', ibid. 359–79; Serbat, *Linguistique latine et linguistique générale*, Louvain 1988, 46–7: 'Nous écarterons donc l'hypothèse d'une origine ergative du nominatif latin (et ie.) qui se heurte à des difficultés trop graves'; Rix 1988 (pre-PIE ergative phase); Lehmann, *Fs. Meid*, 1989, 127: we may abandon the ergative (with Gamkrelidze–Ivanov); Modini, 'Ergative passive', *FoLH* 8, 1989, 351f.; K. H. Schmidt, *HS* 102, 1990, 248 (ergative in Georgian); Bubeník, 'Split ergativity in Indo-Iranian languages', *Diachronica* 6, 1990, 181–212; G. de Boel, 'Les sujets inanimés chez Homère', in Isebaert 1993, 37–69; Back, 'Ergativität und Natürlichkeit', *FoL* 26, 1993, 273–304. For a survey, see J. Seely, 'An ergative historiography', *HL* 4/2, 1977, 191–206 (191: term appears to have been suggested by Adolf Dirr as early as 1912); Rasmussen, *Haeretica*, 1974, 18, 26.

[21] Vaillant, *BSL* 37, 1936, 105f. On *-tt-*>*-ss-*, see also Heller, *Word* 12, 1956, 7; *Lg* 33, 1957, 21 n. 2.

[22] See Benveniste, 'Structure des relations de personne dans le verbe' (1946), 'La nature des pronoms' (1956), 'De la subjectivité dans le langage' (1958), all three now reprinted in his *Problèmes de linguistique générale*, 1966; cf. Kuryłowicz, *Categories* 148; Tláskal, 'La catégorie de la personne en portugais', *FoL* 12, 1980, 367–83 (against Benveniste).

[23] Erhart, *Sbornik Brno* 4, 1955, 11f.; Burrow, *The Sanskrit Language*, 1955, 317; Savčenko, *LPosn* 8, 52–6; Bader, *Word* 24, 1970, 20f. On *-nt-*=participle, see Kieckers (above, 9.7.1.1 n. 1), 12; Benveniste, *Origines* 173; Vaillant, *BSL* 37, 106; Kortlandt, *Studies Hoenigswald*, 1987, 222 (*-nti* originally nom. pl. of participle; for *-i* cf. pronominal **to-i*, **to-i-som*, **to-i-su*, Indo-Uralic plural *-i*); Shields, *HS* 102, 1989, 77 (*-nt* from *-N* x s. *-ti*!); Martinet, *BSL* 86, 1992, 361 (*-n*/*-nt*>*-r*/*-n*). Cuny's view (*Litteris* 7, 1930, 155: *-nto-*=pronouns **no-*+**to-*) was fairly widespread in the 19th cent., e.g. Brugmann, *MU* 1, 1878, 134 (*an-* 'that yonder' +*ta-* 'that').

9.7.1.3

The *perfect endings* (9.2.3 above) appear to stand isolated in the IE system. They are, however, very closely related to certain *passive-middle* endings. For these the following forms were reconstructed above (9.2.2.1):

PE	1	*-(m)ai*	2	*-soi*	3	*-toi*	6	*-ntoi*
SE	1	*-(m)ā*	2	*-so*	3	*-to*	6	*-nto.*

Alongside these, however, there are clearly more archaic forms. The 2nd s. has in Old Indic the secondary ending *-thās*. In the 3rd s. of some verbs an ending *-at* appears instead of *-ta*, e.g. *aduhat* 'milked', *aśayat* 'lay', which stand beside the pres. 3rd s. *duh-ē śay-ē*[1] and therefore are obviously modified from **a-du-ha* **a-śay-a*[2]. In the 3rd pl.

these same verbs have impf. *aduhran aš̄eran* and pres. *duhrē š̄erē*, so that again the imperfect forms are clearly extended with *-n(t)* from **aduhra* **aš̄era*.

The resulting endings of the past tenses

2 *-thās* 3 *-a* 6 *-ra*[3]

have no connection with the endings set out above. They are, however, as Kuryłowicz and Stang have long recognized,[4] manifestly related to the perfect endings

2 *-tha* 3 *-e* 6 *-r*.

It follows that perfect and passive-middle belong closely together. The retention of the old perfect endings in the past tenses is to be explained[5] by their descent from a period in which they, like *-to -nto*, were the primary or rather the primitive endings. This situation is also confirmed by Anatolian, where Luw. 1 *ha*, 3 *ta* serve as secondary endings, but Hitt. 1 *ha-*, 2 *ta-*, 3 *(t)a-* also function as primary endings.

The perfect with its meaning and *o*-grade 3rd s. form in *-e* gives the impression of a noun formation.[6] The forms 1 **woid-Ha*, 2 **woid-tha*, 3 **woid-e*, etc., would then have arisen from **woide-/woido-*, a verbal abstract noun 'knowledge' or verbal adjective 'knowing', by the addition of certain endings which have taken clear shape only in the singular and 3rd plural.[7] This interpretation is again not without difficulties, since **woid-a* **woid-tha* cannot simply be derived from an already established **woido*. We must rather start, therefore, from a root noun **woid-*. But the endings are not entirely clear either: here too personal pronouns would be expected at least in the 1st and 2nd persons, but at best only *-tha* can be connected with **tu*, though not in a straightforward way.[8] These difficulties are not wholly removed even if, in accordance with the general impression, final *-a* is posited for all persons and 3rd s. *-e* regarded as an innovation (see 9.4.3*a* above).[9]

Nevertheless, for an earlier system the following three categories can be set up in the present system:

	Active	Passive-middle	Perfect-middle
2	*-s*	*-so*	*-tha*
3	*-t*	*-to*	*-e*
6	*-nt*	*-nto*	*-r*

A further reduction on the assumption that the second series was constructed on the basis of the 3rd s. *-to* modified from *-e* or *-e/-o*[10] founders on the difficulty of really explaining the origin of *-to*.[11] The above model also does justice to the fact that not all middles are verbs of state; cf. *sek^wetoi* 'follows', **lowetoi* 'washes himself', etc. For the latter type it is surely more probable that their middle derived from the active rather than from the perfect.[12] Transitions between the two groups must doubtless have often occurred on the basis of semantic contacts. In this way a natural explanation of the 1st s. mid. could also be suggested (see 9.2.2.1): *mo* of the passive-middle crossed with *-ha* of the perfect-middle to give *-ma* and *-mai*, *-ho* and *-hoi* respectively.[13] The latter type, i.e. *-ho*, *-t(h)o*, *-o*, seems to be the basis of the Anatolian scheme *-ha -ta -a* (see 9.2.4),[14] while the Hittite *hi*-conjugation represents an innovation from the presentic perfect-middle with *-ha -tha -e*, which under the influence of the *mi*-class became *-hai -thai -ei* and finally *-hi -ti -i*.[15]

A further mutual influence between passive-middle and perfect-middle is to be seen in the celebrated *r*-endings. The Anatolian material shows in the first place that *r* was restricted to the present, secondly that it was limited to the 3rd persons (9.2.2.2). We must go further, however; the ending of the 3rd pl. *-antar*, which arose from the crossing of the 3rd pl. *-anta* and 3rd pl. *-r(o)*, was analogically carried over to the 3rd s. *-a* and *-ta*,[16] and the core portion *-(t)ar/ -antar* or (with *-i* as in the *hi*-conjugation) *-(t)ari/ -antari* became the starting-point for a complete *r*-paradigm – as also in Tocharian (see 9.2.2.2). Italic and Celtic, on the other hand, remained much closer to the initial stage. What the *r*-element is remains as puzzling as ever;[17] the only firm connection would be with the heteroclite nouns in *-r*,[18] but the transition to the 3rd pl. function is even more difficult than in the case of *-nt-*,[19] and its identity with the impersonal *-r* (type OIr. *-berar* 'one carries') has again become questionable.[20] It is clear, however, that its origin lies far back in Indo-European, in that the *r*-inflexion of Italo-Celtic and the eastern group (Hitt., Toch., Phryg.) must surely rest on a common innovation.[21]

The problem of the origin of the 1st s. active ending *-ō* is equally difficult. It is mentioned here because it is often seen as the product of a contraction of thematic *-o-*+perfect *-ha*.[22] But the *o*-timbre of the thematic vowel is not explained by the laryngeal,[23] and there is no basis for an ending *-o* (thus *-ō* from *-e*+*-o*).[24] As the *o*-timbre requires a nasal (9.2.6 above), we are led to *-om*. This will mean that in thematic verbs the 1st s. personal pronoun **em-*, *o*-grade **om-*, with the thematic vowel became *-o-om*, contracted *-ōm*, from which the nasal in final position was lost (5.4.5 above).[25] In this way the problem that thematic and athematic endings are distinguished only in the 1st s. would be eliminated; that this would be desirable is a matter on which Cowgill agrees with Rix and myself.[26]

[1] The verbal forms in *-ē* (1st and 3rd s.) are now collected by Cardona, *Lg* 37, 1961, 338, apparently overlooked by Watkins, *Verb* 88f.

[2] Wackernagel, *KZ* 41, 1907, 309–13; Meillet, *BSL* 24, 1925, 191–4 (*duha* has *e/o*~**woide*); Leumann (above, 9.2.2.2 n. 1), 10f. For Sommer, *Hethiter und Hethitisch*, 1947, 61f., *-at* was original. See also Narten, *Fs. Kuiper*, 1968, 9f.; Watkins, *Verb* 90, 99, 103f.

[3] The OInd. ending *-thās*, with Gr. *θης* and OIr. *-the(r)*, is often traced back to IE *-thēs*, but IE *-thās* (i.e. *-tH₂e+es*) is postulated by Hollifield, *KZ* 92, 1979, 219 (accepted by Cowgill, *Ériu* 34, 1983, 76); on this, see also G. Schmidt, *Fs. Neumann*, 1982, 347f.; Dunkel, in *In Memory of W. Cowgill*, 1987, 26, 34 (*tAo+es>thēs*).

[4] Kuryłowicz, 'Les désinences moyennes de l'ie. et du hittite', *BSL* 33, 1932, 1–4; Stang, 'Perfektum und Medium', *NTS* 6, 1932, 29–39; Safarewicz, 'Les désinences moyennes primaires', 1938, in his *Studia językoznawcze*, 1967, 45–50; cf. Vaillant, 'Les origines du médiopassif', *BSL* 42, 1946, 76–83. To these can be added the more recent discussions in Kuryłowicz, *Apophonie* 41f., *Categories* 58–70, 150; Insler, *IF* 73, 1969, 322f.; Adrados, *Verbo* 100f.; *FoL* 5, 1972, 366–81.

[5] Stang (n. 4 above, 36) has drawn attention to this.

[6] So Brugmann, *Grundriss*², ii/3, 594; *IF* 39, 1920, 139; Vaillant (n. 4 above), 82; Grünenthal, *KZ* 63, 1936, 138 (on this, Lohmann, *KZ* 64, 1937, 42–61, and Grünenthal's reply, ibid. 271–2); Savčenko, *BPTJ* 20, 1961, 117; Kuryłowicz (n. 4 above); Watkins, *Verb* 105f. See also above 9.2.3 n. 1 for Schmalstieg (the perfect is 'completely a nominal form') and Lehmann. Winter, 'Vocative' 219, sees in *-e* a mere supporting vowel.

[7] Kuryłowicz, *Categories* 62; Watkins, *Verb* 107 (**gʷhené* 'occisus'); Puhvel, *PICL* 10/4, 1970, 633 (**louk-Ae, -tAe, -e*, **lēuk-r̥*); Cowgill, in *Heth. und Idg.*, 33f.

[8] Cf. Kuryłowicz, *Apophonie* 44, where the starting-point is still an aoristic base-form **likʷe*.

[9] For *-e*, see further G. Schmidt, *KZ* 85, 1972, 260 n. 108: *-o* is a 'Hirngespinst' ('fantasy').

[10] Kuryłowicz, *Categories* 58 ('mechanism of the introduction of *t*'), and in *Directions* 76f.; Watkins, *Verb* 51 (=*e/o*); Kuryłowicz, *CTL* xi, 1973, 89f.

[11] But in my view *-o* and *-to* are simply the demonstratives; so also Schmalstieg, *FoL* 12, 1980, 355. According to Rix, 'The PIE middle', *MSS* 49, 1988, 101–19, *-o* was a reflexive in the ergative period (cf. *IC* 33, 1989, A 287); Shields, *GL* 24, 1984, 46–55, thinks that *-oi -soi -toi -moi* were datives.

[12] There the reflexive could have formed one of the starting-points, e.g. **lowe-s(w)e* 'wash yourself' becoming **loweso*.

[13] On the 1st s. mid., see also Kuryłowicz, *Categories* 60 (*o+a*); Watkins, *Verb* 130 (*a+om*); Kortlandt, *IF* 86, 1982, 123–36; G. Schmidt, *Fs. Neumann*, 1982, 345–56; and see above 9.2.2.1 n. 4.

[14] On this, see also Ambrosini, 'Ittito *esat* e ai. *aduhat*', *SSL* 6, 1966, 89–95; Neu, *Fachtagung* 7, 1985, 283.

[15] See Sturtevant and Hahn, *Comparative Grammar of the Hittite Language* i², 1951, 131–7; Kronasser, *Etymologie* 373; Puhvel, in *AIED* 243f.; Kammenhuber, *MSS* 24, 1968, 72; 'Hethitisch' 329f.; Meid, *Präteritum* 37f.; Perel'muter, *Obščeie. i grečeskij glagol*, 1977, 200 (perfect not=mid.). Further models of the original IE voice forms are in Neu (n. 14 above, 285, 294) (286: the middle is a contaminated form from active and perfect, e.g. *-to* from *-t -o*); Gamkrelidze–Ivanov, 300f., 330f.; on the latter, see also Szemerényi 1985, 24f., and cf. Yoshida 1990.

[16] For the basics, see Kuryłowicz, *Categories* 69; and esp. Neu (2), 157f.; *IF* 72, 1968, 231; 76, 1972, 244; *Studies Palmer*, 1976, 239–54; and above, 9.2.3 n. 4: Hittite has three forms in *-ar* from IE *-or*; Kuryłowicz, *EC* 12, 1969, 7–20; Eichner, *Fachtagung* 5, 1975, 76; Jasanoff, *Sprache* 23, 1977, 159–70; Katz, *HS* 101, 1988, 26–52. Watkins, *Verb* 51, 175, 180, is inclined to be dismissive and emphasizes in particular (51, 180) that a plural cannot influence the singular. Especially important is Meid's observation (*Fachtagung* 5, 215f.) that of the two extensions of middle *-to*, e.g. **sekʷetoi* and **sekʷetor*, the first is older, since it also appears in the *r*-languages, e.g. in the Hitt. *hi*-conjugation and in the singular of the Lat. perfect (e.g. *nōuī* from **gnōw-a-i*); see Szemerényi 1985, 46.

[17] A particle is postulated by Wagner, *TPS* 1969, 218; Watkins, *Verb* 43, 174, 194; an adverb **H(e)yer(i)* by Georgiev, *BalkE* 18, 1975, 22–3, also *Diachronica* 1, 1984, 74.

[18] e.g. Pisani, *Miscellanea Galbiati* iii, 1951, 31; Martinet, *Word* 11, 1955, 130f.; cf. also Ivanov, *Obščeind.* 123f.; Bader, *Word* 24, 1970, 18f.; Puhvel, *PICL* 10/4, 1970, 631f.; Erhart 1970, 80f.; G. Schmidt, in *Idg. und Kelt.*, 107.

[19] Pedersen, *Hittitisch* 105. A genuine solution would be Vaillant's suggestion (*BSL* 37, 1936, 107 n. 1) that final *-n(t)* became *-r*; unfortunately the sound laws continue to be an obstacle. The same applies to Martinet, *BSL* 86, 1992, 361, cf. above, 7.3.4 n. 2.
[20] On this cf. Schmidt, *IF* 68, 1963, 237.
[21] Kammenhuber, *KZ* 77, 1961, 43f.; *MSS* 24, 1968, 87.
[22] e.g. Savčenko, *LPosn* 8, 1960, 52; Neu, *IF* 72, 1967, 229 (he posits perf. *-o*); Watkins, *Ériu* 21, 1969, 3. A different view (from *o+h*) in Vaillant, *BSL* 38, 1937, 93f.; *Gram. comp.* iii, 20, 141; Pedersen, *Hittitisch* 81; Untermann, *Gedenkschrift Brandenstein*, 1968, 166[3]. See also Oettinger, in Bammesberger 1988, 357; Rasmussen, *Haeretica*, 1974, 20.
[23] See Watkins, *Verb* 108f.; *TPS* 1971, 86; Bader (n. 18 above), 26; Lindeman, in *Heth. und Idg.*, 157 (=156 n. 30).
[24] So Neu (n. 22 above); Specht, *Ursprung* 313.
[25] Cowgill's suggestion (*Fachtagung* 7, 1985, 108) that *-ō* came from *-o-mi* by way of *-ōi* involves unbelievable transformations of *m*; also against it Bammesberger 1986, 157. Other explanations in Erhart, *Sbornik Brno* E 3, 1958, 87f. (*eh^{w}*); Liebert, *Die ie. Personalpronomina*, 1957, 73; Lindeman, *NTS* 21, 1967, 140; Kerns and Schwartz, *Lg* 44, 1969, 718–19; Strunk (below, 9.7.3 n. 1), 301f.
[26] Cowgill, 'The personal endings of thematic verbs in IE', *Fachtagung* 7, 99, 104. See also Neu, *Studies Polomé*, 1988, 465, 470 (*-mi* ousted by *-ō<-oHo*).

9.7.1.4.

In recent times various attempts have been undertaken to recapture earlier stages in the development of the IE verbal system. Particularly thorough is the theory advanced by Schmalstieg, *Studies Polomé* (1988), 591–600. In his view, an early system which opposed an antipassive to an ergative later developed into an opposition of active and medio-passive.

9.7.2.

As regards the *modal formations*, it is remarkable that the *optative* (see 9.3.1.2) takes secondary endings. This could indicate that the optative only secondarily became a mood, that it is properly a past form which acquired the modal use as a secondary function.[1] Thus the optative **pōyēm* of IE **pō(i)-* 'drink' has been explained as originally an *ē*-aorist **pōy-ē-m* which was reinterpreted as **pō-yē-m*.[2] Since an *ē*-aorist has not been proved for Indo-European, this explanation remains in doubt. Others have been induced by the form of the suffix *-yē-* to see in it a verb with the meaning 'go' (derived from **ei-* 'go').[3]

Similarly, attempts are made to trace the *subjunctive* (see 9.3.1.1) to an indicative form.[4] This proceeds without difficulty if the modal use is referred to a future formation,[5] otherwise perhaps not so smoothly. The morphological problem is how *e/o* came to have this function. It has been suggested that the inflexion might be derived from a voluntative form **éy-ō* 'I wish to go' and perhaps a form **éyei* (=*ei+ei*) 'he (one) shall go', in which a thematic type of inflexion was accidentally established.[6]

[1] More than a century ago Curtius maintained (*Zur Chronologie der idg. Sprachforschung*[2], 1873, 54) that 'mood formation . . . developed gradually from tense formation'. And at the

end of the last century Goidànich (reprinted *PICL* 3, 1933, 301f.) stated that the optative represented the perfectivizing (with suffix -*ē*-) of an iterative-durative form.

[2] Kuryłowicz, *Categories* 141; on the use, 143. See also *N. M. Holmer, *Meddelanden från seminarierna för slaviska Språk* 1, 1951, 19–27; 3, 1959, 5–13 (old pret.); Watkins, *Verb* 233f.

[3] e.g. Hirt, *IG* iv, 290f.; vi, 279; vii, 148; Hahn, *Subjunctive* 65. On the SE of the optative, see also Gonda, *Moods* 47; Hoffmann, *Injunctiv* 276.

[4] Kuryłowicz, *Apophonie* 28, 71–4; *Categories* 137f.; Safarewicz, in *Problemy ie. jazykoznanija*, 1964, 15.

[5] Hirt, *IG* iv, 297; Hahn, *Subjunctive passim*.

[6] Risch, *Symbolae Kuryłowicz*, 1965, 238. In my opinion **ei-ei* could at most be a 2nd s. See also Lazzeroni, *Scritti T. Bolelli*, 1985, 171f.

9.7.3

The preceding discussion has been based on the assumption that the IE verbal system is very faithfully reflected by Greek and Indo-Iranian, and that early Indo-European therefore possessed the subjunctive and optative moods and, less certainly, the imperfect and aorist as independent tenses. Within the last two decades, however, serious objections have been raised to a reconstruction of this kind. The evidence of Hittite, which has no subjunctive or optative and in the indicative merely the opposition present–preterite, is no longer seen as proving the loss of once existing categories, but as indicating the retention of an earlier universal stage which did not yet have these categories. Various scholars, especially Wolfgang Meid, have accordingly interpreted the Graeco-Aryan system as a later dialectal innovation in the south-east of the Indo-European area.[1]

When a category is missing, it is naturally very difficult to prove that it has been lost, and much easier to suppose that it never existed at all. What methodological difficulties must, and perhaps can, here be overcome has been shown by K. Strunk, *InL* 9, 1986, 144: on the basis of certain ablaut phenomena the optative must be posited for early Indo-European, whereas the subjunctive is a late innovation.[2]

[1] On this, cf. above, 9.3.1.2 n.1, and Szemerényi 1985, 44f. See also Tischler, 'Relative chronology: the case of PIE', in *In Memory of Ben Schwartz*, 1988, 559–74 (for Meid and his stages I–III); Shields, 'Origins of IE subj. and opt.', ibid. 543–57.

[2] See also Strunk, 'Zur diachronischen Morphosyntax des Konjunktivs', in A. Rijksbaron et al. (eds.), *In the Footsteps of R. Kühner*, 1988, 291–316; Rix 1986, 27; B. Barschel, 'Der Modusbestand des Hethitischen: eine Altertümlichkeit?', *MSS* 47, 1986, 1–21.

9.7.4

A more precise investigation of the tense stems and personal endings thus leads to a progressive *reduction* of the system which at first sight seems so complex. The distinction between *present system* and *aorist system* is certainly of secondary origin, and even in the historical period it is not really possible to tell from the appearance of a stem to which system it belongs: if the personal ending is primary, the decision is easy; if, however, it is secondary, then the answer to the question, imperfect or aorist, depends on whether forms with primary endings are admissible in the language or not.[1]

Further, the position of the *perfect* is now quite different. Whereas in the historical languages it shows fundamentally[2] a relationship with the past (even when merely the result in the present is being considered), it was formerly simply a present. The difference from the 'present system' of the historical period lay not in the tense but in the mode of action: the *-mi* verb expressed *action*, the *-a* verb a *state*.[3] The passive-middle, which is fully formed in late Indo-European, does not yet exist at an earlier stage. This does not mean, however, that we can speak only of one voice, the active, at that stage;[4] there were even then at least two voices: the voices of action and of state.[5]

The great danger of the reductionist method lies precisely in the fact that not the system but a part of it is being considered and yet statements are made about the whole. The reductionist method even leads to the elimination of the category of tense. But it is easily possible that in directing our attention exclusively to the personal endings we overlook certain differences still present in the system, or that a former distinction of tense has been lost. As Kuryłowicz has so well expressed it (*Categories* 58): 'One cannot reconstruct *ad infinitum*. We must be satisfied with the reconstruction of stages bordering the historical reality.'

[1] On this, see Brugmann, *Grundriss*², ii/3, 48; Meillet, *Introduction* 197f., 248; Schwyzer, *GG* i, 640; and cf. Kuryłowicz, *CTL* xi, 1973, 76: 'in all languages . . . the forms of both the preterite and the future result from a revaluation (semantic change) of old *presents*'.

[2] I exclude the intensives (βέβρυχε) and preterite-presents (οἶδα, Goth. *skal*), as they are remnants of a past epoch.

[3] Savčenko, *VJ* 1955 (4), 117; *BPTJ* 20, 1961, 115–18; Safarewicz, in *Problemy ie. jazykoznanija*, 1964, 13–17; Ivanov, *Obščeind.* 137.

[4] Schwyzer, *GG* ii, 224.

[5] On this, see also Perel'muter, 'Zur Entstehung der Kategorie des Tempus im idg. Verbalsystem', *VJ* 1969 (5), 11–21; Meid, *Präteritum* 36; Szemerényi, *Studies A. A. Hill* iii, 1978, 279; Neu (e.g. *Fachtagung* 7, 1985, 285) assumes for the earliest system only the pair active–perfect, from which the later voices gradually developed, e.g. the middle by a contamination of active and perfect (see above, 9.2.7 n.8 and 9.7.1.3 n. 15).

Special Topics

(not indicated in the Table of Contents)

Index